If practice makes perfect, imagine what *better* practice can do . . .

MyWritingLab is an online learning system that provides better writing practice through progressive exercises. These exercises move students from literal comprehension to critical application to demonstration of their ability to write properly. With this better practice model, students develop the skills needed to become better writers!

When asked if they agreed with the following statements, here are how students responded:

97%
The MyWritingLab Student-user Satisfaction Level

"MyWritingLab helped me to improve my writing." 89%

"MyWritingLab was fairly easy to use." 90%

"MyWritingLab helped make me feel more confident about my writing ability." 83%

"MyWritingLab helped me to better prepare for my next writing course." 86%

"MyWritingLab helped me get a better grade." 82%

"I wish I had a program like MyWritingLab in some of my other courses." 78%

"I would recommend my instructor continue using MyWritingLab." 85%

Student Success Story

"The first few weeks of my English class, my grades were at approximately 78%. Then I was introduced to MyWritingLab. I couldn't believe the increase in my test scores. My test scores had jumped from that low score of 78 all the way up to 100% (and every now and then a 99)."

—Exetta Windfield, *College of the Sequoias* (MyWritingLab student user)

If your book did not come with an access code, you may purchase an access code at   www.mywritinglab.com

www.mywritinglab.com

Why Do You Need This New Edition?

If you're wondering why you should buy this new edition of *Along These Lines: Writing Paragraphs and Essays, Fifth Edition*, here are some good reasons!

1. You need to practice the revising and editing skills essential for Composition I and subsequent writing courses. **Every writing chapter includes new exercises** on such skills as choosing the right transitions, combining sentences, using specific details, and improving word choice. (See any writing chapter from 1-11.)

2. You need to develop the critical thinking, reading, and writing skills crucial for success in your future English, humanities, social science, and business courses. (See Chapter 13, "Writing from Reading," for expanded coverage.)

3. You need to read **new articles** containing timely information and advice for students, such as essays about students and credit card debt, students and their use of e-media, and isolation in the suburbs. (See the "Readings" section.)

4. You need **new, expanded coverage of the latest slang and clichés** (and how to avoid them) if you want to complete a job application, write a resume, or do any other type of professional writing that creates a good impression. (See Chapter 32, "Word Choice.")

5. You need to engage in critical thinking by responding to **probing new questions** at the end of every reading selection and by writing about thought-provoking new topics. (See the "Readings" section.)

6. You need to strengthen your research and writing skills by consulting a redesigned chapter that takes you, step-by-step, through the process of incorporating research into your essays. (See Chapter 14, "Using Research to Strengthen Essays.")

7. You need the **new, 2009-2010 guidelines from the Modern Language Association** if you incorporate any research into your writing. (See Chapter 14, "Using Research to Strengthen Essays.")

8. You need more Web-based activities and computer-related writing topics that appeal to computer-savvy learners. (See Chapter 10, the "Writing Your Own Paragraph" section.)

9. You need a "Quick Question" at the beginning of each grammar chapter, a **new feature** that can help you preview the chapter's content. (See the first page of any chapter from 15-29.)

10. You **need the new visual cues** that open each writing chapter, catch your attention, and jumpstart your prewriting. (See the first page of any chapter from 1-11.)

The Homepage . . .

Here is your MyWritingLab HomePage.
You get a bird's eye view of where you are in your course every time you log in.

Your **Course** box shows your class details.

Your **Study Plan** box shows what you last completed and what is next on your **To Do** list.

Your **Gradebook** box shows you a snapshot of how you are doing in the class.

Your **Other Resources** box supplies you with amazing tools such as:

- **Pearson Tutor Services**—click here to see how you can get help on your papers by qualified tutors . . . before handing them in!

- **Research Navigator**—click here to see how this resembles your library with access to online journals for research paper assignments.

- **Study Skills**—extra help that includes tips and quizzes on how to improve your study skills

Now, let's start practicing to become better writers. Click on the Study Plan tab. This is where you will do all your course work.

www.mywritinglab.com

PEARSON mywritinglab

The Study Plan . . .

MyWritingLab provides you with a simple Study Plan of the writing skills that you need to master. You start from the top of the list and work your way down. You can start with the Diagnostic Pre-Tests.

The Diagnostic Pre-Tests contain five exercises on each of the grammar, punctuation, and usage topics. You can achieve mastery of the topic in the Diagnostic Pre-Test by getting four of five or five of five correct within each topic.

After completing the Diagnostic Pre-Test, you can return to your Study Plan and enter any of the topics you have yet to master.

www.mywritinglab.com

Watch, Recall, Apply, Write . . .

Here is an example of a MyWritinglab Activity set that you will see once you enter into a topic. Take the time to briefly read the introductory paragraph, and then watch the engaging video clip by clicking on "Watch: Tense."

```
○ ○ ○                                    MyWritingLab
◄ ► C +   http://www.mywritinglab.com/mel/studyPlan.do?eventName=viewTopic&courseProductFlag=c    Q▾ Google

mywritinglab                              Jeff Montgomery              Settings  Help  Logout
   Course: English 101, Section-1
   Instructor: Stephen Clark                     Home    Study Plan    Gradebook

Home > Study Plan > Tense

Tense

Verb tense tells a reader when something occurred–in the present, past, or future. It is the ending of the verb -s, -ed, -d, or -ing that shows the tense.

The exercises in this module test your knowledge of tense. A watch animation is provided to help you increase your understanding of the concept. Click on "Begin" to start a set of exercises.
```

Review Materials				
❶ Watch: Tense	View			
Activities		**Score**	**Sets Available**	**Sets Taken**
❷ Recall ✳	Begin	N/A	9	0
❸ Grammar Apply ✳	Begin	N/A	2	0
❹ Write	Begin	N/A	1	0

✳ = Required

Return to Study Plan

The video clip provides you with a helpful review.
Now you are ready to start the exercises. There are three types:

- Recall—activities that help you *recall* the rules of grammar

- Apply—activities that help you *apply* these rules to brief paragraphs or essays

- Write—activities that ask you to demonstrate these rules of grammar in your own writing

www.mywritinglab.com

Helping Students Succeed ...

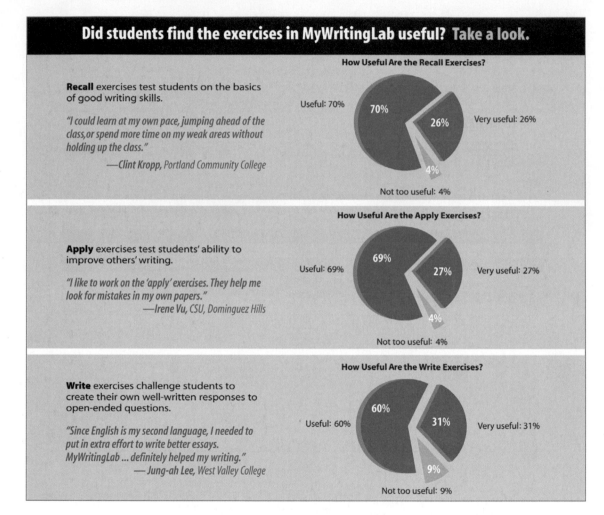

Did students find the exercises in MyWritingLab useful? Take a look.

Recall exercises test students on the basics of good writing skills.

"I could learn at my own pace, jumping ahead of the class, or spend more time on my weak areas without holding up the class."

—*Clint Kropp, Portland Community College*

How Useful Are the Recall Exercises?

Useful: 70%
70%
26% Very useful: 26%
4%
Not too useful: 4%

Apply exercises test students' ability to improve others' writing.

"I like to work on the 'apply' exercises. They help me look for mistakes in my own papers."
—*Irene Vu, CSU, Dominguez Hills*

How Useful Are the Apply Exercises?

Useful: 69%
69%
27% Very useful: 27%
4%
Not too useful: 4%

Write exercises challenge students to create their own well-written responses to open-ended questions.

"Since English is my second language, I needed to put in extra effort to write better essays. MyWritingLab ... definitely helped my writing."
— *Jung-ah Lee, West Valley College*

How Useful Are the Write Exercises?

Useful: 60%
60%
31% Very useful: 31%
9%
Not too useful: 9%

Students just like you are finding MyWritingLab's Recall, Apply, and Write exercises useful in their learning.

PEARSON **mywritinglab**™

Here to Help You ...

Our goal is to provide answers to your MyWritingLab questions as quickly as possible and deliver the highest level of support. By visiting **www.mywritinglab.com/help.html**, many questions can be resolved in just a few minutes. Here you will find help on the following:

☑ System Requirements

☑ How to Register for MyWritingLab

☑ How to Use MyWritingLab

For student support, we also invite you to contact Pearson Customer Technical Support (shown above). In addition, you can reach our Support Representatives online at **http://247.pearsoned.com**. Here you can do the following:

☑ Search Frequently Asked Questions about MyWritingLab

☑ E-mail a Question to Our Support Team

☑ Chat with a Support Representative

www.mywritinglab.com

Along These Lines
Writing Paragraphs and Essays

Why Do You Need This New Edition?

If you're wondering why you should buy this new edition of *Along These Lines: Writing Paragraphs and Essays, Fifth Edition*, here are some good reasons!

1. You need to practice the revising and editing skills essential for Composition I and subsequent writing courses. **Every writing chapter includes new exercises** on such skills as choosing the right transitions, combining sentences, using specific details, and improving word choice. (See any writing chapter from 1-11.)

2. You need to develop the critical thinking, reading, and writing skills crucial for success in your future English, humanities, social science, and business courses. (See Chapter 13, "Writing from Reading," for expanded coverage.)

3. You need to read **new articles** containing timely information and advice for students, such as essays about students and credit card debt, students and their use of e-media, and isolation in the suburbs. (See the "Readings" section.)

4. You need **new, expanded coverage of the latest slang and clichés** (and how to avoid them) if you want to complete a job application, write a resume, or do any other type of professional writing that creates a good impression. (See Chapter 32, "Word Choice.")

5. You need to engage in critical thinking by responding to **probing new questions** at the end of every reading selection and by writing about thought-provoking new topics. (See the "Readings" section.)

6. You need to strengthen your research and writing skills by consulting a redesigned chapter that takes you, step-by-step, through the process of incorporating research into your essays. (See Chapter 14, "Using Research to Strengthen Essays.")

7. You need the **new, 2009-2010 guidelines from the Modern Language Association** if you incorporate any research into your writing. (See Chapter 14, "Using Research to Strengthen Essays.")

8. You need more Web-based activities and computer-related writing topics that appeal to computer-savvy learners. (See Chapter 10, the "Writing Your Own Paragraph" section.)

9. You need a "Quick Question" at the beginning of each grammar chapter, a **new feature** that can help you preview the chapter's content. (See the first page of any chapter from 15-29.)

10. You **need the new visual cues** that open each writing chapter, catch your attention, and jumpstart your prewriting. (See the first page of any chapter from 1-11.)

Along These Lines

Writing Paragraphs and Essays

Fifth Edition
Annotated Instructor's Edition

John Sheridan Biays, professor emeritus of English
Broward College

Carol Wershoven, professor emerita of English
Palm Beach Community College

Prentice Hall
Upper Saddle River   London   Singapore
Toronto   Tokyo   Sydney   Hong Kong   Mexico City

Editorial Director: Leah Jewell
Editor-in-Chief: Craig Campanella
Acquisitions Editor: Blair Zoe Tuckman
Editorial Assistant: David Nitti
VP/Director of Marketing: Tim Stookesbury
Executive Marketing Manager: Megan Galvin-Fak
Marketing Manager: Tom DeMarco
Marketing Assistant: Kyle VanNatter
Senior Operations Supervisor: Sherry Lewis
Operations Specialist: Christina Amato
Assistant Managing Editor: Melissa Feimer
Project Manager: Maureen Benicasa
Text Permissions Specialist: Kathleen Karcher
Senior Art Director: Nancy Wells
Cover & Interior Art Director: Suzanne Duda
Text and Cover Designer: Ximena Tamvakopoulos
Manager, Visual Research: Beth Brenzel
Photo Researcher: Joanne Dippel
Manager, Rights and Permissions: Zina Arabia
Image Permission Coordinator: Nancy Seise
Manager, Cover Visual Research & Permissions: Karen Sanatar
Cover Art: Modern building in Los Angeles by Laurin Rinder/Shutterstock
Full-Service Production and Composition: Black Dot Group
Full-Service Project Management: Sandy Reinhard
Printer/Binder: Webcrafters Inc.
Cover Printer: Lehigh-Phoenix Color Corporation

Credits and acknowledgments borrowed from other sources and reproduced, with permission, in this textbook appear on appropriate page within text (or on page 665).

10 9 8 7 6 5 4 3 2 1

Prentice Hall
is an imprint of

PEARSON

www.pearsonhighered.com

To order the student edition, use
ISBN-13: 978-0-205-64929-7
ISBN-10: 0-205-64929-7

ISBN-13: 978-0-205-64931-0
ISBN-10: 0-205-64931-9

Contents

Preface for Instructors

Our many years of working with beginning writers convinced us that students may gradually come to view writing as a natural process if they engage in a variety of instructional activities (e.g., individual, collaborative, creative, computer-related) that recognizes different learning styles. The *Along These Lines* series is based on this premise, and we are indebted literally to hundreds of instructors who have offered invaluable suggestions for refining our work.

We know all too well that striking a balance between teaching creatively and meeting statewide or departmental "exit-test" objectives can be challenging for composition instructors. On a positive note, however, we are constantly amazed by the tireless efforts of so many developmental educators across the country who remain committed to quality instruction despite severe budget restraints and ever-increasing class sizes. These dedicated instructors simply want their students to succeed, and when these professionals offer advice, we know we should pay close attention.

As you preview this new edition, you may notice several improvements and unique features. Many changes in this edition reflect the collective wisdom of developmental instructors nationwide, and we believe that *Along These Lines: Writing Paragraphs and Essays 5/e* is the most comprehensive, user-friendly, and visually appealing text to date. Thanks very much for your interest in our work and for supporting developmental education along *all* lines.

UNIQUE FEATURES AND IMPROVEMENTS FOR THE FIFTH EDITION

Extensive Visual Enhancements

- A new feature, "Jumping In," opens each writing chapter with an eye-catching, full-color photograph and key questions to prompt student discussion or prewriting about a particular rhetorical pattern.
- Each grammar chapter opens with a "Quick Question" feature and includes an engaging photograph of students thinking, reading, studying, or interacting. Each quick question is related to the grammar principle covered in the chapter and provides an incentive to preview the content.

Focus on Developing Critical Thinking Skills

- Coverage on critical thinking, reading, and writing skills has increased.
- New challenging and timely reading selections include such topics as credit card debt among college students, the loss of community in American suburbs, and student reliance on e-media.
- New critical thinking topics for discussion and writing related to each reading selection provide crucial preparation for future composition courses.

Enhanced Writing Instruction

- Writing assignments now include more suggested Web-based activities and computer-related topics.
- New exercises throughout the writing chapters emphasize the importance of revising and proofreading, skills essential for Composition I and subsequent writing courses.

Expanded Grammar Coverage

- More paragraph editing exercises in each chapter require students to apply the relevant grammar principle to sample writing assignments.
- For instructors seeking additional practice for nonnative learners, the Annotated Instructor's Edition's grammar chapters now include cross-references to the ESL Appendix.
- The ESL Appendix now has twice the number of exercises than the previous edition.
- Increased coverage on avoiding slang, clichés, and wordiness is complemented by lively exercises and comprehensive lists of imprecise, ungrammatical expressions and preferable alternatives.

Expanded Coverage of Research Skills

- A redesigned chapter, "Using Research to Strengthen Essays," introduces students to the basics of research and now includes a user-friendly "At a Glance" box that lists seven common types of Works Cited entries following the new MLA guidelines for documentation.
- Framed samples show how a short essay without research can be developed into one enhanced by documented information. This progression provides a nonthreatening introduction to the research process.
- New exercises cover two research skills: (1) internal citation, including paraphrasing, quoting, and summarizing, and (2) preparation of a Works Cited list for print and online sources.

POPULAR FEATURES RETAINED

In response to suggestions from current users and new reviewers, we have retained these distinctive and popular features:

The Writing Chapters

- Visually appealing checklists, charts, and "Info Boxes".
- A lively conversational tone, including question-and-answer formats and dialogues.
- Boxed examples of an outline, draft, and final version of a writing assignment in each chapter.
- A "Walk-Through" writing assignment at the end of each chapter that guides students, step-by-step, through the stages of the writing process.

- A Peer Review Form in each chapter so students can benefit from a classmate's reaction to their drafts.

The Grammar Chapters

- Three types of grammar exercises—**Practice** (simple reinforcement), **Collaborate** (partner or group work), and **Connect** (application of the grammar principal to paragraphs).
- Grammar concepts taught step-by-step, as in "Two Steps to Check for Fragments."
- A Chapter Test at the end of each grammar chapter, ideal for class review or quick quizzes.

The Reading Sections

- Professional reading selections grouped in one place for easy reference.
- Vocabulary definitions based on the specific context of the writer's intent.
- Writing options sparked by a selection's content and designed to elicit thinking, not rote replication of a model.

OUR PHILOSOPHY

We believe that an effective text should respect students' individuality and their innate desire to learn and succeed. We trust that the *Along These Lines* series will continue to help students flourish within a framework of respect, encouragement, and meaningful interaction as they work through the writing process.

ACKNOWLEDGMENTS

We have been gratified and encouraged by the positive reception the *Along These Lines* series has generated over the years. We are indebted to the following professionals for their frank, comprehensive reviews, which helped us immensely during the revision process:

Jeremy Abad	Chaffey College
Nancy Alexander	Methodist University
Kina Burkett	Jefferson Davis Community College
Beverly Dile	Elizabethtown Community and Technical College
James Fields	Iowa Western Community College
Leona Fisher	Chaffey College
Anita Griffin	Hinds Community College
Carin Halper	Fresno City College
Curtis Harrell	Northwest Arkansas Community College
Aleyenne Johnson-Jonas	Art Institute of California
Billy Jones	Miami Dade College – Kendall Campus
Peter Kearly	Henry Ford Community College
Tracy Lassiter	Eastern Arizona College
Teri Maddox	Jackson State Community College

Jennifer Olds	Chaffey College
Ann Schlumberger	Pima Community College–West Campus
Margaret Wanning	Piedmont Technical College
Tammy White	Forsyth Technical Community College
Brian Wren	Gwinnett Technical College

Debi Doyle and Dave Nitti, editorial assistants, coordinated these reviews with exemplary efficiency and customary good cheer. Somehow, they even managed to keep the red tape and paperwork at bay so we could concentrate on our rounds of revisions.

We are indebted to Craig Campanella, Editor-in-Chief, and Blair Zoe Tuckman, acquisitions editor for Developmental English. Craig is still adept at allaying authors' fears while overseeing Prentice Hall's entire English list. Blair has a passion for "all things developmental" as well as a knack for helping authors navigate through the turbulent waters of today's publishing world. She helped us stay focused and positive.

We were most fortunate to work with Sandy Reinhard and her associates at Black Dot Group. Throughout the copyediting, proofing, and production phases, Sandy kept us intact and relatively sane. She resolved scheduling snags, fixed design problems, met page count mandates, and commiserated with authors. We know we couldn't have been in better–or kinder–hands.

Additionally, we extend thanks to Maureen Benicasa, project manager, whose calm and confident assurance during the production process always boosted our morale. Kudos also to Kathleen Karcher, permissions editor; Edith Bicknell, copy editor; Ximena Tamvakopoulas, designer; Leslie Osher, creative design director; Jon Davies, proofreader; and Leoni McVey, indexer. We are also very grateful to Tom DeMarco, marketing manager, for his enthusiastic support of our series.

Finally, and most importantly, we thank the many students and colleagues who, for over three decades, intrigued, impressed, and inspired us. You made our journey extraordinary along *all* lines.

John Sheridan Biays
Carol Wershoven

Writing in Stages: The Process Approach

INTRODUCTION

Learning By Doing

Writing is a skill, and like any skill, writing improves with practice. This book provides you with ample practice to improve your writing through a variety of individual and group activities. Whether you complete assignments at home or in the classroom, just remember that *good writing takes practice:* you can learn to write well by writing.

Steps Make Writing Easier

Writing is easier if you *do not try to do too much at once.* To make the task of writing easier, *Along These Lines* breaks the process into stages:

PREWRITING

In this stage, you think about your topic, and you gather ideas. You *react* to your own ideas and add even more thoughts. You can also react to other people's ideas as a way of expanding your own.

PLANNING

In this stage, you *examine your ideas* and begin to *focus* them around one main idea or point. Planning involves combing, categorizing, and even eliminating some ideas. Placing your specific details in a logical order often involves *outlining*.

DRAFTING

In this stage, the thinking and planning begin to take shape as a piece of writing. You complete a draft of your work, a *rough version* of the finished product. Then you examine the draft and consider ways to *revise* it, a process that may required extensive *editing* and several versions of your original draft.

POLISHING

In this stage, the final draft of your writing gets one last careful *review* when you are rested and alert. You *proofread* and concentrate on identifying and correcting any mistakes in spelling, mechanics, punctuation, or word choice you may have missed. This stage is the *final check* of your work to make your writing the best it can be.

These four stages in the writing process – prewriting, planning, drafting, and polishing – may overlap. You may be changing your plan even as you work on the draft of your paper. There is no rule that prevents you from returning to an earlier stage. Throughout this book, you will have many opportunities to become familiar with the stages of effective writing. Working individually and with your classmates, you can become a better writer along *all* lines.

CHAPTER 1

Jumping In

*Where do you get your ideas for writing? Do they seem to come at you all at once? Working with a jumble of ideas is often part of the writing process, and one key step is to sort through these ideas. By sorting, you will be working toward one **paragraph** that focuses on one idea or point.*

TEACHING TIP

Tell students that in writing classes, the word "topic" is synonymous with "subject," but that the word "topic" is more often used.

Writing a Paragraph

Usually, students write because they have a writing assignment requiring them to write on some topic or choice of topics, and the writing is due by a certain day. So assume that you get such an assignment and it calls for one paragraph. You might wonder, "Why a paragraph? Why not something large, like a two- or three-page paper? After all, many classes will ask for papers, not just paragraphs."

For one thing, all essays are a series of paragraphs. If you can write one good paragraph, you can write more than one. The **paragraph** is the basic building block of any essay. It is a group of sentences focusing on *one idea* or one point. Keep this concept in mind: *one idea to a paragraph.* Focusing on one idea or one point gives a paragraph **unity**. If you have a new point, start a new paragraph.

You may ask, "Doesn't this mean a paragraph will be short?" How long should a paragraph be, anyway? To convince a reader of one main point, you need to make it, support it, develop it, explain it, and describe it. There will be shorter and longer paragraphs, but for now, you can assume your paragraph will be somewhere between seven and twelve sentences long.

This chapter guides you through each stage of the writing process:

- **Prewriting**—how to generate and develop ideas for your paragraph
- **Planning**—how to organize your ideas
- **Drafting**—how to create, revise, and edit rough drafts
- **Polishing**—how to proofread and make one final check

We give extra emphasis to the prewriting stage in this chapter to give you some extra help in getting started.

BEGINNING THE PREWRITING: GATHERING IDEAS

Suppose your instructor asks you to write a paragraph about your favorite city or town. Writing about your favorite city or town is your general **topic**, but you must choose one city or town to make the topic more specific. With this topic, you already know your **purpose**—to write a paragraph that makes some point about the city or town. You have an **audience** since you are writing this paragraph for your instructor and classmates. Often, your purpose is to write a specific kind of paper for a class. Occasionally, you may have to write with a different purpose or audience, such as writing instructions for a new employee at your workplace, or a letter of complaint to a manufacturer, or a short biographical essay for a scholarship application. Knowing your audience and purpose is important in writing effectively.

Freewriting, Brainstorming, Keeping a Journal

Once you have identified your purpose and audience, you can begin by finding some way to *think on paper*. You can use the techniques of freewriting, brainstorming, or keeping a journal to gather ideas and potential details.

Freewriting Give yourself fifteen minutes to write whatever comes into your mind on your subject. If your mind is a blank, write, "My mind's a blank. My mind's a blank," over and over until you think of something else. The main goal here is to *write without stopping*. Do not stop to tell yourself, "This is stupid," or "I can't use any of this in a paper." Do not stop to correct your spelling or punctuation. Just write. Let your ideas flow. Write *freely*. Here is an example:

Freewriting About a Favorite City or Town

Favorite city or town. City? I like New York. It's so big and exciting. Haven't been there much, though. Only once. My hometown. I like it. It's just another town but comfortable and friendly. Maybe St. Augustine. Lots of fun visits there. Grandparents there. Hard to pick a favorite. Different places are good for different reasons.

Brainstorming This technique is like freewriting because you write whatever comes into your head, but it is a little different because you can pause *to ask yourself questions* that will lead to new ideas. When you brainstorm alone, you "interview" yourself about a subject. You can also brainstorm and ask questions within a group.

TEACHING TIP

As you review prewriting, planning, drafting, and polishing stages, remind students that they can easily become frustrated if they attempt too many tasks simultaneously.

INSTRUCTOR'S NOTE

Prewriting is also called "discovery" or "invention" by some writing instructors and textbooks. For a warm-up activity with word associations, you might ask your students how such terms relate to topic selection (discovery) and development (invention).

TEACHING TIP

Ask students why freewriting might seem awkward at first. Also, if they are "free" to write any thoughts they have on a subject, do they feel less pressure or more pressure than usual? This will be a good time to discuss their fears or frustrations about writing.

TEACHING TIP

Tell your students that freewriting can be done easily on a computer. They can type freely for several minutes, print out what they have typed, and circle ideas they may pursue to help narrow their topic. Stress that the writing should be nonstop to let ideas flow easily.

Brainstorming About a Favorite City or Town

Favorite place.

City or town.

What's the difference between a city and a town?

Doesn't matter. Just pick one. Cities bigger.

How is city life different from town life?

Cities are bigger. More crowded, like Atlanta.

Which do you like better, a city or a town?

Sometimes I like cities.

Why?

There is more to do.

So, what city do you like?

I like New York. St. Augustine.

Is St. Augustine a city?

Yes. A small one.

Do you like towns?

I loved this little town in Mexico.

If you feel like you are running out of ideas in brainstorming, try to form a question out of what you've just written. *Go where your questions and answers lead you.* For example, if you write, "There is more to do in cities," you could form these questions:

> *What is there to do? Sports? Entertainment? Outdoor exercise? Meeting people?*

You could also make a list of your brainstorming ideas, but remember to *do only one step at a time.*

Keeping a Journal A **journal** is a notebook of your personal writing, a notebook in which you write *regularly and often. It is not a diary, but it is a place to record your experiences, reactions, and observations.* In it, you can write about what you have done, heard, seen, read, or remembered. You can include sayings that you would like to remember, news clippings, snapshots—anything that you would like to recall or consider. A journal provides an enjoyable way to practice your writing, and it is a great source of ideas for writing.

Journal Entry About a Favorite City or Town

I'm not going south to see my grandparents this winter. They're coming here instead of me going to St. Augustine. I'd really like to go there. I like the warm weather. It's better than months of snow, ice, and rain here in Easthampton. I'll miss going there. I've been so many times that it's like a second home. St. Augustine is great around Christmas time.

Finding Specific Ideas

Whether you freewrite, brainstorm, or consult your journal, you end up with something on paper. Follow those first ideas; see where they can take you. You are looking for specific ideas, each of which can focus the general topic you started with. At this point, you do not have to choose which specific idea you want to write about. You just want to *narrow your range* of ideas.

You might think, "Why should I narrow my ideas? Won't I have more to say if I keep my topic big?" But remember that a paragraph has one idea; you want to state it clearly and with convincing details for support. If you try to write one paragraph on city life versus town life, for example, you will probably make so many general statements that you will say very little, or you will bore your reader with big, sweeping statements. General ideas are big, broad ones. Specific ideas are smaller, narrower. If you scanned the freewriting example on a favorite city or town, you might underline many specific ideas as possible topics:

> *Favorite city or town. City? I like <u>New York</u>. It's so big and exciting. Haven't been there much, though. Only once. <u>My hometown</u>. I like it. It's just another town but comfortable and friendly. Maybe <u>St. Augustine</u>. Lots of fun visits there. Grandparents there. Hard to pick a favorite. Different places are good for different reasons.*

Consider the underlined terms. They are specific places. You could write a paragraph about any one of these places. Or you could underline specific places in your brainstorming questions and answers:

> *Favorite place.*
> *City or town.*
>
> **What's the difference between a city and a town?**
> *Doesn't matter. Just pick one. Cities bigger.*
>
> **How is city life different from town life?**
> *Cities are bigger. More crowded, like <u>Atlanta</u>.*
>
> **Which do you like better, a city or a town?**
> *Sometimes I like cities.*
>
> **Why?**
> *There is more to do.*
>
> **So, what city do you like?**
> *I like <u>New York</u>. <u>St. Augustine</u>.*
>
> **Is St. Augustine a city?**
> *Yes. A small one.*
>
> **Do you like towns?**
> *I loved this <u>little town in Mexico</u>.*

Each of these specific places could be a topic for your paragraph.

If you reviewed the journal entry on a favorite city or town, you would also be able to underline specific places:

> *I'm not going south to see my grandparents this winter. They're coming here instead of me going to <u>St. Augustine</u>. I'd really like to go there. I like the warm weather. It's better than months of snow, ice, and rain here in*

TEACHING TIP

Devoting the first 5–10 minutes of class (or every other class) to freewriting or writing in a journal can turn a perceived chore into a meaningful period of reflection.

Easthampton. I'll miss going there. I've been so many times that it's like a second home. St. Augustine is great around Christmas time.

Remember, if you follow the steps, they can lead you to specific ideas.

Selecting One Topic

Once you have a list of specific ideas that can lead you to a specific topic, you can pick one topic. Let's say you decided to work with the list of places you gathered through brainstorming:

Atlanta
New York
St. Augustine
a little town in Mexico

Looking at this list, you decide you want to write about St. Augustine as your favorite city.

TEACHING TIP

Groupwork: You can assign a particular topic to several students (or rows) and ask them to work on it collaboratively. If you assign small groups, each group can select its own spokesperson to share the best questions with the rest of the class.

Exercise 1 **Creating Questions for Brainstorming**

Following are several topics. For each one, brainstorm by writing at least six questions related to the topic that could lead you to further ideas. The first topic is done for you:

1. topic: dogs

Question 1. _Why are dogs such popular pets?_

Question 2. _What kind of dog is a favorite pet in America?_

Question 3. _Are dogs hard to train?_

Question 4. _What dog, in your life, do you remember best?_

Question 5. _What's the most famous dog on television?_

Question 6. _Are there dogs as cartoon characters?_

2. topic: food

INSTRUCTOR'S NOTE

Answers will vary. Possible answers shown at right.

Question 1. _What is my favorite food?_

Question 2. _What is the most disgusting food?_

Question 3. _Is junk food really so bad for you?_

Question 4. _Why are there so many food shows on television?_

Question 5. _What country makes the best-tasting food?_

Question 6. _How can eating become a way to improve your mood?_

3. topic: loans

Question 1. _How long does it take to pay back a student loan?_

Question 2. _Why do so many students need large student loans?_

Question 3. *Is it a good idea to take out a car loan?*

Question 4. *What are the alternatives to getting a car loan?*

Question 5. *Have you ever lent money to a friend?*

Question 6. *Is it possible to live loan free?*

Exercise 2 **Finding Specific Details in Freewriting**

Below are two samples of freewriting. Each is a written response to a different topic. Read each sample, and then underline any words and phrases that could become the focus of a paragraph.

Freewriting Reaction to the Topic of Weather

I want to get out of <u>Kansas because I can't stand the weather. Bone-chilling winters</u> when the <u>whole world seems gray.</u> Then the <u>tornadoes</u> in the spring and summer. <u>Just like the tornado in the movie The Wizard of Oz</u> only more frightening. I would like a <u>place without dreary weather.</u> Maybe <u>California</u> or <u>Arizona.</u> I think <u>a desert with hot, dry air</u> or <u>a beach with warm breezes all the time</u> would be great.

INSTRUCTOR'S NOTE

Answers will vary. Possible answers shown at left.

Freewriting Reaction to the Topic of Communication

What's communication? Talking? Or <u>a class in communication,</u> like <u>Speech</u> or <u>Business Communication</u>? I <u>talk constantly.</u> I'm <u>on my cell all the time,</u> too. But I'm <u>terrified of speaking in public,</u> in front of a class. I <u>don't like to talk much to teachers,</u> either.

Exercise 3 **Finding Specific Details in a List**

Below are several lists of words or phrases. In each list, one item is a general term; the others are more specific. Underline the words or phrases that are more specific. The first list is done for you:

1. <u>apple pie</u>
<u>ice cream</u>
desserts
<u>butterscotch pudding</u>
<u>jello</u>
<u>chocolate brownies</u>

2. <u>jars</u>
<u>bags</u>
<u>boxes</u>
<u>buckets</u>
containers

3. <u>street racing</u>
racing
<u>racing movies</u>
<u>NASCAR</u>
<u>horse racing</u>
<u>customized cars</u>

4. <u>sofa</u>
<u>kitchen table</u>
<u>desk</u>
furniture
<u>coffee table</u>
<u>chest of drawers</u>

5. <u>vampire movies</u>
<u>ghost stories</u>
horror movies
<u>escaped maniac movies</u>
<u>zombie movies</u>

6. costs of college
<u>parking stickers</u>
<u>student activities fees</u>
<u>lab fees</u>
<u>tuition</u>
<u>art supplies</u>

Collaborate

Exercise 4 **Finding Topics through Freewriting**

The following exercise must be completed with a partner or a group. Below are several topics. Pick one and freewrite on it for ten minutes. Then read your freewriting to your partner or group. Ask your listener(s) to jot down any words or phrases from your writing that could lead to a specific topic for a paragraph.

Your listener(s) should read the jotted-down words or phrases to you. You will be hearing a collection of specific ideas that came from *your* writing. As you listen, underline the words in your freewriting.

Freewriting topics (pick one):

1. an unexpected pleasure

2. hurt feelings

3. a childhood fear

Freewriting on (name of topic chosen): _____

_____

_____

_____

_____

_____

_____

_____

Adding Details to a Specific Topic

You can develop the specific topic you picked in a number of ways:

1. *Check your list* for other ideas that seem to fit with the specific topic you've picked.
2. *Brainstorm*—ask yourself more questions about your topic, and use the answers as details.
3. *List* any new ideas you have that may be connected to your topic.

One way to add details is to go back and check your brainstorming for other ideas about St. Augustine:

I like St. Augustine.
a small city

Now you can **brainstorm** some questions that will lead you to more details. The questions do not have to be connected to each other; they are just questions that could lead you to ideas and details:

What's a small city?

It doesn't have skyscrapers or freeways or millions of people.

So, what makes it a city?

Thousands of visitors come there every day.

What's so great about St. Augustine?
You can go to the beach nearby.

Is it a clean, big beach?
Sure. And the water is a clear blue.

What else can you do in St. Augustine?
There's lots of history.

Like what?
A fort. The oldest schoolhouse. Old houses.

Another way to add details is to list any ideas that may be connected to your topic. The list might give you more specific details:

grandparents live there
warm in winter
grandparents feed me
I use their car

If you had tried all three ways of adding detail, you would end up with this list of details connected to the topic a favorite city or town:

a small city	*clear blue water*
no freeways	*lots of history*
no skyscrapers	*a fort*
not millions of people	*oldest schoolhouse*
thousands of visitors every day	*grandparents live there*
can always visit family for free	*warm in winter*
beach nearby	*grandparents feed me*
clean, big beach	*I use their car*

INFO BOX: Beginning the Prewriting: A Summary

The prewriting stage of writing a paragraph enables you to gather ideas. This process begins with several steps:

1. **Think on paper and write down any ideas that you have about a topic.** You can do this by freewriting, brainstorming, or by keeping a journal.

2. **Scan your writing for specific ideas that have come from your first efforts.** List these specific ideas.

3. **Pick one specific idea.** Then, by reviewing your early writing, by questioning, and by thinking further, you can add details to the one specific idea.

This process may seem long, but once you have worked through it several times, it will become nearly automatic. When you think about ideas before you try to shape them into a paragraph, you are off to a good start. Confidence comes from having something to say, and once you have a specific idea, you will be ready to begin shaping and developing details that support your idea.

Exercise 5   **Adding Details to a Topic by Brainstorming**

Below are two topics. Each is followed by two or three details. Brainstorm more questions, based on the existing details, that can lead to more details.

INSTRUCTOR'S NOTE

Answers will vary. Possible answers shown at right.

1. topic: advantages of taking public transportation
details: saves money
kind to the environment

Question 1: *How does it save you money?*

Question 2: *Why is it kind to the environment?*

Question 3: *Can you save money on car payments?*

Question 4: *Can you save money by not having to pay for gas?*

Question 5: *Do cars pollute the environment?*

Question 6: *Do fewer cars on the road mean better air quality?*

2. topic: losing your keys
details: causes panic
forces a change of plans
causes embarrassment

Question 1: *Why would anyone panic?*

Question 2: *Why does losing your keys change your plans?*

Question 3: *Why feel embarrassed?*

Question 4: *Does the panic come from a loss of control?*

Question 5: *Does embarrassment come from having to ask for help?*

Question 6: *How do you handle the panic?*

Exercise 6   Adding Details by Listing

INSTRUCTOR'S NOTE

Answers will vary. Possible answers shown at right.

Following are three topics for paragraphs. For each topic, list details that seem to fit the topic.

1. topic: e-mail
details: a. *spam*   c. *lost e-mail*
b. *checking e-mail*   d. *funniest e-mail*

2. topic: a good day at work
details: a. *praise from the boss*   c. *early closing*
b. *a humorous incident*   d. *no impossible demands*

3. topic: nosy neighbors
details: a. *spy on you*   c. *love to gossip*
b. *ask many questions*   d. *peek through curtains*

FOCUSING THE PREWRITING

The next step of writing is to *focus your ideas around some point.* Your ideas will begin to take focus if you re-examine them, looking for *related ideas.* Two techniques that you can use are

- marking a list of related ideas
- mapping related ideas

Listing Related Ideas

To develop a marked list, take another look at the list we developed under the topic of a favorite city or town. The same list is shown below, but you will notice some of the items have been marked with symbols that show related ideas:

N marks ideas about St. Augustine's natural good points
H marks ideas about the St. Augustine's history
F marks ideas about family in St. Augustine

Here is the marked list of ideas related to the topic of a favorite city or town:

a small city	**N** *clear blue water*
no freeways	**H** *lots of history*
no skyscrapers	**H** *a fort*
not millions of people	**H** *oldest schoolhouse*
thousands of visitors every day	**F** *grandparents live there*
F *can always visit family for free*	**N** *warm in winter*
N *beach nearby*	**F** *grandparents feed me*
N *clean, big beach*	**F** *I use their car*

You have probably noticed that some items are not marked: a small city, no freeways, no skyscrapers, not millions of people, thousands of visitors every day. Perhaps you can come back to them later, or you may decide you do not need them in your paragraph.

To make it easier to see what ideas you have and how they are related, try *grouping related ideas,* giving each list a title, like this:

Natural Good Points of St. Augustine

beach nearby	*clear blue water*
clean, big beach	*warm in winter*

History in St. Augustine

lots of history	*oldest schoolhouse*
a fort	

Family in St. Augustine

can always visit family for free	*grandparents live there*
grandparents feed me	*I use their car*

Mapping

Another way to focus your ideas is to mark your first list of ideas, and then cluster the related ideas into separate lists. You can **map** your ideas, like this:

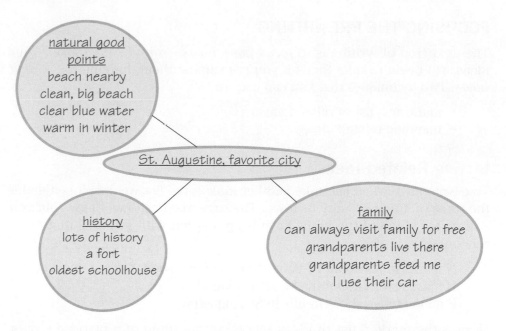

Whatever way you choose to examine and group your details, you are working toward *a focus, a point.* You are asking and beginning to answer the question, "Where do the details lead?" The answer will be the **topic sentence** of your paragraph. It will be the *main idea* of your paragraph.

Forming a Topic Sentence

To form a topic sentence, you can do the following:

1. Review your details and see if you can form some general idea that can summarize the details.
2. Write that general idea as one sentence.

Your sentence that summarizes the details is the **topic sentence**. It makes a general point, and the more specific details you have gathered will support this point.

To form a topic sentence about your favorite city, St. Augustine, review the many details you have listed about the city. It is time to ask questions about those details. You could ask yourself, "What kind of details do I have? Can I summarize them?" You might then write the summary as the topic sentence:

> *I love St. Augustine because it has sun and sea, history, and family.*

Check the sentence against your details. Does it cover the natural good points of St. Augustine? Yes. The topic sentence sums them up as *sun and sea.* Does it cover history and family? Yes. The topic sentence says the place has *history and family.*

Writing Good Topic Sentences

Be careful. *Topics are not the same as topic sentences. Topics are the subjects you will write about.* A topic sentence states the *main idea* you have developed on a topic. Consider the differences between the topics and the topic sentences on the following page:

topic: Why courtesy is important
topic sentence: Courtesy takes the conflict out of unpleasant
encounters.

topic: Dogs and their owners
topic sentence: Many dog owners begin to look like their pets.

Topic sentences *do not announce; they make a point.* Look at the sentences below, and notice the differences between the announcement sentences and the topic sentences.

announcement: I will discuss the process of changing a tire.
topic sentence: Changing a tire is easy if you have the right tools
and follow a simple process.

announcement: An analysis of why recycling paper is important will
be the subject of this paper.
topic sentence: Recycling paper is important because it saves trees,
money, and even certain animals.

Topic sentences can be too big to develop in one paragraph. A topic sentence that is *too broad* may take many paragraphs, even pages of writing, to develop. Look at the very broad sentences below, and then notice how they can be narrowed.

too broad: Athletes get paid too much money. (This sentence is too
broad because the term "athletes" could mean anything from professional boxers to college football players to neighborhood softball teams; "too much money" could mean any fee that basketball
players receive for endorsing products to bonuses that professional
football players get if they make the Super Bowl. The sentence
could also refer to all athletes in the world at any time in history.)
a narrower, better topic sentence: Last year, several professional
baseball players negotiated high but fair salaries.
too broad: I changed a great deal in my last year of high school.
(The phrase "changed a great deal" could refer to physical
changes, intellectual changes, emotional changes, changes in attitude, changes in goals, or just about any other change you can
think of.)
a narrower, better topic sentence: In my last year of high school, I
overcame my shyness.

Topic sentences can be too small to develop in one paragraph. A topic sentence that is *too narrow* cannot be supported by detail. It may be a fact, and facts cannot be developed. A topic sentence that is too narrow leaves you with nothing more to say.

too narrow: I hate broccoli.
an expanded topic sentence: I hate broccoli for two reasons.

too narrow: It takes twenty minutes to get out of the airport parking
lot.
an expanded topic sentence: Congestion at the airport parking lot
is causing problems for travelers.

The prewriting stage begins with free, unstructured thinking and writ-ing. As you work through the prewriting process, your thinking and writing will become more focused.

> **INFO BOX:** **Focusing the Prewriting: A Summary**
>
> The prewriting stage of writing a paragraph enables you to develop an idea into a topic sentence and related details. You can focus your thinking by working in steps.
>
> 1. Try marking a list of related details, or try mapping to group your ideas.
>
> 2. Write a topic sentence that summarizes your details.
>
> 3. Check that your topic sentence is a sentence, not a topic. Make sure that it is not too broad or too narrow and that it is not an announcement. Check that it makes a point and focuses the details you have developed.

Exercise 7   Grouping Related Items in Lists of Details

Below are lists of details. In each list, circle the items that seem to fit into one group; then underline the items that seem to belong to a second group. Some items may not belong in either group. The first list is done for you.

1. topic: blizzards
   underline: power outages   circle: freedom from school
   circle: sit by a warm fire   snows most in February
   circle: drink hot chocolate   underline: travel is hazardous
   circle: snuggle up with loved ones   circle: build a snowman
   weather reports   underline: damage to trees

2. topic: clothes
   jeans   shirts
   circle: evening gown   circle: silk tie
   circle: high heels   sneakers
   underwear   circle: tuxedo
   underline: sweat pants   flip flops

3. topic: listening to gossip
   underline: entertaining   about a friend
   underline: interesting   underline: flattering to be told
   circle: shameful   fear of the teller
   spreads fast   constant gossipers
   circle: petty   circle: unkind

Exercise 8   Writing Topic Sentences for Lists of Details

INSTRUCTOR'S NOTE

Answers will vary. Possible answers shown at right.

Below are lists of details that have no topic sentence. Write an appropriate topic sentence for each one.

1. topic sentence: *In many countries, a teen's transition to adulthood is marked with a celebration.*

   Latino families celebrate *quinceañera*, the fifteenth birthday of their daughters.

   Jewish families celebrate the *bar mitzvah*, or coming of age of thirteen-year-old Jewish boys.

Jewish girls have their own similar ceremony, the *bat mitzvah*.

For many American young women, a sweet sixteen party is a tradition to mark a teen's growth into adulthood.

Every year, thousands of twenty-year-old Japanese men and women come together on one day.

They participate in a traditional ceremony, similar to a graduation ceremony, with speeches and celebrations.

Wealthy parents in England and America celebrate the "coming out" into society of the teenage daughters by holding elaborate debutante balls.

2. topic sentence: *Mrs. Sung gave me tough love when I was a child.*

My neighbor, Mrs. Sung, used to share her dinner with me when my mother came home late.

For my eighth birthday, Mrs. Sung knitted me a warm woolen scarf.

Sometimes she let me hold the leash when she took her Boston terrier for a walk.

If she saw me on the street when it was getting dark, she scolded me and made me come in.

She told me I should have something better to do than hang around in the shadows.

Then she gave me a chore to do, like stacking up her old newspapers.

Of course, she always paid me with cookies.

3. topic sentence: *I never thought English and math would turn my distant roommate into my friend.*

My roommate Etienne is Haitian, so at first I had a hard time understanding his English.

He also seemed very shy.

I didn't see him much, so I figured he was socializing with his own friends and didn't like me.

Then one night I had an important algebra test to study for.

I went to the Tutoring Center to get some help with my math.

Etienne was there, wrapped up in books.

Later, I learned he was there every night, studying English, but also tutoring other people in math.

Etienne and I are good friends now; I help him with English, and he teaches me algebra.

Exercise 9 Turning Topics into Topic Sentences

Below is a list. Some of the items in the list are topic sentences, but a few are topics. Put an X by the items that are topics. On the lines below the list, rewrite the topics into topic sentences.

1. ___X___ Three ways to break up with a partner.

2. _____ The biggest surprise in my life involved a contest.

3. ___X___ Helping a friend overcome shyness and gain self-esteem.

4. _____ Worrying about the future can become an obsession.

5. _____ My father knows just how to make me feel guilty.

6. ___X___ How I got my first chance to play college basketball.

7. _____ A bad dream can be a warning.

8. _____ College costs more money than I ever imagined.

9. ___X___ Why walking is good for your health and your appearance.

10. _____ Most young adults face two difficult choices.

INSTRUCTOR'S NOTE

Answers will vary. Possible answers shown at right.

Rewrite the topics. Make each one into a topic sentence.

1. You can break up with a partner kindly, coldly, or cruelly.

3. Helping a friend overcome shyness and gain self-esteem takes

patience and tact.

6. A lucky accident got me my first chance to play college basketball.

9. Walking is good for your health and appearance.

_____

_____

Exercise 10 Revising Topic Sentences That Are Too Broad

Below is a list of topic sentences. Some of them are too broad to support in one paragraph. Put an X by the ones that are too broad. Then, on the lines below the list, rewrite each broad sentence, making it a topic sentence that could be supported in one paragraph.

1. ___X___ Life is full of coincidences and strange encounters.

2. _____ The worst part of working in an ice cream parlor was developing a hatred of ice cream.

3. ___X___ Talking it out is a good way to solve many problems.

4. ___X___ Khadeem has to learn to go for it if he wants success.

5. _____ Cooper never makes a major decision without consulting his wife.

6. _X_ American families are in danger of falling apart.

7. _____ Eating a family dinner at home is becoming a rare event for my children.

8. _X_ Parents need to watch their children's access to the Internet.

9. _____ Drivers who talk on their cell phones put me in danger.

10. _____ My sister was deeply hurt by nasty e-mail from some of her classmates.

Rewrite the broad sentences. Make each one more limited.

INSTRUCTOR'S NOTE

Answers will vary. Possible answers shown at left.

1. A coincidence brought me face-to-face with an old rival.

3. In my family, my mother insisted no one went to bed angry.

4. If Khadeem wants to own a restaurant, he has to get experience working in restaurants.

6. When parents and children lead overscheduled lives, they have little time to be close.

8. Parents need to be aware that children as young as ten have learned to use the Internet to bully their classmates.

Exercise 11   Making Announcements into Topic Sentences

Below is a list of sentences. Some are topic sentences. Some are announcements. Put an *X* by the announcements. Then, on the lines below the list, rewrite the announcements, making them into topic sentences.

1. _____ Living from paycheck to paycheck is a painful process.

2. _X_ This paper will be about the county's plan to widen Eden Highway to eight lanes.

3. _____ I have three objections to allowing people to smoke on the beach.

4. _____ Sending a greeting card to a friend can be an expensive gesture.

5. _X_ Why I couldn't survive without chocolate is the subject of my essay.

6. _X_ The constantly rising tuition at Adams Technical College is the area to be discussed.

7. _____ If I had more self-confidence, I would start looking for a better job.

8. _____ A bigger public pool could give bored teens a place to socialize in the summer.

9. __X__ This paper concerns the new dress code at Lincoln High School.

10. _____ Mr. Hernandez will be remembered for his generous support of Family Charities in our state.

INSTRUCTOR'S NOTE

Answers will vary. Possible answers shown at right.

Rewrite the announcements. Make each one a topic sentence.

2. The county's plan to widen Eden Highway to eight lanes is a foolish and even dangerous way to deal with our traffic problem.

5. Without chocolate to pick me up physically and emotionally, I couldn't survive.

6. The constantly rising tuition at Adams Technical College is keeping lower-income students from a chance for higher education.

9. The new dress code at Lincoln High School was designed to please parents.

_____

_____

Exercise 12 **Revising Topic Sentences That Are Too Narrow**

Below is a list of topic sentences. Some of them are topics that are too narrow; they cannot be developed with details. Put an *X* by the ones that are too narrow. Then, on the lines below, rewrite those sentences as broader topic sentences that could be developed in one paragraph.

1. _____ Trying to lose weight was a difficult challenge.

2. __X__ My best friend is from Korea.

3. __X__ It took me two hours to get home yesterday.

4. _____ Twenty-four hours of rain caused dangerous flooding in Hilldale.

5. _____ Lillian's Café has the best food in town.

6. __X__ Jack's Bright Lights is an electronics store.

7. _____ Rosalind Okada conquered poverty and bad health to become a psychologist.

8. __X__ Frank Kelly has a million-dollar home in Scottsdale, Arizona.

9. _____ My favorite teacher challenged me to think.

10. _____ Teaching me to drive made my father nervous and crabby.

Rewrite the narrow sentences. Make each one broader.

INSTRUCTOR'S NOTE

Answers will vary. Possible answers shown at left.

2. Because my best friend is from Korea, I have to explain many silly American customs to him.

3. It took me two hours to get home yesterday because the construction on the turnpike is making travel impossible.

6. Jack's Bright Lights is the only local electronics store with a helpful staff.

8. Frank Kelly's million-dollar home in Scottsdale, Arizona, is his reward for years of physical endurance and football injuries.

PLANNING   Devising a Plan for a Paragraph

Checking Your Details

Once you have a topic sentence, you can begin working on an **outline** for your paragraph. The outline is a plan that helps you stay focused in your writing. The outline begins to form when you write your topic sentence and write your list of details beneath the topic sentence. You can now look at your list and ask yourself an important question: "Do I have **enough details** to **support** my topic sentence?" Remember, your goal is to write a paragraph of seven to twelve sentences.

Consider this topic sentence and list of details:

topic sentence: People can be very rude when they shop in super-markets.

details: push in line
express lane
too many items

Does the list contain enough details for a paragraph of seven to twelve sentences? Probably not.

Adding Details When There Are Not Enough

To add details, try brainstorming. Ask yourself some questions like these:

Where else in supermarkets are people rude?
Are they rude in other lanes besides the express lane?
Are they rude in the aisles? How?
Is there crowding anywhere? Where?

By brainstorming, you might come up with these details:

topic sentence: People can be very rude when they shop in super-markets.

details: push in line
express lane

> too many items
> hit my cart with theirs in aisles
> block aisles while they decide
> push ahead in deli area
> will not take a number
> argue with cashier over prices
> yell at the bagger

Keep brainstorming until you feel you have enough details for a seven-to-twelve-sentence paragraph. Remember that it is better to have too many details than too few, for you can always edit the extra details later.

If you try brainstorming and still do not have many details, you can refer to your original ideas—your freewriting or journal—for other details.

Eliminating Details That Do Not Relate to the Topic Sentence

Sometimes, what you thought were good details do not relate to the topic sentence because they do not fit or support your point. Eliminate details that do not relate to the topic sentence. For example, the following list contains a few details that really do not relate to the topic sentence. Those details are crossed out.

topic sentence:	Waiters have to be very patient in dealing with their customers.
details:	customers take a long time ordering
	~~waiter's salary is low~~
	waiters have to explain specials twice
	customers send orders back
	customers blame waiters for any delays
	customers want food instantly
	waiters can't react to sarcasm of customers
	waiters can't get angry if customer gets angry
	~~waiters work long shifts~~
	customers change their mind after ordering

From List to Outline

Take another look at the topic sentence and list of details on a favorite city or town:

topic sentence:	I love St. Augustine because it has sun and sea, history, and family	
details:	a small city	clear blue water
	no freeways	lots of history
	no skyscrapers	a fort
	not millions of people	oldest schoolhouse
	thousands of visitors every day	grandparents live there
	can always visit family for free	warm in winter
	beach nearby	grandparents feed me
	clean, big beach	I use their car

After you scan that list, you are ready to develop the outline of the paragraph.

An outline is a plan for writing, and it can be a type of draft in list form. It sketches what you want to write and the order in which you want to present it. *An organized, logical list will make your writing unified since each item on the list will relate to your topic sentence.*

When you plan, keep your topic sentence in mind:

I love St. Augustine because it has <u>sun</u> and <u>sea</u>, <u>history</u>, and <u>family</u>.

Notice the underlined key words, which lead to three key parts of your outline:

> sun and sea
> history
> family

You can put the details on your list together so that they connect to one of these parts:

sun and sea

> beach nearby, clean, big beach, clear blue water, warm in winter

history

> lots of history, a fort, oldest schoolhouse

family

> can always visit family for free, grandparents live there, grandparents feed me, I drive their car

With this kind of grouping, you have a clearer idea of how to organize a paragraph.

Now that you have grouped your ideas with key words and details, you can write an outline.

An Outline for a Paragraph

topic sentence:	I love St. Augustine because it has sun and sea, history, and family.
details: sun and sea	It is warm in the winter. There is a beach nearby. It is big and clean. The water is clear blue.
history	It has lots of history. There is a fort. The oldest schoolhouse is there.
family	My grandparents live in St. Augustine. I stay at their house. They feed me. I use their car.

As you can see, the outline combined some of the details from the list. Even with these combinations, the details are very rough in style. As you reread the list of details, you will notice places that need more combining, places where ideas need more explaining, and places that are repetitive. Keep in mind that an outline is merely a very rough organization of your paragraph.

As you work through the steps of devising an outline, you can check for the following:

INSTRUCTOR'S NOTE

The outlines for paragraph assignments in this book are simplified, detail-listing formats for easy student reference. In Chapter 11, Writing an Essay, students will be introduced to Roman numeral and Arabic letter outlines.

Checklist: A Checklist for an Outline

✔ **Unity:** Do all the details relate to the topic sentence? If they do, the paragraph will be unified.

✔ **Support:** Do you have enough supporting ideas? Can you add to these ideas with even more specific details?

✔ **Coherence:** Are the details listed in the right order? If the order of points is logical, the paragraph will be coherent.

COHERENCE: PUTTING YOUR DETAILS IN PROPER ORDER

Check the sample outline again, and you will notice that the details are grouped in the same order as the topic sentence: first, details about sun and sea; next, details about history; last, details about family in St. Augustine. Putting the details in an order that matches the topic sentence is a logical order for this paragraph.

Putting the details in logical order makes the ideas in your paragraph easy to follow. The most logical order for a paragraph depends on the subject of the paragraph. If you are writing about an event, you might use **time order** (such as telling what happened first, second, and so forth); if you are arguing some point, you might use **emphatic order** (such as saving your most convincing idea for last); if you are describing a room, you might use **space order** (such as from left to right, or from top to bottom).

The format of the outline helps to organize your ideas. The topic sentence is written above the list of details. This position helps you to remember that the topic sentence is the *main idea*, and the details that support it are written under it. The topic sentence is the most important sentence of the paragraph. You can easily check the items on your list, one by one, against your main idea. You can also develop the *unity* (relevance) and *coherence* (logical order) of your details.

When you actually write a paragraph, the topic sentence does not necessarily have to be the first sentence in the paragraph. Read the paragraphs below, and notice where each topic sentence is placed.

Topic Sentence at the Beginning of the Paragraph

<u>Watching a horror movie on the late show can keep me up all night</u>. The movie itself scares me to death, especially if it involves a creepy character sneaking up on someone in the dark. After the movie, I'm afraid to turn out all the lights and be alone in the dark. Then every little noise seems like the sound of a sinister intruder. Strange shapes seem to appear in the shadows. My closet becomes a place where someone could be hiding. There might even be a creature under the bed! And if I go to sleep, these strange invaders might appear from under the bed or in the closet.

Topic Sentence in the Middle of the Paragraph

The kitchen counters gleamed. In the spice rack, every jar was organized neatly. The sink was polished, and not one spot marred its surface. The stove burners were surrounded by dazzling stainless steel rings. <u>The chef kept an immaculate kitchen</u>. There were no finger marks on the refrigerator door. No sticky spots dirtied the floor. No crumbs hid behind the toaster.

INSTRUCTOR'S NOTE

Some students may have been taught that topic sentences should always be placed at the beginning of a formal paragraph. If they are uncomfortable with options, you can reassure them that many instructors prefer topic sentences at the beginning. Your colleagues or department curriculum/exit test may prefer such a structure.

Topic Sentence at the End of the Paragraph

On long summer evenings, we would play softball in the street. Sometimes we'd play until it was so dark we could barely see the ball. Then our mothers would come to the front steps of the row houses and call us in, telling us to stop our play. But we'd pretend we couldn't hear them. If they insisted, we'd beg for a few minutes more or for just one more game. It was so good to be outdoors with our friends. It was warm, and we knew we had weeks of summer vacation ahead. There was no school in the morning; there would be more games to play. <u>We loved those street games on summer nights</u>.

> Many of your paragraph assignments will require a clear topic sentence, so be sure you follow your own instructor's directions about placement of the topic sentence.

Exercise 13   **Adding Details to Support a Topic Sentence**

The topic sentences below have some—but not enough—details. Write sentences to add details to the list below each topic sentence.

1. **topic sentence:** My coworker is making my job unbearable.

    a. When he is late for work, he expects me to cover up for him.

    b. He also sneaks out early at least twice a week and asks me to lie for him.

    c. I get stuck doing all the work he avoids by being absent.

    d. *He teases me constantly.*

    e. *He makes fun of me in front of the other workers.*

    f. *He spreads nasty rumors about anyone who crosses him.*

    g. *He is a bully.*

INSTRUCTOR'S NOTE

Answers will vary. Possible answers shown at left.

2. **topic sentence:** Sometimes my mother nags me excessively.

    a. She always pushes me to take a shower and dress respectably.

    b. *She constantly reminds me to clean my room.*

    c. *My mother pushes me to call my grandmother.*

    d. *She nags me about skipping breakfast.*

    e. *She lectures me if I come home late.*

    f. *In the car, she always warns me about driving too fast.*

    g. *She cannot stop complaining about my tattoo.*

3. **topic sentence:** Learning to live with a roommate can be stressful.

   a. Roommates may have different sleep schedules.

   b. Sharing a refrigerator can lead to disagreements.

   c. Learning to respect each other's privacy takes time.

   d. *Roommates have to agree on rules for overnight guests.*

   e. *Sharing expenses like rent demands responsibility.*

   f. *Parties in the apartment can test a friendship.*

   g. *"Borrowing" items without permission is not a good idea,*

Exercise 14 Eliminating Details That Do Not Fit

Below are topic sentences and lists of supporting details. Cross out the details that do not fit the topic sentence.

1. **topic sentence:** Gas for my car costs so much that I have cut spending on my social life.

   details: I bought a used SUV, which is big and solid.
   It also guzzles expensive, high-octane gas.
   My gas money is coming from what used to be my funds for fun.
   ~~Everybody needs to have some fun occasionally.~~
   Today, I pick a cheap restaurant when I meet my friends.
   I go to free concerts instead of seeing star performers on tour.
   ~~Everywhere I look, I see people lining up when they spot a bargain at a gas station.~~

2. **topic sentence:** Cell phones offer many distractions.

   details: When people standing in line are bored, they use their cell phones to call their friends.
   ~~Some scientists say cell phones are dangerous to a person's health.~~
   Students who are not interested in class send text messages on their cell phones.
   In some cases, students attending lectures play games on their cell phones.
   ~~Today cell phones offer many kinds of musical rings.~~
   People stuck in traffic make calls on their cell phones to make the time go faster.
   Sometimes, people at a dull meeting use their cell phones to check their e-mail.

Exercise 15 Coherence: Putting Details in the Right Order

These outlines have details that are in the wrong order. In the space provided, number the sentences in the right order: 1 would be the number for the first sentence, and so on.

1. topic sentence: Renewing my driver's license turned out to be a day-long ordeal.

___6___ Once I reached the front of the outdoor line, I was allowed indoors.

___1___ I arrived at the driver's license office half an hour after opening time.

___4___ Guarding the office door was a large person who told me to stay outside and get in line.

___2___ Before I had even found a parking space, I noticed a line of at least fifty people standing outside the office.

___5___ Afraid of the large person, I joined the back of the line and stood outside in the sun for three hours.

___7___ Finally allowed indoors, I joined a huge line of tired and frustrated people.

___3___ From the parking lot, I headed straight to the office, planning to go inside and ask how long the wait would be.

___8___ After two more hours, I reached the front of the inside line and stood in front of a clerk.

___9___ Getting from the clerk to the cashier took only ninety minutes, the shortest part of my long day.

2. topic sentence: Paying bills is an unpleasant chore for me.

___2___ After I gather all the bills, I sort them into the ones I have to pay immediately and the ones I can avoid a little longer.

___4___ Once I have all the bills sorted, I reluctantly pull out my checkbook.

___1___ It starts when I gather all the bills I have scattered in my house.

___5___ Depression leads to determination as I write a check for each urgent bill and put the others aside.

___3___ As I sort, I feel depressed about the money I owe.

___6___ Once the checks and bills are in their envelopes, I search the house for stamps.

___7___ Eventually, I manage to find enough postage to send all the bills.

___8___ As I walk to the mailbox, I congratulate myself on surviving another round of bill paying.

DRAFTING Drafting and Revising a Paragraph

Drafting a Paragraph

The outline is a draft in list form. You are now ready to write the list in paragraph form, to "rough out" a draft of your assignment. This stage of writing is the time to draft, revise, edit, and draft again. You may write several drafts in this stage, but don't think of this as an unnecessary chore or a punishment.

It is a way of taking the pressure off yourself. By revising in steps, you are reminding yourself that the first try does not have to be perfect.

Review the outline on a favorite city or town on page 21. You can create a first draft of this outline in the form of a paragraph. (Remember that the first line of each paragraph is indented). In the draft of the paragraph below, the first sentence of the paragraph is the topic sentence.

A First Draft of a Paragraph

I love St. Augustine because it has sun and sea, history, and family. St. Augustine is warm in the winter. There is a beach nearby. It is clean and big. The water is clear blue. St. Augustine has lots of history. There is an old stone fort. The oldest schoolhouse is there. I can always visit my family for free. My grandparents live in St. Augustine. They feed me. I use their car.

Revising

Once you have a first draft, you can begin to think about revising and editing it. **Revising** means rewriting the draft by making changes in the structure, the order of the sentences, and the content. **Editing** includes making changes in the choice of words, the selection of details, the punctuation, and the pattern and kinds of sentences. It may also include **adding transitions**, which are words, phrases, or sentences that link ideas.

One way to begin revising and editing is to read your work aloud to yourself. Listen to your words, and consider the following questions.

TEACHING TIP

Remind students that revising a first draft can take considerable time. Rearranging the sequence of points and adding more details may require revisiting the outline and changing and extending it. Students should periodically review this checklist as they revise their draft(s).

Checklist: A Checklist for Revising the Draft of a Paragraph (with key terms)

✔ Am I staying on my point? (unity)

✔ Should I take out any ideas that do not relate? (unity)

✔ Do I have enough to say about my point? (support)

✔ Should I add any details? (support)

✔ Should I change the order of my sentences? (coherence)

✔ Is my choice of words appropriate? (style)

✔ Is my choice of words repetitive? (style)

✔ Are my sentences too long? Too short? (style)

✔ Should I combine any sentences? (style)

✔ Am I running sentences together? (grammar)

✔ Am I writing complete sentences? (grammar)

✔ Can I link my ideas more smoothly? (transitions)

If you apply the checklist to the draft of the paragraph on a favorite city or town, you will probably find these rough spots:

- The sentences are very short and choppy.
- Some sentences could be combined.

- Some words are repeated often.
- Some ideas would be more effective if they were supported by more details.
- The paragraph could use a few transitions.

Consider the following revised draft of the paragraph, and notice the changes, underlined, that have been made in the draft:

A Revised Draft of a Paragraph

topic sentence:	I love St. Augustine, <u>Florida</u>, because it has sun and
sentences combined	sea, history, and family. <u>St. Augustine is warm in the win-</u>
transition added	<u>ter, and a big, clean beach with clear blue water is nearby.</u>
sentences combined,	<u>In addition, St. Augustine has lots of history, including an</u>
transition added	<u>old stone fort that looks out on the water.</u> It <u>also</u> has the
details added,	oldest schoolhouse <u>in America, a tiny wooden building</u>.
transition added,	<u>Best of all</u>, my grandparents live in St. Augustine. They are
details added	<u>my favorite relatives</u>, and <u>they make me feel very wel-</u>
sentences combined	<u>come</u>. <u>When I am in St. Augustine, I stay with them,</u> enjoy
	<u>their food, and use their car.</u>

When you are revising your own paragraph, you can use the checklist to help you. Read the checklist several times; then reread your draft, looking for answers to the questions on the list. If your instructor agrees, you can work with your classmates. You can read your draft to a partner or a group. Your listener(s) can react to your draft by applying the questions on the checklist and by making notes about your draft as you read. When you are finished reading aloud, your partner(s) can discuss the notes about your work.

TEACHING TIP

Groupwork: The Peer Review Form on page 37 can help students refine their drafts, and it can reinforce the importance of careful editing. (A Peer Review Form is at the end of each writing chapter.)

Exercise 16   Revising a Draft by Combining Sentences

The paragraph below has many short, choppy sentences. The short, choppy sentences are underlined. Wherever you see two or more underlined sentences clustered next to each other, combine the clustered sentences into one clear, smooth sentence. Write your revised version of the paragraph in the spaces above the lines.

INSTRUCTOR'S NOTE

For more on combining short sentences, see Sentence Variety, Chapter 36.

Paragraph to be revised:

INSTRUCTOR'S NOTE

Answers will vary. Possible answers shown at left.

Joseph, my

Joseph is a great friend to me, but he has one annoying habit. <u>Joseph is my</u>
cousin, is helping me to build an addition to my house.
<u>cousin. He is helping me to build an addition to my house</u>. Without Joseph, I
I can't do the skilled carpentry
would never be able to complete my project. <u>I can't do the skilled carpentry</u>
myself, nor can I afford to pay a carpenter.
<u>myself. I can't afford to pay a carpenter</u>. Joseph works in construction and has
In addition, he is so generous that he won't take
years of experience in carpentry. <u>In addition, he is generous. He won't take</u>
any money from me.
<u>any money from me</u>. All he asks for is lunch or dinner. Unfortunately, Joseph's
I like music, too, but
work costs me my patience. He can't work without music. <u>I like music, too.</u>
Joseph loves one horrible radio station and blasts it for hours.
<u>Joseph loves one horrible radio station. He blasts it for hours.</u> I hear it when he is

working on the roof. I hear it even when he is pounding nails into heavy boards.

Once I have my addition completed, I will love the new space. However, I will

always remember that horrible music.

Collaborate

Exercise 17 Adding Details to a Draft

Complete this exercise with a partner or a group. The paragraph below lacks the kind of details that would make it more interesting. Working with a partner or a group, add the details to the blank spaces provided. When you are finished with the additions, read the revised paragraph to the class.

Paragraph to be revised:

While many college students say they are too busy to watch television, most

have one or two programs they tune into frequently. These programs can be real-

ity shows such as _____ and _____, which have many loyal

viewers. Other students are fans of sports programs and will stay up late to watch

_____ games or _____ tournaments. When it comes to

music programming, shows featuring performers like _____ and

_____ appeal to many viewers age eighteen to twenty-five, while older

viewers may turn to programs with stars such as _____ and _____.

Everyone has his or her favorite comedians, and college students may tune into

comedians like _____ or _____ on programs such as

_____ and _____. Clearly, television may not be a constant

source of entertainment for students, but it offers some escape from the studying,

jobs, and other responsibilities of college life.

POLISHING   Polishing and Proofreading a Paragraph

The final version of your paragraph is the result of careful thinking, planning, and revising. After writing as many drafts as it takes, you read to polish and proofread. You can avoid too many last-minute corrections if you check your last draft carefully. Check that draft for

- spelling errors
- punctuation errors
- word choice
- a final statement

Take a look at the last draft of the paragraph on a favorite city or town. Wherever something is crossed out, the draft has been corrected directly above the crossed-out material. At the end of the paragraph, you will notice a concluding sentence has been added to unify the paragraph.

Correcting the Last Draft of a Paragraph

Florida

I love St. Augustine, ~~Fla.~~, because it has sun and sea, history, and fam-

winter

ily. St. Augustine is warm in the ~~Winter~~, and a large, clean beach with clear

blue   *lots*

~~blew~~ water is nearby. In addition, St. Augustine has ~~lot's~~ of history, includ-

has

ing an old stone fort that looks out on the water. It also ~~have~~ the oldest

schoolhouse in America, a tiny wooden building. Best of all, my grandpar-

ents live in St. Augustine. They are my favorite relatives, and they make me

feel

~~fell~~ very welcome. When I am in St. Augustine, I stay with them, enjoy their

their

food, and use ~~there~~ car. St. Augustine has the perfect natural advantages,

connections

history, and family ~~connection~~ to make it my favorite city.

Giving Your Paragraph a Title

When you prepare the final version of your paragraph, you may be asked to give it a title. The title should be short and should fit the subject of the paragraph. For example, an appropriate title for the paragraph on a favorite city or town could be "My Favorite City" or "The City I Love." Check with your instructor to see if your paragraph needs a title. In this book, the paragraphs do not have titles.

The Final Version of a Paragraph

Following is the final version of the paragraph on a favorite city or town. As you read it, you will notice a few more changes. Even though the paragraph went through several drafts and many revisions, the final copy still reflects some additional polishing: some details have been added, some have been made more specific, and some words have been changed. These changes were made as the final version was prepared. (They are underlined for your reference.)

INSTRUCTOR'S NOTE

Students may mistakenly underline titles, place quotation marks around them, or capitalize each letter. If you require titles on student submissions, remind them about avoiding these pitfalls. For more on punctuating and capitalizing titles, see Chapter 29.

A Final Version of a Paragraph

(Changes from the previous draft are underlined.)

     I love St. Augustine, <u>Florida</u>, because it has sun and sea, history, and family. St. Augustine is warm in the winter, and a <u>wide</u>, clean beach with clear blue water is <u>ten minutes away</u>. In addition, St. Augustine is <u>filled with</u> history, including an old stone fort that looks out on the water. It also has the oldest schoolhouse in America, a tiny wooden building <u>smaller than a two-car garage</u>. Best of all, my grandparents live in St. Augustine. They are my favorite relatives, and they make me feel very welcome. When I am in St. Augustine, I stay with them, enjoy their <u>delicious Spanish</u> food, and use their car. St. Augustine has the natural advantages, history, and family connections to make it my favorite city.

Reviewing the Writing Process

This chapter has taken you through four important stages in writing. As you become more comfortable with them, you will be able to work through them more quickly. For now, try to remember the four stages.

INFO BOX: **The Stages of the Writing Process**

Prewriting: gathering and developing ideas, thinking on paper through freewriting, brainstorming, mapping, or keeping a journal.

Planning: planning the paragraph by combining and dividing details, focusing the details with a topic sentence, listing the supporting details in proper order, and devising an outline.

Drafting: writing a rough draft of the paragraph, then revising and editing it several times.

Polishing: preparing the final version of the paragraph, with one last proofreading check for careless errors in preparation, punctuation, and spelling.

Exercise 18 **Proofreading to Prepare the Final Version**

Following are two paragraphs with the kinds of errors that are easy to overlook when you prepare the final version of an assignment. Correct the errors by writing above the lines. There are twelve errors in the first paragraph and thirteen errors in the second paragraph.

1. My night class is different from my day class in both length and atmosphere.
one   *it's*   *hours*   *listen*
For on thing, its three hour's long, which is a long time to sit and lissen to a teacher
                                                           Fortunately
talk Most of my day classes last an hour and fifteen minutes. Fortunatly, my night

                                                                   ,
instructor gives us a break after the first half of class and in the second half of the
                               activities   *than*
class, we do group work. The group activitys are more interesting then the lecture.

The second difference between my night and day classes is the students. The night
                         no comma needed
students are older, than the day students and more serious. These older students
                  around
don't fool aroun in class; instead, they want to get the job done. I like the studious
                                                       alert
environment in my night class, but I think it is hard to stay allert for three hours.

                               their parents
2. Disrespect for there parent's is spreading among small children. This dis-
                                               whining
respect is not the typical childish behavior of whinning, begging, and acting up to
                                                      When
gain attention. It is rude, open, and insulting defiance. when they cannot get what
                                                              sometimes
they want children as young as four or five call their parents names; some times
                               no comma needed   *is*
these names include dirty words. The new, version of children's tantrums are
                    has
worse. Everyone have seen the typical crying and screaming of a child's tantrum.

biting These

However the new form of tantrum can include kicking, pulling, or biteing. This

tantrums can be very public rebellions in a supermarket, parking lot, or restau-

family

rant. In a restaurant, an angry child may throw food on the floor or at a Family

member. The poor parents caught in this loud demonstration of a child's anger

must feel hidden rage and public shame.

Lines of Detail: A Walk-Through Assignment

This assignment involves working within a group to write a paragraph.

Step 1: Read the three sentences below. Pick the one sentence you
prefer as a possible topic sentence for a paragraph. Fill in the
blank for the sentence you chose.

a. The most frightening movie I've ever seen was

_____ (fill in the title).

b. If money were no problem, the car I'd buy is

_____ (fill in the name of the car).

c. The one food I refuse to eat is _____

(fill in the name of the food).

Step 2: Join a group composed of other students who picked the
same topic sentence you picked. In your class, you'll have
"movie" people, "car" people, and "food" people. Brainstorm
in a group. Discuss questions that could be used to get ideas
for your paragraph.

Collaborate

For the movie topic, sample questions could include,
"What was the most frightening part of the movie?" or "What
kind of movie was it—a ghost story, a horror movie, etc.?" For
the car topic, sample questions could include, "Have you ever
driven this kind of car?" or "Do you know anyone who has
one?" For the food topic, sample questions could include, "Did
you hate this food when you were a child?" or "Where has this
food been served to you?"

As you discuss, write the questions, not the answers,
below. Keep the questions flowing. Do not stop to say, "That's
silly," or "I can't answer that." Try to devise **at least ten
questions.**

Ten Brainstorming Questions:

1. _____

2. _____

3. _____

4. _____

5. _____

6. _____

7. _____

8. _____

9. _____

10. _____

Step 3: Split up. Alone, begin to think on paper. Answer as many questions as you can, or add more questions and answers, or freewrite.

Step 4: Draft an outline of the paragraph. You will probably have to change the topic sentence to fit the details you have gathered. For example, your new topic sentence might be something like

_____ was the most frightening movie I have

ever seen; it creates fear by using _____,

_____, and _____.

or

If money were no problem, I would buy a _____

for its performance, _____, and _____.

or

I refuse to eat _____ because _____.

Remember to look at your details to see where they lead you. The details will help you to refine your topic sentence.

Step 5: Prepare the first draft of the paragraph.

Step 6: Read the draft aloud to your writing group, the same people who met to brainstorm. Ask each member of your group to make at least one positive comment and one suggestion for revision.

Step 7: Revise and edit your draft, considering the group's ideas and your own ideas for improvement.

Step 8: Prepare a final version of the paragraph.

Writing Your Own Paragraph

When you write on any of these topics, follow the four basic stages of the writing process in preparing your paragraph.

1. Begin this assignment with a partner. The assignment requires an interview. Your final goal is to write a paragraph that will introduce a class member, your partner, to the rest of the class. In the final paragraph, you may design your own topic sentence or use one of the topic sentences below, filling in the blanks with the material you have discovered:

Collaborate

There are several details you should know about

_____ (fill in your partner's name).

or

Three unusual events have happened to

_____ (fill in your partner's name).

Before you write the paragraph, follow these steps:

Step 1: Prepare to interview a classmate. Make a list of six questions you might want to ask. They can be questions like, "Where are you from?" or "Have you ever done anything unusual?" Write *at least six questions* before you start the interview. List the questions on the following interview form, leaving room to fill in short answers later.

Interview Form

Question 1: _____

Answer: _____

Question 2: _____

Answer: _____

Question 3: _____

Answer: _____

Question 4: _____

Answer: _____

Question 5: _____

Answer: _____

Question 6: _____

Answer: _____

Additional questions and answers: _____

_____

_____

_____

Step 2: Meet and interview your partner. Ask the questions on your list. Jot down brief answers. Ask *any other questions* you think of as you are talking; write down the answers on the additional lines at the end of the interview form.

Step 3: Change places. Let your partner interview you.

Step 4: Split up. Use the list of questions and answers about your partner as the prewriting part of your assignment. Work on the planning and draft steps.

Step 5: Ask your partner to read the draft version of your paragraph, write any comments or suggestions for improvement below the paragraph, and mark any spelling or grammar errors in the paragraph itself.

Step 6: When you have completed a final version of the paragraph, read the paragraph to the class.

2. Below are some topic sentences. Select one and use it to write a paragraph.

I am easily irritated by _____.

My first experience with college registration was _____.

High school students should never forget that _____.

3. Write a paragraph on one of the topics below. Create your own topic sentence; explain and support it with specific details.

a favorite activity   a dreaded chore   a challenging class
a special song   a treasured toy   a patriotic moment

4. Examine the two photographs of families on the next page. After you have looked at them carefully, write a paragraph with this topic sentence:

Families can be as varied as their members.

You can write about many kinds of families, not just the kinds shown in the photographs.

5. Examine the photograph of the dog above. After you have looked at it carefully, write a paragraph with this topic sentence:

   Some owners treat their pets like people.

   The details of the photograph can provide you with some details, but come up with other details on your own.

> **Note:** Additional writing options can be found after the professional reading "Getting Carded," which begins on page 599.

How Do I Get a Better Grade?

Visit www.mywritinglab.com for audio-visual lectures and additional practice sets about writing a paragraph.

Get a better grade with MyWritingLab!

Name: _____   Section: _____

Peer Review Form for a Paragraph

After you have written a draft of your paragraph, let a writing partner read it. When your partner has completed the form below, discuss the comments. Then repeat the same process for your partner's paragraph.

The topic sentence of this paragraph is _____

_____

_____

_____

The detail that I liked best begins with the words _____

_____

The paragraph has _____ (enough, too many, too few) details to support

the topic sentence.

A particularly good part of the paragraph begins with the words _____

_____

I have questions about or would like to know more about _____

_____

Other comments on the paragraph: _____

_____

_____

_____

_____

_____

_____

_____

_____

Reviewer's Name: _____

CHAPTER 2

Jumping In

School spirit can be exhibited in a variety of ways, including fans' enthusiastic support of athletic teams. Is school spirit evident at your institution? Are there silly ways students express school spirit? Are there major events? By answering such questions, you will be **illustrating** ways students exhibit pride in their school.

INSTRUCTOR'S NOTE

The writing term *illustration* is synonymous with *exemplification*. Beginning writing students may grasp the former term more easily since they will *illustrate* their main idea by providing specific examples.

Illustration

WHAT IS ILLUSTRATION?

Illustration uses specific examples to support a general point. In your writing, you often use illustration because you frequently want to support a point by providing a specific example.

Hints for Writing an Illustration Paragraph

Knowing What Is Specific and What Is General A *general* statement is a broad point. The following statements are general:

> Traffic can be bad on Hamilton Boulevard.
> Car insurance costs more today than it did last year.
> It is difficult to meet people at my college.

You can support a general statement with specific examples:

general statement: Traffic can be bad on Hamilton Boulevard.
specific examples: During the morning rush hour, the exit to First Avenue is jammed.
If there is an accident, cars can be backed up for a mile.

general statement:	Car insurance costs more today than it did last year.
specific examples:	Last year I paid $150 a month; this year I pay $200 a month.
	My mother, who has never had a traffic ticket, has seen her insurance premium rise 50 percent.
general statement:	It is difficult to meet people at my college.
specific examples:	After class, most students rush to their jobs.
	There are very few places to sit and talk between classes.

When you write an illustration paragraph, be careful to support a general statement with specific examples, not with more general statements:

NOT THIS: general statement:	College is harder than I thought it would be.
~~**more general statements:**~~	~~It is tough to be a college student.~~ ~~Studying takes a lot of my time.~~
BUT THIS: general statement:	College is harder than I thought it would be.
specific examples:	I cannot afford to miss any classes.
	I have to study at least two hours a day.

If you remember to illustrate a broad statement with specific examples, you will have the key to this kind of paragraph.

Exercise 1 Recognizing Broad Statements

Each list below contains one broad statement and three specific examples. Underline the broad statement.

1. Between classes, I spend money at the vending machines.

A parking sticker for my car cost money.

I have to pay to use a printer at the computer lab.

College expenses include many unexpected items.

2. My ex-boyfriend felt obligated to tell me all my faults.

Sometimes tact is more useful than complete honesty.

When a friend asked me for an honest opinion of his looks, I gave it and lost the friend.

I began to dislike a friend who told me the nasty gossip she heard about me.

3. Single parents face particular challenges in daily life.

Single parents need to find reliable, affordable child care if they want to go to school or work.

The responsibilities of raising a child alone can overwhelm a parent.

A single parent has to struggle to find time for a social life.

4. Airlines charge more for tickets when fuel costs rise.

Food prices rise because delivery to supermarkets costs more.

<u>A rise in oil prices affects everybody.</u>

For many homeowners, home heating costs increase.

 Exercise 2   **Distinguishing the General Statement From the Specific Example**

Each general statement below is supported by three items of support. Two of these items are specific examples; one is too general to be effective. Underline the one that is too general.

1. **general statement:**   If you walk a dog, you will get to know everyone in the neighborhood.
   support: Other dog owners will stop to talk.
   <u>Neighbors will become acquainted with you.</u>
   Children will want to pet your dog.

2. **general statement:**   Asian food is becoming increasingly popular.
   support: Prepackaged sushi is available at the supermarket.
   <u>Everybody likes some form of Asian food.</u>
   Noodles (from noodle shops or in instant packets) are as popular as spaghetti.

3. **general statement:**   Grandparents can hold families together.
   support: Several generations gather at the grandparents' house regularly.
   <u>Without grandparents, some families would fall apart.</u>
   Some grandparents are raising their grandchildren.

4. **general statement:**   Teenage girls love jewelry.
   support: <u>Adolescent females crave jewelry.</u>
   Thirteen-year-old girls adore beads around their necks and wrists.
   Girls can't wait to pierce their ears and wear stylish earrings.

Collaborate

Exercise 3   **Adding Specific Examples to a General Statement**

With a partner or group, add four specific examples to each of the following general statements.

1. **general statement:**   Many children have typical childhood fears.

   examples: _Some children are afraid of the dark._

   Others are afraid of going in the water.

   Children may also be frightened of monsters.

   Some are afraid of dogs.

2. **general statement:**   These days, pizza toppings can include almost anything.

   examples: _Barbecued or buffalo chicken tops pizza._

   There are pizzas topped with shrimp.

Some pizzas are covered with vegetables.

Other pizzas have lasagna toppings.

3. general statement: People have a number of ways of saying "I'm sorry" without actually saying those words.

examples: *Some just say, "Oops!"*

Others say, "My fault."

"Excuse me" is another way of apologizing.

Others say, "What a dumb thing for me to do!"

4. general statement: Men are likely to receive the same birthday gifts every year.

examples: *Fathers are likely to receive sweaters.*

Boyfriends are used to receiving cologne.

Husbands may get sport shirts.

Almost every man gets gadgets.

WRITING THE ILLUSTRATION PARAGRAPH IN STEPS

PREWRITING   Gathering Ideas: Illustration

Suppose your instructor asks you to write a paragraph about some aspect of **clothes**. You can begin by thinking about your subject to gather ideas and to find a focus for your paragraph. Looking through entries in your journal might lead you to the following underlined entry:

Journal Entry About Clothes

I went to the mall yesterday to look for some <u>good shoes</u>. What a crowd! Some big sale was going on, and the stores were packed. Everybody was pushing and shoving. I just left. I'll go when it's not so crowded. I hate <u>buying clothes and shoes</u>. Wish I could just wear <u>jeans and tee shirts</u> all the time. But even then, the <u>jeans have to have the right label</u>, or you're looked down on. There are <u>status labels on the tee shirts</u>, too. Not to mention <u>expensive athletic shoes</u>.

The underlined terms can lead you to a list:

good shoes   jeans have to have the right label
buying clothes and shoes   status labels on tee shirts
jeans and tee shirts   expensive athletic shoes

Consider the underlined terms. Many of them are specific ideas about clothes. You could write a paragraph about one item or about several related items on the list.

Adding Details to an Idea

Looking at the list on the page 41, you might decide you want to write something about this topic: *tee shirts*. To add details, you decide to brainstorm:

Who wears tee shirts?

Athletes, children, teens, movie stars, musicians, parents, older people, restaurant workers.

How much do they cost?

Some are cheap, but some are expensive.

What kinds of tees are there?

Sports tees, concert tees, college names on tees, designer tees, ads on tees.

Why do people wear tees?

They're comfortable and fashionable.

What ads are on tees?

Beer, sporting goods.

What else do you see on tees?

Mickey Mouse, seascapes, political slogans, souvenir pictures or sayings.

You now have this list of ideas connected to the topic of tee shirts:

status labels on tees	*concert tees*
athletes	*college names on tees*
children	*designer tees*
teens	*ads on tees*
movie stars	*comfortable*
musicians	*fashionable*
parents	*beer*
older people	*sporting goods*
restaurant workers	*Mickey Mouse*
cheap	*seascapes*
expensive	*political slogans*
sports tees	*souvenir pictures or sayings*

Creating a Topic Sentence

If you examine this list, looking for *related ideas*, you can create a topic sentence. The ideas on the list include (1) details about the kinds of people who wear tee shirts, (2) details about the cost of tee shirts, and (3) details about what is pictured or written on tee shirts. Not all the details fit into these three categories, but many do.

Grouping the related ideas into the three categories can help you focus your ideas into a topic sentence.

Kinds of People Who Wear Tee Shirts

athletes	*movie stars*	*older people*
children	*musicians*	*restaurant workers*
teens	*parents*	

The Cost of Tee Shirts

cheap	*some expensive*

What Is Pictured or Written on Tee Shirts

ads on tees	beer ads	seascapes
concert tees	sporting goods	political slogans
college names	Mickey Mouse	souvenir pictures or sayings

You can summarize these related ideas in a topic sentence:

People of various backgrounds and ages wear all kinds of tee shirts.

Check the sentence against your details. Does it cover the people who wear tees? Does it cover what is on the shirts?

Yes. The topic sentence says, "*People of various backgrounds and ages* wear *all kinds* of tee shirts." The topic sentence has given you a focus for your illustration paragraph.

Exercise 4 Finding Specific Ideas in Freewriting

Following are two samples of freewriting. Each is a response to a broad topic. Read each sample, and then underline any words that could become a more specific topic for a paragraph.

Freewriting Reaction to the Topic of Health

What about health? Am I healthy? I guess so, except <u>what does it mean to be healthy?</u> Does it mean eating <u>health food</u>? Or <u>going to the doctor</u> often? <u>I hate going to the doctor</u> because it makes me start to worry about my health. Also about money. I don't have <u>health insurance</u>. Why are there so many <u>people without health insurance?</u> And <u>prescriptions</u>. They <u>cost too much.</u>

Freewriting Reaction to the Topic of Noise

I am surrounded by noise. I work next to <u>a building</u> that is <u>under construction</u> so I hear <u>pounding</u> and <u>drilling</u> and <u>sawing</u> all day. <u>Not all noise bothers me. I study with music on. Other people's music can make me crazy.</u> What's <u>the worst noise?</u> I'm not sure. I don't like it to be <u>too quiet</u>, like it is in a scary movie just before a horrible scene.

Exercise 5 Finding Specific Ideas in Lists

Following are two lists. Each list is a response to a broad topic. Read each list; then underline any phrases that could become a more specific topic for a paragraph.

Topic: children

children and family	<u>being a stepchild</u>
children and crime	<u>babysitting twin boys</u>
<u>dangerous toys</u>	children's needs
<u>privileges of the oldest child</u>	<u>toddler's temper tantrums</u>
childhood diseases	international aid to children

Topic: animals

modern zoos	<u>litter-box training a cat</u>
hunting in America	<u>ferrets and the law</u>
<u>the perfect fishing spot</u>	<u>service dogs in police work</u>
dangerous African animals	types of snakes and reptiles
<u>famous cartoon animals</u>	animal rescue

Exercise 6 **Grouping Related Ideas in Lists of Details**

Following are lists of details. In each list, circle the items that seem to fit into one group; then underline the items that seem to fit into a second group. Some items may not fit into either group.

1. **topic:** victories
   (surviving cancer)   winning the Super Bowl
   earning an Olympic medal   war victories
   (recovering from addiction) astronauts on the moon
   the lottery winner   (triumphing over abuse)
   (defeating poverty)   being first in the Daytona 500

2. **topic:** games
   checkers   (soccer)
   The Olympics   scrabble
   Monopoly   children's games
   (softball)   game shows
   a trophy   (hockey)

3. **topic:** taking summer classes in college
   can earn credits quickly   (less time for a summer job)
   (not all courses are offered) (more to learn in shorter time)
   able to focus on one class students' summer wardrobe
   student parking is available smaller classes in summer school
   summer graduation ceremony Saturday classes

Exercise 7 **Writing Topic Sentences for Lists of Details**

Following are lists of details that have no topic sentences. Write an appropriate topic sentence for each one.

1. **topic sentence:** *Your car can be like a little home on wheels.*

In a car, you can talk on your cell phone.

You can eat and drink in your car.

If your car is parked at your school or job, it's a good place for a quick nap.

Right before class, you can study in your car.

You can store your books, clothes, beach chair, and sports equipment in your car.

You can listen to music in your car.

You can even watch a DVD in some cars.

2. **topic sentence:** *People have discovered a variety of ways to deal with stress.*

Some people relieve stress by working out at a gym.

Others run to get rid of tension.

Talking to a sympathetic partner or friend can restore calm.

Becoming absorbed in a hobby can help a person leave stress behind.

Another way to conquer stress is to go for a walk, to a movie, or to a park.

Listening to music can transport a person to a tranquil place.

An activity like dancing or playing basketball can lower stress levels, too.

3. topic sentence: *My mother's life has been tough but inspiring.*

My mother came to this country when she was seven years old.

She could not speak the language, and she went to school only when she wasn't needed to work in the fields.

At sixteen, she gave birth to my older brother.

Although her childhood was difficult, she managed to earn her high school equivalency diploma at nineteen.

At twenty-one, she was working two jobs and raising two children alone.

Today, she goes to college with me and is studying to be a computer programmer.

I hope that some day I will be as strong as she is.

Exercise 8   Choosing the Better Topic Sentence

Following are lists of details. Each list has two possible topic sentences. Underline the better topic sentence for each list.

1. possible topic sentences:

a. Busy people spend too much money on fast food.

b. Living on fast food can be expensive and unhealthy.

People in a rush to get to work think they don't have time to make coffee.
So instead of a quick cup of instant coffee at home, they wind up buying an expensive latte or cappuccino.
Lunchtime is another money-making time for fast-food outlets.
Many workers in a hurry pay a hefty price for the yogurt, sandwich, or salad they could have brought from home.
College students racing between classes grab a small but expensive bag of chips and a soda.
For the same price, they could have bought a large bag of chips and two or three cans of soda at the supermarket.
Students and workers (especially those with children) drive home late and feel too tired to cook.
Their answer is more fast food: pizza or burgers picked up on the way home instead of cooked at home for less money.

2. Possible topic sentences:

a. Scales can help a person who wants to lose weight.

b. <u>The way people check their weight can affect weight loss.</u>

Some people check their weight several times a day.
Such constant checking can leave dieters impatient and disappointed.
People who go on the scale after a big meal will be horrified at signs of a weight gain.
On the other hand, the scale will give a lower weight when a person has an empty stomach.
Many dieters believe in using the scale weekly, at the same time of day each week.
The weekly weigh-in can give a more accurate picture of gradual weight loss.
Other weight-conscious people swear that they never use a scale at all.
They check their progress by the tightness or looseness of their clothes.
They claim their way involves less stress than relying on a scale.

3. Possible topic sentences:

a. Friends can be strange sometimes.

b. <u>Being a good friend takes work.</u>

In middle school I had a best friend named Colin.
Colin was funny, smart, and bold.
We played and explored the neighborhood every day.
Unfortunately, Colin liked to exaggerate.
He would convince me to explore a haunted house that was really somebody's old tool shed.
He dragged us to watch a gang fight that turned out to be two boys arguing about football.
Colin's wild stories infuriated me but I tolerated them because he was my friend.
In high school, my closest friend had a great sense of humor, generosity, and charm.
Gradually, I realized he also had a drinking problem.
He was furious when I tried to help him stop drinking.
For months, he refused to speak to me.
When he finally went for help, I was there to support him.

PLANNING   Devising a Plan: Illustration

When you plan your outline, keep your topic sentence in mind:

People of <u>various backgrounds</u> and <u>ages</u> wear <u>all</u> kinds of tee shirts.

Notice the underlined key words that lead to three key phrases:

people of various backgrounds
people of various ages
all kinds of tee shirts

Assign each detail to **one** of the key phrases.

people of various backgrounds

athletes, movie stars, musicians, restaurant workers

people of various ages

children, teens, parents, older people

all kinds of tee shirts

concert tees, college names on tees, beer ads, sporting goods, Mickey
Mouse shirts, surfer tees, souvenir tees, political slogans

With this kind of grouping, you have a clearer idea of how to organize a
paragraph.

An Outline for an Illustration Paragraph

topic sentence:	People of various backgrounds and ages wear all kinds of tee shirts.
details:	
various backgrounds	Athletes wear tee shirts. Movie stars are seen in them. Musicians perform in tee shirts. Restaurant workers wear tee shirts.
various ages	Children and teens wear tee shirts. Parents and older people wear them.
kinds of tees	There are tee shirts sold at concerts. Some shirts have the names of colleges on them. Others advertise a brand of beer or sporting goods. Mickey Mouse is a favorite character on them. Surfers' tee shirts have seascapes on them. Some shirts are souvenirs. Others have political slogans.

As you can see, the outline combined some of the details from the list. You
can combine other details, avoid repetition, and add more details as you
draft your essay.

Exercise 9 **Adding Details to an Outline**

Collaborate

Below are three partial outlines. Each has a topic sentence and some
details. Working with a partner or group, add more details that support the
topic sentence.

1. **topic sentence:** When a rainy weekend destroys your outdoor plans,
      you can enjoy some indoor activities.

   a. Make popcorn and watch a great DVD.

   b. Play cards with some friends.

   c. Go bowling.

   d. *Paint your room a dramatic color.*

INSTRUCTOR'S NOTE

Answers will vary. Possible answers shown at right.

    e. *Call an old friend and catch up.*

    f. *Take a child to a roller-skating rink.*

    g. *Put old photos of your former loves into an album.*

2. **topic sentence:** Many people hate their hair.

    a. They think it's too straight.

    b. They think it's too frizzy.

    c. They hate the color.

    d. *They think it's too curly.*

    e. *They wish it were thicker.*

    f. *They think it's too thick.*

    g. *They are afraid they are losing their hair.*

3. **topic sentence:** People who love their cars may spend their cash on personalizing or improving their autos.

    a. Some pay for fancy paint jobs.

    b. Many have the windows tinted.

    c. Others have slogans or cartoon characters painted on the windows.

    d. *Some rebuild the engines.*

    e. *Others buy expensive wheel rims or hubcaps.*

    f. *A few restore classic cars.*

    g. *Many install elaborate sound systems.*

Exercise 10 **Eliminating Details That Are Repetitive**

In the following outlines, some details use different words to repeat an example given earlier in the list. Cross out the repetitive details.

1. **topic sentence:** Sitting can be uncomfortable or worse.

    Sitting too long in a tiny classroom desk is confining.

    A long family dinner in straight-backed chairs hurts a person's bones.

    ~~A person's body starts to ache after an hour in a student desk.~~

    Even though a dentist's chair looks comfortable, the patient sitting through dental work is not at ease.

    The folding chairs used at many ceremonies were not designed for real human beings.

    ~~Being stuck in a rigid chair at an endless family meal is hard on a person's back.~~

    A sofa with itchy fabric can make sitting unpleasant.

    Nothing is worse than being crammed for hours in the seat of an airplane.

2. topic sentence: Complaining can unite people, but it can also isolate
an individual.

Sometimes neighbors get to know each other because they
have similar complaints about the neighborhood or the landlord.

Students sometimes join forces to complain about a college
policy or rule.

~~People who live near one another may start a friendship by
venting their dissatisfaction with the neighborhood.~~

Many workers like to get together to complain about their boss.

Sometimes complaining gets boring and even depressing.

The constant complainer's negativity is not attractive.

~~Nobody likes to be around someone who complains too often.~~

~~The person who complains too much can lose friends.~~

3. topic sentence: Everybody has some advice for fighting a cold.

My mother thinks vitamin C tablets will help.

My grandmother believes in chicken soup with a good dash of
pepper.

My uncle says the only way to shake a cold is to go to bed and
sleep it off.

"Drink plenty of liquids," says my neighbor.

~~My roommate urges bed rest.~~

My sister, who is interested in alternative medicine, urges me to
try an herbal tea.

~~At school, my instructor told me to take lots of fluids.~~

My boss says there is an old saying, "Starve a cold and feed a
fever," which means that I shouldn't eat too much.

DRAFTING   **Drafting and Revising: Illustration**

Review the outline on tee shirts on page 47. You can create a first draft of
this outline in the form of a paragraph. At this point, you can combine some
of the short, choppy sentences of the outline, add details, and add transitions to link your ideas. You can revise your draft using the following checklist.

Checklist: A Checklist for Revising an Illustration Paragraph

✔ Should some of the sentences be combined?

✔ Do I need more or better transitions?

✔ Should I add more details to support my points?

✔ Should some of the details be more specific?

Transitions

As you revise your illustration paragraph, you may find places where one idea ends and another begins abruptly. This problem occurs when you forget to add **transitions**, which are words, phrases, or sentences that connect one idea to another. Using transitions effectively will make your writing clear and smooth. When you write an illustration paragraph, you will need some transitions that link one example to another and other transitions to link one section of your paragraph to another section. Here are some transitions you may want to use in writing an illustration paragraph.

INFO BOX: Transitions for an Illustration Paragraph		
another example	in the case of	other kinds
a second example	like	such as
for example	one example	the first instance
for instance	one instance	another instance
in addition	other examples	to illustrate

Look carefully at the following draft of the paragraph on tee shirts, and note how it combines sentences, add details, and uses transitions to transform the outline into a clear and developed paragraph.

A Draft of an Illustration Paragraph

topic sentence

       People of various backgrounds and ages wear all kinds of tee shirts. Athletes and movie

sentences combined

sentences combined

details added

stars are seen in them. Musicians often perform in them, and restaurant workers sometimes work in tee shirts marked with the

sentences combined

name of the restaurant. Children, teens, their parents, and older people all wear tee shirts.

transition sentence added

details added

Almost anything can be printed or pictured on a tee shirt. At concerts, fans can buy tee shirts stamped with the name of the group on stage. College students can wear the name of their college on a shirt. Some shirts

details added

details added

advertise a brand of beer, like Bud, or a sporting goods company, like Nike. Mickey Mouse is a favorite character on tee shirts.

transition added

sentences combined

Other kinds of shirts include shirts with seascapes on them, and souvenir shirts, like the ones that say, "My folks visited Philadel-

details added, transition, details added

phia, and all I got was this lousy tee shirt." Other shirts have political slogans, like "Save the Whales."

Exercise 11 Revising a Draft by Combining Sentences

The paragraph below has many short, choppy sentences, which are underlined. Wherever you see two or more underlined sentences clustered next to each other, combine them into one clear, smooth sentence. Write your revised version of the paragraph in the spaces above the lines.

Unlike

My mother never stops talking. As soon as she wakes up, she starts talking. <u>She is</u>
most people, she starts the day by talking in complete sentences.
<u>not like most people. She starts the day by talking. She talks in complete sentences.</u>
While I am trying to wake up, she
I try to avoid having breakfast with my mother. <u>I am trying to wake up. She hits me</u>
hits me with one question after another.
<u>with one question after another.</u> For instance, she wants to know when I am leav-
During the day, my
ing for work, when I will be home, and what I want for dinner. <u>During the day, my</u>
mother calls me several times to ask more questions about what am I doing, how
<u>mother calls me several times to ask more questions. She asks questions about</u>
my day is going, and why I haven't called.
<u>what I am doing, how my day is going, and why I haven't I called.</u> Then she tells

me about her day and her activities. People tell me that my mother has always
In fact, her nonstop talking once surprised the doctors at the
been a talker. <u>In fact, her nonstop talking once surprised the doctors and nurses at</u>
hospital where she was giving birth to me.
<u>a hospital. It was the place where she was giving birth to me.</u>

Exercise 12 Revising a Draft by Adding Transitions

The paragraph below needs some transitions. Add appropriate transitions (words or phrases) to the blanks.

I enjoy being with others, but sometimes I prefer to be alone. ____*For example,*____

I prefer to study by myself because I can concentrate better when I have no one to

distract me. ____*In addition,*____ I like the quiet of studying in solitude.

In another instance, I like to make phone calls in private so that I can express

myself more fully. If I am talking to family members about a problem, I do not want

strangers around to hear. Sometimes I just want time alone to think about chal-

lenges ____*such as*____ doing well in college and paying my bills. Solitude gives

me the chance to think through a problem so that it doesn't become a crisis.

Exercise 13 Adding Details to a Draft

Collaborate

The paragraph on the following page lacks the kind of details that would make it more interesting. Working with a partner or group, add details to the blank spaces provided. When you are finished, read the revised paragraph to the class.

The clothes people wear to work depend on their positions. The average college student who works at a restaurant is likely to wear _____ or _____ on the job. Men who work behind the counter of an expensive men's clothing store may be required to dress in _____, while women who sell makeup in department stores often have to wear _____ and perfect makeup. If a person works as a teller in a bank, he or she cannot come to work in _____. Instead, appropriate dress is _____ and _____. Executives in financial corporations are often expected to dress in _____, _____, and _____. On the other hand, people in creative fields such as music or film production can wear almost anything from _____ to _____ when they work.

POLISHING   ## Polishing and Proofreading: Illustration

As you prepare the final version of your illustration paragraph, make any changes in word choice or transitions that can refine your writing. Following is the final version of the paragraph on tee shirts. As you read it, you will notice a few more changes: some details have been added, some have been made more specific, and a transition has been added. In addition, a concluding sentence has been added to unify the paragraph. These changes were made as the final version was prepared.

A Final Version of an Illustration Paragraph

(Changes from the last draft are underlined.)

People of various backgrounds and ages wear all kinds of tee shirts. Athletes and movie stars are seen in them. Musicians often perform in <u>ragged tees</u>, and restaurant workers sometimes work in tee shirts marked with the name of the restaurant. Children, teens, their parents, and <u>older people</u> all wear tee shirts. Almost anything can be painted or pictured on a tee shirt. At concerts, <u>for example</u>, fans can buy tee shirts stamped with the name of the group on stage. College students can wear the name of their college on a shirt. Some <u>popular</u> shirts advertise a brand of beer, like Bud, or a sporting goods company, like Nike. Mickey Mouse is a favorite character on tee shirts. Other kinds of tee shirts include <u>surfer</u> shirts with seascapes on them and souvenir shirts, like the <u>surly</u> ones that say, "My folks visited Philadelphia, and all I got was this lousy tee shirt." Other shirts have political slogans, like "Save the Whales." <u>What is written or pictured on tee shirts is as varied as the people who wear them.</u>

Before you prepare the final version of your illustration paragraph, check your latest draft for errors in spelling, punctuation, typing, and copying.

> **For your information:** A sample illustration essay based on the same topic and following the same writing steps can be found in Chapter 12, on pages 273–279.

Exercise 14   **Proofreading to Prepare the Final Version**

Following are two illustration paragraphs with the types of errors that are easy to overlook when you prepare the final version of an assignment. Correct the errors by writing above the lines. There are twelve errors in the first paragraph and ten errors in the second paragraph.

        asking

1. Today, when people say they want a drink of water, they could be axsing

   course   *many*

for a number of drinks. Of coarse, there is water right from the faucet, but manny

     bottled   ,

people drink bottle water. There are dozens of brands of bottled water and there

         kinds

are also two basic kind of water in bottles. One kind is fizzy, and one kind is flat.

  addition

In edition, there are many new types of water, such as water with vitamins, water

        flavored   *supermarket*

with caffeine, and Flavored water. These days, a whole row in the suppermarket

            varieties

can be filled with ten or twenty variety of water, and restaurants may offer a

                       kinds   ,

choice of water, from free tap water to expensive kins of bottled water. As a result

a person who asks for a glass of water has to be very specific.

          Mrs.

2. I once thought Mrs Deon was the nastiest teacher in the world. She was

  fourth   ,

my forth grade teacher and she had her eye on me from the first day of class. As

                         grinning   .

soon as I walked in the door, she told me to stop grining at her She said she

                                       every

would soon wipe that smile off my face. For an entire year, she jumped on me evry

time I even thought about misbehaving. For example, she pulled the gum out of

my mouth before I had even started chewing it. Every day, she walked around the

classroom   ,

class room to check on each student. She praised many boys and girls but she

never praised me. When she got to me, she screamed some command. For

                                     sit

instance, she told me to get my feet off the desk in front of me and set up straight.

                      respect

Mrs. Deon was a mean lady, but today I respeck her. In her own way, she was try-

ing to turn a wild boy into a student.

Lines of Detail: A Walk-Through Assignment

Your assignment is to write an illustration paragraph about music.

    Step 1: Freewrite or brainstorm on this broad topic for ten minutes.

Step 2: Review your freewriting or brainstorming. Underline any parts that are specific ideas related to the broad topic, music.

Step 3: List all the specific ideas. Choose one as the narrowed topic for your paragraph.

Step 4: Add related ideas to your chosen, narrowed topic. Do this by reviewing your list for related ideas and by brainstorming for more related ideas.

Step 5: List all your related ideas and review their connection to your narrowed topic. Then write a topic sentence for your paragraph.

Step 6: Write a first draft of your paragraph.

Step 7: Revise your first draft. Be sure it has enough details and clear transitions. Combine any choppy sentences.

Step 8: After a final check for any errors in punctuation, spelling, and word choice, prepare the final version of the paragraph.

Writing Your Own Illustration Paragraph

When you write on any of these topics, follow the four basic stages of the writing process in preparing your illustration paragraph.

Collaborate

Computer

1. Begin this assignment with a partner or group. Together, write down as many old sayings as you can. (Old sayings include statements like, "It's not whether you win or lose; it's how you play the game that's important," or "Money can't buy happiness.") If anyone in your group speaks a second language, ask him or her to translate and explain any old sayings from that language. To review quotations categorized by topics, visit **<http://www.quoteland.com>.**

    Once you have a long list of sayings, split up. On your own, pick one saying; then write a paragraph on that saying. Your paragraph should give several examples that prove the truth of the saying.

2. Below are some topic sentences. Select one and write a paragraph in which you use examples to support (illustrate) the topic sentence.

    _____ makes me nervous.

    _____ takes great courage.

    A snowstorm forces me to _____.

    A rainy day is a good day to catch up on indoor chores.

    The friendliest store in my neighborhood is _____.

3. Select one of the topics listed below. Write a paragraph on some narrowed part of the topic. If you choose the topic of jobs, for example, you might narrow the topic to illustrate the benefits or drawbacks of your job.

jobs	fears	dreams	mistakes
stress	money	television	mysteries
computers	children	celebrities	surprises
fashion	challenges	memories	holidays

4. Examine the photograph on the next page. After you have looked at it carefully, write a paragraph using the following topic sentence:

    Fast food restaurants appeal to a variety of ages and tastes.

(The photograph may help you think of examples to support the topic sentence.)

5. Examine the image below. After you have looked at it carefully, write a paragraph with this topic sentence:

Whenever I am delayed by a traffic jam on a major highway, I can react in several ways.

Note: Additional writing options suitable for illustration-related assignments can be found after the professional reading, "Spanglish," which begins on page 603.

How Do I Get a Better Grade?

Visit www.mywritinglab.com for audio-visual lectures and additional practice sets about illustration.

Name: _____   Section: _____

Peer Review Form for an Illustration Paragraph

After you have written a draft of your illustration paragraph, let a writing partner read it. When your partner has completed the form below, discuss the comments. Then repeat the same process for your partner's paragraph.

The examples in this paragraph relate to this topic sentence: _____

_____

_____

_____

The paragraph has _____ (enough, too few) details to support the topic sentence.

The most effective example was the one about _____

_____

Three words or phrases of specific detail in the paragraph are _____

_____

_____

Two transitions (words or phrases) in the paragraph are _____

_____

I have questions about or would like to know more about _____

_____

Other comments: _____

_____

_____

_____

_____

_____

_____

_____

_____

Reviewer's Name:_____

CHAPTER 3

Jumping In

*What is your strongest impression of this scene? Does the scene stir up feelings of power? Excitement? Anxiety? Examining the scene carefully, along with your reactions, will help you **describe** it effectively.*

Description

WHAT IS DESCRIPTION?

Description shows a reader what a person, place, thing, or situation is like. When you write description, you try to *show, not tell*, about something. You want to make the reader see that person, place, or situation, and then, perhaps, to make the reader think about or act on what you have shown.

Hints for Writing a Descriptive Paragraph

Using Specific Words and Phrases Using specific words and phrases will help the reader "see" what you are describing. If a word or phrase is *specific*, it is *exact and precise*. The opposite of specific language is language that is vague, general, or fuzzy. Think of the difference between specific and general in this way:

TEACHING TIP

To help your students understand the importance of using specific details, ask them about their experience working with the public. Are their customers or guests often vague or unclear about what they want? What kinds of details do customers need to provide? (Students may be eager to share or vent frustrations about ineffective communication.)

57

Imagine that you are browsing through a used car lot. A salesman approaches you.

"Can I help you?" the salesman asks.
"I'm looking for a good, reliable car," you say.
"Well, what kind of car did you have in mind?" asks the salesman.
"Not too old," you say.
"A sports car?" asks the salesman.
"Maybe," you say.

The conversation could go on and on. You are being very general in saying that you want a "good, reliable" car. The salesman is looking for specific details: How old a car do you want? What model of car?

In writing, if you use words like "good" or "nice" or "bad" or "interesting," you will not have a specific description or a very effective piece of writing. Whenever you can, try to use a more precise word instead of a general term. To find a more explicit term, ask yourself such questions as, "What type?" or "How?" The examples below show how a general term can be replaced by a more specific one.

general word: hat (Ask "What type?")
more specific words: beret, fishing hat, baseball cap

general word: lettuce (Ask "What type?")
more specific words: iceberg, romaine, arugula

general word: ran (Ask "How?")
more specific words: raced, sprinted, loped

general word: nice (Ask "How?")
more specific words: friendly, outgoing, courteous

Exercise 1 **Identifying General and Specific Words**

INSTRUCTOR'S NOTE

For more on specific language, see Chapter 32 on word choice.

Below are lists of words. Put an "X" by the one term in each list that is more general than the others. The first one is done for you.

List 1

__X__ science
_____ botany
_____ biology
_____ astronomy
_____ geology

List 2

__X__ medical worker
_____ surgeon
_____ nurse
_____ physical therapist
_____ radiologist

List 3

_____ uncle
__X__ relative
_____ cousin
_____ niece
_____ brother

List 4

_____ peach
_____ banana
_____ orange
__X__ fruit
_____ apple

Exercise 2 **Ranking General and Specific Items**

On the next page are lists of items. In each list, rank the items from the most general (1) to the most specific (4).

List 1

___2___ car accessories

___4___ fancy wheel rims

___1___ cars

___3___ luxury car accessories

List 2

___1___ law enforcement

___3___ state road enforcement

___4___ highway patrol

___2___ state law enforcement

List 3

___1___ cartoons

___2___ cartoons on television

___3___ cartoons about a family

___4___ The Simpsons

List 4

___2___ sweet food

___1___ food

___3___ candy

___4___ chocolate bar

Exercise 3 **Interviewing for Specific Answers**

To practice being specific, interview a partner. Ask your partner to answer the questions below. Write his or her answers in the spaces provided. When you have finished, change places. In both interviews, your goal is to find specific answers, so you should both be as explicit as you can in your answers.

Collaborate

Interview Questions

1. What is your favorite flavor of ice cream? _____

2. What did you eat and drink for breakfast this morning? _____

   _____

3. What is your favorite professional sports team? _____

   _____

4. What television personality do you most dislike?_____

   _____

5. If you were painting your room, what color would you choose?_____

   _____

6. What fabric do you think is the softest? _____

7. When you think of a fierce dog, what breed comes to mind? _____

   _____

8. When you think of a fast car, what car do you picture? _____

   _____

9. What specific items of clothing are your most comfortable clothes?

   _____

10. What is the most enjoyable city or town you have visited? _____

   _____

Exercise 4 **Finding Specific Words or Phrases**

List four specific words or phrases beneath each general one. You may use brand names where they are appropriate. The first word on List 1 is done for you.

List 1:

general word: green

specific word or phrase: *olive green*

lime green

blue green

mint green

List 2:

general word: said

specific word or phrase: *whispered*

screeched

murmured

screamed

List 3:

general word: relationship

specific word or phrase: *friendship*

love affair

business partnership

marriage

List 4:

general word: snack

specific word or phrase: *granola bar*

doughnut

apple

Pop Tart

Exercise 5 **Identifying Sentences That Are Too General**

Below are lists of sentences. In each group, put an "X" by one sentence that is general and vague.

1. a. __X__ Movies are my passion.

   b. _____ I see four movies a week.

   c. _____ Last year I spent a thousand dollars on movies.

2. a. _____ She constantly brags about her money and looks.

   b. _____ She checks her appearance in every mirror she finds.

   c. __X__ She is full of herself.

3. a. __X__ You should go for it.

   b. _____ You should audition for the television talent show.

   c. _____ You should enter the marathon.

4. a. _____ In my night class, we listen to lectures all night.

  b. __X__ My night class is boring.

  c. _____ In my night class, the teacher reads the book aloud.

Using Sense Words in Your Descriptions

One way to make your description specific and vivid is to use *sense words*. As you plan a description, ask yourself,

> What does it **look** like?
> What does it **sound** like?
> What does it **smell** like?
> What does it **taste** like?
> What does it **feel** like?

The sense details can make the description vivid. Try to include details about the five senses in your descriptions. Often you can brainstorm sense details more easily if you focus on specific details that relate to each sense.

INFO BOX: Devising Sense Details

For the sense of	think about
sight	colors, light and dark, shadows, brightness, shape, or size
hearing	noise, silence, or the kinds of sounds you hear
smell	fragrance, odors, scents, aromas, or perfume
taste	bitter, sour, sweet, or compare the taste of one thing to another
touch	the feel of things: texture, hardness, softness, roughness, smoothness

---

Exercise 6   **Brainstorming Sense Details for a Descriptive Paragraph**

Collaborate

With a partner or a group, brainstorm on the following ideas for a paragraph. For each topic, list at least six questions and answers that could help you find sense details. Be prepared to read your completed exercise to another group or to the class.

  1. topic: The man was dangerous.
        Brainstorm questions and answers:

  Q: *What made him look dangerous? A: He was big.* _____

  Q: *How big was he? A: Over six feet tall.* _____

  Q: *What about his weight? A: At least two hundred pounds.* _____

  Q: *Did he carry a weapon? A: Just his huge, scarred fists.* _____

  Q: *What was his face like? A: He had hard, cold eyes.* _____

  Q: *Did he have any scars? A: He had a big slash across his chin.* _____

2. topic: The empty classroom was weird at night.
Brainstorm questions and answers:

Q: *What was so weird? A: The shadows and the darkness outside.*

Q: *Didn't you have lights on? A: Yes, but outside was all black.*

Q: *What else seemed strange? A: The silence.*

Q: *Was the silence frightening? A: A little.*

Q: *Why? A: Because classrooms are usually full of noisy people.*

Q: *What else was weird? A: Seeing the rows of empty seats.*

3. topic: The drinking water was disgusting.
Brainstorm questions and answers:

Q: *What color was it? A: A cloudy beige.*

Q: *Was there anything in the water? A: Silt.*

Q: *What did the water feel like? A: Like water with sand in it.*

Q: *Where did the water come from? A: A rusty faucet.*

Q: *Where was this faucet? A: In a deserted farmhouse.*

Q: *What did the water taste like? A: Like sour mud.*

| Exercise 7 | **Writing Sense Words** |

Write sense descriptions for the items below.

1. Write four words or phrases to describe the texture of a brick wall:

hard, scratchy, rough, raw

2. Write four words or phrases to describe what a lizard looks like:

a little dinosaur, a flash of lime green, a noble head and steady tail, a

dragon

3. Write four words or phrases to describe the sounds of a class that has just ended:

notebooks snap shut, desks rattle, chairs scrape the floor, feet shuffle

WRITING THE DESCRIPTIVE PARAGRAPH IN STEPS

| PREWRITING | Gathering Ideas: Description |

Writing a descriptive paragraph begins with thinking on paper, looking for specific details and sense descriptions. You can think by brainstorming, freewriting, or writing in a journal. For example, you might decide to write about your brother's bedroom. Brainstorming might lead you to something like the following list of ideas:

Brainstorming a List for a Descriptive Paragraph

- *older brother Michael—got a big bedroom*
- *I shared with my little brother*
- *stars pasted on the ceiling*
- *took a long time to fix it up the way he wanted it*
- *lots of books about science fiction in two bookcases*
- *movie posters of <u>AI: Artificial Intelligence</u> and <u>The Matrix</u>*
- *old videos like <u>Raiders of the Lost Ark</u> in bookcases*
- *his bed had no headboard, made to look like a couch*
- *<u>Star Trek</u> pillows on the bed*

The Dominant Impression

When you think you have enough details, you can begin to think about focusing them. Look over these details and consider where they are taking you. If you were to look at the list above, you might identify ideas that keep appearing in the details:

- stars pasted on the ceiling
- lots of books about science fiction in two bookcases
- movie posters of <u>AI: Artificial Intelligence</u> and <u>The Matrix</u>
- old videos like <u>Raiders of the Lost Ark</u> in bookcases
- <u>Star Trek</u> pillows on the bed

Reading over this list, you realize that all the specific titles of films or television shows are related to fantasy or science fiction. Therefore, one main idea about your brother's bedroom relates to his interest in fantasy or science fiction. This idea is the **dominant impression**, or the main point of the description. In a descriptive paragraph, the dominant impression is the topic sentence. For example, the topic sentence could be

> *My brother's bedroom reflected his fascination with fantasy and science fiction.*

Once you have a dominant impression, you are ready to add more ideas to explain and support it. You should try to make the added details specific by using sense description where appropriate.

Exercise 8   **Adding Details to a Dominant Impression**

Following are sentences that could be used as a dominant impression in a descriptive paragraph. Add more details. Some details to explain and support the dominant impression are already given.

1. **dominant impression:**   Jennifer's hair was a disaster.

   details: a. *She had colored it red.*

   b. *The red was the color of a Raggedy Ann doll's hair.*

   c. *Her hair was stiff and straight.*

   d. *It fell straight to chin length.*

   e. *It felt like straw.*

TEACHING TIP

To help students develop supporting details, tell students to ask, "How?" or "To what extent?" after identifying the dominant impression. (For example, *How* disastrous was her hair?) Quick questions can lead to additional and more specific details in their writing.

INSTRUCTOR'S NOTE

Answers will vary. Possible answers shown at left.

2. dominant impression: The boy had been playing happily in mud puddles.

details: **a.** *His hair was crusted with dried mud.*

         b. *Streaks of dirt smeared his smiling face.*

         c. *His once blue shirt was now blue and brown.*

         d. *His knees were caked with dirt.*

         e. *The laces of his sneakers were stiff with mud.*

3. dominant impression: The noise in the club made my head ache.

details: **a.** *Music with a booming bass pounded into the room.*

         b. *To be heard, people screamed over the music.*

         c. *Other people shouted into their cell phones.*

         d. *Someone with a microphone shouted above the music.*

         e. *A few fireworks outside the door sounded like a gun.*

Exercise 9   **Creating a Dominant Impression from a List of Details**

INSTRUCTOR'S NOTE

Answers will vary. Possible answers shown at right.

Following are lists of details. For each list, write one sentence that could be used as the dominant impression created by the details.

1. dominant impression: *The arrival of the soldiers was a joyful scene.*

details: The soldiers back from the war grinned as they entered the airport terminal.

Young women holding babies began to smile and cry.

Soon soldiers were holding the babies and the women in tight hugs.

Other soldiers kissed their girlfriends and boyfriends.

Some people rushed up to give the soldiers flowers and flags.

Parents, brothers, and sisters of the soldiers grabbed their loved ones in a group embrace.

In between hugs, everyone took pictures of this moment.

2. dominant impression: *Emilio was a nervous person.*

details: Emilio bit his nails down to the skin on his fingers.

He was startled whenever he heard a sudden noise.

When he sat, his left leg jiggled uncontrollably.

At night, he would suddenly tremble in his sleep.

Sometimes he would cry out in his sleep, too.

Emilio's eyes had a haunted look, as if he were remembering terrible events.

3. dominant impression: *The Siamese cat looked like a princess of the cat world.*

details: The Siamese cat had a sleek coat of cream fur with chocolate accents at the ears, paws, and tail.

The expression in her eyes was knowing and mysterious.

She sat up elegantly, her posture straight and her tail wrapped perfectly around her body.

When she moved, she glided past other cats as if they were of no interest to her.

She walked on long, slender legs, so lightly that she appeared to be moving above the ground.

The cat was not cold or friendly; she was content in her own world.

PLANNING Devising a Plan: Description

You can use the sentence you created as the dominant impression as the topic sentence of your outline. Beneath the topic sentence, list the details you have collected. Once you have this rough list, check the details by asking,

Do all the details relate to the topic sentence?
Are the details in logical order?

Following are the topic sentence and list of details for the paragraph describing a brother's bedroom. The details that are crossed out don't "fit" the topic sentence.

topic sentence: My brother's bedroom reflected his fascination with fantasy and science fiction.

- ~~older brother Michael got a big bedroom~~
- ~~I shared with my little brother~~
- stars pasted on the ceiling
- ~~took a long time to fix it up the way he wanted it~~
- lots of books about science fiction in two bookcases
- movie posters of <u>AI: Artificial Intelligence</u> and <u>The Matrix</u>
- old videos like <u>Raiders of the Lost Ark</u> in bookcases
- ~~his bed had no headboard, made to look like a couch~~
- <u>Star Trek</u> pillows on the bed

Notice what is crossed out. The details about the size of Michael's bedroom, the little brother's bedroom, the time it took Michael to fix up his bedroom, and the bed that looked like a couch do not really have much to do with the topic sentence. The topic sentence is about Michael's fascination with science fiction and fantasy. It is about how his bedroom revealed that fascination.

Remember that as you write and revise, you may decide to eliminate other ideas, to reinsert ideas you once rejected, or even to add new ideas. Changing your mind is a natural part of revising.

Once you have decided upon your best list of details, check their order. Remember, when you write a description, you are trying to make the reader *see*. It will be easier for the reader to imagine what you see if you put your description in a simple, logical order. You might want to put descriptions in order by **time sequence** (first to last), by **spatial position** (top to bottom, or right to left), or by **similar types** (for example, all about the flowers, then all about the trees in a park).

If you are describing a house, for instance, you may want to start with the outside of the house and then describe the inside. You do not want the details to shift back and forth, from outside to inside and back to outside. If you are describing a person, you might want to group all the details about his or her face before you describe his or her body. You might describe a meal from first course to dessert.

Look again at the details describing the bedroom. It is logical to use three categories to create a simple order: from the ceiling, to the walls, and to the furniture. Now look at the following outline and notice how this order works.

An Outline for a Descriptive Paragraph

topic sentence: My brother's bedroom reflected his fascination with fantasy and science fiction.

details:

ceiling
- Stars were pasted on the ceiling.
- At night, they glowed in the dark.
- The room appeared to be covered by a starry sky.

walls
- Movie posters covered the walls.
- There was a poster of Steven Spielberg's film, <u>AI: Artificial Intelligence</u>.
- Another poster, of <u>The Matrix</u>, was framed.

furniture
- There were lots of books about science fiction in two bookcases.
- I remember <u>Fahrenheit 451</u> and <u>The War of the Worlds</u>.
- Old videos like <u>Raiders of the Lost Ark</u> were also stacked on the bookshelves.
- The bed was piled high with <u>Star Trek</u> pillows.

You probably noticed that the outline has more details than the original list. These details help to make the descriptions more specific. You can add them to the outline and to the drafts of your paragraph.

Once you have a list of details focused on a topic sentence and arranged in some logical order, you can begin writing a draft of your description paragraph.

Exercise 10 **Finding Details That Do Not Relate**

Survey the following lists. Each includes a topic sentence and several details. In each list, cross out the details that do not relate to the topic sentence.

1. **topic sentence:** Jacy's is the perfect place to take young children.
   details: Jacy's is an Italian restaurant that sells only what children love: pizza.
   It has every kind of pizza from pepperoni pizza to chocolate dessert pizza.

It sells the pizza in tiny slices that small hands find easy to pick up and that are just enough to satisfy a child's appetite.

~~Parents always caution their children not to take more food than the children can finish.~~

Jacy's also entertains children.

It has games for children to play while their parents eat, talk, or enjoy a break.

In one game, children use mechanical claws to fish for a small toy.

~~This game entices children because it looks easy but is nearly impossible.~~

A variety of other games, including video games, amuse the children who come to Jacy's for food and fun.

2. topic sentence: My sister Briana has been a screamer since the day she was born.

details: My mother says Briana was born kicking and crying so loudly the doctor was surprised.

When she learned to talk, Briana shouted her words.

~~On the other hand, I have a soft voice.~~

She never raised her hand in first grade but just yelled at the teacher.

She startled the teacher and scared the children.

By the time she was ten, Briana could frighten grown men with her loud voice.

In a crowd of noisy people, Briana could always be heard.

~~She was a small girl with big eyes and long, thin legs.~~

When Briana was fourteen, her voice became her biggest asset.

She became a singer in a girl group.

Today, her powerful voice is heard on the radio.

3. topic sentence: Elite Furniture is the perfect store for people on a budget.

details: From the outside, Elite furniture looks like a large building with chipped paint and big, dirty windows.

~~Elite Furniture is in a strip mall full of run-down or closed stores.~~

Inside, Elite Furniture is full of good deals.

Right inside the entrance, the store is full of living room furniture in discontinued styles.

The couches, chairs, end tables, and coffee tables are reduced as much as 50 percent.

There are bargains in leather and fabric couches and wooden tables.

Further into the store are the bedroom sets.

A queen-size bed or a chest of drawers may be available for as little as $150.

At the back of the store is the hidden treasure.

It is a giant room full of used furniture.

~~Many student apartments are furnished entirely in used furniture.~~

At Elite Furniture, a person could furnish a small apartment with less than five hundred dollars' worth of used furniture.

Exercise 11 Putting Details in Order

Following are lists that start with a topic sentence. The details under each topic sentence are not in the right order. Put the details in logical order by labeling them, with 1 being the first detail, 2 the second, and so forth.

1. topic sentence: The decor in the store was designed to give anyone a headache.
(Arrange the details from walls to ceiling.)

details: *3* Some of the frames included carved and gilded faces of monsters.

1 The walls were painted a glaring lime green.

2 On top of the painted walls were huge mirrors in a variety of frames.

4 On the ceiling, blinding track lighting reached into every corner of the room.

5 The blinding light was painful, and the pain was intensified by the effect of green walls multiplied in the mirrors.

2. topic sentence: A visit to a new friend turned out to be creepy.
(Arrange the details from beginning to end.)

details: *4* Looking for a safe place away from Amber, I sank into a nearby couch.

3 I declined his offer to get friendly with the snake.

1 When my friend Ali opened the front door, he had a snake draped over his shoulder.

2 He asked me if I wanted to pet the snake, whose name was Amber.

5 Once I felt safe on the couch, I leaned my head back, only to see Ali's pet tarantula an inch from my face.

3. topic sentence: The new coffee house seemed strange and enticing.
(Arrange the details from outside to inside.)

details: *2* Inside the door, a person had to get used to the dark.

3 Eventually, the light from a giant television screen led a person to a small coffee bar.

1 Six tiny tables and chairs crowded the sidewalk.

_____4_____ At the bar, people ordered exotic coffees from South and Central America.

_____5_____ Beyond the bar was a huge couch where people lounged and listened to new music.

Exercise 12 Creating Details Using a Logical Order

The following lists include a topic sentence and indicate a required order for the details. Write five sentences of details in the required order.

1. **topic sentence:** For Halloween, my four-year-old son dressed as Mickey Mouse.
   (Arrange the details from head to foot.)

   a. _He wore large black mouse ears._

   b. _His face was painted with big eyes and whiskers._

   c. _He wore a bow tie on his neck._

   d. _He wore short pants with suspenders._

   e. _His big shoes looked like Mickey's._

2. **topic sentence:** The sights and sounds at the midnight electronics sale gave me a headache.
   (Describe the sights; then describe the sounds.)

   a. _Waiting for the store to open, people pushed against the glass doors._

   b. _As soon as the doors opened, bargain hunters stampeded._

   c. _Shoppers began fighting over cameras and televisions._

   d. _The frenzy for bargains erupted in a roar._

   e. _Above the roar came screams of pain and fury._

3. **topic sentence:** Our drive to Hillcrest was boring.
   (Describe the drive from beginning to end.)

   a. _We began our drive through miles of factories and dirty warehouses._

   b. _After an hour, we hit a long stretch of farmland._

   c. _Soon, we were drowsy from looking at endless miles of cows._

   d. _Then we couldn't find a good radio station and were desperate for amusement._

   e. _As we drove into Hillcrest, we saw more dreary factories._

DRAFTING   Drafting and Revising: Description

After you have an outline, the next step is to create a first rough draft of the paragraph. At this point, you can begin combining some of the ideas in your outline, making two or more short sentences into one longer one. You can also write your first draft in short sentences and combine the sentences later. Your goal is simply to put your ideas in paragraph form so that you can see how they look and check to see what needs to be improved.

The first draft of a paragraph will not be perfect. If it were perfect, it wouldn't be a first draft. Once you have the first draft, check it, using the following list:

Checklist: A Checklist for Revising a Descriptive Paragraph

✓ Are there enough details?

✓ Are the details specific?

✓ Do the details use sense words?

✓ Are the details in order?

✓ Is there a dominant impression?

✓ Do the details connect to the dominant impression?

✓ Have I made my point?

A common problem in writing description is creating a fuzzy, vague description. Take a look at the following fuzzy description:

> The football fans were rowdy and excited. They shouted when their team scored. Some people jumped up. The fans showed their support by cheering and stomping. They were enjoying every minute of the game.

The description could be revised so that it is more specific and vivid:

TEACHING TIP

Remind students that these details answer the questions "How?" and "To what extent?" the fans were rowdy and excited.

> The football fans were rowdy and excited. When their team scored, they yelled, "Way to go!" or "Stomp 'em! Crush 'em!" until they were hoarse. Three fans, wearing the team colors of blue and white on their shirts, shorts, and socks, jumped up, spilling their drinks on the teenagers seated below them. During timeouts, the fans chanted rhythmically, and throughout the game they stomped their feet in a steady beat against the wooden bleachers. As people chanted, whooped, and woofed, they turned to grin at each other and thrust their clenched fists into the air.

The vivid description meets the requirements of the checklist. It has sufficient specific details. The details use sense words to describe what the fans looked and sounded like. The details also support a dominant impression of rowdy, excited fans. The vivid, specific details make the point.

Exercise 13 **Revising a Paragraph, Finding Irrelevant Sentences**

Following are two descriptive paragraphs. In each, there are sentences that are irrelevant, meaning they do not have anything to do with the first sentence, the topic sentence. Cross out the irrelevant sentences in the paragraphs below.

1. Pedro always seemed too friendly to be genuine. ~~Everybody needs friends.~~ I hardly knew Pedro when he started asking me questions about my classes, my family, and my friends. My answers always led to a generous offer from Pedro. If I said I was broke, he offered to lend me money. If I said I had to spend the weekend studying, he said he would meet me at the library and help me study. He smiled frequently and spoke in a sympathetic

tone that made me uncomfortable. I think he wanted to be my counselor, like a television psychologist. ~~I am so sick of those talk shows where couples fight on television and an expert comes out and advises them.~~ Pedro was always kind, helpful, and positive. He smiled, laughed, and listened to my gripes. Unfortunately, I couldn't get close to him. I felt that he was too good to be true.

2. The student cafeteria is not a place to study. It is always crowded, so it is impossible to find a quiet nook for reading. The noise level is high. People blast their music, shout to one another across the tables, and fight over their games of cards and dominoes. ~~There is a patio outside, but nobody ever uses it.~~ Students bump into one another and jostle the tables as they try to make their way through the crowds. In addition, there is always some special activity going on. For instance, one club sells flowers on Valentine's Day, and several student organizations sell candy. ~~I think all those sales belong in high school.~~ Anyone who wants to do homework or cram for a test will find it hard to concentrate in the cafeteria.

Exercise 14   Revising a Paragraph for More Specific Details

INSTRUCTOR'S NOTE

Answers will vary. Possible answers shown at left.

In the following paragraphs, the details that are underlined are not specific. Change the underlined sentences to create more specific descriptions. Write the new descriptions in the lines below each paragraph.

1. The Caribbean Festival ended with a delicious island dinner. To begin, banana bread and spicy conch fritters were served. The main course included snapper marinated in lime juice, broiled golden on the outside and tender white on the inside. Crispy coconut shrimp, pigeon peas and rice, and mango relish completed this course. <u>The meal ended with a great dessert.</u>

revisions: *Piña colada ice cream ended the meal.*

2. My first car was a piece of junk, but it was a status symbol to me. The car tires were so old that they were a pale, dusty gray. Only two wheels had hubcaps, and one of those hubcaps had a large dent. The trunk of the car wouldn't close properly, so I had to hold the trunk together with strong rope. <u>The paint job was awful.</u> Inside, the vinyl dashboard was cracked, and so was the cheap plastic upholstery. Mangled stuffing popped out of the seats. On the floor, empty French fries cartons and burger wrappings added a rancid odor. The car was smelly, old, and ugly, but it was mine. Now that I owned it, I, not others, would decide when and where I would go.

revisions: *The paint, a faded red, had cracked and peeled to reveal a layer of dirty greenish rust.*

Transitions

As you revise your description paragraph, you may notice places in the paragraph that seem choppy or abrupt. That is, one sentence may end, and another may start, but the two sentences don't seem to be connected. Reading your paragraph aloud, you may sense that it is not very smooth.

You can make the writing smoother and make the content clearer by using **transitions**, which are words or phrases that link one idea to another idea. They tell the reader what he or she has just read and what is coming next. Here are some transitions you may want to use in writing a description:

INSTRUCTOR'S NOTE

For more on sentence combining options that incorporate transitions, see Chapter 16 on coordination and Chapter 18 on subordination.

INFO BOX: **Transitions for a Descriptive Paragraph**

To show ideas brought together:

and	also	in addition	next

To show a contrast:

although	however	on the contrary	unlike
but	in contrast	on the other hand	yet

To show a similarity:

all	each	like	similarly
both			

To show a time sequence:

after	first	next	then
always	second, third (etc.)	often	when
before	meanwhile	soon	while

To show a position in space:

above	beside	in front of	over
ahead of	between	inside	there
alongside	beyond	near	toward
among	by	nearby	under
around	close	next to	underneath
away	down	on	up
below	far	on top of	where
beneath	here	outside	

There are many other transitions you can use, depending on what you need to link your ideas. Take a look at a draft of the description paragraph of a bedroom. Compare it to the outline on page 66. You will notice that more sense details have been added. Transitions have been added, too. Pay particular attention to the transitions in this draft.

INSTRUCTOR'S NOTE

Remind students that movie titles are underlined in student papers because movies are considered major works. They are not, of course, transitions.

A Draft of a Descriptive Paragraph

(Transitions are underlined.)

My brother's bedroom reflected his fascination with fantasy and science fiction. Stars were pasted on the ceiling <u>where</u>, at night, they glowed in the dark. <u>Then</u> the room appeared to be covered by a starry sky. Movie posters covered the walls. A poster of Steven Spielberg's film <u>AI: Artificial Intelligence</u> hung <u>next to</u> a poster of <u>The Matrix</u> in a shiny chrome frame. <u>Below</u> the posters, two steel bookcases had lots of books about science fiction. I remember <u>Fahrenheit 451</u> and <u>The War of the Worlds</u>. Old videos like <u>Raiders of the Lost Ark</u> were also stacked on the bookshelves. The bed was piled high with <u>Star Trek</u> pillows.

Exercise 15 **Recognizing Transitions**

Underline the transitions in the paragraph below.

Waiting for my bus, I felt like a stranger in the scene. <u>Under</u> the roof of the small bus shelter, I was all alone. <u>In front of</u> me was a strip of dead grass littered with soft drink cans and cigarette butts. A six-lane highway was <u>beyond</u> the grass patch. Cars and trucks sped <u>by</u> me, focused on passing each other, making the green light, and getting somewhere fast. The drivers did not have time to notice me. A few cars in the outside lane swerved <u>toward</u> me as they temporarily lost control. <u>Far ahead of</u> me, <u>on the other side</u> of the highway, tall buildings with blank glass fronts stared. Maybe they were staring at me, the only human being who was not enclosed in metal or glass.

Exercise 16 **Combining Sentences and Using Transitions**

The following description has some choppy sentences that could be combined to create a smoother paragraph. Combine each pair of underlined sentences using appropriate transitions, and write the revised sentence above the original pair.

The food court at Pine Tree Mall entices many hungry shoppers. *The smell of* <u>One odor calls</u> *fresh-baked chocolate chip cookies calls to shoppers first.* <u>to shoppers first. It is the smell of fresh-baked chocolate chip cookies.</u> Next is a restaurant devoted to every version of fried chicken: chicken tenders, chicken sandwiches, white-meat chicken, chicken wings, and chicken legs. *Nearby is pizza* <u>Pizza is nearby.</u> *with a thick, soft crust, glistening layers of cheese, and bright red pepperoni.* <u>It has a thick, soft, crust, glistening layers of cheese, and bright red pepperoni.</u>

The spicy smells of a Chinese restaurant fill the air just beyond the pizza parlor. *Shoppers can feast on creations from a wok or an endless variety of egg rolls.* <u>Shoppers can feast on creations from a wok. Here there is also an endless variety of egg rolls.</u> The food court ends with the greatest temptation of all. *It is an ice* <u>It is an ice</u> *cream store, but not just any ice cream store.* <u>cream store. It is not just any ice cream store.</u> This store offers thirty flavors of ice cream, mix-ins, frozen yogurt, soft ice cream, and ice cream cakes. The food court offers tasty choices to those with a sweet tooth or those who crave chicken, pizza, *Few hungry shoppers can ignore the food at Pine Tree Mall* or Chinese food. <u>Few hungry shoppers can ignore the food at Pine Tree Mall. They</u> *because they can't get past all the sights and smells.* <u>can't get past all the sights and smells.</u>

POLISHING   **Polishing and Proofreading: Description**

In preparing the final version of a descriptive paragraph, you add the finishing touches to your paragraph, making changes in words, changing or adding transitions, and sharpening details. In the final version of the description paragraph, you will notice these changes:

- The phrase "had lots of books" has been changed to "were crammed with books." The phrases "lots of" and "a lot" are not specific, and some writers use them repetitively. Try not to use them.
- "My brother" has been identified by name, Michael.
- A few more sense details have been added.
- Another specific name of a video has been added.
- In the draft paragraph, the ending of the paragraph is a little sudden. The paragraph needs a sentence that pulls all the details together and reminds the reader of the topic sentence. The final version has an added sentence that unifies the paragraph.

A Final Version of a Descriptive Paragraph

(Changes from the draft are underlined.)

My brother <u>Michael's</u> bedroom reflected his fascination with fantasy and science fiction. Stars were pasted on the ceiling where, at night, they glowed in the dark. Then the room appeared to be covered by a starry sky. Movie posters covered the walls. A poster of Stephen Spielberg's <u>AI: Artificial Intelligence</u> hung next to a poster of <u>The Matrix</u> in a shiny chrome frame. Below the posters, two <u>black</u> steel bookcases <u>were crammed with books</u> about science fiction. I remember <u>Fahrenheit 451</u> and <u>The War of the Worlds</u>. Old videos like <u>Raiders of the Lost Ark</u> and <u>Alien</u> were also stacked on the bookshelves. The bed was piled high with <u>huge, soft</u> Star Trek pillows. <u>Anyone entering the room would know at once that Michael liked to escape to fantastic and futuristic places.</u>

Before you prepare the final copy of your own descriptive paragraph, check your last draft for errors in spelling, punctuation, typing, and copying.

For your information: A sample descriptive essay based on the same topic and following the same writing steps can be found in Chapter 12, on pages 279–284.

Exercise 17   **Proofreading to Prepare the Final Version**

Following are two descriptive paragraphs with the kinds of errors it is easy to overlook when you write the final version of an assignment. Correct the errors, writing above the lines. There are nine errors in the first paragraph and twelve errors in the second.

disgraceful

1. My most comfortable shoes are dilapidated and disgraceful. They are sneak-

. stitching

ers that are so old I cannot remember when I bought them? The stiching around the

toes

top of each shoe is gone, and every day I expect one of my toe's to pop out. The

flexible   soles

leather is all cracked and dirty, but to me, the leather is soft and flexible. The souls *are*

of the shoes is worn down about three layers. The soles are so thin that walking in

puddles wets my feet all the way through. However, those soles have been shaped to

fit my feet, and I like them. My friends say, "When are you going to get rid of those

?"   *no comma needed*

shoes"? I just say, "Never." They don't realize that, it would take years to break in

another pair of sneakers and make them as comfortable as my old ones.

         an   *throw*

    2. My father has a old reclining chair that he will not trow away because of

its   *no comma needed*

it's memories. The chair is creaky and battered. It is so old, that most of its stuff-

    The

ing is flat. the cloth covering the chair used to be shiny but now is dull. However,

                                    used

my father hangs on to the old recliner. When I was a baby, I use to sit on my

father's lap in the chair. He would read me the sports pages of the newspaper.

Even though   *idea*

Eventhough I had no Idea what he was saying, I liked the soothing sound of his

                gave

voice. In the winter, my mother give my father an old plaid blanket so that he

would be comfortable in his chair. When I was a little boy and felt sad, I some-

times snuggled alone under the blanket in the chair. Several times, I saw my father

asleep in his chair in the early morning. Years later, I realized that sometimes he

    too   *Then*

had been to tired to get up from the chair and go to bed. Than the chair became a

                               No comma needed

sad object to me. Now I am a man, and I see the chair differently. Now, I smile

when I see my father hold my baby son and rock him in the chair.

Lines of Detail: A Walk-Through Assignment

Your assignment is to write a paragraph describing a popular place for socializing. Follow these steps.

Step 1: To begin, freewrite about a place where people socialize. For example, you could write about a place where people go to eat, or dance, or swim, or just "hang out."

Step 2: Read your freewriting. Underline all the words, phrases, and sentences of description.

Step 3: List everything you underlined, grouping the ideas in some order. Maybe the details can be listed from inside to outside, or maybe they can be put into categories, like walls, floor, and furniture, or scenery and people.

Step 4: After you've surveyed the list, write a sentence about the dominant impression of the details.

Step 5: Using the dominant impression as your topic sentence, write an outline. Add specific details where you need them. Concentrate on details that appeal to the senses.

Step 6: Write a first draft of your paragraph. Be sure to check the order of your details. Combine short sentences and add transitions.

Step 7: Revise your first draft version, paying particular attention to order, specific details, and transitions.

Step 8: After a final check for punctuation, spelling, and word choice, prepare the final version of the paragraph.

Writing Your Own Descriptive Paragraph

When you write on any of the following topics, work through the stages of the writing process in preparing your descriptive paragraph. Be sure that your paragraph is based on a dominant impression, and put the dominant impression into your topic sentence.

1. Write a paragraph that describes one of the items below:

a favorite piece of clothing	a hospital waiting room
a popular exotic food	an eccentric friend
a favorite relative	a messy car
a very young baby	an irritating customer
a peaceful place	a person who changed your life
your first impression of a school	the contents of your purse or wallet

2. Describe a place that creates one of these impressions:

peace	tension	friendliness
cheerfulness	danger	safety

3. Describe a person who conveys one of these impressions:

confidence	warmth	pride
fear	style	shyness
intelligence	conformity	strength

Computer

4. Visit the Web site of your local newspaper, and find a photograph of a local event involving two or more individuals. Describe where the people are, what the event is, what the people are doing, what their facial expressions suggest, and anything you find unique about the setting. You may have to look through the archives of the Web site until you find a photograph that prompts such details. Be sure your details relate to a dominant impression of the scene, and be sure to select a photograph that you find interesting or unique. Attach the photograph to the completed paragraph.

Collaborate

5. Interview a partner so that you and your partner can gather details and then write a description paragraph with the title "My Ideal Room."

First, prepare a list of at least six questions to ask your partner. Write down the answers your partner gives and use those answers to form more questions. For example, if your partner says her ideal room would be a game room, ask her what games she'd like to have in it. If your partner says his ideal room would be a workshop, ask him what kind of workshop.

When you've finished the interview, switch roles. Let your partner interview you. Feel free to add more questions or to follow up on previous ones.

Give your partner his or her interview responses. Take your own responses and use them as the basis for gathering as many details as you can on your perfect room. Then go on to the outline, draft, and final version of your paragraph. Be prepared to read your completed paragraph to your partner.

6. Study the photograph below. Then write a paragraph that describes and explains the dominant impression of this scene.

7. Look carefully at the face in the photograph. Write a description that focuses on the aura of the face. Does the face give an impression of wisdom? Pain? Sorrow? Peace? Strength? You decide, and then support your decision by describing the details of the photograph.

How Do I Get a Better Grade?

Visit www. mywritinglab. com for audio-visual lectures and additional practice sets about description.

Get a better grade with MyWritingLab!

Note: Additional writing options suitable for description-related assignments can be found after the professional reading "A Present for Popo," which begins on page 607.

Name: _____   Section: _____

Peer Review Form for a Descriptive Paragraph

After you've written a draft of your descriptive paragraph, let a writing partner read it. When your partner has completed the form below, discuss the comments. Then repeat the same process for your partner's paragraph.

The dominant impression of the paragraph is this sentence: _____

_____

_____

The details of the description are in a specific order. That order is (for example, top to bottom, time order, etc.) _____

The part of the description I liked best begins with the words _____

_____

The part that could use more or better details begins with the words _____

_____

I have questions about or would like to know more about _____

_____.

I noticed these transitions: _____

_____.

A place where transitions could be added or improved is right before the words _____

_____.

Other comments on the paragraph: _____

_____

_____

_____

_____

_____

_____

_____

Reviewer's name: _____

CHAPTER 4

Jumping In

*What do you think happened just before this dramatic scene? Can you imagine what led to the tense atmosphere? There must be a story behind this picture, and if you write the story, you will be writing a **narrative** paragraph.*

Narration

WHAT IS NARRATION?

Narration means telling a story. Everybody tells stories; some people are better storytellers than others. When you write a **narrative** paragraph, you can tell a story about something that happened to you or to someone else, or about something that you saw or read.

A narrative, like a description, relies on specific details, but it is also different from a description because it covers events in a time sequence. While a description can be about a person, a place, or an object, a narrative is always about happenings: events, actions, incidents.

Interesting narratives do more than just tell what happened. They help the reader become involved in the story by providing vivid details. These details come from your memory, your observation, or your reading. Using good details, you don't just tell the story; you *show* it.

Give the Narrative a Point

We all know people who tell long stories that seem to lead nowhere. These people talk on and on; they recite an endless list of activities and soon become boring. Their narratives have no point.

TEACHING TIP

As a warm-up activity, ask students if they've recently told a narrative without realizing it. Could narratives be part of someone's job (for example, a trial lawyer addressing a jury, a police officer writing an incident report, a reporter writing an article about a kidnapping, etc.)?

The difficult part of writing a narrative is making sure that it has a point. That point will be included in the topic sentence. The point of a narrative is the meaning of the incident or incidents you are writing about. To get to the point of your narrative, ask yourself questions like these:

What did I learn?
What is the meaning of this story?
What is my attitude toward what happened?
Did it change me?
What emotion did it make me feel?
Was the experience a good example of something (such as unfairness, kindness, generosity, or some other quality)?

The answers to such questions can lead you to a point. An effective topic sentence for a narrative is

not this: I'm going to tell you about the time I flunked my driving test. (This is an announcement; it does not make a point.)
but this: When I failed my driving test, I learned not to be overconfident.
not this: Yesterday my car stalled in rush-hour traffic. (This identifies the incident but does not make a point. It is also too narrow to be a good topic sentence.)
but this: When my car stalled in rush-hour traffic, I was annoyed and embarrassed.

The topic sentence, stating the point of your narrative paragraph, can be placed in the beginning, middle, or end of the paragraph. You may want to start your story with the point so that the reader knows exactly where your story is headed, or you may want to conclude your story by leaving the point until last. Sometimes the point can even fit smoothly into the middle of your paragraph.

Consider the narrative paragraphs below. The topic sentences are in various places.

Topic Sentence at the Beginning

<u>When I was five, I learned how serious it is to tell a lie.</u> One afternoon, my seven-year-old friend Tina asked me if I wanted to walk down the block to play ball in an empty lot. When I asked my mother, she said I couldn't go because it was too near dinner time. I don't know why I lied, but when Tina asked me if my mother had said yes, I nodded my head in a lie. I wanted to go play, and I did. Yet as I played in the dusty lot, a dull buzz of guilt or fear distracted me. As soon as I got home, my mother confronted me. She asked me whether I had gone to the sandlot and whether I had lied to Tina about getting permission. This time, I told the truth. Something about my mother's tone of voice made me feel very dirty and ashamed. I had let her down.

Topic Sentence in the Middle

When I was little, I was afraid of diving into water. I thought I would go down and never come back up. Then one day, my father took me to a pool where we swam and fooled around, but he never forced me to try a dive. After about an hour of playing, I walked round and round the edge of the pool, trying to get the courage to dive in. Finally, I did it.

TEACHING TIP

Students often need to be reminded that topic sentences should not be announcements. Some students may have developed the habit in speech classes, in informal presentations, or in high school classes that rewarded content over structure.

TEACHING TIP

For students who say they have always been taught that topic sentences of paragraphs must be at the beginning, reassure them that they can follow the pattern in the first example.

When I made that first dive, I felt blissful because I had done something I had been afraid to do. As I came to the surface, I wiped the water from my eyes and looked around. The sun seemed more dazzling, and the water sparkled. Best of all, I saw my father looking at me with a smile. "You did it," he said. "Good for you! I'm proud of you."

Topic Sentence at the End

It seemed like I'd been in love with Reeza for years. Unfortunately, Reeza was always in love with someone else. Finally, she broke up with her boyfriend Nelson. I saw my chance. I asked Reeza out. After dinner, we talked and talked. Reeza told me all about her hopes and dreams. She told me about her family and her job, and I felt very close to her. We talked late into the night. When she left, Reeza kissed me. "Thanks for listening," she said. "You're like a brother to me." Reeza meant to be kind, but she shattered my hopes and dreams.

Exercise 1 Finding the Topic Sentence in a Narrative Paragraph

Underline the topic sentence in each narrative paragraph below.

Paragraph 1

When I drive home from work, I take the same route every day. It is not a freeway or even a crowded road. However, one day I had a frightening near-accident on this road. I was driving in the inside lane when suddenly a small white car changed lanes right in front of me. The car was about to hit me, so I swung my steering wheel to the left. Immediately, my car rotated in a circle, first slipping and skidding on the grass median and then facing the wrong direction in my original lane. The terror of the experience was the sudden loss of control. I could not have prevented the white car from swinging in front of me. I could not stop the direction of my car. I could not stop my car at all. After an instant of shock, I looked around me. Fortunately, no car was near enough to hit me. Shaken and dazed, I turned my car around and drove home.

Paragraph 2

When the police showed up at our party, we knew the fun had gone too far. My parents had gone away for the weekend, so my brother and I told a few friends to come over on Saturday night for a get-together. Unfortunately, those friends must have told other friends because our house was full of people by 10:00 p.m. Meanwhile, cars full of strangers kept circling the block, looking for places to park. I tried to keep the noise down, but each car arrived with speakers blasting. By midnight, trash covered the front yard, and cars blocked all the driveways on the street. Within minutes, two officers arrived and told us our neighbors had complained. We were actually relieved because the arrival of the police gave us an excuse to get rid of some of the weird people who had invaded our space.

Paragraph 3

My sister can be irritating. She is four years older than I am, so she feels free to hand out advice. Because she is married and a parent, she feels she knows the world better than I do. Last week, she was scolding me about my lack of a social life. Meanwhile, I noticed how tired she was as she tried to comfort the baby on her shoulder and prevent her toddler from climbing onto the windowsill. I saw the piles of laundry on the sofa and the diaper bags, plastic toys, and stroller on the floor. As she urged me to explore my options, meet new people, and have some fun, my sister paced back and forth, holding her heavy, wailing baby. Then her husband called to say he would be late, and my sister sat down, staring into space. <u>Suddenly I realized that my sister was not a superior being, but a woman trying to cope with her own loneliness.</u>

Exercise 2 Writing the Missing Topic Sentences in Narrative Paragraphs

Following are three paragraphs. If the paragraph already has a topic sentence, write it in the lines provided. If it does not have a topic sentence, create one. (Two of the paragraphs have no topic sentence.)

Paragraph 1

I postponed taking a required Fundamentals of Speech class because it terrified me. It involved speaking alone in front of the class. Once I enrolled in the class, I sat through every lecture in fear, waiting for the day when I would have to speak. When the instructor asked the students to sign up for a date to deliver a short speech, I signed up for the latest possible day. Of course, postponing my speech made me more nervous because I had to listen to the early speakers, who all seemed calm and confident. During the week before I was scheduled to speak, I worried, I planned, I even practiced in front of a friend. I expected to make a fool of myself. On the night before my speech, I could not sleep. On the morning of my speech, I considered skipping the class, but a small bit of courage made me show up. As I waited for my turn, the blood pounded in my head. Finally, when I stood at the podium, I wondered if everyone saw my body shaking. I do not know how I delivered my speech. All I know is that everyone applauded when it was over. Stunned, I returned to my seat and felt the fear go away.

INSTRUCTOR'S NOTE

Paragraph 2 has a topic sentence. Answers for paragraphs 1 and 3 will vary. Possible answers are shown.

If the paragraph already has a topic sentence, write it here. If it does not have a topic sentence, create one. *By facing my fears, I was able to speak in public.*

Paragraph 2

Once I joined the computer club, I felt like a part of the college. I am a basically shy person, and my first months at college were unhappy ones. I went to class and went home again, never talking to anyone. Then one day, I saw a notice posted about the computer club. I love my computer and am fascinated by anything online or digital. Gathering up my courage, I went to the next meeting of the club. As I entered the room, I felt like running out immediately. Everyone seemed to know everyone else, and I didn't know where to sit. I decided to sit next to two people who were talking about laptops and notebooks. I became so interested in the conversation that I was drawn into it. By the end of the first meeting, I had met five people and had arranged to get together for coffee with three of them. Suddenly, school did not seem like such a lonely place.

If the paragraph already has a topic sentence, write it here. If it does not have a topic sentence, create one. *Once I joined the computer club, I felt like a part of the college.*

Paragraph 3

Last week I was cat-sitting for a family who had to go out of town for a few days. The cat, Archie, is an affectionate gray cat with only one wish: to explore. Because he is an indoor cat, I knew I would have to be extremely careful while Archie was a guest in my house. I was very careful until the third day. On that day, the mail carrier came to drop off a package. I was so excited to receive an unexpected package that I left the door open a little too long. Just before I shut the door, I saw a flash of gray cross the threshold. I panicked. I raced outside, calling, "Archie! Archie!" I combed the small, fenced front yard, but Archie was nowhere to be found. Then I examined every bush and tree in the backyard. Meanwhile, I imagined the horror of having to tell my friends I had lost their cat. Then I thought of all the terrible things that could happen to the adventurous Archie. Finally, I returned to my front door, which, in my panic, I had left open. Sitting calmly in the doorway was Archie.

If the paragraph already has a topic sentence, write it here. If it does not have a topic sentence, create one. *Even adventurers have to come home sometime.*

Hints for Writing a Narrative Paragraph

Everyone tells stories, but some people tell stories better than others. When you write a story, be sure to

- Be clear.
- Be interesting.
- Stay in order.
- Pick a topic that is not too big.

1. Be clear. Put in all the information the reader needs in order to follow your story. Sometimes you need to explain the time or place or the relationships of the people in your story in order to make the story clear. Sometimes you need to explain how much time has elapsed between one action and another. This paragraph is not clear:

> I've never felt so stupid as I did on my first day of work. I was stocking the shelves when Mr. Cimino came up to me and said, "You're doing it wrong." Then he showed me how to do it. An hour later, he told me to call the produce supplier and check on the order for grapefruit. Well, I didn't know how to tell Mr. Cimino that I didn't know what phone to use or how to get an outside line. I also didn't know how to get the phone number of the produce supplier, or what the order for the grapefruit was supposed to be and when it was supposed to arrive. I felt really stupid asking these questions.

What is wrong with the paragraph? It lacks all kinds of information. Who is Mr. Cimino? Is he the boss? Is he a produce supervisor? And, more importantly, what kind of place is the writer's workplace? The reader knows the place has something to do with food, but is it a supermarket, or a fruit market, or a warehouse?

2. Be interesting. A boring narrative can make the greatest adventure sound dull. Here is a dull narrative:

> I had a wonderful time on prom night. First, we went out to dinner. The meal was excellent. Then we went to the dance and saw all our friends. Everyone was dressed up great. We stayed until late. Then we went out to breakfast. After breakfast we watched the sun come up.

Good specific details are the difference between an interesting story and a dull one.

3. Stay in order. Put the details in a clear order so that the reader can follow your story. Usually, time order is the order you follow in narration. This narrative has a confusing order:

> My impatience cost me twenty dollars last week. There was a pair of shoes I really wanted. I had wanted them for weeks. So, when payday came around, I went to the mall and checked the price on the shoes. I had been checking the price for weeks before. The shoes were expensive, but I really wanted them. On payday, my friend, who works at the shoe store, told me the shoes were about to go on sale. But I was impatient. I bought them at full price, and three days later, the shoes were marked down twenty dollars.

There's something wrong with the order of events here. Tell the story in the order it happened: first, I saw the shoes and wanted them; second, the shoes were expensive; third, I checked the price for several weeks; fourth, I got paid; fifth, I checked the price again; sixth, my friend told me the shoes were about to go on sale; seventh, I paid full price right away; eighth, the shoes went on sale. A clear time sequence helps the reader follow your narrative.

4. Pick a topic that is not too big. If you try to write about too many events in a short space, you run the risk of being superficial. You cannot describe anything well if you cover too much. This paragraph covers too much:

> Starting my sophomore year at a new high school was a difficult experience. Because my family had just moved to town, I didn't know anybody at school. On the first day of school, I sat by myself at lunch. Finally, two students at another table started a conversation with me. I thought they were just feeling sorry for me. At the end of the first week, it seemed like the whole school was talking about exciting plans for the weekend. I spent Friday and Saturday night at home, doing all kinds of things to keep my mind off my loneliness. On Monday, people casually asked, "Have a good weekend?" I lied and said, "Of course."

This paragraph would be better if it discussed one shorter time period in greater depth and detail. It could cover the first day at school, or the first lunch at school, or the first Saturday night at home alone, when the writer was doing "all kinds of things" to keep from feeling lonely.

Using a Speaker's Exact Words in Narrative

Some of the examples of narrative that you have already seen have included the exact words someone said. You may want to include part of a conversation in your narrative. To do so, you need to know how to punctuate speech.

A person's exact words get quotation marks around them. If you change the words, you do not use quotation marks.

> **exact words:** "You're being silly," he told me.
> **not exact words:** He told me that I was being silly.

> **exact words:** My sister said, "I'd love to go to the party."
> **not exact words:** My sister said she would love to go to the party.

INSTRUCTOR'S NOTE

For more on punctuating dialogue (direct quotes), students can review Chapter 29.

There are a few other points to remember about punctuating a person's exact words. Once you've started quoting a person's exact words, periods and commas generally go inside the quotation marks. Here are two examples:

> Richard said, "Nothing can be done."
> "Be careful," my mother warned us.

When you introduce a person's exact words with phrases like *She said*, or *The teacher told us*, put a comma before the quotation marks. Here are two examples:

> She said, "You'd better watch out."
> The teacher told us, "This will be a challenging class."

> If you are using a person's exact words and have other questions about punctuation, read about the use of quotation marks in Chapter 29 of the grammar section of this book.

WRITING THE NARRATIVE PARAGRAPH IN STEPS

PREWRITING Gathering Ideas: Narration

Finding something to write about can be the hardest part of writing a narrative paragraph because it is usually difficult to think of anything interesting or significant that you have experienced. By answering the following questions you can gather topics for your paragraph.

Exercise 3 Questionnaire for Gathering Narrative Topics

Collaborate

Answer the questions below and list details in the spaces provided. Then read your answers to a group. The members of the group should then ask you follow-up questions. Write your answers on the lines provided; the answers will add details to your list.

Finally, ask each member of your group to circle one topic or detail on your questionnaire that could be developed into a narrative paragraph. Discuss the suggestions. Repeat this process for each member of the group.

Narrative Questionnaire

1. Did you ever have a close call? When?

   _____

   Write four details you remember about it:

   a. _____

   b. _____

   c. _____

   d. _____

   Additional details, to be added after working with the group:

   _____

   _____

2. Have you ever lost an item that was important to you? Write four details about what happened before, during, and after:

   a. _____

   b. _____

   c. _____

   d. _____

   Additional details, to be added after working with the group:

   _____

   _____

3. Have you ever had a day when everything went wrong? Write four details about that day:

   a. _____

   b. _____

   c. _____

   d. _____

   Additional details, to be added after working with the group:

   _____

   _____

Freewriting for a Narrative Topic

One good way to discover something to write about is to freewrite. For example, if your instructor asks you to write a narrative paragraph about something that changed you, you might begin by freewriting.

Freewriting for a Narrative Paragraph

Topic: Something That Changed Me

Something that changed me. I don't know. What changed me? Lots of things happened to me, but I can't find one that changed me. Graduating from high school? Everybody will write about that, how boring, and anyway, what was the big deal? I haven't gotten married. No big change there. Divorce. My parents' divorce really changed the whole family. A big shock to me. I couldn't believe it was happening. I was really scared. Who would I live with? They were really calm when they told me. I've never been so scared. I was too young to understand. Kept thinking they'd just get back together. They didn't. Then I got a stepmother. The year of the divorce was a hard time for me. Kids suffer in divorce.

Narrowing and Selecting a Suitable Narrative Topic

After you freewrite, you can assess your writing, looking for words, phrases, or sentences that you could expand into a paragraph. The sample writing has several ideas for a narrative:

> *high school graduation*
> *learning about my parents' divorce*
> *adjusting to a stepmother*
> *the year of my parents' divorce*

Looking for a topic that is not too big, you could use

> *high school graduation*
> *learning about my parents' divorce*

Since the freewriting has already called graduation a boring topic, the divorce seems to be a more attractive subject. In the freewriting, you already have some details related to the divorce; add to these details by brainstorming. Follow-up questions and answers might include the following:

How old were you when your parents got divorced?

I was seven years old when my mom and dad divorced.

Are you an only child?

My sister was ten.

Where did your parents tell you? Did they both tell you at the same time?

They told us at breakfast, in the kitchen. Both my folks were there. I was eating toast. I remember I couldn't eat it when they both started talking. I remember a piece of toast with one bite out of it.

What reasons did they give?

They said they loved us, but they couldn't get along. They said they would always love us kids.

If you didn't understand, what did you <u>think</u> was happening?

At first I just thought they were having another fight.

Did you cry? Did they cry?

I didn't cry. My sister cried. Then I knew it was serious. I kept thinking I would have to choose which parent to live with. Then I knew I'd really hurt the one I didn't choose. I felt so much guilt about hurting one of them.

What were you feeling?

I felt ripped apart.

Questions can help you form the point of your narrative. After brainstorming, you can go back and survey all the details. Do they lead you to a point? Try asking yourself the questions listed earlier in this chapter: What did I learn? What is the meaning of this story? What is my attitude toward what happened? Did it change me? What emotion did it make me feel? Was the experience a good example of something (like unfairness, or kindness, or generosity)?

For the topic of the divorce, the details mention a number of emotions: confusion, pain, shock, disbelief, fear, guilt. The *point* of the paragraph cannot list all these emotions, but it could be stated this way:

When my parents announced they were divorcing, I felt confused by all my emotions.

Now that you have a point and several details, you can move on to the outlining stage of writing a narrative paragraph.

Exercise 4　**Distinguishing Good Topic Sentences from Bad Ones in Narration**

Below are sentences. Some would make good topic sentences for a narrative paragraph. Others would not: they are too big to develop in a single paragraph, or they are so narrow they can't be developed, or they make no point about an incident or incidents. Put an *X* by the sentences that would not make good topic sentences.

1. __X__ I was born in a small town in Haiti.

2. _____ I became anxious after my neighbor's house was burglarized last week.

3. __X__ A semester of Art Appreciation taught me about centuries of great art.

4. _____ My first day of work at an auto parts warehouse made me want to quit.

5. __X__ This is the story of my heart surgery.

6. _____ I discovered what I wanted to do with my life when I visited a hospital for sick children.

7. __X__ Last week my brother scored a touchdown for his college team.

8. __X__ Alcohol is a problem for my mother and my stepfather.

9. __X__ Yesterday I got my driver's license.

10. _____ I never felt jealousy until I saw Christina talking to a handsome stranger.

Exercise 5　**Developing a Topic Sentence from a List of Details**

Following are two lists of details. Each has an incomplete topic sentence. Read the details carefully; then complete each topic sentence.

1. **topic sentence:** A talk with _my aunt_____ helped me to

understand _my father's behavior toward me._____

INSTRUCTOR'S NOTE

Answers will vary. Possible answers shown at left.

details: My father has always been strict with me.

Until I was in my teens, he never let me go outside after dark to meet my buddies on the street.

He also insisted on knowing all my friends.

Yesterday, I became upset with my father's constant questioning and surveillance.

I complained to my Aunt Angela.

My aunt said my father had a secret.

In his teens, my father had been in a gang.

He had been involved in fights.

"That scar on his neck is from a knife fight," my aunt said.

She added that my father had been in prison.

"He is not proud of his past," my aunt said, "so he hides it from you."

"He feels that he must be hard on you," Aunt Angela added, "to keep you safe."

I felt that my aunt was talking about a stranger, but at least the stranger cared about me.

2. **topic sentence:** My last meeting with Melissa was a _shocking_____ time for me.

details: Melissa and I had been going out for about a year.

We had a routine of spending part of each weekend together.

We went to the movies, to the mall, or to a coffee shop.

Sometimes we just drove around.

When we talked, we talked mostly about our jobs, music, sports, or video games.

I was comfortable with her, and I thought she was happy with our relationship.

Last Saturday night, as she got into my car, I asked her what she wanted to do.

Melissa didn't really answer my question.

Instead, she said she didn't want to see me anymore.

When I asked her why, she became angry.

"It's been a year," she said, "and you've never talked about marrying me."

I didn't know what to say.

"I don't have any more time to waste on you," she snarled.

She left, slamming the car door.

I just sat there.

PLANNING   **Devising a Plan: Narration**

The topic of how an experience changed you has led you to a point and a list of details. You can now write a rough outline, with the point as the topic sentence. Once you have the rough outline, check it for these qualities:

Relevance: Do all the details connect to the topic sentence?
Order: Are the details in a clear order?
Development: Does the outline need more details? Are the details specific enough?

Your revised outline might look like the following:

An Outline for a Narrative Paragraph

topic sentence:	When my parents announced that they were divorcing, I felt confused by all my emotions.
details: **background of the narrative**	I was seven when my mom and dad divorced. My sister was ten. Both my folks were there. They told us at breakfast, in the kitchen. I was eating toast. I remember I couldn't eat anything when they started talking. I remember a piece of toast with one bite out of it.
story of the divorce announcement	My parents were very calm when they told us. They said they loved us but couldn't get along. They said they would always love us kids. It was a big shock to me.
my reactions at each stage	I couldn't believe it was happening. At first I just thought they were having another fight. I was too young to understand. I didn't cry. My sister cried. Then I knew it was serious. I kept thinking I would have to choose which parent to live with. I knew I'd really hurt the one I didn't choose. I felt so much guilt about hurting one of them. I felt ripped apart.

Once you have a revised outline, you're ready to write a draft of the narrative paragraph.

Exercise 6 Finding Details That Are Out of Order in a Narrative Outline

The outlines below have details that are out of order. Put the details in correct time order by numbering them 1, 2, and so forth.

1. **topic sentence:** After yesterday's experience, I will never sit on my patio again.

   details: ___1___ Yesterday was a beautiful day with a cool breeze and a cloudless sun.

   ___3___ While I sat on a lawn chair, reading the newspaper, my hyperactive terrier explored the bushes around the patio.

   ___2___ Once I saw how great the weather was, I decided to enjoy the outdoors on my small patio.

_7_   Once I felt sure that my dog was not getting into any mischief, I fell asleep.

_4_   Soon the sun made me drowsy, so I dropped the newspaper.

_5_   Drowsiness led me to the idea of a nap.

_6_   Before I fell asleep, I checked on my dog, who was running happily in the bushes.

_8_   I woke to the sound of my dog barking furiously at me—or at my lawn chair.

_10_   It was a long, shiny black snake that my dog had chased under the seat of the chair.

_9_   Looking down at my chair, I saw something beneath the seat.

2. topic sentence: A woman at my checkout counter made me feel as if I didn't exist.

details: _2_   I said, "Hello, how are you today?" as I always do.

_1_   It all began as it usually does when a customer steered her cart into my checkout aisle.

_3_   When she didn't reply to my greeting, I noticed that she was talking on her cell phone.

_8_   I handed her the receipt and asked her if she needed help carrying her groceries.

_9_   She ignored me, pushed her cart full of bagged groceries, continued her phone conversation, and walked away.

_4_   She continued talking, louder now, and using her free hand, she unloaded the groceries.

_5_   Soon I totaled the amount and announced what she owed me.

_6_   The woman acted as if she hadn't heard the amount.

_7_   Instead of reacting, she just swiped her credit card through the cardholder, still talking loudly on the phone.

Exercise 7   Recognizing Irrelevant Details in a Narrative Outline

Below are two outlines. One of them has details that are not relevant to the topic sentence. Cross out the details that do not fit.

1. topic sentence: The worst part of our trip was the tollbooth.

details: Last weekend, my wife and I drove for three hours to visit my parents in Orlando.

~~It's also fun to go to the theme parks in Orlando.~~

We sailed through light traffic and good weather until we had only twenty minutes to go.

Then we suffered the frustrations of a turnpike tollbooth.

We joined the shortest lane at the toll plaza.

~~Sometimes it is hard to figure out which lane will be the fastest moving.~~

Ahead of us were only two cars, so we expected a quick ride through the lane.

After about five minutes, we realized that the car next to the booth was not moving.

Instead, the driver of that car was having a long conversation with the attendant.

The conversation got longer, and I got impatient.

I wanted to blow the car horn, but my wife stopped me.

Ten minutes went by, and we still were not moving. Then the attendant left the booth to talk to the attendant at the next booth.

I began shouting, "Come on! Let's move!"

After what seemed like an hour, the toll booth attendant returned.

The two cars ahead of us began to move.

~~I'm always afraid of losing the card that indicates how much toll to pay.~~

Still feeling frustrated, I paid my toll and left.

2. topic sentence: My mother received a welcome surprise in the mail on Saturday.

details: She went out to check the mailbox, not expecting anything exciting.

In fact, she was expecting bills.

Times have been hard for her lately; she lost her job, and the bills have been piling up.

When she returned to the house carrying a bunch of envelopes, she looked discouraged.

"More bills," she said.

She flipped through envelopes from two credit card companies, the electric company, and the water department.

"Well," she said, "I guess I might as well open them and face the bad news."

Just as she expected, the electric company and the credit card companies wanted money.

However, the letter from the water department contained a check for fifty dollars.

The water company said it had made an error and overcharged my mother several months ago.

"What do you know?" my mother said. "Maybe this means my luck is turning!"

DRAFTING   Drafting and Revising: Narration

After you have a revised outline for your narration paragraph, you can begin working on a rough draft of the paragraph. As you write your first draft, you can combine some of the short sentences of the outline. Once you have a draft, you can check it for places you would like to improve. The list below may help you to check your draft.

> **Checklist: A Checklist for Revising the Draft of a Narrative Paragraph**
>
> ✓ Is my narrative vivid?
>
> ✓ Are the details clear and specific?
>
> ✓ Does the topic sentence fit all the details?
>
> ✓ Are the details written in a clear order?
>
> ✓ Do the transitions make the narrative easy to follow?
>
> ✓ Have I made my point?

Revising for Sharper Details

A good idea for a narrative can be made better if you revise for sharper details. In the paragraph below, the underlined words and phrases could be revised to create better details. In the following example, see how the second draft has more vivid details than the first draft.

First Draft: Details Are Dull

A woman at the movies showed me just how rude and selfish people can be. It all started when I was in line with <u>a lot</u> of other people. We had been waiting <u>a long time</u> to buy our tickets. We were outside, and it <u>wasn't pleasant.</u> We were impatient because time was running out and the movie was about to start. Some people were <u>making remarks</u>, and <u>others were pushing</u>. Then <u>a woman cut to</u> the front of the line. The cashier at the ticket window <u>told</u> the woman there was a line and she would have to go to the end of it. The woman <u>said she didn't want to wait because her son didn't want to miss the beginning of the movie.</u>

Second Draft: Better Details

A woman at the movies showed me just how rude and selfish people can be. It all started when I was in line with <u>forty or fifty other people</u>. We had been waiting to buy our tickets for <u>twenty minutes</u>. We were outside, <u>where the temperature was about 90 degrees, and it looked like rain</u>. We were all getting impatient because time was running out and the movie was about to start. <u>I heard two people mutter about how ridiculous the wait was, and someone else kept saying, "Let's go!" The man directly behind me kept pushing me, and each new person at the end of the line pushed the whole line forward, against the ticket window.</u> Then a woman <u>with a loud voice and a large purse thrust her purse and her body in front of the ticket window.</u> The cashier <u>politely</u> told the woman there was a line and she had to go to the end of it. But the woman answered <u>indignantly.</u> <u>"Oh no," she said, "I'm with my son Mickey. And Mickey really wants to see this martial arts movie. And he hates to miss the first part of any movie. So I can't wait. I've got to have those tickets now."</u>

Checking the Topic Sentence

Sometimes you think you have a good idea, a good topic sentence, and specific details, but when you write the draft of the paragraph, you realize the

TEACHING TIP

Have students jot down the underlined words in the first draft and then match them with the additional details in the second draft (in two columns). Ask them what details they find effective. Why? This activity will help them understand the difference between vague and specific.

topic sentence does not quite fit all the details. When that happens, you can either revise the details or *rewrite the topic sentence.*

In the following paragraph, the topic sentence (underlined) does not quite fit all the details, so the topic sentence should be rewritten.

> <u>I didn't know what to do when a crime occurred in front of my house.</u> At 9:00 p.m., I was sitting in my living room, watching television, when I heard what sounded like a crash outside. At first I thought it was a garbage can that had fallen over. Then I heard another crash and a shout. I ran to the window, and I looked out into the dark. I couldn't see anything because the streetlight in front of my house was broken. But I heard at least two voices, and they sounded angry and threatening. I heard another voice, and it sounded like someone moaning. I was afraid. I ran to the telephone. I was going to call 911, but then I froze in fear. What if the police came, and people got arrested? Would the suspects find out I was the one who had called the police? Would they come after <u>me</u>? Would I be a witness at a trial? I didn't want to get involved. So I just stood behind the curtain, peeking out and listening. Pretty soon the shouting stopped, but I still heard sounds like hitting. I couldn't stand it any more. I called the police. When they came, they found a young teenager, badly beaten, in the street. They said my call may have saved his life.

The paragraph above has good details, but the story has more of a point than "I didn't know what to do." The person telling the story finally did do something. Following is a better topic sentence that covers the whole story.

topic sentence rewritten: I finally found the courage to take the proper action when a crime occurred in front of my house.

> **Exercise 8**   **Combining Sentences in a Draft of a Narrative**

The following paragraph contains some short, choppy sentences, which are underlined. Wherever you see two or more underlined sentences clustered next to each other, combine them into one clear, smooth sentence. Write your revised versions above the original sentences.

INSTRUCTOR'S NOTE

Answers will vary. Possible answers shown at right.

I had just entered the

Helping an elderly man brought me a rush of satisfaction. <u>I had just entered the</u>

hall of my apartment building when I saw several envelopes and flyers on the

<u>hall of my apartment building. I saw several envelopes and flyers. They were on</u>

floor near the mailboxes.

<u>the floor. They were near the mailboxes.</u> Then I saw a person lying face down on

the floor. Instinctively, I leaned down to check on the person. A gray-haired man

spoke to me. "I came to get my mail, and I slipped," he said. "Now I can't get

I was glad that the man was conscious and speaking.

myself back up." <u>I was glad that the man was conscious. Hearing him speak made</u>

<u>me feel relieved.</u> Without thinking about my strength and the man's condition, I

At that moment, I understood what it is like to lift a person who

tried to lift him. <u>At that moment, I understood what it is like to lift a person. The</u>

can't help himself.

<u>person can't help himself.</u> Fortunately, another resident came down the hall and

We lifted the old man, carried him between us, got him into his

helped me out. <u>We lifted the old man. We carried him between us. We got him into</u>

apartment, and rested him on the sofa.

<u>his apartment. We got him resting on his sofa.</u> His wife, who hadn't realized he had

fallen, greeted us like we were heroes. "Oh, thank you, thank you," she said. Then

she began to cry. When I left, I seemed to be walking in a happy daze. Without hes-

Because of me, two people were safe and happy.

itating, I had done the right thing. <u>Two people were happy. Because of me, they</u>

<u>were safe.</u> In a way, I had been tested and had passed my own test.

Exercise 9   Adding Better Details to a Draft of a Narrative

The following paragraph has some details that could be more vivid. Rewrite
the paragraph in the lines below it, replacing the underlined details with
more vivid words, phrases, or sentences.

     I almost lost a friendship because of my own insecurity. Tanya
and I have been friends <u>for a long time</u>, ever since we met at the
restaurant where we both worked. Working with Tanya made the job
fun because we joked and gossiped together. <u>We did things</u> outside of
work, too. Recently, I noticed that Tanya was <u>acting strange</u>. I began
to think that she wasn't interested in being my friend anymore. Feeling hurt and insulted, I began <u>acting crazy around her</u>. The situation
escalated when Tanya began to react to my cold behavior and sarcastic tone. Fortunately, Tanya was brave enough to confront me.
"What's the matter?" she asked. "Have I done anything to hurt you?" I
accused her of <u>some stuff</u>, but Tanya was patient enough not to get
angry. She explained that she had been preoccupied lately because
her brother Fareed was in the hospital, undergoing a series of tests. I
believed that Tonya had been cold to me, but she had really been concerned for her brother. Once I understood Tanya's situation, I felt
<u>stupid</u>. All I could do was apologize to my friend and promise to <u>do</u>
<u>better</u>.

Rewrite: *I almost lost a friendship because of my own insecurity. Tanya and*

*I have been friends **for two years**, ever since we met at the restaurant where*

we both worked. Working with Tanya made the job fun because we joked and

*gossiped together. We **met for coffee or for a meal** outside of work, too.*

*Recently, I noticed that Tanya was **ignoring me and brushing off my***

***questions with one-word answers**. I began to think that she wasn't interested*

*in being my friend anymore. Feeling hurt and insulted, I began **speaking to***

***her in a cutting tone, using as few words as possible**. The situation escalated*

when Tanya began to react to my cold behavior and sarcastic tone. Fortunately,

Tanya was brave enough to confront me. "What's the matter?" she asked.

*"Have I done anything to hurt you?" I accused her of **treating me as if I***

***didn't exist**, but Tanya was patient enough not to get angry. She explained*

that she had been preoccupied lately because her brother Fareed was in the hospital, undergoing a series of tests. I believed that Tonya had been cold to

me, but she had really been concerned for her brother. Once I understood

*Tanya's situation, I felt **selfish and immature**. All I could do was apologize to*

*my friend and promise to **trust our friendship**.*

Exercise 10   Writing a Better Topic Sentence for a Narrative

The paragraphs below could use better topic sentences. (In each paragraph, the current topic sentence is underlined.) Read each paragraph carefully, then write a new topic sentence for it in the space provided.

Paragraph 1

<u>My old boyfriend called me last week.</u> I had not seen him in three years. At our last meeting, he had left me feeling hurt and worthless. I felt that I had lost my only chance at love and that he had rejected me because I just wasn't good enough to meet his standards. Now, I suddenly heard his voice and froze. I was not prepared to speak to him. He filled up the blank spaces, however. He told me of his accomplishments: his great new job and his new apartment. He never asked how I was or what I had been doing. Instead he went on and on, telling me of his travels to Mexico and Arizona, his sports car, and his flat-screen television. His bragging was empty and sad. Suddenly, I was grateful that I had never become one of that man's possessions. "You sound like you have everything you want," I said, and I knew that he had nothing I wanted.

New topic sentence: *A call from an old boyfriend brought me a valuable*

insight.

Paragraph 2

<u>Ari and I locked ourselves out of our apartment yesterday.</u> Ari had rushed out to grab his algebra textbook from his car, and he left the apartment door wide open. In the meantime, Ari's girlfriend, Sabrina, called and said she needed to talk to Ari immediately. I ran outside to tell him. Unfortunately, just as I reached the parking lot and found Ari, a huge gust of wind slammed our apartment door shut. It was not just shut; it was locked shut. "Do you have your key?" I asked Ari. "No," he said, "Don't you have yours?" We tried pushing the door open, but of course the only result was a scary creaking-splitting sound around the door frame. Then we got another idea: we would try sliding a credit card between the lock and the door frame. We had seen many television detectives use this method, but they must have been smarter than we were. So far, the only result of our efforts was to create suspense among some of the neighbors, who thought we were burglars. Irritated, frustrated, and impatient, Ari and I were exchanging insults and accusations when Sabrina rescued us. Sick of waiting for Ari to come to the phone, she had driven over to confront him. Sabrina was furious, but she was also our hero, for Ari had given her a key to our apartment.

New topic sentence: *When Ari and I locked ourselves out of our apartment,*

we were trapped in our own helplessness.

Using Transitions Effectively in Narration

When you tell a story, you have to be sure that your reader can follow you as you move through the steps of your story. One way to make your story easier to follow is to use transitions. Most of the transitions in narration have to do with time. Below is a list of transitions writers often use in writing narration.

INFO BOX: Transitions for a Narrative Paragraph

after	before	in the meantime	soon after
again	during	later	still
always	finally	later on	suddenly
at first	first	meanwhile	then
at last	second (etc.)	next	until
at once	frequently	now	when
at the same time	immediately	soon	while

The Draft

Below is a draft of the paragraph on divorce. As you read it, you will notice that some ideas from the outline on page 90 have been combined, the details have been put in order, and transitions have been added. Exact words of dialogue have been used to add vivid details.

A Draft of a Narrative Paragraph

(Transitions are underlined.)

When my parents announced that they were divorcing, I felt confused by all my emotions. At the time of their announcement, I was seven and my sister was ten. Both my folks were there to tell us. They told us at breakfast, in the kitchen. I was eating toast, but I remember I couldn't eat anything when they started talking. I remember a piece of toast with one bite taken out of it. My parents were very calm when they told us. "We love both you kids very much," my dad said, "but your mother and I aren't getting along." They said they would always love us. The announcement was such a shock to me that I couldn't believe it was happening. At first, I just thought they were having another fight. Because I was too young to understand, I didn't cry. Suddenly, my sister started to cry, and then I knew it was serious. I kept thinking I would have to choose which parent to live with. I knew I'd really hurt the one I didn't choose, so I felt so much guilt about hurting one of them. I felt ripped apart.

Exercise 11 Recognizing Transitions in a Narrative Paragraph

Underline the transitions in the following paragraph.

Our race to catch a plane must have looked like a scene from an action movie. Alejandro and I were supposed to have an hour at the airport between our first and second flights, but our first flight was late in arriving. As a result, we had only fifteen minutes to catch the second flight. When we got off the first plane, we raced to the departures schedule board to check the gate number for the next flight. The gate was far away, and, even worse, it was on another concourse. Immediately, we began running to the moving sidewalk. Soon we were sprinting down the slow-moving sidewalk, passing the calm people standing still. <u>Next,</u> we waited anxiously for the train that would take us to our concourse. <u>Meanwhile,</u> we heard a loudspeaker announce our flight's departure. <u>Then</u> the train arrived. We pushed our way into a crowded compartment. <u>Finally,</u> we used our last bit of strength to stagger to the departure gate. We leaped toward the gate, flashing our boarding passes at the startled flight attendant seconds <u>before</u> the plane's door was shut.

TEACHING TIP

This exercise will be a good place to note that transitions do not necessarily have to be placed at the beginning of sentences.

Exercise 12 **Adding the Right Transitions to a Narrative Paragraph**

In the following paragraph, circle the correct transition in each of the pairs.

⟨When⟩/After I was twelve, I was obsessed with getting a tattoo. I felt that having a tattoo would make me look sophisticated and even dangerous at school. The only problem with my achieving this goal was that my grandmother would kill me if I showed up with a tattoo. To convince her that I badly needed to mark and paint my skin, I tried many tactics. Before/⟨At first,⟩ I claimed that everyone had tattoos. I told her that athletes, musicians, and even middle-aged ladies had them. My grandmother was not impressed. ⟨Immediately⟩/Again I switched to another tactic. "Tattoos are works of art," I told Granny. "You are not going to wear art on your body," she insisted. ⟨Next⟩/Last I tried bribing her. I promised Granny that if she let me get a tattoo, I would never again cause her any trouble. My solemn promise didn't even tempt her. Always/⟨Finally⟩ I resorted to the most childish way of persuading an adult. I whined. "Please, please, Granny," I cried. "I really want a tattoo. Please." "You can have your tattoo," my grandmother said. ⟨At last⟩/Frequently I felt that I had won my battle. However, my grandmother wasn't finished with me. "You can have your tattoo," she repeated, "when you are a man and old enough to pay for your own foolishness."

POLISHING **Polishing and Proofreading: Narration**

As you prepare the final version of the narration paragraph, make any minor changes in word choice or transitions that can refine your writing. Below is the final copy of the narrative paragraph on divorce. Notice these changes in the final version:

- The draft version used both formal and informal words like "folks" and "parents" and "dad." The final version uses only "parents" and "father."
- A few details have been added.
- A few details have been changed.
- A transition has been added.

A Final Version of a Narrative Paragraph

(Changes from the draft are underlined.)

When my parents announced that they were divorcing, I felt confused by all my emotions. At the time of the announcement, I was seven and my sister was ten. Both <u>my parents</u> were there to tell us. They told us at breakfast, in the kitchen. I was eating toast, but I remember I couldn't eat anything when they started talking. <u>In fact,</u> I remember <u>staring at</u> a piece of toast with one bite taken out of it. My parents were very calm when they told us. "We both love you very much," my

<u>father</u> said. "But your mother and I aren't getting along." They said they would always love us. The announcement was such a shock to me that I couldn't believe it was happening. At first, I just thought they were having another fight. Because I was too young to understand, I didn't cry. Suddenly, my sister started to cry, and then I knew it was serious. I kept thinking I would have to choose which parent to live with. I knew I'd really hurt the one I didn't choose, so I felt <u>terrible</u> guilt about hurting one of them. I felt ripped apart.

Before you prepare the final version of your narrative paragraph, check your latest draft for errors in spelling, punctuation, typing, and copying.

> **For your information:** A sample narrative essay based on this topic and following the same writing steps can be found in Chapter 12, on pages 284–287.

Exercise 13   Proofreading to Prepare the Final Version

Following are two narrative paragraphs with the kinds of errors that are easy to overlook when you prepare the final version of an assignment. Correct the errors, writing above the lines. There are fourteen errors in the first paragraph and thirteen in the second.

Paragraph 1

        night   *no comma needed*
My Friday nite was spoiled, when I had to deal with an angry and aggressive

woman. She arrived late at night at the Peaceful Inn, where I work. She came with
                                    checked
her pet, a large barking dog named Chanel. When the woman check in, she wanted
  no quotation mark   *third*
to know "why I had put her on the 3rd floor, the floor for smokers. I explained that

the third floor was the only floor where dogs could stay with their owners. "I'm

not a smoker," the woman complained, "so why should I have to breathe the
                      response   *smokers*
smokers' polluted air?" I managed to stifle my responce that the poor smoker's
                                      had
would have to listen to Chanel barking all night. After the woman have lost the
                           inn
battle of the third floor, she demanded cookies. When I told her the Inn had no

cookies, she reminded me of the Peaceful Inn's advertising, which promised fresh-

baked cookies every day. Then I had to explain to her that the cookies were baked

only in the afternoon. "Why can't you bake me some cookies now?" she insisted.

"You don't have anything else to do in the middle of the night." Finally, after more
                barking   *However*
of her complaining and Chanel's Barking, the woman left for her room. however,
                ten
my troubles were not over. Within 10 minutes, my angry guest called. Even nastier
                        no comma needed
than before, she wanted me to bring her a new ice bucket, because hers looked

dirty. Twenty minutes later, she called again, this time to complain that the vend-

ing machine had no Diet Coke. Thanks to this unhappy women, this was one night
                                                          woman

when the Peaceful Inn was not peaceful for me.

Paragraph 2

                                   class   *wonderful*
   Last week in my painting Class, I received a wonderfull gift. I took the class

only because I needed an art, music, or theater class in order to graduate. Art
                         than
seemed easier then singing, dancing, or acting, so I signed up for a painting class. I
             conscious   *someone*
was really self-conscience at first, for I hated the idea of some one watching over
                              tried
my shoulder while I tried to paint. After a few days, I calmed down a little because

the teacher was helpful, not critical. At the same time, I developed a real fear of

the other students They seemed so talented and confident as they laughed and
                                                     You're
talked. I hunched over my painting and worried. "Your not an artist," I told myself,
     you've
"and You've never been good at anything." I imagined the other students feeling
                                             loser
sorry for me, the poor untalented losser. Then, last Tuesday, the teacher said he
     an
had a announcement. Two paintings from our art class had been selected for a

local exhibition. Immediately, I stopped listening. I wondered who the lucky stu-
                           ,
dents would be but I never thought I had a chance. Suddenly, I heard my name
                                             felt
called. When I realized there was no mistake, I feel shocked by my happiness. At

last, I knew I could be good at something.

INSTRUCTOR'S NOTE:

For lists and exercises covering words that sound alike/look alike, see Chapter 31.

Lines of Detail: A Walk-Through Assignment

Write a paragraph about an incident in your life that embarrassed, amused, frightened, saddened, or angered you. In writing the paragraph, follow these steps:

Step 1: Begin by freewriting. Then read your freewriting, looking for both the details and focus of your paragraph.

Step 2: Brainstorm for more details. Then write all the freewriting and brainstorming as a list.

Step 3: Survey your list. Write a topic sentence that makes a point about the details.

Step 4: Write an outline. As you write the outline, check that your details fit the topic sentence and are in clear order. As you revise your outline, add details where they are needed.

Step 5: Write and revise a draft of your paragraph. Revise until your details are specific and in a clear order and your transitions are smooth. Combine any sentences that are short and choppy. Add a speaker's exact words if they will make the details more specific.

Step 6: In preparing the final version, check for punctuation, spelling, and word choice.

Writing Your Own Narrative Paragraph

When you write on any of the following topics, be sure to work through the stages of the writing process in preparing your narrative paragraph.

1. Write about some surprising event you saw that you will never forget. Begin by freewriting. Then read your freewriting, looking for both the details and the focus of your paragraph.

   If your instructor agrees, ask a writing partner or group to (a) listen to you read your freewriting, (b) help you focus it, and (c) help you add details by asking questions.

2. Write a narrative paragraph about a mistake you made at your first job. Include how that mistake proved to be a valuable lesson.

3. Write a narrative paragraph about the couple in the photograph on page 101. Look carefully at their expressions and body language, and write about events you imagine happened before, during, and after this scene. You may want to include some dialogue in your paragraph.

Collaborate

4. Interview an older family member or friend. Ask him or her to tell you an interesting story about his or her past. Ask questions as the person speaks. Take notes. If you have a recorder, you can record the interview, but take notes as well.

When you've finished the interview, review the information with the person you've interviewed. Ask the person if he or she would like to add anything. If you wish, ask follow-up questions.

Next, on your own, find a point to the story. Work through the stages of the writing process to turn the interview into a narrative paragraph.

Computer

5. Visit the Web site of your local newspaper, and find a news article about a crime that involved a sequence of events leading to a confrontation, arrest, or escape. Write the details of the story in time order, and be sure to use effective transitions. Your topic sentence should state what type of crime occurred as well as the outcome of it. (As you take notes from the article, be aware that newspaper accounts are not written in time order, so you will have to do some reordering of events.) Include a copy of the article with your paragraph.

6. Have you ever been judged unfairly because of your age, race, or appearance? Write a narrative about the incident and include the emotions you experienced at the time.

7. Write a narrative about the hurricane in the photograph. You can include events you imagine happened to the family before, during, and after the dramatic scene in the photograph.

How Do I Get a Better Grade?

mywritinglab

Visit www.mywritinglab.com for audio-visual lectures and additional practice sets about narration.

Get a better grade with MyWritingLab!

Note: Additional writing options suitable for narrative-related assignments can be found after the professional reading "The Good Father," which begins on page 610.

Name: _____   Section: _____

Peer Review Form for a Narrative Paragraph

After you have written a draft of your narrative paragraph, let a writing partner read it. When your partner has completed the form below, discuss the responses. Repeat the same process for your partner's paragraph.

I think the topic sentence of this paragraph is _____

_____

_____

_____

I think the topic sentence (a) states the point well, (b) could be revised. (Choose one.)

The part of the narrative I liked best begins with the words _____

_____

_____

The part that could use more or better details begins with the words _____

_____

An effective transition was _____

_____

I have questions about or would like to know more about _____

_____

I would like to take out the part about _____

_____

I think the narrative is (a) easy to follow, (b) a little confusing. (Choose one.)

_____

Other comments: _____

_____

_____

_____

Reviewer's Name   _____

CHAPTER 5

Jumping In

Could you teach a person who has never used a digital camera how to take photos with it? How would you start your explanation? How many steps would your instructions take? Teaching in steps involves one kind of *process*.

Process

WHAT IS PROCESS?

Process writing explains how to do something or describes how something happens or is done. When you tell the reader how to do something (a **directional process**), you speak directly to the reader, giving clear, specific instructions about how to perform some activity. Your purpose is to explain an activity so that a reader can do it. For example, you may have to leave instructions telling a new employee how to close the cash register or use the copy machine. A directional process uses "you," or in the way it gives directions, the word "you" is understood.

When you describe how something happens or is done (an **informational process**), your purpose is to explain an activity without telling a reader how to do it. For example, you can explain how a boxer trains for a fight or how a special effect for a movie was created. Instead of speaking directly to the reader, an informational process speaks about "I," "he," "she," "we," "they," or about a person by his or her name.

A Process Involves Steps in Time Order

Whether a process is directional or informational, it describes something that is done in steps, and these steps are in a specific order: a **time order**.

The process can involve steps that are followed in minutes, hours, days, weeks, months, or even years. For example, the steps in changing a tire may take minutes, whereas the steps taken to lose ten pounds may take months.

You should keep in mind that a process involves steps that *must follow a certain order*, not just a range of activities that can be placed in any order. This sentence *signals a process*:

> Learning to search the Internet is easy if you follow a few simple directions. (Using the Internet involves following steps in order; that is, you cannot search before you turn on the computer.)

This sentence *does not signal a process*:

> There are several ways to get a person to like you. (Each way is separate; there is no time sequence here.)

Telling a person, in a conversation, how to do something or how something is done gives you the opportunity to add important points you may have overlooked or to throw in details you may have skipped at first. Your listener can ask questions if he or she does not understand you. Writing a process, however, is more difficult. Your reader is not there to stop you, to ask you to explain further, or to question you. In writing a process, you must be organized and clear.

Hints for Writing a Process Paragraph

1. **In choosing a topic, find an activity you know well.** If you write about something familiar to you, you will have a clearer paragraph.

2. **Choose a topic that includes steps that must be done in a specific time sequence.**

   not this: I find lots of things to do on a rainy day.
   but this: I have a plan for cleaning the garage.

3. **Choose a topic that is fairly small.** A complicated process cannot be covered well in one paragraph. If your topic is too big, the paragraph can become vague, incomplete, or boring.

   too big: There are many stages in the process of a bill before Congress becoming a law.
   smaller and manageable: Willpower and support were the most important elements in my struggle to quit smoking.

4. **Write a topic sentence that makes a point.** Your topic sentence should do more than announce. Like the topic sentence for any paragraph, it should have a point. As you plan the steps of your process and gather details, ask yourself some questions: What point do I want to make about this process? Is the process hard? Is it easy? Does the process require certain tools? Does the process require certain skills, like organization, patience, or endurance?

   an announcement: This paragraph is about how to change the oil in your car.
   a topic sentence: You do not have to be a mechanic to change the oil in your car, but you do have to take a few simple precautions.

5. **Include all of the steps.** If you are explaining a process, you are writing for someone who does not know the process as well as you

TEACHING TIP

1. Ask students to list the steps involved in preparing for an important event (e.g., a ceremony, a party, a trip). This will generate several ideas.
2. Have they observed how someone else completes the steps of a process (e.g., a friend who trains for a sports competition, a family member who prepares for a job interview)?

do. Keep in mind that what seems clear or simple to you may not be clear or simple to the reader, and be sure to tell what is needed before the process starts. For instance, what ingredients are needed to cook the dish? Or what tools are needed to assemble the toy?

TEACHING TIP

1. Tell students they can be objective "reporters" as they analyze the steps they or others undertake to complete a process.
2. If students have difficulty elaborating about a step, tell them they can emphasize the importance of each step in a process by examining what would happen (or go wrong) if the step was neglected or not completed correctly.

6. **Put the steps in the right order.** Nothing is more irritating to a reader than trying to follow directions that skip back and forth. Careful planning, drafting, and revision can help you get the time sequence right.

7. **Be specific in the details and steps.** To be sure you have sufficient details and clear steps, keep your reader in mind. Put yourself in the reader's place. Could you follow your own directions or understand your steps?

If you remember that a process explains how to do something or how something is done, you will focus on being clear. Now that you know the purpose and strategies of writing a process, you can begin the prewriting stage.

Exercise 1 Recognizing Good Topic Sentences for Process Paragraphs

If a sentence is a good topic sentence for a process paragraph, put OK on the line provided. If a sentence has a problem, label that sentence with one of these letters:

A This is an announcement; it makes no point.

B This sentence covers a topic that is too big for one paragraph.

S This sentence describes a topic that does not require steps.

1. _OK_ If you follow a simple plan, you can get the best deal on a checking account.

2. _A_ How I learned to drive an all-terrain vehicle is the subject of this paragraph.

3. _B_ The process of adopting a child is complicated.

4. _S_ There are several tips for selling your car.

5. _OK_ Making a good first impression on your boyfriend's or girlfriend's parents means using the first meeting to gain their trust gradually.

6. _B_ The art of customizing an automobile developed over the years.

7. _A_ This paper is about the way you can make homemade chili.

8. _S_ Many things go into the preparation for a glamorous party.

9. _OK_ When my nephew was born, my brother learned the right way to change a diaper.

10. _OK_ I found an easy way to clean up the mess under the kitchen sink.

Collaborate

Exercise 2 Including Necessary Materials in a Process

Following are three possible topics for a process paragraph. For each topic, work with a partner or a group and list the items (materials, ingredients, tools, utensils, supplies) the reader would have to gather before he or she began the process. When you've finished the exercise, compare your lists with another group's lists to see if you've missed any items.

INSTRUCTOR'S NOTE

Answers will vary. Possible answers shown at left.

   1. topic: brewing a pot of coffee

   needed items: _a coffeepot, a paper coffee filter, water, a packet or can_

   of ground coffee, a spoon

   2. topic: washing a dog

   needed items: _a large tub filled with warm water, many clean towels, a_

   washcloth or sponge, a bucket of water (for rinsing) or a hose, dog shampoo

   3. topic: painting a room

   needed items: _paint, paintbrushes and/or rollers and roller pans, extension_

   poles for paint rollers, tape, drop cloth, ladder

WRITING THE PROCESS PARAGRAPH IN STEPS

PREWRITING   Gathering Ideas: Process

The easiest way to start writing a process paragraph is to pick a small topic, one that you can cover well in one paragraph. Then you can gather ideas by listing or freewriting or both.

If you decide to write about how to find the right apartment, you might begin by freewriting.

Then you might check your freewriting, looking for details that have to do with the process of finding an apartment. You can underline those details, as in the example that follows.

Freewriting for a Process Paragraph

Topic: Finding the right apartment

You have to <u>look around</u>. <u>Don't pick the first apartment you see</u>. Sean did that, and he wound up with a dump. <u>Look at a bunch</u>. But <u>not too many</u>, or you'll get confused. <u>The lease</u>, too. <u>Check it carefully</u>. <u>How much is the security deposit</u>? <u>Do you want a one bedroom</u>? <u>Friends can help</u> if they know of any nice apartments. I found my place that way. Maybe somebody you know lives in <u>a good neighborhood</u>. A <u>convenient location can be more expensive</u>. But <u>can save you money on transportation</u>.

Next, you can put what you've underlined into a list, in correct time sequence:

   before the search

   Do you want a one bedroom?
   Friends can help

a good neighborhood
a convenient location can be more expensive
Can save you money on transportation

during the search

look around
Don't pick the first apartment you see.
Look at a bunch.
But not too many

after the search

Check the lease carefully.
How much is the security deposit?

Check the list. Are some details missing? Yes. A reader might ask, "What other ways (besides asking friends) can help you find apartments? What else should you do before you search? When you're looking at apartments, what should you be looking for? What questions should you ask? After the search, how do you decide which apartment is best? And what, besides the security deposit, should you check on the lease?" Answers to questions like these can give you the details needed to write a clear and interesting directional process.

Writing a Topic Sentence for a Process Paragraph

Freewriting and a list can now help you focus your paragraph by identifying the point of your process. You already know what the subject of your paragraph is: finding the right apartment. But what's the point? Is it easy to find the right apartment? Is it difficult? What does it take to find the right apartment?

Maybe a topic sentence could be

Finding the right apartment takes planning and careful investigation.

Once you have a topic sentence, you can think about adding details that explain your topic sentence and you can begin the planning stage of writing.

Exercise 3   Finding the Steps of a Process in Freewriting

Read the following freewriting, then reread it, looking for all the words, phrases, or sentences that have to do with steps. Underline all those items. Then once you've underlined the freewriting, put what you've underlined into a list in a correct time sequence.

INSTRUCTOR'S NOTE

Answers will vary. Possible answers shown at right.

How to Make a Turkey Sandwich: Freewriting

   Get smoked turkey in the deli, or you may like slices of freshly cooked turkey. Thanksgiving is the time to use the freshly cooked turkey leftovers. You have to have lots of mayonnaise, too. You also need a knife to spread the mayonnaise. The mayonnaise goes on the bread. First, you need bread or a large roll. Then—after the mayonnaise, put the turkey on the bread. You can pick your choice of toppings on the turkey. You can put lettuce and tomato. Some people like to put cheese on the turkey. But does cheese belong in a traditional turkey sandwich like the ones you make after Thanksgiving? Other people put cranberry sauce on. After you've put on your choice of toppings, squeeze the sandwich shut and enjoy.

Your List of Steps in Time Sequence

1. *First, you need bread or a large roll.*

2. *Get smoked turkey in the deli or slices of freshly cooked turkey.*

3. *You have to have lots of mayonnaise.*

4. *You need a knife to spread the mayonnaise.*

5. *You can pick your choice of toppings (lettuce and tomato, cheese, or cranberry sauce).*

6. *The mayonnaise goes on the bread.*

7. *Then put the turkey on the bread.*

8. *Put on your choice of toppings.*

9. *Squeeze the sandwich shut and enjoy.*

PLANNING Devising a Plan: Process

Using the freewriting and topic sentence on finding an apartment, you can make an outline. Then you can revise it, checking the topic sentence and improving the list of details where you think they could be better. A revised outline on finding the right apartment is shown below.

An Outline for a Process Paragraph

topic sentence:	Finding the apartment you want takes planning and careful investigation.
details:	Decide what you want.
	Ask yourself, "Do I want a one bedroom?" "What can I afford?"
before	A convenient location can be expensive.
the	It can also save you money on transportation.
search	Friends can help you with names of nice apartments.
	Maybe somebody you know lives in a good neighborhood.
	Check the classified advertisements in the newspapers.
	Look around.
	Don't pick the first apartment you see.
	Look at several.
during	But don't look at too many.
the	Check the cleanness, safety, plumbing, and appliances of
search	each one.
	Ask the manager about the laundry room, additional storage, parking facilities, and maintenance policies.
	Compare the two best places you saw.
after	Consider the price, location, and condition of the
the	apartments.
search	Check the leases carefully.
	Check the requirements for first and last month's rent
	deposits.

The following checklist may help you revise an outline for your own process paragraph.

Checklist: A Checklist for Revising a Process Outline

✔ Is my topic sentence focused on some point about the process?

✔ Does it cover the whole process?

✔ Do I have all the steps?

✔ Are they in the right order?

✔ Have I explained the steps clearly?

✔ Do I need better details?

Exercise 4 **Revising the Topic Sentence in a Process Outline**

The topic sentence below doesn't cover all the steps of the process. Read the outline several times; then write a topic sentence that covers all the steps of the process and has a point.

topic sentence: If you want to clean out the inside of your car, be prepared with the right tools.

details: First, you need a large, sturdy garbage bag.

You also need a car vacuum or a small regular vacuum.

A bucket of soapy water and a washcloth are also necessary.

Also bring a spray bottle of window cleaner, a spray bottle of furniture polish, and two clean cloths.

Finally, bring an air deodorizer.

Now that you have the tools, clean with vigor and determination.

First, throw all the junk in your car—food wrappers, empty soda cans and water bottles, newspapers—into the garbage bag.

Then vacuum the car, paying particular attention to the floor.

Clean the dirty surfaces of the car, such as a sticky dashboard or console, with soap and water.

At this point you may be sick of cleaning, but stay focused on the final steps.

Use the window cleaner to wipe the grime off the inside of the car windows.

With your last bit of energy, clean any vinyl or leather parts of the car with furniture polish.

Maintain the new-car smell of the furniture polish by popping an air deodorizer in the car.

Now enjoy the product of your hard work: a clean, attractive car.

Revised Topic Sentence: _If you want to clean the inside of your car, be_ _prepared with the right tools, energy, and determination._

INSTRUCTOR'S NOTE

Answers will vary. Possible answer shown at left.

Exercise 5 **Revising the Order of Steps in a Process Outline**

The steps in each of these outlines are out of order. Put numbers in the spaces provided, indicating what step should be first, second, and so on.

1. **topic sentence:** My sister has developed a smart routine that allows her to communicate with her children.

   details: _8_ Because they have had their mother's attention before dinner, Chris and Callie are calm and happy at the evening meal.

   _3_ As they work on their homework, they ask questions, and my sister is there to help and encourage.

   _1_ An hour before dinner, my sister brings her two children, seven-year-old Chris and six-year-old Callie, into the kitchen.

   _2_ While my sister begins to make dinner, the children work on their homework.

   _4_ Once the children have finished their homework, my sister asks for their help.

   _5_ As they help, they get to mix the ingredients of a salad or taste a sauce.

   _7_ By the time dinner is ready, my sister and her children have had a long conversation about the children's day and thoughts.

   _6_ While dinner cooks, the children stay in the kitchen, feeling part of the family ritual.

2. **topic sentence:** My roommate has the same wake-up routine every morning.

   details: _8_ Once he has his coffee, he drags himself to the bathroom.

   _10_ Finally, he returns to the bedroom, scoops some clothes off the floor, and puts them on.

   _6_ He is too impatient to wait for the kettle to boil, so he just pours some of its warm water into his mug.

   _5_ He turns on the kettle.

   _1_ As soon as the alarm clock goes off, he knocks it onto the floor.

   _2_ Fifteen minutes after the alarm rings, he stumbles out of bed.

   _3_ With his eyes shut, he staggers from the bedroom to the kitchen.

_7_　　He stirs the mess with his finger and gulps.

_9_　　In the bathroom, he brushes his teeth; then combs his hair with his fingers.

_4_　　In the kitchen, he grabs the jar of instant coffee and shakes about three tablespoons of coffee powder into a dirty mug.

3. topic sentence: Mr. Corelli, my College Algebra teacher, has a perfect system for calming students' fears.

details:　_2_　　Once a student hears that invitation, he or she feels welcome.

_1_　　At the first class meeting, Mr. Corelli invites every student who wants extra help to visit him in his office.

_9_　　Laughing and reassured, the student leaves the office.

_3_　　When a student comes to the office, Mr. Corelli is friendly.

_4_　　First, he asks the student to sit down.

_6_　　Once he understands the student's problem, Mr. Corelli works patiently with the student.

_5_　　As soon as the student sits down, Mr. Corelli listens closely as the student describes his or her confusion.

_7_　　Often, Mr. Corelli breaks up the office session with a joke.

_8_　　When the student feels more confident about the challenges of algebra, Mr. Corelli ends with a funny story about his own student days.

Exercise 6　**Listing All of the Steps in an Outline**

Following are three topic sentences for process paragraphs. Write all the steps needed to complete an outline for each sentence. After you've listed all the steps, number them in the correct time order.

INSTRUCTOR'S NOTE

Answers will vary. Possible answers shown at right.

1. topic sentence: If you plan early, you can relax when a storm threatens to cut off the power and water in your area.

steps:　*1. Before storm season begins, make a list of the supplies and food you will need.*

2. Go shopping early at a large discount store that sells everything you need.

3. First, get the items that sell fast during the storm season: batteries, battery-powered lights and radios, ice chests, and paper towels.

4. Next, get the essential food items such as water, canned food, soft drinks or juice, crackers, and peanut butter.

5. Buy a few items that can help you pass the time after the storm: board games, playing cards, and books.

6. Store your purchases at home and keep them for emergencies.

7. Relax. You won't have to join long, frantic lines of shoppers when a storm threatens.

2. topic sentence: There are a few simple steps for cooking a hamburger.

steps: 1. You will need one hamburger patty, some cooking oil or butter, salt and pepper, a frying pan, and a metal burger flipper.

2. Shake salt and pepper on the burger.

3. Place the frying pan on a stove burner.

4. Turn the heat to high.

5. Immediately place a pat of butter or a drop of oil into the pan.

6. When the butter or oil begins to sizzle, put the burger into the pan.

7. Watch the burger carefully.

8. When you see the bottom of the burger begin to turn brown, flip the burger.

9. Continue frying the burger until it has reached the stage you want: rare, medium, or well done.

3. topic sentence: To produce a crisply ironed shirt, follow a few simple steps.

steps: 1. You need an ironing board with a padded cover, a steam iron (or a nonsteam iron and a spray bottle of water), a clean shirt, and a hanger.

2. Open the ironing board.

3. Turn on the iron and set the correct temperature for the fabric of the shirt.

4. Add water to the small opening on the steam iron, or place a spray bottle of water nearby.

5. Place the shirt on the ironing board and spray a little water from the iron or the spray bottle as you iron each part of the shirt.

6. Iron the back of the shirt collar first, keeping the collar smooth and flat.

7. Iron the shoulders of the shirt.

8. Then iron the back of the shirt.

9. Iron the front and sides.

10. Iron the sleeves and cuffs.

11. Turn off the iron and hang your crisp shirt on a hanger.

DRAFTING　Drafting and Revising: Process

You can take the outline and write it in paragraph form, and you'll have a first draft of the process paragraph. As you write the first draft, you can combine some of the short sentences from the outline. Then you can review your draft and revise it for organization, details, clarity, grammar, style, and word choice.

Using the Same Grammatical Person

Remember that the *directional* process speaks directly to the reader, calling him or her "you." Sentences in a directional process use the word "you," or they imply "you."

> **directional:** *You* need a good paint brush to get started.
> Begin by making a list. ("You" is implied.)

Remember that the *informational* process involves somebody doing the process. Sentences in an informational process use words like "I," "we," "he," "she," or "they" or a person's name.

> **informational:** *Chip* needed a good paint brush to get started.
> First, *I* can make a list.

One problem in writing a process is shifting from describing how somebody did something to telling the reader how to do an activity. When that shift happens, the two kinds of processes get mixed. That shift is called a **shift in person**. In grammar, the words "I" and "we" are considered to be in the first person, "you" is in the second person, and "he," "she," "it," and "they" are in the third person.

If these words refer to one, they are *singular*; if they refer to more than one, they are *plural*. The following list may help.

INFO BOX:　A List of Persons

1st person singular:	I
2nd person singular:	you
3rd person singular:	he, she, it, or a person's name
1st person plural:	we
2nd person plural:	you
3rd person plural:	they, or the names of more than one person

---

In writing your process paragraph, decide whether your process will be directional or informational, and stay with one kind.

Below are two examples of a shift in person. Look at them carefully and study how the shift is corrected.

> **shift in person:**　After *I* preheat the oven to 350 degrees, *I* mix the egg whites and sugar with an electric mixer set at high speed. *Mix* until stiff peaks form. Then *I* put the mixture in small mounds on an ungreased cookie sheet. ("Mix until stiff peaks form" is a shift to the "you" person.)

shift corrected: After *I* preheat the oven to 350 degrees, *I* mix the egg whites and sugar with an electric mixer set at high speed. *I* mix until stiff peaks form. Then *I* put the mixture in small mounds on an ungreased cookie sheet.

shift in person: A *salesperson* has to be very careful when a customer tries on clothes. *The clerk* can't hint that a suit may be a size too small. *You* can insult a customer with a hint like that. (The sentences shifted from "salesperson" and "clerk" to "you.")

shift corrected: A *salesperson* has to be very careful when customers try on clothes. *The clerk* can't hint that a suit may be a size too small. *He or she* can insult a customer with a hint like that.

Using Transitions Effectively

INSTRUCTOR'S NOTE

For more on shifts in person, see Chapter 27.

As you revise your draft, you can add transitions. Transitions are particularly important in a process paragraph because you are trying to show the steps in a *specific sequence*, and you are trying to show the *connections* between steps. Effective transitions will also keep your paragraph from sounding like a choppy, boring list.

Following is a list of some of the transitions you can use in writing a process paragraph. Be sure that you use transitional words and phrases only when it is logical to do so, and try not to overuse the same transitions in a paragraph.

INFO BOX: **Transitions for a Process Paragraph**

after	during	later	then
afterward	eventually	meanwhile	to begin
as	finally	next	to start
as he/she is	first, second, etc.	now	until
as soon as	first of all	quickly	when
as you are	gradually	sometimes	whenever
at last	in the beginning	soon	while
at the same time	immediately	suddenly	while I am . . .
before	initially	the first step,	
begin by	last	the second step, etc.	

When you write a process paragraph, you must pay particular attention to clarity. As you revise, keep thinking about your audience to be sure your steps are easy to follow. The following can help you revise your draft.

> **Checklist: A Checklist for Revising a Process Paragraph**
>
> ✔ Does the topic sentence cover the whole paragraph?
>
> ✔ Does the topic sentence make a point about the process?
>
> ✔ Is any important step left out?
>
> ✔ Should any step be explained further?
>
> ✔ Are the steps in the right order?
>
> ✔ Should any sentences be combined?
>
> ✔ Have I used the same person throughout the paragraph to describe the process?
>
> ✔ Have I used transitions effectively?

Exercise 7   Correcting Shifts in Person in a Process Paragraph

Below is a paragraph that shifts from being an informational to a directional process in several places. Those places are underlined. Rewrite the underlined parts directly above the original text so that the whole paragraph is an informational process.

Aaron hates feeling like a stranger in class, so he has developed a system

for making friends in the early days of the term. He starts at the first class meet-
He looks
ing. You look around to see who appears friendly and open. Sometimes he can

identify potential friends by their expressions or body language. For example,

someone smiling and looking around the room is more likely to be friendly than
he comes
someone staring straight ahead, stone faced. At the next class meeting, you
finds   *He doesn't*
come early and find a seat near one of the friendly people. You don't even have
He just makes   *offers*
to be the one to start a conversation. Just make eye contact and offer a subtle
he looks   *his*
smile. Next, look to the other side of your desk. A warm and open person might
he has
be sitting there. Soon, someone makes a remark. Then you have to keep the con-

versation going. He tries to involve another person or two in the talk. Once

Aaron has made the initial contact, he can look forward to developing friend-

ships as the term continues.

Exercise 8   Revising Transitions in a Process Paragraph

The transitions in this paragraph could be better. Rewrite the underlined transitions directly above the original ones so that the transitions are smoother.

You have to be extremely careful when you make a U-turn on a busy high-

To start,

way. <u>First,</u> look far ahead for an opening in the road. Looking far ahead will give

Next,

you time to make the turn. <u>Second,</u> slowly and carefully ease into the lane closest

When you are near the opening,   *Then*

to the opening. <u>Third,</u> put on your directional signals. <u>Fourth,</u> enter the opening.

Now

<u>Fifth,</u> look to the left and right of the oncoming traffic to determine its speed and

your chances of entering the stream of cars. As you are looking, check for a

Afterward,   *Eventually,*

nearby traffic light. <u>Sixth,</u> wait patiently. <u>Seventh,</u> turn carefully and slowly.

Finally,

<u>Eighth,</u> do not speed up on the highway; instead, drive at the same speed as the

traffic that now surrounds you.

INSTRUCTOR'S NOTE

Answers will vary. Possible answers shown at left.

Exercise 9   **Combining Sentences in a Process Paragraph**

The following paragraph has many short, choppy sentences, which are underlined. Wherever you see two or more underlined sentences clustered next to each other, combine them into one clear, smooth sentence. Write your revised versions of those sentences in the space above the original.

It

My brother has found a foolproof way to distract, annoy, and manipulate me. <u>It</u>

begins at night when I am studying.

<u>begins at night. Night is the time when I am studying</u>. First, Corey sticks his head

in the kitchen doorway and pretends to be surprised to see me at the kitchen table.

Then he leaves, looking guilty

"Oops, sorry," he says. "Are you studying again?" <u>Then he leaves. He looks guilty.</u>

and apologetic.

<u>He also looks apologetic</u>. About five minutes pass before Corey returns. This time

he comes into the room. "Did I interrupt you?" he says. "I really didn't mean to

bother you." Meanwhile, I am waiting for his next move. Soon, it arrives. He asks

I am sure

me a silly question or opens the refrigerator and stares at its contents. <u>I am sure</u>

this step is planned to get my complete attention.

<u>this step is deliberate. It is planned to get my complete attention</u>. Now he has it, but

He

I am still determined to get back to my work. Eventually, Corey goes away. <u>He</u>

leaves to find another way to invade my space.

<u>leaves to come up with another strategy. He wants to find a way to invade my</u>

<u>space</u>. Meanwhile, I am not concentrating on my studies because I am waiting for

Corey to strike again. After about twenty minutes, he returns. During this invasion

He reminds me of an errand or a chore I

of my privacy, he begins cleverly. <u>He reminds me of a something I wanted to do. It</u>

wanted to do.

<u>could be an errand. It could be a chore I wanted to do</u>. "Yes," I say. "I planned to do

that soon." I do not even look up from my books. I just want him to leave. "I could

INSTRUCTOR'S NOTE

Answers will vary. Possible answers shown at left.

I toss him my car keys, which
do it for you, right away," he says, "if I had a car." <u>I toss him my car keys. He</u>
he wanted all along, and blame myself for falling for Corey's tricks again.
<u>wanted them all along. I blame myself for falling for Corey's tricks again.</u>

The Draft

Below is a draft of the process paragraph on finding an apartment. This draft has more details than the outline on page 109. Some short sentences have been combined, and transitions (which are underlined) have been added.

A Draft of a Process Paragraph

Finding the apartment you want takes planning and investigation. <u>First of all,</u> you must decide what you want. Ask yourself, "Do I want a one bedroom apartment?" or "Do I want a studio apartment?" Most important, ask yourself, "What can I afford?" A convenient location can be expensive; on the other hand, that location can save you money on transportation. <u>Before</u> you start looking for a place, do some research. Friends can help you with the names of nice apartments. Be sure to check the classified advertisements in the newspaper. <u>Once you begin</u> your search, don't pick the first place you see. You should look at several places, but looking at too many can make your search confusing. Just be sure to check each apartment's cleanness, safety, plumbing, and appliances. <u>Then</u> ask the manager about the laundry room, additional storage, parking facilities, and maintenance policies. <u>After</u> you've completed your search, compare the two best places you saw. Consider each one's price, location, and condition. Carefully check each lease, studying the amount of the security deposit and deposit for first and last month's rent.

POLISHING Polishing and Proofreading: Process

Before you prepare the final copy of your process paragraph, you can check your latest draft for grammar, word choice, and style that need revising.

Following is the final version of the process paragraph on finding the apartment you want. You'll notice that it contains several changes from the previous draft.

- The word "nice" has been changed to "suitable" to make the description more specific.
- The sentence that began, "You should look" has been rewritten so that it follows the pattern of the preceding sentences. Three sentences in a row now include the parallel pattern of "Be sure," "don't pick," and "Look at."
- The second use of "be sure" has been changed to "remember," to avoid repetition.
- New details about what to check for in the leases have been added.
- A final sentence that relates to the topic of the paragraph has been added.

A Final Version of a Process Paragraph

(Changes from the draft are underlined.)

> Finding the apartment you want takes planning and investigation. First of all, you must decide what you want. Ask yourself, "Do I want a one bedroom apartment?" or "Do I want a studio apartment?" Most important, ask yourself, "What can I afford?" A convenient location can be expensive; on the other hand, that location can save you money on transportation. Before you start looking for a place, do some research. Friends can help you with the names of <u>suitable</u> apartments. Be sure to check the classified advertisements in the newspaper. Once you begin your search, don't pick the first place you see. <u>Look at</u> several places, but <u>be aware that</u> looking at too many can make your search confusing. <u>Just remember</u> to check each apartment's cleanness, safety, plumbing, and appliances. Then ask the manager about the laundry room, additional storage, parking facilities, and maintenance policies. After you've completed your search, compare the two best places you saw. Consider each one's price, location, and condition. Carefully check each lease, studying the amount of the security deposit, the deposit for first and last month's rent, <u>and the rules for tenants.</u> <u>When you've completed your comparison, you're ready to choose the apartment you want.</u>

As you prepare the final copy of your process paragraph, check carefully for errors in spelling, punctuation, typing, and formatting.

> **For your information:** A sample process essay based on this topic and following the same writing steps can be found in Chapter 12, pp. 289–293.

Exercise 10   Proofreading to Prepare the Final Paragraph

Following are two process paragraphs with the kinds of errors that are easy to overlook when you prepare the final version of an assignment. Correct the errors, writing above the lines. There are twelve errors in the first paragraph and thirteen in the second paragraph.

1. After year's *(years)* of shopping the wrong way, I figured out the rite *(right)* way to shop for food. Ever since I had my own apartment, I considered foodshopping *(food shopping)* a frustrating chore. To me, it involved searching the aisles for items, backtracking through same *(the)* aisles as I suddenly remembered another item, and forgetting several items on each trip. My new system takes the frustration out of a trip to the Supermarket *(supermarket)*. To begin, I put a small pad, *(no comma needed)* and pencil near the refrigerator. Every time I found *(find)* myself using the last of the milk, potato chips, or some other food, I write the item on a page of the pad. I list the food items in columns that match the aisles in the store. For example milk and eggs go in the same column because they

take
share an aisle in the store. When I am ready to shop, I took my list along. Once I
shop *I*
enter the store, I shopp aisle by aisle, according to my list. With this system, i for-

get fewer groceries, save time, and make fewer trips to the supermarket. Now,
shopping
shop for food is almost as easy as eating food.

2. The best way to deal with cockroaches is never to give up. Let's say you
night *of*
get up in the nite for a glass on water. Suddenly, when you turn on the light, an
your *bare*
enormous roach skitters across you're bear feet. Of course, the first thing you do
no comma needed
is scream, as if an ax murderer were at the window. Next, you begin to plan an
.
extermination You grab a newspaper and swat at the insect just as the ugly bug

slips between the sink and the kitchen counter. You've missed it. Immediately, you
you
begin a search for the can of insect spray that You keep for emergencies. Eventu-
, *no comma needed*
ally you find it, and spray the entire kitchen. You spray so much that every roach
twenty miles *you've*
within twenny mile should be dead. Unfortunately, you don't know if youv'e killed

the roach that crossed your toes in your kitchen. Now is the time to persevere.

Never go back to bed in defeat. Instead, stand guard in the kitchen until one big
into
roach staggers out in to the open. Then claim a victory for cockroach hunters

everywhere.

Lines of Detail: A Walk-Through Assignment

Your assignment is to write a paragraph on how to plan a special day. Follow these steps:

Step 1: Focus on one special day. If you want to, you can begin by using your own experience. Ask yourself such questions as, "Have I ever planned a birthday party? A baby or wedding shower? A surprise party? A picnic? A reunion? A barbecue? A celebration of a religious holiday? Have I ever seen anyone else plan such a day? If so, how would I teach a reader about planning for such a day?"

Step 2: Once you have picked the day, freewrite. Write anything you can remember about the day and how you or someone else planned it.

Step 3: When you've completed the freewriting, read it. Underline all the details that refer to steps in planning that event. List the underlined details, in time order.

Step 4: Add to the list by brainstorming. Ask yourself questions that can lead to more details. For example, if an item on your list is, "Send out invitations early," ask questions like, "How early?" and "How do I decide whom to invite?"

Step 5:   Survey your expanded list. Then write a topic sentence that makes some point about your planning for this special day. To reach a point, think of questions like these: "What makes a plan successful?" or "If I am planning for a special day (birthday, barbecue, surprise party, and so forth), what must I remember?"

Step 6:   Use the topic sentence to prepare an outline. Be sure that the steps in the outline are in the correct time order.

Step 7:   Write a first draft of the paragraph, adding details and combining short sentences.

Step 8:   Revise your draft. Be careful to use smooth transitions, and check that you have included all the necessary steps.

Step 10:   Prepare and proofread the final version of your paragraph.

Writing Your Own Process Paragraph

When you write on one of these topics, be sure to work through the stages of the writing process in preparing your process paragraph. Also, be sure to write from your own experience.

1. Write a **directional** or **informational process** about one of these topics:

packing a suitcase	fixing a clogged drain
preparing for a garage sale	changing the oil in a car
painting a room	waxing a car
taking a test	breaking a specific habit
losing weight	gaining weight
training a roommate	giving a pet a bath
coping with rejection	walking for better health
doing holiday shopping in one day	getting up in the morning
getting good tips as a server	preparing for a job interview
performing a family ritual	asking for a raise

2. Write about the wrong way to do something, or the wrong way you (or someone else) did it. You can use any of the topics in the list above, or you can choose your own topic.

3. Imagine that a relative who has never been to your state is coming to visit. This relative will arrive at the nearest airport, rent a car, and drive to your house. Write a paragraph giving your relative clear directions for getting from the airport to your house. Be sure to have an appropriate topic sentence.

4. Interview one of the counselors at your college. Ask the counselor to tell you the steps for applying for financial aid. Take notes or tape the interview, get copies of any forms that are included in the application process, and ask questions about these forms.

   After the interview, write a paragraph explaining the process of applying for financial aid. Your explanation is directed at a high school senior who has never applied for aid.

Collaborate

5. Interview someone whose cooking you admire. Ask that person to tell you the steps involved in making a certain dish. Take notes or tape the interview. After the interview, write a paragraph, *not* a recipe, explaining how to prepare the dish. Your paragraph will explain the process to someone who is a beginner at cooking.

Computer

6. Brainstorm about a particular task or function of a word-processing program that took considerable practice for you to master. (For example, you could write about moving text, highlighting, finding or creating a file, and so forth.) Write a paragraph that explains how to master this specific skill. Conclude your paragraph by stressing the benefits and/or practical uses of this skill.

Computer

7. Visit your college's Web site and follow any links that are associated with your campus bookstore. After reviewing the information about shopping for books and supplies, and based on your own experience, write a paragraph that explains the most efficient way to avoid long lines and waiting periods. If your college bookstore offers online purchasing, be sure to include the steps involved in this option.

8. Study the photograph below, and notice the connection between the dog and the man. Then write a process paragraph on how to train a dog to catch a ball or a Frisbee in midair.

9. Examine the photograph below, and then write a paragraph on how an athlete can focus his or her concentration for maximum benefit.

Note: Additional writing options suitable for process-related assignments can be found after the professional reading "Breath of Life," which begins on page 614.

How Do I Get a Better Grade?

mywritinglab

Visit www.mywritinglab.com for audio-visual lectures and additional practice sets about process.

Get a better grade with MyWritingLab!

Name: _____   Section: _____

Peer Review Form for a Process Paragraph

After you've written a draft of your process paragraph, let a writing partner read it. When your partner has completed the form below, discuss the responses. Repeat the same process for your partner's paragraph.

The steps that are most clearly described are _____

_____

_____

I'd like more explanation about this step: _____

_____

Some details could be added to the part that begins with the words _____

_____

I noticed these transitions: _____

_____

A transition could be added to the part that begins with the words _____

_____

I have questions about _____

The best part of this paragraph is _____

_____

Other comments: _____

_____

_____

_____

_____

_____

_____

_____

Reviewer's name: _____

Comparison and Contrast

WHAT IS COMPARISON? WHAT IS CONTRAST?

To **compare** means to point out *similarities*. To **contrast** means to point out *differences*. **When you compare or contrast, you need to come to some conclusion.** It's not enough to say, "These two things are similar," or "They are different." Your reader will be asking, "So what? What's your point?" You may be showing the differences between two restaurants to explain which is the better buy:

> *If you like Mexican food, you can go to either Café Mexicana or Juanita's, but Juanita's has lower prices.*

Or you may be explaining the similarities between two family members to explain how people with similar personalities can clash:

> *My cousin Bill and my brother Karram are both so stubborn they can't get along.*

Hints for Writing a Comparison or Contrast Paragraph

1. Limit your topic. When you write a comparison or contrast paragraph, you might think that the easiest topics to write about are broad ones with many similarities or differences. However, if you make your topic too large, you will not be able to cover it well, and your paragraph will be full of very large, boring statements.

Here are some topics that are too large for a comparison or contrast paragraph: two countries, two periods in history, two kinds of addiction, two wars, two economic or political systems, two presidents.

2. Avoid the obvious topic. Some people think it is easier to write about two items if the similarities or differences between them are obvious, but with an obvious topic, you will have nothing new to say, and you will risk writing a boring paragraph.

Here are some obvious topics: the differences between high school and college, the similarities between *Saw* and *Saw II*. If you are drawn to an obvious topic, *try a new angle* on the topic. Write about the unexpected, using the same topic. Write about the similarities between high school and college, or the differences between *Saw* and *Saw II*. You may have to do more thinking before you come up with ideas, but your ideas may be more interesting to write about and to read.

3. Make your point in the topic sentence of your comparison or contrast paragraph. Indicate whether the paragraph is about similarities or differences in a topic sentence like this:

> Because he is so reliable and loyal, Michael is a much better friend to me than Stefan. (The phrase "much better" indicates differences.)
> My two botany teachers share a love of the environment and a passion for protecting it. (The word "share" indicates similarities.)

4. Do not announce in the topic sentence. The sentences below are announcements, not topic sentences:

> This paper will explain the similarities between my two botany teachers.
> Let me tell you how Michael is a different kind of friend than Stefan.

5. Make sure your topic sentence has a focus. It should indicate similarities or differences; it should focus on the specific kind of comparison or contrast you will make.

> **not focused:** My old house and my new one are different.
> **focused:** My new home is bigger, brighter, and more comfortable than my old one.

6. In the topic sentence, cover both subjects to be compared or contrasted.

> **covers only one subject:** The beach at Santa Lucia was dirty and crowded.
> **covers both subjects:** The beach at Santa Lucia was dirty and crowded, but the beach at Fisher Bay was clean and private.

Be careful. It is easy to get so carried away by the details of your paragraph that you forget to put both subjects into one sentence.

Exercise 1 Identifying Suitable Topic Sentences for a Comparison or Contrast Paragraph

Following is a list of possible topic sentences for a comparison or contrast paragraph. Some would make good topic sentences. The ones that wouldn't make good topic sentences have one or more of these problems: they are announcements; they don't indicate whether the paragraph will be about similarities or differences; they don't focus on the specific kind of comparison or contrast to be made; they cover subjects that are too big to write about in one paragraph; or they don't cover both subjects.

Mark the problem sentences with an *X*. If a sentence would make a good topic sentence for a comparison or contrast paragraph, mark it OK.

1. __*OK*__ My last day of work at Bell's Restaurant was more stressful than the first.

2. __*OK*__ Mr. Carcetti gives more tests and assigns more homework than Mrs. Reilly does.

3. __*X*__ On the one hand, there is the Cadillac Escalade, and on the other hand, there is the Lincoln Navigator.

4. __*X*__ Cats and dogs have different physical needs, physical abilities, and evolutionary histories.

5. __*X*__ This essay will explore the similarities between Forest High School and Pacific College.

6. __*X*__ Hollybrook Apartments offer better parking and more recreation facilities.

7. __*X*__ Mexico and Jamaica have an exotic flavor, a rich history, and natural beauty.

8. __*OK*__ The Cadillac Escalade and the Lincoln Navigator share an image of power, strength, and aggression.

9. __*X*__ There are two sociology teachers, Mr. Carcetti and Mrs. Reilly.

10. __*X*__ My friends Suzanne and Selena are very different.

INSTRUCTOR'S NOTE

Before analyzing the exercises and reviewing sample paragraphs, you may want students to preview the various topics they could write about. Sample topics for a comparison or contrast paragraph are on pp. 148-150.

Organizing Your Comparison or Contrast Paragraph

Whether you decide to write about similarities (to compare) or differences (to contrast), you will have to decide how to organize your paragraph. You can choose between two patterns of organization: subject-by-subject or point-by-point.

Subject-by-Subject Organization In the subject-by-subject pattern, you support and explain your topic sentence by first writing all your details on one subject and then writing all your details on the other subject. If you choose a subject-by-subject pattern, be sure to discuss the points for your second subject *in the same order* as you did for the first subject. For example, if your first subject is an amusement park and you cover (1) the price of admission, (2) the long lines at rides, and (3) the quality of the rides, when you discuss the second subject, another amusement park, you should write about its prices, lines, and quality of rides *in the same order*.

Look carefully at the outline and comparison paragraph below for a subject-by-subject pattern.

A Comparison Outline: Subject-by-Subject Pattern

> **topic sentence:** Once I realized that my brother and my mother are very much alike in temperament, I realized why they don't get along.

details:

subject 1, James—temper unkind words	My brother James is a hot-tempered person. It is easy for him to lose control of his temper. When he does, he often says things he later regrets.
stubbornness	James is also very stubborn. In an argument, he will never admit he is wrong. Once we were arguing about baseball scores. Even when I showed him the right score, printed in the paper, he wouldn't admit he was wrong. He said the newspaper had made a mistake. James' stubbornness overtakes his common scnsc.
subject 2, mother—temper	James has inherited many of his character traits from our mother. She has a quick temper, and anything can provoke it. Once, she got angry because she had to wait too long at a traffic light.
unkind words	She also has a tendency to use unkind words when she's mad.
stubbornness	She never backs down from a disagreement or concedes she was wrong. My mother even quit a job because she refused to admit she'd made a mistake in taking inventory. Her pride can lead her into foolish acts. After I realized how similar my brother and mother are, I understood how such inflexible people are likely to clash.

A Comparison Paragraph: Subject-by-Subject Pattern

	Once I realized that my brother and my mother are very much alike in temperament, I realized why they don't get along.
subject 1, James—temper	My brother James is a hot-tempered person. It is easy for him to lose control of his temper,
unkind words, stubbornness	and when he does, he often says things he regrets. James is also very stubborn. In an argument, he will never admit he is wrong. I remember one time when we arguing about baseball scores. Even when I showed him the right scores, printed in the newspaper, he wouldn't admit he was wrong. James insisted that the newspaper must have made a mistake in printing the score. As this example shows, sometimes James' stubbornness overtakes his common sense. It took me a while to realize that my stubborn brother James has inherited many of his traits from our mother. Like
subject 2, mother temper	James, she has a quick temper, and almost anything can provoke it. She once got angry

unkind words	because she had to wait too long at a traffic light. She also shares James' habit of saying unkind things when she's angry. And just as James refuses to back down when he's wrong,
stubbornness	my mother will never back down from a disagreement or concede she's wrong. In fact, my mother once quit a job because she refused to admit she'd made a mistake in taking inventory. Her pride is as powerful as James' pride, and it can be just as foolish. After I realized how similar my mother and brother are, I understood how such inflexible people are likely to clash.

Look carefully at the paragraph in the subject-by-subject pattern, and you'll note that it

- begins with a topic sentence about both subjects—James and his mother,
- gives all the details about one subject—James,
- then gives all the details about the second subject—his mother—in the same order.

Point-by-Point Organization In the point-by-point pattern, you support and explain your topic sentence by discussing each point of comparison or contrast, switching back and forth between your subjects. You explain one point for both subjects, then explain another point for both subjects, and so on.

Look carefully at the outline and the comparison paragraph below for the point-by-point pattern.

A Comparison Outline: Point-by-Point Pattern

topic sentence:	Once I realized that my brother and my mother are very much alike in temperament, I realized why they don't get along.
details:	
point 1, temper— James and mother	My brother James is a hot-tempered person. It is easy for him to lose control of his temper. My mother has a quick temper, and anything can provoke it. Once she got angry because she had to wait too long at a traffic light.
point 2, unkind words— James and mother	When my brother gets mad, he often says things he regrets. My mother has a tendency to use unkind words when she's mad.
point 3, stubbornness— James and mother	James is very stubborn. In an argument, he will never admit he is wrong. Once we were arguing about baseball scores. Even when I showed him the right score, printed in the newspaper, he wouldn't admit he was wrong. He said the newspaper had made a mistake. James' stubbornness overtakes his common sense.

My mother will never back down from a disagreement or admit she is wrong. She even quit a job because she refused to admit she'd made a mistake in taking inventory. She was foolish in her stubbornness. After I realized how similar my mother and brother are, I understood how such inflexible people are likely to clash.

A Comparison Paragraph: Point-by-Point Pattern

point 1, temper—James and mother	Once I realized that my brother and my mother are very much alike in temperament, I realized why they don't get along. My brother is a hot-tempered person, and it is easy for him to lose control of his temper. My mother shares James' quick temper, and anything can provoke her anger. Once, she got angry because she had to wait too long at a traffic light.
point 2, unkind words—James and mother	When my brother gets mad, he often says things he regrets. Similarly, my mother is known for the unkind things she's said in anger. James is a very stubborn person. In an
point 3, stubbornness—James and mother	argument, he will never admit he's wrong. I can remember one argument we were having over baseball scores. Even when I showed him the right score, printed in the newspaper, he wouldn't admit he had been wrong. He simply insisted the paper had made a mistake. At times like that, James' stubbornness overtakes his common sense. Like her son, my mother will never back down from an argument or admit she was wrong. She even quit a job because she refused to admit she'd made a mistake in taking inventory. In that case, her stubbornness was as foolish as James'. It took me awhile to see the similarities between my brother and mother. Yet after I realized how similar these two people are, I understood how two inflexible people are likely to clash.

Look carefully at the paragraph in the point-by-point pattern, and you'll note that it

- begins with a topic sentence about both subjects—James and his mother,
- discusses how both James and his mother are alike in these points: their quick tempers, the unkind remarks they make when they are angry, and their often foolish stubbornness,
- switches back and forth between the two subjects.

The subject-by-subject and point-by-point patterns can be used for either a comparison or a contrast paragraph. But whatever pattern you choose, remember these hints:

1. Be sure to use the same points to compare or contrast two subjects. If you are contrasting two cars, you can't discuss the price and safety features of one, then the styling and speed of the other. You must discuss the price and safety features of both, or the styling and speed of both.

You don't have to list the points in your topic sentence, but you can include them, like this: "My old Ford turned out to be a cheaper, safer, and faster car than my boyfriend's new Mazda."

2. Be sure to give roughly equal space to both subjects. This rule doesn't mean you must write the same number of words—or even sentences—on both subjects. It does mean you should be giving fairly equal attention to the details of both subjects.

Since you will be writing about two subjects, this type of paragraph can involve more details than other paragraph formats. Thus, a comparison or contrast paragraph may be longer than twelve sentences.

Using Transitions Effectively for Comparison or Contrast

How and when you use transitions in a comparison or contrast paragraph depend on the answers to two questions:

1. Are you writing a comparison or contrast paragraph?

   - When you choose to write a *comparison* paragraph, you use transitional words, phrases, or sentences that point out *similarities*.
   - When you choose to write a *contrast* paragraph, you use transitional words, phrases, or sentences that point out *differences*.

2. Are you organizing your paragraph in the point-by-point or subject-by-subject pattern?

   - When you choose to organize your paragraph in the point-by-point pattern, you need transitions *within* each point and *between* points.
   - When you choose to organize in the subject-by-subject pattern, you need *most of your transitions* in the *second half* of the paragraph to remind the reader of the points you made in the first half.

Here are some transitions you can use in writing comparison or contrast. Many others you may think of will also be appropriate for your ideas.

INFO BOX: **Transitions for a Comparison or Contrast Paragraph**

To show similarities:

additionally	both	in the same way	similar to
again	each of	just like	similarly
also	equally	like	so
and	furthermore	likewise	too
as well as	in addition		

To show differences:

although	even though	instead of	though
but	except	nevertheless	unlike
conversely	however	on the other hand	whereas
despite	in contrast to	otherwise	while
different from	in spite of	still	yet

Writing a comparison or contrast paragraph challenges you to make decisions: Will I compare or contrast? Will I use a point-by-point or a subject-by-subject pattern? Those decisions will determine what kind of transitions you will use and where you will use them.

Writing Appropriate Transitions for a Comparison or Contrast Paragraph

Below are pairs of sentences. First, decide whether each pair shows a comparison or contrast. Then combine the two sentences into one, using an appropriate transition (either a word or a phrase). You may have to rewrite parts of the original sentences to create one smooth sentence. The first pair is done for you.

1. My mother loves to go out dancing.
   My father has danced only once: at his wedding.

   combined: *My mother loves to go out dancing, yet my father has danced*

   only once: at his wedding.

2. Scout, my golden retriever, loves to play with other dogs.
   Ripley, my collie, prefers the company of humans.

   combined: *Scout, my golden retriever, loves to play with other dogs; on the*

   other hand, Ripley, my collie, prefers the company of humans.

3. Getting sufficient rest can help a person fight the flu.
   People with the flu should drink plenty of liquids.

   combined: *Getting sufficient rest, in addition to drinking plenty of liquids,*

   can help a person fight the flu.

4. Small children are anxious to grow up.
   Many adults miss the pleasures of childhood.

   combined: *Although small children are anxious to grow up, many adults*

   miss the pleasures of childhood.

5. Professor Wu challenged me to think before I wrote my essays.
   Professor Farrell urged me to use my head in solving math problems.

   combined: *Professor Wu challenged me to think before I wrote my essays;*

   in the same way, Professor Farrell urged me to use my head in solving math

   problems.

6. My high school football coach was tough but never had favorites.
   At college, the coach of the football team was extremely hard on me yet still fair.

   combined: *Both my high school and college football coaches were tough*

   but fair.

WRITING THE COMPARISON OR CONTRAST PARAGRAPH IN STEPS

PREWRITING   Gathering Ideas: Comparison or Contrast

One way to get started on a comparison or contrast paragraph is to list as many differences or similarities as you can on one topic. Then you can see whether you have more similarities (comparisons) or differences (contrasts), and decide which approach to use. For example, if you are asked to compare or contrast two restaurants, you could begin with a list like the one that follows.

List for Two Restaurants: Victor's and The Garden

similarities
both offer lunch and dinner
very popular
nearby

differences

Victor's	The Garden
formal dress	informal dress
tablecloths	placemats
food is bland	spicy food
expensive	moderate
statues, fountains, fresh flowers	dark wood, hanging plants

Getting Points of Comparison or Contrast

Whether you compare or contrast, you are looking for points of comparison or contrast, items you can discuss about both subjects.

If you surveyed the list on the two restaurants and decided you wanted to contrast the two restaurants, you'd see that you already have these points of contrast:

    dress   food
    decor   prices

To write your paragraph, start with several points of comparison or contrast. As you work through the stages of writing, you may decide you don't need all the points you've jotted down, but it is better to start with too many points than with too few.

Exercise 3   Developing Points of Comparison or Contrast

Collaborate

Do this exercise with a partner or a group. Following are some topics that could be used for a comparison or contrast paragraph. Underneath each topic, write three points of comparison or contrast. Be ready to share your answers with another group or with the class. The first topic is done for you.

1. topic: Compare or contrast two popular singers (or singing groups). Points of comparison or contrast:

a. _the kinds of songs they sing_

b. _the kinds of fans they attract_

c. _how long they have been popular_

2. topic: Compare or contrast two rooms. Points of comparison or contrast:

a. _what they are used for_

b. _their size_

c. _their furniture_

3. topic: Compare or contrast two kinds of pizza. Points of comparison or contrast:

a. _the taste_

b. _the toppings_

c. _the price_

4. topic: Compare or contrast two cell phones. Points of comparison or contrast:

a. _their cost_

b. _their features_

c. _their popularity_

Exercise 4 **Finding Differences in Subjects That Look Similar**

Following are pairs of subjects that seem very similar but that do have differences. List three differences for each pair.

1. subjects: ballpoint pens and felt-tip pens
differences:

a. _their uses_

b. _their popularity_

c. _their cost_

2. subjects: paper napkins and paper towels
differences:

a. _their strength_

b. _their colors_

c. _the variety of sizes_

3. subjects: hair gel and hair spray
differences:

a. _their texture_

b. _their uses_

c. _the types of people who use them_

4. subjects: rearview mirror and side mirror
differences:

a. *their angle of vision*

b. *their ease of adjustment*

c. *the frequency of use*

Exercise 5 **Finding Similarities in Subjects That Look Different**

Following are pairs of subjects that are different but have some similarities.
List three similarities for each pair.

1. subjects: starting college and graduating from college
similarities:

a. *a sense of achievement*

b. *hope for new opportunities*

c. *fear of the unknown*

INSTRUCTOR'S NOTE

Answers will vary. Possible
answers shown at left.

2. subjects: being a student and being a teacher
similarities:

a. *must keep to a class schedule*

b. *look forward to vacations*

c. *must be prepared for class*

3. subjects: parents and children
similarities:

a. *love each other*

b. *irritate each other*

c. *challenge each other's attitudes and values*

4. subjects: driving to your destination and taking a plane
similarities:

a. *you can be delayed*

b. *you can face bad weather*

c. *you should wear a seat belt*

Adding Details to Your Points

Once you have some points, you can begin adding details to them. The details
may lead you to more points. If they do not, they will still help you develop the
ideas of your paragraph. If you were to write about the differences in restaurants, for example, your new list with added details might look like this:

List for a Contrast of Restaurants

Victor's	*The Garden*
dress—formal	*informal dress*
men in jackets, women in dresses	*all in jeans*
decor—pretty, elegant	*place mats, on table is a card*
statues, fountains,	*listing specials, lots of dark wood,*

fresh flowers on tables, *tablecloths*	*brass, green hanging plants*
food—bland tasting *traditional, broiled fish or* *chicken, traditional steaks,* *appetizers like shrimp cocktail,* *onion soup*	*spicy and adventurous* *pasta in tomato sauces, garlic* *in everything, curry,* *appetizers like tiny tortillas,* *ribs in honey-mustard sauce*
price—expensive *everything costs extra,* *like appetizer, salad*	*moderate* *price of dinner includes* *appetizer and salad*

Reading the list about restaurants, you might conclude that some people may prefer The Garden to Victor's. Why? There are several hints in your list. The Garden has cheaper food, better food, and a more casual atmosphere. Now that you have a point, you can put it into a topic sentence. A topic sentence contrasting the restaurants could be

> *Some people would rather eat at The Garden than at Victor's because The Garden offers better, cheaper food in a more casual environment.*

Once you have a possible topic sentence, you can begin working on the planning stage of your paragraph.

Exercise 6 **Writing Topic Sentences for Comparison or Contrast**

Below are lists of details. Some lists are for comparison paragraphs; some are for contrast paragraphs. Read each list carefully; then write a topic sentence for each list.

1. topic sentence: *Rain and snow come from the same source and have a similar ability to cause damage and disrupt daily life.*

List of Details

rain	**snow**
source—water falls in drops from the sky	frozen water falls from the sky
ability to do damage—flooding hurts people, property, and nature	blizzards can destroy homes, lives, and the environment
ability to disrupt daily life—games rained out, flights delayed, outdoor festivals and concerts canceled	airlines delay flights, schools closed, roads closed, power outages

2. topic sentence: *Rain and snow have different relations to sports, the seasons, and nature.*

List of Details

rain	**snow**
relation to sports—no sports require rain	winter sports like skiing and snowboarding require snow

| relation to seasons—it can rain in any season | snow falls mostly in winter |
| relation to nature—rain is needed for plants and crops to grow | plants and crops do not grow in the snow |

3. topic sentence: *Chocolate and vanilla are both extremely popular, come in several varieties, and mix well with other flavors and foods.*

List of Details

chocolate	**vanilla**
popularity—one of the most popular flavors in foods	extremely popular flavor in desserts and beverages
varieties—milk chocolate, dark chocolate, white chocolate	French vanilla, vanilla bean, plain vanilla
capacity for blending—ice creams: chocolate fudge, chocolate marshmallow, chocolate cherry, rocky road, chocolate amaretto, chocolate raspberry, chocolate fudge, chocolate brownie chunk; other foods: mocha coffee, hot chocolate, chocolate cake, brownies, cookies	ice creams: vanilla fudge, raspberry vanilla, cherry vanilla, vanilla chocolate chip, vanilla with strawberries, cookies and cream, vanilla with peaches, vanilla with M&M's®; other foods: vanilla pudding, cake, cookies

4. topic sentence: *Chocolate has a more exciting image, is more versatile in its uses, and comes in more forms than vanilla.*

List of Details

chocolate	**vanilla**
image—associated with self-indulgence and a special treat	often referred to as "plain vanilla," not as exciting
versatility—chocolate-flavored medicines, chocolate-dipped fruit, chocolate bunnies, chocolate fountains	flavors for cakes, cookies, coffee, more traditional uses
forms—comes in bars, melted, powder (cocoa), chips	a liquid essence carries the flavor

PLANNING   Devising a Plan: Comparison or Contrast

With a topic sentence, you can begin to draft an outline. Before you can write an outline, however, you have to make a decision: What pattern do you want to use in organizing your paragraph? Do you want to use the subject-by-subject or the point-by-point pattern?

The following is an outline of a contrast paragraph in point-by-point form.

An Outline of a Contrast Paragraph: Point-by-Point Pattern

topic sentence:	Some people would rather eat at The Garden than at Victor's because The Garden offers better, cheaper food in a more casual environment
details:	Food at Victor's is bland tasting and traditional.
	The menu has broiled fish, chicken and traditional steaks.
	The spices used are mostly parsley and salt.
	The food is the usual American food, with a little French food on the list.
point 1—food	Appetizers are the usual things like shrimp cocktail or onion soup.
	Food at The Garden is more spicy and adventurous.
	There are many pasta dishes in tomato sauce.
	There is garlic in just about everything.
	The Garden serves four different curry dishes.
	It has all kinds of ethnic food.
	Appetizers include items like tiny tortillas and hot honey-mustard ribs.
point 2—prices	The prices of the two restaurants differ.
	Victor's is expensive.
	Everything you order costs extra.
	An appetizer and a salad costs extra.
	Food at The Garden is more moderately priced.
	The price of a dinner includes an appetizer and a salad.
point 3— **environment**	Certain diners may feel uncomfortable in Victor's, which has a formal environment.
	Everyone is dressed up, the men in jackets and ties and the women in dresses.
	Less formal diners would rather eat in a more casual place.
	People don't dress up to go to The Garden; they wear jeans.
conclusion	Many people prefer a place where they can relax, with reasonable prices and unusual food, to a place that's a little stuffy, with a traditional and expensive menu.

Once you've drafted an outline, check it. Use the following checklist to help you review and revise your outline.

Checklist: A Checklist for an Outline of a Comparison or Contrast Paragraph

✔   Do I have enough details?

✔   Are all my details relevant?

✔   Have I covered all the points on both sides?

✔   If I'm using a subject-by-subject pattern, have I covered the points in the same order on both sides?

✔   Have I tried to cover too many points?

✔   Have I made my main idea clear?

Using this checklist as your guide, compare the outline with the prewriting list on page 135–136. You may notice several changes:

- Some details on decor in the list have been omitted because there were too many points.
- A concluding sentence has been added to reinforce the main idea.

Exercise 7 **Adding a Point and Details to a Comparison or Contrast Outline**

The following outline is too short. Lengthen it by adding a point of comparison and details to both subjects to develop the comparison.

topic sentence: Those looking for a gift for a child should know that battery-operated toys and non-battery-operated toys share risks and rewards.

details: Whether it has a battery inside or not, a toy can break.
Nothing is worse than inserting a battery into the toy, giving the toy to a child, and watching the toy stop operating after a few minutes.
When given a toy without a battery, a child can destroy even the simplest toy by chewing it, throwing it, or pulling it to pieces.
Anyone who gives a toy, no matter how complicated, to a child risks witnessing the child lose interest within minutes.
A battery-operated toy can grab a child's attention because a child has seen it advertised on television.
However, the toy that seemed so exciting on television may be a disappointment.
Toys without batteries are usually for younger children, and younger children may tire of a toy more quickly.

Add a new point of comparison, and details, about battery-operated toys and non-battery-operated toys:

Both kinds of toys can prove to be a great success with a child.

Some children are fascinated with the moving parts of a battery operated toy and will study it for hours.

The simplest toy, one without any need for a battery, can have an enormous appeal for a child who likes to use his or her imagination.

Exercise 8 **Finding Irrelevant Details in a Comparison or Contrast Outline**

The following outline contains some irrelevant details. Cross out the details that don't fit.

topic sentence: Paper towels and paper napkins are not meant to do the same tasks.

details: Paper towels are stronger than paper napkins.
The towels have a thick, coarse texture.
The napkins are thinner and finer in texture.
Paper towels and paper napkins are not used the same way in the kitchen.
The towels can wipe up spills or absorb grease beneath food, like bacon, cooked in the microwave.
~~It is best to keep a roll of paper towels handy in the kitchen.~~
Paper napkins are too thin to wipe up much liquid or be useful in the microwave.
However, the thinness of paper napkins makes them perfect for diners who want to wipe their mouths.
Paper napkins are also important in protecting diners' laps.
Napkins ~~always seem to slip to the floor.~~
In other parts of the house, paper towels' strength makes them more useful than paper napkins.
Paper towels and window cleaner work well together.
Paper towels can be used to dust wood or clean tile.
~~In the car, paper towels are useful for quick cleanups.~~
A paper napkin would soon shred if it were used to clean a window.
Paper napkins are so thin that they cannot collect much dust or dirt.
~~Paper napkins are almost like toilet tissue.~~
Two paper products, paper towels and paper napkins, are useful in any home, but not for the same purposes.

Exercise 9   Revising the Order in a Comparison or Contrast Outline

Below is an outline written in the subject-by-subject pattern. Rewrite the part of the outline that is in italics so that the points in the second half follow the order of the first half. You do not have to change any sentences; just rearrange them.

topic sentence: Smooth peanut butter and crunchy peanut butter are different in texture, in taste, and in combination with other foods.

details: Smooth peanut butter is so common that it is usually referred to as "peanut butter" because it has the texture people expect.
When it is spread on bread, smooth peanut butter shows no grit, only swirls.
It has an even consistency.
Its texture relates to its taste.
The taste is pure and smooth, never interrupted by a gritty peanut fragment.
Smooth peanut butter is like applesauce with no apple chunks.
Smooth peanut butter can combine well with certain foods.
Chocolate peanut butter frosting, for example, should be smooth, so crunchy peanut fragments don't belong in the frosting.
The traditional peanut butter and grape jelly sandwich combines sleek jelly and smooth peanut butter.
Crunchy peanut butter mixes well in certain foods.

*Chocolate chip cookies, for example, can be made with
crunchy peanut butter for extra flavor and texture.
Similarly, crunchy peanut butter brownies are tasty.
The texture of crunchy peanut butter gives it a unique taste.
The combination of smooth and rough makes this peanut
butter seem more natural than smooth peanut butter.
Eating it is like eating applesauce with pieces of real apple.
People may not be as familiar with the texture of crunchy
peanut butter.
When it is spread on bread, it looks like a swirl of smooth-
ness and sand.*

Rewritten order: *1. People may not be as familiar with the texture of*

crunchy peanut butter.

2. When it is spread on bread, it looks like a swirl of smoothness and sand.

3. The texture of crunchy peanut butter gives it a unique taste.

4. The combination of smooth and rough makes this peanut butter seem

more natural than smooth peanut butter.

5. Eating it is like eating applesauce with pieces of real apple.

6. Crunchy peanut butter mixes well in certain foods.

7. Chocolate chip cookies, for example, can be made with crunchy peanut

butter for extra flavor and texture.

8. Similarly, crunchy peanut butter brownies are tasty.

INSTRUCTOR'S NOTE

Answers will vary. Possible
answers shown at left.

DRAFTING ## Drafting and Revising:
Comparison or Contrast

When you've revised your outline, you can write the first draft of the restaurant paragraph. After making a first draft, you may want to combine more
sentences, rearrange your points, fix your topic sentence, or add vivid
details. You may also need to add transitions.

The Draft

Here is a draft version of the paragraph on contrasting two restaurants. As
you read it, notice the changes from the outline on page 138: the order of
some details in the outline has been changed, sentences have been combined, and transitional devices have been added.

A Draft of a Contrast Paragraph, Point-by-Point Pattern

(Transitions are underlined.)

    Some people would rather eat at The Garden than at Victor's because The
Garden offers better and cheaper food in a more casual environment. The food at
Victor's is bland tasting and traditional. The menu has broiled fish, chicken, and
traditional steaks. The food is the usual American food with a little French food on

continued

the list. Appetizers are the usual things like shrimp cocktail and onion soup. The spices used are mainly parsley and salt. Food at The Garden, <u>however,</u> is more spicy and adventurous. The restaurant has all kinds of ethnic food. There are many pasta dishes with tomato sauce. The menu has four kinds of curry on it. The appetizers include items like tiny tortillas and hot honey-mustard ribs. <u>And if parsley is the spice of choice at Victor's,</u> garlic is the favorite spice at The Garden. The prices at the restaurants differ, <u>too.</u> Victor's is expensive because everything you order costs extra. An appetizer or a salad costs extra. Food at The Garden, <u>in contrast,</u> is more moderately priced because the price of a dinner includes an appetizer and a salad. <u>Price and menu are important, but the most important difference between the restaurants has to do with environment.</u> Certain diners may feel uncomfortable at Victor's, which has a formal kind of atmosphere. Everyone is dressed up, the men in jackets and ties and the women in dresses. The less formal diners would rather eat in a more casual place like The Garden, where everyone wears jeans. Many people prefer a place where they can relax, with reasonable prices and unusual food, to a place that is a little stuffy, with a traditional and expensive menu.

The checklist below may help you to revise your own draft.

**Checklist: A Checklist for Revising the Draft of a Comparison
          or Contrast Paragraph**

✔ Did I include a topic sentence that covers both subjects?

✔ Is the paragraph in a clear order?

✔ Does it stick to one pattern, either subject-by-subject or point-by-point?

✔ Are both subjects given roughly the same amount of space?

✔ Do all the details fit?

✔ Are the details specific and vivid?

✔ Do I need to combine any sentences?

✔ Are transitions used effectively?

✔ Have I made my point?

Exercise 10   **Revising the Draft of a Comparison or Contrast Paragraph
                    by Adding Vivid Details**

INSTRUCTOR'S NOTE

Answers will vary. Possible
answers shown at right.

You can do this exercise alone, with a writing partner, or with a group. The following contrast paragraph lacks the vivid details that could make it interesting. Read it; then rewrite the underlined parts in the space above them. Replace the original words with more vivid details.

In three ways, learning to dance was a different experience than I had

expected. My girlfriend had dared me to enter a local ballroom dancing contest, so

I felt that I needed a few dance lessons first. Before I began the lessons, I imag-

how to tango and meringue
ined myself in a room full of snobby dancers. They would know <u>how to do stuff</u>

clumsy
and be shocked at how <u>bad</u> I was. I also expected the dance instructors to be
critical   *cold and sarcastic*
<u>mean</u>. I was sure they would be <u>awful</u> as they tried to teach me to dance. Most of
          make many mistakes   *slipping, tripping, and*
all, I expected to <u>mess up</u> on the dance floor. I could see myself <u>doing lots of silly</u>
sliding
<u>things</u> in front of the other dancers and the instructors. To my surprise, learning to
                                                                    friendly
dance was nothing like what I had feared. First, the other dancers were <u>nice</u>. Most

of them were beginners like me, and they were not critical of my first attempts.

Even the more experienced dancers accepted me. Second, the dance instructors

worked hard to make me feel comfortable. Instead of criticizing every mistake,
          develop my natural ability.
they encouraged me to <u>do well</u>. My biggest surprise was my realization that I

could actually learn to dance. Each lesson gave me more confidence because I

could see my own improvement. I know I'll never be dancing with the stars, but at

least I won't embarrass my girlfriend at the local contest.

Exercise 11   Revising a Draft by Combining Sentences

The paragraph below has many short, choppy sentences, which are underlined. Whenever you see two or more underlined sentences clustered next
to each other, combine them into one smooth, clear sentence.

INSTRUCTOR'S NOTE

Answers will vary. Possible
answers shown at left.

                                                    Like a dictator, my
   I love my father, but in his home he behaves like a dictator. <u>A dictator gives all</u>
father gives all the orders.
<u>the orders. My father gives all the orders</u>. Sometimes these orders are petty

demands such as telling me to get my feet off the coffee table. At other times he
                                    For example, he insists that I follow
makes unfair demands that limit my freedom. <u>For example, he insists that I follow</u>
a curfew and forces me to give some of my salary to my mother to pay for
<u>a curfew. He forces me to give some of my salary to my mother. She can use the</u>
household expenses.
<u>money to pay for household expenses</u>. Like the worst kind of dictator, he accepts
                        He won't listen when I tell him that I am too old
no challenges to his authority. <u>When I tell him that I am too old to have a curfew,</u>
for a curfew or have a right to spend my own money.
<u>he refuses to listen. He won't listen when I say I have a right to spend all of my</u>

<u>own money</u>. His policy is that as long as I live in his house, I must follow his rules.

Worst of all, my father, like any dictator, assumes that he is always right. Since he

was raised by a strict father, my father assumes that a good father acts like a dic-
          He is blind to changes in society that give more freedom to teens.
tator. <u>He is blind to changes in society. These changes give more freedom to teens</u>.

I know that my father is doing what he thinks is right, but I wish he could be more

modern in his thinking.

POLISHING   ## Proofreading and Polishing: Comparison or Contrast

Contrast Paragraph: Point-by-Point Pattern

Following is the final version of the paragraph contrasting restaurants, using a point-by-point pattern. When you read it, you'll notice several changes from the draft on pages 141–142.

- "Usual" or "usually" was used too often, so synonyms were substituted.
- "Onion soup" became "<u>French</u> onion soup," to polish the detail.
- "Everything <u>you</u> order" was changed to "everything <u>a person</u> orders," to avoid sounding as if the reader is ordering food at Victor's.
- "A formal <u>kind of atmosphere</u>" became "a formal environment," to eliminate extra words.

A Final Version of a Contrast Paragraph: Point-by-Point Pattern

(Changes from the draft are underlined.)

Some people would rather eat at The Garden than at Victor's because The Garden offers better and cheaper food in a more casual environment. The food at Victor's is bland tasting and traditional. The menu has broiled fish, chicken, and traditional steaks. The food is <u>typical</u> American food with a little French food on the list. Appetizers are <u>standard</u> things like shrimp cocktail and <u>French</u> onion soup. The spices are mostly parsley and salt. Food at The Garden, however, is more spicy and adventurous. The restaurant has all kinds of ethnic food. There are many pasta dishes with tomato sauce. The menu has four kinds of curry on it. The appetizers include items like tiny tortillas and hot honey-mustard ribs. And if parsley is the spice of choice at Victor's, garlic is the favorite spice at The Garden. The prices at the restaurants differ, too. Victor's is expensive because everything <u>a person</u> orders costs extra. An appetizer or a salad costs extra. Food at The Garden, in contrast, is more moderately priced because the price of a dinner includes an appetizer and a salad. Price and menu are important, but the most important difference between the two restaurants has to do with environment. Certain diners may feel uncomfortable at Victor's, which has a formal <u>environment</u>. Everyone is dressed up, the men in jackets and ties and the women in dresses. Less formal diners would rather eat in a more casual place like The Garden, where everyone wears jeans. Many people prefer a place where they can relax, with reasonable prices and unusual food, to a place that is a little stuffy, with a traditional and expensive menu.

Before you prepare the final copy of your comparison or contrast paragraph, check your latest draft for errors in spelling, punctuation, typing, and formatting.

> **For your information:** A sample point-by-point contrast essay based on this topic and following the same writing steps can be found in Chapter 12, pp. 293–299.

The Same Contrast Paragraph: Subject-by-Subject

To show you what the same paragraph contrasting restaurants would look like in a subject-by-subject pattern, the outline, draft, and final version are shown below.

An Outline: Subject-by-Subject Pattern

topic sentence:	Some people would rather eat at The Garden than at Victor's because The Garden offers better, cheaper food in a more casual environment.
details:	Food at Victor's is bland tasting and traditional.
	The menu has broiled fish, chicken, and traditional steaks.
	The spices used are mostly parsley and salt.
	The food is the usual American food, with a little French food on the list.
subject 1, Victor's	Appetizers are the usual things like shrimp cocktail and onion soup.
	Victor's is expensive.
	Everything you order costs extra.
	An appetizer or salad costs extra.
	Certain diners may feel uncomfortable at Victor's, which has a formal environment.
	Everyone is dressed up, the men in jackets and ties and the women in dresses.
	Food at The Garden is more spicy and adventurous.
	There are many pasta dishes in tomato sauce.
	There is garlic in just about everything.
	The Garden serves four different curry dishes.
subject 2, The Garden	It has all kinds of ethnic food.
	Appetizers include items like tiny tortillas and hot honey-mustard ribs.
	Food at The Garden is moderately priced.
	The price of a dinner includes an appetizer and a salad.
	The Garden is casual.
	People don't dress up to go there; they wear jeans.
conclusion	Many people prefer a place where they can relax, with reasonable pries and unusual food, to a place that's a little stuffy, with a traditional and expensive menu.

A Draft: Subject-by-Subject Pattern

(Transitions are underlined.)

Some people would rather eat at The Garden than at Victor's because The Garden offers better, cheaper food in a more casual environment. The food at Victor's is bland tasting and traditional. The menu has broiled fish, chicken, and traditional steaks on it. The food is the usual American food, with a little French food on the list. Appetizers are the usual things like shrimp cocktail and

continued

onion soup. At Victor's, the spices are mostly parsley and salt. Eating traditional food at Victor's is expensive, since everything you order costs extra. An appetizer or a salad, for instance, costs extra. Victor's prices make some people nervous, and the restaurant's formal environment makes them uncomfortable. At Victor's, everyone is dressed up, the men in jackets and ties and the women in dresses. <u>The formal atmosphere, the food, and the prices attract some diners, but others would rather go to The Garden for a meal</u>. The food at The Garden is more spicy and adventurous <u>than the offerings at Victor's</u>. The place has all kinds of ethnic food. There are many pasta dishes in tomato sauce, and The Garden serves four different curry dishes. Appetizers include items like tiny tortillas and hot honey-mustard ribs. <u>If Victor's relies on parsley and salt to flavor its food</u>, The Garden sticks to garlic, which is in just about everything. Prices are lower at The Garden <u>than they are at Victor's</u>. The Garden's meals are more moderately priced because, <u>unlike Victor's</u>, The Garden includes an appetizer and a salad in the price of a dinner. <u>And in contrast to Victor's</u>, The Garden is a casual restaurant. People don't dress up to go to The Garden; everyone wears jeans. Many people prefer a place where they can relax, with unusual food at reasonable prices, to a place that's a little stuffy, with a traditional and expensive menu.

A Final Version: Subject-by-Subject Pattern

(Changes from the draft are underlined.)

Some people would rather eat at The Garden than at Victor's because The Garden offers better, cheaper food in a more casual environment. The food at Victor's is bland tasting and traditional. The menu has broiled fish, chicken, and traditional steaks on it. The food is typical American food, with a little French food on the list. Appetizers are the <u>standard</u> things like shrimp cocktail and <u>French</u> onion soup. At Victor's, the spices are mostly parsley and salt. Eating traditional food at Victor's is expensive because everything <u>a person</u> orders costs extra. An appetizer or a salad, for instance, costs extra. Victor's prices make some people nervous, and the restaurant's formal environment makes them uncomfortable. At Victor's, everyone is dressed up, the men in jackets and ties and the women in dresses. The formal <u>environment</u> and the prices attract some diners, but others would rather go to The Garden for a meal. The food at The Garden is more spicy and adventurous than the offerings at Victor's. The place has all kinds of ethnic food. There are many pasta dishes in tomato sauce, and The Garden serves four different curry dishes. Appetizers include items like tiny tortillas and hot honey-mustard ribs. If Victor's relies on parsley and salt to flavor its food, The Garden sticks to garlic, which is in just about everything. Prices are lower at The Garden than they are at Victor's. The Garden's meals are moderately priced because, unlike Victor's, The Garden includes an appetizer and a salad in the price of a dinner. And in contrast to Victor's, The Garden is a casual restaurant. People don't dress up to go to The Garden; everyone wears jeans. Many people prefer a place where they can relax, with unusual food at reasonable prices, to a place that's a little stuffy, with a traditional and expensive menu.

Exercise 12 Proofreading to Prepare the Final Version

Following are two comparison or contrast paragraphs with the kinds of errors it is easy to overlook in a final copy of an assignment. Correct the

errors, writing your corrections above the lines. There are thirteen errors in
the first paragraph and fifteen in the second.

1. Most people occasionally sleep late, but do they sleep <u>too</u> late? Sleeping late
                                                    no comma needed
is significantly different from sleeping too late. People, who sleep late tend to stay in
              an
bed a half hour or hour after their usual wake-up time. Maybe they sleep late because
                                schedule
of a change in their work or school skedule. Such people wake up fully rested and
              They   *extra*
even energized. they are grateful for the Extra sleep because it restores their

                                ,
strength. On the other hand people who sleep too late tend to stay in bed for

hours beyond their normal schedule. Usually, they have a free day or have skipped

work and decided to spend most of their time asleep. Unfortunately, they wake up
feeling tired
filling tire, even drugged, from all the sleep. They find it difficult to get out of bed.

Another difference between the two kinds of late sleeping is the level of guilt.

Sleeping a half hour or an hour late can make people feel a bit guilty, but not
            guilty
extremely guilt. After all, late sleepers still have most of the day ahead of them.

However, those who sleep too late may feel they have wasted most of the day.

Terrible guilt can strike the sleepers who had a few plans for the day, slept through

half of it, and woke with no energy to do anything. Guilt about sleeping can be
          worse   .
made worst by the reaction of others Late sleepers may have a parent, partner, or

roommate comment, "Sleeping late? It must be nice," with a hint of envy. Those

who sleep too late are likely to hear such accusations as, "Are you finally getting
      "
up? or "Do you know what time it is?" Sleeping late draws a little envy, but sleep-
      too
ing to late has a higher price.

2. My current girlfriend is turning out to be a copy of my last girlfriend. My last
                                            thought
girlfriend, Dina, was deeply in love with me for about a month. She tought every-
            said
thing I did or say was great, and she loved to sit at home with me and watch televi-

sion. But after about six weeks, I noticed Dina was complaining more and more.
    said   *didn't*   *sit*
She say she di'nt want to set around the house anymore; she wanted to go out to
clubs   *parties*
club and attend partys. I got sick of her complaining, so I stopped seeing her as

much. I went out with my friends instead. One night at a party, I met a beautiful

woman
women named Cherisse. When Dina found out, she gave me a choice: I could

see her, or I could see Cherisse. That is how I wound up with my current girl-

                                            lovely   *no comma needed*
friend, Cherisse. Like Dina, Cherisse was sweet and lovley for a while. She said,
                              private
she was happy to spend privite time with me, watching television and talking.
                                                whine
Then, in the same way Dina did, Cherisse started to wine. She said I never took
                    claimed
her anywhere. She claim I must be ashamed of her. She insisted she wanted to

meet my friends. When I brought some friends over, she didn't like them. As a

result, I started socializing with my friends more. Cherisse was even angrier that I
wasn't   *no comma needed*
wasnt taking her out. One day she discovered, that I had been seen at a club with

another woman. The next day, just like Dina, she gave me a choice. I don't know

what I'll do this time because I don't seem to have much luck with women!

Lines of Detail: A Walk-Through Assignment

Write a paragraph that compares or contrasts any experience you've heard about with the same experience as you lived it. For example, you could compare or contrast what you heard about starting college with your actual experience of starting college. You could compare or contrast what you heard about falling in love with your experience of falling in love, or what you heard about playing a sport with your own experience playing that sport. To write your paragraph, follow these steps:

Step 1: Choose the experience you will write about; then list all the similarities and differences between the experience as you heard about it and the experience as you lived it.

Step 2: To decide whether to write a comparison or contrast paragraph, survey your list to see which has more details, the similarities or the differences.

Step 3: Add details to your comparison or contrast list. Survey your list again, and group the details into points of comparison or contrast.

Step 4: Write a topic sentence that includes both subjects, focuses on comparison or contrast, and makes a point.

Step 5: Decide whether your paragraph will be in the subject-by-subject or point-by-point pattern. Write your outline in the pattern you choose.

Step 6: Write a draft of your paragraph. Revise your draft, checking the transitions, the order of the points, the space given to each subject, and the relevance and vividness of details. Combine any short, choppy sentences.

Step 7: Before you prepare the final copy of your paragraph, edit for word choice, spelling, punctuation, and transitions.

Writing Your Own Comparison or Contrast Paragraph

When you write on one of these topics, be sure to follow the stages of the writing process in preparing your comparison or contrast paragraph.

1. Compare or contrast what is most important in your life now to what was most important to you as a child. You might want to brainstorm about your values then and now before narrowing your focus to specific similarities or differences.

2. Compare or contrast any of the following:

two pets	two relatives	two college Web sites
two gifts	two jobs	two apartment complexes
two supervisors	two role models	two discount stores
two clubs	two athletic teams	two flat-screen televisions

   If your instructor agrees, you may want to brainstorm points of comparison or contrast with a writing partner or a group.

3. Imagine that you are a reporter who specializes in helping consumers get the best for their money. Imagine that you are asked to rate two brands of the same supermarket item. Write a paragraph advising your readers which is the better buy. You can rate two brands of cola, yogurt, potato chips, toothpaste, ice cream, chocolate chip cookies, or paper towels—any item you can get in a supermarket.

   Be sure to devise *enough* points to contrast. You can't, for example, do a well-developed paragraph on just the taste of two cookies. But you can also discuss texture, color, smell, price, fat content, calories, number of chocolate chips, and so on. If your instructor agrees, you may want to brainstorm topics or points of contrast with a group as a way of beginning the writing process. Then work on the outline, drafts, and final version on your own.

4. Compare or contrast your taste in music, dress, or ways of spending leisure time, with that of another generation.

5. If you have ever shopped online for sales or bargains offered by your favorite department store, contrast this experience with shopping inside the store itself. Select one specific store for this assignment, but be sure to contrast the specific differences between the two shopping choices. You should include three points of contrast in your paragraph.

6. Interview a person of your age group who comes from a different part of the country. (Note: There may be quite a few people from different parts of the country in your class.) Ask him or her about similarities or differences between his or her former home and this part of the country. You could ask about similarities or differences in dress, music, dating, nightlife, ways to spend leisure time, favorite entertainers, or anything else that you like.

   After the interview, write a paragraph that either shows how people of the same age group, but from different parts of the country, have different tastes in something like music or dress or share

Collaborate

the same tastes in music, dress, etc. Whichever approach you use, use details you collected in the interview.

7. Examine the photograph of the two buildings. Then write a paragraph contrasting them. You can start by asking such questions as the following: Which is more elegant? Seems less impressive? Is more serene? Is more modern? Use the details of the photograph to support your topic sentence.

8. Look carefully at the photograph of the two boys. Write a paragraph contrasting the mood of the boys with the atmosphere of the background.

Note: Additional writing options suitable for comparison or contrast–related assignments can be found after the professional reading "Honesty and Dishonesty," which begins on page 617.

How Do I Get a Better Grade?

PEARSON
mywritinglab

Visit www.mywritinglab.com for audio-visual lectures and additional practice sets about comparison and contrast.

Get a better grade with MyWritingLab!

Name: _____   Section: _____

Peer Review Form for a Comparison or Contrast Paragraph

After you've written a draft of your paragraph, let a writing partner read it. When your partner has completed the form below, discuss the comments. Then repeat the same process for your partner's paragraph.

I think the topic sentence of this paragraph is _____

_____

_____

The pattern of this paragraph is (a) subject by subject, (b) point by point. (Choose one.)

The points used to compare or contrast are _____

_____

_____

The part of the paragraph I liked best is about _____

_____

The comparison or contrast is (a) easy to follow, (b) a little confusing. (Choose one.)

I have questions about or would like to know more about _____

I would like to see a few more details about _____

I would like to take out the part about _____

I would like to add or change a transition in front of the words _____

_____

Other comments: _____

_____

_____

_____

_____

_____

_____

_____

_____

Reviewer's name _____

Jumping In

*If you were hungry, which one of the foods in the photographs would you prefer to eat? Are the foods all equally fattening? If not, which is the most fattening? Which is the least? If you can rank the foods from least to most fattening, you will be using a technique called **classification**.*

CHAPTER 7

Classification

WHAT IS CLASSIFICATION?

When you **classify**, you divide something into different categories, and you do it according to some basis. For example, you may classify the people in your neighborhood into three types: those you know well, those you know slightly, and those you don't know at all. Although you may not be aware of it, you have chosen a basis for this classification. You are classifying the people in your neighborhood according to *how well you know them*.

Hints for Writing a Classification Paragraph

1. Divide your subject into three or more categories or types. If you are thinking about classifying DVD players, for instance, you might think about dividing them into cheap players and expensive players. Your basis for classification would be the price of DVD players. But you would need at least one more type—moderately priced players. Using at least three types helps you to be reasonably complete in your classification.

2. Pick one basis for classification and stick with it. If you are classifying DVD players by price, you cannot divide them into cheap, expensive, and Japanese. Two of the categories relate to price, but "Japanese" does not.

TEACHING TIP

Emphasize the difference between a category (or type) and an example (or details) within a category. Students may initially confuse the two until they see that a category is a larger concept than an example within a category.

In the following examples, notice how one item does not fit its classification and has been crossed out.

fishermen

fishermen who fish every day
weekend fishermen
~~*fishermen who own their own boat*~~

(If you are classifying fishermen on the basis of how often they fish, "fishermen who own their own boat" does not fit.)

tests

essay tests
objective tests
~~*math tests*~~
combination essay and objective tests

(If you are classifying tests on the basis of the type of questions they ask, "math tests" does not fit, because it describes the subject being tested.)

3. Be creative in your classification. While it is easy to classify drivers according to their age, your paragraph will be more interesting if you choose another basis for comparison, such as how drivers react to a very slow driver in front of them.

4. Have a reason for your classification. You may be classifying to help a reader understand a topic, or to help a reader choose something, or you may be trying to prove a point, to criticize, or to attack.

A classification paragraph must have a unifying reason behind it, and the detail for each type should be as descriptive and specific as possible. Determining your audience and deciding why you are classifying can help you stay focused and make your paragraph more interesting.

| Exercise 1 | **Finding a Basis for Classifying**

Write three bases for classifying each of the following topics. The first topic is done for you.

1. topic to classify: cats
You can classify cats on the basis of

a. *their age*

b. *their color*

c. *how friendly they are*

2. topic to classify: cell phones
You can classify cell phones on the basis of

a. *their price*

b. *their size*

c. *their features*

3. **topic to classify:** superhero movies
   You can classify superheroes movies on the basis of

   a. *the appeal of the superhero*

   b. *the level of the superhero's power*

   c. *the quality of the action scenes*

4. **topic to classify:** hamburgers
   You can classify hamburgers on the basis of

   a. *their toppings*

   b. *their size*

   c. *cooking methods*

Exercise 2 **Identifying What Does Not Fit the Classification**

In each list below, one item does not fit because it is not classified on the same basis as the others on the list. First, determine the basis for the classification. Then cross out the one item on each list that does not fit.

1. **topic:** fish

   basis for classification: *how it is cooked*

   list: broiled fish
         ~~frozen fish~~
         fried fish
         baked fish

2. **topic:** fences

   basis for classification: *what they are made of*

   list: wooden fences
         ~~electrified fences~~
         chain-link fences
         iron fences

3. **topic:** complainers

   basis for classification: *how often they complain*

   list: constant complainers
         frequent complainers
         occasional complainers
         ~~angry complainers~~

4. **topic:** spoons

   basis for classification: *purpose*

   list: soup spoon
         iced-tea spoon
         ~~wooden spoon~~
         coffee spoon

Exercise 3 **Finding Categories That Fit One Basis for Classification**

In the lines under each topic, write three categories that fit the basis of classification that is given. The first one is done for you.

1. topic: cartoons on television
basis for classification: when they are shown
categories:

a. *Saturday morning cartoons*

b. *weekly cartoon series shown in the evening*

c. *cartoons that are holiday specials*

INSTRUCTOR'S NOTE

Answers will vary. Possible answers shown at right.

2. topic: professional basketball coaches
basis for classification: how popular they are with the public
categories:

a. *extremely popular*

b. *somewhat popular*

c. *unpopular*

3. topic: paper
basis for classification: its purpose
categories:

a. *wrapping paper*

b. *graph paper*

c. *crepe paper*

4. topic: horses
basis for classification: their job
categories:

a. *race horses*

b. *horses for mounted police officers*

c. *carriage horses*

WRITING THE CLASSIFICATION PARAGRAPH IN STEPS

PREWRITING Gathering Ideas: Classification

First, pick a topic for your classification. The next step is to choose some basis for your classification.

Brainstorming a Basis for Classification

Sometimes the easiest way to choose one basis is to brainstorm about different types related to your topic and to see where your brainstorming leads you. For example, if you were to write a paragraph classifying phone calls, you could begin by listing anything about phone calls that occurs to you:

Phone Calls

sales calls at dinnertime	*people who talk too long*
short calls	*calls I hate getting*
calls in the middle of the night	*wrong numbers*
long-distance calls	*waiting for a call*

The next step is to survey your list. See where it is leading you. The list on phone calls seems to have a few items about *unpleasant phone calls:*

> *sales calls at dinnertime*
> *wrong numbers*
> *calls in the middle of the night*

Maybe you can label these "Calls I Do Not Want," and that will lead you toward a basis for classification. You might think about calls you *do not* want and calls you *do* want. You think further and realize that you want or do not want certain calls because of their effect on you.

You decide to use the effect of the calls on you as the basis for classification. Remember, however, that you need at least three categories. If you stick with this basis for classification, you can come up with three categories:

> *calls that please me*
> *calls that irritate me*
> *calls that frighten me*

By brainstorming, you can then gather details about your three categories:

Added Details for Three Categories

calls that please me

from boyfriend

good friends

catch-up calls—someone I haven't talked to for a while

make me feel close

calls that irritate me

sales calls at dinnertime

wrong numbers

calls that interrupt

invade privacy

calls that frighten me

emergency call in the middle of the night

"let's break up" call from boyfriend

change my life, indicate some bad change

Matching the Points within the Categories

As you begin thinking about details for each of your categories, try to write about the same points in each type. For instance, in the list on phone calls, each category includes some details about who made the call:

> *calls that please me—from good friends, my boyfriend*
> *calls that irritate me—from salespeople, unknown callers*
> *calls that frighten me—from the emergency room, my boyfriend*

Each category also includes some details about why you react to them in a specific way:

calls that please me—make me feel close
calls that irritate me—invade privacy
calls that frighten me—indicate some bad change

You achieve unity by covering the same points for each category.

Writing a Topic Sentence for a Classification Paragraph

The topic sentence for a classification paragraph should do two things:

1. It should mention what you are classifying.
2. It should indicate the basis for your classification by stating the basis or by listing your categories, or both.

Consider the details on phone calls. To write a topic sentence about the details,

1. mention what you are classifying: phone calls; and
2. indicate the basis for classifying by (a) stating the basis (their effect on me), or (b) listing the categories (calls that please me, calls that irritate me, and calls that frighten me). You may also state both the basis and the categories in the topic sentence.

Following these guidelines, you can write a topic sentence like this:

I can classify phone calls according to their effect on me.

or

Phone calls can be grouped into the ones that please me, the ones that irritate me, and the ones that frighten me.

Both of these topic sentences state what you're classifying and give some indication of the basis for the classification. Once you have a topic sentence, you are ready to begin the planning stage of writing the classification paragraph.

Collaborate

| Exercise 4 | Creating Questions to Get Details for a Classification Paragraph |

Do this exercise with a partner or group. Each list below includes a topic, the basis for classifying that topic, and three categories. For each list, think of three questions that you could ask to get more details about the types. The first list is done for you.

1. **topic:** moviegoers
   basis for classification: how they behave during the movie
   categories: the quiet moviegoers, the irritating moviegoers, the obnoxious moviegoers
   questions you can ask:

   a. *Does each type use a cell phone?*

   b. *Does each type talk during the movie?*

   c. *Does each type come and go during the movie?*

2. topic: sports fans expressing support for a team
   basis for classification: how supportive they are
   categories: loyal fans, extremely loyal fans, fanatic fans
   questions you can ask:

   a. *How will team support be expressed on each type's car?*

   b. *How much team-related clothing will each type wear to a game?*

   c. *How will each type's support be reflected in body decoration?*

INSTRUCTOR'S NOTE

Answers will vary. Possible answers shown at left.

3. topic: people in line at the post office
   basis for classification: what they are carrying
   categories: the one-envelope people, the several-boxes people, the people with a plastic carrier box of messy mail
   questions you can ask:

   a. *What is each type's purpose?*

   b. *How does each type behave in line?*

   c. *How long will each type be at the post office?*

4. topic: people who send flowers
   basis for classification: their motives for sending flowers
   categories: the romantic, the thoughtful, the guilty
   questions you can ask:

   a. *On what occasions will each type send flowers?*

   b. *What kind of flowers will each type send?*

   c. *What message will each type write on the card?*

Exercise 5 **Writing Topic Sentences for a Classification Paragraph**

Review the topics, bases for classification, and categories in Exercise 4. Then, using that material, write a good topic sentence for each topic.

Topic Sentences

   for topic 1: *Moviegoers can be classified on the basis of how they behave during the movie.*

   for topic 2: *Sports fans expressing support for a team can be grouped into the loyal fans, the extremely loyal fans, and the fanatic fans.*

   for topic 3: *People in line at the post office can be categorized according to what they are carrying.*

TEACHING TIP

Groupwork: This exercise can be done in groups to practice collaborative brainstorming and peer revision for precise wording of these topic sentences.

INSTRUCTOR'S NOTE

Answers will vary. Possible answers shown at left.

for topic 4: *People who send flowers can be classified into the romantic, the thoughtful, and the guilty.*

PLANNING   Devising a Plan: Classification

Effective Order in Classifying

After you have a topic sentence and a list of details, you can create an outline. Think about which category you want to write about first, second, and so on. The order of your categories will depend on what you're writing about. If you're classifying ways to meet people, you can save the best for last. If you're classifying three habits that are bad for your health, you can save the worst one for last.

If you list your categories in the topic sentence, list them in the same order you will use to explain them in the paragraph.

Following is an outline for a paragraph classifying phone calls. The details have been put into categories. The underlined sentences have been added to clearly define each category before the details are given.

An Outline for a Classification Paragraph

topic sentence: Phone calls can be grouped into the ones that please me, the ones that irritate me, and the ones that frighten me.

category 1, details

There are some calls that please me.
They make me feel close to someone.
I like calls from my boyfriend, especially when he calls just to say he is thinking of me.
I like to hear from good friends.
I like catch-up calls.
These are calls from people I haven't talked to in a while.

category 2, details

There are some calls that irritate me.
These calls invade my privacy.
Sales calls always come at dinnertime.
They offer me newspaper subscriptions or "free" vacations.
I get at least four wrong-number calls each week.
All these calls irritate me, and I have to interrupt what I'm doing to answer them.

category 3, details

There are some calls that frighten me.
They are the calls that tell me about some bad change in my life.
I once got a call in the middle of the night.
It was from a hospital emergency room.
The nurse said my brother had been in an accident.
I once got a call from a boyfriend.
He said he wanted to break up.

You can use the following checklist to help you revise your own classification outline.

Checklist: A Checklist for Revising the Classification Outline

✓   Do I have a consistent basis for classifying?

✓   Does my topic sentence mention what I am classifying and indicate the basis for classification?

✓   Do I have enough to say about each category in my classification?

✓   Are the categories presented in the most effective order?

✓   Am I using clear and specific details?

With a revised outline, you can begin writing your draft.

Exercise 6   **Recognizing the Basis for Classification within the Topic Sentence**

The topic sentences below do not state a basis for classification, but you can recognize the basis nevertheless. After you've read each topic sentence, write the basis for classification on the lines provided. The first one is done for you.

1. topic sentence: People at the supermarket can be classified into those who qualify for the express lane, those who push a moderately filled cart, and those who drag overloaded carts.

basis for classification: _how much they have in their carts_

2. topic sentence: When it comes to car owners, there are those who never clean their cars, those who occasionally use the drive-through car wash, and those who wash, wax, and polish their cars every weekend.

basis for classification: _how often they clean their cars_

3. topic sentence: Dogs can be grouped into shy, friendly, and extremely social.

basis for classification: _how friendly they are_

4. topic sentence: Cousins fall into three types: the ones who are like siblings, the ones who are casual friends, and the ones who are rivals.

basis for classification: _how close they are_

Exercise 7   **Adding Details to a Classification Outline**

Collaborate

Do this exercise with a partner or group. In this outline, add details where the blank lines indicate. Match the points covered in the other categories.

topic sentence: My experiences at the dentist's office can be classified into routine visits, unpleasant encounters, and nightmare occasions.

INSTRUCTOR'S NOTE

Answers will vary. However, they must cover the following: a second detail about (a) the kind of dental work that occurs at an unpleasant encounter, (b) the kind of dental work that occurs on a nightmare occasion, and (c) the duration of the pain on a nightmare occasion.

details: Most of my visits to the dentist's office are routine.

They are for regular checkups, cleaning, and X-rays.

The cleaning involves some painful moments of scraping, scratching, and probing.

The X-ray hurts because I have a painful piece of cardboard wedged in my mouth that is also uncomfortable.

However, by the time I get home from a routine visit, I feel fine.

Unpleasant encounters usually involve a more complicated procedure.

Sometimes I need special work on my gums.

At other times, the dentist finds, cleans, and fills cavities.

Even with a little anesthetic, these procedures hurt as the dentist hits a nerve or cuts too deeply.

They hurt after I leave the dentist's office, but I recover quickly.

Nightmare occasions are few but unforgettable.

One of them involved an impacted wisdom tooth.

Another involved a broken tooth.

In both cases, the surgery in the office had me clutching the dental chair in pain.

I went home in pain and suffered for several days.

The only kind of visit to the dentist that I can tolerate is routine, slightly painful, and quickly forgotten.

DRAFTING   **Drafting and Revising: Classification**

You can transform your outline into a first draft of a paragraph by writing the topic sentence and the details in paragraph form. As you write, you can begin combining some of the short sentences, adding details, and inserting transitions.

Transitions in Classification

Various transitions can be used in a classification paragraph. The transitions you select will depend on what you are classifying and the basis you choose for classifying. For example, if you are classifying roses according to how pretty they are, you can use transitions like, "*one lovely kind* of rose," and "*another, more beautiful kind,*" and "*the most beautiful kind.*" In other classifications you can use transitions like, "the first type," "another type," or "the final type." In revising your classification paragraph, use the transitions that most clearly connect your ideas.

As you write your own paragraph, you may want to refer to a "kind" or a "type." For variety, try such other words as "class," "group," "species," "form," or "version" if it is logical to do so.

After you have a draft of your paragraph, you can revise and review it. The checklist below may help you with your revisions.

> **Checklist: A Checklist for Revising the Draft of a Classification Paragraph**
>
> ✓ Does my topic sentence state what I am classifying?
>
> ✓ Does it indicate the basis of my classification?
>
> ✓ Should any of my sentences be combined?
>
> ✓ Do my transitions clearly connect my ideas?
>
> ✓ Should I add more details to any of the categories?
>
> ✓ Are the categories presented in the most effective order?

Following is a draft of the classification paragraph on phone calls. Compare these changes to the outline on page 160:

- An introduction has been added, in front of the topic sentence, to make the paragraph smoother.
- Some sentences have been combined.
- Some details have been added.
- Transitions have been added.
- A final sentence has been added so that the paragraph makes a stronger point.

TEACHING TIP

For this draft, have students find each of the changes listed and then discuss the changes with them. Reviewing the additional details and transitions is especially relevant at this stage in the writing process. Students will see that the wording in a draft often differs from the wording in an outline. Stress that wording evolves over *several* drafts.

A Draft of a Classification Paragraph

I get many phone calls, but they fit into three types. Phone calls can be grouped into the ones that please me, the ones that irritate me, and the ones that frighten me. There are some calls that please me because they make me feel close to someone. I like calls from my boyfriend, especially when he calls just to say he is thinking of me. I like to hear from my good friends. I like catch-up calls, the calls from people I haven't talked to in a while that fill me in on what friends have been doing. There are also calls that irritate me because they invade my privacy. Sales calls, offering me newspaper subscriptions and "free" vacations, always come at dinnertime. In addition, I get at least four wrong-number calls each week. All these calls irritate me, and I have to interrupt what I'm doing to answer them. The more serious calls are the ones that frighten me. They are the calls that tell me about some bad change in my life. Once, in the middle of the night, a call from a hospital emergency room told me my brother had been in an accident. Another time, a boyfriend called to tell me he wanted to break up. When I get bad news by phone, I realize that the telephone can bring frightening calls as well as friendly or irritating ones.

Exercise 8   **Combining Sentences for a Better Classification Paragraph**

The following paragraph has some short sentences that would be more effective if they were combined. Combine each pair of underlined sentences into one sentence. Write the new sentence in the space above the old ones.

INSTRUCTOR'S NOTE

Answers will vary. Possible answers shown at right.

INSTRUCTOR'S NOTE

For more on combining short sentences, see Chapter 33 on sentence variety.

In my experience, the three kinds of sleep are deep sleep, ordinary sleep, and

Deep sleep is a rare and wonderful type of sleep.

minimal sleep. <u>Deep sleep is a wonderful type of sleep. It is rare.</u> Deep sleep

I am likely to enjoy

begins almost as soon as I get into bed, and it lasts for hours. <u>I am likely to enjoy</u>

deep sleep when I am physically exhausted, extremely calm, or quietly happy.

<u>deep sleep when I am physically exhausted. It may also come when I am</u>

<u>extremely calm. In addition, I am likely to experience it when I am quietly happy.</u>

Normal sleep is the kind of sleep I experience most nights. A night of normal sleep

begins with a period of stress or worry and eventually leads to a fairly calm sleep

The stress can be a reaction to the challenges of the past day;

of about six hours. <u>The stress can</u> be a <u>reaction to the challenges of the past day.</u>

in contrast, the worry can come from my anxieties about the next day.

<u>The worry can come from several sources. These sources are my anxieties about</u>

<u>the next day.</u> The third kind of sleep, minimal sleep, strikes me only occasionally.

It takes me hours to get minimal sleep, and the sleep lasts only an hour or two. I

I cannot

find it almost impossible to sleep after a sad or frightening experience. <u>I cannot</u>

take sleep for granted because I may sleep a long, deep sleep, a normal, fairly

<u>take sleep for granted. It can be a long, deep sleep. It is usually a normal, fairly</u>

calm one, or a horrible, minimal one.

<u>calm sleep. Minimal sleep can give a person a horrible night.</u>

Exercise 9 **Identifying Transitions in a Classification Paragraph**

Underline all the transitions in the paragraph below. The transitions may be words or groups of words.

I can classify compliments according to how valuable they are to me. The <u>first kind</u>, the phony compliment, is easily recognized. Someone who dislikes or fears a person may feel obliged to give that person a phony compliment. Such compliments include, "That shirt looks great on you," a statement from someone who has seen the shirt a thousand times, or praise such as, "Nice work!" given by a rival full of resentment. <u>Another kind</u>, the automatic compliment, usually comes from a well-meaning person. Unfortunately, this person is trying to be supportive but can actually hurt a friend. <u>One version</u> of this compliment is saying, "You look great!" to a person with the red nose and teary eyes of the flu. <u>The best and rarest type</u> of compliment is the meaningful one. Meaningful compliments are rare because the person giving the compliment is likely to be demanding, highly respected, and even loved. <u>This class of compliment</u> includes, "I'm so proud of you!" said by a tough and often silent father to a son who just received a diploma, and, "You have a real gift for music," spoken by a demanding music teacher to a struggling artist. Compliments come in a variety of <u>forms</u>, but everyone recognizes and appreciates the meaningful ones.

POLISHING Polishing and Proofreading: Classification

Following is the final version of the classification paragraph on phone calls. Compare the draft of the paragraph on page 163 to the final version and you'll notice these changes:

- The first sentence has been rewritten so that it is less choppy, and a word of transition, "My," links the second sentence to the first.
- Some words have been eliminated and sentences rewritten so that they are not too wordy.
- The word choice has been refined: "bad change" has been replaced by "crisis," "someone" has been changed to "a person I care about" to make the detail more precise, and "irritate" has been changed to "annoy" to avoid repetition.

TEACHING TIP

Have several students read aloud different portions of the final version. If their assigned portion includes an underlined section, have them identify the type of editing change (i.e., transitional link, less wordy, more-precise details, less repetition). They should cross reference this final version with the draft on page 163. Stress that a final version is often the result of multiple drafts.

A Final Version of a Classification Paragraph

(Changes from the draft are underlined.)

    <u>I get many phone calls, but most of them fall into one of three types.</u> <u>My</u> phone calls can be grouped into the ones that please me, the ones that irritate me, and the ones that frighten me. There are some calls I want to receive because they make me feel close to <u>a person I care about.</u> I like calls from my boyfriend, especially when he calls just to say he is thinking of me. I like to hear from my good friends. I like catch-up calls from <u>friends</u> I haven't talked to in a while. There are also calls I don't want because they invade my privacy. Sales calls, offering me newspaper subscriptions and "free" vacations, always come at dinnertime. In addition, I get at least four wrong-number calls each week. All these calls <u>annoy me,</u> and I have to interrupt what I'm doing to answer them. The more serious calls are the ones I really don't want to receive. They are the calls that tell me about some <u>crisis</u> in my life. <u>I once got a midnight call from a hospital emergency room, informing me my brother had been in an accident.</u> Another time, a boyfriend called to tell me he wanted to break up. When I get bad news by phone, I realize that the telephone can bring frightening calls as well as friendly or irritating ones.

Before you prepare the final version of your own classification paragraph, check your latest draft for errors in spelling, punctuation, word choice, and typing.

For your information: A sample classification essay based on this topic and following the same writing steps can be found in Chapter 12, pp. 300–304.

Exercise 10   Proofreading to Prepare the Final Version

Following are two classification paragraphs with the kind of errors it is easy to overlook when you prepare the final version of an assignment. Correct the errors, writing above the lines. The first paragraph has thirteen errors; the second has eleven errors.

Paragraph 1

Meals

Meal's eaten at home fall into three categories, and they are those eaten in the

dining

living room, those eaten in the kitchen, and those eaten in the dinning room.

Meals eaten in the living room are the least formal of meals. Eating in the living

is

room are likely to mean eating in front of the television, so the food is usually

placed on a coffee table or on the diner's lap. Often, the food is not on a plate

sandwich no comma needed   chips

because the meal is a sanwich, or a bag of Chips. In such cases, the food is simply

usually

handheld. Meals eaten in the kitchen are usual more formal. The food is on a

The

kitchen table, and two or more people sitting on chairs eat at the table. the

kitchen setting often involves family members, and someone sets plates, silver-

ware, and glasses on the table. Food served in the kitchen is likely to be prepared

in some way; it is cooked or at least warmed up in a microwave. The third class of

formal

meals is the most foremal class. Meals eaten at a dining room table are family

gatherings and can include guests The table is often set with more and better

plates, silverware, and glasses than a meal in the kitchen involves. A meal in the

rolls

dining room may include a greater variety of food, including desserts, roles,

soups, or salads. Most likely, some of the food will be homemade. Each kind of

meal has its benefits. A meal in the living room is quick, casual, and easy while a

slightly more formal kitchen meal offers social interaction and better food. For

the best food and a more social atmosphere, a meal eaten in the dining room can

memories

leave special memmries.

Paragraph 2

desserts

For those who love chocolate treats, there are three kinds of deserts: mildly

chocolate

chocolate, real chocolate, and extreme chocolate. Mildly choclate desserts have a *light*

chocolate flavor, but they are lite on satisfaction. Such desserts include chocolate-

no comma needed

flavored popsicles or chocolate-covered marshmallow cookies. These desserts,

are not rich enough in deep chocolate flavor. Real chocolate desserts have more

of that essential ingredient In this category, there are chocolate layer cakes, fudge

no comma needed

brownies, and chocolate cream pies. These goodies offer a more, chocolate expe-

rience. For those who can never have enough chocolate, there is a third type of

dessert, in the extreme chocolate class. Extreme chocolate desserts come with

names like Death by Chocolate or Chocolate Overload. They contain multiple

no comma needed

forms of chocolate such as, layers of cake, chocolate chips, chocolate icing, bits

of fudge, chunks of brownies, chocolate ice cream, chocolate pudding, and

covered   *say*

chocolate-cover nuts. The names of these desserts says it all. These goodies must

be eaten in small portions because chocolate lovers could die of happiness if they

too   .

ate to much

Lines of Detail: A Walk-Through Assignment

Write a paragraph that classifies bosses on the basis of how they treat their employees. To write the paragraph, follow these steps:

Step 1: List all the details you can remember about bosses you have worked for or known.

Step 2: Survey your list. Then list three categories of bosses, based on how they treat their employees.

Step 3: Now that you have three categories, study your list again, looking for matching points for all three categories. For example, all three categories could be described by this matching point: where the boss works.

Step 4: Write a topic sentence that (a) names what you are classifying and (b) states the basis for classification or names all three categories.

Step 5: Write an outline. Check that your outline defines each category, uses matching points for each category, and puts the categories in an effective order.

Step 6: Write a draft of the classification paragraph. Check the draft, revising it until it has specific details, smooth transitions, and effective word choice.

Step 7: Before you prepare the final copy of your paragraph, check your last draft for any errors in punctuation, spelling, word choice, or mechanics.

Writing Your Own Classification Paragraph

When you write on any of these topics, be sure to work through the stages of the writing process in preparing your classification paragraph.

Collaborate

1. Write a classification paragraph on any of the topics listed below. As a first step, you will need to narrow the topic. For example, instead of classifying all cars, you can narrow the topic to *sports* cars, or fears to *irrational* fears. If your instructor agrees, brainstorm with a partner or a group to come up with (a) a basis for your classification, (b) categories related to the basis, and (c) points you can make to give details about each of the categories.

cartoon heroes	jewelry	hair
horror movies	drivers	restaurants
romantic movies	birthdays	dates
children	cars	scams
parents	cell phone options	salespeople
students	fans at a concert	fears
professors	fans at a sports event	weddings
coaches	rumors	excuses
cameras	shoes	hobbies

2. Below are some topics. Each one already has a basis for classification. Write a classification paragraph on one of these choices. If your instructor agrees, work with a partner or group to brainstorm categories, matching points and details for the categories.

Classify

a. exams on the basis of how *difficult* they are.
b. weekends on the basis of how *busy* they are.
c. valentines on the basis of how *romantic* they are.
d. breakfasts on the basis of how *healthy* they are.
e. skin divers (or some other recreational athletes) on the basis of how *experienced* they are.
f. singers on the basis of the *kind of audience* they appeal to.
g. television commercials on the basis of what *time of day or night* they are broadcast.
h. radio stations on the basis of what *kind of music* they play.
i. urban legends on the basis of how *illogical* they are.

3. Look carefully at the photograph below. Then use its details to write a classification paragraph with this topic sentence:

College students can be classified according to the way they react to a professor's explanation of a concept.

Note: Additional writing options suitable for classification-related assignments can be found after the professional reading "Three Disciplines for Children," which begins on page 620.

How Do I Get a Better Grade?

Visit www.mywritinglab.com for audio-visual lectures and additional practice sets about classification.

Get a better grade with MyWritingLab!

Name: _____ Section: _____

Peer Review Form for a Classification Paragraph

After you've written a draft of your classification paragraph, let a writing partner read it. When your partner has completed the form below, discuss his or her comments. Then repeat the same process for your partner's paragraph.

This paragraph classifies _____ (write the topic).

The basis for the classification is _____

_____

The matching points are _____

_____

The part that could use more or better details is _____

_____

I have questions about or would like to know more about _____

_____

I would like to see more specifics about _____

_____

I would like to take out the part about _____

_____

The part of this paragraph I like best is _____

_____

Other comments: _____

_____

_____

_____

_____

_____

_____

_____

Reviewer's Name: _____

CHAPTER 8

Jumping In

Can you define the expression on this child's face in one word? Why did you use that word? What does that word mean to you? By exploring such questions, you are now working toward a personal **definition.**

Definition

WHAT IS DEFINITION?

A **definition** paragraph is one that explains *what a term means to you.* You can begin thinking about what a term means by consulting the dictionary, but your paragraph will include much more than a dictionary definition. It will include a personal definition.

You can select several ways to explain the meaning of a term. You can give examples, you can tell a story, or you can contrast your term with another term. If you were writing a definition of perseverance, for example, you could do one or more of the following: you could give examples of people you know who have persevered, you could tell a story about someone who persevered, or you could contrast perseverance with another quality, like impatience. You could also write about times when perseverance is most needed or about the rewards of perseverance.

TEACHING TIP

Point out that in everyday conversation, we often ask others what they mean. For example, a clothing sales-clerk might tell a customer that a particular color of pants is too harsh to match a navy jacket. The customer might ask, "What exactly do you mean by 'harsh'?"

Hints for Writing a Definition Paragraph

1. Pick a word or phrase that has a personal meaning for you and that allows you room to develop your idea. Remember that you will be writing a full paragraph on this term. Therefore, a term that can be defined quickly and in only one way is not a good choice. For example, you would not have much to say about terms like "cauliflower" or "dental floss" unless you have strong personal feelings about cauliflower or dental floss. If you don't have such feelings, your paragraph will be very short.

When you think about a term to define, you might think about some personal quality you admire or dislike. If some quality provokes a strong reaction in you, you will probably have something to write about that term.

2. The topic sentence should have three parts. Include these items:

- the *term* you are defining
- the broad *class* or *category* into which your term fits
- the specific *distinguishing characteristics* that make the term different from all the others in the class or category

Each of the following topic sentences could be a topic sentence for a definition paragraph because it has the three parts.

| term | category | distinguishing characteristics |

Resentment is the *feeling* that *life has been unfair.*

| term | category | distinguishing characteristics |

A *clock-watcher* is a *worker* who *is just putting in time, not effort.*

3. Select an appropriate class or category when you write your topic sentence.

not this: Resentment is a thing that makes you feel life has been unfair. (Resentment is a feeling or an attitude. Say so.)

not this: Resentment is when you feel life has been unfair. ("When" is a word that refers to a time, like noon or 7:00 p.m. Resentment is a feeling, not a time.)

not this: Resentment is where a person feels life has been unfair. ("Where" is a word that refers to a place, like a kitchen or a beach. Resentment is not a place; it is a feeling.)

but this: Resentment is the feeling that life has been unfair.

4. Express your attitude toward the term you are defining in the "distinguishing characteristics" part of the topic sentence. Make that attitude clear and specific.

not this: Resentment is the feeling that can be bad for a person. (Many feelings can be bad for a person. Hate, envy, anger, and impatience, for instance, can all be bad. What is special about resentment?)

not this: Resentment is an attitude of resenting another person or a circumstance. (Do not define a word with another form of the word.)

but this: Resentment is the feeling that life has been unfair.

5. Use specific and concrete examples to explain your definition. *Concrete* terms refer to things you can see, touch, taste, smell, or hear. Using concrete terms and specific examples will make your definition interesting and clear.

You may be asked to define an *abstract* idea like happiness. Even though an abstract idea cannot be seen, touched, tasted, smelled, or heard directly, you can give a personal definition of it by using concrete terms and specific examples:

not this: Happiness takes place when you feel the joy of reaching a special goal. ("Joy" and "special goal" are abstract terms. Avoid defining one abstract term by using other abstract terms.)

but this: I felt happiness when I saw my name at the top of the list of athletes picked for the team. Three months of daily, six-hour practices had paid off, and I had achieved more than I had set out to do. (The abstract idea of happiness is linked to a specific, concrete example of feeling happiness.)

If you remember to show, not tell, your reader what your term means, you'll have a better definition. Be especially careful not to define a term with another form of that term.

Exercise 1   **Recognizing Abstract and Concrete Words**

In the list below, put an *A* by the abstract words and a *C* by the concrete words.

1. _A_ pride
2. _C_ helicopter
3. _A_ liberty
4. _C_ laughter
5. _A_ suspicion
6. _A_ personality
7. _C_ stadium
8. _C_ friend
9. _A_ destiny
10. _A_ confidence

11. _A_ sympathy
12. _C_ lightning
13. _A_ virtue
14. _C_ mansion
15. _C_ pineapple
16. _A_ determination
17. _A_ ambition
18. _C_ magazine
19. _A_ generosity
20. _A_ imagination

Exercise 2   **Completing a Topic Sentence for a Definition**

Following are unfinished topic sentences for definition paragraphs. Finish each sentence so that the sentence expresses a personal definition of the term and has the three requirements for a definition's topic sentence.

1. A teen idol is a celebrity who *is worshiped and imitated by the young.*

_____

2. A road hog is a driver who *violates another driver's boundaries.*

_____

3. A bargain is an item that *is bought at a lower than expected price.*

4. A raw deal is treatment that *seems unfair or harsh.*

5. A nightmare is a dream that *terrifies the dreamer.*

6. A drive-through window is an opening in a restaurant wall that *allows people in cars to order and receive food.*

7. A role model is a person who *sets an example for a younger or less-experienced person.*

8. A starter home is a residence that *people who have never owned a house can afford.*

9. The head of the family is the relative who *has the most authority over the other family members.*

10. A pack rat is a person who *cannot throw anything away.*

Exercise 3   **Recognizing Problems in Topic Sentences for Definition Paragraphs**

Review the three components that should be included in the topic sentence for a definition paragraph. Then read the topic sentences below, put an *X* next to each sentence that has a problem, and underline the part of the sentence that is faulty.

1. _____ A sense of humor is a gift for seeing the funny side of conflicts and setbacks.

2. __*X*__ Suspicion is a tendency to <u>suspect</u> others.

3. _____ Greed is a hunger that cannot be satisfied.

4. _____ Concentration is the ability to focus on one idea.

5. _____ Maturity is the stage at which people take responsibility for their own choices.

6. __*X*__ Hostility is <u>when</u> someone feels that another person is his or her enemy.

7. __*X*__ Joy is an emotion that appears in sudden, <u>joyous</u> moments.

8. _____ An overachiever is a person who constantly strives to reach new and difficult goals.

9. __*X*__ Hope is a <u>thing</u> that helps people get by.

10. __*X*__ Financial security is <u>where</u> a person has enough money to pay bills and save for the future.

Exercise 4   **Writing Examples for Definition Paragraphs**

Below are incomplete statements from definition paragraphs. Complete them in the spaces below by writing specific examples. When you have completed the statements, share your work with a group. After each group member has read his or her examples aloud, discuss the examples. Which examples did you like best? Which are the clearest and most specific? Do some examples lead to a different definition of a term than other examples do?

INSTRUCTOR'S NOTE

Answers will vary. Possible answers shown at left.

The first part of each sentence has been started for you.

1. I first saw betrayal in action when *my little brother told my mother* *about my secret crush on our babysitter. My mother laughed and made* *me feel ridiculous. I lost trust in my brother for a long time.*

   Another example of betrayal was my experience with *some friends* *in middle school. Four of us had skipped school one day and later tried* *to sneak into the movies. When the manager discovered us at the* *back door of the movies, my friends all ran and left me to face the* *consequences.*

2. The greediest action I ever saw was *an incident in first grade. Before* *the teacher could stop him, one little boy grabbed a handful of cookies at* *a class party and stuffed them into his mouth.*

   It was greedy because *the little boy had taken so many cookies that* *there were not enough left for the other children.*

   A person in the news that I think is greedy is *a developer in my town* _____ because he/she *is building more and more houses on land* *that used to be where wildlife lived. He wants to make more money.*

3. The person who represents patience to me is *my grandmother* because this person *works hard to keep her family together but never* *complains.*

   I was called on to show patience when *I sat in the emergency room* *while my brother was treated for a brain injury. I had to sit, wait, and* *trust in the work of the doctors.*

4. A situation when a person must be tactful is *during a friend's divorce.* *A person must be supportive of the friend but not offer too much advice* *or ask too many questions.*

   I saw tact in action when *my teacher told me I had failed a test.* *She waited until all the other students had left the room and did not* *embarrass me.*

WRITING THE DEFINITION PARAGRAPH IN STEPS

PREWRITING Gathering Ideas: Definition

To pick a topic for your definition paragraph, begin with some personality trait or type of person. For instance, you might define "the insecure person." If you listed your first thoughts, your list might look like this:

the insecure person
someone who is not emotionally secure
wants (needs?) other people to make him or her feel good
no self-respect

Using Questions to Get Details

Often, when you look for ideas to define a term, you get stuck with big, general statements or abstract words, or you simply cannot come up with enough to say. If you are having trouble getting ideas, think of questions about your term. Jot these questions down without stopping to answer them. One question can lead you to another question. Once you have five or more questions, you can answer them, and the answers will provide details for your definition paragraph.

If you were writing about the insecure person, for example, you could begin with questions like these:

What are insecure people like?
What behavior shows a person is insecure?
How do insecure people dress or talk?
What makes a person insecure?
Why is insecurity a bad trait?
How do insecure people relate to others?
Does insecurity hurt the insecure person? If so, how?
Does the insecure person hurt others? If so, how?

By scanning the questions and answering as many as you can, you can add details to your list. Once you have a longer list, you can review it and begin to group the items on the list. Following is a list of grouped details on the insecure person.

Grouped Details on the Insecure Person

wants (needs?) other people to make him or her feel important
no self-respect

insecure people have to brag about everything
a friend who brags about his car
they tell you the price of everything

they put others down
saying bad things about other people makes insecure people feel better

insecure people can never relax inside
can never enjoy being with other people
other people are always their competitors
must always worry about what others think of them

The Topic Sentence

Grouping the details can help you arrive at several main ideas. Can they be combined and revised to create a topic sentence? Following is a topic sentence on the insecure person that meets the requirements of naming the term, placing it in a category, and distinguishing the term from others in the category:

term   *category*   *distinguishing characteristics*

The *insecure person* is *someone* who *needs other people to make him or her feel respected and important.*

Once you have a topic sentence, you can begin working on the planning stage of the paragraph.

Exercise 5 **Designing Questions to Gather Details**

Following are terms that could be defined in a paragraph. For each term, write five questions that could lead you to details for the definition. The first one has been done for you as an example.

1. term: arrogance

questions:
a. *Do I know anyone who displays arrogance?*
b. *Is there any celebrity I think is arrogant?*
c. *What is an arrogant action?*
d. *What kind of remark is an example of arrogance?*
e. *Why are people arrogant?*

TEACHING TIP

Groupwork: This exercise works well as a small group activity.

2. term: the borrower

questions:
a. *What kind of things does a borrower ask for?*
b. *Isn't everyone a borrower at some time?*
c. *When does a borrower become annoying?*
d. *Why do some people become constant borrowers?*
e. *How can a person say "no" to a borrower?*

INSTRUCTOR'S NOTE

Answers will vary. Possible answers shown at left.

3. term: anxiety

questions:
a. *Isn't everyone anxious at one time or another?*
b. *What does anxiety feel like?*
c. *What does an anxious person look like?*
d. *Is some anxiety worse than another anxiety?*
e. *How can a person deal with anxiety?*

4. term: insight

questions:
a. *Why is insight valuable?*
b. *Do I know anyone with insight?*
c. *Can people develop insight?*
d. *Can people have insight into themselves?*
e. *What careers demand insight?*

Exercise 6   **Grouping Related Ideas for a Definition Paragraph**

Following is a list of ideas for a definition paragraph. Read the list several times; then group all the ideas on the list into one of the three categories below. Put the letter of the category next to each idea.

Categories:

G = how criticism can be **good**

B = how criticism can be **bad**

D = **dealing** with criticism

List

1. _G_ Constructive criticism is meant to help a person do better, and the person offering the criticism has good intentions.

2. _B_ Criticism given by a jealous or spiteful person can sting and shatter the recipient's confidence.

3. _D_ A person who remembers only the criticism and not the praise is developing an unrealistic and dark self-image.

4. _B_ When an angry person criticizes, his or her words are intended to hurt.

5. _D_ Learning to recognize each critic's motives is a good way to tell genuine, helpful suggestions from negative remarks.

6. _B_ Parents who are too critical of their children may erode their children's confidence.

7. _G_ Children need some criticism so that they do not grow up overprotected.

8. _B_ Most gossip is a mean and cowardly form of criticism.

9. _G_ A secure and ambitious person needs a mentor to offer honest assessments that include criticism.

10. _G_ An athlete would not improve much without the tough criticism of a caring coach.

PLANNING   **Devising a Plan: Definition**

To make an outline for a definition paragraph, start with the topic sentence and list the grouped details. Often, a first outline does not have many examples or concrete, specific details. A good way to be sure you put specific details and concrete examples into your paragraph is to include shortened versions of them in your revised outline. If you compare the following outline to the grouped list of details on page 176, you will see how specific details and concrete examples have been added.

An Outline for a Definition Paragraph

topic sentence:	The insecure person is someone who needs other people to make him or her feel respected and important.
details:	Insecure people have to brag about everything.
	An insecure friend may brag about his car.
added detail	Insecure people wear expensive jewelry and tell you what it costs.
added detail	They brag about their expensive clothes.
added detail	They make sure they wear clothes with trendy labels, another kind of bragging.
	Insecure people put others down.
	Saying bad things about others makes insecure people feel better.
added example	When some friends were talking about Susan's great new job, Jill had to make mean remarks about Susan.
	Jill hated having Susan look like a winner.
	Insecure people can never relax inside.
	They can never enjoy being with other people.
	Other people are always their competitors.
added example	Luke can't enjoy any game of basketball unless he is the star.
	Insecure people must always worry about what others think of them.

When you prepare your own definition outline, use the following checklist to help you revise it.

Checklist: A Checklist for Revising a Definition Outline

✓ Does my topic sentence include a category and the characteristics that show how my term is different from others in the category?

✓ Have I defined my term so that it is different from any other term?

✓ Am I being concrete and specific in the details?

✓ Do I have enough examples?

✓ Do my examples relate to the topic sentence?

✓ Are my details in the most effective order?

With a revised outline, you are ready to begin writing a rough draft of your definition paragraph.

Exercise 7 Rewriting a Topic Sentence for a Definition Paragraph

Following is an outline in which the topic sentence does not make the same point as the rest of the outline. Rewrite the topic sentence so that it relates to the details.

topic sentence:	Burnout is a feeling of tiredness.
details:	My father was experiencing burnout at work.
	He went to work feeling hopeless and angry.

The hours were long, and the demands were endless.

His only motivation for working was to earn a salary.

He didn't care about doing his best because no one ever noticed.

An athlete can earn many honors and still feel burned out.

The stress of constant training and the pressure to win can hurt an athlete as much as a physical injury.

A burned-out athlete may go through the motions of training and competing.

Even famous athletes can become beaten down by the demands of fame.

Mothers who try to juggle work and childcare responsibilities are candidates for burnout.

Most working mothers want to do well at work.

However, work outside the home isn't their only work.

At every moment away from home, a working mother is thinking of her children.

She is also remembering the responsibilities waiting for her at home.

When two jobs become too much to handle, working mothers can fall apart.

Rewrite the Topic Sentence: *Burnout is extreme exhaustion brought on by too much pressure.*

Exercise 8 **Revising an Example to Make It More Concrete and Specific**

The following outline contains one example that is too abstract. In the lines provided, rewrite the example that is too abstract, using more specific, concrete details.

topic sentence:	A sixth sense is a way of knowing what cannot be explained by science.
details:	When I first met Emma, my wife, I disliked her.
example 1	She was not the type of woman I usually found attractive.
	I thought she was loud and bossy.
	Although I felt no attraction to her, I could not stop thinking about her.
	Two years later, after several failed romances with others, I began seeing Emma.
	We married in six months and are extremely happy.
example 2	My grandfather's sixth sense led him to an important business decision.
	When he was a young man, he was about to invest all the money he had in a business.
	A childhood friend was going to be his partner.
	Everybody encouraged my grandfather to sign a contract.

He felt something inside telling him not to enter the partnership.

He did not, and he avoided something bad.

example 3   The most remarkable example of the power of a sixth sense involved a child.

When I was seven, I was playing near an abandoned house in the neighborhood.

A little girl named Leah was playing ball with me.

Eventually, we became bored.

I decided to explore the overgrown yard around the old house.

Soon I had reached the steps of the old house.

"Don't go in there," Leah said, in a stern voice.

When I asked why, she insisted, "Don't go."

For some reason, I obeyed her.

A few days later, the police found an escaped convict who had been living in the house for some time.

INSTRUCTOR'S NOTE

Answers will vary. Possible answer shown at left.

The Revised Example: _My grandfather's sixth sense led him to an important_

decision.

At twenty-five, he planned to invest all his money in a bakery.

Adam, a childhood friend, was going to be his partner.

My grandfather's parents and sister encouraged my grandfather to

sign a contract.

The day before my grandfather was to sign the partnership agreement,

he felt dizzy and sick.

As he lay down, he saw disaster ahead.

He refused to sign the papers, and Adam found another partner.

Within a year, Adam was arrested for fraud.

He had stolen and spent all the money invested in the bakery.

DRAFTING   Drafting and Revising: Definition

To write the first draft of your definition paragraph, you can rewrite the outline in paragraph form, combining some of the short sentences and adding more details. Remember that your purpose in this definition paragraph is to explain your personal understanding of a term. Therefore, you want to be sure that your topic sentence is clear and that your explanation connects your details to the topic sentence. A careful use of transitions will link your details to your topic sentence.

Transitions

Since you can define a term in many ways, you can also use many transitions. If you are listing several examples in your paragraph, you can use transitions like "first," "second," and "finally." If you are contrasting your term with another, you can use transitions like "on the other hand" or "in contrast." You may want to alert or remind the reader that you are writing a definition paragraph by using phrases like "can be defined as," "can be considered as," "means that," or "implies that."

Because many definitions rely on examples, the transitions below are ones you may want to use.

TEACHING TIP

Remind students not to include transitional words/phrases just to have them. Students too often think that the more transitions they use, the better. Stress that such links should be logical rather than forced.

INFO BOX: Transitions for a Definition Paragraph

a classic case of ____ is ____	in fact	another time
another case	in one case	sometimes
for example	in one instance	specifically
for instance	one time	

The Draft

Following is a draft of the definition paragraph on the insecure person. When you read it, you'll notice several changes from the outline on page 179.

- Transitions have been added in several places. Some transitions let the reader know an example is coming; some transitions link one point about the topic to another point; other transitions connect an example to the topic sentence.
- Examples have been made concrete and specific.
- The word choice has been improved.

INSTRUCTOR'S NOTE

This draft may be a good place to point out that the use of *you* here is a shift in person. It is corrected in the final version of this sample paragraph on page 187.

A Draft of a Definition Paragraph

(Transitions are underlined.)

The insecure person is someone who needs other people to make him or her feel respected and important. The insecure person loves to brag about everything. <u>For instance</u>, a friend may brag about his car. He tells everyone he meets that he drives a Honda S2000 sports car. An insecure person tells you the price of everything. He wears expensive jewelry and tells you what it costs, <u>like</u> the person who always flashes his Rolex watch. <u>Another</u> insecure person will brag about her expensive clothes or make sure she always wears clothes with trendy labels, <u>another kind</u> of bragging. <u>Bragging is not the only way an insecure person tries to look good</u>; he or she may put other people down. Saying bad things about other people can put the insecure person on top. <u>For instance</u>, some friends were recently talking about another friend, Susan, who had just started a great new job. Jill had to add some mean remarks about how lucky Susan had been to get the job since Susan really wasn't qualified for it. Jill hated having Susan look like a winner. The insecure person can hurt others <u>but also</u> suffers inside. <u>Such a person</u> can never relax because he or she always sees other people as competitors. <u>An example of this attitude is</u> seen in Luke, a college acquaintance who always plays pickup basketball games. Even though the games are just for fun, Luke can't enjoy any game unless he is the star. Luke is a typically insecure person, for he must always worry about what others think of him.

The following checklist may help you to revise the draft of your own definition paragraph.

Checklist: A Checklist for Revising the Draft of a Definition Paragraph

✓ Is my topic sentence clear?

✓ Have I written enough to define my term clearly?

✓ Is my definition interesting?

✓ Could it use another example?

✓ Could it use more details?

✓ Do I need to combine any sentences?

✓ Do I need any words, phrases, or sentences to link the examples or details to the topic sentence?

✓ Do I need any words, phrases, or sentences to reinforce the topic sentence?

Exercise 9 Adding Examples to a Draft of a Definition Paragraph

Paragraphs 2 and 3 that follow need examples with concrete, specific details to explain their points. On the blank lines, write examples with concrete, specific details. Each example should be at least two sentences long. The first paragraph is done for you.

Paragraph 1

Listlessness is the feeling that nothing is worth starting. After a hectic week, I often wake up on Saturday morning feeling listless. I just do not have the energy to do the things I intended to do. *I may have planned to wash my car, for example, but I cannot bring myself to get going. I cannot put together the bucket, detergent, brushes, and window cleaner I need to start the process. I tell myself, "Why wash the car? It will probably rain anyway."* Another time I feel listless is when I am faced with a big assignment. *For instance, I hate to start a term paper because there is so much to do. I have to think of a topic, do research, read, take notes, plan, write, and revise. When I am faced with so many things to do, I don't do anything. I tell myself it is not worth starting because I will probably get a bad grade on the paper anyway.* I put off getting started. I let listlessness get the better of me.

Paragraph 2

Comforters are people who help others deal with disappointment or loss. Comforters are needed in competitive sports. *A comforter tells the members of the losing team that they played a good game. He or she reminds the players of their moments of glory in the game and insists that the next game will end in victory.* Someone who loses a job needs a comforter. *A comforter listens to the sad or infuriating story of the job loss and sympathizes. Then a comforter assures the newly unemployed person that the job wasn't worth having. In addition, a comforter says that a better job will turn up soon.* The worst loss of all, a death, is more bearable when a comforter is near. *At that time, a comforter may say nothing at all. He or she will just be near. A comforter will stay near through the difficult stages of grief, and this closeness is the greatest support of all.* The world would be a colder, tougher place without comforters.

Paragraph 3

Road rage is a dangerous expression of the frustrations of driving. Crowded roads, long commutes, and personal stress can provoke a person to express road rage. Common expressions of road rage involve language or car signaling. *An angry driver may shout "you idiot" at someone who cannot even hear the words. Another way to signal disgust is to honk the horn loudly or flash the car lights at the driver who violates one's space.* Some road rage gets more personal. *Drivers have been known to start fistfights over a parking space. An angry driver may stop at a red light, leave his car, and pound on the car windows of the driver who offended him or her.* Road rage can even become deadly. *An unstable and overstressed driver can interpret a rude or careless act as a personal attack. The unstable person may respond by attacking with his or her car, ramming the victim's car or running it off the road. In some cases, an infuriated driver has used a gun.* Then the foolishness of road rage becomes tragic.

Exercise 10 Identifying the Words That Need Revision in a Definition Paragraph

INSTRUCTOR'S NOTE

Answers will vary. Possible choices for vague words shown at left.

The following paragraph has too many vague, abstract words. Underline the words that you think should be replaced with more specific or concrete words or examples.

Greed is the endless desire for more. Most people think of greed as the desire for money, but there are other kinds of greed. Celebrities who cannot endure being ignored are greedy for attention. They live to be seen at trendy clubs and <u>places like that.</u> Other people, who may have had a quiet life, can become greedy for new experiences. These people want to climb a mountain, sail across an ocean, or <u>do other exciting things</u> before they die. Everyone has a bit of greed in him or her. Some people are greedy eaters; they cannot resist the last brownie on the plate or <u>whatever is around.</u> Music lovers crave the latest CD from their favorite group and strive to own <u>lots of music.</u> The worst part of greed is its endlessness. Greedy people can never be satisfied. If they get <u>something,</u> for example, they cannot appreciate it because they are already thinking about <u>the next one</u> they want. Enjoyment and greed don't really go together.

Exercise 11 Combining Sentences in a Definition Paragraph

INSTRUCTOR'S NOTE

For more on sentence combining practice, see Chapter 33 on sentence variety.

The following definition paragraph has some short, choppy sentences that could be combined. These pairs or clusters of sentences are underlined. Combine each pair or cluster into one smooth sentence, and write the new sentence in the space above the original ones.

INSTRUCTOR'S NOTE

Answers will vary. Possible answers shown at left.

A people pleaser is a person who cannot feel comfortable until those around him or her are content. A people pleaser in a room full of strangers can sense the

For example, if a group of airline passengers waiting to board a

atmosphere. <u>For example, a group of airline passengers may be waiting to board a</u>

plane looks sullen and impatient, a people pleaser will make a joke to lighten the

<u>plane. The people look sullen and impatient. A people pleaser will make a joke to</u>

atmosphere.

<u>lighten the atmosphere.</u> A people pleaser is even more sensitive to the mood of

At a family dinner, the pleaser can tell at once if a son is angry

family or friends. <u>At a family dinner, the pleaser can tell at once if a son is angry at</u>

at a father and even guess what caused the anger.

<u>a father. In addition, the pleaser can even guess what caused the anger.</u> The

people pleaser will not rest until the ugly silences of the father and son and the

nervousness of the rest of the family have disappeared. In a peacemaking role, a

However, people pleasers have another,

people pleaser can be helpful and kind. <u>However, people pleasers have another</u>

less attractive side.

<u>side. It is not so attractive.</u> A people pleaser likes to be liked and badly needs

To get this approval, a people pleaser may stretch the truth in order to

approval. <u>To get this approval, a people pleaser may stretch the truth. The people</u>

tell others what they want to hear.

<u>pleaser may do this because he or she wants to tell others what they want to hear.</u>

For example, a people pleaser will take a friend's side in an argument rather than

be honest about the friend's mistakes. People pleasers also face constant anger

and disappointment. It comes from those who will never be happy, no matter how

hard the people pleaser tries. Worse, people pleasers themselves are likely to

People pleasers

become frustrated and angry at those who refuse to be content. <u>People pleasers</u>

face a hard and endless struggle that will last until they realize that no one can

<u>face a hard and endless struggle. This struggle will last until they realize that no</u>

make another person happy.

<u>one can make another person happy.</u>

Exercise 12   **Adding the Right Transitions to a Definition Paragraph**

In the following paragraph, circle the correct transition in each of the pairs.

Nerve is boldness that can impress or infuriate others. In fact/(For example,)

observers may say, "It took nerve for that seventy-year-old man to try skydiving on

his birthday." They admire the daring of an older person attempting a dangerous

sport for the first time. One time/(Another time) when nerve gains approval involves

wish fulfillment. The ambitious young person who approaches a famous multimil-

lionaire on the street and asks for a job has this kind of nerve. When the young per-

son is hired and the story appears on television, many people secretly think, "I wish

I had the guts to do that." However, nerve brings disapproval as often as it buys

admiration. (Sometimes)/Another case a person with nerve crosses the line into vio-

lating another person's rights. (In fact)/ In contrast, examples of this kind of nerve

can be seen every day on the highway when one driver recklessly cuts in front of

another. "What colossal nerve!" complains the driver who has been cut off and is

now feeling road rage. (Another case)/ In one case of nerve that provokes fury is

related to romance. Nothing makes a person angrier than discovering that a best

friend has stolen a lover. Nerve is powerful, but because a person can misuse this

power, nerve should be reserved for the right occasion.

POLISHING   Polishing and Proofreading: Definition

Before you prepare the final version of your definition paragraph, check your latest draft to see if it needs a few changes. You may want to check for good transitions, appropriate word choice, and effective details. If you compare the draft on page 182 to the following final version of the paragraph on the insecure person, you will see a few more revisions:

- The wording has been improved so that it is more precise.
- Transitions have been added to reinforce the topic sentence.
- The word "you" has been taken out so that the paragraph is consistent in person.

TEACHING TIP

Tell students that just a few seemingly minor changes can make a paragraph read much more smoothly.

A Final Version of a Definition Paragraph

(Changes from the draft are underlined.)

>   The insecure person is someone who needs other people to make him or her feel respected and important. To get respect, the insecure person loves to brag about everything. For instance, a friend may brag about his car. He tells everyone he meets that he drives a Honda S2000 sports car. An insecure person tells people the price of everything. He wears expensive jewelry and tells people what it costs, like the man who always flashes his Rolex watch. Another insecure person will brag about her expensive clothes or make sure she wears clothes with trendy labels, another kind of bragging. Bragging isn't the only way an insecure person tries to look good; he or she may also criticize other people. Criticizing others can put the insecure person on top. For instance, some friends were recently talking about another friend, Susan, who had just started a great new job. Jill had to add some mean remarks about how lucky Susan had been to get the job since Susan really wasn't qualified for it. Jill couldn't stand to have Susan look like a winner. The insecure person like Jill can hurt others but also suffers inside. Such a person can never relax because he or she always sees other people as competitors. An example of this attitude can be seen in Luke, a college acquaintance who always plays pickup basketball games. Even though the games are just for fun, Luke can't enjoy any game unless he is the star. Luke is a typically insecure person, for he must always worry about what others think of him.

As you prepare the final version of your definition paragraph, check your latest draft for any errors in spelling, punctuation, typing, and formatting.

> **For your information:** A sample definition essay based on this topic and following the same writing steps can be found in Chapter 12, pp 305–310.

Exercise 13   Correcting Errors in the Final Version of a Definition Paragraph

Following are two definition paragraphs with the kind of errors it is easy to overlook in a final version. Correct the errors by writing above the lines. There are thirteen errors in the first paragraph and twelve in the second paragraph.

experiences

1. Anticipation is the excited feeling a person experences before a happy event.

no comma needed

The best example, of anticipation is the jittery joy of a child about to celebrate his

whose

or her birthday. People who's jobs require a traditional Monday-through-Friday

, and it (no comma after "and")

schedule experience anticipation on Friday morning and, it builds during the rest

filled

of the day. Students are fill with expectation weeks before summer vacation

high school

begins, and High School seniors anticipate graduation for nearly a year. Anticipa-

;

tion can make events better, for instance, Halloween would not be as much fun

costumes

without the planning of extravagant custumes and buying of special candy. There

occasions

are even occassions that are so exciting they include lively preliminary events. For

example, people have baby showers before the birth of a baby and family dinners

night   *Everyone*   *forward*

the nite before a wedding. Every one likes to look foreward to life's high points;

therefore, anticipation can brighten many dull days.

2. Self-pity is a focus on what has gone wrong in one's life. Everyone pities him-

herself   *no comma needed*

self or her self at one time because bad luck, and misery are part of every life.

,   *weeks*

When my brother lost his job for example, he spent week's in shock, hiding in the

house and staring at the television. It took months for him to talk about anything

but the unfairness of his situation, but eventually he got up, out, and into the

cannot

struggle for another job. However, some people canot get past the stage of feeling

sorry for themselves. They would rather stay in the dark, dangerous world of self-

lives

pity. Once people choose to see only the sadness and suffering in their lifes, their

best friend

chances to improve their lives disappear. My bestfriend, for example, spent a

year recovering from a terrible accident. During that time, he was unable to move

He

past the pain and horror of the amputation of his arm. he could not stop thinking

about his losses: his loss of physical ability, his loss of physical image, and his loss

of job prospects. No matter how other's who cared about him tried to comfort

others

Christopher, he refused to hope. Fortunately, he finally found the inner strength to

Focusing   *no comma needed*

fight his negative attitude. Focussing on possibilities instead of pain is, a struggle

no comma needed

for my friend. Christopher is my hero, because he no longer gives in to self-pity.

Lines of Detail: A Walk-Through Assignment

Write a paragraph that gives a personal definition of a secure person. To write the paragraph, follow these steps:

Step 1: List all your ideas about a secure person.

Step 2: Write at least five questions that can add details about a secure person. Answer the questions as a way of adding details to your list.

Step 3: Group your details; then survey the groups.

Step 4: Write a topic sentence that includes the term you are defining, puts the term into a category, and distinguishes the term from others in the category.

Step 5: Write an outline. Begin by writing the topic sentence and the groups of details. Then add more details and specific examples.

Step 6: Write a draft of your paragraph. To revise, check that you have enough examples, that your examples fit your definition, and that the examples are in an effective order. Combine any choppy sentences and add transitions.

Step 7: Before you prepare the final version of your definition paragraph, check the punctuation, word choice, transitions, and grammar of your latest draft.

Writing Your Own Definition Paragraph

When you write on any of these topics, be sure to work through the stages of the writing process in preparing your definition paragraph.

Collaborate

1. Define an abstract term using concrete, specific details. Choose from the list below. You can begin by looking up the term in a dictionary to be sure you understand the dictionary meaning. Then write a personal definition.

   You can begin by freewriting. If your instructor agrees, you can read your freewriting to a group for reactions and suggestions. If you prefer, you can begin by brainstorming a list of questions to help you define the term. Again, if your instructor agrees, you can work with a group to develop brainstorming questions. Here is the list of abstract terms:

ambition	envy	prejudice
anger	failure	self-deception
betrayal	generosity	self-discipline
bliss	initiative	selfishness
boredom	irritation	shame
charisma	loneliness	style
charity	loyalty	success
charm	persistence	suspicion

2. Write a definition of a type of person. Develop your personal definition with specific, concrete details. You can choose one of the types listed below or choose your own type.

Freewriting on the topic is one way to begin. If your instructor agrees, you can read your freewriting to a group for reactions and suggestions. You can also begin by brainstorming a list of questions to help you define your term. If your instructor agrees, you can work with a group to develop brainstorming questions. Following is the list of types.

the achiever	the daredevil	the manipulator
the apologizer	the dreamer	the old reliable friend
the bodybuilder	the fan	the organizer
the braggart	the fitness fanatic	the neatness fanatic
the buddy	the Mr./Ms. Fixit	the procrastinator
the bully	the inventor	the two-timer
the chocaholic	the jock	the whiner
the compulsive liar	the joker	the workaholic

3. Think of one word that best defines you. In a paragraph, define that word, using yourself as a source of examples and details. To begin, you may want to freewrite about several words that define you; then you can select the most appropriate one.

4. Using Google™ or a similar search engine, type in the words "Web log" and "blog."

Investigate as many definitions as you can of the term "blog." Based on this information, write a definition of this term and assume that your audience is a group of adults who have never read or written a blog. Your definition may include examples of blogs from the fields of politics, entertainment, news, business, and education.

5. Study the photograph below. Then write a paragraph that defines (a) combat stress or (b) courage under fire.

How Do I Get a Better Grade?

Note: Additional writing options suitable for definition-related assignments can be found after the professional reading "Breaking the Bonds of Hate," which begins on page 624.

Name _____ Section _____

Peer Review Form for a Definition Paragraph

After you've written a draft of your definition paragraph, let a writing partner read it. When your partner has completed the form below, discuss the comments. Then repeat the same process for your partner's paragraph.

In the topic sentence, the term being defined is placed in this category or class: _____

_____

In the topic sentence, the characteristic(s) that make(s) the term different from others in its class or category is/are _____

_____

The most enjoyable or interesting part of this definition starts with the words _____

_____

The part that could use a clear example or more details starts with the words _____

_____

I have questions about or would like to know more about _____

_____

I would like to take out the part about _____

_____

Other comments: _____

_____

_____

_____

_____

_____

_____

_____

_____

Reviewer's name: _____

CHAPTER 9

Jumping In

*What do you think may have helped this individual get this far in college? How can his college experience help him face new challenges? Answers to these questions focus on the **causes** and **effects** of his college success.*

TEACHING TIP

Here might be a good time to remind students of the difference between "effect" (noun) and "affect" (verb). Such distinctions and other homonyms can be found in Chapter 31, "Words That Sound Alike/Look Alike."

Cause and Effect

WHAT IS CAUSE AND EFFECT?

Almost every day, you consider the causes or effects of events so that you can make choices and take action. In writing a paragraph, when you explain the **reasons** for something, you are writing about **causes**. When you write about the **results** of something, you are writing about **effects**. Often in writing, you consider both the causes and effects of a decision, an event, a change in your life, or change in society, but in this chapter, you will be asked to *concentrate on either causes (reasons)* or *effects (results)*.

Hints for Writing a Cause or Effect Paragraph

1. Pick a topic you can handle in one paragraph. A topic you can handle in one paragraph is one that (a) is not too big and (b) doesn't require research.

Some topics are so large that you probably can't cover them in one paragraph. Topics that are too big include ones like

Why People Get Angry
Effects of Unemployment on My Family

Other topics require you to research the facts and to include the opinions of experts. They would be good topics for a research paper, but not for a one-paragraph assignment. Topics that require research include ones like

The Causes of Divorce
The Effects of Television Viewing on Children

When you write a cause or effect paragraph, choose a topic you can write about by using what you already know. That is, make your topic smaller and more personal. Topics that use what you already know are ones like

Why Children Love Animal Cartoon Characters
The Causes of My Divorce
What Enlistment in the Navy Did for My Brother
How Alcoholics Anonymous Changed My Life

2. Try to have at least three causes or effects in your paragraph. Be sure you consider immediate and remote causes or immediate and remote effects. Think about your topic and gather as many causes or effects as you can *before* you start drafting your paragraph.

An event usually has more than one cause. Think beyond the obvious, the **immediate cause**, to more **remote causes**. For example, the immediate cause of your car accident might be the other driver who hit the rear end of your car. But more remote causes might include the weather conditions or the condition of the road.

Situations can have more than one result, too. If you take Algebra I for the second time and you pass the course with a "C," an **immediate result** is that you fulfill the requirements for graduation. But there may be other, **more remote results**. Your success in Algebra I may help to change your attitude toward mathematics courses, or may build your confidence in your ability to handle college work, or may lead you to sign up for another course taught by the same teacher.

3. Make your causes and effects clear and specific. If you are writing about why short haircuts are popular, don't write, "Short haircuts are popular because everybody is getting one" or "Short haircuts are popular because they are a trend." If you write either of those statements, you have really said, "Short haircuts are popular because they are popular."

Think further. Have any celebrities been seen with this haircut? Write the names of actors, athletes, or musicians who have the haircut, or the name of the movie and the actor who started the trend. By giving specific details that explain, illustrate, or describe a cause or effect, you help the reader understand your point.

4. Write a topic sentence that indicates whether your paragraph is about causes or effects. You should not announce, but you can *indicate.*

not this: The effects of my winning the scholarship are going to be discussed. (an announcement)
but this: Winning the scholarship changed my plans for college. (indicates effects will be discussed)

TEACHING TIP

Ask students about some positive event or change they have observed in their neighborhood (or apartment or town). A rally, a walk-a-thon for a worthy cause, a new park, a street widening, etc., are possibilities. Focusing the discussion on causes/effects of a positive event or trend can help students analyze without resorting to complaining.

TEACHING TIP

If students have trouble grasping the concept of "remote," ask them to list the immediate benefits of taking a CPR class (or similar safety class) and then list the long-range benefits. Some of your students, especially if they are training to be health professionals, paramedics, or firefighters, will be well aware of the positive effects of taking such a class.

You can *list* a short version of all your causes or effects in your topic sentence, like this:

> The high price of concert tickets has enriched a few performers and promoters, excluded many fans, and threatened the future of live entertainment.

You can just *hint* at your points by summarizing them, like this:

> The high price of concert tickets has brought riches to a few but hurt many others.

Or you can use words that *signal* causes or effects.

words that signal causes: reasons, why, because, motives, intentions

words that signal effects: results, impact, consequences, changed, threatened, improved

Exercise 1   Selecting a Suitable Topic for a Cause or Effect Paragraph

Below is a list of topics. Some are suitable for a cause or effect paragraph. Some are too large to handle in one paragraph, some would require research, and some are both too large and would require research. Put an "X" next to any topic that is not suitable.

1. __X__ The Impact of Rising Insurance Rates on Homeowners

2. __X__ The Causes of Alcoholism

3. __X__ Why Internet Predators Are a Growing Threat

4. _____ How a Cell Phone Saved My Daughter's Life

5. __X__ The Effects of Pollution on Our Society

6. __X__ The Causes of Divorce in Low-Income Families

7. __X__ The Impact of Technology in High School Classrooms

8. _____ Reasons I Decided to Major in Accounting

9. __X__ Effects of Anorexia

10. _____ Why My Child Fears Large Dogs

Exercise 2   Recognizing Cause and Effect in Topic Sentences

In the list below, if the topic sentence is for a cause paragraph, put "C" next to it. If the sentence is for an effect paragraph, put "E" next to it.

1. __E__ Blogging is changing my social life.

2. __C__ My brother's experiences in prison are the key to understanding his depression.

3. __E__ Getting married had an impact on my spending habits.

4. __C__ During the holidays, people overspend to please others, to make an impression, and to feel part of a crowd.

5. __C__ College freshmen need a support system because they are confused, insecure, and anxious about the demands of college life.

6. __E__ My husband's giant-sized television has changed his
evenings, weekends, and vacation time.

7. __C__ Professor Stein has three motives for beginning each class
with a quiz.

8. __C__ I joined the army to earn money for college, learn a job
skill, and serve my country.

9. __E__ Ethan's move to Nebraska had unexpected consequences
for him.

10. __E__ Once I started volunteering at a shelter for battered
women, I realized how small kindnesses can change
lives.

WRITING THE CAUSE OR EFFECT PARAGRAPH IN STEPS

PREWRITING Gathering Ideas: Cause or Effect

Once you've picked a topic, the next—and very important—step is getting
ideas. Because this paragraph will contain only causes *or* effects, and
details about them, you must be sure you have enough causes or effects to
write a developed paragraph.

Freewriting on a Topic

One way to get ideas is to freewrite on your topic. Since causes and effects
are so clearly connected, you can begin by freewriting about both and then
choose one, causes or effects, later.

If you were thinking about writing a cause or effect paragraph on owning a car, you could begin by freewriting something like this:

Freewriting on Owning a Car

*A car of my own. Why? I needed it. Couldn't get a part-time job without one. Because I
couldn't get to work. Needed it to get to school. Of course I could have taken the bus to
school. But I didn't want to. Feel like a grown-up when you have a car of your own.
Freedom to come and go. I was the last of my friends to have a car. Couldn't wait. An old
Nissan. But I fixed it up nicely. Costs a lot to maintain. Car payments, car loan. Car
insurance.*

Now you can review the freewriting and make separate lists of the
causes and effects you wrote down:

causes (reasons)

needed to get a part-time job
needed to get to school
my friends had cars

effects (results)

feel like a grown-up
freedom to come and go

> *costs a lot to maintain*
> *car payments*
> *car loan*
> *car insurance*

Because you have more details on the effects of owning a car, you decide to write an effects paragraph.

Your list of effects can be used several ways. You can add to it if you think of ideas as you are reviewing your list. You can begin to group ideas in your list and then add to it. Following is a grouping of the list of effects; grouping helps you see how many effects and details you have.

> ***effects of getting my own car***
>
> *effect 1:*   *I had to pay for the car and related expenses*
> *details:*   *costs a lot to maintain*
>   *car payments*
>   *car loan*
>   *car insurance*
>
> *effect 2:*   *I had the freedom to come and go.*
> *details:*   *none*
>
> *effect 3:*   *I felt like a grown-up.*
> *details:*   *none*

Will these effects work in a paragraph? One way to decide is to try to add details to the ones that have no details. Ask questions to get those details.

> *effect 2: I had the freedom to come and go.*
>
> **What do you mean?**
>
> *Well, I didn't have to beg my father for his truck any more. I didn't have to get rides from friends. I could go to the city when I wanted. I could ride around just for fun.*
>
> *effect 3: I felt like a grown-up.*
>
> **What do you mean, "like a grown-up"?**
>
> *Adults can go where they want, when they want. They drive themselves.*

If you look carefully at the answers to the questions above, you'll find that the two effects are really *the same.* By adding details to both effects, you'll find that both are saying that owning a car gives you the adult freedom to come and go.

So the list needs another effect of owning a car. What else happened? How else did things change when you got your car? You might answer:

> *I worried about someone hitting my car.*
> *I worried about bad drivers.*
> *I wanted to avoid the scratches you get in parking lots.*

With answers like these, your third effect could be

> *I became a more careful driver.*

Now that you have three effects and some details, you can rewrite your list. You can add details as you rewrite.

List of Effects of Getting My Own Car

effect 1:   *I had to pay for the car and related expenses.*
details: *costs a lot to maintain*

            car payments

            car loans

            car insurance

effect 2:   *I had the adult freedom to come and go.*
details: *didn't have to beg my father for his truck*

            didn't have to get rides from friends

            could go to the city when I wanted

            could ride around for fun

effect 3:   *I became a more careful driver.*
details: *worried about someone hitting the car*

            worried about bad drivers

            wanted to avoid the scratches cars get in parking lots

Designing a Topic Sentence

With at least three effects and some details for each effect, you can create a topic sentence. The topic sentence for this paragraph should indicate that the subject is the *effects* of getting a car. You can summarize all three effects in your topic sentence, or you can just hint at them. A possible topic sentence for the paragraph can be

> *Owning my own car cost me money, gave me freedom, and made me more careful about how I drive.*

or

> *Once I got a car of my own, I realized the good and bad sides of ownership.*

With a topic sentence and a fairly extensive list of details, you are ready to begin the planning stage in preparing your paragraph.

Exercise 3 **Designing Questions for a Cause or Effect Paragraph**

Collaborate

Below are four topics for cause or effect paragraphs. For each of the following topics, write five questions that could lead you to ideas on the topic. (The first one is completed for you.) After you've written five questions for each topic, give your list to a member of your writing group. Ask him or her to add one question to each topic and then to pass the exercise on to the next member of the group. Repeat the process so that each group member adds to the lists of all the other members.

Later, if your instructor agrees, you can answer the questions (and add more questions and answers) as a way to begin writing a cause or effect paragraph.

1. **topic:** the effects of camera phones on crime
   questions that can lead to ideas and details:

   a. *Are unsuspecting people photographed and blackmailed?*

   b. *Can the cameras be used to photograph confidential documents?*

c. *Are the cameras being used by Peeping Toms?*

d. *Can criminals use the camera phones to photograph banks?*

e. *Can citizens photograph a crime in progress?*

additional questions: *Can citizens photograph a suspect or perpetrator?*

Can police use the cameras in surveillance?

2. **topic:** why many people prefer to shop online
   questions that can lead to ideas and details:

a. *Does online shopping save gas?*

b. *Are there more choices online?*

c. *Is it easy to save money online?*

d. *Does online shopping save time?*

e. *Can online shopping be done at work?*

additional questions: *Is online shopping fun?*

Is online shopping easier than walking through a mall?

Does online shopping make last-minute purchases easy?

3. **topic:** the effects of overcrowded highways on commuters
   questions that can lead to ideas and details:

a. *Are people driving less?*

b. *Are they carpooling?*

c. *Are they taking the bus?*

d. *Are they leaving for work earlier?*

e. *Are they taking the train?*

additional questions: *Are they driving more cautiously?*

Are they looking for jobs closer to home?

Are they involved in more accidents?

4. **topic:** why Americans want DVD players in their cars
   questions that could lead to ideas and details:

a. *Are the players just another electronic toy for the car?*

b. *Are they a status symbol?*

c. *Do parents want them to amuse bored children?*

d. *Are families taking more long trips?*

e. *Has the car become a second home for many people?*

additional questions: *Do passengers need constant stimulation?*

Do babies like the sound and movement of DVDs?

Do young adults like the car DVD?

Exercise 4   **Creating Causes or Effects for Topic Sentences**

For the topic sentences below, create three causes or effects, depending on what the topic sentence requires. The first one is completed for you.

1. **topic sentence:** Sticking to an exercise routine has both improved and complicated my life.

   a. *I am in better physical shape than I have been in years.*

   b. *The physical exercise also gives me a mental boost.*

   c. *I now have to find time to fit my routine into my busy schedule.*

2. **topic sentence:** There are several reasons why many people are willing to spend several dollars on a cup of coffee.

   a. *The coffee comes in special flavors.*

   b. *The coffee is fresh.*

   c. *Expensive coffee can be a status symbol.*

INSTRUCTOR'S NOTE

Answers will vary. Possible answers shown at left.

3. **topic sentence:** The popularity of tattoos has had surprising effects.

   a. *The image of tattoos has changed from sleazy to stylish.*

   b. *Everyone from teens to their parents is getting one or more tattoos.*

   c. *Small children enjoy wearing temporary tattoos.*

4. **topic sentence:** Taking a course or two in a short summer term can be rewarding for college students.

   a. *Students who use a summer term to concentrate on one challenging course may find the focus brings good grades.*

   b. *Students just starting college can get used to college routines and policies in a less stressful atmosphere.*

   c. *Students who complete a summer term feel less pressured to load their semester schedule with too many classes.*

PLANNING   **Devising a Plan: Cause or Effect**

With a topic sentence and a list of causes (or effects) and details, you can draft an outline of your paragraph. Once you have a rough outline, you can work on revising it. You may want to add to it, to take out certain ideas, to rewrite the topic sentence, or to change the order of the ideas. The following checklist may help you to revise your outline.

Checklist: A Checklist for Revising the Outline of a Cause or Effect Paragraph

✓   Does my topic sentence make my point?

✓   Does it indicate whether my paragraph is about causes or effects?

✓   Does the topic sentence fit the rest of the outline?

✓   Have I included enough causes or effects to make my point?

✓   Have I included enough details?

✓   Should I eliminate any ideas?

✓   Is the order of my causes or effects clear and logical?

The Order of Causes or Effects

Looking at a draft outline can help you decide on the best order for your causes or effects. There is no single rule for organizing causes or effects. Instead, you should think about the ideas you are presenting and decide on the most logical and effective order.

For example, if you are writing about some immediate and some long-range effects, you might want to discuss the effects in a **time order**. You might begin with the immediate effect, then discuss what happens later, and end with what happens last of all. If you are discussing three or four effects that are not in any particular time order, you might save the most important effect for last, for an **emphatic order**. If one cause leads to another, then use the **logical order** of discussing the causes.

Compare the following outline on owning a car to the list of effects on page 197. Notice that, in the outline, the carefree side of owning a car comes first, and the cares of owning a car, the expense and the worry, come later. The topic sentence follows the same order.

An Outline for an Effects Paragraph

revised topic sentence:	Owning my own car gave me freedom, cost me money, and made me careful about how I drive.
effect 1 **details**	⎰ I had the adult freedom to come and go. I didn't have to beg my father for his truck. I didn't have to get rides from my friends. I could go to the city when I wanted. ⎱ I could ride around for fun.
effect 2 **details**	⎰ I had to pay for the car and related expenses. A car costs a lot to maintain. I had car payments. I had a car loan to pay. ⎱ I had car insurance.

continued

effect 3
details
{
I became a more careful driver.
I worried about someone hitting the car.
I worried about bad drivers.
I wanted to avoid the scratches cars can get in a parking lot.
}

Once you have a revised outline of your cause or effect paragraph, you are ready to begin writing your draft.

Exercise 5 Writing Topic Sentences for Cause or Effect Outlines

Following are two outlines. They have no topic sentences. Read the outlines carefully several times. Then write a topic sentence for each.

1. **topic sentence:** *An argument with my parents has long-lasting results for me.*

INSTRUCTOR'S NOTE

Answers will vary. Possible answers shown at left.

   details: After I argue with my parents, I cannot calm down for hours.
I relive each part of the conflict, feeling the rage and frustration again.
I torment myself by thinking of all the clever remarks I could have made.
The next day, I find it impossible to look my mother in the eye.
The anger of the argument is too fresh.
I avoid my father because I am afraid he will offer more criticism.
Days later, when my parents and I have begun talking to each other again, I have still not recovered.
Resentment of their attitudes lingers inside me.
I also feel misunderstood and alone in the family.

2. **topic sentence:** *I fell in love with Mia because she was pretty, she was funny, and she loved me.*

   details: Mia was an attractive woman.
When she walked by, men noticed.
Her large, dark eyes seemed flirtatious.
Mia always made me laugh.
She had a smart comeback to any of my teasing remarks.
She saw the silly side of my obsession with cars and NASCAR.
The main reason I fell in love with Mia was that she loved me.
No one had ever been interested in me the way that Mia was.
She listened as if my words were important.
When I was with Mia, I felt safe and valued.

Exercise 6   **Revising the Order of Causes or Effects**

Below are topic sentences and lists of causes or effects. Reorder each list according the directions given at the end of the list. Put "1" by the item that would come first, and so forth.

1. **topic sentence:** Nicole decided to major in business for three reasons.

   _1_ She had always been interested in hearing about money and the successful people who made it.

   _3_ She was expected to take over her father's pool-maintenance business in a few years.

   _2_ She did well in business-related classes in high school.

   Use this order: From least important to most important.

2. **topic sentence:** My aunt's fear of dogs changed the way she lived.

   _3_ Her fear grew so intense that she refused to leave her apartment at all.

   _2_ She would not leave the apartment unless she could get right into a taxi and avoid encountering a dog.

   _1_ She moved into an apartment building that did not allow dogs.

   Use this order: Time order.

3. **topic sentence:** Living on my own has had negative and positive effects on me.

   _1_ I missed my family and always having someone to talk to.

   _3_ I eventually began to enjoy my own privacy.

   _2_ I gradually learned to depend on my own inner resources.

   Use this order: The order indicated by the topic sentence, from bad to good.

Exercise 7   **Developing an Outline**

The following outlines need one more cause or effect and details for that cause or effect. Fill in the missing parts.

1. **topic sentence:** Falling in love can be both wonderful and terrifying.

   effect 1:   The moment I fell in love for the first time, the rush of my emotions made the world seem a better place.

   details: Even if it was raining, the weather seemed perfect.
   Strangers seemed friendly and approving.
   Every pleasant sensation, like warmth or comfort, seemed magnified.

   effect 2:   Being in love seems to give a person a purpose in life.

   details: My brother thought about his girlfriend day and night.
   He kept planning their future.
   He would replay every encounter with her and enjoy every detail.

effect 3: *Unfortunately, love brings new and strange emotions that can be frightening.*

details (at least two sentences): *From the very beginning of my first love, I was afraid it would not last.*

In contrast, my brother felt that being in love was costing him his freedom.

INSTRUCTOR'S NOTE

Answers will vary. Possible answers shown at left.

2. topic sentence: People give many reasons for drinking too much.

cause 1: Some swear that they need a drink or two to relax at the end of the day.

details: They may claim that their jobs are extremely stressful.
They may say that being home with children all day is nerve-wracking.
Some insist that they cannot get to sleep without a couple of drinks.

cause 2: Others complain that alcohol is a part of their family history.

details: Some say that they grew up with parents who regularly drank at meals.
Others might blame their drinking on alcoholic parents.
A few blame their alcohol problem on parents who allowed their young children to taste alcohol.

cause 3: *Many heavy drinkers swear that they drink only to be social.*

details (at least two sentences): *They argue that people at parties are expected to celebrate with alcohol.*

They complain that peer pressure leads them to drink at bars.

They say that it is rude to refuse the offer of a drink.

D R A F T I N G **Drafting and Revising: Cause or Effect**

Once you have an outline in good order, with a sufficient number of causes or effects and a fair amount of detail, you can write a first draft of the paragraph. When the first draft is complete, you can read and reread it, deciding how you'd like to improve it. The following checklist may help you revise.

> **Checklist: A Checklist for Revising the Draft of a Cause or Effect Paragraph**
>
> ✓ Does my topic sentence indicate cause or effect?
>
> ✓ Does it fit the rest of the paragraph?
>
> ✓ Do I have enough causes or effects to make my point?
>
> ✓ Do I have enough details for each cause or effect?
>
> ✓ Are my causes or effects explained clearly?
>
> ✓ Is there a clear connection between my ideas?
>
> ✓ Have I shown the links between my ideas?
>
> ✓ Do I need to combine sentences?
>
> ✓ Do I need an opening or closing sentence?

Linking Ideas in Cause or Effect

When you write about how one event or situation causes another, or about how one result leads to another, you have to be very clear in showing the connections between events, situations, or effects.

One way to be clear is to rely on transitions. Some transitions are particularly helpful in writing cause or effect paragraphs.

> **INFO BOX:** **Transitions for a Cause or Effect Paragraph**
>
> **For cause paragraphs:**
>
> | | | | |
> |---|---|---|---|
> | because | for | for this reason | since |
> | due to | | | |
>
> **For effect paragraphs:**
>
> | | | | |
> |---|---|---|---|
> | as a result | hence | so | therefore |
> | consequently | in consequence | then | thus |

Making the Links Clear

Using the right transition is not always enough to make your point. Sometimes you have to write the missing link in your line of thinking so that the reader can understand your point. To write the missing link means writing phrases, clauses, or sentences that help the reader follow your point.

> **Not this:** Many mothers are working outside the home. Consequently, microwave ovens are popular.
>
> **But this:** Many mothers are working outside the home and have less time to cook. Consequently, microwave ovens, which can cook food in minutes, are popular.

The hard part of making clear links between ideas is that you have to put yourself in your reader's place. Remember that your reader cannot read your mind, only your paper. Connections between ideas may be very clear in your mind, but you must spell them out on paper.

Revising the Draft

Below is a draft of the paragraph on owning a car. When you read it, you'll notice many changes from the outline on pages 200–201:

- The details on "car payments" and "a car loan" said the same thing, so the repetition has been cut.
- Some details about the costs of maintaining a car and about parking have been added.
- The order of the details about the costs of a car has been changed. Now, paying for a car comes first; maintaining it comes after.
- Sentences have been combined.
- Transitions have been added.

A Draft of an Effects Paragraph

(Transitions are underlined.)

   Owning my own car gave me freedom, cost me money, and made me more careful about how I drive. <u>First of all,</u> my car gave me the adult freedom to come and go. I didn't have to beg my father for his truck or get rides from my friends anymore. I could go to the city or even ride around for fun when I wanted. <u>On the negative side,</u> I had to pay for the car and related expenses. I had to pay for the car loan. I also paid for car insurance. <u>A car costs a lot to maintain, too.</u> I paid for oil changes, tune-ups, tires, belts, and filters. <u>With so much of my money put into my car,</u> I became a more careful driver. I worried about someone hitting the car and watched out for bad drivers. <u>In addition,</u> I wanted to avoid the scratches a car can get in a parking lot, so I always parked far away from other cars.

Exercise 8 Making the Links Clear

Following are ideas that are linked, but their connection is not clearly explained. Rewrite each pair of ideas, making the connection clear.

1. I wanted to take an easy course in summer school. Therefore, I signed up for Ancient History.

   Rewritten: *I wanted to take an easy course in summer school. Since I*
   had always done well in history classes, I signed up for Ancient History.

   _____

   _____

   (**Hint:** Is history easy for you?)

2. Michael had all the mannerisms of my brother Dave. Consequently, I distrusted Michael from the moment we met.

   Rewritten: *Michael had all the mannerisms of my brother Dave, who hurt*
   and betrayed me. Consequently, I distrusted Michael from the moment
   we met.

   _____

   _____

   (**Hint:** Did you distrust your brother Dave? Why?)

3. Terrence was running out of money, so he wanted to eat at Chili Castle.

Rewritten: *Terrence was running out of money, so he wanted to eat at Chile Castle, which is an inexpensive restaurant.*

(**Hint:** Is Chile Castle an inexpensive restaurant?)

4. In the past three months, ten houses in my neighborhood have experienced break-ins. As a result, many neighbors are getting dogs.

Rewritten: *In the past three months, ten houses in my neighborhood have experienced break-ins. As a result, many neighbors are getting dogs, whose barking may scare burglars away.*

(**Hint:** How will the dogs prevent break-ins?)

Exercise 9 **Revising a Paragraph by Adding Details**

Each of the following paragraphs is missing details. Add at least two sentences of details to each paragraph.

1. I have three important motives for wanting to improve my English. First, I am a recent immigrant to the United States, and I need to learn more English so that I can do well in my classes. Although I studied English for many years in Nigeria, I have a hard time in college. The professors speak very fast, and I get lost trying to follow them. Reading the textbooks is also difficult, and I need a dictionary by my side. I also want to improve my English skills so that I can find a good job. I know that in business, technology, or science, a knowledge of English is essential. This knowledge will help me find work in many countries, not just in English-speaking ones. Most important, I am eager to learn better English so that I can make friends in the United States. *Even though Americans seem very friendly, I am lonely in this country. Everyone says "Hello" and "How are you doing?" but I am too insecure to answer with many words. I need to know more English in order to feel confident enough to have a real conversation.*

INSTRUCTOR'S NOTE

Answers will vary. Possible answers are shown.

I believe that by learning more English, I will make friends, succeed in college, and find opportunities in employment.

2. Surviving a hurricane has had a great impact on me. When a major hurricane devastated my community, it first brought me stunned horror. My apartment was blown apart, my car was crushed, and my neighborhood was without power or water for weeks. I couldn't even call my family because my cell phone wasn't working. Gradually, I felt myself becoming stronger and more determined. Government relief workers and volunteers arrived, and weeks turned into months of slow recovery. I drew hope from small incidents, like the volunteer who distributed bags of ice in the searing heat, and later from large events, like the reconstruction of my apartment building. However, the most important and lasting effect of the hurricane was my new gratitude for the simple joys of being alive. *Today, instead of complaining about another gray day, I enjoy the pattern of the clouds. When I am stuck in traffic, I focus on the music on the car radio. On a busy day, I take a minute to enjoy the taste of ice cream or the sound of my cat purring.*

Living through a hurricane was horrible, but it taught me how to appreciate daily life.

Exercise 10 Revising a Draft by Combining Sentences

Combine the underlined sentences in the following paragraph. Write your combinations in the space above the original sentences.

My family and friends expected

My first job had some surprising effects on me. <u>My family and friends expected</u> *me to hate working at a huge discount store, but I actually liked the job.* <u>me to hate working. I was working at a huge discount store. I actually liked the job.</u>

In fact, the first effect of the job was the pride I felt in being able to do the work.

I had been terrified when I started. The assistant manager made me stock some

I was afraid I would

shelves in the kitchen wares section, and I was nervous. <u>I was afraid I would</u>

INSTRUCTOR'S NOTE

Answers will vary. Possible answers are shown.

INSTRUCTOR'S NOTE

For more on combining sentences, see Chapter 16 on coordination and Chapter 18 on subordination.

forget to fill a high shelf, drop a coffeemaker, or knock a row of glasses onto the
<u>forget to fill a high shelf. Maybe I would drop a coffeemaker. Possibly, I could</u>
floor.
<u>knock a row of glasses onto the floor.</u> Avoiding such disasters was my first victory.

I'm known for being a reckless spender,
The second surprise involved my salary. <u>I'm known for being a reckless spender.</u>
the kind who can't walk into a mall without buying something.
<u>I'm the kind who can't walk into a mall without buying something.</u> However, I

actually put half of my salary in the bank and left it there. I felt that I had worked

hard to earn that money and didn't want to waste it. The most shocking result of

my first job was my new understanding of what it means to work. I had always

assumed that my mother, father, and older sister went to a job and sat around all

Working is hard,
day. Even my part-time work was enough to open my eyes. <u>Working is hard. Stress</u>
stressful, and exhausting.
<u>is involved. Work will exhaust a person.</u> Now, when a family member comes home

from work, I ask, "How was your day?", and I can understand their complaints.

POLISHING   **Polishing and Proofreading: Cause or Effect**

Following is the final version of the paragraph on owning a car. When you contrast the final version with the draft on page 205, you'll notice several changes:

- An introductory sentence has been added.
- Some sentences have been combined.
- Transitions have been revised.
- Some words have been changed so that the language is more precise.

Changes in style, word choice, sentence variety, and transitions can all be made before you decide on the final version of your paragraph. You may also want to add an opening or closing sentence to your paragraph.

A Final Version of an Effects Paragraph

(Changes from the draft are underlined.)

    <u>When I bought my first car, I wasn't prepared for all the changes it made in my life.</u> Owning my own car gave me freedom, cost me money, and made me careful about how I drive. First of all, my car gave me the adult freedom to come and go. I didn't have to beg my father for his truck or get rides from my friends anymore. I could go to the city or even ride around for fun when I wanted. On the negative side, I had to pay for the car and related expenses. <u>I had to pay for both the car loan and car insurance.</u> A car costs <u>money</u> to maintain, too. I paid for oil changes, tune-ups, tires, belts, and filters. With so much of my money put into my car, I became a more careful driver. I worried about someone hitting the car, and watched out for bad drivers. <u>To avoid dangers in the parking lot as well as on the road,</u> I always parked <u>my car far</u> away from other cars, <u>keeping my car safe from scratches.</u>

Before you prepare the final version of your cause or effect paragraph, check your latest draft for errors in spelling, punctuation, typing, and formatting.

> **For your information:** A sample effects essay based on this topic and following the same writing steps can be found in Chapter 12, pp. 313-315

Exercise 11 Correcting a Final Copy of a Cause or Effect Paragraph

Following are two paragraphs—one cause and one effect—with the kinds of errors that are easy to overlook when you prepare the final version of an assignment. Correct the errors, writing above the lines. There are thirteen errors in the first (effects) paragraph and twelve errors in the second (cause) paragraph.

                           has   *father*

1. Making a decision to lose weight have changed my Father physically and

emotionally   *father's*

emotional. First, my fathers' plan for losing weight began with a healthy diet. Once

he began to follow the diet, he began to feel more alive. Because he was no longer

         hours   *and*

spending hour's in front of the television, drinking gallons of soda an eating

snacks full of fat, he lost ten pounds and his sluggish attitude. He was willing to

try new experiences and go to new places. As a result, my mother was able to con-

                                      no comma needed

vince him to join a group of neighbors who walked for a mile, or two early in the

                      ,   *lose*

morning. After he joined this group; he began to loose more weight. In addition,

he began to gain a network of friends. The neighbors dedicated to morning exer-

cise shared news and views as they walked. The final effect on my father was a

       confidence.

growing confident He had improved his health and his social life, so he felt proud.

                         television anymore

My father doesn't slump in front of the Television any more. He doesn't rely on

                               life

food for comfort. Today he is a healthy man with a fuller live.

                       three

2. I gave my grandmother a cat for tree reasons. The first reason was necessity.

                                                  ,

I found a poor, thin kitten in an alley near my school last week and I couldn't leave

her there. On the other hand, I couldn't bring her home. My apartment manager

doesn't

don't allow pets. As I searched for a home for the cat, I thought of my

                 grandmother

grandmother. My Grandmother recently lost my grandfather, and she has been

feeling   *depressed*

filling very depress. It was hard for her to get out of bed and face the day alone. I

no comma needed
wanted to help her, and to cheer her up. If she had a cat to feed, she would have to
morning *would*
get up in the mourning, I thought. In addition, a curious kitten wood give my

grandmother someone to play with and even to talk to. My final reason was self-

ish. I loved that kitten. I couldn't bring it to a shelter and never know its fate. With
grandmother's , *three dashes*
the kitten in my grandmother house, I could visit often and all 3 of us (my
or commas are also correct
grandmother, the cat, and I) would be happy.

Lines of Detail: A Walk-Through Assignment

Write a paragraph on this topic: The Effects of Overcrowded Highways on Commuters. To write your paragraph, follow these steps:

Step 1: Go back to Exercise 3 on pages 197–198. Topic 3 is the same topic as this assignment. If you have already done that exercise, you have five or more questions that can lead you to ideas and details. If you haven't done the exercise, do topic 3 now.

Step 2: Use the answers to your questions to prepare a list of ideas and details. Put the items on your list into groups of effects and related details. Add to the groups until you have at least three effects (and related details) of overcrowded highways on commuters.

Step 3: Write a topic sentence that fits your effects.

Step 4: Write an outline. Check that your outline has sufficient details and that you have put the effects in the best order.

Step 5: Write a rough draft of your paragraph. Revise it until you have enough specific details to explain each effect and the links between your ideas are smooth and clear. Check whether any sentences should be combined and whether your paragraph could use an opening sentence or a concluding one.

Step 6: Before you prepare the final copy of your paragraph, check your latest draft for word choice, punctuation, transitions, and spelling.

Writing Your Own Cause or Effect Paragraph

When you write on any of the following topics, be sure to work through the stages of the writing process in preparing your cause or effect paragraph.

1. Write a cause paragraph on one of the following topics. You create the topic by filling in the blanks.

   Why I Chose _____

   Why I Stopped _____

   Why I Enjoy _____

Why I Started _____

Why I Bought _____

2. Write a one-paragraph letter of complaint to the manufacturers of a product you bought or to the company that owns a hotel, restaurant, airlines, or some other service you used. In your letter, write at least three reasons why you (a) want your money refunded or (b) want the product replaced. Be clear and specific about your reasons. Be sure your letter has a topic sentence.

   Collaborate

   If your instructor agrees, read a draft of your letter to a writing partner while your partner pretends to be the manufacturer or the head of the company. Afterward, ask your partner to point out where your ideas are not clear or convincing and where you make your point effectively.

3. Think of a current fad or trend. The fad can be a popular style of clothing, type of movie, style of music, a sport, a pastime, a kind of food or drink, an athlete, a gadget, an invention, an appliance, and so on. Write a paragraph on the causes of this fad or trend or the effects of it.

   Collaborate

   If your instructor agrees, begin by brainstorming with a group. Create a list of three or four fads or trends. Then create a list of questions to ask (and answer) about each fad or trend. If you are going to write about **causes**, for example, you might ask questions like these:

   What changes in society have encouraged this trend?
   Have changes in the economy helped to make it popular?
   Does it appeal to a specific age group? Why?
   Does it meet any hidden emotional needs? For instance, is it a way to gain status or to feel safe or powerful?

   If you are going to write about **effects**, you might ask questions like these:

   Will this trend last?
   Has it affected competitors?
   Is it spreading?
   Is the fad changing business, or education, or the family?
   Has it improved daily life?

4. If you have a vivid memory of one of the following experiences, write a paragraph about the experience's effects on you.

moving to a new place	losing a friend
making a new friend	losing a job
being a victim of a crime	breaking a bad habit
winning a contest	entering a relationship
undergoing surgery	ending a relationship

5. If you currently use a computer for drafting your writing assignments, write a paragraph that summarizes the effects of relying on the computer for composing most, if not all, of your writing assignments. Remember that the effects may be both positive and negative, so you will need to brainstorm or freewrite first. Be sure your final version of the paragraph reflects logical organization of details and appropriate transitions.

   Computer

6. After looking at the photograph above, write a paragraph on why joining an exercise group can have social benefits.

7. After looking at the photograph above, write a paragraph on the positive effects of a young person and an old person creating a bond.

Note: Additional writing options suitable for cause- or effect-related assignments can be found after the professional reading "Students in Shock," which begins on page 628.

How Do I Get a Better Grade?

visit www.mywritinglab.com for audio-visual lectures and additional practice sets about cause and effect.

Get a better grade with MyWritingLab!

Name: _____   Section: _____

Peer Review Form for a Cause or Effect Paragraph

After you've written a draft of your cause or effect paragraph, let a writing partner read it. When your partner has completed the form below, discuss the comments. Then repeat the same process for your partner's paragraph.

This is **a cause paragraph** / **an effect paragraph**. (Circle one.)

In this paragraph, the causes or effects are (briefly list all of them) _____

_____

_____

_____

The topic sentence uses these words to indicate cause or effect: _____

_____ (Write the exact words.)

The cause or effect that is most clearly explained is _____

_____

I would like to see more details added to _____

_____

I have questions about _____

I would like to take out the part about _____

Other comments on the paragraph: _____

_____

_____

_____

_____

_____

_____

_____

_____

Reviewer's name: _____

CHAPTER 10

Argument

WHAT IS ARGUMENT?

A written **argument** is an attempt to *persuade* a reader to think or act in a certain way. When you write an argument paragraph, your goal is to get people to see your point so that they are persuaded to accept it and perhaps to act on it.

In an argument paragraph, you take a stand. Then you support your stand with reasons. In addition, you give details for each reason. Your goal is to persuade your reader by making a point that has convincing reasons and detail.

Hints for Writing an Argument Paragraph

1. Pick a topic you can handle. Your topic should be small enough to be covered in one paragraph. For instance, you can't argue effectively for world peace in just one paragraph.

2. Pick a topic you can handle based on your own experience and observation. Topics like legalizing drugs, gun control, capital punishment, or air pollution require research into facts, figures, and expert opinions to make a complete argument. They are topics you can write

INSTRUCTOR'S NOTE

Chapter 13, "Writing from Reading," contains information on the importance of critical thinking skills, pp. 337–339. This overview may be useful for future argument essays based on your reading assignments.

about convincingly in a longer research paper, but for a one-paragraph argument, pick a topic based on what you've experienced yourself.

> **not this topic:** Organized Crime
> **but this topic:** Starting a Crime Watch Program in My Neighborhood

3. Do two things in your topic sentence: name the subject of your argument and take a stand. The following topic sentences do both.

> subject   takes a stand
> The college cafeteria should serve more healthy snacks.

> subject   takes a stand
> High school athletes who fail a course should not be allowed to play on a school team.

You should take a stand, but *don't* announce it:

> **not this:** This paragraph will explain why Springfield needs a teen center.
> **but this:** Springfield should open a teen center. (This is a topic sentence with a subject and a stand.)

4. Consider your audience. Consider why these people should support your points. How will they be likely to object? How will you get around these objections? For instance, you might want to argue to the residents of your community that the intersection of Hawthorne Road and Sheridan Street needs a traffic light. Would anyone object?

INSTRUCTOR'S NOTE

For a list of argument topics that ask students to consider their audience of readers, see pp. 232–233 in this chapter.

At first, you might think, "No. Why would anyone object? The intersection is dangerous. There's too much traffic there. People risk major accidents getting across the intersection." However, if you think further about your audience, which is the people in your community, you might identify these objections: (1) some town residents may not want to pay for a traffic signal, and (2) some drivers may not want to spend extra time waiting for a light to change.

There are several ways to handle objections:

DISCUSSION QUESTION

Students who have taken a speech course may have studied ways to refute a point or ways to "consider the opposition." Ask whether any of them can discuss stands on topics they have debated or researched for other classes.

> You can *refute* an objection. To refute it means to prove that it isn't valid; it isn't true. For instance, if someone says that a light wouldn't do any good, you might say that a new light has already worked in a nearby neighborhood.
>
> Sometimes it's best to admit the other side has a point. You have to *concede* that point. For instance, traffic lights do cost money, and waiting for a light to change does take time.
>
> Sometimes you can *turn an objection into an advantage.* When you acknowledge the objection and yet use it to make your own point, you show that you've considered both sides of the argument. For instance, you might say that the price of a traffic signal at the intersection is well worth the expense because that light will buy safety for all the drivers who try to cross Hawthorne Road and Sheridan Street. As an alternative, you might say that waiting a few moments for the light to change is better than waiting many minutes for an opening in the heavy traffic of the intersection.

5. Be specific, clear, and logical in your reasons. As always, think before you write. Think about your point and your audience. Try to come up with at least three reasons for your position.

Be careful that your reasons do not overlap. For instance, you might write the following:

> topic sentence: *College students should get discounts on movie tickets.*
> audience: *Owners of movie theaters.*
> reasons: *1. Many college students can't afford current ticket prices.*
> *2. The cost of tickets is high for most students.*
> *3. More people in the theater means more popcorn and candy sold at the concession stand.*

But reasons 1 and 2 overlap; they are really part of the same reason.

Be careful not to argue in a circle. For instance, if you say, "One reason for having an after-school program at Riverside Elementary School is that we need one there," you've just said, "We need an after-school program because we need an after-school program."

Finally, be specific in stating your reasons.

> **not this:** One reason to start a bus service to and from the college is to help people.
> **but this:** A bus service to and from the college would encourage students to leave their cars at home and use travel time to study.

Exercise 1   **Recognizing Good Topic Sentences for an Argument Paragraph**

Some of the topic sentences below are appropriate for an argument paragraph. Some are for topics that are too large for one paragraph, and some are for topics that would require research. Some are announcements. Some do not take a stand. Put *OK* next to the sentences that would work well in an argument paragraph.

1. _____ Politicians should be more concerned about early childhood education for all children over the age of three.

2. _____ The need for a community park in Keaton Heights is the subject of this essay.

3. _____ Financial aid debt is a heavy burden for many college graduates.

4. _OK_ Parenting classes should be offered at Madison High School at night and on weekends.

5. _____ Why trans fats should be banned at restaurants is the topic to be discussed.

6. _____ Something must be done about Internet crime.

7. _OK_ The county courthouse needs a parking garage with free parking.

8. _____ We must take action to fight the growth of global warming.

9. _____ Iguanas invading South Florida are a growing problem.

10. _OK_ Homeowners in the Sand Hills neighborhood must be responsible for maintaining the appearance of their houses.

Collaborate

Exercise 2 **Recognizing and Handling Objections**

Below are the topic sentences of arguments. Working with a group, list two possible objections to each argument that might come from the specific audience identified. Then think of ways to handle each objection by refuting it, conceding it, or trying to turn it to your advantage. On the lines provided, write the actual sentence(s) you would use in a paragraph.

1. **topic sentence:** Triton College should provide an all-night study area for its students.

   audience: the deans, vice president, and president of the college

   possible objections from this audience:

   a. *Students in the study area would be vulnerable to crime.*

   b. *Few students would use the area after 11:00 p.m.*

   answering objections:

   a. *The area could be located near the campus police office so that campus police could check on it regularly.*

   b. *A pilot program could monitor the number of students and most popular times for use after the initial opening.*

2. **topic sentence:** Residents of Rose Hill should spend some of their tax money on a skate park.

   audience: residents of Rose Hill who do not have skateboarders in their families

   possible objections from this audience:

   a. *Skate parks are extremely noisy.*

   b. *Teens who gather at skate parks may commit crimes.*

   answering objections:

   a. *It is better to contain the noise of skateboarders in one park than to spread it through neighborhoods and malls.*

   b. *Teens with nowhere to go are more likely to get into trouble than teens socializing at a skate park.*

3. **topic sentence:** Private citizens in Midland Township should be banned from owning exotic pets (such as tigers and alligators).

   audience: Midland Township owners of exotic pets

   possible objections from this audience:

   a. *Many exotic pets are rescued animals who need a haven.*

   b. *This law shows a hatred of animals.*

   answering objections:

   a. *Rescued animals deserve a better home than a cage in someone's backyard.*

   b. *The exotic pet who escapes can be a danger to itself or others.*

WRITING THE ARGUMENT PARAGRAPH IN STEPS

PREWRITING   Gathering Ideas: Argument

Imagine that your instructor has given you this assignment:

> Write a one-paragraph letter to the editor of your local
> newspaper. Argue for something in your town that needs to be
> changed.

One way to begin is to **brainstorm** for some specific thing that you can write about.

Is there a part of town that needs to be cleaned up?
Should something be changed at a school?
What do I notice on my way to work or school that needs improvement?
What could be improved in my neighborhood?

By answering these questions, you may come up with one topic, and then you can list ideas on it.

topic

Cleaning Up Roberts Park

ideas

dirty and overgrown
benches are all cracked and broken
full of trash
could be fixed up
people work nearby
they would use it

You can consider your audience and possible objections:

audience

local people of all ages who read the local paper

possible objections from this audience

would cost money
more important things to spend money on

answering objections

Money would be well spent to beautify the downtown.
City children could play there in the fresh air and in nature; workers could eat lunch there.

Grouping Your Ideas

Once you have a list, you can start grouping the ideas on your list. Some of the objections you wrote down may actually lead you to reasons that support your argument. That is, by answering objections, you may come up with reasons that support your point. Following is a list with a point to argue, three supporting reasons, and some details about cleaning up Roberts Park.

A List for an Argument Paragraph

point:	*We should fix up Roberts Park*
reason:	*Improving the park would make the downtown area more attractive to shoppers.*
details:	*Shoppers could stroll in the park or rest from their shopping.*
	Friends could meet in the park for a day of shopping and lunch.
reason:	*City children could play in the park.*
details:	*They could get fresh air.*
	They could play in a natural setting.
reason:	*Workers could eat lunch outdoors.*
details:	*Several office complexes are nearby.*
	Workers would take a break outdoors.

With three reasons and some details for each, you can draft a topic sentence. Remember that your topic sentence for an argument should (1) name your subject and (2) take a stand. Below is a topic sentence about Roberts Park that does both.

      subject   **takes a stand**

Roberts Park should be cleaned up and improved.

With a topic sentence, you are ready to move on to the planning stage of preparing an argument paragraph.

Exercise 3 **Distinguishing between Reasons and Details**

Each list below has three reasons and details for each reason. Put *Reason 1*, *Reason 2*, and *Reason 3* next to the reasons on each list. Then put *Detail for 1*, *Detail for 2*, or *Detail for 3* by the items that give details about each reason. There may be more than one sentence of detail connected to one reason.

1. **topic sentence:** Physical exercise should be a part of every school day at Emerson Elementary School.

reason 1	Physical exercise is good for children's health.
reason 2	Children who take a break for exercise are more likely to pay attention in class.
detail for 1	Exercise can develop young children's coordination.
detail for 2	Exercise helps to release energy that must be stifled in the classroom.
detail for 3	Games can encourage teamwork.
detail for 1	Childhood obesity is a problem, and exercise is one solution.
reason 3	Exercise helps children to learn social skills.
detail for 3	Even individual forms of exercise like stretching or bending get children to talk and laugh together.

detail for 2   Physical exercise can keep students alert.

detail for 2   There is less restlessness and fidgeting in class when students know they will have a break.

2. topic sentence: The broken streetlights on Milton Avenue need to be repaired immediately.

reason 1   The lack of lighting makes the street unattractive.

detail for 3   An elderly man was mugged at 8:00 p.m. last week as he carried his groceries home on Milton Avenue.

reason 2   Dark streets can lead to accidents.

detail for 1   Without streetlights, Milton Avenue appears dirty and rundown.

detail for 2   Pedestrians can trip and fall when they can't see a curb or a large crack in a sidewalk.

reason 3   An unlighted street is an invitation to criminals.

detail for 3   In the past month, three nighttime smash-and-grab crimes have occurred on Milton Avenue.

detail for 1   The merchandise in store windows appears ugly and cheap if there are no streetlights to illuminate it.

detail for 2   One section of Milton Avenue is so dark that a person could walk into a wire fence.

detail for 2   One driver tried to park on Milton Avenue and hit the bumper of another parked car because he could not see the bumper in the darkness.

Exercise 4	**Finding Reasons to Support an Argument**

Give three reasons that support each point. In each case, the readers of your local newspaper will be the audience for an argument paragraph.

1. point: Bus stops in Garfield should be transformed into bus shelters.

reasons: a. _The weather in Garfield can be brutally hot or cold._

b. _Shelters would encourage residents to try public transportation and cut down on traffic._

c. _Today, elderly people with failing driving skills must keep driving or wait for a bus in the snow._

2. point: The owners of Lakeview Apartments need to get rid of the speed bumps in the parking lot.

reasons: a. _The speed bumps are annoying to careful drivers._

b. _The bumps are so large and high that they have damaged the underside of several cars._

INSTRUCTOR'S NOTE

Answers will vary. Possible answers shown at left.

c. *The winding roads of the apartment complex make speeding impossible even without speed bumps.*

3. **point:** Parking at Hawthorne College should be free to all.

   reasons: a. *Taxpayers already pay for the buildings and parking lots at this public college.*

   b. *Allowing free parking for all would eliminate the cost of preparing several varieties of parking decals.*

   c. *Fewer campus police would be needed since they would not have to patrol the parking lots and issue traffic tickets.*

PLANNING   **Devising a Plan: Argument**

With a topic sentence and a list of reasons and details, you can draft an outline. Then you can review it, making whatever changes you think it needs. The checklist below may help you to review and revise your outline.

Checklist: A Checklist for Revising an Argument Outline

✓ Does my topic sentence make my point? Does it state a subject and take a stand?

✓ Have I considered the objections to my argument so that I am arguing intelligently?

✓ Do I have all the reasons I need to make my point?

✓ Do any reasons overlap?

✓ Are my reasons specific?

✓ Do I have enough details for each reason?

✓ Are my reasons in the best order?

The Order of Reasons in an Argument

When you are giving several reasons, it is a good idea to keep the most convincing or most important reason for last. Saving the best for last is called using **emphatic order**. For example, you might have these three reasons to tear down an abandoned building in your neighborhood: (1) The building is ugly. (2) Drug dealers are using the building. (3) The building is infested with rats. The most important reason, the drug dealing, should be used last, for an emphatic order.

Following is an outline on improving Roberts Park. When you look at the outline, you'll notice several changes from the list on page 220:

- Since the safety of children at play is important, it is put as the last detail.
- Some details have been added.

- A sentence has been added to the end of the outline. It explains why improving the park is a good idea even to people who will never use the park themselves. It is a way of answering these people's objections.

An Outline for an Argument Paragraph

topic sentence: Roberts Park should be cleaned up and improved.

reason: Improving the park would make the downtown area more attractive to shoppers.

details: Shoppers could stroll through the park or rest there after shopping.
Friends could meet at the park for a day of shopping and lunch.

reason: Workers from nearby offices and stores could eat lunch outdoors.

details: Several office complexes are nearby.
An hour outdoors is a pleasant break from work.

reason: City children could play there.

details: They would get fresh air.
They would play on grass, not on asphalt.
They would not have to play near traffic.

final idea: An attractive park improves the city, and all residents benefit when the community is beautified.

Exercise 5   Working with the Order of Reasons in an Argument Outline

Below are topic sentences and lists of reasons. For each list, put an *X* by the reason that is the most significant, the reason you would save for last in an argument paragraph.

1. **topic sentence:** School buses must be equipped with heating and air-conditioning.

    reason 1: __X__ Students with allergies can suffer sudden breathing problems in a hot, humid bus.

    reason 2: _____ Stifling heat can make students and their driver irritable and impatient.

    reason 3: _____ Not all students have the warm clothes needed for a ride on an unheated bus.

2. **topic sentence:** Anderson Hospital needs to expand its emergency-room services.

    reason 1: _____ Waiting time in the emergency room can be as long as three hours.

    reason 2: _____ More and more uninsured sick people choose the emergency room as their only source of health care.

reason 3: __X__ Last month, an elderly man who got lost in the crowd at the Anderson emergency room nearly died there.

3. **topic sentence:** College students should receive free annual flu shots at their colleges.

reason 1: _____ Flu keeps people of all ages from work or school.

reason 2: _____ Classrooms, lecture halls, or labs are perfect places for the flu to spread.

reason 3: __X__ People die of the flu every year.

Exercise 6   Recognizing Reasons That Overlap

Below are topic sentences and lists of reasons. In each list, two reasons overlap. Put an X by the two reasons that overlap.

1. **topic sentence:** Petrocelli's Pizza should offer a delivery service.

   a. __X__ Petrocelli's is located in a traffic-filled part of town and is hard to get to.

   b. _____ Many students in college dormitories a few miles from Petrocelli's love pizza but don't have cars.

   c. __X__ Some people like Petrocelli's pizza but go to another pizzeria in an area with less traffic congestion.

   d. _____ After a long day at work, some people drag themselves home and suddenly realize they want pizza delivered.

2. **topic sentence:** All college courses should include at least one class review session before final exams.

   a. _____ Many students miss a class or two during the term and need to catch up on the material they missed.

   b. __X__ A review during class time is convenient for all the people enrolled in the class.

   c. _____ A class review can be a way for students to structure and focus their studying for final exams.

   d. __X__ Not all students have time to schedule an appointment to review with their instructors, so a class meeting devoted to a review is an easy solution.

3. **topic sentence:** The new classroom building at the college should put benches in the halls.

   a. _____ Students who come early to class need a place to sit while the previous class ends.

   b. __X__ On cold and rainy days, students and teachers need shelter indoors between classes.

   c. _____ Benches would make the wide hallways more people-friendly.

   d. __X__ Benches would welcome students who come inside in bad weather.

Exercise 7   Identifying a Reason That Is Not Specific

For each of the following lists, put an *X* by the reason that is not specific.

1. **topic sentence:** The advanced swimming class should hold a swim party for disabled children.

   a. __*X*__ Water is good for many disabled children.

   b. _____ Exercise in water is an important part of rehabilitation for many disabled children.

   c. _____ Members of the swim class are skilled enough to assist children in the water.

   d. _____ The children would enjoy a place where they could be themselves, make new friends, and splash their old friends.

2. **topic sentence:** Millennium Mall needs a bigger food court.

   a. _____ The court can hold only six stalls, so there is little variety in food choices.

   b. _____ There are so few tables and chairs that some people wait fifteen minutes for a place to sit and eat.

   c. __*X*__ Many of the unpleasant aspects of the food court would disappear if the court were larger.

   d. _____ Too many people crammed into too little space creates unbearable noise.

3. **topic sentence:** Manufacturers should minimize the use of hard, clear plastic to wrap small, cheap items.

   a. _____ It's impossible to open an item sealed in this kind of plastic and cardboard without a strong, heavy pair of scissors.

   b. _____ A person who cuts into this plastic risks a cut on his or her hand.

   c. _____ Wrapping a cheap item such as a hairbrush in this elaborate packaging only raises the price of the item.

   d. *X* Trying to remove an item from the stiff, hard packaging is aggravating.

Exercise 8   Adding Details to an Outline

Following is part of an outline. It includes a topic sentence and three reasons. Add at least two sentences of details to each reason. Your details may be examples or descriptions.

topic sentence: Adult moviegoers should not bring children under six into movies meant for adults.

reason: It is no fun for a young child to sit through a grown-up movie.

details: *Children quickly become bored by a screen full of adults talking.*

details: *Even car chases and stunts cannot hold children's attention for ninety minutes to two hours.*

TEACHING TIP

Groupwork: This exercise can work well with groups of 3–4 students working through each part.

INSTRUCTOR'S NOTE

Answers will vary. Possible answers shown.

reason: Adults in the audience suffer when children become bored and unhappy.

details: *Those in the audience who came without children resent the noise of unhappy, restless children.*

details: *Those who brought the children feel embarrassed and angry.*

_____

reason: Small children can get upset when they're at a movie meant for adults.

details: *They become anxious when their family members tell them to sit still or be quiet.*

details: *Scenes of graphic violence shown on a huge screen can haunt children for years.*

DRAFTING   Drafting and Revising: Argument

Once you are satisfied with your outline, you can write the first draft of your paragraph. When you have completed it, you can begin revising the draft so that your argument is as clear, smooth, and convincing as it can be. The checklist below may help you with your revisions.

Checklist: A Checklist for Revising a Draft of an Argument Paragraph

✓ Do any of my sentences need combining?

✓ Have I left out a serious or obvious reason?

✓ Should I change the order of my reasons?

✓ Do I have enough details?

✓ Are my details specific?

✓ Do I need to explain the problem or issue I am writing about?

✓ Do I need to link my ideas more clearly?

✓ Do I need a final sentence to stress my point?

Checking Your Reasons

Be sure that your argument has covered all the serious or obvious reasons. Sometimes writers get so caught up in drafting their ideas that they forget to mention something very basic to the argument. For instance, if you were arguing for a leash law for your community, you might state that dogs who run free can hurt people and damage property. But don't forget to mention another serious reason to keep dogs on leashes: dogs who are not restrained can get hurt or killed by cars.

One way to see if you have left out a serious or obvious reason is to ask a friend or classmate to read your draft and to react to your argument. Another technique is to put your draft aside for an hour or two and then read it as if you were a reader, not the writer.

Explaining the Problem or the Issue

Sometimes your argument discusses a problem so obvious to your audience that you do not need to explain it. On the other hand, sometimes you need to explain a problem or issue so that your audience can understand your point. If you tell readers of your local paper about teenage vandalism at Central High School, you probably need to explain what kind of vandalism has occurred and how often. Sometimes it is smart to convince readers of the seriousness of a situation by explaining it a little so that they will be more interested in your argument.

Transitions That Emphasize Your Reasons

In writing an argument paragraph, you can use any transition, depending on how you arrange your reasons and details. However, no matter how you present your reasons, you will probably want to *emphasize* one of them. Below are some transitions that can be used for emphasis.

INFO BOX: Transitions to Use for Emphasis

above all	finally	most important	most significant
especially	mainly	most of all	primarily

For example, by saying, "*Most important*, broken windows at Central High School are a safety problem," you put the emphasis for your audience on this one idea.

Revising a Draft

Following is a draft of the argument paragraph on Roberts Park. When you read it, you'll notice these changes from the outline on page 223:

- A description of the problem has been added.

- Details have been added.

- Short sentences have been combined.

- Transitions, including two sentences of transition, have been added. "Most important" and "Best of all"—transitions that show emphasis—have been included.

TEACHING TIP

Remind students about the effectiveness of emphatic order (arranging supporting reasons and details in the order of least to most important) in argument/persuasive paragraphs and essays.

A Draft of an Argument Paragraph

(Transitions are underlined.)

Roberts Park was once a pretty little park, but today it is overgrown with weeds, cluttered with trash and rusty benches. Roberts Park should be cleaned up and improved. Improving the park would make the downtown area more attractive to shoppers. Shoppers could stroll through a renovated park or rest there after shopping. Friends could also meet there for a day of shopping and lunch. <u>Shoppers are not the only ones who could enjoy the park.</u> Workers from nearby offices and stores could eat lunch outdoors. Several office complexes are near the park, and workers from these offices could bring their lunch to work and eat outside in good weather. I think many people would agree that an hour spent

continued

outdoors is a pleasant break from work. <u>Most important</u>, city children could play in an improved Roberts Park. They would get fresh air while they played on grass, not asphalt. <u>Best of all</u>, they would not have to play near traffic. <u>Children, shoppers, and workers would benefit from a cleanup of Roberts Park, but so would others</u>. An attractive park improves the city, and all residents benefit when a community is beautified.

Exercise 9 **Adding an Explanation of the Problem to an Argument Paragraph**

This paragraph could use an explanation of the problem before the thesis. Write a short explanation of the problem in the lines provided.

INSTRUCTOR'S NOTE

Answers will vary. Possible answer shown at right.

The players and coaches at Glendale High School work hard. They win a fair

number of games, but they don't get much attention. Working hard without much

notice can be hard on a team's morale, and even the team mascot, an eagle

dressed like a Roman soldier, looks tired.

The Glendale High School football team needs a new mascot. A new mascot would create pride among the players. A strong, new image would be a sign to the team members that the coaches and school staff respect and value the Glendale Conquerors. The time spent to choose and design a mascot would represent some needed attention to a neglected team. In addition, a new mascot could rally the students and create new support for the players and the games. Support would turn into an increase in school spirit as the bleachers began to fill with fans. One last reason to create a new mascot involves the community. A change in mascots would be news in this small town. Drawing attention to the school, the new mascot might interest more residents in going to the games and supporting the team. The team could once again become a source of pride for the community. A simple change of team mascot could lead to high spirits for the team, school spirit for the student body, and civic pride for the community.

Exercise 10 **Recognizing Transitions in an Argument Paragraph**

Underline all the transitions—words, phrases, or sentences—in the paragraph below. Put a double line under any transitions that emphasize.

I like my college classes; I even look forward to several of them. <u>However</u>, there is one part of most classes that I resent: the coffee. I am sick of the students (and sometimes professors) who stroll into the classroom balancing a huge paper cup of latte or double vanilla mocha on top of their books and papers. I believe that coffee drinkers should get their caffeine outside the classroom. <u>First of all</u>, coffee drinks distract me. I can smell their brew of coffee and cinnamon or chocolate or cream. The odor is attractive and overwhelming. <u>More important</u>, I have to keep an eye on the coffee in case it spills near me or on me. <u>Even when</u> I manage to avoid coffee spills, they are ever-present. The classroom floors are sticky with spilled coffee, cream, and sugar. If I put my books on the floor under my desk, I risk picking up a sticky stack of textbooks and notebooks at the end of class. Once I sat at a desk coated with a glaze of coffee and sugar. <u>Most important,</u> coffee spills in the classroom are not only dirty; they are unsanitary. The old buildings at our campus attract cockroaches and mice. The sticky, sometimes sweet remains of coffee on the floor or in discarded paper cups invite these creatures. <u>Finally,</u> I understand that the hard work of college can exhaust students and teachers, but I wish they would drink their pick-me-ups before class.

Exercise 11   Revising a Draft by Combining Sentences

In the following paragraph, combine each cluster of underlined sentences into one clear, smooth sentence. Write your combinations in the space above the original sentences.

Star Supermarket should sell all of its fruit and vegetables loose instead of

For example,

packaged. Packaged fruit or vegetables often conceal spoiled pieces. <u>For example,</u>
strawberries in clear plastic boxes sometimes look ripe and large on the top layer,
<u>strawberries in clear plastic boxes sometimes look ripe and large on the top layer.</u>
but in the middle, the boxes hide pale green or mushy fruit.
<u>In the middle the boxes hide pale green fruit. Sometimes there is mushy fruit.</u>

Bags of onions have been known to contain rotten ones. Also, loose produce

would appeal to the customers who want small quantities of fruit or vegetables. A

Similarly, a person who

single person does not need a five-pound bag of potatoes. <u>Then there is the person</u>
shops every day may want only one fresh tomato.
<u>who shops every day. This person many want only one tomato. The tomato must</u>

<u>be fresh.</u> Finally, loose produce is appealing because shoppers enjoy picking

Some people want

through a selection of produce to find what they want most. <u>Some people want</u>
soft, ripe peaches while others want firm ones.
<u>soft, ripe peaches. Firm ones are the choice for other people.</u> As for potatoes, peo-

Packaged produce can

ple like big ones for baking and smaller ones for boiling. <u>Packaged produce can</u>
hide the flaws in food, make shoppers buy more than they need, or force them to
<u>hide the flaws in food. Also, it can make shoppers buy more than they need. Some</u>
settle for less.
<u>shoppers have to settle for less than what they wanted.</u> Loose produce gives shop-

pers more of a choice.

INSTRUCTOR'S NOTE

Answers will vary. Possible answers shown at left.

POLISHING   Proofreading and Polishing: Argument

Following is the final version of the argument paragraph on Roberts Park. When you read it, you'll notice several changes from the draft on pages 227–228:

- Some words have been changed to improve the details.
- The first sentence has been changed so that it is more descriptive and uses a parallel pattern for emphasis.

INSTRUCTOR'S NOTE

For more on parallelism, see Chapter 20.

A Final Version of an Argument Paragraph

(Changes from the draft are underlined.)

Roberts Park was once a pretty little park, but today it is overgrown with weeds, <u>littered with trash, and cluttered with rusty benches.</u> Roberts Park should be cleaned up and improved. Improving the park would make the downtown area more attractive to shoppers. Shoppers could stroll through a <u>restored</u> park or rest there after shopping. Friends could also meet <u>at the park</u> for a day of shopping and lunch. Shoppers are not the only ones who could enjoy the park. Workers from nearby offices and stores could eat lunch outdoors. Several office complexes are near the park, and workers from these offices could bring <u>a bag</u> lunch to work and eat outside in good weather. I think many people would agree that an hour spent outdoors is a pleasant break from work. Most important, city children could play in an improved Roberts Park. They would get fresh air while they played on grass, not asphalt. Best of all, they would not have to play near traffic. Children, shoppers, and workers would benefit from a cleanup of Roberts Park, but so would others. An attractive park improves the city, and all residents benefit when a community is beautified.

Before you prepare the final version of your argument paragraph, check your latest draft for errors in spelling, punctuation, typing, and formatting.

> **For your information:** A sample argument essay based on this topic and following the same writing steps can be found in Chapter 12, pp. 316–322.

Exercise 12 Proofreading to Prepare the Final Version

Following are two paragraphs with the kinds of errors that are easy to overlook when you prepare the final version of an assignment. Correct the errors, writing above the lines. There are eleven errors in the first paragraph and ten in the second paragraph.

Paragraph 1

College students, like everyone else, has financial problems and sometime *have* *sometimes*

need help with these problems. This help should be available on campus in the

form of financial counciling. If it began at student Orientation, financial counsel- *counseling* *orientation*

ing could actually prevent some problem's. Orientation usually includes informa- *problems*

tion about financial aid, but a few warnings about financial temptation should be

issued to new students. For example, new students need to be prepared for all

the credit card offers that will come their way. A student who has been through

no comma needed

the experience, of having too many credit cards and too much debt would make a

convincing speaker. In addition, financial advisors should be available all term,

problem

just as academic counselors are. Often, an academic prolem is related to a money

classes

conflict. One student may miss a number of class because he or she has been

sick, has no health insurance, and needs to find a free or low-cost clinic. Another

student may need advice about collecting unemployment benefits. Finally, finan-

cial advice can move beyond solving a problem to planning a future. An advisor

design   *An*

can help a student dezine a budget or learn to save a little each week. A advisor

can read a lease and explain it before a student signs it. For many students, learn-

ing to handle money is a major lesson and advisors could help students avoid

learning it the hard way.

Paragraph 2

an

Our local animal shelter does a excellent job of caring for homeless animals

their

and finding them loving homes It is time for local veterinarians to do there part.

Local veterinarians should be asked to volunteer three months of free care for

owners

each pet adopted from the shelter. Free care would really help the pet owner's. A

shelter pet often needs shots and a checkup and they are expensive. Some people

who would love to have a pet might not adopt one because they cannot afford the

medical costs. If the initial medical costs were free, people might be more likely to

take home a great dog or cat. The veterinarians who volunteered their services

benefit

would benifit, too. The shelter could announce the names of the participating vet-

doctors

erinarians, giving these pet doctor's free, positive publicity. In addition the grateful

no comma needed

pet owners would probably remain loyal to these generous veterinarians, and

continue to visit them long after the three-month free period is over. As a result,

the veterinarians would gain many new clients. Finally, the biggest winners in this

scheme would be the pets. Shelter pets have faced many trials and uncertain

they

times. When they begin a better life in a caring home, They should start it in good

health.

Lines of Detail: A Walk-Through Assignment

Write a one-paragraph letter to the editor of your local newspaper. Argue for some change you want for your community. You could argue for a traffic light, turn signal, or stop sign at a specific intersection. Or you could argue for bike paths in certain places, a recycling program, more bus service, or for any other specific change you feel is needed. To write your paragraph, follow these steps:

Step 1: Begin by listing all the reasons and details you can about your topic. Survey your list and consider any possible objections. Answer the objections as well as you can, and see if the objections can lead you to more reasons.

Step 2: Group your reasons, listing the details that fit under each reason. Add details where they are needed and check to see if any reasons overlap.

Step 3: Survey the reasons and details and draft a topic sentence. Be sure that your topic sentence states the subject and takes a stand.

Step 4: Write an outline. Then revise it, checking that you have enough reasons to make your point. Also check that your reasons are specific and in an effective order. Make sure that you have sufficient details for each reason. Check that your outline includes answers to any significant objections.

Step 5: Write a draft of your argument. Revise the draft until it includes any necessary explanations of the problem being argued, all serious or obvious reasons, and sufficient specific details. Also check that the most important reason is stated last. Add all the transitions that are needed to link your reasons and details.

Step 6: Before you prepare the final copy of your paragraph, decide whether you need a final sentence to stress your point and whether your transitions are smooth and logical. Refine your word choice. Then check for errors in spelling, punctuation, and grammar.

Writing Your Own Argument Paragraph

When you write on any of the topics below, be sure to work through the stages of the writing process in preparing your argument paragraph.

1. Write a paragraph for readers of your local newspaper, arguing for one of the following:
   a. a ban on all advertising of alcohol
   b. mandatory jail terms for those convicted of drunk driving
   c. eliminating soft drinks from the vending machines at local high school(s)
   d. a fine for all dog or cat owners who have not had their animals neutered, to be used to support animal shelters

2. In a paragraph, argue one of the following topics to the audience specified. If your instructor agrees, brainstorm your topic with a group before you start writing. Ask the group to "play audience," by reacting to your reasons, raising objections, and asking questions.

topic a. Early-morning classes should be abolished at your college.
audience: the dean of academic affairs

topic b. College students should get discounts at movie theaters.
audience: the owner of your local movie theater

topic c. Your college should provide a day-care facility for students with children.
audience: the president of your college

topic d. Businesses should hire more student interns.
audience: the president of a company (name it) you'd like to work for

3. Write a paragraph for or against any of the following topics. The audience for this argument is your classmates and your instructor.

For or Against

a. seat belt laws
b. hidden cameras to catch drivers who run red lights
c. dress codes in high school
d. uniforms in elementary schools
e. mandatory student activities fees for commuter students at colleges and universities
f. a law requiring a month waiting period between buying a marriage license and getting married
g. a higher tax on cigarettes to be used to pay the health costs of smokers with smoking-related illnesses

4. Visit your state's Department of Motor Vehicles Web site. Review the penalties for DUI (Driving Under the Influence of Alcohol) or DWI (Driving While Intoxicated). Argue for or against one of these penalties, and be sure to be as logical as possible. As an alternative, argue in favor of stricter penalties for either DUI or DWI in your city or state.

Computer

5. Some educators and parents are very concerned about the potentially harmful effects of violent video games on children. Using a search engine such as Google™ or Alta Vista™, type in the words "video games" and "action." See if you can find the manufacturer's description of a video game you have played, and find the targeted age range. Using this information, argue for or against this point: (*Name of the video game*) is suitable for children ages ___ to ___.

Computer

6. Study the photograph at the top of the next page. Then argue for some way to solve this congestion. You may want to argue for widening the road, better public transportation, carpooling, staggered work hours, or another solution.

7. Study the photograph below. Pretend this alley is near your home, and argue for a way to keep it clean.

Note: Additional writing options suitable for argument-related assignments can be found after the professional reading, "Sidewalks Can Make a Town a Neighborhood," which begins on page 632 .

How Do I Get a Better Grade?

Name: _____ Section: _____

Peer Review Form for an Argument Paragraph

After you've written a draft of your argument paragraph, let a writing partner read it. When your partner has completed the form below, discuss the comments. Then repeat the same process for your partner's paragraph.

The topic sentence has this subject: _____

_____

It takes this stand: _____

_____

The most convincing part of the paragraph started with the words _____

_____and ended with the words_____

_____

After reading this paragraph, I can think of an objection to this argument. The objection is _____

_____

_____

The paragraph has/has not handled this objection. (Choose one.)

The part of the argument with the best details is the part about _____

_____

The part that could use more or better details is the part about _____

_____

The order of the reasons (a) is effective (b) could be better. (Choose one.)

I have questions about _____

_____

Other comments: _____

_____

_____

_____

_____

_____

Reviewer's name: _____

CHAPTER 11

Jumping In

The construction of a well-built home requires careful designing, a solid foundation, and sturdy framing. Similarly, an effective **essay** *stems from careful planning, a solid foundation of well-constructed paragraphs, and meticulous attention to details.*

Writing an Essay

WHAT IS AN ESSAY?

You write an essay when you have more to say than can be covered in one paragraph. An **essay** can consist of one paragraph, but in this book, we take it to mean a writing of more than one paragraph. An essay has a main point, called a *thesis*, supported by subpoints. The subpoints are the *topic sentences*. Each paragraph in the *body*, or main part, of the essay has a topic sentence. In fact, each paragraph in the body of the essay is like the paragraphs you've already written because each one makes a point and then supports it.

Comparing the Single Paragraph and the Essay

Read the paragraph and the essay that follow, both about Bob, the writer's brother. You will notice many similarities.

A Single Paragraph

I think I'm lucky to have a brother who is two years older than I am. For one thing, my brother Bob fought all the typical child-parent battles, and I was the real winner. Bob was the one who made my parents understand that seventeen-year-olds shouldn't have an 11:00 p.m. curfew on weekends. He fought for his rights. By the time I turned seventeen, my parents had accepted the later curfew, and I didn't have to fight for it. Bob also paved the way for me at school. He was such a great athlete that I benefited from his reputation. When I tried out for the basketball team, I had an advantage before I hit the court. I was Bob Cruz's younger brother, so the coach thought I had to be pretty good. At home and at school, my big brother was a big help to me.

An Essay

Some people complain about being the youngest child or the middle child in the family. These people believe older children get all the attention and grab all the power. I'm the younger brother in my family, and I disagree with the complainers. I think I'm lucky to have a brother who is two years older than I am.

For one thing, my brother Bob fought all the typical child-parent battles, and I was the real winner. Bob was the one who made my parents understand that seventeen-year-olds shouldn't have an 11:00 p.m. curfew on weekends. He fought for his rights, and the fighting wasn't easy. I remember months of arguments between Bob and my parents as Bob tried to explain that not all teens on the street at 11:30 are punks or criminals. Bob was the one who suffered from being grounded or who lost the use of my father's car. By the time I turned seventeen, my parents had accepted the later curfew, and I didn't have to fight for it.

Bob also paved the way for me at school. Because he was so popular with the other students and the teachers, he created a positive image of what the boys in our family were like. When I started school, I walked into a place where people were ready to like me, just as they liked Bob. I remember the first day of class when the teachers read the new class rolls. When they got to my name, they asked, "Are you Bob Cruz's brother?" When I said yes, they smiled. Bob's success opened doors for me in school sports, too. He was such a great athlete that I benefited from his reputation. When I tried out for the basketball team, I had an advantage before I hit the court. I was Bob Cruz's younger brother, so the coach thought I had to be pretty good.

I had many battles to fight as I grew up. Like all children, I had to struggle to gain independence and respect. In my struggles at home and at school, my big brother was a big help to me.

If you read the two selections carefully, you noticed that they make the same main point, and they support that point with two subpoints.

main point: I think I'm lucky to have a brother who is two years older than I am.

subpoints: 1. My brother Bob fought all the typical child-parent battles, and I was the real winner.

2. Bob also paved the way at school.

You also noticed that the essay is longer because it has more details and examples to support the points.

ORGANIZING AN ESSAY

INSTRUCTOR'S NOTE

Throughout this chapter, the terms "thesis" and "thesis statement" are used interchangeably.

TEACHING TIP

Tell students that the thesis statement is the controlling idea for the essay much like a topic sentence is the controlling idea for a paragraph.

When you write an essay of more than one paragraph, the **thesis** is the focus of your entire essay; it is the major point of your essay. The other important points that relate to the thesis are in topic sentences.

> **Thesis:** Working as a salesperson has changed my character.
>
> **Topic sentence:** I have learned patience.
>
> **Topic sentence:** I have developed the ability to listen.
>
> **Topic sentence:** I have become more tactful.

Notice that the thesis expresses a bigger idea than the topic sentences below it and is supported by the topic sentences. The essay has an introduction, a body, and a conclusion.

1. **Introduction:** The first paragraph is usually the introduction. The thesis is included in this paragraph.
2. **Body:** This central part of the essay is the part where you support your main point (the thesis). Each paragraph in the body of the essay has its own topic sentence.
3. **Conclusion:** Usually one paragraph long, the conclusion reminds the reader of the thesis.

Writing the Thesis

There are several characteristics of a thesis:

1. It is expressed in a sentence. A thesis is *not* the same as the topic of the essay or the title of the essay:

   topic: quitting smoking
   title: Why I Quit Smoking
   thesis: I quit smoking because I was concerned for my health, and I wanted to prove to myself that I could break the habit.

INSTRUCTOR'S NOTE

Some students will have difficulty breaking the habit of "announcing" what the essay will be about.

2. A thesis *does not announce*; it makes a point about the subject.

   announcement: This essay will explain the reasons why young adults should watch what they eat.
   thesis: Young adults should watch what they eat so that they can live healthy lives today and prevent future health problems.

3. A thesis *is not too broad.* Some ideas are just too big to cover well in an essay. A thesis that tries to cover too much can lead to a superficial or boring essay.

   too broad: People all over the world should work on solving their interpersonal communications problems.
   acceptable thesis: As a southerner, I had a hard time understanding that some New Yorkers think slow speech is ignorant speech.

4. A thesis *is not too narrow.* Sometimes, writers start with a thesis that looks good because it seems specific and precise. Later, when they try to support such a thesis, they can't find anything to say.

   too narrow: My sister pays forty dollars a week for a special formula for her baby.
   acceptable thesis: My sister had no idea what it would cost to care for a baby.

Hints for Writing a Thesis

1. Your thesis can **mention the specific subpoints** of your essay. For example, your thesis might be

   I hated *The Revenge of the Shark People* because the film's plot was disorganized, its conflict was unrealistic, and its scenes were overly violent.

   With this thesis, you have indicated the three subpoints of your essay: *The Revenge of the Shark People* had a disorganized plot, it had an unrealistic conflict, and it had overly violent scenes.

2. You can **make a point** without listing your subpoints. For example, you can write a thesis like this:

   I hated *The Revenge of the Shark People* because it was a bloody mess.

   With this thesis, you can still use the subpoints stating that the movie had a disorganized plot, an unrealistic conflict, and overly violent scenes. You just don't have to mention all your subpoints in the thesis.

Exercise 1 Recognizing Good Thesis Sentences

Following is a list of thesis statements. Some are acceptable, but others are too broad or too narrow. Some are announcements; others are topics, not sentences. Put a *G* next to the good thesis sentences.

TEACHING TIP

Ask students if they can spot which statements are actually fragments and thus not suitable for a thesis statement (2 and 7).

1. __*G*__ My brother spent some time in prison, but he has turned that experience into a mission to help the children of prisoners.

2. _____ The emotions that keep me from succeeding in a career.

3. _____ Alcoholism is a factor in the breakup of many marriages.

4. __*G*__ A basketball coach taught me three ways to stay healthy.

5. __*G*__ Next semester's increase in tuition will affect my plans for graduating in the spring.

6. _____ The price of oil affects the economy of nations across the globe.

7. _____ Why burglary is increasing at the Liberty Mall.

8. _____ Treating our veterans with care and respect is an issue in our country today.

9. _____ My employer suddenly changed the rules on overtime pay.

10. _____ How fathers can find fun and free activities to share with their children will be explained in this essay.

Exercise 2 Selecting a Good Thesis Sentence

In each pair of thesis statements following, put a *G* next to the good one.

1. a. __*G*__ Several local agencies are happy to accept donations of old clothes and furniture and make donating simple.

   b. _____ What to do with old clothes and furniture is the subject of this essay.

2. a. _____ David went to Houston last week.

   b. _G_ David went to Houston last week because he is looking for a job with a future and for a city lifestyle.

3. a. _G_ The psychological rewards of volunteering include a sense of purpose, an increase in self-esteem, and an opportunity to connect to others.

   b. _____ The psychological rewards of volunteering will be discussed in this essay.

4. a. _____ Global warming is such a threat to the earth that every nation must take immediate action to protect future generations from disaster.

   b. _G_ Our college should sponsor a series of lectures to introduce the community to some simple ways to reduce global warming.

5. a. _G_ Standardized state exit tests put some high school seniors in a difficult situation.

   b. _____ Standardized state exit tests and the problems of some high school seniors.

Exercise 3 Writing a Thesis That Relates to the Subpoints

Following are lists of subpoints that could be discussed in an essay. Write a thesis for each list. Remember that there are two ways to write a thesis: you can write a thesis that includes the specific subpoints, or you can write one that makes a point without listing the subpoints. As an example, the first one is done for you, using both kinds of thesis sentences.

1. **one kind of thesis:** *If you want a pet, a cat is easier to care for than a dog.*

   _____

   another kind of thesis: *Cats make better pets than dogs because cats don't need to be walked, don't mind being alone, and don't make any noise.*

   subpoints: a. Cats don't have to be walked and exercised, like dogs do.
   b. Cats are independent and don't mind being home alone, but a dog gets lonely.
   c. Cats are quieter than dogs.

INSTRUCTOR'S NOTE

Answers will vary. Possible answers shown.

2. **thesis:** *An office romance can be fun but risky.*

   _____

   subpoints: a. An office romance can make going to work fun for the lovers.
   b. An office romance gone wrong can poison the atmosphere at the workplace.

3. **thesis:** *Working together will naturally result in some office romances.*

   _____

   subpoints: a. People who work together can get to know each other well over the many hours spent together.

    b. They often become friends and allies.

    c. The shared experiences and close friendship of the job can develop mutual trust and understanding.

    d. Workers who spend long hours together, trust each other, and feel comfortable together can easily fall in love.

4. thesis: _Cousins can play the roles of sisters, brothers, parents, or best friends._

subpoints:

    a. For an only child, cousins can take the place of sisters or brothers.

    b. Older cousins can play the role of parents.

    c. Cousins can also become best friends.

WRITING THE ESSAY IN STEPS

In an essay, you follow the same steps you learned in writing a paragraph—prewriting, planning, drafting, and polishing—but you adapt them to the longer essay form.

> **PREWRITING**   Gathering Ideas: An Essay

Often, you begin by _narrowing a topic_. Your instructor may give you a large topic so that you can find something smaller, within the broad one, that you would like to write about.

    Some students think that because they have several paragraphs to write, they should pick a big topic, one that will give them enough to say. But big topics can lead to boring, superficial, general essays. A smaller topic can challenge you to find the specific, concrete examples and details that make an essay effective.

    If your instructor asked you to write about college, for instance, you might _freewrite_ some ideas as you narrow the topic:

narrowing the topic of college

what college means to me—too big, and it could be boring
college vs. high school—everyone might choose this topic
college students—too big
college students who have jobs—better!
problems of working and going to college—OK!

In your freewriting, you can consider your _purpose_—to write an essay about some aspect of college—and _audience_—your instructor and classmates. Your narrowed topic will appeal to this audience because many students hold jobs and instructors are familiar with the problems of working students.

Listing Ideas

Once you have a narrow topic, you can use whatever process works for you. You can brainstorm by writing a series of questions and answers about your topic, you can freewrite on the topic, you can list ideas on the topic, or you can do any combination of these processes.

    Following is a sample listing of ideas on the topic of the problems of working and going to college.

problems of working and going to college

early classes	*weekends only time to study*
too tired to pay attention	*no social life*
tried to study at work	*apartment a mess*
got caught	*missed work for makeup test*
got reprimanded	*get behind in school*
slept in class	*need salary for tuition*
constantly racing around	*rude to customers*
no sleep	*girlfriend ready to kill me*
little time to do homework	

Clustering the Ideas

By clustering related items on the list, you'll find it easier to see the connections between ideas. The following items have been clustered (grouped), and they have been listed under a subtitle.

Problems of Working and Going to College: Ideas in Clusters

problems at school	*problems at work*
early classes	*tried to study at work*
too tired to pay attention	*got caught*
slept in class	*got reprimanded*
little time to do homework	*missed work for makeup test*
get behind in school	*rude to customers*

problems outside of work and school

weekends only time to study
no social life
apartment a mess
girlfriend ready to kill me

TEACHING TIP

This is a good place to remind students that thesis statements are often not segmented. However, students should be advised that some writing instructors prefer a segmented thesis statement because it provides students with the direction and organization of the essay's body paragraphs.

When you surveyed the clusters, you probably noticed that some of the ideas from the original list were left out. These ideas—on racing around, not getting enough sleep, and needing tuition money—could fit into more than one place and might not fit anywhere. You might come back to them later.

When you name each cluster by giving it a subtitle, you move toward a focus for each body paragraph of your essay. And by beginning to focus the body paragraphs, you start thinking about the main point, the thesis of the essay. Concentrating on the thesis and on focused paragraphs helps you to *unify* your essay.

Reread the clustered ideas. When you do so, you'll notice that each cluster is about problems at a different place. You can incorporate that concept into a thesis with a sentence like this:

> *Students who work while they attend college face problems at school, at work, and at home.*

Once you have a thesis and a list of details, you can begin working on the planning part of your essay.

Exercise 4 Narrowing Topics

Collaborate

Working with a partner or a group, narrow these topics so that the new topics are related, but smaller and suitable for short essays between four and six paragraphs long. The first topic is narrowed for you.

1. **topic:** summer vacation
   smaller, related topics:

   a. *a car trip with children* _____

   b. *finding the cheapest flight to Mexico* _____

   c. *my vacation job* _____

2. **topic:** sports
   smaller, related topics:

   INSTRUCTOR'S NOTE

   Answers will vary. Possible answers shown at left.

   a. *breaking my nose playing ice hockey* _____

   b. *Super Bowl commercials* _____

   c. *living with a soccer fanatic* _____

3. **topic:** fear
   smaller, related topics:

   a. *conquering my fear of heights* _____

   b. *why my best friend fears looking ridiculous* _____

   c. *a new mother's fear for her child* _____

4. **topic:** money
   smaller, related topics:

   a. *what to do with loose change* _____

   b. *giving a child an allowance* _____

   c. *saving money on car insurance* _____

Exercise 5 Clustering Related Ideas

Following are two topics, each with a list of ideas. Mark all the related items on the list with the same number (1, 2, or 3). Not all items will get a number. When you've finished marking the list, write a title for each number that explains the cluster of ideas.

1. **topic:** a sleepless night

   __*1*__ a loud party going on in the apartment upstairs

   __*3*__ I lay there and thought about my early morning math exam

   __*3*__ became stressed about sleeping through the alarm

   __*1*__ car horns blared all night

   _____ saw car lights coming through the window

   __*2*__ my air conditioner broke down

   __*3*__ started obsessing about my grades

   __*1*__ doors slammed and car alarms screamed

   __*2*__ I was sweating into a damp pillow

   __*2*__ the sheets stuck to my clammy skin

INSTRUCTOR'S NOTE

Title answers will vary. Possible answers shown at right.

The ideas marked 1 can be titled _noises_

The ideas marked 2 can be titled _heat_

The ideas marked 3 can be titled _worries_

    2. topic: why Valentine's Day can be stressful

       _1_   getting cards in elementary school a popularity contest

       _2_   adults search for the right gift for a loved one

       _2_   adults hope their loved one will remember them

       _3_   florists compete to make money

       _3_   jewelers face a huge selling season

       _1_   school children get teased for secret crushes

       _3_   candy stores struggle to sell the most chocolate

       _2_   lonely men and women feel unloved

       _3_   red bows on teddy bears offer love for sale in every drugstore

       _1_   some children cannot afford to give cards

The items marked 1 can be titled _pressure on children_

The items marked 2 can be titled _pressure on adults_

The items marked 3 can be titled _commercial pressures_

PLANNING   **Devising a Plan: An Outline for an Essay**

In the next stage of writing your essay, draft an outline. Use the thesis to focus your ideas. There are many kinds of outlines, but all are used to help a writer organize ideas. When you use a **formal outline**, you show the difference between a main idea and its supporting detail by *indenting* the supporting detail. In a formal outline, Roman numerals (numbers I, II, III, and so on) and capital letters are used. Each Roman numeral represents a paragraph, and the letters beneath the numeral represent supporting details.

The Structure of a Formal Outline

first paragraph	I. Thesis
second paragraph	II. Topic sentence
	A.
	B.
details	C.
	D.
	E.
third paragraph	III. Topic sentence
	A.
	B.
details	C.
	D.
	E.

TEACHING TIP

Tell students that the thesis will be only one sentence (statement) and that they should expect to develop some general statements to lead into the thesis statement. (See "Hints for Writing the Introduction" on pp. 250–252.)

fourth paragraph	IV.	Topic sentence
		A.
		B.
details		C.
		D.
		E.
fifth paragraph	V.	Conclusion

Hints for Outlining

Developing a good, clear outline now can save you hours of confused, dis-organized writing later. The extra time you spend to make sure your outline has sufficient details and that *each paragraph stays on one point* will pay off in the long run.

1. Check the topic sentences. Keep in mind that each topic sentence in each body paragraph should support the thesis sentence. If a topic sentence is not carefully connected to the thesis, the structure of the essay will be confusing. Here are a thesis and a list of topic sentences; the topic sentence that does not fit is crossed out:

thesis:	I.	A home-cooked dinner can be a rewarding experience for the cook and the guests.
topic	II.	Preparing a meal is a satisfying activity.
sentences:	III.	It is a pleasure for the cook to see guests enjoy the meal.
	IV.	~~Many recipes are handed down through generations.~~
	V.	Dinner guests are flattered that someone cooked for them.
	VI.	Dining at home is a treat for everyone at the table or in the kitchen.

Since the thesis of this outline is about the pleasure of dining at home for the cook and the guests, topic sentence IV doesn't fit: it isn't about the joy of cooking *or* of being a dinner guest. It takes the essay off track. A careful check of the links between the thesis and the topic sentences will help keep your essay focused.

2. Include enough details. Some writers believe that they don't need many details in the outline. They feel they can fill in the details later, when they actually write the essay. Even though some writers do manage to add details later, others who are in a hurry or who run out of ideas will have problems.

For example, imagine that a writer has included very few details in an outline, like this outline for a paragraph:

II. A burglary makes the victim feel unsafe.
  A. The person has lost property.
  B. The person's home territory has been invaded.

The paragraph created from that outline might be too short, lack specific details, and look like this:

A burglary makes the victim feel unsafe. First of all, the victim has lost property. Second, a person's home territory has been invaded.

If you have difficulty thinking of ideas when you write, try to tackle the problem in the outline. The more details you put into your outline, the more detailed and effective your draft essay will be. For example, suppose the same outline on the burglary topic had more details, like this:

II. A burglary makes the victim feel unsafe.

more details about burglary
- A. The person has lost property.
- B. The property could be worth hundreds of dollars.
- C. The victim can lose a television or camera or DVD player.
- D. The burglars may take cash.
- E. Worse, items with personal value, like family jewelry or heirlooms, can be stolen.

more details about safety concerns
- F. Even worse, a person's territory has been invaded.
- G. People who thought they were safe know they are not safe.
- H. The fear is that the invasion can happen again.

You will probably agree that the paragraph will be more detailed, too.

3. Stay on one point. It is a good idea to check the outline of each body paragraph to see whether the paragraph stays on one point. Compare each topic sentence, which is at the top of the list for the paragraph, against the details indented under it. Staying on one point gives each paragraph unity.

Below is the outline for a paragraph that has problems staying on one point. See if you can spot the problem areas.

III. Sonya is a generous person.

A. I remember how freely she gave her time when our club had a car wash.
B. She is always willing to share her lecture notes with me.
C. Sonya gives 10 percent of her salary to her church.
D. She is a member of Big Sisters and spends every Saturday with a disadvantaged child.
E. She can read people's minds when they are in trouble.
F. She knows what they are feeling.

The topic sentence of the paragraph is about generosity. However, sentences E and F talk about Sonya's insight, not her generosity.

When you have a problem staying on one point, you can solve the problem two ways:

1. Eliminate details that do not fit your main point.
2. Change the topic sentence to cover all the ideas in the paragraph.

For example, you could cut out sentences E and F about Sonya's generosity, getting rid of the details that do not fit. As an alternative, you could change the topic sentence in the paragraph so that it relates to all the ideas in the paragraph. A better topic sentence is "Sonya is a generous and insightful person."

Revisiting the Prewriting Stage

Writing an outline can help you identify undeveloped places in your plan, places where your paragraphs will need more details. You can get these details in two ways:

1. Go back to the writing you did in the prewriting stage. Check whether items on a list, or ideas from prewriting, can lead you to more details for your outline.

2. Brainstorm for more details by a question-and-answer approach. For example, if the outline includes "My apartment is a mess," you might ask, "Why? How messy?" Or if the outline includes "I have no social life," you might ask, "What do you mean? No friends? No activities? Or what about school organizations?"

The time you spend writing and revising your outline will make it easier for you to write an essay that is well developed, unified, and coherently structured. The checklist below may help you to revise.

Checklist: A Checklist for Revising the Outline of an Essay

✓ **Unity:** Do the thesis and topic sentences all lead to the same point? Does each paragraph make one, and only one, point? Do the details in each paragraph support the topic sentence? Does the conclusion unify the essay?

✓ **Support:** Do the body paragraphs have enough supporting details?

✓ **Coherence:** Are the paragraphs in the most effective order? Are the details in each paragraph arranged in the most effective order?

A sentence outline on the problems of working and going to college follows. It includes the thesis in the first paragraph. The topic sentences have been created from the titles of the ideas clustered earlier. The details have been drawn from ideas in the clusters and from further brainstorming. The conclusion has just one sentence that unifies the essay.

An Outline for an Essay

paragraph 1	I. Thesis: Students who work while going to college face problems at school, at work, and at home.
paragraph 2 **topic sentence** **details**	II. Trying to juggle job and school responsibilities creates problems at school. A. Early classes are difficult. B. I am too tired to pay attention. C. Once I slept in class. D. I have little time to do homework. E. I get behind in school assignments.
paragraph 3 **topic sentence** **details**	III. Work can suffer when workers attend college. A. I tried to study at work. B. I got caught by my boss. C. I was reprimanded. D. Sometimes I come to work very tired. E. When I don't have enough sleep, I can be rude to customers. F. Rudeness gets me in trouble. G. Another time, I had to cut work to take a makeup test.

continued

paragraph 4
topic sentence
details

IV. Working students suffer outside of classes and the workplace
    A. I work nights during the week.
    B. The weekends are the only time I can study.
    C. My apartment is a mess since I have no time to clean it.
    D. Worse, my girlfriend is ready to kill me because I have no social life.
    E. We never even go to the movies anymore.
    F. When she comes over, I am busy studying.

paragraph 5
conclusion

V. I have learned that working students have to be very organized to cope with their responsibilities at college, work, and home.

Exercise 6   Completing an Outline for an Essay

Following is part of an outline that has a thesis and topic sentences, but no details. Add the details and write in complete sentences. Write one sentence for each capital letter. Be sure that the details are connected to the topic sentence.

  I. Thesis: Automobiles today offer many features that drivers could not have imagined thirty years ago.

  II. Automobiles offer equipment to make driving and navigation easier.

INSTRUCTOR'S NOTE

Answers will vary. Possible answers shown at right.

    A. *Some cars have the capacity to parallel park themselves.*

    B. *Some have a sensor to warn of rear objects as drivers back out.*

    C. *Some offer an electronic tire gauge on the dashboard.*

    D. *One navigation system displays maps to any location.*

    E. *One includes voice commands for driving to a location.*

  III. Cars are more comfortable than ever before.

    A. *Dual air conditioning and heating zones control climate.*

    B. *Sun roofs can be shaded to moderate the sun's rays.*

    C. *Some cars offer heated seats.*

    D. *Some cars offer power seats for setting preferred positions.*

    E. *Some cars offer extra padding on the armrests.*

  IV. The options for entertainment and information have increased dramatically.

    A. *Satellite radio is becoming increasingly popular.*

    B. *Sound systems are more elaborate.*

    C. *DVD players offer music.*

D. *Screens offer movie DVDs.*

E. *Hands-free telephone systems are available.*

V. Today's automobiles are easier to drive, more luxurious to ride in, and more connected to entertainment and information sources.

Exercise 7   **Focusing an Outline for an Essay**

The outline below has a thesis and details, but it has no topic sentences for the body paragraphs. Write the topic sentences.

I. Thesis: I'll never buy Oliver Bennington clothes again.

II. *Oliver Bennington clothes are popular because of their image.*

INSTRUCTOR'S NOTE

Answers will vary. Possible answers shown at left.

A. Famous rappers wear the clothes.

B. Rich celebrities, living wild, glamorous lives and dressed in the latest Oliver Bennington styles, are often photographed for the tabloids.

C. Music videos show gorgeous women dancing in Oliver Bennington jeans and tee shirts.

D. A famous model appears in the Oliver Bennington advertisements.

E. The model and the advertisements are on giant billboards in Times Square.

F. The high price of Oliver Bennington clothes also makes them seem like quality products for special people.

III. *In reality, I found out the hard way that Oliver Bennington clothes have no quality at all.*

A. When I got an unexpected bonus at work, I decided to spend the money on some classy clothing.

B. Like many other people, I wanted a wardrobe with a famous label.

C. I quickly bought a jacket, two pairs of jeans, and two shirts with the famous Oliver Bennington label.

D. The first time I wore one of the shirts, it rained, and the color in the shirt bled into my skin.

E. The stitching on the jeans began to unravel after a couple of washings.

F. After I had worn the jacket for a month, the leather began to look dull and cracked.

IV. Thanks to my experience with Oliver Bennington clothes, I realized that the image of a product has nothing to do with its quality.

DRAFTING   Drafting and Revising: An Essay

When you are satisfied with your outline, you can begin drafting and revising the essay. Start by writing a first draft of the essay, which includes these parts: introduction, body paragraphs, and conclusion.

WRITING THE INTRODUCTION

Where Does the Thesis Go?

The **thesis** should appear in the introduction of the essay, in the first paragraph. But most of the time, it should not be the first sentence. In front of the thesis, write a few (three or more) sentences of introduction. Generally, the thesis is the *last sentence* in the introductory paragraph.

Why put the thesis at the end of the first paragraph? First of all, writing several sentences in front of your main idea gives you a chance to lead into it, gradually and smoothly. This will help you build interest and gain the reader's attention. Also, by placing the thesis after a few sentences of introduction, you will not startle the reader with your main point.

Finally, if your thesis is at the end of the introduction, it states the main point of the essay just before that point is supported in the body paragraphs. Putting the thesis at the end of the introduction is like putting an arrow pointing to the supporting ideas in the essay.

Hints for Writing the Introduction

There are a number of ways to write an introduction.

1. You can begin with some general statements that gradually lead to your thesis:

general statements	Students face all kinds of problems when they start college. Some students struggle with a lack of basic math skills; others have never learned to write a term paper. Students who were stars in high school have to cope with being just another social security number at a large institution. Students with small children have to find a way to be good parents and good students, too. Although all these problems are common, I found an even more typical conflict. <u>My biggest problem in college was learning to organize my time.</u>
thesis at end	

2. You can begin with a quotation that smoothly leads to your thesis. The quotation can be from someone famous, or it can be an old saying. It can be something your mother always told you, or it can be a slogan from an advertisement or the words of a song.

quotation	Everybody has heard the old saying, "Time flies," but I never really thought about that statement until I started college. I expected college to challenge me with demanding coursework. I expected it to excite me with the range of people I would meet. I even thought it might amuse me with the fun and intrigue of dating and romance.

thesis at end
But I never expected college to exhaust me. I was surprised to discover that <u>my biggest problem in college was learning to organize my time.</u>

> **Note:** You can add transition words or phrases to your thesis, as in the sample above.

3. You can tell a story as a way of leading into your thesis. You can open with the story of something that happened to you or to someone you know, a story you read about or heard on the news.

story
My friend Phyllis is two years older than I am, and so she started college before I did. When Phyllis came home from college for the Thanksgiving weekend, I called her with plans for fun, but Phyllis told me she planned to spend most of the weekend sleeping. I didn't understand her when she told me she was worn out. When I started college myself, I understood her perfectly. Phyllis was a victim of that old college ailment: not knowing how to handle time. I

thesis at end
developed the same disease. <u>My biggest problem in college was learning to organize my time.</u>

4. You can explain why this topic is worth writing about. Explaining could mean giving some background on the topic, or it could mean discussing why the topic is an important one.

explain
I do not remember a word of what was said during my freshman orientation, and I wish I did. I am sure somebody somewhere warned me about the problems I would face in college. I am sure somebody talked about getting organized. Unfortunately, I didn't listen, and I had to learn the hard way. I hope other students will listen and learn and be spared my hard lesson

thesis at end
and my big problem. <u>My biggest problem in college was learning to organize my time.</u>

5. You can use one or more questions to lead into your thesis. You can open with a question or questions that will be answered by your thesis. Or you can open with a question or questions that catch the reader's attention and move toward your thesis.

question
Have you ever stayed up all night to study for an exam, then fallen asleep at dawn and slept right through the time of the exam? If you have, then you were probably the same kind of college student I was. I was the student who always ran into class three minutes late, the one who begged for an extension on the term paper, the one who pleaded with the teacher to postpone the test. I just could not get things

thesis at end
done on schedule. <u>My biggest problem in college was learning to organize my time.</u>

6. You can open with a contradiction of your main point as a way of attracting the reader's interest and leading to your thesis. You can begin with an idea that is the opposite of what you will say in your thesis. The opposition of your opening and your thesis creates interest.

contradiction	People who knew me in my freshman year probably felt really sorry for me. They saw a girl with dark circles under her bloodshot eyes, a girl who was always racing from one place to another. Those people probably thought I was exhausted from overwork. But they were wrong. My problem in college was definitely not too much work; it was the way I
thesis at end	handled my work. <u>My biggest problem in college was learning to organize my time.</u>

Exercise 8 **Writing an Introduction**

Below are five thesis sentences. Pick one. Then write an introductory paragraph on the lines provided. Your last sentence should be the thesis sentence. If your instructor agrees, read your introduction to others in the class who wrote an introduction to the same thesis, or read your introduction to the entire class.

Thesis Sentences

1. Television should focus on how young adults really live.

2. Many people regularly participate in some form of gambling.

3. Cell phones can be an annoying piece of technology.

4. Three sports heroes represent what it means to be a true winner.

5. Standing up to a bully takes a special kind of person.

(Write an introduction) _____

_____

_____

_____

_____

_____

_____

WRITING THE BODY OF THE ESSAY

In the body of the essay, the paragraphs *explain*, *support*, and *develop* your thesis. In this part of the essay, each paragraph has its own topic sentence. The topic sentence in each paragraph does two things:

1. It focuses the sentences in the paragraph.

2. It makes a point connected to the thesis.

The thesis and the topic sentences are ideas that need to be supported by details, explanations, and examples. You can visualize the connections among the parts of an essay like this:

Introduction with Thesis

Body
{
Topic Sentence
   Details
Topic Sentence
   Details
Topic Sentence
   Details

Conclusion

When you write topic sentences, refer to the checklist below to help you organize your essay.

Checklist: A Checklist for the Topic Sentences of an Essay

✓   Does the topic sentence give the point of the paragraph?

✓   Does the topic sentence connect to the thesis of the essay?

How Long Are the Body Paragraphs?

Remember that the body paragraphs of an essay are the place where you explain and develop your thesis. Those paragraphs should be long enough to explain your points, not just list them. To do this well, try to make your body paragraphs *at least seven sentences* long. As you develop your writing skills, you may find that you can support your ideas in fewer than seven sentences.

Developing the Body Paragraphs

You can write well-developed body paragraphs by following the same steps you used in writing single paragraphs for the earlier assignments in this course. By working through the stages of gathering ideas, outlining, drafting, revising, editing, and proofreading, you can create clear, effective paragraphs.

To focus and develop the body paragraphs, ask the questions below as you revise:

Checklist: A Checklist for Developing Body Paragraphs for an Essay

✓   Does the topic sentence cover everything in the paragraph?

✓   Do I have enough details to support the topic sentence?

✓   Do all the details in the paragraph explain, develop, or illustrate the topic sentence?

Exercise 9   **Creating Topic Sentences**

Following are thesis sentences. For each thesis, write topic sentences (as many as indicated by the numbered blanks). The first one is done for you.

1. **thesis:** Cats make good pets.

   topic sentence 1: *Cats are independent and don't mind being home alone.*

   topic sentence 2: *Cats are easy to litter-train.*

   topic sentence 3: *Cats are fun to play with.*

2. **thesis:** My son is a curious and friendly toddler.

   topic sentence 1: *He loves to explore any new environment.*

   topic sentence 2: *He welcomes new children at his preschool.*

INSTRUCTOR'S NOTE

Answers will vary. Possible answers shown at right.

3. **thesis:** When students see a "Class Meeting Cancelled" notice posted on the classroom door, they have several reactions.

   topic sentence 1: *Many are happy to have a free hour or more.*

   topic sentence 2: *Some are irritated that they traveled to school for no reason.*

   topic sentence 3: *Some wonder if the instructor is ill.*

4. **thesis:** Joining the military can offer opportunities, but it can also present challenges.

   topic sentence 1: *Military service can provide a person with a chance for an education.*

   topic sentence 2: *Many young people develop maturity by serving in the military.*

   topic sentence 3: *Military training can be tough and brutal.*

   topic sentence 4: *Military life demands self-discipline.*

WRITING THE CONCLUSION

The last paragraph in the essay is the **conclusion**. It does not have to be as long as a body paragraph, but it should be long enough to unify the essay and remind the reader of the thesis. You can use any of these strategies in writing the conclusion

1. You can restate the thesis, in new words. Go back to the first paragraph of your essay and reread it. For example, this could be the first paragraph of an essay:

| introduction | Even when I was a child, I did not like being told what to do. I wanted to be my own boss. When I grew up, I figured that the best way to be my own boss was to own my own business. I thought that being in charge would be easy. I now know how difficult being an independent businessperson can be. |
| thesis at end | Independent business owners have to be smart, highly motivated, and hard-working. |

The thesis, underlined above, is the sentence that you can restate in your conclusion. Your task is to *keep the point but put it in different words.* Then work that restatement into a short paragraph, like this:

| restating the thesis | People who own their own business have to be harder on themselves than any employer would ever be. Their success is their own responsibility; they cannot blame company policy or rules because they set the policy and make the rules. If the business is to succeed, their intelligence, drive, and effort are essential. |

2. You can make a judgment, valuation, or recommendation. Instead of simply restating your point, you can end by making some comment on the issue you've described or the problem you've illustrated. If you were looking for another way to end the essay on owning one's own business, for example, you could end with a recommendation.

| ending with a recommendation | People often dream of owning their own business. Dreaming is easy, but the reality is tough. Those who want to succeed in their own venture should find a role model. Studying a role model would teach them how ambition, know-how, and constant effort lead to success. |

3. You can conclude by framing your essay. You can tie your essay together neatly by *using something from your introduction* as a way of concluding. When you take an example, or a question, or even a quotation from your first paragraph and refer to it in your last paragraph, you are "framing" the essay. Take another look at the introduction to the essay on owning your own business. The writer talks about not liking to be told what to do, being one's own boss, and believing that being in charge would be easy. The writer also mentions the need to be smart, highly motivated, and hard working. Now consider how the ideas of the introduction are used in this conclusion:

| frame frame | Children who do not like to take directions may think that being their own boss will be easy. Adults who try to start a business busi- ness soon discover that they must be totally |

frame	self-directed; that is, they must be strong
frame	enough to <u>keep learning,</u> to <u>keep pushing for-</u> <u>ward,</u> and to <u>keep working.</u>

Exercise 10   Choosing a Better Way to Restate the Thesis

Following are four clusters. Each cluster consists of a thesis sentence and two sentences that try to restate the thesis. Each restated sentence could be used as part of the conclusion to an essay. Put *B* next to the sentence in each pair that is a better restatement. Remember that the better choice repeats the same idea as the thesis but does not rely on too many of the same words.

1. **thesis:** Many people turn to the Internet because they are lonely.

    restatement 1: _____ When they are lonely, many people go to the Internet.

    restatement 2: _*B*_ Those who feel isolated can find company on the Internet.

2. **thesis:** Walking a dog is a good way to get exercise and meet people.

    restatement 1: _____ One way to get exercise and meet people is to walk a dog.

    restatement 2: _*B*_ Walking a dog is a healthy and social activity.

3. **thesis:** Gossiping is wrong, but everybody gossips.

    restatement 1: _*B*_ Gossip is a nasty but universal activity.

    restatement 2: _____ Everybody gossips even though gossiping is wrong.

4. **thesis:** Children are secure when they live in a family with a regular routine and consistent discipline.

    restatement 1: _____ Every child feels secure when his or her family follows a regular routine and uses consistent discipline.

    restatement 2: _*B*_ When a family lives by a regular schedule and consistent rules, children feel safe.

Revising the Draft

Once you have a rough draft of your essay, you can begin revising it. The following checklist may help you to make the necessary changes in your draft.

Checklist: Checklist for Revising the Draft of an Essay

✓   Does the essay have a clear, unifying thesis?

✓   Does the thesis make a point?

✓   Does each body paragraph have a topic sentence?

✓   Is each body paragraph focused on its topic sentence?

✓   Are the body paragraphs roughly the same length?

✓   Do any of the sentences need combining?

> ✓   Do any of the words need to be changed?
>
> ✓   Do the ideas seem to be smoothly linked?
>
> ✓   Does the introduction catch the reader's interest?
>
> ✓   Is there a definite conclusion?
>
> ✓   Does the conclusion remind the reader of the thesis?

Transitions within Paragraphs

In an essay, you can use two kinds of transitions: those within a paragraph and those between paragraphs.

Transitions that link ideas *within a paragraph* are the same kinds you used earlier. Your choice of words, phrases, or even sentences depends on the kind of connection you want to make. Here is a list of some common transitions and the kinds of connections they express.

INFO BOX: **Common Transitions within a Paragraph**

To join two ideas:

again	another	in addition	moreover
also	besides	likewise	similarly
and	furthermore		

To show a contrast or a different opinion:

but	instead	on the other hand	still
however	nevertheless	or	yet
in contrast	on the contrary	otherwise	

To show a cause-and-effect connection:

accordingly	because	for	therefore
as a result	consequently	so	thus

To give an example:

for example	in the case of	such as	to illustrate
for instance	like		

To show time:

after	first	recently	subsequently
at the same time	meanwhile	shortly	then
before	next	soon	until
finally			

Transitions between Paragraphs

When you write something that is more than one paragraph long, you need transitions that link each paragraph to the others. There are several effective ways to link paragraphs and remind the reader of your main idea and of how the smaller points connect to it. Restatement and repetition are two of these ways:

1. **Restate an idea** from the preceding paragraph at the start of a new paragraph. Look closely at the two paragraphs below and notice how the

second paragraph repeats an idea from the first paragraph and provides a link.

> If people were more patient, driving would be less of an ordeal. If, for instance, the driver behind me didn't honk his horn as soon as the traffic light turned green, both he and I would probably have lower blood pressure. He wouldn't be irritating himself by pushing so hard. Also, I wouldn't be reacting by slowing down, trying to irritate him even more, and getting angry at him. When I get impatient in heavy traffic, I just make a bad situation worse. My hurry doesn't get me to my destination any faster; it just stresses me out.

transition
restating an idea
> <u>The impatient driver doesn't get anywhere; neither does</u> the impatient customer at a restaurant. Impatience at restaurants doesn't pay. I work as a hostess at a restaurant, and I know that the customer who moans and complains about waiting for a table won't get one any faster than the person who makes the best of the wait. In fact, if a customer is too aggressive or obnoxious, the restaurant staff may actually slow down the process of getting that customer a table.

2. Use synonyms and repetition as a way of reminding the reader of an important point. For example, in the two paragraphs below, notice how certain repeated words, phrases, and synonyms all remind the reader of a point about facing fear. The repeated words and synonyms are underlined.

> Some people just <u>avoid</u> whatever they fear. I have an uncle who is <u>afraid</u> to fly. Whenever he has to go on a trip, he does anything he can to <u>avoid</u> getting on an airplane. He will drive for days, travel by train, take a bus trip. Because he is so <u>terrified</u> of flying, he lives with <u>constant anxiety</u> that someday he may have to fly. He is always thinking of the one emergency that could force him to <u>confront what he most dreads.</u> Instead of <u>dealing directly with his fear,</u> he lets it <u>haunt</u> him.
>
> Other people are even worse than my uncle. He won't <u>attack his fear</u> of something external. But there are people who won't <u>deal with their fear</u> of themselves. My friend Sam is a good example of this kind of person. Sam has a serious drinking problem. All of Sam's friends know he is an alcoholic. But Sam <u>will not admit</u> his addiction. I think he is <u>afraid to face</u> that part of himself. So he <u>denies</u> his problem, saying he can stop drinking any time he wants to. Of course, until Sam has the courage to <u>admit what he is most afraid of,</u> his alcoholism, he won't be able to change.

A Draft Essay

Below is a draft of the essay on working and going to college. As you read it, you'll notice many changes from the outline on pages 247–248:

- An introduction has been added, written in the first person, "I," to unify the essay.
- Transitions have been added within and between paragraphs.
- General statements have been replaced by more specific ones.
- Word choice has been improved.
- A conclusion has been added. Some of the ideas added to the conclusion came from the original list of ideas about the topic of work and school. They are ideas that do not belong in the body paragraphs but are useful in the conclusion.

A Draft of an Essay

(Thesis and topic sentences are underlined.)

I work thirty hours a week at the front desk of a motel in Riverside. When I first signed up for college classes, I figured college would be fairly easy to fit into my schedule. After all, college students are not in class all day, as high school students are. So I thought the twelve hours a week I'd spend in class wouldn't be too much of a load. But I was in for a big surprise. <u>My first semester at college showed me that students who work while going to school face problems at school, at work, and at home.</u>

<u>First of all, trying to juggle job and school responsibilities creates problems at school.</u> Early morning classes, for example, are particularly difficult for me. Because I work every weeknight from 6:00 p.m. to 12:00 a.m., I don't get home until 1:00 a.m., and I can't fall asleep until 2:00 a.m. or later. I am too tired to pay attention in my 8:00 a.m. class. Once, I even fell asleep in that class. My work hours create other conflicts. They cut into my study time, so I have little time to do all the assigned reading and papers. I get behind in these assignments, and I never seem to have enough time to catch up. Consequently, my grades are not as good as they could be.

Because I both work and go to school, I have problems doing well at school. But <u>work can also suffer when workers attend college.</u> Students can bring school into the workplace. One night I tried to study at work, but my boss caught me reading my biology textbook at the front desk. I was reprimanded, and now my boss doesn't trust me. Sometimes I come to work very tired. When I don't get enough sleep, I can be rude to motel guests who give me a hard time. Then the rudeness can get me into trouble. I remember one particular guest who reported me because I was sarcastic to her. She had spent a half hour complaining about her bill, and I had been too tired to be patient. Once again, my boss reprimanded me. Another time, school interfered with my job when I had to cut work to take a makeup test. I know my boss was unhappy with me then, too.

As a working student, I run into trouble on the job and at college. <u>Working students also suffer outside of college and the workplace.</u> Since I work nights during the week, the weekends are the only time I can study. Because I have to use my weekends to do schoolwork, I can't do other things. My apartment is a mess since I have no time to clean it. Worse, my girlfriend is ready to kill me because I have no social life. We never even go to the movies anymore. When she comes over, I am busy studying.

continued

With responsibilities at home, work, and college, I face a cycle of stress. I am constantly racing around, and I can't break the cycle. I want a college education, and I must have a job to pay my tuition. The only way I can manage is to learn to manage my time. <u>I have learned that working students have to be very organized to cope with their responsibilities at college, work, and home.</u>

Exercise 11 Identifying the Main Points in the Draft of an Essay

Below is the draft of a four-paragraph essay. Read it, then reread it and underline the thesis and the topic sentences in each body paragraph and in the conclusion.

DISCUSSION QUESTION

This essay is about what one volunteer learned by working with children. Ask students if they have worked with youngsters and what aspects of the experience they find memorable. This discussion could spark ideas for potential essay topics.

Until this year, I had never considered spending my free time helping others in my community. Volunteer work, I thought, was something retired folks and rich people did to fill their days. Just by chance, I became a volunteer for the public library's Classic Connection, a group that arranges read-a-thons and special programs for elementary school children. <u>Although I don't receive a salary, working with some perceptive and entertaining third graders has been very rewarding in other ways.</u>

<u>Currently, I meet with my small group of four girls and three boys each Saturday morning from ten to eleven o'clock, and they have actually taught me more than I ever thought possible.</u> I usually assign the children various passages in an illustrated children's classic like <u>The Little Prince</u>, and I help them with the difficult words as they read aloud. When I occasionally read to them, they follow right along, but when it's their turn, they happily go off track. I've learned that each child has a mind of his or her own, and I now have much more respect for day-care workers and elementary school teachers who must teach, entertain, and discipline thirty rowdy children all day long. I'm tired after one hour with just seven children.

<u>I have also learned the value of careful planning.</u> I arrive at each session with a tape recorder and have the children record sound effects related to the story we'll be reading. At certain points during the session, we stop to hear the sound effects. They love to hear themselves and seem more focused on reading when I use this method. I feel more relaxed when I am well prepared and the sessions go smoothly.

<u>I have enjoyed making several new friends and contacts through the Classic Connection.</u> I've become friendly with the parents of the kids in my reading group,

and one of the fathers has offered me a good-paying job at his printing business.
He even mentioned he could be flexible about my schedule. I asked him if he
could help me put a collection together of the group's most outrageous original
stories, and he said he'd be glad to do it in his free time. I've thus learned that the
spirit of volunteerism is indeed contagious.

 I plan to keep volunteering for the Classic Connection's programs and look
forward to a new group that should be starting soon. I don't know if I'm ready to
graduate to an older group. <u>After all, third graders still have much to teach me.</u>

Exercise 12   Adding Transitions to an Essay

The following essay needs transitions. Add the transitions where indicated,
and add the kind of transition—word, phrase, or sentence—indicated.

 When I started college, I hoped to make the kind of friends who would join
me for wild parties and daring adventures. I met several of these people and had
plenty of fun and excitement. At the same time, I met three people who, over time,
became close friends. None of the three is the kind of person I would have chosen
for a friend in high school. *However* (add a word or phrase), all of them are now
my friends and heroes.

 The first (add a word or phrase), Robinson Emile, was a puzzle to me, and it
took a long time for me to figure him out. He was in my English class, but for about a
month I barely noticed him because he never said a word. One day, when I was bored
in class and scanning the room, I saw a serious, focused person. This person was
Robinson, and he never took his eyes off the instructor. At the end of class, we spoke.
He was shy and had a foreign accent. I felt sorry for him because he seemed lonely. I
do not feel sorry for him anymore. I learned that he had come to the United States
from Haiti. After three years, Robinson had learned English, gotten two jobs, and
made his way to college. Today, I know that he is smart, funny, and generous with his
time. When he isn't working at his two jobs or going to school, he tutors me in algebra.

 Robinson is my quiet, determined friend and role model

(add a sentence). A different type of friend and hero is Mia Morales. Mia is
definitely not shy or even studious. In fact, I have to remind her about upcoming

INSTRUCTOR'S NOTE

For this exercise, students
may want to refer to the "Info
Box" on transitions on page
257.

INSTRUCTOR'S NOTE

Answers will vary. Possible
answers shown.

assignments or tests. I met Mia when we were in the same discussion group in child psychology class. Most of the group members were reluctant to talk, _but_ (add a word or phrase), Mia took charge. Within minutes, her bubbly style got us all participating. Mia is always cheerful and lively at school. _In addition_ (add a word or phrase), she is a devoted mother of three and a caring nursing assistant. Mia is always short of time and money. _However_ (add a word or phrase), she has enough positive energy for at least two people.

Mia and Robinson became my friends after we met in class (add a sentence). I met my third friend and hero in college, but not in class. He is Mr. Wells, and he is a counselor. _In fact_ (add a word or phrase), he is the busiest counselor at school. To see him, students line up outside his office. Even during the busy days of registration, Mr. Wells manages to calm, soothe, advise, and motivate each student. In my first semester at college, I wanted to drop out. Fortunately, a friend told me to see Mr. Wells. Mr. Wells never really advised or warned me. Instead, he listened. _Furthermore_ (add a word or phrase), he listened without criticizing me. Somehow, I left his office with new hopes for academic success. I still see Mr. Wells, just to talk. Recently, he told me that he had to try college three times before he truly committed to staying in school. I felt better after I heard that. I would like to have Mr. Wells' power to help people.

Most students expect college to improve their social lives and expand their group of friends. _On the other hand_ (add a word or phrase), few students expect to make friends like Mr. Wells, Mia, and Robinson. I think I'm lucky that these three came into my life.

| Exercise 13 | Recognizing Synonyms and Repetition Used to Link Ideas in an Essay |

In the following essay, underline all the synonyms and repetition (of words or phrases) that help remind the reader of the thesis sentence. (To help you, the thesis is underlined.)

I am a social person. I like to be with my family and friends. I enjoy their company at meals, sports events, parties, and college. I enjoy a long road trip with my brothers or my best friend. <u>However, there are times when I need to be by myself.</u>

Unless I am <u>alone,</u> I cannot really study. I have tried studying in a quiet area at the campus library, but I get distracted by looking at and listening to other people. I envy the students who can sprawl on the floor outside the classroom, focus on a textbook, and cram last-minute information before a test. <u>I could never concentrate in a hallway full of anxious people.</u> Even a study group where students share notes and help each other offers too much stimulation for me. I study <u>in solitude</u> at home.

<u>People come between me and my ability to study; they also block my appreciation of nature.</u> A day at the beach with friends is wonderful, but for me, a full experience of a sunset over the ocean <u>must be solitary.</u> Similarly, I like a <u>solo</u> walk in the rain and the <u>private</u> pleasure of sitting on my patio early in the morning, listening to the birds. On my break at work, I go off <u>by myself,</u> find a big tree, sit, and watch the squirrels play.

<u>I most need time away from others</u> when I try to solve a problem. I usually discuss any major problem with a friend or two first, and we might even consider my options. However, <u>I need to choose the best solution for me without depending on others.</u> Working through my conflicts, my needs, and the consequences of each choice is a complicated process. I have learned that I cannot rush to a quick or easy solution. For me, finding a way to deal with a problem takes thinking, but also patience. If I am patient and <u>alone,</u> I can discover what I should do. Digging deep inside my head and heart takes <u>self-reliance.</u>

Dealing with conflict, connecting to nature, and studying are very different activities. Yet they all require an intense concentration that helps me explore and connect ideas, experiences, and even emotions. Whether it is comprehending the connections in science or history, feeling the power of nature, or making the best personal choice, the <u>activity demands that I work alone.</u>

POLISHING Polishing and Proofreading: An Essay

Creating a Title

TEACHING TIP

Tell students that an essay title should be a phrase and not a sentence. Many students are tempted to reuse their thesis statement for the title.

When you are satisfied with the final version of your essay, you can begin preparing a good copy. Your essay will need a title. Try to think of a short title that is connected to your thesis. Since the title is the reader's first contact with your essay, an imaginative title can create a good first impression. If you can't think of anything clever, try using a key phrase from your essay.

The title is placed at the top of your essay, about an inch above the first paragraph. Always capitalize the first word of the title and all major words such as nouns, pronouns, verbs, adjectives, and adverbs. Minor words such as articles ("the," "an," "a"), prepositions ("of," "in," "between"), and coordinating conjunctions ("and," "but," "so") arc not capitalized unless they are the first or last words of the title. *Do not* underline or put quotation marks around your title.

The Final Version of an Essay

INSTRUCTOR'S NOTE

Remind students that this sample final version of an essay is reduced to fit within a textbook, and that in their essays, the title should be about one inch (or three lines) above the first paragraph.

Following is the final version of the essay on working and going to college. When you compare it to the draft on pages 259–260, you will notice some changes:

- In the first paragraph, the words "I thought" have been added to make it clear that the statement is the writer's opinion.
- One topic sentence, in paragraph 2, has been revised so that it includes the word "students" and the meaning is more precise.
- Words have been changed to sharpen the meaning.
- Transitions have been added.

A Final Version of an Essay

(Changes from the draft are underlined.)

Problems of the Working College Student

I work thirty hours a week at the front desk of a motel in Riverside. When I first <u>registered</u> for college classes, I figured college would be fairly easy to fit into my schedule. After all, <u>I thought,</u> college students are not in class all day, as high school students are. So I <u>assumed that</u> the twelve hours a week I'd spend in class wouldn't be too much of a load. But I was in for a big surprise. My first semester at college showed me that students who work while going to college face problems at school, at work, and at home.

First of all, <u>students who try</u> to juggle job and school responsibilities <u>find trouble at school</u>. Early morning classes, for example, are particularly difficult for me. Because I work every weeknight from 6.00 p.m. to 12.00 a.m., I don't get home until 1:00 a.m., and I can't fall asleep until 2:00 a.m., or later. <u>Consequently,</u> I am too tired to pay attention in my <u>eight o'clock class</u>. Once, I even fell asleep in that class. My work hours create other conflicts. They cut into my study time, so I have little time to do all the assigned reading and papers. I get behind in the assignments, and I never seem to have enough time to catch up. <u>As a result,</u> my grades are not as good as they could be.

Because I both work and go to school, I have problems doing well at school. But work can also suffer when workers attend college. Students can bring school into the workplace. <u>I've been guilty of this practice and have paid the price.</u> One night I tried to study at work, but my boss caught me reading my biology textbook at the front desk. I was reprimanded, and now my boss doesn't trust me. Sometimes I come to work very tired, <u>another problem.</u> When I don't get enough sleep, I can be rude to motel guests who give me a hard time. Then the rudeness can get me into trouble. I remember one particular guest who reported me because I was sarcastic to her. She had spent a half hour complaining about her bill, and I had been too tired to be patient. Once again, my boss reprimanded me. Another time, school interfered with my job when I had to cut work to take a makeup test. I know my boss was unhappy with me then, too.

As a working student, I run into trouble on the job and at college. Working students also suffer outside of classes and the workplace. <u>My schedule illustrates the conflicts of trying to juggle too many duties.</u> Since I work nights during the week, the weekends are the only time I can study. Because I have to use my weekends to do schoolwork, I can't do other things. My apartment is a mess since I have no time to clean it. Worse, my girlfriend is ready to kill me because I have no social life. We never even go to the movies anymore. When she comes over, I am busy studying.

With responsibilities at home, work, and college, I face a cycle of stress. I am constantly racing around, and I can't break the cycle. I want a college education, and I must have a job to pay my tuition. The only way I can manage is to learn to manage my time. <u>In my first semester at college, I've realized</u> that working students have to be very organized to cope with the responsibilities of college, work, and home.

Before you prepare the final copy of your essay, check your latest draft for errors in spelling, punctuation, typing, and formatting.

Exercise 14   Proofreading to Prepare the Final Version

Following are two essays with the kinds of errors that are easy to overlook when you prepare the final version of an assignment. Correct the errors, writing above the lines. There are twelve errors in the first essay and fifteen in the second.

Essay 1
The Best Times of My Day
"The Best Times of My Day"

Most of my life is routine. I go to work, I go to school, and I come home. This is

my schedule for most of the week. Even on weekends, I go to work and find
                                                            no comma needed
myself back at school, studying in the library. Even though, routines can be

boring, there are certain times of each day that I enjoy.
                                  occurs
One of the best parts of my day occur right after my alarm goes off. At that

moment, I feel wonderful. My bed is warm, and I am resting my head on soft

pillows and my body on a firm mattress. I am coming out of the deepest sleep of

Sometimes,

the night. Some times, I am half inside a terrific dream. Unfortunately, this part of

my day is short since I have to get up.

Another part of the day that I enjoy is my ten-minute break. I buy a large cup of

ten   *,*

coffee and relax. For 10 minutes, I don't study I don't call anyone on my cell

phone, and I don't even talk to anyone. I find a quiet corner at work and tune out

the world. I refuse to focus on my obligations and chores. Concentrating only on

the taste and warmth of the coffee, I recharge my batteries for the rest of the day.

The end of my day is my favorite time. Once again, I am alone. I stretch out on

,

the couch and listen to music. Sometimes my cat joins me curling up against my

motorcycle   *feel*

leg and purring like a motor cycle. I look back on my day and fill that I have

accomplished what I set out to do. At last, I can let go of my worries.

longs

Everybody long for those special holidays, vacations, or celebrations that are

never forgotten. I want them too, but I have realized that even the most ordinary

its pleasures

day has it's pleasure's. In fact, I can find three of these moments every day.

Essay 2

and

Children, Parents, And Respect

Everyone has experienced the bad behavior of others. Strangers cut ahead in

line, drivers tailgate in traffic, and diners leave no tip for a hardworking waiter.

members

Even family member's can be nasty. They gossip about each other, carry on end-

surprising

less feuds, and bring up old complaints at family gatherings. The most suprising

Children

bad behavior comes from children. children are expected to misbehave in small

ways, but today's children have a terrible lack of respect for their parents and

their parents' rules.

Most parents expect their children to act up at home. It is natural for little girls

and boys to be cranky when they are tired or bored after a long day at home.

Small children have not learned table manners, so parents expect the children to

spit out food they do not like or toss their Cheerios on the floor. However, today's

such as a

parents put up with much worse. They are used to constant defiance such a refusal to come to the table, to go to bed, or to stop hitting a sister or brother.

Today's children want what they want, and when they don't get it, they fight their

wear
enemies: their parents. When they where their parents down, the children feel an

uneasy victory.

no comma needed
  The same open defiance can be seen at restaurants. Parents suffer humiliation,

when their children refuse to sit still, be quiet, or stay in their seats. Any attempt

to restrain the boys and girls leads to shouting or screaming. The children, furious

restrained
that they have been restrain, begin to fight with their parents or with each other.

Even when the food arrives, some of it becomes a missile launched at a family

member. Since the poor parents do not want to look like monsters in front of the

diners
other dinncrs, they do little to calm their offspring. Meanwhile, the children push

harder to claim their parent's attention.

  Bad behavior becomes dangerous when children and parents move to more

open spaces. A child who has not learned to respect his parents may not respect

animals either, and may grab a dog by the ears or tail. That child may get bitten. A

child used to ignoring the word "no" can run into the street. A child who will not

come when called can wander off in a park or at the mall. Thirty seconds is

no comma needed
enough time, for a parent to lose a child who is exploring alone.

  Not every mischievous child is going to get lost, bitten, or injured Children

need to test boundaries as a part of maturing. Parents are caught in a bind. They

want their children to feel pure, unconditional love. They do not want to hurt a

boy girl   ,
small Boy or Girl by using harsh words or punishment yet they need to be in

children's
charge. By insisting on their childrens respect for rules, parents will give their

children the security of knowing the family limits.

Lines of Detail: A Walk-Through Assignment

Choose two radio stations that are popular with people your age. They can
be two stations that broadcast music or two stations that broadcast talk

programs. Write a four-paragraph essay describing who listens to each station. To write the essay, follow these steps:

Step 1: Begin with some investigation. Listen to two stations, talk or music, popular with your age group. Before you listen, prepare a list of at least six questions. The questions will help you gather details for your essay. For any radio station, you can ask:

What kinds of products, restaurants or services are advertised?

Does the station offer any contests?

Does the station sponsor any events?

For two music stations, your questions might include these:

What groups or solo artists does the station play?

What kind of music does it play?

For two talk-radio stations, your questions might include these:

What are the talk-show hosts like? Are they funny or insulting or serious?

What topics are discussed?

What kind of people call in?

Listen to the stations you chose, and as you listen, take notes. Answer your own questions, and write down anything about each station that catches your interest or that seems relevant.

Step 2: Survey your notes. Mark the related ideas with the same number. Then cluster the information you have gathered, and give each cluster a title.

Step 3: Focus all your clusters around one point. To find a focus, ask yourself whether the listeners of the two stations are people of the same social class, with the same interests, the same educational background, and the same ethnic or racial background.

Try to focus your information with a thesis like one of these:

_____ (station name) and _____ (station name) appeal

to the same audience.

_____ (station name) and _____ (station name) appeal

to different audiences.

_____ (station name) and _____ (station name) use

different strategies to appeal to the same kind of listeners.

_____ (station name) appeals to young people

who _____, but _____ (station name) appeals to young

people who _____.

While _____ (station name) is popular with middle-aged

listeners interested in _____, _____ (station name)

appeals to middle-aged listeners who like _____.

Step 4: Once you have a thesis and clustered details, draft an outline. Revise your draft outline until it is unified, expresses the ideas in a clear order, and has enough supporting details.

Step 5: Write a draft of your essay. Revise the draft, checking it for balanced paragraphs, relevant and specific details, a strong conclusion, and smooth transitions.

Step 6: Before you prepare the final version of your essay, check for spelling, word choice, punctuation, and mechanical errors. Also, give your essay a title.

Writing Your Own Essay

When you write on any of these topics, be sure to work through the stages of the writing process in preparing your essay.

1. Take any paragraph you have already written for this class and develop it into an essay of four or five paragraphs. If your instructor agrees, read the paragraph to a partner or group, and ask your listener(s) to suggest points inside the paragraph that could be developed into paragraphs of their own.

Collaborate

2. Write an essay using one of the following thesis statements:

If I won a million dollars, I know what I would do with it.
Most families waste our natural resources every day, simply by going through their daily routines.
Television's coverage of football [or basketball, or tennis, or any other sport you choose] could be improved by a few changes.
All bad romances share certain characteristics.
If I could be someone else, I'd like to be _____ for several reasons.

3. Write an essay on earliest childhood memories. Interview three classmates to gather detail and to focus your essay. Ask each one to tell you about his or her earliest childhood memory. Before you begin interviewing, make a list of questions like these: What is your earliest memory? How old were you at the time? What were you doing? Do you remember other people or events in that scene? If so, what were the others doing? Were you indoors? Outdoors? Is this a pleasant memory? Why do you think this memory has stayed with you? Use the details collected at the interviews to write a five-paragraph essay with a thesis sentence like one of the following:

Collaborate

Childhood memories vary a great deal from person to person.
The childhood memories of different people are surprisingly similar.
Although some people's first memories are painful, others remember a happy time.
Some people claim to remember events from their infancy, but others can't remember anything before their third (or fourth, fifth, etc.) birthday.

4. Freewrite for ten minutes on the two best days of your life. After you've completed the freewriting, review it. Do the two days have much in common? Or were they very different? Write a four-para-graph essay based on their similarities or differences, with a thesis like one of these:

The two best days of my life were both _____. (Focus on

similarities.)

While one of the best days of my life was _____, the other great

day was _____. (Fill in with differences.)

5. Write a five-paragraph essay on one of the following topics:

Three Careers for Me	Three Wishes
Three Decisions for Me	Three Workplace Friends
Three Family Traditions	Three Workplace Hazards
Three Lucky People	The Three Worst Jobs

6. Narrow one of the following topics and then write an essay on it. Remember that brainstorming and freewriting can help you narrow your focus.

animals	dreams	games	money	secrets
books	family	habits	music	students
celebrities	fashion	health	nature	teachers
crime	fears	lies	romance	travel

Computer

7. Many people are turning to online dating services as a way to meet people and potential partners. Find an online dating service and investigate its methods, claims, and fees. Based on your research, write an essay that takes a stand on the following statement:

_____, an online dating service, is ethical/unethical (choose

one) in its promises.

If you or someone you know has ever used an online dating serv-ice, write an essay based on the following statement:

Finding a suitable mate through an online dating service can be

a(n) _____ experience.

8. Look closely at the top photograph on page 271. Write a five-paragraph essay in which you describe a situation that the picture may represent. In one body paragraph, you can write about how these two people met and decided to head for New York; in another paragraph, about what they are hoping for as they stand together hitchhiking; and in another paragraph, about what may happen to them next.

9. Look closely at the photograph below. Write a four-paragraph essay in which you describe the relationship between the people in the photograph. You can use your imagination, but try to base your imaginings on the facial expressions and body language of the people.

Note: Additional writing options suitable for essay assignments can be found after three professional readings: "The Longest Day," which begins on page 635, "A Brother's Murder," which begins on page 643, and "Navajo Code Talkers: The Century's Best Kept Secret," which begins on page 647.

How Do I Get a Better Grade?

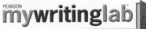

Visit www.mywritinglab.com for audio-visual lectures and additional practice sets about writing an essay.

Get a better grade with MyWritingLab!

Name: _____ Section: _____

Peer Review Form for an Essay

After you've written a draft of your essay, let a writing partner read it. When your partner has completed the form below, discuss the comments. Then repeat the same process for your partner's essay.

The thesis of this essay is _____

_____

The topic sentences for the body paragraphs are _____

_____

_____

_____

The topic sentence in the conclusion is _____

_____

The best part of the essay is the _____ (first, second, third, etc.) paragraph.

I would like to see details added to the part about _____

I would take out the part about _____

The introduction is (a) good or (b) could be better. (Choose one.)

The conclusion is (a) good or (b) could be better. (Choose one.)

I have questions about _____

Other comments: _____

_____

_____

_____

_____

_____

_____

_____

_____

Reviewer's name: _____

CHAPTER 12

Different Essay Patterns

You can write essays in a number of patterns, but any pattern will develop more easily if you follow the writing steps in preparing your essay. The examples in this chapter take you through the steps of preparing an essay in each pattern. Each sample essay expands on its related paragraph pattern in an earlier chapter of this book.

ILLUSTRATION

Hints for Writing an Illustration Essay

1. Use specific examples to support a general point. Remember that a *general* statement is a broad point, and a *specific* example is narrow.

general statement: The weather was terrible yesterday.
specific example: It rained for six hours.

general statement: I am having trouble in my math class.
specific example: I can't understand the problems in Chapter 12.

Jumping In

*Snowflakes come in an infinite variety of shapes and sizes, and while no two flakes are identical, they do share basic elements. Similarly, essays can be structured in **different patterns** and still share basic writing elements. Which pattern of writing covered in previous chapters (illustration, description, narration, etc.) did you find most effective for developing a paragraph? Do you think this pattern could also work well if you expanded your paragraph into an essay?*

2. Be sure that you support a general statement by using specific examples instead of merely writing another general statement.

> **not this: general statement:** The weather was terrible yesterday.
> **more general statements:** ~~It was awful outside.~~
> ~~Yesterday brought nasty weather.~~

> **but this: general statement:** The weather was terrible yesterday.
> **specific examples:** It rained for six hours.
> Several highways were flooded.

3. Be sure that you have sufficient examples and that you develop them well. If you use one or two examples and do not develop them effectively, you will have a skimpy paragraph. You can use fewer examples and develop each one, or you can use more examples and develop them less extensively.

not this: a skimpy paragraph:

The weather was terrible yesterday. It rained for six hours. Several highways were flooded.

but this: a paragraph with a few examples, each one well developed:

The weather was terrible yesterday. It rained for six hours. The rain was heavy and harsh, accompanied by high winds that lashed the trees and signs on stores and restaurants. The downpour was so heavy that several highways were flooded. Drivers who usually take the Collins Road Expressway were diverted to a narrow city street and crawled home at 30 mph. Additionally, traffic on the interstate highway was at a standstill because drivers slowed to gawk at the numerous accidents caused by the lack of visibility and water-slicked roads.

or this: a paragraph developed with more examples:

The weather was terrible yesterday. It rained for six hours, and several highways were flooded. Cedar Forest Elementary School closed early because of a leak in the auditorium's roof. The standing water also collected in low-lying residential areas where some children put on their swimsuits and splashed in four to six inches of water. Their parents, meanwhile, were trying to sweep the water out of porches and patios and praying that more rain would not seep into their houses. The high winds that accompanied the rain snapped tree branches and littered the area with debris. Two small For Sale signs were blown into the drive-through window at Burger King.

WRITING THE ILLUSTRATION ESSAY IN STEPS

PREWRITING Gathering Ideas: Illustration Essay

If you were asked to write an illustration essay about some aspect of clothes, you might first freewrite to narrow the topic and then decide to write about *tee shirts*. Brainstorming and listing your ideas about tee shirts might lead you to group your ideas into three categories:

Listing and Grouping Ideas for an Illustration Paragraph

Topic: Tee Shirts

kinds of people who wear tee shirts

athletes	*movie stars*	*older people*
children	*musicians*	*restaurant workers*
teens	*parents*	

the cost of tee shirts

cheap	*some expensive*

what is pictured or written on tee shirts

ads on tees	*beer ads*	*seascapes*
concert tees	*sporting goods*	*political slogans*
college names	*Mickey Mouse*	*souvenir pictures or sayings*

You can summarize these ideas in a thesis sentence:

> *People of various backgrounds and ages wear all kinds of tee shirts.*

This thesis sentence contains three parts: (1) people of various backgrounds, (2) people of all ages, and (3) all kinds of tee shirts. The part about the cost of tee shirts has been left out of the thesis. As you work toward a thesis, you can decide what to include and what to leave out. The three parts of the thesis may lead you to topic sentences for your outline.

With a thesis sentence and a list of ideas, you are now ready to write an outline for your essay.

PLANNING Devising a Plan: Illustration Essay

Following is an outline for an illustration essay on tee shirts.

An Outline for an Illustration Essay

paragraph 1	I. Thesis: People of various backgrounds and ages wear all kinds of tee shirts.
paragraph 2 **topic sentence** **and details** **people of** **various** **backgrounds**	II. The rich and poor, famous and unknown all wear tee shirts. A. Famous athletes can be seen in tee shirts, signing autographs after a game. B. Members of the local Little League team wear tees. C. Movie stars are seen in them. D. Musicians perform in tee shirts. E. Restaurant workers wear tee shirts. F. Famous political leaders work out in tee shirts.
paragraph 3 **topic sentence** **and details** **people of all** **ages**	III. Every age group feels comfortable in tee shirts. A. Mothers dress their babies in soft little tees. B. Older children wear a favorite tee shirt until it falls apart. C. A teen wardrobe would not be complete without the latest style in tee shirts.

continued

D. Parents wear them to clean and do chores.

E. Older people can be seen jogging or gardening in tees.

paragraph 4
topic sentence
and details
all kinds of
tee shirts

IV. Almost anything can be printed or pictured on a tee shirt.

A. There are tees sold at concerts.

B. Some shirts have the names of colleges on them.

C. Others advertise a brand of beer or sporting goods.

D. Mickey Mouse is a favorite character on them.

E. Surfers' tee shirts have seascapes on them.

F. Some shirts are souvenirs.

G. Others have political slogans.

paragraph 5
conclusion

V. Anyone can find a tee shirt suited to his or her age and lifestyle, and that shirt can carry almost any message.

The outline combined some of the details from the list with new details gathered during the outlining process. As you write and revise your draft, you can continue to add details. You can also combine sentences, add transitions, and work on word choice.

DRAFTING Drafting and Revising: Illustration Essay

Following is a draft of the essay on tee shirts. As you read it, you'll notice many changes from the outline.

- An introduction has been added.
- Transitions have been added within and between paragraphs.
- Details have been added.
- Sentences have been combined.
- A concluding paragraph has been added.

A Draft of an Illustration Essay

(Thesis and topic sentences are underlined.)

Fashion fads come and go. One year, everyone wears ripped jeans, and another year, striped soccer shirts are in. Whatever is most popular this year will most likely be out of style by next year. However, there is one piece of clothing that never goes out of style: the tee shirt. People of various backgrounds and ages wear all kinds of tee shirts.

The rich and poor, famous and unknown all wear tee shirts. While famous athletes dressed in tees sign autographs after a big game, children of the local Little League proudly sport their team shirts. Movie stars wear tees to their movie premieres. Musicians, both famous and struggling, perform in tee shirts. Meanwhile, many restaurant workers wear the restaurant's name or logo on their uniform tee. Even famous politicians have been photographed jogging or working out in tee shirts.

Tees appeal to all classes, and they also appeal to all generations. Every age group feels comfortable in tee shirts. Mothers dress their babies in soft little tee shirts. Older children often become so attached to a favorite tee that they wear it until it falls apart. In addition, a teen wardrobe would not be complete without the latest style in tee shirts. Parents wear them to clean the house, do the shopping, and wash the car. Older people in tees can be seen jogging through the neighborhood or gardening in their front yard.

All kinds of people wear tees, just as the shirts themselves come in all varieties. <u>Almost anything can be pictured or printed on a tee shirt.</u> At concerts, tee shirts with the performer's name on them cost a lot of money. Another popular kind of tee carries the name of a college. Other tees advertise a brand of beer, like Bud, or a sporting goods company, like Nike. Mickey Mouse is a favorite character on tee shirts, and not just on children's tees. Still other kinds of shirts include surfer tee shirts with seascapes on them and souvenir tees, like the ones that say, "My folks visited Philadelphia, and all I got was this lousy tee shirt." Some shirts have political slogans, like "Save the Whales."

Fads can fade, but the tee shirt is everywhere. It has become so popular that it is almost a uniform. Its popularity is connected to its variety. <u>Anyone can find a tee shirt suited to his or her age and lifestyle, and that shirt can carry almost any message.</u>

| POLISHING | ## Polishing and Proofreading: Illustration Essay |

Following is the final version of the essay on tee shirts. When you compare it to the draft, you will notice some changes:

- Some of the word choice has been polished to make a description more precise or to eliminate an awkward phrase.
- One phrase, "cost a lot of money," was changed to "can be expensive" to eliminate the use of "a lot," a phrase that some writers rely on too heavily.
- A transition was added to the conclusion.
- The conclusion includes a new, final sentence, to stress the link between tee shirts' popularity and their variety.
- A title has been added.

A Final Version of an Illustration Essay

(Changes from the draft are underlined.)

Tee Shirts Galore

Fashion fads come and go. One year, everyone wears ripped jeans, and another year, striped soccer shirts are in. Whatever is most popular this year will most likely be out of style by next year. However, there is one piece of clothing that never goes out of style: the tee shirt. People of various backgrounds and ages wear all kinds of tee shirts.

The rich and poor, famous and unknown all wear tee shirts. While famous athletes dressed in tees sign autographs after a big game, children of the local Little League proudly sport their team shirts. Movie stars wear tees to their <u>glamorous</u> movie premieres. Musicians, both famous and struggling, perform in tee shirts. Meanwhile, many restaurant workers wear the restaurant's name or logo on their uniform tee. Even famous politicians have been photographed jogging or working out in tee shirts.

Tees appeal to all classes, and they also appeal to all generations. Every age group feels comfortable in tee shirts. Mothers dress their babies in soft little tee

continued

shirts. Older children often become so attached to a favorite tee that they wear it until it falls apart. In addition, a teen wardrobe would not be complete without the latest style in tee shirts. Parents wear them to clean the house, do the shopping, and wash the car. Older people in tees can be seen jogging through the neighborhood or gardening in their front yard.

All kinds of people wear tees, just as the shirts themselves come in all varieties. Almost anything can be pictured or printed on a tee shirt. At concerts, tee shirts with the performer's name on them <u>can be expensive</u>. Another popular kind of tee carries the name of a college. Other tees advertise a brand of beer, like Bud, or a sporting goods company, like Nike. Mickey Mouse is a favorite character on tee shirts <u>for all ages</u>. Still other kinds of shirts include surfer tee shirts with seascapes on them, and souvenir tees, like the ones that say, "My folks visited Philadelphia, and all I got was this lousy tee shirt." Some shirts have political slogans, like "Save the Whales."

Fads can fade, but the tee shirt is everywhere. It has become so popular that it is <u>like a uniform</u>. <u>Yet</u> its <u>universal appeal</u> is connected to its variety. Anyone can find a tee shirt suited to his or her age and lifestyle, and that shirt can carry almost any message. <u>Therefore, each tee shirt is a uniform that reflects the person who wears it.</u>

TOPICS FOR WRITING AN ILLUSTRATION ESSAY

When you write on any of these topics, work through the stages of the writing process in preparing your essay.

1. Complete one of the following statements and use it as the thesis for an illustration essay.

   Finding a job can be _____.

   People in love often _____.

   Students under pressure sometimes _____.

   A sense of humor can _____.

   Fitting in is _____.

   In a crisis, there are always people who _____.

2. Choose one of the following topics. Narrow it to a more specific topic and then write a thesis statement about it. Use that thesis to write an illustration essay.

adolescents	families	nature
babies	health	technology
change	laws	weddings
crime	loneliness	young adults

Collaborate

3. To begin this assignment, work with two or three classmates. Brainstorm as many typical, general statements as you can. You are looking for the kinds of generalizations we have all heard or even said. For example, "Your college years are the best years of your life," or "Old people are the worst drivers on the road." List as many as you can. Then split up. Pick one of the general statements and write a thesis that challenges the truth of the statement. For

example, your thesis could be, "The college years are not the best years of a person's life," or "Old people are not always bad drivers." Use the thesis for an illustration essay.

4. To begin this assignment, look around your classroom. Now, write a general statement about some aspect of the classroom: the furniture, the colors used to decorate, the condition of the room, what the students carry to class, the students' footwear, facial expressions, hair styles, and so forth. Write a five-paragraph essay using that general statement as your thesis and supporting it with specific examples from your observation.

DESCRIPTION

Hints for Writing a Descriptive Essay

1. Use many specific details.   Because an essay is usually longer than one paragraph, you will need more details to develop an essay. To ensure that your details create an effective description, make them specific.

2. Decide on a clear order.   Without a clear order, a descriptive essay will become a jumble of details spread over several paragraphs. Decide on a clear order (from inside to outside, from top to bottom, and so forth) and stick to it. Each body paragraph can focus on one part of that order.

WRITING THE DESCRIPTIVE ESSAY IN STEPS

PREWRITING   Gathering Ideas: Descriptive Essay

If you were going to write an essay describing your brother's bedroom, you might first brainstorm a list.

Brainstorming a List for a Descriptive Essay

Topic: My Brother's Bedroom

- *older brother Michael—got a big bedroom*
- *I shared with my little brother*
- *stars pasted on the ceiling*
- *took a long time to fix it up the way he wanted it*
- *lots of books about science fiction in two bookcases*
- *movie posters of <u>AI: Artificial Intelligence</u> and <u>The Matrix</u>*
- *old videos like <u>Raiders of the Lost Ark</u> in bookcases*
- *his bed had no headboard, made to look like a couch*
- *<u>Star Trek</u> pillows on the bed*

After surveying the list, you want to think about what point it makes. The main point of the list is the *dominant impression.* For this list, the dominant impression could be this sentence:

My brother's bedroom reflected his fascination with fantasy and science fiction.

This sentence could be the thesis sentence of the descriptive essay.

PLANNING   **Devising a Plan: Descriptive Essay**

Following is an outline for a descriptive essay on a brother's bedroom.

An Outline for a Descriptive Essay

paragraph 1

I. Thesis: My brother's bedroom reflected his fascination with fantasy and science fiction.

paragraph 2
topic sentence
and details
the ceiling

II. The ceiling created a fantasy.
  A. Stars were pasted on the ceiling.
  B. In the daylight, they were nearly invisible.
  C. At night, they glowed in the dark.
  D. The room appeared to be covered by a starry sky.
  E. On many nights, my brother and I would lie on the floor.
  F. We would pretend his room was a spaceship and the stars were the planets.

paragraph 3
topic sentence
and details
the walls

III. The walls were the most obvious sign of my brother's interests.
  A. They were covered in movie posters from fantasy or science fiction films.
  B. There was a poster of Steven Spielberg's film <u>AI: Artificial Intelligence.</u>
  C. My brother had seen the movie five times.
  D. At a garage sale, he had found an old poster of <u>ET</u>.
  E. It was also on the wall.
  F. Another poster, of <u>The Matrix</u>, was framed.
  G. The walls made me feel as if I were in the lobby of a movie theater.

paragraph 4
topic sentence
and details
the furniture

IV. The furniture was ordinary, but it had some fantastic touches.
  A. There were two battered old bookcases ready for the junk pile.
  B. They were full of books about science fiction.
  C. I remember <u>Fahrenheit 451</u> and <u>The War of the Worlds</u>.
  D. Old videos like <u>Raiders of the Lost Ark</u> were also stacked on the bookshelves.
  E. My brother had the same standard single bed that I had.
  F. His was piled high with <u>Star Trek</u> pillows.

paragraph 5
conclusion

V. My brother created his own fantastic world in his room.

The outline combined some of the details from the list with new details gathered during the planning process. As you write and revise your draft, you can continue to add details. You can also combine sentences, add transitions, and work on word choice.

DRAFTING Drafting and Revising: Descriptive Essay

Following is a draft of the essay on a brother's bedroom. As you read it, you'll notice many changes from the outline on page 280.

- An introduction has been added.
- Transitions have been added within and between paragraphs.
- Details have been added.
- Sentences have been combined.
- A concluding paragraph has been written.

A Draft of a Descriptive Essay

(Thesis and topic sentences are underlined.)

Whenever my older brother and I would watch television, we would fight over what to watch. I always wanted to watch wrestling, but my brother was bigger than I was, so we ended up watching Deep Space Nine or Alien 2. He would watch even the oldest reruns of The Twilight Zone because he loved the strange, the unreal, and the scientific. Even my brother's bedroom reflected his fascination with fantasy and science fiction.

The ceiling of his room created a fantasy. Stars were pasted on the ceiling. In the daylight, they were nearly invisible. In the night, they glowed in the dark so that the room appeared to be covered by a starry sky. On many nights, my brother and I would lie on the floor. We would pretend his room was a spaceship and the stars were the planets.

Although the ceiling gave a hint of my brother's dreams, and that hint was visible at night, there was another hint. The walls were the most visible sign of my brother's interests. They were covered in movie posters from fantasy or science fiction films. There was a poster of Steven Spielberg's film AI: Artificial Intelligence. My brother had seen the movie five times, and the poster hung over his bed. At a garage sale, he found an old poster of ET. It and the AI poster hung over his bed. Another poster, of The Matrix, was framed and covered the opposite wall. The posters made me feel as if I were in the lobby of a movie theater.

Unlike the wall decorations, the furniture was ordinary, but my brother had given it some fantastic touches. He had two battered old bookcases ready for the junk pile. They were like any other boy's furniture except that they were full of books about science fiction. I particularly remember Fahrenheit 451 and The War of the Worlds. Old videos like Raiders of the Lost Ark were also stacked on the bookshelves. And even though my brother had the same standard single bed that I had, his was different. It was piled high with Star Trek pillows.

Any boy's room reveals his interests. However, few boys are as determined as my brother was in transforming his room into something else. My brother created his own fantastic world in his room.

POLISHING Polishing and Proofreading: Descriptive Essay

Following is a final version of the essay on a brother's bedroom. When you compare it to the draft, you will notice some changes:

- The introduction used the word "even" twice, an awkward repetition. A change in word choice and a new transition to the thesis statement eliminated the repetition.

- A final sentence was added to the second paragraph. The paragraph needed a few more details, and the new sentence helped to reinforce the thesis, too.
- A change in word choice in the third paragraph eliminates the repetition of "visible."
- The third paragraph also repeated the detail that the *AI* poster hung over the bed. The repetition was cut.
- New details were added to the third paragraph.
- A sentence of specific details was added to the conclusion; so were other details.
- A title has been added.

A Final Version of a Descriptive Essay

(Changes from the draft are underlined.)

My Brother's Heavenly Bedroom

Whenever my older brother and I would watch television, we would fight over what to watch. I always wanted to watch wrestling, but my brother was bigger than I was, so we ended up watching <u>Deep Space Nine</u> or <u>Alien 2</u>. He would watch the oldest reruns of <u>The Twilight Zone</u> because he loved the strange, the unreal, and the scientific. <u>This love was so strong that</u> even my brother's bedroom reflected his fascination with fantasy and science fiction.

The ceiling of his room created a fantasy. Stars were pasted on the ceiling. In the daylight, they were nearly invisible. In the night, they glowed in the dark so that the room appeared to be covered by a starry sky. On many nights, my brother and I would lie on the floor. We would pretend his room was a spaceship and the stars were the planets. <u>At these moments, I became a partner in his imaginary world.</u>

Although the ceiling gave a hint of my brother's dreams, and that hint was <u>apparent</u> at night, there was another, <u>stronger</u> hint. The walls were the most visible sign of my brother's interests. They were covered in movie posters from fantasy or science fiction films. There was a poster of Steven Spielberg's film <u>AI: Artificial Intelligence</u>. My brother had seen the movie five times. At a garage sale, he found an old, ragged poster of <u>ET</u>. <u>He cut the poster's ragged edges and covered it in plastic.</u> It and the <u>AI</u> poster hung over his bed. Another poster, <u>a dark vision</u> of <u>The Matrix</u>, was framed and covered the opposite wall. The posters made me feel as if I were in the lobby of a movie theater.

Unlike the wall decorations, the furniture was ordinary, but my brother had given it some fantastic touches. He had two battered old bookcases ready for the junk pile. They were like any other boy's furniture except that they were full of books of science fiction. I particularly remember <u>Fahrenheit 451</u> and <u>The War of the Worlds.</u> Old videos like <u>Raiders of the Lost Ark</u> were also stacked on the bookshelves. And even though my brother had the same standard single bed that I had, his was different. It was piled high with <u>Star Trek</u> pillows.

Any boy's room reveals his interests. <u>There may be a basketball, some video games, and a poster or two.</u> However, few boys are as determined as my brother was in transforming his room into <u>his private space.</u> My brother created his own fantastic world in his room.

TOPICS FOR WRITING A DESCRIPTIVE ESSAY

When you write on any of these topics, work through the stages of the writing process in preparing your essay.

Collaborate

1. Begin this essay with a partner. Describe your ideal man or woman to your partner. Ask your partner to (1) jot down the details of your description and (2) help you come up with specific details by asking you follow-up questions each time you run out of ideas. Work together for at least ten minutes. Then change roles. Let your partner describe his or her ideal man or woman to you and take notes for your partner. Then split up and use the details you collected to write an essay.

2. Describe a place you would never want to return to. Be sure to use specific details that explain why this place is terrible, unpleasant, or unattractive.

3. If you were allowed to take only three items (furniture, pictures, photographs, jewelry, and so forth) from your home, what would these things be? Write an essay describing them and their importance to you.

4. Describe one of the following:

   a place that you loved when you were a child
   a room that makes you feel comfortable
   a place you go to when you feel stressed
   a favorite pet
   your workplace
   your favorite place outdoors
   the place you go to study

5. Describe someone you know well and who has two sides to him or her. These sides may be the private and the public sides, the happy and sad sides, the calm and angry sides, and so forth. Give specific details for both sides of this person.

6. We all associate certain people with certain rooms. For instance, you may associate your mother with her kitchen or her home office, or your brother with the garage, where he works on his car. You may picture your father in the den, where he likes to relax. Choose a person you know well, and then decide which room you associate with this person. Then write an essay showing how the details of that room relate to the person's personality, interests, and goals.

NARRATION

Hints for Writing a Narrative Essay

1. Give the essay a point and stick to it. A narrative essay tells a story. A story without a point becomes a list of moments that lead nowhere. Once you have your point, check that your use of details does not lead you away from the point.

2. Divide your narrative into clear stages. In an essay, you divide your narrative into several paragraphs. Check that each body paragraph has a clear focus (in the topic sentence) and that you have a clear reason for your division. You may decide to divide your body paragraphs into (a) before, during, and after, or (b) the first part of the story, the middle part, and the ending.

WRITING THE NARRATIVE ESSAY IN STEPS

PREWRITING   Gathering Ideas: Narrative Essay

If you were asked to write a narrative essay about something that changed you, you might begin by freewriting.

Freewriting for a Narrative Essay

Topic: Something That Changed Me
Something that changed me. I don't know. What changed me? Lots of things happened to me, but I can't find one that changed me. Graduating from high school? Everybody will write about that, how boring, and anyway, what was the big deal? I haven't gotten married. No big change there. Divorce. My parents' divorce really changed the whole family. A big shock to me. I couldn't believe it was happening. I was really scared. Who would I live with? They were real calm when they told me. I've never been so scared. I was too young to understand. Kept thinking they'd just get back together. They didn't. Then I got a stepmother. The year of the divorce was a hard time for me. Kids suffer in divorce.

Reviewing your freewriting, you decide to write on the topic of your parent's divorce. Once you have this topic, you begin to brainstorm about your topic, asking yourself questions that can lead to further details about the divorce.

With more details, you can decide that your essay will focus on the announcement of your parents' divorce and the emotions you felt. You devise the following topic sentence:

> *When my parents announced that they were divorcing, I felt confused by all my emotions.*

PLANNING   Devising a Plan: Narrative Essay

Following is an outline for a narrative essay on the announcement of your parent's divorce and the emotions you felt. As you read it, note how it divides the announcement into three parts: (1) the background of the announcement, (2) the story of the divorce announcement, and (3) the emotions connected to the announcement.

An Outline for a Narrative Essay

paragraph 1	I. Thesis: When my parents announced that they were divorcing, I felt confused by all my emotions.
paragraph 2 topic sentence and details background of	II. I will never forget how one ordinary day suddenly became a terrible one. A. I was seven when my mom and dad divorced. B. My sister was ten.

the announcement
C. Both of my parents were there.
D. They told us at breakfast, in the kitchen.
E. I was eating toast.
F. I remember I couldn't eat anything after they started talking.
G. I remember a piece of toast with one bite out of it.

paragraph 3
topic sentence
and details
story of the
announcement
III. When my parents first spoke, I was in shock.
A. They were very calm when they told us.
B. They said they loved us, but they couldn't get along.
C. They said they would always love us kids.
D. It was an unreal moment to me.
E. I couldn't believe it was happening.
F. At first I just thought they were having another fight.
G. I was too young to understand.
H. I didn't cry.

paragraph 4
topic sentence
and details
my emotions
IV. When the reality hit me, my emotions overwhelmed me.
A. My sister cried.
B. Then I knew it was serious.
C. I kept thinking I would have to choose which parent to live with.
D. I knew I would really hurt the one I didn't choose.
E. I loved them both.
F. I felt so much guilt about leaving one of them.
G. I also needed both of them.
H. I felt ripped apart.

paragraph 5
conclusion
V. When my parents' marriage fell apart, so did I.

The outline combined some of the details from the freewriting with other details gathered through brainstorming and during the outlining process. As you write and revise your draft, you can continue to add details. You can also combine sentences, add transitions, and work on word choice.

DRAFTING Drafting and Revising: Narrative Essay

Following is a draft of the essay on an announcement of divorce. As you read it, you'll notice many changes from the outline.

- An introduction has been added.
- Transitions within the paragraphs have been added.
- Details have been added.
- Some dialogue has been added.
- A concluding paragraph has been added.

A Draft of a Narrative Essay

(Thesis and topic sentences are underlined.)

Divorce can be really hard on children. <u>When my parents announced that they were divorcing, I felt confused by all my emotions.</u>

continued

<u>I will never forget how one ordinary day suddenly became a terrible one.</u> I was seven, and my sister was ten on that day. Both of my parents told us at breakfast, in the kitchen. I clearly remember that I was eating toast, but once they started talking, I couldn't eat anything. I can still recall holding a piece of toast with one bite out of it. I stared at the toast stupidly as I listened to what they had to say.

<u>When my parents first spoke, I was in shock.</u> They were very calm when they told us. "We love both of you very much," my dad said, "but your mother and I aren't getting along." "But we will always love you," my mother added. The announcement was such an unreal moment that I couldn't believe it was happening. My parents used to fight a lot, so at first I just thought they were having another fight. I was too young to understand. In fact, I didn't even cry.

<u>When the reality hit me, my emotions overwhelmed me.</u> My sister began to cry, and I suddenly knew it was serious. I kept thinking I would have to choose which parent to live with, and I knew I would really hurt the one I didn't choose. I loved them both. I was filled with guilt about hurting one. I also needed both parents so much that I dreaded separating from one of them. I believed that the one I didn't choose would hate me. I felt ripped apart.

In one morning, my world changed. One minute, I was an ordinary seven-year-old having breakfast with his family. The next, I was experiencing powerful emotions no child should feel. <u>When my parents' marriage fell apart, so did I.</u>

POLISHING   Polishing and Proofreading: Narrative Essay

Following is the final version of the essay on an announcement of divorce. When you compare it to the draft, you will notice some changes:

- The introduction has been developed and improved.
- More specific details have been added.
- The word "dad" has been replaced with "father" so that the language is more formal.
- The phrase "a lot" was changed to "often" since "a lot" is an overused phrase.
- The word "fight" was replaced by "argument" so that "fight" does not appear twice in one sentence.
- The first word in paragraph 4 has been changed from "When" to "Then" so that the openings of paragraphs 3 and 4 are not repetitive.
- The word "it" in paragraph 4 has been replaced by "the situation" so that the sentence is clearer.
- To improve the style in paragraph 4, some sentences have been combined.
- A title has been added.

A Final Version of a Narrative Essay

(Changes from the draft are underlined.)

An Emotional Morning

<u>No childhood is perfect, and part of growing up is facing disappointment, change, and loss. However, there is one loss that can be overwhelming.</u> Divorce can be really hard on children. When my parents announced that they were divorcing, I felt confused by all my emotions.

I will never forget how one ordinary day suddenly became a terrible one. I was seven, and my sister was ten on that day. Both of my parents told us at breakfast, in the kitchen. I clearly remember that I was eating toast, but once they started talking, I couldn't eat anything. I can still recall holding a piece of <u>whole wheat</u> toast with one bite out of it. I stared at the toast stupidly as I listened to what they had to say.

When my parents first spoke, I was in shock. They were very calm when they told us. "We love both of you very much," my <u>father</u> said, "but your mother and I aren't getting along." "But we will always love you," my mother added. The announcement was such an unreal moment that I couldn't believe it was happening. My parents used to fight <u>often</u>, so at first I just thought they were having another <u>argument</u>. I was too young to understand. In fact, I didn't even cry.

<u>Then</u> the reality hit me, and my emotions overwhelmed me. My sister began to cry, and I suddenly knew <u>the situation</u> was serious. I kept thinking I would have to choose which parent to live with, and I knew I would really hurt the one I didn't choose. Because I loved them both, I was filled with guilt about hurting one. I also needed both parents so much that I dreaded separating from one of them. I believed that the one I didn't choose would hate me. I felt ripped apart.

In one morning, my world changed. One minute, I was an ordinary seven-year-old having breakfast with his family. The next, I was experiencing powerful emotions no child should feel. When my parents' marriage fell apart, so did I.

TOPICS FOR WRITING A NARRATIVE ESSAY

When you write on any of these topics, work through the stages of the writing process in preparing your essay.

1. This assignment begins with an interview. Ask one (or both) of your parents to tell you about the day you were born. Be prepared to ask questions. (For example, were you expected that day, or did you surprise your family? Was there a rush to the hospital?) Get as many details as you can. Then write a narrative essay about that day.

2. Write about a time you learned an important lesson. Use the events of the time to explain how you learned the lesson.

3. Write the story of an argument (one you were involved in or one you observed) and its consequences.

4. Write about a crime you witnessed or were a victim of. Be sure to include details about what happened after the crime was committed.

5. Write about an incident in your life that seemed to be fate (that is, seemed to be meant to happen).

6. Write the story of an accident. The accident can be one you were involved in or one you observed. It can be any kind of accident: a car accident, a sports injury, and so forth.

7. Write on any of the following topics:

your first day at work	your first day at school
the best day of your life	the worst day of your life
the day you witnessed a victory	a day you made a friend
a day you lost a friend	a day with a pleasant surprise

PROCESS

Hints for Writing a Process Essay

1. Remember that there are two kinds of process essays: a **directional** process essay tells the reader how to do something; an **informational** process essay explains an activity without telling the reader how to do it. Whether you write a directional or process essay, be sure to make a point. That point is expressed in your thesis.

When you write a process essay, it is easy to confuse a topic with a thesis.

> **topic:** How to change the oil in your car.
>
> **thesis:** You don't have to be an expert to learn how to change the oil in your car.
>
> **topic:** How gardeners squirrel-proof their backyards.
>
> **thesis:** Gardeners have to think like squirrels to keep the critters away from plants and trees.

2. Find some logical way to divide the steps into paragraphs. If you have seven steps, you probably don't want to put each one into a separate paragraph, especially if they are short steps. You would run the risk of having a list instead of a well-developed essay. To avoid writing a list, try to cluster your steps according to some logical division.

For instance, if you are writing about how to prepare for a successful party, you could divide your steps into groups like (1) what to do a week before the party, (2) what to do the day before the party, and (3) what to do the day of the party. Or if you are writing about how to make a carrot cake, you could divide the steps into (1) assembling the ingredients, (2) making the cake, and (3) baking and frosting the cake.

3. Develop your paragraphs by explaining each step thoroughly and by using details. If you are explaining how to make a cake, you can't simply tell the reader to mix the combined ingredients well. You need to explain how long to mix and whether to mix with a fork, spoon, spatula, or electric mixer. Fortunately, an essay gives you the time and space to be clear. And you will be clear if you put yourself in the reader's place and anticipate his or her questions.

WRITING THE PROCESS ESSAY IN STEPS

PREWRITING Gathering Ideas: Process

If you were writing a process essay about finding an apartment, you might first freewrite your ideas on the topic. Brainstorming and listing your ideas might lead you to group your ideas into three categories, organized in time order:

Listing and Grouping Ideas for a Process Essay

Topic: Finding an Apartment

Before the Search

Do you want a one bedroom?

Friends can help.

A good neighborhood

A convenient location can be more expensive.

Can save you money on transportation

During the Search

Look around.

Don't pick the first apartment you see.

Look at a bunch.

But not too many

After the Search

Check the lease carefully.

How much is the security deposit?

After some more thinking, you could summarize these ideas in a thesis:

Finding the apartment you want takes planning and careful investigation.

With a thesis sentence and some ideas clustered in categories, you can write an outline for your essay.

PLANNING   **Devising a Plan: Process Essay**

Following is an outline for a process essay on finding an apartment.

An Outline for a Process Essay

paragraph 1

    I. Thesis: Finding the apartment you want takes planning and careful investigation.

paragraph 2
topic sentence
and details
before the
search

    II. You can save yourself stress by doing some preliminary work.

        A. Decide what you want.

        B. Ask yourself, "Do I want a one bedroom?" and "What can I afford?"

        C. Weigh the pros and cons of your wishes.

        D. A convenient location can be expensive.

        E. It can also save you money on transportation.

        F. Friends can help you with the names of nice apartments.

        G. Maybe somebody you know lives in a good neighborhood.

        H. Check the classified advertisements in the newspapers.

paragraph 3
topic sentence
and details
during the
search

    III. On your search, be patient, look carefully, and ask questions.

        A. Look around.

        B. Don't pick the first apartment you see.

        C. Look at several.

        D. But don't look at too many.

        E. Check the cleanness, safety, plumbing, and appliances of each one.

continued

F. Ask the manager about the laundry room, additional storage, parking facilities, and maintenance policies.

paragraph 4
topic sentence
and details
after the
search

IV. When you've seen enough apartments, take time to examine your options.
  A. Compare the two best places you saw.
  B. Consider the price, locations, and condition of the apartments.
  C. Check the leases carefully.
  D. Are pets allowed?
  E. Are there rules about getting roommates?
  F. Check the amount of the security deposit.
  G. Check the requirements for the first and last month's rent deposit.

paragraph 5
conclusion

V. With the right strategies and a thorough search, you can get the apartment that suits you.

The outline used each cluster of steps as one body paragraph. A topic sentence for each body paragraph made some point about that group of steps. It also added many new details gathered during the outlining process. As you write and revise your draft, you can continue to add details. You can also combine sentences, add transitions, and work on word choice.

DRAFTING Drafting and Revising: Process Essay

Following is a draft of the essay on finding an apartment. As you read it, you'll notice many changes from the outline.

- An introduction has been added.
- Transitions have been added within and between paragraphs.
- Details have been added.
- Sentences have been combined.
- A concluding paragraph has been added.

A Draft of a Process Essay

(Thesis and topic sentences are underlined.)

Some people drive around a neighborhood until they see an apartment complex with a Vacancy sign. They talk to the building manager, visit the apartment, and sign a lease. Soon they are residents of their new apartment, and often they are unhappy with their home. These people went about their search the wrong way. They did not realize that finding the apartment you want takes planning and careful investigation.

You can save yourself stress by doing some preliminary work. First of all, decide what you want. Ask yourself, "Do I want a one-bedroom apartment?" and "What can I afford?" Weigh the pros and cons of your wishes. You may want a convenient location, but that can be expensive. On the other hand, that location can save you money on transportation. When you've decided what you want, rely on friends to help you with your search. They can help you with the names of nice apartments. Maybe somebody you know lives in a good neighborhood and can help you find an apartment. In addition, check the classified advertisements in the newspapers. They are full of possibilities.

<u>In your search, be patient, look carefully, and ask questions.</u> It's important to look around and not to pick the first apartment you see. Look at several so that you can get a sense of your options. However, don't look at so many apartments that they all become a blur in your memory. As you visit each apartment, check its cleanness, safety, plumbing, and appliances. You don't want an apartment that opens onto a bad area or one with a leaky refrigerator. Be sure to ask the apartment manager whether there are a laundry room, a storage area, and sufficient assigned parking and guest parking. Check to see if a maintenance person lives on the premises.

<u>When you've seen enough apartments, take the time to examine your options.</u> First, compare the two best places you saw. Now that you have narrowed your search, consider the price, location, and condition of each apartment. Check the leases carefully. If you have or are thinking of getting a pet, check to see if pets are allowed. Check the rules about roommates, too. Next, check to see how much money you will have to put up initially. Does the lease specify the amount of the security deposit? Does it require a payment of first and last month's rent? The answers to these questions can help you reach a decision.

Once you have followed the steps of the process, you are ready to make your choice. While these steps take more time than simply picking the first place you see on the street, they are worth it. <u>With the right strategies and a thorough search, you can get the apartment that suits your needs.</u> All that remains is to settle into your new home.

POLISHING   **Polishing and Proofreading: Process Essay**

Following is the final version of the essay on finding an apartment. When you compare it to the draft, you will notice some changes:

- A transition has been added to the beginning of paragraph 2 for smoother movement from the thesis at the end of paragraph 1 to the topic sentence of paragraph 2.
- The words "nice," "good," and "bad" have been changed to more specific descriptions.
- More details have been added to the end of paragraph 3.
- A title has been added.

A Final Version of a Process Essay

(Changes from the draft are underlined.)

How to Find a Suitable Apartment

Some people drive around a neighborhood until they see an apartment complex with a Vacancy sign. They talk to the building manager, visit the apartment, and sign a lease. Soon they are residents of their new apartment, and often they are unhappy with their home. These people went about their search the wrong way. They did not realize that finding the apartment you want takes planning and careful investigation.

<u>When it comes to choosing an apartment</u>, you can save yourself stress by doing some preliminary work. First of all, decide what you want. Ask yourself, "Do I want a one-bedroom apartment?" and "What can I afford?" Weigh the pros and cons of your wishes. You may want a convenient location, but that can be expensive. On the other hand, that location can save you money on transportation.

continued

When you've decided what you want, rely on friends to help you with your search. They can help you with the names of <u>suitable</u> apartments. Maybe somebody you know lives in an <u>attractive</u> neighborhood and can help you find an apartment. In addition, check the classified advertisements in the newspapers. They are full of possibilities.

In your search, be patient, look carefully, and ask questions. It's important to look around and not to pick the first apartment you see. Look at several so that you can get a sense of your options. However, don't look at so many apartments that they all become a blur in your memory. As you visit each apartment, check its cleanness, safety, plumbing, and appliances. You don't want an apartment that opens onto a <u>dark and deserted</u> area or one with a leaky refrigerator. Be sure to ask the apartment manager whether there are a laundry room, a storage area, and sufficient assigned parking and guest parking. Check to see if a maintenance person lives on the premises <u>or if a rental agency handles emergencies</u> and <u>repairs</u>.

When you've seen enough apartments, take the time to examine your options. First, compare the two best places you saw. Now that you have narrowed your search, consider the price, location, and condition of each apartment. Check the leases carefully. If you have or are thinking of getting a pet, check to see if pets are allowed. Check the rules about roommates, too. Next, check to see how much money you will have to put up initially. Does the lease specify the amount of the security deposit? Does it require a payment of first and last month's rent? The answers to these questions can help you reach a decision.

Once you have followed the steps of the process, you are ready to make your choice. While these steps take more time than simply picking the first place you see on the street, they are worth it. With the right strategies and a thorough search, you can get the apartment that suits your needs. All that remains is to settle into your new home.

TOPICS FOR WRITING A PROCESS ESSAY

When you write on any of these topics, work through the stages of the writing process in preparing your essay.

1. Write a directional or informational process essay about one of these topics:

applying for a loan	learning to ski
childproofing a room	learning to surf
cutting and styling hair	overcoming shyness
finding the best airfare	painting a room
finding a roommate	proposing marriage
getting a good night's sleep	registering for class
giving yourself a manicure	selling a car
having a pleasant first date	setting up a new computer
installing a car's sound system	teaching someone to drive
learning to dance	trying out for a team
learning to skateboard	writing a thank-you note

2. You may work through some process at work. For example, you may have to open or close a store, clean a piece of machinery, fill out a report, use a specific computer program, or follow a process in making telemarketing calls. You may have to maintain the appearance of a work area (like aisles in a supermarket), or follow

a procedure in dealing with complaints. If you follow a process at work, write an essay that teaches the process to a new employee.

3. Think of a time when you had to make an important decision. Write an essay about how you reached that decision. You can write about the circumstances that led to your having to make a choice and about the steps you took to come to a decision. That is, what did you consider first? Did you weigh the good and bad points of your options? What was your first choice? Did you stick with that decision or change your mind? Trace the steps of your thought process.

4. Is there someone you know who has an irritating habit or is hard to live with? For instance, you may be living with someone who leaves the kitchen a mess, or working with someone who always loses items (staplers, pens) and borrows yours. Write an essay in which you teach this person the steps to breaking the bad habit or changing the annoying behavior.

COMPARISON AND CONTRAST

Hints for Writing a Comparison or Contrast Essay

1. Use the thesis of your comparison or contrast to make a statement. Your essay must do more than explain the similarities or differences between two people, places, or things. It must make some statement about the two. For instance, if you are writing about the differences between your first and second semester of college, your thesis may be that a person can change radically in a short time.

2. Use your points of comparison or contrast as a way to organize your body paragraphs. A comparison or contrast essay needs points; each point focuses on a specific similarity or difference. For example, you might use three points to compare two dogs: their appearance, their temperament, and their abilities. You can write one body paragraph on each of these points of comparison.

3. Use a point-by-point pattern. That is, each body paragraph can explain one point of comparison or contrast. The topic sentence can summarize the point, and the details about the two subjects (people, places, or things you are comparing) can support the topic sentence. These details can be grouped so that you first discuss one subject, and then the other. You might, for example, compare the appearance of two dogs. An outline for one body paragraph might look like the following:

topic sentence	II. My German shepherd and my border collie are similar in appearance.
point: appearance subject 1: my German shepherd	A. Max, my shepherd, has long, shiny black and brown hair. B. His ears stand up as if he is always alert. C. His eyes are dark and intelligent.
subject 2: my border collie	D. Sheba, my collie, has glossy black and white hair. F. Her pointed ears make it seem as if she is always listening to something. G. Her black eyes are knowing and wise.

WRITING THE COMPARISON OR CONTRAST ESSAY IN STEPS

PREWRITING   Gathering Ideas: Comparison or Contrast Essay

One way to get started on a comparison or contrast essay is to list as many differences or similarities as you can on one topic. Then you can see whether you have more similarities (comparisons) or differences (contrasts), and decide which approach to use. For example, if you decide to compare or contrast two restaurants, you could begin with a list like this:

Listing Ideas for a Comparison or Contrast Essay

Topic: Two restaurants: Victor's and The Garden

Similarities

both offer lunch and dinner

very popular

nearby

Differences

Victor's	The Garden
formal dress	informal dress
tablecloths	place mats
food is bland	spicy food
expensive	moderate
statues, fountains, fresh flowers	dark wood, hanging plants

Getting Points of Comparison or Contrast

Whether you compare or contrast, you are looking for points of comparison or contrast, items you can discuss about both subjects.

If you surveyed the list on the two restaurants and decided you wanted to contrast the two, you'd see that you already have these points of contrast:

dress   food
decor   prices

To write your essay, start with several points of comparison or contrast. As you work through the stages of writing, you may decide you don't need all the points you've jotted down, but it is better to start with too many points than with too few.

Once you have some points, you can begin adding details to them. The details may lead you to more points. If they do not, they will still help you develop the ideas of your paragraph. If you were to write about the differences in restaurants, for example, your new list with added details might look like this:

Listing Ideas for a Contrast Essay

Topic: Two Restaurants

Victor's	*The Garden*
dress—formal	*informal dress*
men in jackets, women in dresses	*all in jeans*
decor—pretty, elegant	*place mats, on table is a card listing specials,*
statues, fountains,	*lots of dark wood, brass,*
fresh flowers on tables,	*green hanging plants*
tablecloths	
food—bland tasting	*spicy and adventurous*
traditional, broiled fish or	*pasta in tomato sauces, garlic in everything,*
chicken, traditional steaks,	*curry,*
appetizers like shrimp cockail,	*appetizers like tiny tortillas, ribs in honey-*
onion soup	*mustard sauce*
price—expensive	*moderate*
everything costs extra,	*price of dinner includes*
like appetizer, salad	*appetizer and salad*

Reading the list about the two restaurants, you might conclude that some people may prefer The Garden to Victor's. Why? There are several hints in your list. The Garden has cheaper food, better food, and a more casual atmosphere. Now that you have a point, you can put it into a thesis sentence. A thesis contrasting the restaurants could be as follows:

> *Some people would rather eat at The Garden than at Victor's because The Garden offers better, cheaper food in a more casual environment.*

Once you have a possible thesis, you can begin working on the planning stage of your essay.

PLANNING   **Devising a Plan: Contrast Essay**

Following is an outline for a contrast essay on two restaurants.

An Outline for a Contrast Essay

paragraph 1	I. Thesis: Some people would rather eat at The Garden than at Victor's because The Garden offers better, cheaper food in a more casual environment.
paragraph 2 **topic sentence** **and details** **food** **Victor's**	II. The menus at the two restaurants reveal significant differences. A. Food at Victor's is bland tasting and traditional. B. The menu has broiled fish, chicken, and traditional steaks. C. The spices used are mostly parsley and salt. D. The food is the usual American food, with a little French food on the list.

continued

The Garden

    E. Food at The Garden is more spicy and adventurous.

    G. There are many pasta dishes in tomato sauce.

    H. There is garlic in just about everything.

    I. The Garden serves five different curry dishes.

    J. It has all kinds of ethnic food.

    K. Appetizers include items like tiny tortillas and hot honey-mustard ribs.

paragraph 3

topic sentence

and details

price

Victor's

The Garden

III. There is a contrast in prices at the two restaurants.

    A. Victor's is expensive.

    B. Everything you order costs extra.

    C. An appetizer or a salad costs extra.

    D. Even a potato costs extra.

    E. Food at The Garden is more moderately priced.

    G. The price of a dinner includes an appetizer and a salad.

    H. All meals come with a potato, pasta, or rice.

paragraph 4

topic sentence

and details

environment

Victor's

The Garden

IV. At Victor's and The Garden, meals are served in opposing environments.

    A. Certain diners may feel uncomfortable in Victor's, which has a formal atmosphere.

    B. Everyone is dressed up, the men in jackets and ties and the women in dresses.

    C. Even the children in the restaurant are in their best clothes and sit up straight.

    D. Less formal diners would rather eat in a more casual place.

    E. People don't dress up to go The Garden; they wear jeans.

    F. Some come in shorts and sandals.

    G. The children often wear sneakers and caps.

    H. They wriggle in their seats and even crawl under the table.

paragraph 5

conclusion

V. Many people prefer a place where they can relax, with reasonable prices and unusual food, to a place that's a little stuffy, with a traditional and expensive menu.

The outline added some new details gathered during the outlining process. The topic sentences of the body paragraphs are based on the points of contrast on the earlier list. One point of contrast, the decor of the restaurants, has been omitted. The details about decor may be useful in the introduction or conclusion of the essay.

As you write and revise your draft, you can continue to add details. You can also combine sentences, add transitions, and work on word choice.

DRAFTING   Drafting and Revising: Contrast Essay

Following is a draft of the essay on two restaurants. As you read it, you'll notice many changes from the outline.

- An introduction has been added, and it contains some of the details on decor gathered earlier.

- Transitions have been added within and between paragraphs.
- Details have been added.
- Sentences have been combined.
- The word choice has been improved.
- A concluding paragraph has been added.

A Draft of a Contrast Essay

(Thesis and topic sentences are underlined.)

There are two well-known restaurants in town. One, Victor's, is an elegant place with white linen tablecloths and fresh flowers on each table. The other, The Garden, has paper place mats on the tables. The only other item on the tables is a small card listing the day's specials. While it might seem that Victor's is a more attractive setting for a meal, The Garden has its advantages. <u>Some people would rather eat at The Garden than at Victor's because The Garden offers better, cheaper food in a more casual environment.</u>

<u>The menus at the two restaurants reveal significant differences.</u> Food at Victor's is bland tasting and traditional. The menu offers broiled fish, baked chicken, and typical steaks like T-bone and sirloin. The spices used are mostly parsley and salt. Victor's serves standard American food with a little French food on the list; for example, the appetizers include an American favorite, shrimp cocktail, and French onion soup. While food at Victor's relies on old, safe choices, food at The Garden is more spicy and adventurous. There are many pasta dishes in tomato sauce. Garlic appears in just about everything from mashed potatoes to pork roasts. The Garden serves five different curry dishes. In fact, it has all kinds of ethnic food; tiny tortillas and ribs dipped in honey and hot Chinese mustard are the most popular appetizers.

Food choice is not the only difference between Victor's and The Garden; <u>there is also a contrast in prices at the two restaurants.</u> Victor's is expensive. Everything you order, such as an appetizer or a salad, costs extra. Even a baked potato costs extra. An entree like a steak, for example, comes on a platter with a sprig of parsley. If you want a potato or a vegetable, you have to pay extra for it. Food at The Garden is more moderately priced. The price of a dinner includes an appetizer and a salad; in addition, all meals come with a potato, pasta, or rice, so there are few pricey extras to pay for.

The cost of a meal at Victor's is different from one at The Garden, and the atmosphere in which the meal is enjoyed is different, too. <u>At the two places, meals are served in opposing settings.</u> Certain diners may feel uncomfortable in Victor's, which has a formal atmosphere. Everyone is dressed up, the men in jackets and ties, and the women in dresses. Even the children at Victor's are dressed in their best and sit straight up in their chairs. Less formal diners would rather eat in a more casual place, like The Garden. People don't dress up to go to The Garden; they wear jeans or shorts and sandals. The children often wear sneakers and baseball caps. They wriggle in their seats and even explore under the table.

Sometimes adults want to let go, just as children do. They want to sit back, not up, stretch their legs in casual clothes, not jackets and ties or dresses, and explore new food choices, not the same old standards. The Garden appeals to that childlike need for physical comfort and adventurous dining, at a moderate cost. <u>People</u> choose it over Victor's because they <u>prefer a place where they can relax, with reasonable prices and unusual food, to a place that's a little stuffy, with a traditional and expensive menu.</u>

POLISHING　Polishing and Proofreading: Contrast Essay

Following is a final version of the essay on two restaurants. When you compare it to the draft on page 297, you will notice some changes:

- More specific details have been added.
- Two sentences in paragraph 3 have been revised so that the shift to "you" is eliminated.
- The phrase "explore under the table" in paragraph 4 has been changed to "explore the spaces under the table" for clarity.
- One sentence in the conclusion has been revised so that it has a stronger parallel structure.
- A title has been added.

A Final Version of a Contrast Essay

(Changes from the draft are underlined.)

Victor's and The Garden: Two Contrasting Restaurants

There are two well-known restaurants in town. One, Victor's, is an elegant place with white linen tablecloths and fresh flowers on each table. The other, The Garden, has paper place mats on the tables. The only other item on the tables is a small card listing the day's specials. While it might seem that Victor's is a more attractive setting for a meal, The Garden has its advantages. Some people would rather eat at The Garden than at Victor's because The Garden offers better, cheaper food in a more casual environment.

The menus at the two restaurants reveal significant differences. Food at Victor's is bland tasting and traditional. The menu offers broiled fish, baked chicken, and typical steaks like T-bone and sirloin. The spices used are mostly parsley and salt; <u>pepper, garlic, and curry are nowhere to be found.</u> Victor's serves standard American food with a little French food on the list; for example, the appetizers include an American favorite, shrimp cocktail, and French onion soup. While food at Victor's relies on old, safe choices, food at The Garden is more spicy and adventurous. There are many pasta dishes, <u>from linguini to lasagna,</u> in <u>a rich</u> tomato sauce. Garlic appears in just about everything from mashed potatoes to pork roasts. The Garden serves five different curry dishes. In fact, it has all kinds of ethnic food; tiny tortillas and ribs dipped in honey and hot Chinese mustard are the most popular appetizers.

Food choice is not the only difference between Victor's and The Garden; there is also a contrast in prices at the two restaurants. Victor's is expensive. Everything <u>a person orders</u>, such as an appetizer or a salad, costs extra. Even a baked potato costs extra. An entree like a steak, for example, comes on a platter with a sprig of parsley. <u>Anyone who wants</u> a potato or a vegetable has to pay extra for it. Food at The Garden is more moderately priced. The price of a dinner includes an appetizer and a salad; in addition, all meals come with a potato, pasta, or rice, so there are few pricey extras to pay for.

The cost of a meal at Victor's is different from one at The Garden, and the atmosphere in which the meal is enjoyed is different, too. At the two places, meals are served in opposing settings. Certain diners may feel uncomfortable in Victor's, which has a formal atmosphere. Everyone is dressed up, the men in jackets and ties, and the women in <u>fancy</u> dresses. Even the children at Victor's are dressed in their best and sit straight up in their chairs. Less formal diners would rather eat in a more casual place, like The Garden. People don't dress up to go to The Garden; they wear jeans or shorts and sandals. The children often wear sneakers and baseball caps. They wriggle in their seats and even explore <u>the spaces</u> under the table.

Sometimes adults want to let go, just as children do. They want to sit back, not up, stretch their legs in casual clothes, <u>not hold their breath in tight ties or fancy dresses</u>, and explore new food choices, not <u>settle for</u> the same old standards. The Garden appeals to that childlike need for physical comfort and adventurous dining, at a moderate cost. People choose it over Victor's because they prefer a place where they can relax, with reasonable prices and unusual food, to a place that's a little stuffy, with a traditional and expensive menu.

TOPICS FOR WRITING A COMPARISON OR CONTRAST ESSAY

When you write on any of these topics, work through the stages of the writing process in preparing your essay.

1. Compare or contrast any of the following:

two holidays	satellite and cable television
two video games	two Internet providers
two personal goals	two clothing styles
two weddings	two surprises
two movie theaters	two role models
two expensive purchases	two houses you've lived in
two coworkers	two assignments

2. Find a baby picture of yourself. Study it carefully; then write an essay about the similarities between the baby and the adult you are today. You can use physical similarities or similarities in personality or attitude (as expressed in the photo). If your instructor agrees, you can ask a classmate to help you find physical resemblances between you as you are today and the baby in the picture.

Collaborate

3. Compare or contrast the person you were two years ago to the person you are today. You might consider such points of comparison as your worries, fears, hopes, goals, or relationships.

4. Begin this assignment by working with a partner or group. Brainstorm to make a list of four or five top performers (singers, actors, comedians) popular with one age group (young teens, high school students, college students, people in their twenties, thirties, and so forth—your group can decide on the age group). Once you have the list, write individual essays comparing or contrasting two of the people on the list.

Collaborate

5. Compare or contrast the way you spend a weekday with the way you spend a day off. You can consider what you do in the morning, afternoon, and evening, as points of comparison or contrast.

CLASSIFICATION

Hints for Writing a Classification Essay

1. Be sure to have a point in your classification. Remember that you need to do more than divide something into three or more types, according to some basis, and explain and describe these types. You must have a reason for your classification. For example, if you write about three types of digital cameras, you may be writing to evaluate them, and your point may state which type is the best buy. If you are classifying weight-loss programs, you may be studying each type so that you can prove that two types are dangerous.

2. A simple way to structure your classification essay is to explain each type in a separate body paragraph. Then use the same kind of details to describe each type. For instance, if you describe the medical principles, food restrictions, and results of one type of weight-loss program, describe the medical principles, food restrictions, and results of the other types of weight-loss programs.

WRITING THE CLASSIFICATION ESSAY IN STEPS

PREWRITING   Gathering Ideas: Classification Essay

First, pick a topic for your classification. The next step is to choose some basis for your classification. For example, if you were to write a paragraph classifying phone calls, you could write about phone calls on the basis of their effect on you. With this basis for classification, you can come up with three categories:

> *calls that please me*
>
> *calls that irritate me*
>
> *calls that frighten me*

By brainstorming, you can then gather details about your three categories:

Added Details for Three Categories of a Classification Essay

Topic: Phone Calls

calls that please me
from boyfriend
good friends
catch-up calls—someone I haven't talked to for a while
make me feel close

calls that irritate me
sales calls at dinner time
wrong numbers
calls that interrupt
invade privacy

calls that frighten me
emergency call in the middle of the night
"let's break up" call from boyfriend
change my life, indicate some bad change

With these categories and details, you can write a thesis that (1) mentions what you are classifying and (2) indicates the basis for your classifying by listing all three categories or by stating the basis, or both. Here is a thesis that follows the guidelines:

> *Phone calls can be grouped into the ones that please me, the ones that irritate me, and the ones that frighten me.*

This thesis mentions what you are classifying: *phone calls*. It indicates the basis for classification, the effect of the phone calls, by listing the types: *the ones that please me, the ones that irritate me, and the ones that frighten me.* Here is another thesis that follows the guidelines:

> *I can classify phone calls according to their effect on me.*

This thesis also mentions what you are classifying, *phone calls*, but it mentions the basis for classification, *their effect on me*, instead of listing the types.

Once you have a thesis sentence and a list of ideas, you are ready to begin the planning stage of writing the classification essay.

PLANNING   Devising a Plan: Classification Essay

Following is an outline for a classification essay on phone calls.

An Outline for a Classification Essay

paragraph 1	I. Thesis: Phone calls can be grouped into the ones that please me, the ones that irritate me, and the ones that frighten me.

paragraph 2
topic sentence
and details
pleasing calls
	II. Calls that please me make me feel close to someone.
	  A. I like calls from my boyfriend, especially when he calls to say he is thinking of me.
	  B. I like to hear from good friends.
	  C. My two best friends call me at least twice a day.
	  D. I like catch-up calls.
	  E. These are calls from people I haven't talked to in a while.
	  F. A friend I hadn't seen in a year called me from Ecuador to say "Happy Birthday."
	  G. We talked for a long time.

paragraph 3
topic sentence
and details
irritating calls
	III. Some calls irritate me because they invade my privacy.
	  A. Sales calls always come at dinner time.
	  B. They offer me newspaper subscriptions or "free" vacations.

continued

C. The calls start with a friendly voice, talking fast.

D. By the time I find out what the caller is selling, my dinner is cold.

E. I get at least four wrong-number calls each week.

F. Some of the callers don't even apologize.

G. These calls annoy me because I have to interrupt what I'm doing to answer them.

paragraph 4
topic sentence
and details
frightening calls

IV. The calls that tell me about some bad change in my life frighten me.

A. I once got a call in the middle of the night.

B. It was from a hospital emergency room.

C. The nurse said my brother had been in an accident.

D. That was the most terrifying call of my life.

E. I once got a call from a boyfriend.

F. He said he wanted to break up.

G. His words hurt me.

paragraph 5
conclusion

V. A phone is just an instrument; its effect on the person who receives a call makes it a good or bad instrument.

The outline combined some of the details from the list with new details gathered during the writing process. It used the three categories as the basis for the topic sentences for the body paragraphs. Each topic sentence has two parts: (1) the name of the category, like pleasing calls, and (2) the effect of calls in this category. For example, here is one topic sentence:

1. the category   *2. the effect of calls in this category*

Calls that please me make me feel close to someone.

Since the point of the essay is to show the effect of different kinds of calls, this topic sentence is effective.

As you write and revise your draft, you can continue to add details. You can also combine sentences, add transitions, and work on word choice.

DRAFTING   Drafting and Revising: Classification Essay

Following is a draft of the essay on phone calls. As you read it, you'll notice many changes from the outline.

- An introduction has been added.
- Transitions have been added within and between paragraphs.
- Details have been added.
- Sentences have been combined.
- A concluding paragraph has been added.

A Draft of a Classification Essay

(Thesis and topic sentences are underlined.)

I am lost without a phone. My friends swear that I must have been born holding a tiny phone to my ear. Although I am constantly talking on the phone, I am not always enjoying the process. Not all my phone calls are enjoyable. In fact, <u>the calls can be grouped into the ones that please me, the ones that irritate me, and the ones that frighten me.</u>

<u>Calls that please me make me feel close to someone.</u> For example, I like calls from my boyfriend, especially when he calls to say that he is thinking of me. I also like to hear from good friends. My two best friends call me at least twice a day, and it is amazing that we can always find something to talk about. Catch-up calls, calls from people I haven't seen in a while, are another kind of call I enjoy. Recently, a friend I hadn't seen in a year called me from Ecuador to say "Happy Birthday." It was so good to hear from her that we talked for a long time.

The ring of a phone can bring me warm feelings, but it can sometimes bring irritation. <u>Calls that irritate me invade my privacy.</u> Sales calls, for instance, always come at dinner time. They offer me newspaper subscriptions or "free" vacations that always have a hidden cost. This kind of call always starts with a friendly voice, talking fast. By the time I figure out what the caller is selling, my dinner is cold. Also in this category are wrong-number calls. I get at least four of these a week, and some of the callers don't even apologize for bothering me. These calls annoy me because I have to interrupt what I'm doing to answer them.

Finally, there are the worst calls of all. <u>The calls that frighten me tell me about some bad change in my life.</u> I once got a call in the middle of the night. It was from a hospital emergency room; the nurse told me my brother had been in an accident. That was the most terrifying call of my life. Another time, a boyfriend called to say he wanted to break up. His cold words surprised and hurt me.

I rely on the telephone, but it is not always good to me. Ever since I received the call about my brother's accident, I tremble when the phone rings late at night. However, I have come to realize that <u>a phone is just an instrument; its effect on the person who receives a call makes it a good or bad instrument.</u>

POLISHING | ## Polishing and Proofreading: Classification Essay

Following is the final version of the essay on phone calls. When you compare it to the draft, you will notice some changes:

- Some of the word choice has been polished to make details more specific, to eliminate repetition, or to eliminate an awkward phrase.
- A final sentence has been added to paragraph 4 to reinforce the point that both examples in the paragraph are about a life-changing phone call.
- The last sentence in the concluding paragraph has been revised to make a more precise statement about the basis for the classification: the effect of each type of phone call.
- A title has been added.

A Final Version of a Classification Essay

(Changes from the draft are underlined.)

Phone Calls: Good, Bad, and Ugly

I am lost without a phone. My friends swear that I must have been born holding a tiny phone to my ear. Although I am constantly talking on the phone, I am not always enjoying the process. Not all <u>the conversations</u> are <u>pleasant</u>. In fact, the calls can be grouped into the ones that please me, the ones that irritate me, and the ones that frighten me.

continued

Calls that please me make me feel close to someone. For example, I like calls from my boyfriend, especially when he calls to say that he is thinking of me. I also like to hear from good friends. My two best friends call me at least twice a day, and it is amazing that we can always find something to talk about. Catch-up calls, calls from people I haven't seen in a while, are another kind of call I enjoy. Recently, a friend I hadn't seen in a year called me from Ecuador to say "Happy Birthday." It was so good to hear from her that we talked for <u>an hour</u>.

The ring of a phone can bring me warm feelings, but it can sometimes bring irritation. Calls that irritate me invade my privacy. Sales calls, for instance, always come at dinner time. They offer me newspaper subscriptions or "free" vacations that always have a hidden cost. This kind of call always starts with a friendly voice, talking fast. By the time I figure out what the caller is selling, my dinner is cold. Also in this category are wrong-number calls. I get at least four of these a week, and some of the callers don't even apologize for bothering me. These calls annoy me because I have to interrupt what I'm doing to answer them.

Finally, there are the worst calls of all. The calls that frighten me tell me about some <u>crisis</u> in my life. I once got a call in the middle of the night. It was from a hospital emergency room; the nurse told me my brother had been in an accident. That was the most terrifying call of my life. Another time, a boyfriend called to say he wanted to break up. His cold words surprised and hurt me. <u>Both of these calls brought me news that changed my life, and the news was totally unexpected.</u>

I rely on the telephone, but it is not always good to me. Ever since I received the call about my brother's accident, I tremble when the phone rings late at night. However, I have come to realize that a phone is just an instrument; <u>it conveys a message</u>. Its effect on the person who receives <u>that message</u> makes it a <u>welcome, annoying, or dreaded</u> instrument.

TOPICS FOR WRITING A CLASSIFICATION ESSAY

When you write on any of these topics, work through the stages of the writing process in preparing your essay.

Collaborate

1. Write a classification essay on any of the topics below. If your instructor agrees, brainstorm with a partner or group to come up with a basis for your classification and categories related to the basis.

bargains	recipes	workouts
cartoon heroes	snacks	your clothes
discount stores	talk shows	your coworkers
ghost stories	teen idols	your dreams
gossip	visits to the dentist	your mistakes
music videos	war movies	your relatives
photographs	Web sites	your travels

2. You may not know it, but you are probably an expert on something. For example, you may work in a jewelry store and know all about diamonds. You may be a paramedic and know about medical emergencies. If you are a veterinarian's assistant, you know about cats and dogs. If you collect Barbie dolls, you are an expert on these toys. Consider what you know best, through your work, hobbies, education, or leisure activities, and write a classification essay about a subject in that area. If you know about diamonds, you can

classify engagement rings. If you work at a veterinarian's office, you can classify pet owners or poodles.

3. Below are some topics. Each one already has a basis for classification. Write a classification essay on one of the choices.

Classify
a. babysitters on the basis of how competent they are
b. small children on the basis of their sleeping habits
c. teenage boys or girls on the basis of their favorite sport
d. government offices (like the driver's license office, courthouse) on the basis of how efficient they are
e. roads on the basis of how safe they are
f. fads on the basis of how long they last
g. auto repair shops on the basis of their reliability
h. classrooms on the basis of how comfortable they are
i. uniforms on the basis of how attractive they are
j. uniforms on the basis of how comfortable they are

4. This assignment requires a little research. Write an essay that classifies some product according to price. That is, you can classify home computers (or hair dryers, bookbags, hiking boots, motorcycles, and so forth) according to their cost. Pretend that you are writing to advise readers who may want to buy this product and want the best deal for their money. Research the details of this product in different price ranges; for example, explain what the most expensive computer includes and how useful these features are, and then explain what mid-priced and low-priced computers offer for their price. Use your essay to recommend the best deal for the money.

DEFINITION

Hints for Writing a Definition Essay

1. Write a personal definition, not a dictionary definition. To develop a definition essay, you need to define a term that can be explained by more than the words in the dictionary. You can develop your essay with concrete terms and specific examples that help define the term.

> **terms that won't work in a personal definition:** photosynthesis, DNA, the Colt Revolver, the Renaissance

> **terms that will work in a personal definition:** self-pity, patience, the team player, the pessimist

2. Include in your thesis (1) the term you are defining, (2) the broad class or category into which your term fits, and (3) the specific distinguishing characteristics that make the term different from all others in the class or category. Each of the following sentences could be the thesis for a definition essay.

> *term   category distinguishing characteristics*
>
> *Envy is the desire for what others have.*
>
> *term   category distinguishing characteristics*
>
> *A nitpicker is a person who worries excessively about minor details.*

3. Form your body paragraphs from different aspects of your term; for example, if you defined *patience*, you might write one paragraph on the times when patience is necessary and another on the times when people need to stop being patient and take action. If you write about *temptation*, you might write one paragraph on how to resist temptation and another on when to give in to temptation.

WRITING THE DEFINITION ESSAY IN STEPS

PREWRITING   Gathering Ideas: Definition Essay

To pick a topic for your definition essay, you can begin with some personality trait or type of person. For instance, you might define "the insecure person." If you listed your first thoughts, your list might look like this:

> *the insecure person*
> *someone who is not emotionally secure*
> *wants (needs?) other people to make him or her feel good*
> *no self-respect*

Often, when you look for ideas to define a term, you get stuck with big, general statements or abstract words, or you simply cannot come up with enough to say. If you are having trouble getting ideas, think of questions about your term. Jot these questions down without stopping to answer them. One question can lead you to another question. Once you have five or more questions, you can answer them, and the answers will provide details for your definition paragraph.

If you were writing about the insecure person, for example, you could begin with questions like these:

> *What are insecure people like?*
> *What behavior shows a person is insecure?*
> *How do insecure people dress or talk?*
> *What makes a person insecure?*
> *Why is insecurity a bad trait?*
> *How do insecure people relate to others?*
> *Does insecurity hurt the insecure person? If so, how?*
> *Does the insecure person hurt others? If so, how?*

By scanning the questions and answering as many as you can, you can add details to your list. Once you have a longer list, you can review it and begin to group the items on the list. Following is a list of grouped details on the insecure person.

Grouped Details for a Definition Essay

Topic: The Insecure Person

wants (needs?) other people to make him or her feel important
no self-respect

insecure people have to brag about everything
a friend who brags about his car
they tell you the price of everything

they put others down

saying bad things about other people makes insecure people feel better

insecure people can never relax inside

can never enjoy being with other people

other people are always their competitors

must always worry about what others think of them

Grouping the details can help you arrive at several main ideas. Can they be combined and revised to create a topic sentence? Following is a topic sentence on the insecure person that meets the requirements of naming the term, placing it in a category, and distinguishing the term from others in the category:

term   *category*   *distinguishing chararcteristics*

The insecure person is someone who needs other people to make him or her feel respected and important.

Once you have a thesis sentence, you can begin working on the planning stage of the essay.

PLANNING   **Devising a Plan: Definition Essay**

Following is an outline for a definition essay on the insecure person.

An Outline for a Definition Essay

paragraph 1

I.   Thesis: The insecure person is someone who needs other people to make him or her feel respected and important.

paragraph 2
topic sentence
and details
bragging

II. Insecure people have to brag about everything.
  A. An insecure friend may have to brag about his car.
  B. He is sure to tell you how fast it can go.
  C. Insecure people wear expensive jewelry and tell you what it cost.
  D. A man will tell you what his ring cost; a woman will tell you what her boyfriend paid for her ring.
  E. They make sure they wear clothes with trendy labels.
  F. They have to have shirts with the designer's logo on the pocket and jackets with the designer's name spread across the front.
  G. This is another kind of bragging.

paragraph 3
topic sentence
and details
putting others
down

III. Insecure people put others down.
  A. They make mean remarks about other people's looks, clothes, or style.
  B. Saying bad things about others makes insecure people feel better.
  C. When some friends were talking about Susan's great new job, Jill had to make mean remarks about Susan.
  D. Jill hated having Susan look like a winner.
  E. Jill wanted all the attention and admiration for herself.

continued

F. I work with a man who is always spreading cruel gossip.

G. His attacks on others are a cowardly way of making himself look good.

paragraph 4
topic sentence
and details
never relaxing

IV. Insecure people can never relax inside.
A. They can never enjoy being with other people.
B. Other people are always their competition.
C. Luke plays pickup basketball games.
D. He can't enjoy any game of basketball unless he is the star.
E. When someone on his team scores, he is not pleased.
F. Instead, he becomes aggressive and selfish.
G. Another person I know is always loud and crude at parties.
H. He is so desperate to be liked that he turns himself into an obnoxious character that he thinks is the life of the party.

paragraph 5
conclusion

V. Insecure people must always worry about what others think about them.

The outline combined some of the details from the list with new details and examples gathered during the outlining process. As you write and revise your draft, you can continue to add details. You can also combine sentences, add transitions, and work on word choice.

DRAFTING   Drafting and Revising: Definition Essay

Following is a draft of the essay on the insecure person. As you read it, you'll notice many changes from the outline.

- An introduction has been added.
- Transitions have been added within and between paragraphs.
- Details have been added.
- Sentences have been combined.
- A concluding paragraph has been added.

A Draft of a Definition Essay

(Thesis and topic sentences are underlined.)

Everybody knows at least one person who seems to feel so superior that no one could ever reach his or her status. Sometimes this person annoys others; at other times, this person hurts them. While it seems to be pride that motivates this person to irritate and belittle others, it is really insecurity disguised as ego. The insecure person is someone who needs other people to make him or her feel respected and important.

One sign of the insecure person is bragging. Insecure people have to brag about everything. An insecure friend may have to brag about his car and will be sure to tell everyone that he drives a Honda S2000 sports car. Some insecure people wear expensive jewelry and tell you what it cost. A man may boast about what his ring cost; a woman will mention what her boyfriend paid for her ring. Others filled with insecurity brag about their expensive clothes. They make sure they wear clothes with trendy labels. They have to have shirts with the designer's logo on the pocket or jackets with the designer's name spread across the front. This is another kind of bragging.

   Insecure people not only like to build themselves up, but they also have to put others down. They make mean remarks about other people's looks, clothes, and style. Saying bad things about others makes insecure people feel better. Recently, some friends were talking about our classmate Susan's great new job. While most of us were happy for Susan, Jill had to add some comments about how lucky Susan had been to get the job since Susan was not qualified for it. Because she wants all the attention and admiration for herself, Jill hated having Susan looking like a winner. Another insecure person is a man I work with who is always spreading cruel gossip. His attacks on others are his cowardly way of making himself look good.

   The constant need to shine in other people's opinion means that insecure people can never relax inside. Other people are always their competition for attention or approval. One such person is Luke, a college acquaintance who always plays on our pickup basketball games. Even though the games are just for fun, Luke can't enjoy any game of basketball unless he is the star. When someone on his team scores, he isn't pleased. Instead, he becomes aggressive and selfish. He wants to win every game single-handed. Another person who is eager to shine is always loud and crude at parties. He is so desperate to be liked that he turns himself into an obnoxious character that he thinks is the life of the party.

   Insecure people can be mean and obnoxious, but they are mainly sad. Insecure people must always worry about what others think of them. Because they care so much about others' opinions, they cannot be spontaneous or open. They must get very tired of hiding their fears behind their bragging and criticizing. They must also be very lonely.

POLISHING   Polishing and Proofreading: Definition Essay

Following is the final version of the essay on the insecure person. When you compare it to the draft, you will notice some changes:

- Sentences in paragraph 2 have been combined for a smoother style.
- The word "this" in the last sentence of paragraph 2 has been replaced with a more specific phrase: "This obsession with designer clothes."
- Some of the word choice has been polished to avoid repetition or to be precise.
- A specific example has been added to paragraph 4.
- A title has been added.

A Final Version of a Definition Essay

(Changes from the draft are underlined.)

The Insecure Person

   Everybody knows at least one person who seems to feel so superior that no one could ever reach his or her status. Sometimes this person annoys others; at other times, this person hurts them. While it seems to be pride that motivates this

continued

person to irritate and belittle others, it is really insecurity disguised as ego. The insecure person is someone who needs other people to make him or her feel respected and important.

<u>One sign of the insecure person is bragging, for insecure people have to brag about everything.</u> An insecure friend may have to brag about his car and will be sure to tell everyone that he drives a Honda S2000 sports car. Some insecure people wear expensive jewelry and brag about what it cost. A man may boast about what his ring cost; a woman will mention what her boyfriend paid for her ring. Others filled with insecurity <u>show off</u> their expensive clothes. They make sure they wear clothes with trendy labels. They have to have shirts with the designer's logo on the pocket or jackets with the designer's name spread across the front. This <u>obsession with designer clothes</u> is another kind of bragging.

Insecure people not only like to build themselves up, but they also have to put others down. They make mean remarks about other people's looks, clothes, and style. <u>Making nasty comments</u> about others makes insecure people feel better. Recently, some friends were talking about our classmate Susan's great new job. While most of us were happy for Susan, Jill had to add some comments about how lucky Susan had been to get the job since Susan was not qualified for it. Because she wants all the attention and admiration for herself, Jill hated having Susan looking like a winner. Another insecure person is a man I work with who is always spreading cruel gossip. His attacks on others are his cowardly way of making himself look good.

The constant need to shine in other people's opinion means that insecure people can never relax inside. Other people are always their competition for attention or approval. One such person is Luke, a college acquaintance who always plays on our pickup basketball games. Even though the games are just for fun, Luke can't enjoy any game of basketball unless he is the star. When someone on his team scores, he isn't pleased. Instead, he becomes aggressive and selfish. He wants to win every game single-handed. Another person who is eager to shine is <u>my cousin Jamie, a generally good-natured person who</u> is always loud and crude at parties. He is so desperate to be liked that he turns himself into an obnoxious character that he thinks is the life of the party.

Insecure people can be mean and obnoxious, but they are mainly sad. Insecure people must always worry about what others think of them. Because they care so much about others' opinions, they cannot be spontaneous or open. They must get very tired of hiding their fears behind their bragging and criticizing. They must also be very lonely.

TOPICS FOR WRITING A DEFINITION ESSAY

When you write on any of these topics, work through the stages of the writing process in preparing your essay.

1. What is the one quality you most admire in other people? Is it courage, kindness, drive, or another character trait? Choose a quality and write an essay defining it.

2. Define any of the terms below, using specific details and examples. You can begin by looking up the term in a dictionary to make sure you understand the dictionary meaning. Then write a personal definition.

boldness	compassion	contentment
brotherhood	confidence	generosity

guilt	perseverance	sympathy
longing	satisfaction	trust
nerve	shyness	willpower
paranoia	stress	worry

3. Write a definition of a specific type of person. Develop your definition by using specific details and examples. Following is a list of types.

the big brother/sister	the hypochondriac	the patriot
the computer geek	the ideal mate	the planner
the control freak	the loner	the rebel
the critic	the lost soul	the sneak
the good sport	the nagger	the tattletale
the guardian angel	the natural athlete	the tightwad

4. We often use terms that we assume everyone knows, but that may not have clear definitions. Write your definition of such a term. Examples of these terms are listed below, but you can also choose your own term.

alpha male	negative vibes	people skills
comfort zone	a people person	personal issues
fashion sense	people pleaser	street smarts

CAUSE AND EFFECT

Hints for Writing a Cause or Effect Essay

1. **Choose either causes or effects.** If you try to do both in a short essay, you will make your task more difficult. In addition, you need a longer and more complex essay to cover both causes and effects adequately.

2. **You can use each cause or effect as the focus of one body paragraph.** You can develop the paragraph by explaining and describing that cause or effect.

WRITING THE CAUSE OR EFFECT ESSAY IN STEPS

PREWRITING   Gathering Ideas: Cause or Effect Essay

If you were thinking about writing a cause or effect essay on owning a car, you could begin by freewriting something like this:

Freewriting for a Cause or Effect Essay

Topic: Owning a Car

A car of my own. Why? I needed it. Couldn't get a part-time job without one. Because I couldn't get to work. Needed it to get to school. Of course I could have taken the bus to school. But I didn't want to. Feel like a grown-up when you have a car of your own. Freedom to come and go. I was the last of my friends to have a car. Couldn't wait. An old Camaro. But I fixed it up nicely. Costs a lot to maintain. Car payments, car loan. Car insurance.

Now you can review the freewriting and make separate lists of causes and effects you wrote down:

causes (reasons)
needed to get a part-time job
needed to get to school
my friends had cars

effects (results)
feel like a grown-up
freedom to come and go
costs a lot to maintain
car payments
car loan
car insurance

Because you have more details on the effects of owning a car, you decide to write an effects essay.

After brainstorming questions to help you gather more effects and details, you are ready to write another list:

List of Effects for a Effect Essay

Topic: Owning a Car

effect 1: I had to pay for the car and related expenses.

details: *costs a lot to maintain*
              car payments
              car loans
              car insurance

effect 2: I had the adult freedom to come and go.

details: *didn't have to beg my father for his truck*
              didn't have to get rides from friends
              could go to the city when I wanted
              could ride around for fun

effect 3: I became a more careful driver.

details: *worried about someone hitting the car*
              worried about bad drivers
              wanted to avoid the scratches cars get in parking lots

---

With at least three effects and some details for each effect, you can create a thesis. The thesis for this essay should indicate that the subject is the *effects* of getting a car. You can summarize all three effects in your thesis, or you can just hint at them. A possible thesis sentence for the essay can be

Owning my own car cost me money, gave me freedom, and made me more careful about how I drive.

The thesis summarizes all three effects. Another possible thesis hints at the effects:

Once I got a car, I realized the good and bad sides of ownership.

With a thesis sentence, three effects, and a list of details, you are ready to write an outline for your essay.

PLANNING **Devising a Plan: Effects Essay**

Following is an outline for an effects essay on owning a car.

An Outline for an Effects Essay

paragraph 1	I. Thesis: Owning my own car gave me freedom, cost me money, and made me a more careful driver.

paragraph 2
topic sentence
and details
effect 1
freedom
	II. The wonderful part of owning a car was the adult freedom it gave me.
	  A. I didn't have to beg my father for his truck.
	  B. Every time I asked him, he seemed reluctant to lend it to me.
	  C. He was always worried that I would get the interior dirty.
	  D. I didn't have to get rides from my friends.
	  E. I was really tired of begging rides from my buddies, and I am sure they were sick of driving me around.
	  F. I could go to the city whenever I wanted.
	  G. I could even ride around for fun.

paragraph 3
topic sentence
and details
effect 2
costs
	III. I had to pay for the car and related expenses.
	  A. A car costs a lot to maintain.
	  B. There are oil changes and tune-ups.
	  C. My car needed new tires.
	  D. I had car payments.
	  E. I had a car loan to pay.
	  F. I had car insurance.
	  G. I had to work overtime to pay the insurance bills.

paragraph 4
topic sentence
and details
effect 3
cautiousness
	IV. I became a more careful driver.
	  A. I worried about someone hitting the car.
	  B. I could see my beautiful car dented and dinged.
	  C. I began to worry about bad drivers.
	  D. I became more nervous on the road.
	  E. I worried about parking lots.
	  F. I wanted to avoid the scratches cars can get in parking lots.
	  G. I parked at the end of the row, away from other cars.

paragraph 5 conclusion	V. Owning a car gave me adult freedom, but it gave me adult responsibilities and worries, too.

The outline put each effect into a separate body paragraph. It combined some of the details from the list with details gathered during the outlining process. As you write and revise your draft, you can continue to add details. You can also combine sentences, add transitions, and work on word choice.

DRAFTING   Drafting and Revising: Effects Essay

Following is a draft of the essay on owning a car. As you read it, you'll notice many changes from the outline on page 313.

- An introduction has been added.
- Transitions have been added within and between paragraphs.
- Details have been added.
- Sentences have been combined.
- A concluding paragraph has been added.

A Draft of an Effects Essay

(Thesis and topic sentences are underlined.)

Ever since I was six years old, I have dreamed of owning my own car. The day I got my driver's license was one of the happiest days of my life. All that was left, I thought, was having a car of my own. That day came, too, and it changed my life. <u>Owning my own car gave me freedom, cost me money, and made me a more careful driver.</u>

<u>The wonderful part of owning a car was the adult freedom it gave me.</u> First of all, I didn't have to beg my father for his truck anymore. Every time I asked him, he seemed reluctant to lend it to me. He was always worried that I would get the interior dirty. Second, I no longer had to get rides from my friends whenever I wanted to go somewhere. I was really tired of begging rides from my buddies, and I am sure they were sick of driving me around. With my own car, I could go to the city whenever I wanted. I could even ride around for fun.

On the more serious side, <u>I had to pay for the car and related expenses.</u> A car costs a lot to maintain. There are oil changes and tune-ups to keep the car in good running condition. Two months after I got my car, I had to buy four new and very expensive tires. Of course, I had monthly payments on my car loan. I also had to pay for car insurance, which, because of my young age, was unbelievably expensive. My insurance cost so much that I had to work overtime to pay it.

Now that I was paying for the car I drove, <u>I became a more careful driver.</u> I became worried about someone hitting the car; I could imagine my beautiful car dented and dinged. These thoughts made me worry about bad drivers and become more nervous on the road. Parking lots made me nervous, too. To avoid the scratches cars can get in parking lots, I parked at the end of the row, away from other cars.

<u>Owning a car gave me adult freedom, but it gave me adult responsibilities and worries, too.</u> Even with the stress of car payments, insurance payments, and car maintenance, I would never give up my car. My fear of dents and scratches can't keep me from the joy of driving whenever and wherever I want. I'm happy to accept the responsibilities that come with being on the road in my own car.

POLISHING   Polishing and Proofreading: Effects Essay

Following is the final version of the essay on owning a car. When you compare it to the draft, you will notice some changes:

- Some of the word choice has been polished, replacing a vague term like "costs a lot" with the more specific "costs hundreds of dollars" and avoiding repetition of words like "worry" and "expensive."

- Details have been added; for instance, in paragraph 2 there are new details about what makes a car dirty and about how friends feel ("acting like a taxi service") when they are constantly asked for rides.
- A sentence has been added to paragraph 4 to support the topic sentence. The focus of the paragraph is on careful driving, and the body of the paragraph gives many examples of the fears of a new car owner, but it needed one more detail to show the change in the owner's driving.
- A title has been added.

A Final Version of an Effects Essay

(Changes from the draft are underlined.)

Owning a Car: My New Lease on Life

Ever since I was six years old, I have dreamed of owning my own car. The day I got my driver's license was one of the happiest days of my life. All that was left, I thought, was having a car of my own. That day came, too, and it changed my life. Owning my own car gave me freedom, cost me money, and made me a more careful driver.

The wonderful part of owning a car was the adult freedom it gave me. First of all, I didn't have to beg my father for his truck anymore. Every time I asked him, he seemed reluctant to lend it to me. He was always worried that I would dirty the interior with food wrappers and empty soda cans. Second, I no longer had to get rides from my friends whenever I wanted to go somewhere. I was really tired of begging rides from my buddies, and I am sure they were sick of acting like a taxi service. With my own car, I could go to the city whenever I wanted. I could even ride around for fun.

On the more serious side, I had to pay for the car and related expenses. A car costs hundreds of dollars to maintain. There are oil changes and tune-ups to keep the car in good running condition. Two months after I got my car, I had to buy four new and very expensive tires. Of course, I had monthly payments on my car loan. I also had to pay for car insurance, which, because of my young age, was unbelievably high. My insurance cost so much that I had to work overtime to pay the bill.

Now that I was paying for the car I drove, I became a more careful driver. I became worried about someone hitting the car; I could imagine my beautiful car dented and dinged. These thoughts made me fear bad drivers and become more nervous on the road. I began to drive more defensively, and instead of challenging aggressive drivers, I began to avoid them. Parking lots made me nervous, too. To avoid the scratches cars can get in parking lots, I parked at the end of the row, away from other cars.

Owning a car gave me adult freedom, but it gave me adult responsibilities and worries, too. Yet even with the stress of car payments, insurance payments, and car maintenance, I would never give up my car. My fear of dents and scratches can't keep me from the joy of driving whenever and wherever I want. I'm happy to accept the responsibilities that come with being on the road, in my own car.

TOPICS FOR WRITING A CAUSE OR EFFECT ESSAY

When you write on any of these topics, work through the stages of the writing process in preparing your essay.

1. Think of a time when you had to make an important choice. Then write an essay explaining the reasons for your choice. Your essay can include an explanation of your options as well as the reasons for your choice.

2. Write an essay about the effects one of the following experiences had on you (or someone you know well).

learning to swim	learning to read
learning a new language	learning to use a computer
learning to dance	learning to sing
learning to play a new sport	learning to meditate
learning to play a musical instrument	

3. Write an essay on one of the following topics:

Why Some Students Are Nervous about Speaking in Class
Why Most Children No Longer Walk or Ride Bicycles to School
Why Many High School Students Have Part-Time Jobs
Why Many _____ (teens, young people, families, older people, Hispanics, Chinese, Canadians—you name the group) like to watch _____ (you name the television show).
Why College Students May Feel Lonely

4. Think of a singer, rapper, singing group, or musician that is popular with people of your age and background. Write an essay explaining that person or group's popularity.

5. Explain why a certain kind of car has become much more popular than it used to be.

ARGUMENT

Hints for Writing an Argument Essay

1. **Pick a topic based on your own experience and observation.** Although you may not realize it, you have a wide range of experience because you play many roles: consumer, student, parent, child, husband or wife, worker, driver, pet owner, athlete. These and many other roles may fit you. In each of your roles, you may have noticed or experienced something that can lead to a topic.

2. **Be sure to take a stand in your thesis.** That is, don't merely state a problem, but make a point about how to solve or eliminate it.

> **not this:** The potholes on Johnson Road are terrible.
>
> **but this:** The Department of Public Works must fix the potholes on Johnson Road immediately.
>
> **not this:** Skateboarders have nowhere to go in Mason Heights.
>
> **but this:** Mason Heights needs a skateboard park.

3. **Use the reasons in your argument as a way to focus your body paragraphs.** If you have three reasons, for instance, you can write three body paragraphs.

4. Consider your audience's objections. Always ask yourself who the audience is for your argument. If you are arguing that your office needs a new copier, you will probably be writing to your supervisor. If you are arguing for an after-school program at your child's elementary school, you will probably be writing to the school board. Think about why your audience should support your points and how they might object.

There are several ways to handle objections. If you can *refute* an objection—that is, prove that it isn't valid—you have removed a major obstacle. Sometimes you may have to admit the other side has a valid objection by *conceding* it. Even by conceding, however, you win confidence by showing that you know both sides of the argument and are open-minded enough to consider another point of view.

Another way to handle an objection is to *turn an objection into an advantage*. That is, you can admit the objection is valid but use it to reinforce your own point. If you are arguing for a new copier and your supervisor says it is too expensive, you can agree that it is expensive but that the office is losing time and money by constantly repairing the old copier. Turning an obstacle into an advantage shows that you are informed, open-minded, and quick-thinking.

Even if you do not openly refer to objections in your argument essay, being aware of possible objections helps you to frame your points effectively, with your audience in mind.

WRITING THE ARGUMENT ESSAY IN STEPS

PREWRITING Gathering Ideas: Argument Essay

Imagine that your instructor has given you this assignment:

> Write a letter to the editor of your local newspaper. Argue for something in your town that needs to be changed.

One way to begin is to brainstorm for some specific issue that you can write about. You can ask questions such as these: Is there a part of town that needs to be cleaned up? Should something be changed at a school? What do I notice on my way to work or school that needs improvement? What could be improved in my neighborhood?

By answering these questions, you may come up with one topic, and then you can list ideas on it.

topic
Cleaning Up Roberts Park

ideas
dirty and overgrown
benches are all cracked and broken
full of trash
could be fixed up
people work nearby
they would use it

You can consider your audience and possible objections:

audience
local people of all ages who read the local paper

possible objections from this audience
would cost money
more important things to spend money on

answering objections
Money would be well spent to beautify the downtown.
City children could play there in the fresh air and in nature; workers could eat lunch there.

Once you have a list, you can start grouping the ideas on your list. Some of the objections you wrote down may actually lead you to reasons that support your argument. That is, by answering objections, you may come up with reasons that support your point. Following is a list with a point to argue, three supporting reasons, and some details about cleaning up Roberts Park.

A List for an Argument Essay

Topic: Cleaning Up a Park

point: *We should fix up Roberts Park*

reason: *Improving the park would make the downtown area more attractive to shoppers.*

details: *Shoppers could stroll in the park or rest from their shopping.*
Friends could meet in the park for a day of shopping and lunch.

reason: *City children could play in the park.*

details: *They could get fresh air.*
They could play in a natural setting.

reason: *Workers could eat lunch outdoors.*

details: *Several office complexes are nearby.*
Workers would take a break outdoors.

With your reasons and details, you can draft a thesis sentence:

Roberts Park should be cleaned up and improved.

With a thesis sentence, three reasons, and details, you are ready to move on to the planning stage of preparing an argument essay.

> **PLANNING**   Devising a Plan: Argument Essay

Following is an outline for an argument essay on cleaning up a park.

An Outline for an Argument Essay

paragraph 1	I. Thesis: Roberts Park should be cleaned up and improved.
paragraph 2 **topic sentence** **and details**	II. Improving the park would make the downtown area more attractive to shoppers.
	A. If the city could clean, landscape, and refurnish the park, it would be a natural refuge for shoppers.
reason 1	B. It is located in the middle of the shopping district.
a place for **shoppers**	C. Those who already shop in the city could stroll through the park or rest there after shopping.

D. Soon, shoppers would tell their friends about the attractive, new-looking park.
E. Eventually, friends could agree to meet at the park for a day of shopping and lunch.
F. City shops and department stores would see business improve.
G. Business would be good for restaurants, too.

paragraph 3
topic sentence
add details

reason 2
a place for
workers

III. Workers from nearby offices and stores could eat lunch outdoors.
A. Several office buildings are nearby.
B. During the lunch break, many people, even those who bring their lunch, want to get out of the office or store.
C. Everyone wants to get up and forget the job for a little while.
D. Some want fresh air.
E. Others want to read a book or magazine while they eat.
F. Others want to get some exercise by walking a little.
G. Others just want to observe nature and people.
H. An improved park could meet all these needs.

paragraph 4
topic sentence
and details

reason 3
a place for
children

IV. City children could play there.
A. City children live in apartments.
B. They don't have backyards to enjoy.
C. They are reduced to playing in dangerous streets or on narrow sidewalks.
D. Many aren't allowed outside at all.
E. They go from sitting all day at school to sitting at home.
F. In the park, children could interact rather than sit alone inside, watching television and playing video games.
G. They could play on grass, not asphalt.
H. They would not have to play near traffic.

paragraph 5
conclusion

V. Roberts Park used to be the city's landmark, and it could be, once again.

The outline combined some of the details from the list with new details gathered during the planning process. It focused each body paragraph on one reason to clean up the park. As you write and revise your draft, you can continue to add details to each reason. You can also combine sentences, add transitions, and work on word choice.

DRAFTING   **Drafting and Revising: Argument Essay**

Following is a draft of the essay on cleaning up a park. As you read it, you'll notice many changes from the outline on pages 318–319.

- An introduction has been added.
- Transitions have been added within and between paragraphs.
- Details have been added.
- A concluding paragraph has been added.

A Draft of an Argument Essay

(Thesis and topic sentences are underlined.)

Roberts Park was once a pretty little park with a fountain, dark wood benches, carefully landscaped paths, and lush trees and flowers. Today, however, the fountain is cracked and dry, the benches are faded and splintered, and the paths are overgrown. Trash fills the flowerbeds. <u>Roberts Park should be cleaned up and improved.</u>

There are several reasons why a better park would make a better city. <u>First, improving the park would make the downtown area more attractive to shoppers.</u> If the city could clean, landscape, and refurnish the park, it would be a natural refuge for shoppers. It is right in the middle of the shopping district, making it convenient for those who already shop in the city to stroll through the park or rest there. Soon, shoppers might tell their friends about the attractive, new-looking park. Eventually, friends could agree to meet at the park for a day of shopping and lunch. City shops and department stores would see an increase in business, and restaurants would benefit, too.

Those who do business in the city would appreciate a renovated park as well. <u>Workers from nearby offices and stores could eat lunch outdoors.</u> Several high-rise office buildings are nearby, full of office workers. During their lunch break, many people, even those who bring their lunch, want to get out of the office or store. Everyone wants to get up and forget the job for a little while. Some want fresh air while others want to read a book or magazine while they eat. The more ambitious want to get some exercise by walking a little; however, many people just want to observe nature and people. An improved park could meet all these needs.

The most important reason to clean up the park is to help children. <u>City children could play in Roberts Park.</u> City children, who live in apartments, don't have backyards to enjoy. If they go outside, they are reduced to playing in dangerous streets or on narrow sidewalks. Many aren't allowed outside at all. They go from sitting all day at school to sitting at home. In a restored park, children could interact rather than sit alone inside, watching television and playing video games. They could play on grass, not asphalt. Best of all, they would not have to play near traffic.

Today, the words "Roberts Park" describe a rundown, ragged plot of broken benches, weeds, and trash. But the place could be a haven for children, shoppers, and workers. Once the park was green, the fountain shimmered, and the benches shone. <u>Roberts Park used to be the city's landmark, and it could be, once again.</u>

POLISHING ## Polishing and Proofreading: Argument Essay

Following is the final version of the essay on cleaning up a park. When you compare it to the draft on page 320, you will notice some changes:

- The introduction needed a transition from the description of the park to the thesis.
- A transition sentence has been added.
- One sentence in paragraph 2 has been revised to eliminate extra words.

- Also in paragraph 2, the words "shop," "shoppers," and "shopping" became repetitive, so one phrase, "these people," replaced one use of "shoppers."
- Some details have been added and word choice improved.
- A new sentence of details has been added to paragraph 4.
- A transition has been added to paragraph 4.
- A title has been added.

A Final Version of an Argument Essay

(Changes from the draft are underlined.)

The Case for Renovating Roberts Park

Roberts Park was once a pretty little park, with a <u>bubbling</u> fountain, dark wood benches, carefully landscaped paths, and lush trees and flowers. Today, however, the fountain is cracked and dry, the benches are faded and splintered, and the paths are overgrown. Trash fills the flowerbeds. <u>It is time to make this place parklike again.</u> Roberts Park should be cleaned up and improved.

There are several reasons why a better park would make a better city. First, improving the park would make the downtown area more attractive to shoppers. If the city could clean, landscape, and refurnish the park, it would be a natural refuge for shoppers. <u>Because it is right in the middle of the shopping district, those who already shop in the city would be likely to stroll through the park or rest there.</u> Soon, <u>these people</u> might tell their friends about the attractive, new-looking park. Eventually, friends could agree to meet at the park for a day of shopping and lunch. City shops and department stores would see an increase in business, and restaurants would benefit, too.

Those who do business in the city would appreciate a renovated park as well. Workers from nearby offices and stores could eat lunch outdoors. Several high-rise office buildings are nearby, full of office workers. During their lunch break, many people, even those who bring their lunch, want to get out of the office or store. Everyone wants to get up and forget the job for a little while. Some want fresh air while others want to read a book or magazine while they eat. The more ambitious want to get some exercise by walking a little; however, many people just want to observe nature and people. An improved park could meet all these needs.

The most important reason to clean up the park is to help children. City children could play in Roberts Park. City children, who live in apartments, don't have backyards to enjoy. If they go outside, they are reduced to playing in dangerous streets or on narrow sidewalks. Many aren't allowed outside at all. They go from sitting all day at school to sitting at home. In a restored park, children could interact rather than sit alone inside, watching television and playing video games. <u>They would get some much-needed exercise. In addition</u>, they could play on grass, not asphalt. Best of all, they would not have to play near traffic.

Today, the words "Roberts Park" describe a rundown, ragged <u>site full of</u> broken benches, weeds, and trash. But the place could be a haven for children, shoppers, and workers. Once the park was green, the fountain shimmered, and the benches shone. Roberts Park used to be the city's landmark, and it could be, once again.

TOPICS FOR WRITING AN ARGUMENT ESSAY

When you write on any of these topics, work through the stages of the writing process in preparing your essay.

1. Write an essay for readers of your local newspaper, arguing for or against one of the following:

   a. city-wide curfew for every person under 18
   b. video surveillance cameras that record all activity in high-crime areas
   c. ban on using a cell phone while driving
   d. an online traffic school

2. As a consumer, you purchase a number of products and services. Think of one product (like toothpaste, a calculator, or a pair of athletic shoes) or a service (like a flight on a plane, car repair, or a meal in a restaurant) that you feel needs improvement. Write an essay in the form of a letter to the president of the company that produces the product or offers the service. Argue for the improvement you want. Be specific. For example, if you are dissatisfied with a brand of cereal, you might want less deceptive packaging, or a lower price, or less sugar in the cereal.

3. Write to the president of a company whose advertising offends you. The advertising can be television or print advertising. In an essay in the form of a letter, argue for removing that advertising.

4. Argue for one of the following college issues. (Your audience will be the president, vice presidents, and deans at your college).

   a. open parking (with the exception of handicapped spaces) at your college
   b. a laptop (at a minimal rental fee and with a security deposit) for each registered student
   c. a twenty-four-hour study area with computers available
   d. security escorts for all evening students who ask to be accompanied to their cars

5. If you are a parent, a husband or wife, a partner, an employee, an employer, a student, a pet lover, a driver, or a traveler, you have most likely noticed something (in one of your roles) that has irritated or upset you. Write an argument essay about how to change that place, rule, policy, procedure, situation, and so forth.

CHAPTER 13

Writing from Reading

WHAT IS WRITING FROM READING?

One way to find topics for writing is to draw on your ideas, memories, and observations. Another way is to write from reading you have done. You can *react* to it; you can *agree* or *disagree* with something you have read. In fact, many college assignments and tests ask you to write about an assigned reading: an essay, a chapter in a textbook, an article in a journal. This kind of writing requires an active, involved attitude toward your reading. Such reading is done in steps:

1. Preread
2. Read
3. Reread with a pen or pencil

After you have completed these three steps, you can write from your reading. You can write about what you have read, or you can react to what you have read.

AN APPROACH TO WRITING FROM READING

Attitude

Before you begin the first step of this reading process, you need to have a certain **attitude**. That attitude involves thinking about what you will read as half of a conversation. The writer has opinions and ideas; he or she makes points, just like you do when you write or speak. The writer supports his or her points with specific details. If the writer were speaking to you in a conversation, you would respond to his or her opinions or ideas. You would agree, disagree, or question. You would jump into the conversation, linking or contrasting your ideas with those of the other speaker.

The right attitude toward reading demands that you read the way you'd converse: *you become involved*. In doing this, you "talk back" as you read, and later you react in your own writing. Reacting as you read will keep you focused on what you are reading. If you are focused, you will remember more of what you read. With an active, involved attitude, you can begin the step of prereading.

Prereading

Before you actually read an assigned essay, a chapter in a textbook, or an article in a journal, magazine, or newspaper, take a few minutes to look it over, and be ready to answer the following questions:

Checklist: A Checklist for Prereading

✓ How long is this reading?

✓ Will I be able to read it in one sitting, or will I have to schedule several time periods to finish it?

✓ Are there any subheadings in the reading? Do they give any hints about the reading?

✓ Are there any charts? Graphs? Boxed information?

✓ Are there any photographs or illustrations with captions? Do the photos or captions give me any hints about the reading?

✓ Is there any introductory material about the reading or its author? Does the introductory material give me any hints about the reading?

✓ What is the title of the reading? Does the title hint at the point of the reading?

✓ Are any parts of the reading underlined, italicized, or emphasized in some other way? Do the emphasized parts hint at the point of the reading?

WHY PREREAD?

Prereading takes very little time, but it helps you immensely. Some students believe it is a waste of time to scan an assignment; they think they should jump right in and get the reading over with. However, spending just a few minutes on preliminaries can save hours later. Most importantly, prereading helps you to become a *focused reader*.

If you scan the length of an assignment, you can pace yourself. And if you know how long a reading is, you can alert yourself to its plan. A short reading, for example, has to come to its point fairly soon. A longer essay may take more time to develop its point and may use more details and examples.

Subheadings, charts, graphs, illustrations, boxed or other highlighted material are important enough that the author wants to emphasize them. Looking over that material *before* you read gives you an overview of the important points the reading will contain.

Introductory material or introductory questions will also help you know what to look for as you read. Background on the author or on the subject may hint at ideas that will come up in the reading. Sometimes even the title of the reading will give you the main idea.

You should preread so that you can start reading the entire assignment with as much knowledge about the writer and the subject as you can get. Then, when you read the entire assignment, you will be reading *actively*, for more knowledge.

Forming Questions Before You Read

If you want to read with a focus, it helps to ask questions before you read. Form questions by using the information you gained from prereading.

Start by noting the title and turning it into a question. If the title of your assigned reading is "Reasons for the Alien and Sedition Acts," you can turn that title into a question: "What were the reasons for the Alien and Sedition Acts?"

You can turn subheadings into questions. If you are reading an article on beach erosion, and one subheading is "Artificial Reefs," you can ask, "How are artificial reefs connected to beach erosion?"

You can form questions from graphs and illustrations. If a chapter in your history book includes a photograph of a Gothic cathedral, you can ask, "How are Gothic cathedrals connected to this period in history?" or "Why are Gothic cathedrals important?" or "What is Gothic architecture?"

You can write down these questions, but it's not necessary. Just forming questions and keeping them in the back of your mind helps you read actively and stay focused.

An Example of the Prereading Step

Take a look at the article below. Don't read it; *preread* it.

A Ridiculous Addiction

by Gwinn Owens

Gwinn Owens, a retired editor and columnist for the Baltimore Evening Sun, *writes this essay about his experiences in parking lots, noting that the American search for a good parking space "transcends logic and common sense."*

Words You May Need to Know (Corresponding paragraph numbers are in parentheses.)

preening (2): primping, making oneself appear elegant

perusing (2): reading

stymied (3): hindered, blocked, defeated

addiction (5): a compulsive habit

coveted (6): desired, eagerly wished for

transcends (6): rises above, goes beyond the limits of

atavistically (7): primitively
acrimonious (8): bitter, harsh
holy grail (8): a sacred object that the Knights of the Round Table devoted years to finding
antithesis (9): opposite

ensconced (10): securely sheltered
idiocy (11): foolish behavior
contempt (13): scorn, lack of respect
emporium (14): store

1   Let us follow my friend Frank Bogley as, on the way home from work, he swings into the shopping mall to pick up a liter of Johnny Walker, on sale at the Bottle and Cork. In the vast, herringboned parking area there are, literally, hundreds of empty spaces, but some are perhaps as much as a forty-second walk from the door of the liquor store. So Bogley, a typical American motorist, feels compelled to park as close as possible.

2   He eases down between the rows of parked cars until he notices a blue-haired matron getting into her Mercedes. This is a prime location, not more than twenty-five steps from the Bottle and Cork. Bogley stops to await her departure so as to slip quickly into the vacated slot. She shuts the door of her car as Bogley's engine surges nervously. But she does not move. She is, in fact, preening her hair and perusing a magazine she just bought.

3   The stymied Bogley is now tying up traffic in that lane. Two more cars with impatient drivers assemble behind him. One driver hits his horn lightly, then angrily. Bogley opens his window and gives him the finger, but reluctantly realizes that the Mercedes isn't about to leave. His arteries harden a little more as, exasperated, he gives up and starts circling the lot in search of another space, passing scores of empty ones which he deems too far from his destination. Predictably, he slips into the space for the handicapped. "Just for a moment," he says to his conscience.

4   The elapsed time of Bogley's search for a convenient parking space is seven minutes. Had he chosen one of the abundant spaces only a few steps farther away, he could have accomplished his mission in less than two minutes, without frazzled nerves or skyrocketing blood pressure—his as well as those who were backed up behind him. He could have enjoyed a little healthful walking to reduce the paunch that is gestating in his middle.

5   Frank Bogley suffers an acute case of parking addiction, which afflicts more Americans than the common cold. We are obsessed with the idea that it is our constitutional right not to have to park more than ten steps from our destination.

6   Like all addictions, this quest for the coveted spot transcends logic and common sense. Motorists will pursue it without concern over the time it takes, as if a close-in parking space were its own sweet fulfillment. They will park in the fire lane, in the handicapped space or leave the car at the curb, where space is reserved for loading.

7   The quest atavistically transcends politeness and civility. My local paper recently carried a story about two motorists who, seeing a third car

about to exit a spot, both lusted for the vacancy. As soon as the departing vehicle was gone, one of the standbys was a little faster and grabbed the coveted prize. The defeated motorist leaped from his car, threw open his rival's door and punched him in the snoot. He was charged with assault. Hell hath no fury like a motorist who loses the battle for a close-in parking space.

8   The daily obsession to possess the coveted slot probably shortens the life of most Americans by at least 4.2 years. This acrimonious jockeying, waiting, backing, maneuvering for the holy grail of nearness jangles the nerves, constricts the arteries and turns puppylike personalities into snarling mad dogs.

9   I know a few Americans who have actually kicked the habit, and they are extraordinarily happy people. I am one, and I owe my cure to my friend Lou, who is the antithesis of Frank Bogley. One day I recognized Lou's red Escort in the wallflower space of the parking lot of our local supermarket. There was not another vehicle within eighty feet.

10   In the store I asked him why he had ensconced his car in lonely splendor. His answer made perfect sense: "I pull in and out quickly, nobody else's doors scratch my paint and I get a short walk, which I need." Lou, I might point out, is in his 60s and is built like 25—lean and fit.

11   These days, I do as Lou does, and a great weight has been lifted. Free of the hassle, I am suddenly aware of the collective idiocy of the parking obsession—angry people battling for what is utterly without value. I acquire what does have value: saving of time, fresh air, peace of mind, healthful exercise.

12   The only time I feel the stress now is when I am a passenger with a driver who has not yet taken the cure. On one recent occasion I accepted a ride with my friend Andy to a large banquet at which I was a head-table guest. The banquet hall had its own commodious parking lot, but Andy is another Frank Bogley.

13   He insisted on trying to park near the door "because it is late." He was right, it *was* late, and there being no slots near the door, he then proceeded to thread his way through the labyrinth of the close-in lot, as I pleaded that I didn't mind walking from out where there was plenty of space. He finally used five minutes jockeying his big Lincoln into a Honda-size niche. Thanks to Andy's addiction, I walked late into the banquet hall and stumbled into my conspicuous seat in the midst of the solemn convocation. My attitude toward him was a mixture of pity and contempt, like a recovering alcoholic must feel toward an incipient drunk.

14   These silly parking duels, fought over the right not to walk more than 15 steps, can be found almost anywhere in the fifty states. They reach their ultimate absurdity, however, at my local racquet and fitness club. The battle to park close to the door of the athletic emporium is fought as aggressively as

at the shopping mall. Everyone who parks there is intending to engage in tennis, squash, aerobic dancing, muscle building or some other kind of athletic constitutional. But to have to exercise ahead of time by walking from the lot to the door is clearly regarded by most Americans as unconstitutional.

The Results of Prereading By prereading the article, you might notice the following:

> The title is "A Ridiculous Addiction."
> The author is a former newspaper writer from Baltimore.
> There are many vocabulary words you may need to know.
> The essay is about parking lots.
> The introductory material says Americans' search for a desirable parking space goes beyond the limits of common sense.

You might begin reading the article with these questions in mind:

> What is the addiction?
> How can an addiction be ridiculous? An addiction is usually considered something very serious, like an addiction to drugs.
> What do parking spaces have to do with addiction?
> What is so illogical about looking for a good parking space?

Reading

The first time you read, try to get a sense of the whole piece you are reading. Reading with questions in mind can help you do this. If you find that you are confused by a certain part of the reading selection, go back and reread that part. If you do not know the meaning of a word, check the vocabulary list to see if the word is defined for you. If it is not defined, try to figure out the meaning from the way the word is used in the sentence.

If you find that you have to read more slowly than the way that you usually do, don't worry. People vary their reading speed according to what they read and why they are reading it. If you are reading for entertainment, for example, you can read quickly; if you are reading a chapter in a textbook, you must read more slowly. The more complicated the reading selection, the more slowly you will read it.

An Example of the Reading Step

Now read "A Ridiculous Addiction." When you've completed your first reading, you will probably have some answers, like those below, to the prereading questions you formed.

Answers to Prereading Questions

> The author says that the ridiculous addiction is the need to find the best parking space.
> He means it's ridiculous because it makes parking a serious issue, and because people do silly things to get good parking spots.
> People are illogical in getting parking because they'll even be late for an event in order to get a good space. Or they get upset.

Rereading with Pen or Pencil

The second reading is the crucial one. At this point, you begin to *think on paper* as you read. In this step, you make notes or write about what you read. Some students are reluctant to do this, for they are not sure *what* to note or write. Think of making these notes as a way of learning, thinking, reviewing, and reacting. Reading with a pen or pencil in your hand keeps you alert. With that pen or pencil, you can do the following:

Mark the main point of the reading.
Mark other points.
Define words you don't know.
Question parts of the reading you're not sure of.
Evaluate the writer's ideas.
React to the writer's opinions or examples.
Add ideas, opinions, or examples of your own.

There is no single system for marking or writing as you read. Some readers like to underline the main idea with two lines and to underline other important ideas with one line. Some students like to put an asterisk (a star) next to important ideas, while others like to circle key words.

Some people use the margins to write comments like, "I agree!" or "Not true!" or "That's happened to me." Sometimes readers put questions in the margin; sometimes they summarize a point in the margin next to its location in the essay. Some people make notes in the white space above the reading and list important points, and others use the space at the end of the reading. Every reader who writes while he or she reads has a personal system; what these systems share is an attitude. *If you write as you read, you concentrate on the reading selection, get to know the writer's ideas, and develop ideas of your own.*

As you reread and write notes, don't worry too much about noticing the "right" ideas. Think of rereading as the time to jump into a conversation with the writer.

An Example of Rereading with Pen or Pencil

For "A Ridiculous Addiction," your marked article might look like the following:

A Ridiculous Addiction

Gwinn Owens

Let us follow my friend Frank Bogley as, on the way home from work, he swings into the shopping mall to pick up a liter of Johnny Walker, on sale at the Bottle and Cork. In the vast, herringboned parking area there are, literally, hundreds of empty spaces, but some are perhaps as much as a forty-second walk from the door of the liquor store. So Bogley, <u>a typical American motorist, feels compelled to park as close as possible.</u>   *the bad habit*

He eases down between the rows of parked cars until he notices a blue-haired matron getting into her Mercedes. This is a prime location, not more than twenty-five steps from the Bottle and Cork. Bogley stops to await her departure so as to slip quickly into the vacated slot. She shuts the door of her car as Bogley's engine surges nervously. But she does not move. She is, in fact, preening her hair and perusing a magazine she just bought.

The stymied Bogley is now tying up traffic in that lane. Two more cars with impatient drivers assemble behind him. One driver hits his horn lightly, then angrily. Bogley opens his window and gives him the finger, but reluctantly realizes that the Mercedes isn't about to leave. His arteries harden a little more as, exasperated, he gives up and starts circling the lot in search of another space, passing scores of empty ones which he deems too far from his destination. <u>Predictably, he slips into the space for the handicapped.</u> "Just for a moment," he says to his conscience.

I hate this!

<u>The elapsed time of Bogley's search for a convenient parking space is seven minutes.</u> Had he chosen one of the abundant spaces only a few steps farther away, <u>he could have accomplished his mission in less than two minutes, without frazzled nerves or skyrocketing blood pressure—his as well as those who were backed up behind him.</u> He could have enjoyed a little healthful walking to reduce the paunch that is gestating in his middle.

wasted time

irritation

Frank Bogley suffers an acute case of parking addiction, which afflicts more Americans than the common cold. <u>We are obsessed with the idea that it is our constitutional right not to have to park more than ten steps from our destination.</u>

<u>Like all addictions, this quest for the coveted spot transcends logic and common sense.</u> Motorists will pursue it without concern over the time it takes, as if a close-in parking space were its own sweet fulfillment. <u>They will park in the fire lane, in the handicapped space or leave the car at the curb, where space is reserved for loading.</u>

The quest atavistically <u>transcends politeness and civility.</u> My local paper recently carried a story about two motorists who, seeing a third car about to exit a spot, both lusted for the vacancy. As soon as the departing vehicle was gone, one of the standbys was a little faster and grabbed the coveted prize. The defeated motorist leaped from his car, threw open his rival's door and punched him in the snoot. He was charged with assault. Hell hath no fury like a motorist who loses the battle for a close-in parking space.

example

The daily obsession to possess the coveted slot probably shortens the life of most Americans by at least 4.2 years. This acrimonious jockeying, waiting, backing, maneuvering for the holy grail of nearness jangles the nerves, constricts the arteries and turns puppylike personalities into snarling mad dogs.

I know a few Americans who have actually kicked the habit, and they are extraordinarily happy people. I am one, and I owe my cure to my friend Lou, who is the (antithesis) of Frank Bogley. One day I recognized Lou's red Escort in the wallflower space of the parking lot of our local supermarket. There was not another vehicle within eighty feet.

opposite

In the store I asked him why he had ensconced his car in lonely splendor. His answer made perfect sense: "<u>I pull in and out quickly, nobody else's doors scratch my paint and I get a short walk, which I need.</u>" Lou, I might point out, is in his 60s and is built like 25—lean and fit.

breaking the habit:

the advantages

These days, I do as Lou does, and a great weight has been lifted. Free of the hassle, I am suddenly aware of the collective idiocy of the parking obsession—angry people battling for what is utterly without value. I acquire what does have value: <u>saving of time, fresh air, peace of mind, healthful exercise.</u>

more advantages

The only time I feel the stress now is when I am a passenger with a driver who has not yet taken the cure. On one recent occasion I accepted a ride with my friend Andy to a large banquet at which I was a head-table guest. The banquet hall had its own commodious parking lot, but Andy is another Frank Bogley.

He insisted on trying to park near the door "because it is late." He was right, it *was* late, and there being no slots near the door, he then proceeded to thread his way through the labyrinth of the close-in lot, as I pleaded that I didn't mind walking from out where there was plenty of space. <u>He finally used five minutes jockeying his big Lincoln into a Honda-size niche.</u> Thanks to Andy's addiction, I walked late into the banquet hall and stumbled into my conspicuous seat in the midst of the solemn convocation. My attitude toward him was a mixture of pity and contempt, like a recovering alcoholic must feel toward an incipient drunk.

how true!

<u>These silly parking duels, fought over the right not to walk more than fifteen steps, can be found almost anywhere in the fifty states.</u> They reach their ultimate absurdity, however, at my local racquet and fitness club. The battle to park close to the door of the athletic emporium is fought as aggressively as at the shopping mall. Everyone who parks there is intending to engage in tennis, squash, aerobic dancing, muscle building or some other kind of athletic constitutional. But to have to exercise ahead of time by walking from the lot to the door is clearly regarded by most Americans as unconstitutional.

What the Notes Mean

In the sample above, the underlining indicates sentences or phrases that seem important. The words in the margin are often summaries of what is underlined. The words "wasted time," "irritation," and "effects," for instance, are like subtitles or labels in the margin.

Some words in the margin are reactions. When Owens describes a man who parked illegally in a handicapped spot, the reader notes, "I hate this!" When the writer talks about a Lincoln trying to fit into a Honda-sized spot, the reader writes, "How true!" One word in the margin is a definition. The word "antithesis" in the selection is defined as "opposite" in the margin.

The marked-up article is a flexible tool. You can go back and mark it further. You may change your mind about your notes and comments and find other, better, or more important points in the article.

You write as you read to involve yourself in the reading process. Marking what you read can help you in other ways, too. If you are to be tested on the reading selection or asked to discuss it, you can scan your markings and notations at a later time for a quick review.

Exercise 1 **Reading and Making Notes**

Following is the last paragraph of "A Ridiculous Addiction." First, read it. Then reread it and make notes on the following:

1. Underline the sentence that begins the long example in the paragraph.

2. Circle a word you don't know and define it in the margin.

3. In the margin, add your own example of a place where people fight for parking spaces.

4. At the end of the paragraph, summarize the point of the paragraph.

Paragraph from "A Ridiculous Addiction"

These silly parking duels, fought over the right not to walk more than fifteen steps, can be found almost anywhere in the fifty states. <u>They reach their ultimate absurdity, however, at my local racquet and fitness club.</u> The battle to park close to the door of the athletic emporium is fought as aggressively as at the shopping mall. Everyone who parks there is intending to engage in tennis, squash, aerobic dancing, muscle building, or some other kind of athletic constitutional. But to have to exercise ahead of time by walking from the lot to the door is clearly regarded by most Americans as unconstitutional.

INSTRUCTOR'S NOTE

Answers for the main point of the paragraph will vary. Possible answer shown at right.

Main point of the paragraph: *People on their way to a health club show*

how silly it is to fight for a parking space.

TEACHING TIP

Tell students that summarizing an essay can help them remember its main points. It is a valuable study technique even if they are not doing it for an assignment.

WRITING A SUMMARY OF A READING

There are a number of ways you can write about what you've read. You may be asked for a summary of an article or chapter, or for a reaction to it, or to write about it on an essay test. For each of these, this chapter will give you guidelines, so that you can follow the stages of the writing process.

A **summary** of a reading tells the important ideas in brief form. It includes (1) the writer's main idea, (2) the ideas used to explain the main idea, and (3) some examples used to support the ideas.

NOTE:

For advice on "Writing for an Essay Test," see pp. 341–342.

When you preread, read, and make notes on the reading selection, you have already begun the prewriting stage for a summary. You can think further, on paper, by listing the points (words, phrases, sentences) you've already marked on the reading selection.

INSTRUCTOR'S NOTE

If you prefer to have students use reading selections as prompts for reacting to key points rather than summarizing them, you can skip to "Writing a Reaction to a Reading" on page 337.

PREWRITING Gathering Ideas: Summary

Marking a List of Ideas

To find the main idea for your summary and the ideas and examples connected to the main idea, you can mark related items on your list. For example, the expanded list below was made from "A Ridiculous Addiction." Four symbols are used:

K marks the **kinds** of close spots people will take.

X marks all **examples** of what can happen when people want a good spot.

− marks the **negative** effects of the close-parking habit.

+ marks the **advantages** of breaking the habit.

A List of Ideas for a Summary of "A Ridiculous Addiction"

K *no close spots, takes handicapped*

X *seven minutes looking for close spot*

− *wasted time, could have found*
  another in two minutes

X *got mad*

X *made others wait*

X *they got angry*

  Americans obsessed with right
  to good spot

  transcends logic

  no common sense

K *park in fire lane*

K *leave car at curb*

K *loading zone*

− *impolite*

X *an assault over a spot*

− *jangles nerves, constricts arteries, and*
  makes people mad dogs

  kicking the habit

+ *get in and out fast*

+ *no scratched car doors*

+ *good exercise*

+ *saving time*

+ *fresh air*

+ *peace of mind*

+ *healthful exercise*

X *late for big dinner*

X *fitness clubs the silliest—won't walk*

The marked list could be reorganized, like this:

kinds of close spots people will take

handicapped
fire lane
curb
loading zone

examples of what can happen when people want a good spot

seven minutes of wasted time
others, waiting behind, get mad
an assault over a spot
late for a big dinner
members of the fitness club won't walk

negative effects of the close-parking habit

wasted time
impolite
jangles nerves, constricts arteries
makes people mad dogs

advantages of breaking the habit

get in and out fast
no scratched car doors
good exercise
saving time
fresh air
peace of mind
healthful exercise

Selecting a Main Idea

The next step in the process is to select the idea you think is the writer's main point. If you look again at the list of ideas, you'll note a cluster of ideas that are unmarked:

1. Americans obsessed with the right to a good spot
2. transcends logic
3. no common sense

You might guess that they are unmarked because they are more general than the other ideas. In fact, these ideas are connected to the title of the essay: "A Ridiculous Addiction," and they are connected to some of the questions in the prereading step of reading: "What's the addiction?" and "How can an addiction be ridiculous?"

Linking the ideas may lead you to a main idea for the summary of the reading selection:

Americans' obsession with finding a good parking spot makes no sense.

Once you have a main idea, check that main idea to see if it fits with the other ideas in your organized list. *Do the ideas in the list connect to the main idea?* Yes. "Kinds of close spots people take" explains how silly it is to break the law. "Examples of what can happen" and "negative effects" show why the habit makes no sense, and "advantages of breaking the habit" shows the reasons to conquer the addiction.

Once you have a main point that fits an organized list, you can move to the planning stage of a summary.

Exercise 2   **Marking a List of Ideas and Finding the Main Idea for a Summary**

Below is a list of ideas from an article called "How to Land the Job You Want." Read the list, and then mark the items on the list with one of these symbols:

X   **examples** of people looking for or getting jobs

S   **steps** in getting a job

A   **advice** from employers

After you've marked all the ideas, survey them, and think of a main idea. Try to focus on an idea that connects to the title, "How to Land the Job You Want."

List of Ideas

___X___ Laid-off engineer used his personality to get a sales job.

___A___ Insurance company manager says applicants can walk in without appointment.

___S___ Find the hidden job market.

___X___ Unemployed teacher found a job through his insurance agent.

___X___ Bank worker got a job through his club.

___S___ Prepare specifically for each interview.

___S___ Locate hidden openings.

_A_ Company director says a good letter of application is crucial.

_S_ Make resume strong and polished.

_S_ Put yourself in employer's place in writing a resume.

_X_ Cabinetmaker checked phone books of nine cities for companies in his field.

_S_ Use the library to research job opportunities.

Main idea: _You can land the job you want if you are willing to work hard at_

your job search.

INSTRUCTOR'S NOTE

Answers for the main idea will vary. Possible answer shown at left.

PLANNING Devising a Plan: Summary

Below is a sample of an outline for a summary of "A Ridiculous Addiction."
As you read it, you'll notice that the main idea of the prewriting stage has
become the topic sentence of the outline, and the other ideas have become
the details.

An Outline for a Summary of "A Ridiculous Addiction"

topic sentence:	Americans' obsession with finding a good parking spot makes no sense.
details:	
examples	Many bad or silly things can happen when people try for a good spot. One person wasted seven minutes. He made other drivers angry. Someone else got involved in an assault. Someone else was late for a big dinner. Silly people, on their way to a fitness club, will avoid the walk in the fitness club parking lot.
negative effects	Looking for a close spot can make people impolite or turn them into mad dogs. It can jangle drivers' nerves or constrict arteries. Some people will even break the law and take handicapped spots or park in a fire lane or loading zone.
advantages of breaking the habit	If people can give up the habit, they can gain advantages. A faraway spot is not popular, so they can get in and out of it fast. Their cars won't be scratched. They get exercise and fresh air by walking.

In the preceding outline, some ideas from the original list have been left out
(they were repetitive), and the order of some points has been rearranged.
That kind of selecting and rearranging is what you do in the planning stage
of writing a summary.

DRAFTING Drafting and Revising: Summary

Attributing Ideas in a Summary

INSTRUCTOR'S NOTE

Since your students may not have much experience with proper attribution, this may be a good time to tell them that giving proper credit to authors/sources is an integral part of many college courses. For more on proper attribution, see Chapter 14, "Using Research to Strengthen Essays."

The draft of your summary paragraph is the place where you combine all the material into one paragraph. This draft is much like the draft of any other paragraph, with one exception: When you summarize another person's ideas, be sure to say whose ideas you are writing. That is, *attribute the ideas to the writer.* Let the reader of your paragraph know

1. the author of the selection you are summarizing, and
2. the title of the selection you are summarizing.

You may wish to do this by giving your summary paragraph a title like this:

A Summary of "A Ridiculous Addiction," by Gwinn Owens

(Note that you put the title of Owens' essay in quotation marks.)

On the other hand, you may want to put the title and author into the paragraph itself. Following is a draft of a summary of "A Ridiculous Addiction" with the title and author incorporated into the paragraph.

A Draft of a Summary of "A Ridiculous Addiction"

"A Ridiculous Addiction" by Gwinn Owens says that Americans' obsession with finding a good parking spot makes no sense. Many bad or silly things can happen when people try for a good spot. One person wasted seven minutes. He made other drivers angry. Someone else got involved in an assault. Someone else was late for a big dinner. Silly people, on their way to a fitness club, will avoid the walk in the club parking lot. Looking for a close spot can make people impolite or turn them into mad dogs. It can be stressful. Some people even break the law and take handicapped spots or park in a fire lane or loading zone. If people can give up the habit, they can gain advantages. A faraway spot is not popular, so they can get in and out of it fast. Their cars won't be scratched. They get exercise and fresh air by walking.

When you review this draft and read it aloud, you may notice a few problems:

- It is wordy.
- In some places, the word choice could be better.
- Some of the sentences are choppy.
- It might be a good idea to mention that the examples in the summary were Gwinn Owens'.

Revising the draft means rewriting to eliminate some of the wordiness, to combine sentences or smooth out ideas, and to insert the point that the author, Gwinn Owens, gave the examples used in the summary. When you state that Owens created the examples, you are being clear in giving the author credit for his ideas. Giving credit is a way of attributing ideas to the author.

Note: When you refer to an author in something that you write, use the author's first and last name the first time you make a reference. For example, you write "Gwinn Owens" the first time you refer to this author. Later in the paragraph, if you want to refer to the same author, use only his or her last name. Thus, a second reference would be to "Owens."

POLISHING Proofreading and Polishing: Summary

Look carefully at the final version of the summary. Notice how the sentences have been changed and words added or taken out. "Owens" is used to show that the examples given came from the essay.

A Final Version of a Summary of "A Ridiculous Addiction"

"A Ridiculous Addiction" by Gwinn Owens says that Americans' obsession with finding a good parking spot makes no sense. Owens gives many examples of the unpleasant or silly things that can happen when people try for a good spot. One person wasted seven minutes and made the other drivers angry. Someone else got involved in an assault; another person was late for an important dinner. At fitness club parking lots, people coming for exercise are missing out on the exercise of walking through the parking lot. Looking for a good spot can turn polite people into impolite ones or even into mad dogs. The search is not only stressful; it can also lead people to break the law by taking handicapped, fire lane, or loading zone spots. If people broke the habit and took spots farther away from buildings, they would have several advantages. No one wants the far-away spots, so drivers can get in and out fast, without any scratches on their cars. In addition, people who break the habit get exercise and fresh air.

Writing summaries is good writing practice, and it also helps you develop your reading skills. Even if your instructor does not require you to turn in a polished summary of an assigned reading, you may find it helpful to summarize what you have read. In many classes, midterms or other exams cover assigned readings. If you make short summaries of each reading as it is assigned, you will have a helpful collection of focused, organized material to review.

WRITING A REACTION TO A READING

A summary is one kind of writing you can do after reading, but there are other kinds. You can react to a reading by agreeing or disagreeing with some idea within the reading or by writing on a topic related to the reading. The effectiveness of your reaction will depend on your careful evaluation of the reading selection.

The Role of Critical Thinking As You Read

When you start forming opinions based on what you observe, hear, read, or discuss, you are applying **critical thinking skills**. Thinking critically as you read involves examining an issue from different sides as well as evaluating the validity, or truthfulness, of the information presented.

Applying the critical thinking process to evaluate what you are reading requires that you ask yourself the following questions:

- What is the writer's main idea or proposal?
- Is the main idea supported by facts? Personal experience? Expert opinion(s)?

- Does the writer reach logical conclusions based on his or her evidence?

Sharpening your critical thinking skills by using this type of questioning as you read can enable you to form reasonable opinions and express them confidently. Reading critically can help you succeed in all of your college classes, and it will be especially beneficial in your future composition courses.

Developing Points of Agreement or Disagreement

One way to use a reading selection to lead you to a topic is to review the selection and jot down any statements that provoke a strong reaction in you. You will be looking for sentences with which you agree or disagree. If you already marked "A Ridiculous Addiction" as you read, you might list these statements as points of agreement or disagreement:

Points of Agreement or Disagreement

"Hell hath no fury like a motorist who loses the battle for a close-in parking space."—agree

"This quest for the coveted spot transcends logic and common sense."—disagree

---

Then you might pick one of the statements and agree or disagree with it in writing, examining why or to what extent you agree or disagree with the author's point. If you disagreed with the second statement that "this quest for the coveted spot transcends logic and common sense," you might develop the prewriting part of writing by listing your own ideas. You might focus on why a close parking space is important to you. With a focus and a list of reasons, you could move to the planning part of writing from reading.

> **PLANNING**　Devising a Plan: Agree or Disagree

An outline might look like the one below. As you read it, notice that the topic sentence and ideas are your opinion, not the ideas of the author of "A Ridiculous Addiction." You used his ideas to devise your own thoughts.

An Outline for an Agree or Disagree Paragraph

Topic sentence:	Sometimes a close parking spot is important.
details:	
convenience	{ I may have heavy bags to carry from the store.
car safety	{ Cars can be vandalized. Vandalism and burglary are more likely if the car is parked at a distance.
personal safety	{ I can be attacked in a parking lot. Attacks are more likely at night. Muggings are more likely if I am parked far away.

DRAFTING   Drafting and Revising: Agree or Disagree

If your outline provides you with enough good points to develop, you are on your way to a paragraph. If you began with the ideas above, for example, you could develop them into a paragraph like this:

A Draft for an Agree or Disagree Paragraph

Sometimes a close parking spot is important. The short distance to a store can make a difference if I have heavy bags or boxes to carry from the store to my car. Convenience is one reason for parking close. A more important reason is safety. In my neighborhood, cars are often vandalized. Sometimes, cars get broken into. Cars are more likely to get vandalized or burglarized if they are parked far from stores. Most of all, I am afraid to park far from stores or restaurants because I am afraid of being attacked in a parking lot, especially at night. If I am far away from buildings and other people, I am more likely to be mugged.

POLISHING   Polishing And Proofreading: Agree or Disagree

When you read the paragraph above, you probably noticed some places where it could be revised:

- It could use more specific details.
- It should attribute the original idea about parking to Gwinn Owens, probably in the beginning.
- Some sentences could be combined.

Following is the final version of the same paragraph. As you read it, notice how a new beginning, added details, and combined sentences make it a smoother, clearer, and more developed paragraph.

A Final Version for an Agree or Disagree Paragraph

Gwinn Owens says that people who look for close parking spaces are foolish, but I think that sometimes a close parking spot is important. The short distance to a store can make a difference if I have heavy bags or boxes to carry from the store to my car. Convenience is one reason for parking close, but the more important reason is safety. In my neighborhood, cars are often vandalized. Antennas get broken off; the paint jobs get deliberately scratched. Sometimes, cars get broken into. Radios and MP3 players are stolen. Cars are more likely to get vandalized or burglarized if they are parked far from stores. Most of all, I am afraid to park far from stores or restaurants because I am afraid of being attacked in a parking lot, especially at night. If I am far away from buildings or other people, I am more likely to be mugged.

Reading critically can give you many ideas for your own writing. Developing these ideas into a polished paragraph requires the same writing process as does any piece of good writing, a process that takes you through the stages of prewriting, planning, drafting, and polishing.

Writing on a Related Idea

Another type of writing requires critical thinking and writing. Your instructor might ask you to react by writing about some idea connected to your reading. For example, your instructor might ask you to react to "A Ridiculous Addiction" by writing about some practice or habit that irritates you. You can begin to gather ideas by freewriting.

> PREWRITING   Gathering Ideas: Reaction

Freewriting

You can freewrite in a reading journal, if you wish. To freewrite, you can do the following

- Write key points made by the author.
- Write about whatever you remember from the reading selection.
- Write down any of the author's ideas that you think you might want to write about someday.
- List questions raised by what you have read.
- Connect the reading selection to other things you have read or heard or experienced.
- Write any of the author's exact words that you might like to remember, putting them in quotation marks.

Freewriting that reacts to "A Ridiculous Addiction" might look like this:

Freewriting for a Reaction to a Reading

"A Ridiculous Addiction"—Gwinn Owens
People are silly in fighting for parking spaces. Owens says these are "silly parking duels." They get mean. Take handicapped spots. Angry. They fight over spots. Get angry when people sit in their cars and don't pull out of a spot. They jam big cars in small spaces, cars get damaged. They're "angry people battling for what is utterly without value." Why? To make a quick getaway?

Freewriting helps you review what you've read; it can also lead you to a new writing topic that can be developed differently than a summary or an agree/disagree paragraph.

Brainstorming

After you freewrite, you can brainstorm. You can ask yourself questions to lead you toward a topic for your own paragraph. For instance, brainstorming on the idea, "angry people battling for what is utterly without value" could look like this:

Brainstorming after Freewriting

Owens says people fighting for spaces are "battling for what is utterly without value." So why do they do it? Is there any other time drivers battle for what has no value?
Sure. On the highway. All the time.

How?
They weave in and out. They cut me off. They tailgate. They speed.

What are they fighting for?

They want to gain a few minutes. They want to get ahead. Driving is some kind of contest to them.

Then don't they get some kind of satisfaction in the battle?

Not really. I often see them at the same red light I've stopped at. And their driving is very stressful for them. It raises their blood pressure, and it makes them angry and unhappy. They can't really win.

Could you write a paragraph on drivers who think of driving as a contest? If so, your brainstorming, based on your critical reading and freewriting, has lead you to a topic. Once you have arrived at your own topic, you can focus and develop it by working through the stages of the writing process.

WRITING FOR AN ESSAY TEST

Most essay questions require a form of writing from reading. That is, your instructor asks you to write about an assigned reading. Usually, an essay test requires you to write from memory, not from an open book or notes. Such writing can be stressful, but breaking the task into steps can eliminate much of the stress.

Before the Test: The Steps of Reading

If you work through the steps of reading days before the test, you are halfway to your goal. First, *prereading* helps to get you focused; second, *reading* the selection will give you a sense of the whole selection; and third, *rereading with a pen or pencil* can be particularly helpful when you a preparing for a test. Most essay questions will ask you to summarize a reading selection or to react to it. In either case, you must be familiar with the reading's main idea, supporting ideas, examples, and details. If you note these by marking the selection, you are teaching yourself about the main point, supporting ideas, and structure of the reading selection.

Shortly before the test, review the marked reading assignment. Your notes will help you to focus on the main point and the supporting ideas.

During the Test: The Stages of Writing

Answering an essay question for a test may seem very different from writing at home. After all, on a test, you must rely on your memory and write within a time limit, and these restrictions can make you feel anxious. However, by following the stages of the writing process, you can meet that challenge calmly and confidently.

Prewriting Before you begin to write, think about the question: Is the instructor asking for a summary of a reading selection? Or is he or she asking you to react to a specific idea in the reading, by describing or developing that idea with examples, or by agreeing or disagreeing? For example, if you were to answer an essay question about "A Ridiculous Addiction," you might be asked (1) to explain what Gwinn Owens thinks are the advantages and disadvantages of seeking a close parking space (a summary), or (2) to explain what he means when he says fighting for parking turns drivers into mad dogs (a reaction, where you develop and explain one part of the reading), or (3) to agree or disagree that close spaces are utterly without value (a reaction, where you have to be aware of what Owens said on this point).

Once you've thought about the question, freewrite or make a list of your first ideas about the question. At this time, don't worry about how "right" or "wrong" your writing is—just write your first thoughts.

Planning Your writing will be clear if you follow a plan. Remember that your audience for this writing is your instructor and that he or she will be evaluating how well you stick to the subject, make a point, and support it. Your plan for making a point about the subject and supporting that point can be written in a brief outline.

First, reread the question. Next, survey your list or freewriting. Does it contain a main point that answers the question? Does it contain supporting ideas and details?

Next, write a main point; then list supporting ideas and details under the main point. Your main point will be the topic sentence of your answer. If you need more support, try brainstorming.

Drafting Write your point and supporting ideas in paragraph form. Remember to use effective transitions and to combine short sentences.

Polishing You will probably not have time to copy your answer, but you can review it, proofread it, and correct any errors in spelling, punctuation, and word choice. This final check can produce a more refined answer.

Organize Your Time

Some students skip steps: without thinking or planning, they immediately begin writing their answer to an essay question. Sometimes they find themselves stuck in the middle of a paragraph, panicked because they have no more ideas. At other times, they find themselves writing in a circle, repeating the same point over and over. Occasionally, they even forget to include a main idea.

You can avoid these hazards by spending time on each of the stages. Planning is as important as writing. For example, if you have 30 minutes to write an essay, you can divide your time like this:

> 5 minutes: thinking, freewriting, listing
> 10 minutes: planning, outlining
> 10 minutes: drafting
> 5 minutes: reviewing and proofreading

Focusing on one step at a time can make you more confident and your task more manageable.

Lines of Detail: A Walk-Through Assignment

Here are two ideas from "A Ridiculous Addiction":

1. The typical American has a compulsion about finding a convenient parking space.
2. People who search for good parking spots become mean and nasty.

Pick one of the ideas with which you agree or disagree. Write a paragraph explaining why you agree or disagree. Follow these steps:

> **Step 1:** Begin by listing at least two reasons why you agree or disagree. Use your own experience with parking lots to come up

with your reasons. For example, for statement 1, you could ask yourself these questions: Are all Americans concerned with parking spaces? How do you know? Is it a compulsion or just practical behavior? For statement 2, you might ask questions like these: Have you ever seen nastiness in parking lots? Have you ever experienced it? What actions were mean? Answering such questions can help you come up with your reasons for agreement or disagreement.

Step 2: Read your list to a partner or group. With the help of your listener(s), you can add reasons or details to explain the reasons.

Collaborate

Step 3: Once you have enough ideas, transform the statement you agreed or disagreed with into a topic sentence.

Step 4: Write an outline by listing your reasons and details below the topic sentence. Check that your list is in a clear and logical order.

Step 5: Write a draft of your paragraph. Check that you have attributed Gwinn Owens' statement, that you have enough details, and that you have combined any choppy sentences. Revise your draft until the paragraph is smooth and clear.

Step 6: Before you prepare the final copy, check your last draft for errors in spelling, punctuation, and word choice.

Writing Your Own Paragraph

When you write on one of these topics, be sure to work through the stages of the writing process in preparing your paragraph.

1. Gwinn Owens writes about Americans' addiction to the close-in parking space. Write about another addiction that Americans have. Instead of writing about a topic such as drug or alcohol addiction, follow Owens' example and write about a social habit that is hard to break. You might, for instance, write about people's habit of

driving while talking on a phone	tailgating
weaving in and out of traffic	speeding
driving too slowly	pushing in line
running yellow traffic lights	littering
talking during a movie	gossiping

Once you've chosen a habit, brainstorm, alone or with a partner, for details. Think about details that could fit these categories:

why the habit is foolish	where and when people act this way
why the habit is dangerous	advantages of breaking the habit

Ask yourself questions, answer them, and let the answers lead to more questions. Once you've collected some good details, work through the stages of writing a paragraph.

2. Gwinn Owens writes about a great invention, the car, and about the parking problems caused by cars. Below are several other recent inventions that can cause problems. Your goal is to write a paragraph about *the problems one of these inventions can cause.*

Collaborate

To start, pick two of the inventions below. Alone, or with a partner or group, brainstorm both topics: ask questions, answer them, and add details so that each topic can lead you to enough ideas for a paragraph.

After you've brainstormed, pick the topic you like better and work through the stages of preparing a paragraph.

Brainstorm on problems that could be caused by two of the following:

voicemail	lasers	passwords	hybrid cars
blogs	credit cards	e-mail	chat rooms

Computer

3. Do some online research about one of the inventions listed in topic 2, and see if you can find the original purpose of the invention and how its current uses differ from the way it was first used. (For example, the Internet was originally intended for communication among scientists but is widely used by the general public today.) Write a paragraph about how this invention has developed different uses over the years.

4. Buying merchandise via Web sites or by phone has never been easier. Based on your observations or through personal experience, explain why shopping online or through television channels, such as the Home Shopping Network and QVC, can become as addictive as the parking obsession that Gwinn Owens describes. Examine the lure of this particular means of shopping, how or why the consumer may become hooked, and ways that one can recognize whether he or she has become an obsessive online or cable television shopper.

Topics for Critical Thinking and Writing

1. Much interaction in our daily lives occurs when we are stressed. People who feel pressured by too many responsibilities and too little time may become impatient on the road or in the parking lot. Consider the stresses behind other conflicts such as parents shouting at their children in public places, children misbehaving in day care, passengers becoming angry or agitated on airplanes, or parents becoming angry at coaches at children's Little League games.

2. Have you ever seen a movie or a television show in which the hero breaks rules that most of us are expected to follow? For example, does the main character smash into other peoples' cars, leap over people waiting in line, or snatch items from a market or store? How is the audience expected to feel about such behavior? What do the creation of a rule-breaking hero and the audience's reaction to the hero say about our secret wishes?

How Do I Get a Better Grade?

PEARSON
mywritinglab

Visit www.mywritinglab.com for audio-visual lectures and additional practice sets about writing from reading.

Get a better grade with MyWritingLab!

Name: _____ Section: _____

Peer Review Form for Writing from Reading

After you've written a draft version of your paragraph, let a writing partner read it. When your partner has completed the form below, discuss the comments. Repeat the same process for your partner's paragraph.

This paragraph (1) summarizes (2) agrees or disagrees (3) writes about an idea connected to a reading selection. (Choose one.)

I think this paragraph needs/does not need to include the title and author of the reading selection. Why or why not? _____

_____

_____

The topic sentence of this paragraph is _____

_____

_____

The best part of this paragraph started with the words _____

_____

_____

One suggestion to improve this paragraph is _____

_____

_____

Other comments: _____

_____

_____

_____

_____

_____

_____

_____

_____

Reviewer's name: _____

CHAPTER 14

Using Research to Strengthen Essays

THE ROLES OF RESEARCH

During your college experience, you will no doubt use research techniques in your coursework as well as in your daily life. Even if you have not yet written a formal paper involving research, you probably have already employed various research techniques to solve problems or make crucial decisions. For example, deciding about what college or technical school to attend and learning about financial aid opportunities may have involved contacting professionals and taking careful notes. Similarly, if you are a parent who has investigated community day-care options or family insurance plans, you are well aware of the importance of thorough research. Asking key questions and organizing your findings are research skills that can serve you well in college and in life.

Most of the writing assignments you have completed thus far have probably been based on your own experiences, observations, or opinions. By writing regularly, you now know the importance of purpose, audience, organization, supporting details, and revision in producing a polished, final version of an essay. By appreciating the basics of effective writing, you can also recognize how essays can be strengthened through research. This chapter will show how a student writer can strengthen his or her original essay by smoothly incorporating supporting material from outside sources.

Starting with a Basic Outline and Essay

The following outline and short essay about dog-rescue groups are based solely on the writer's own experience and knowledge about dog-rescue operations. You may notice that the outline is in the same format as the outlines you reviewed in Chapter 11, "Writing an Essay." The writer's thesis is that such groups perform a humane service by rescuing homeless dogs and by carefully matching potential adopters with suitable pets. (Later in this chapter, you will see how the writer smoothly incorporated information from five sources into an outline, draft, and final version of the essay.)

An Outline for an Essay without Research

I. Dog-rescue organizations perform a humane service by saving homeless dogs and matching responsible adopters with a devoted new family member.

II. Dog-rescue volunteers play several roles.
   A. Some volunteers are "spotters" who look for specific breeds at local shelters.
   B. Experienced rescue volunteers may become coordinators and arrange assistance from various sources.
   C. Volunteers work with national organizations such as Save-A-Pet and Petfinder.com, which maintain databases of adoptable dogs from rescue groups throughout the United States and Canada.
   D. Volunteers assist at rescue-dog "Adoption Days" hosted by pet supply chains such as Petco and PetSmart.

III. Rescue groups provide important information and benefits for prospective adopters.
   A. By viewing a rescue group's Web site, potential adopters can read about a dog's age, temperament, adoption fee, and any special medical conditions.
   B. If a potential adopter does not find a suitable dog, he or she can still complete an online application.
   C. On an application, a potential adopter can list his or her preferences for the age, gender, and size of the dog.
   D. Although some dogs are puppies rescued from abusive situations, most are adult dogs already socialized and housebroken.

IV. Careful screening often results in a successful adoption.
   A. Rescue groups routinely conduct home visits to check the living conditions and the neighborhood.
   B. The applicant must have access to veterinary care.
   C. The applicant must agree to return the dog to the rescue organization if he or she can no longer care for the animal.
   D. A foster parent can fully inform the adoptive parent about potential adjustment problems.
   E. Careful attention to such details leads to a winning adoption process.

V. Rescue groups not only provide care for homeless dogs; they also remind us of the joy made possible by compassionate adoption.

An Essay without Research

The following essay, written from the outline you have just reviewed, contains no research from outside sources; it is based solely on the writer's own knowledge and experience. As you read it, you will notice how the points in the outline have been developed through the use of specific details, effective sentence combining, and key transitions. You may also notice that some of the original words and phrases in the outline have been changed for better style.

The Humane Work of Dog-Rescue Groups

Although the United States is generally regarded as a country that loves and pampers its pets, animal shelters are often filled to capacity with dogs that have been abandoned, abused, or surrendered by their owners. Sadly, some shelters routinely euthanize healthy dogs if no one claims or adopts them after a grace period ranging from just days to a few weeks. Fortunately, however, many shelters work closely with dog-rescue organizations that find loving, temporary homes where foster parents can provide care and, if necessary, rehabilitation. Staffed by dedicated volunteers, rescue groups perform a humane service by saving homeless dogs and enabling responsible adopters to gain a devoted new family member.

From rescuing retired greyhounds to saving mini "mutts," dog-rescue volunteers play several roles.

For example, they often serve as "spotters" at local shelters, looking for specific dogs that can be fostered by individuals who specialize in specific breeds such as boxers and golden retrievers. Experienced volunteers may become coordinators who arrange for assistance from a variety of sources, including local veterinarians, groomers, transporters, and Web site designers. Many rescue groups work closely with national organizations such as Save-A-Pet and Petfinder.com whose Web sites publish comprehensive lists of adoptable rescue dogs throughout the United States and Canada. On weekends, rescue volunteers can be seen helping out during "Adoption Days" sponsored by national chains, including Petco and PetSmart.

Rescue groups provide both crucial information and welcome benefits for potential adopters. When one becomes interested in a specific dog on a rescue group's Web site, he or she can read about the animal's medical needs, age, temperament, and adoption fee. Even if he or she does not spot a suitable dog but remains interested in adopting one from rescue, he or she can fill out an application and list preferences regarding a dog's age, gender, and size. Although rescue groups occasionally receive puppies and young dogs that have been picked up during police raids of abusive puppy mills and backyard breeders, the majority of dogs available for adoption are older ones. Any pet owner who has experienced the aggravation of sleepless nights and numerous house-training "accidents" can appreciate the benefits of adopting an older, socialized, and housebroken dog.

Although the adoption process may take several weeks or even months to find the best match, careful screening improves the chances for a successful adoption. Rescue groups routinely conduct home visits of prospective dog owners to see if both the living conditions and the neighborhood will be suitable for the dog's size, temperament, and exercise needs. In addition, the applicant must have access to veterinary care and agree to return the dog to the rescue organization if he or she can no longer properly care for it. A foster parent can fully inform the adoptive parent about a dog's potential adjustment problems because the animal's behavior has been observed over a period of weeks--if not months--in a home setting. Careful attention to such details leads to a winning adoption process.

Whichever way a dog comes to a rescue group--by an owner surrender, a good Samaritan, or even by a police

raid of an illegal breeding operation--it will have an
opportunity to live out the rest of its life free from
harm and neglect. Rescue groups not only provide care
for homeless dogs; they also remind us of the joy made
possible by compassion, commitment, and unconditional
love.

FINDING RESEARCH TO STRENGTHEN ESSAYS

Locating Material in Your College Library

The Online Catalog If you decide to use research to strengthen an essay, you can take advantage of a number of options. Your college library probably has an online catalog system that lists all of the library's books and major holdings. You can search the online catalog by a key word related to your subject, or, if you already have information about authors who deal with your subject, you can search by the author's last name or the title of an author's book. An online catalog can provide you with a list of sources, the call number of each source (the number that will help you find the book on the library shelves), and information regarding the availability of the source. If your college has more than one campus, the online catalog can tell you which campus has a copy of the book you want. Be sure to take advantage of any "Help" menu the system provides as well as any library orientation offered on your campus.

Popular Periodical Indexes College libraries commonly subscribe to several index services that provide access to complete articles (called "full-text" articles) from periodicals (magazines, journals, and newspapers). Some of the most widely used periodical indexes include the following: *EBSCOhost, InfoTrac, LexisNexis, NewsBank, Reader's Guide to Periodical Literature,* and *WilsonWeb.*

Always preview articles carefully to see if they contain useful information for your research essay. Scan articles online, and print copies of the pages that will be useful for highlighting and note-taking later. Also, copy the first and last page of the article, which include information you will need for giving credit to the author and the source of the article. Be sure to ask your instructor if he or she will require copies of entire articles or just the pages you used in your essay.

Internet Search Engines The World Wide Web is the largest component of the Internet, and every Web site has an address, or **URL (uniform resource locator)**. Many students now use search engines that help users locate specific Web sites and potential sources if they do not know URL addresses. Here are some of the more popular search engines, along with their URLs:

AltaVista	http://www.altavista.com
Google	http://www.google.com
HotBot	http://www.hotbot.com
Yahoo!	http://www.yahoo.com

Unfortunately, some links posted on Web sites may be unavailable, and students will have to conduct searches carefully. Also, outdated information may remain posted on a Web site indefinitely, so students need to be cautious about using statistics or expert opinions that are several years old.

Checking for Validity of Sources

The writer of the dog-rescue essay decided to strengthen his paper by adding material from outside sources. The instructor required students to incorporate information from at least one print publication (magazine, newspaper, or book) and two valid electronic (online) sources. *While a traditional research paper involves a more comprehensive use of outside sources and a lengthier planning and research process, a short essay can often be enhanced by adding relevant material from experts. Regardless of the scope of any research assignment, the sources used must be valid.*

The student began his Internet search by typing the key phrase "dog rescue organizations" into the Google search function. This initial search resulted in a list of several hundred potential sources. After consulting with his instructor about the validity of his sources, the student was able to narrow his list to several dozen suitable sources.

Although the Internet and popular search engines are valuable tools to use for research, students are often tempted to use information from a Web site without checking for accuracy or validity. Students should check the author's credentials, such as educational background and professional experience, and other significant connections. In addition, students should locate any information about the background of the company or individuals responsible for a Web site. For example, if a student is investigating dog-rescue groups, the words of a veterinarian or background information from a nonprofit organization such as the Humane Society of the United States can generally be considered reliable. Since the veterinarian and the non-profit group are experienced and have no financial ties to the selling of dogs, their information is more valid than opinions from a pet shop owner, who makes money selling pets, or from a chat room popular with pet owners, who may know very little about dog-rescue groups.

Similarly, print sources need to be evaluated just as carefully. For example, a brochure advertising quick or foolproof dog training programs would not be as reliable as an article from a magazine endorsed by the American Society for the Prevention of Cruelty to Animals (ASPCA). Many colleges offer library orientations that include suggestions for determining the validity of a Web site's information and of a print source's reliability.

If you have any doubt about a source's validity, check with your instructor or seek advice from a campus librarian. At the very least, see if an article lists the title or credentials of the author. If you have found an unsigned article, see if the organization responsible for the material lists its history and/or purpose. Also, check for the publication date of the article, the original place of publication, the tone of the article (i.e., Does it avoid slang? Does it appear serious?), and the proper use of statistics and expert opinion. Using valid sources will lend credibility to your work.

INCOPORATING AND ACKNOWLEDGING YOUR SOURCES

Gathering and Organizing Sources

Once you have previewed your potential sources and have selected the ones best suited for your topic, you will need printouts of any online article (or at least the necessary pages) for highlighting and note-taking. If you are using a book or a magazine in its original form, you will need to photocopy the relevant pages. To keep track of all the sources you are using, you should staple or paper clip the pages of each source and label each one clearly.

If you have narrowed your search to eight sources (e.g., three magazine articles, two newspaper articles, and one book), you could organize your sources alphabetically by the authors' last names. If an article does not list its author, you can use the first major word of the title in place of the author's last name. Then you can label your sources as Source #1, Source #2, and so forth. This type of labeling will be useful for you later as you develop an outline that includes references to your sources.

Your instructor may want to see a preliminary list of your potential sources, and he or she may also require that your notes from sources be written on lined 4″ × 6″ note cards. Be sure you follow your instructor's specific guidelines and directions.

Taking Notes and Acknowledging Your Sources

When you take notes from one of your sources and use the information in your paper, you must acknowledge the source. This acknowledgment is called **documentation** because you are documenting, or giving credit, to the author and the work that provided the information. When you provide documentation within a research essay, you are using what is called **internal citation**. "Citation" means "giving credit," and "internal" means "inside," or "within," the paper. At the end of your essay, you list all the sources you cited within the paper. This list is called the **Works Cited**. The list of works cited is on a separate page from the rest of the essay, and it is the last numbered page of the essay.

Avoiding Plagiarism

Plagiarism occurs when you use a source's words or ideas and fail to give proper credit to the author and/or source of the work. Even if you paraphrase (state someone else's ideas in your own wording), you must give credit to the original source.

Whether you summarize material from an outside source, quote directly from it, or even paraphrase from it, you must acknowledge the source. Failure to do so is a form of academic theft. Depending on departmental or college policy, the penalties for plagiarism can be severe, ranging from receiving a failing grade on the plagiarized paper or failing a course, to expulsion. Some departments now use special software programs to check all student papers for plagiarism, and it is simply not worth the risk to submit research assignments without proper documentation.

Options for Acknowledging Your Sources

The Modern Language Association (MLA) System of Documentation
The Modern Language Association (MLA) system of documentation is preferred by English instructors, and you may find that humanities instructors on your campus also want you to follow MLA guidelines. In other departments, such as psychology and social sciences, instructors may ask you to follow the American Psychological Association (APA) system of documentation. Be sure to follow your instructor's directions regarding documentation requirements for your research assignments. There are many handbooks available that contain both MLA and APA styles of documentation, and most

freshman composition courses require that students purchase a handbook. You may want to check with your instructor to find out which handbook is used for freshman composition on your campus.

Over the next several pages, you will see how MLA documentation is used for summarizing, paraphrasing, and directly quoting information from sources. **You will also see how books, periodicals, and electronic sources should be listed on a Works Cited page that conforms to the new MLA guidelines that took effect in the 2009–2010 school year.**

MLA Internal ("In-text") Citation When using internal citation, you have several options for incorporating and giving credit to the source of your information. If you use a combination of techniques, your paper will read more smoothly. The following examples of summarizing, directly quoting, paraphrasing, and combining a direct quotation and paraphrase will provide you with sufficient documentation options as you draft your essay. Notice that authors and/or page numbers appear in parentheses, and this form is called **parenthetical documentation**.

A Summary of an Entire Book

One at a Time: A Week in an American Animal Shelter describes the fate of seventy- five animals who passed through a local shelter in Northern California over a seven-day period (Leigh and Geyer).

Note: No page numbers are included in this brief summary because the entire work is summarized. New MLA rules (effective in the 2009–2010 school year) require the use of italics rather than underlining for all titles of independently published works.

A Direct Quotation

According to Leigh and Geyer, "The safest and most reliable identification is provided by a combination of an ID tag, which is easily visible, and a microchip, which is permanent" (2).

Note: If you do not introduce the author before you quote from his or her work, you must put the author's name in parentheses at the end of the quoted material. In this case, there are two authors. Both of their names could be placed in parentheses, as follows: (Leigh and Geyer 2). Notice that the period goes after the parentheses.

A Paraphrase

A clearly marked ID tag, along with a permanent microchip, provides an animal with the best and safest means of identification (Leigh and Geyer 2).

A Combination of a Direct Quote and a Paraphrase

Leigh and Geyer emphasize that the best means of identification for an animal is "provided by a combination of an ID tag, which is easily visible, and a microchip, which is permanent" (2).

A Source Quoted in Another Author's Work

Kathy Nicklas-Varraso, author of *What to Expect from Breed Rescue*, notes that adopters will "most often get an adult whose chewing phase, housebreaking phase, and general puppy wildness are gone" (qtd. in Mohr).

Note: Nicklas-Varraso is the author being quoted; her comment was found in an online magazine article by Mohr. Mohr is the source that the student writer found. Therefore, Mohr is the source cited in parentheses. No page numbers are cited when the article comes from an online magazine.

Signal Phrases

In two of the preceding examples, **signal phrases** have been used to introduce quoted or paraphrased material. Signal phrases such as "Leigh and Geyer emphasize" and "According to Leigh and Geyer" are phrases that enable you to lead smoothly into documented information. Here are some of the more commonly used signal phrases, using Smith as the author:

According to Smith,   Smith reports that
As Smith notes,   Smith claims that
Smith suggests that   Smith points out that
Smith emphasizes that   Smith contends that

Documenting Information from a Source with an Unknown Author

If there is no author listed for a source, you can introduce the full title of the work after a signal phrase or place an abbreviation of the title in parentheses at the end of the information cited. For example, you can choose either of the following forms:

As the article "The Rules of Local Zoning Boards" notes, many counties prohibit businesses from operating out of garages in residential communities (C1).

or

Many counties prohibit businesses from operating out of garages in residential communities ("Rules" C1).

Note: When your source is a newspaper article, as in the examples above, give the section of the newspaper and the page number, as in C1, which stands for section C, page 1. Article titles are placed within quotation marks; book titles are placed in italics according to new MLA rules.

Exercise 1 **Paraphrasing from Sources**

Paraphrase each of the short excerpts following and include the appropriate parenthetical documentation. Use a signal phrase in at least one of the excerpts you paraphrase. The first excerpt is done for you and shows two options.

1. "A dog's sense of smell is not only exquisitely sensitive, but it communicates with a brain that can make fine discriminations among scents and learn new ones when they become important." (from *How Dogs Think* by Stanley Coren, page 63)

Paraphrase (no signal phrase): *Dogs have a keen sense of smell that enables the brain to distinguish between scents and remember new ones (Coren 63).*

or

Paraphrase (with a signal phrase): *Coren notes that dogs have a very sensitive sense of smell that enables the brain to recognize and remember important scents (63).*

2. "The world is full of damaged dogs who desperately need homes. Lots of wonderful people rescue them, and those people deserve our heartfelt appreciation. Patience and hard work can go a long way to rehabilitate dogs damaged in their youth by unstable environments." (from *For the Love of a Dog* by Patricia O'Connelly, page 87)

Paraphrase: *Neglected and abused dogs are common throughout the world, and individuals who rescue them deserve much recognition for their patience and hard work during the rehabilitation process (O'Connelly 87).*

3. "The sniffing ritual is designed in part to help dogs establish who has the more forceful personality and deserves extra respect. This is an essential component of all of their introductions as well as the interactions that follow." (from *The Secret Lives of Dogs* by Jane Murphy, page 64)

Use a combination of paraphrasing and direct quoting: *According to Jane Murphy, the "sniffing ritual" among dogs helps them determine whose personality is more dominating and thus deserving of more respect. Sniffing is "an essential component of all of their introductions" and interactions (64).*

4. "Grieving dogs experience symptoms similar to those experienced by a grieving pet owner. They may show signs of stress or restlessness. They may stop eating and lose weight or become listless and depressed. They may also have trouble sleeping or howl pitifully over the loss of their companion." (from *What's Your Dog's IQ?* by Sue Owens Wright, page 155)

Paraphrase: *A dog can grieve the loss of a companion much like humans grieve the loss of a loved one. Restlessness, insomnia, weight loss, and even mournful howling are symptoms of the animal's depression (Wright 155).*

Works Cited Entries: MLA Format

The Works Cited list of sources contains only the works you cited in your paper. This alphabetized list starts on a separately numbered page after the essay itself. **On the Works Cited page, entries should be double spaced, and the second and subsequent lines of each entry should be indented five spaces. Double spacing should also be used between each entry. Starting in 2009, MLA requires that the medium of publication (print, Web, CD, performance, etc.) be listed for all Works Cited entries.** For easy reference, a list of seven of the most common types of Works Cited entries follows. (A more complete list of sample Works Cited entries follows the "At a Glance" quick reference pages.)

AT A GLANCE: Seven Common Types of Works Cited Entries

Book

| author | title | city where published | publisher | date |

Stevens, Paul Drew. *Real Animal Heroes*. New York: Signet, 1997. Print.

Magazine Article

| author | article title | name of magazine |

Boks, Ed. "The Dirty Little Secret in Your Community." *Newsweek*

| date | page |

27 June 2005: 15. Print.

Newspaper Article

| author | article title | name of newpaper |

Caldwell, Tanya. "Boca Names Its New Dog Park." *South Florida*

| name of newspaper | date | year | section and page number |

Sun Sentinel 10 Aug. 2005: B1. Print.

Journal Article

| author | article title | name of journal |

Newkirk, Thomas. "The Dogma of Transformation." *College Compo-*

| name of journal | volume and issue number | year | pages |

sition and Communication 56.2 (2004): 251–71. Print.

Note: Page numbers are not listed for online articles because different printers will affect the page numbering of the printed article. *Exception:* If an article is contained within a PDF file, page numbers can be listed because numbers will be consistent regardless of the system used.

Article from an Online Magazine

author   *article title*
Woolf, Norma Bennett. "Getting Involved in Purebred Rescue."

name of magazine   *date published*   *date of access*
Dog Owner's Guide 18 May 2005. Web. 20 June 2005.

URL address
<http://www.canismajor.com/dog/rescinv.html>.

Article from an Online Database Subscription Service

author   *article title*   *publication*
Foss, Brad. "No Braking for Higher Prices." *South Florida*

date published *section, page* *subscription service* *library used*
Sun-Sentinel 11 Aug. 2005: D1. *NewsBank*. Broward County

location   *date of access*
Lib., Fort Laderdale, FL. Web. 16 Aug. 2005.

URL address
<http://www.newsbank.com>.

Note: Occasionally, the URL address will appear on its own line because some word processing programs will not split the site's address.

An Entire Web Site (No Named Author)

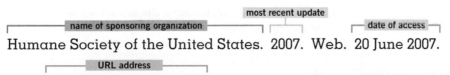

name of sponsoring organization   *most recent update*   *date of access*
Humane Society of the United States. 2007. Web. 20 June 2007.

URL address
<http://www.hsus.org>.

Note: The first date is the year listed for the Web site's most recent update. The second date is the date of access by the user. The name of the Web site here is also the sponsoring organization and group author.

WORKS CITED ENTRIES: A COMPREHENSIVE LIST (MLA)

Books

Book by One Author

Stevens, Paul Drew. *Real Animal Heroes*. New York: Signet, 1997. Print.

> **Note:** New York is the place of publication, Signet is the publisher, and 1997 is the
> year of publication. Short forms of the publisher's name should be used, so
> "Inc." and "Co." can be omitted.

Book by Two Authors

Leigh, Diane, and Marilee Geyer. *One at a Time: A Week in an American Animal*

   Shelter. Santa Cruz: No Voice Unheard, 2003. Print.

> **Note:** When two or three authors are listed, the name of the first author is listed
> last name first, and the other author(s) are listed in regular order. If there
> are more than three authors, the name of the first author is listed last name
> first and followed by the Latin phrase *et al.*, which means *and others*.

A Short Work in an Anthology

Wong, Edward. "A Long Overdue Apology." *Tales from the Times*. Ed. Lisa Belkin.

   New York: St. Martin's Griffin, 2004. 29–34. Print.

> **Note:** An anthology is a book-length collection of short works such as articles,
> essays, poems, or short stories. It usually has at least one editor who com-
> piles and organizes all of the short works, which are by different authors.
> When you are citing from an anthology, begin with the author of the short
> work and its title; then list the name of the anthology and its editor. At the
> end of the entry, list the page numbers of the short work.

Introduction from a Book

Curtis, Jamie Lee. Foreword. *Second Chances: More Tales of Found Dogs*. By

   Elise Lufkin. Guilford: Lyons, 2003. ix–x. Print.

> **Note:** Sometimes a book will contain either an introduction, preface, or foreword
> written by someone other than the author of the book. When citing from
> such introductory material, begin with the author of this material, followed
> by the word "Introduction" (not in quotes) (or "Preface" or "Foreword"), the
> name of the book, the author of the book, place of publication, publisher,
> date of publication, and the page numbers of the introduction, which will
> usually be in small Roman numerals.

Dictionary or Encyclopedia

"Luxate." *The American Heritage College Dictionary*. Third Edition. New York:

  Houghton Mifflin, 1993. Print.

Note: "Luxate" is the word you defined by using this dictionary.

Periodicals

Periodicals are newspapers, magazines, and scholarly journals. In Works
Cited listings, all months except May, June, and July are abbreviated.

Newspaper Article

Caldwell, Tanya. "Boca Names Its New Dog Park." *South Florida Sun-Sentinel*

  10 Aug. 2005: B1+. Print.

Note: B1 refers to the section (B) and page number (1) of the article. The plus sign
  (+) means that the article was continued on another page.

Newspaper Editorial

"Disaster Aid." Editorial. *South Florida Sun-Sentinel* 9 Aug. 2005: A10. Print.

Note: Newspaper editorials do not list an author.

Magazine Article (from a Monthly or Bimonthly Publication)

Richard, Julie. "The Lost Tigers of China." *Best Friends* Mar. 2005: 27–29. Print.

Magazine Article (from a Weekly Publication)

Boks, Ed. "The Dirty Little Secret in Your Community." *Newsweek* 27 June

  2005: 15. Print.

Journal Article

Newkirk, Thomas. "The Dogma of Transformation." *College Composition and*

  Communication 56.2 (2004): 251–71. Print.

Note: The number 56 is the volume number, 2 is the issue number, and 2004 is the
  year of publication.

Electronic Sources

Electronic sources can include professional Web sites, online periodicals, works from subscription services (such as *NewsBank*), e-mails, and even CD-ROMs.

When you list a Web site as one of your sources, you should include as many of the following items as you can find on the site:

1. Author or group author's name
2. Title of the site
3. Date of publication or date of latest update
4. The company or organization that sponsors the Web site (if it is different from the group author)
5. Date you accessed the Web site
6. Include the URL (list with angle brackets) if readers would be unable to locate the source without this Web address.

Entire Web Site

Human Society of the United States. 2007. Web. 20 June 2007. <http://www.hsus.org>.

Note: In this example, the sponsoring organization, the Humane Society of the United States, is also the group author of the site. 2007 is the date of the Web site's most recent update. The second date is the date of access by the user.

Article or Short Work

Mohr, Lori. "Adopting from a Breed Rescue Group." *Animal Forum*. Web. 23 June

2005. <http://www.animalforum.com/dbreedrescue.htm>.

Note: In this example, no date of publication was available, so the only date given in this listing is the date the article was accessed by the student writer.

Article from an Online Magazine

Woolf, Norma Bennett. "Getting Involved in Purebred Rescue." *Dog Owner's Guide*

18 May 2005. Web. 20 June 2005. <http://www.canismajor.com/dog/rescinv>.

Article from an Online Subscription Service

Foss, Brad. "No Braking for Higher Prices." *South Florida Sun Sentinel* 11 Aug.

2005: D1. *NewsBank*. Broward County Lib., Fort Lauderdale, FL. Web. 16 Aug.

2005. <http://www.newsbank.com>.

Note: If you use one of your library's online subscription services, you can first follow the same format as a print periodical, but you will need to add the name of the subscription service, the library you used, the date you accessed the article, and the URL address (if available).

E-mail

Brown, Vernon. "Re: Answers to Your Questions." Message to Jason Roberts. 15 July

2005. E-mail.

Other Sources: Nonprint

Personal Interview

Carter, Michael. Personal interview. 17 Mar. 2005.

Radio or Television Program

"Babies Having Babies." *Live on Five Series.* Narr. Harry Anderson. NBC. WPTV,

West Palm Beach. 6 Aug. 2004. Television.

Exercise 2   Listing Works Cited Entries in MLA Format

Arrange the items from the basic sources below in correct MLA format. Consult the "Works Cited Entries" on 356–358 for proper form and punctuation.

1. Book

City where published: New York
Publisher: Free Press
Author: Stanley Coren
Title: How Dogs Think
Year published: 2002

Coren, Stanley. *How Dogs Think.* New York: Free Press, 2002. Print.

_____

2. Newspaper Article

Newspaper: Gainesville Sun
Article title: A Message That Lives On
Section of newspaper: A
Date: January 16, 2008
Author: Alice Wallace
Pages: 1 and 4

Wallace, Alice. "A Message That Lives On." *Gainesville Sun* 16 Jan. 2008:

A1+. Print.

3. Magazine Article (from a monthly publication)

Article: The Pug Who Came to Dinner
Author: Gail MacMillan
Magazine: Bark

Pages: 67–69
Month: March
Year: 2007

Macmillan, Gail. "The Pug Who Came to Dinner." *Bark* Apr. 2007: 67–69.

Print.

4. Journal Article

Journal: Journal of Communication
Article: Dialogue about the American Family on Television
Volume: 50
Issue number: 4
Year published: 2000
Pages: 79–110
Author: Kelly F. Albada

Albada, Kelly F. "Dialogue about the American Family on Television."

Journal of Communication 50.4 (2000): 79–110. Print.

Incorporating Research into Your Outline

After you have compiled all of your notes from your sources, you need to determine what information you will use and where it bests fits into your essay. The best way to do this is to work with your original outline before you draft a research version of your essay. Here again is the outline for the dog-rescue essay, but it is a bit different from the outline on pages 347–348. This version now includes references to sources; key information from these sources will be the research that strengthens the essay.

Notice that the headings "Introduction" and "Conclusion" have been added to the outline. In this version, the writer wanted to include some relevant research in both the introductory and concluding paragraphs as well as in the body paragraphs, so he expanded his outline. By placing research references in the outline, the student writer will know where the new information will be included when he prepares the drafts and final version of his research essay.

Note: The references to the added research appear in bold print so that you can compare this outline to the previous one.

An Outline for an Essay with Research

I. Introduction
    A. Six to eight million dogs and cats are placed in shelters each year; three to four million are euthanized. **See Humane Society, source #2.**
    B. Some shelters euthanize animals routinely. **See Leigh and Geyer, source #3.**
    C. Some shelters work with rescue groups.

Thesis Statement: Dog-rescue organizations perform a humane service by saving homeless dogs and

matching responsible adopters with a devoted new
family member.

II. Dog-rescue volunteers play several roles.
   A. Some volunteers are "spotters" who look for
      specific breeds at local shelters.
   B. Experienced rescue volunteers may become coor-
      dinators and arrange assistance from various
      sources. **See Woolfe, source #5.**
   C. Volunteers work with national organizations
      such as Save-A-Pet and Petfinder.com which
      maintain databases of adoptable dogs from
      rescue groups throughout the United States
      and Canada.
   D. Volunteers assist at rescue-dog "Adoption
      Days" hosted by pet supply chains such as
      Petco and PetSmart.

III. Rescue groups provide important information and
    benefits for prospective adopters.
   A. By viewing a rescue group's Web site, poten-
      tial adopters can read about a dog's age,
      temperament, adoption fee, and any special
      medical conditions.
   B. If a potential adopter does not find a suit-
      able dog, he or she can still complete an
      online application.
   C. On an application, a potential adopter can
      list his or her preferences for the age, gen-
      der, and size of the dog.
   D. Although some dogs are puppies rescued from
      abusive situations, most are adult dogs
      already socialized and housebroken. **See
      Nicklas-Varraso in Mohr, source #4.**

IV. Careful screening often results in a successful
    adoption.
   A. Rescue groups routinely conduct home visits to
      check the living conditions and the neighbor-
      hood.
   B. The applicant must have access to veterinary
      care.
   C. The applicant must agree to return the dog to
      the rescue organization if he or she can no
      longer care for the animal.
   D. A foster parent can fully inform the
      adoptive parent about potential adjustment
      problems.
   E. Careful attention to such details leads to a
      winning adoption process.

> V. Conclusion
>   A. Rescue groups provide an opportunity for a dog to live out the rest of its life free from harm and neglect.
>   B. We should "embrace non-lethal strategies" to show we are a humane society. **See Bok, source #1.**
>
> Concluding Statement: Rescue groups not only provide care for homeless dogs; they also remind us of the joy made possible by compassionate adoption.

A Draft of an Essay with Research

The following is a rough version of the original essay on dog-rescue groups; it has been strengthened with some material from outside sources. (The material is underlined so that you can spot it easily.) The marginal annotations will alert you to (1) places where the information is directly quoted or paraphrased and (2) places where revisions are necessary to achieve a better style.

The Humane Work of Dog-Rescue Groups

Although the United States is generally regarded as a country that loves and pampers its pets, animal shelters are often filled to capacity with dogs that have been abandoned, abused, or surrendered by their owners. *statistic and paraphrased statement from online source as part of introduction* <u>Each year, six to eight million dogs and cats are placed in shelters, and three to four million of them are euthanized (Humane Society).</u> Sadly, some shelters routinely euthanize healthy dogs if no one claims or adopts them after a grace period ranging from just days to a few weeks. *direct quotation from the preface of a book with two authors* <u>These dogs have only "about a fifty percent chance of getting out alive" (Leigh and Geyer viii).</u> Fortunately, however, many shelters work closely with dog-rescue organizations that find loving, temporary homes where foster parents can provide care and, if necessary, rehabilitation. Staffed by dedicated volunteers, rescue groups perform a humane service by saving homeless dogs and enabling responsible adopters to gain a devoted new family member.

From rescuing retired greyhounds to saving mini "mutts," dog-rescue volunteers play several roles. For example, they often serve as "spotters" at local shelters, looking for specific dogs that can be fostered by individuals who specialize in specific breeds such as boxers and golden retrievers. Experienced volunteers may become coordinators who arrange for assistance from a variety of sources, including local veterinarians, groomers, transporters, and Web site designers. <u>Norma Bennett Woolf writes for the online magazine *Dog Owner's Guide*. Woolf states, "There's always room for more foster homes, fund-raisers, dog spotters, kennels, public relations workers, and trainers."</u> Many rescue groups work closely with national organizations such as Save-A-Pet and Petfinder.com whose Web sites publish comprehensive lists of adoptable rescue dogs throughout the United States and Canada. On weekends, rescue volunteers can be seen helping out during "Adoption Days" sponsored by national chains, including Petco and PetSmart.

direct quotation from an online magazine, sentence combining needed

Rescue groups provide both crucial information and welcome benefits for potential adopters. When one becomes interested in a specific dog on a rescue group's Web site, he or she can read about the animal's medical needs, age, temperament, and adoption fee. Even if he or she does not spot a suitable dog but remains interested in adopting one from rescue, he or she can fill out an application and list preferences regarding a dog's age, gender, and size. Although rescue groups occasionally receive puppies and young dogs that have been picked up during police raids of abusive puppy mills and backyard breeders, the majority of dogs available for adoption are older ones. <u>Kathy Nicklas-Varraso wrote *What to Expect From Breed Rescue*. This writer says, "You'll most often get an adult whose chewing phase, housebreaking phase, and general puppy-wildness are gone" (qtd. in Mohr).</u> Any pet owner who has experienced the aggravation of sleepless nights and numerous house-training "accidents" can appreciate the benefits of adopting an older, socialized, and house-broken dog.

a source quoted in another author's work; needs to be more smoothly blended

Although the adoption process may take several weeks or even months to find the best match, careful screening improves the chances for a successful adoption. Rescue groups routinely conduct home visits of prospective dog owners to see if both the living conditions and the neighborhood will be suitable for the dog's size, temperament, and exercise needs. In addition, the applicant must have access to veterinary care and agree to return the dog to the rescue organization if he or she can no longer properly care for it. A foster parent can fully inform the adoptive parent about a dog's potential adjustment problems because the animal's behavior has been observed over a period of weeks--if not months--in a home setting. <u>Nicklas-Varraso states,</u>

direct quote; needs a transition

"<u>Borderline pets are offered for adoption within strict guidelines, such as no other pets or fenced yards only</u>" <u>(qtd. in Mohr)</u>. Careful attention to such details leads to a winning adoption process.

  However a dog finds its way to a rescue group--by an owner surrender, a good Samaritan, or even by a police raid of an illegal breeding operation--it will have an opportunity to live out the rest of its life free from harm and neglect. <u>Ed Bok is director of Animal Care and Control for New York City. He believes that we should embrace preventive, non-lethal strategies that reveal that at our core we truly are a humane humane society (15)</u>. Rescue groups not only follow <u>Bok's advice</u> by providing care for homeless dogs; they also remind us of the joy made possible by compassion, commitment, and unconditional love.

print source is a magazine; sentence combining needed; put Bok's name in a signal phrase

Note: A Works Cited page will be included in the final version of this essay.

PREPARING THE FINAL VERSION OF AN ESSAY WITH RESEARCH

Making Final Changes and Refinements

The final version of the research essay includes the refinements suggested in the margins of the previous draft. You will notice that the final essay reflects proper MLA documentation and page numbering format. Other improvements relate to the style of the essay. Changes from the previous draft include the following:

- The title has been changed to be more descriptive and appealing.
- Information from sources has been more smoothly blended by sentence combining and the use of signal phrases.
- An awkward repetition of "he or she" has been changed to the more specific term "a potential adopter," in the third paragraph.
- The word "humane" has been added in the last paragraph to reinforce the idea of compassionate care for animals.
- To conform to MLA format, the writer has placed his name, his instructor's name, the course title, and the date in the upper left-hand corner of the first page.
- Again following MLA guidelines, the writer has placed his last name and page number in the upper right-hand corner of each page of the essay.
- A Works Cited page, in proper MLA format, is included and appears as the last page of the essay.

Note: Pages in the sample paper are not 8½ × 11 standard size. MLA format requires margins of at least one inch but no more than an inch and a half on all sides of the page.

Roberts 1

Jason Roberts

Professor Alvarez

English 100

7 December 2008

Crusading for Canines:

Dog-Rescue Groups and Winning Adoptions

Although the United States is generally regarded as a country that loves and pampers its pets, animal shelters are often filled to capacity with dogs that have been abandoned, abused, or surrendered by their owners. Each year, six to eight million dogs and cats are placed in shelters, and three to four million of them are euthanized (Humane Society). Sadly, some shelters routinely euthanize healthy dogs if no one claims or adopts them after a grace period ranging from just days to a few weeks. These dogs have only "about a fifty percent chance of getting out alive" (Leigh and Geyer viii). Fortunately, however, many shelters work closely with dog-rescue organizations that find loving, temporary homes where foster parents can provide care and, if necessary, rehabilitation. Staffed by dedicated volunteers, rescue groups perform a humane service by saving homeless dogs and enabling responsible adopters to gain a devoted new family member.

From rescuing retired greyhounds to saving mini "mutts," dog-rescue volunteers play several roles. For example, they often serve as "spotters" at local shelters, looking for specific dogs that can be fostered by individuals who specialize in specific breeds such as boxers and golden retrievers. Experienced volunteers may become coordinators who arrange for assistance from a variety of sources, including local veterinarians, groomers, transporters, and Web site designers. As Norma Bennett Woolf suggests in the online magazine *Dog Owner's Guide*, "There's always room for more foster homes, fund-raisers, dog-spotters, kennels, public relations workers, and trainers." Many rescue groups work closely with national organizations such as Save-A-Pet and Petfinder.com whose Web sites publish comprehensive lists of adoptable rescue dogs throughout the United States and Canada. On weekends, rescue volunteers can be seen helping out during "Adoption Days" sponsored by national chains, including Petco and PetSmart.

Rescue groups provide both crucial information and welcome benefits for potential adopters. When one becomes interested in a specific dog on a rescue group's Web site, he or she can read about the animal's medical needs, age, temperament, and adoption fee. Even if a potential adopter does not spot a suitable dog but remains interested in adopting one from rescue, he or she can fill out an application and list preferences regarding a dog's age, gender, and size. Although rescue groups occasionally receive puppies and young dogs that have been picked up during police raids of abusive puppy mills and backyard breeders, the majority of dogs available for adoption are older ones. Kathy Nicklas-Varraso, author of *What to Expect from Breed Rescue*, notes that adopters will "most often get an adult whose chewing phase, housebreaking phase, and general puppy wildness are gone" (qtd. in Mohr). Any pet owner who has experienced the aggravation of sleepless nights and numerous house-training "accidents" can appreciate the benefits of adopting an older, socialized, and housebroken dog.

Although the adoption process may take several weeks or even months to find the best match, careful screening improves the chances for a successful adoption. Rescue groups routinely conduct home visits of prospective dog owners to see if both the living conditions and the neighborhood will be suitable for the dog's size, temperament, and exercise needs. In addition, the applicant must have access to veterinary care and agree to return the dog to the rescue organization if he or she can no longer properly care for it. A foster parent can fully inform the adoptive parent about a dog's potential adjustment problems because the animal's behavior has been observed over a period of weeks--if not months--in a home setting. Nicklas-Varraso stresses that the "borderline pets are offered for adoption within strict guidelines, such as no other pets or fenced yards only" (qtd. in Mohr). Careful attention to such details leads to a winning adoption process.

However a dog finds its way to a rescue group--by an owner surrender, a good Samaritan, or even by a police raid of an illegal breeding operation--it will have an opportunity to live out the rest of its life free from harm and neglect. Ed Boks, director of Animal Care and Control for New York City, urges us to "embrace preventive, non-lethal strategies that reveal that at our core, we truly are a humane society" (15). Rescue groups not only provide humane care for homeless dogs; they also remind us of the joy made possible by compassion, commitment, and unconditional love.

Roberts 4

Works Cited

Boks, Ed. "The Dirty Little Secret in Your Community." *Newsweek* 27 June 2005: 15. Print.

Humane Society of the United States. 2007. 20 June
2007. Web. <http://www.hsus.org>.

Leigh, Diane, and Marilee Geyer. Preface. *One at a
Time: A Week in an American Animal Shelter*.
Santa Cruz: No Voice Unheard, 2003. vii–viii.
Print.

Mohr, Lori. "Adopting from a Breed Rescue Group."
Animal Forum. Web. 23 June 2005. <http://www.
animalforum.com/dbreedrescue.htm>.

Woolf, Norma Bennett. "Getting Involved in
Purebred Rescue." *Dog Owner's Guide* 18 May
2005. Web. 20 June 2005. <http://www.canismajor
.com/dog/rescinv.html>.

How Do I Get a Better Grade?

Visit www. mywritinglab. com
for audio-visual lectures
and additional practice sets
about using research to
strengthen essays.

*Get a better grade with
MyWritingLab!*

Grammar for Writers

INTRODUCTION

Overview

In this section, you'll be working with the basics of grammar that you need to be a clear writer. If you are willing to memorize certain rules and work through the activities here, you will be able to apply grammatical rules automatically as you write.

Using "Grammar for Writers"

Since this section of the textbook is divided into self-contained segments, it does not have to be studied in sequence. Your instructor may suggest you review specific rules and examples, or you may be assigned various segments as either a class or group assignment. Various approaches are possible, and thus you can regard this section as a "user-friendly" grammar handbook for quick reference. Mastering the practical parts of grammar will improve your writing, helping you to become more sure of yourself and better prepared for future composition courses.

Contents

True or (False:) In a sentence, the verb always comes after the subject.
(After you study this chapter, you will be confident of your answer.)

The Simple Sentence

Identifying the crucial parts of a sentence is the first step in many writing decisions: how to punctuate, how to avoid sentence fragments, how to be sure that subjects and verbs "agree" (match). To move forward to these decisions requires a few steps back—to basics.

RECOGNIZING A SENTENCE

Let's start with a few basic definitions. A basic unit of language is a **word**.

examples: *car, dog, sun*

Tell students that if a word group has a subject and a verb and does not make sense by itself (i.e., is not a dependent clause), it is one type of sentence fragment.

372

A group of related words can be a **phrase**.

> **examples:** *shiny new car; snarling, angry dog; in the bright sun*

When the group of words contains a subject and a verb, it is called a **clause**. When the word group has a subject and a verb and makes sense by itself, it is called a **sentence** or an **independent clause**. When the word group has a subject and a verb but does not make sense by itself, it is called a **dependent clause**.

If you want to check to see whether you have written a sentence, and not just a group of related words, you first have to check for a subject and a verb. Locating the verbs first can be easier.

RECOGNIZING VERBS

Verbs are words that express some kind of action or being. Verbs about the five senses—sight, touch, smell, taste, sound—are part of the group called **being verbs**. Look at some examples of verbs as they work in sentences:

> **action verbs:**
> We *walk* to the store every day.
> The children *ran* to the playground.

> **being verbs:**
> My mother *is* a good cook.
> The family *seems* unhappy.
> The soup *smells* delicious.

Exercise 1 **Recognizing Verbs**

Underline the verbs in each of the following sentences.

1. A loud cry <u>woke</u> me out of a sound sleep.
2. This game <u>appears</u> simple.
3. You <u>are</u> the hardest worker at the restaurant.
4. Two brave joggers <u>run</u> in the coldest weather.
5. The soldier <u>saluted</u> his mother.
6. Distrust <u>keeps</u> the brothers apart.
7. Vanessa and Chris <u>were</u> my neighbors in Providence.
8. Emilio <u>sounds</u> thrilled about the new baby.
9. On warm days, the cat <u>dozed</u> in the sun.
10. My boss <u>starts</u> each day with a joke.

More on Verbs

The verb in a sentence can be more than one word. First of all, there can be **helping verbs** in front of the main verb, the action or being verb. Here is a list of some frequently used helping verbs: *is, am, are, was, were, do, must, might, have, has, shall, will, can, could, may, should, would.*

> I *was watching* the Super Bowl. (The helping verb is *was*.)
> You *should have called* me. (The helping verbs are *should* and *have*.)

INSTRUCTOR'S NOTE

If your students need help understanding the difference between sentences and fragments, refer to Chapter 19 on sentence fragments.

ESL NOTE

Two-word verbs (e.g., *turn in, turn off, hand in,* etc.) can be particularly confusing for nonnative speakers. For a list of such verbs, see "Two-Word Verbs" on page 60 of the ESL Appendix.

The president *can select* his assistants. (The helping verb is *can*.)
Leroy *will graduate* in May. (The helping verb is *will*.)

Helping verbs can make the verb in a sentence more than one word long. But there can also be more than one main verb:

Andrew *planned* and *practiced* his speech.
I *stumbled* over the rug, *grabbed* a chair, and *fell* on my face.

Collaborate

| **Exercise 2** | **Writing Sentences with Helping Verbs** |

Complete this exercise with a partner or a group. First, ask one person to add at least one helping verb to the verb given. Then work together to write two sentences using the main verb and the helping verb(s). As a final step, appoint one spokesperson for your group to read all your sentences to the class. Notice how many combinations of main verb and helping verb you hear.

The first one is done for you.

1. **verb:** named

   verb with helping verb(s): *was named*

   sentence 1: *I was named after my father.*

   sentence 2: *Washington, D.C., was named after the first president.*

INSTRUCTOR'S NOTE

Answers will vary. Possible answers shown at right.

2. **verb:** staring

   verb with helping verb(s): *must be staring*

   sentence 1: *That good-looking girl must be staring at you.*

   sentence 2: *At this moment, Tommy must be staring at his e-mail.*

3. **verb:** forget

   verb with helping verb(s): *should forget*

   sentence 1: *You should forget about that old quarrel.*

   sentence 2: *Keith should forget his old girlfriend.*

4. **verb:** hurt

   verb with helping verb(s): *can hurt*

   sentence 1: *A sharp remark can hurt a vulnerable person.*

   sentence 2: *I can hurt my feet on the rocky beach.*

5. **verb:** included

   verb with helping verb(s): *was included*

   sentence 1: *An appetizer was included in the price of dinner.*

   sentence 2: *Jacob's first wife was included among the wedding guests.*

RECOGNIZING SUBJECTS

TEACHING TIP

Tell students that an easy way to spot an action verb in a sentence is to remember that it tells what a subject <u>does</u> (present tense), <u>did</u> (past tense), or <u>will do</u> (future tense). (For example: He cleans his room; he cleaned his room; he will clean his room.)

After you can recognize verbs, finding the subjects of sentences is easy because subjects and verbs are linked. If the verb is an action verb, for example, the subject will be the word or words that answer the question, "Who or what is doing that action?"

The truck stalled on the highway.

Step 1: Identify the verb: *stalled*

Step 2: Ask, "Who or what stalled?"

Step 3: The answer is the subject: The *truck* stalled on the highway. *Truck* is the subject.

If your verb expresses being, the same steps apply to finding the subject.

Spike was my best friend.

Step 1: Identify the verb: *was*

Step 2: Ask, "Who or what was my best friend?"

Step 3: The answer is the subject: *Spike* was my best friend. *Spike* is the subject.

Just as there can be more than one word to make up a verb, there can be more than one subject.

examples: *David* and *Leslie* planned the surprise party.
My *father* and *I* worked in the yard yesterday.

Exercise 3   **Recognizing the Subjects in Sentences**

Underline the subjects in the following sentences.

1. Nobody has been taking out the trash lately.

2. Something is happening at our neighbor's house.

3. After my last exam, worry and hope battled in my brain.

4. Sometimes shopping offers an escape from my troubles.

5. Airports are becoming more crowded with holiday travelers.

6. Confidence can be an asset for a job seeker.

7. On Mondays, Chris, Bill and I meet for coffee before class.

8. With great joy, the lost dog greeted its owner.

9. We can finish our conversation in a few minutes.

10. Aunt Teresa could have misunderstood my directions to the house.

More about Recognizing Subjects and Verbs

When you look for the subject of a sentence, look for the core word or words; don't include descriptive words around the subject. The idea is to look for the subject, not for the words that describe it.

The dark blue *dress* looked lovely on Anita.
Dirty *streets* and grimy *houses* destroy a neighborhood.

The subjects are the core words *dress*, *streets*, and *houses*, not the descriptive words *dark blue*, *dirty*, and *grimy*.

PREPOSITIONS AND PREPOSITIONAL PHRASES

Prepositions are usually small words that often signal a kind of position or possession, as shown in the following list:

INFO BOX: **Some Common Prepositions**

about	before	beyond	inside	on	under
above	below	during	into	onto	up
across	behind	except	like	over	upon
after	beneath	for	near	through	with
among	beside	from	of	to	within
around	between	in	off	toward	without
at					

A prepositional phrase is made up of a preposition and its object. Here are some prepositional phrases. In each one, the first word is the preposition; the other words are the object of the preposition.

TEACHING TIP

Listing prepositional phrases that have become clichés or slang can be an enjoyable way for students to spot prepositional phrases. (For example: *under the weather*, *down on his luck*, *up in the air*.)

Prepositional Phrases

about the movie	of mice and men
around the corner	off the record
between two lanes	on the mark
during recess	up the wall
near my house	with my sister and brother

There is an old memory trick to help you remember prepositions. Think of a chair. Now, think of a series of words you can put *in front of* the chair:

around the chair	*off* the chair
behind the chair	*on* the chair
between the chairs	*near* the chair
by the chair	*to* the chair
from the chair	*under* the chair
of the chair	*with* the chair

Those words are prepositions.

You need to know about prepositions because they can help you identify the subject of a sentence. There is an important grammar rule about prepositions:

Nothing in a prepositional phrase can ever be the subject of the sentence.

Prepositional phrases describe people, places, or things. They may describe the subject of a sentence, but they never include the subject. Whenever you are looking for the subject of a sentence, begin by putting parentheses around all the prepositional phrases.

> The restaurant (around the corner) makes the best fried chicken (in town).

The prepositional phrases are in parentheses. Since *nothing* in them can be the subject, once you have eliminated the prepositional phrases, you can follow the steps to find the subject of the sentence:

> What is the verb? *makes*
> Who or what makes the best fried chicken? The *restaurant*.
> *Restaurant* is the subject of the sentence.

By marking off the prepositional phrases, you are left with the *core* of the sentence. There is less to look at.

ESL NOTE
(1) ESL students may need help with the prepositions of time and space. See the "Prepositions" section on pp. 662–665 of the ESL Appendix. (2) Nonnative speakers often have difficulty understanding the meaning of some colloquial prepositional phrases. Examining literal interpretations of some expressions can be an amusing yet practical examination of prepositions.

> (Behind the park), a *carousel* (with gilded horses) delighted children (from all the neighborhoods).
> subject: *carousel*

> The *dog* (with the ugliest face) was the winner (of the contest).
> subject: *dog*

Exercise 4   **Recognizing Prepositional Phrases, Subjects, and Verbs**

Put parentheses around all the prepositional phrases in the following sentences. Then underline the subject and verb and put an *S* above each subject and a *V* above each verb.

1. Alicia has been wondering about her chances for a job in nursing at a hospital near the military base.

2. An argument between my mother and father affected all the children in the family.

3. Elderly people in our neighborhood are becoming substitute grandparents to many children without older relatives in the area.

4. At the top of his lungs, the toddler screamed for his mother and stretched his arms toward her.

5. Nothing in the refrigerator except a few potato chips looks edible to me.

6. Before dinner, I can run to the bakery and get some cookies for dessert.

7. The girl with the long dark hair sat near me during the pep rally inside the gym.

8. A couple of raindrops fell on Cody's newly waxed car and left tiny water marks.

9. Over the weekend, a silly argument caused a serious feud between two families in the neighborhood.

$$(\qquad)(\qquad)\ \ S \qquad V$$

10. From the first day of the term, <u>Charlie</u> <u>has been worrying</u>

$$(\qquad)(\qquad)$$

about his grade in this class.

Collaborate

Exercise 5   **Writing Sentences with Prepositional Phrases**

Complete this exercise with a partner. First, add one prepositional phrase to the core sentence. Then ask your partner to add a second prepositional phrase to the same sentence. For the next sentence, switch places. Let your partner add the first phrase; you add the second. Keep reversing the process throughout the exercise. When you have completed the exercise, be ready to read the sentences with two prepositional phrases to the class. The first one has been done for you as a sample.

1. **core sentence:** Rain fell.

   Add one prepositional phrase: *Rain fell on the mountains.*

   Add another prepositional phrase: *From a dark sky, rain fell on the mountains.*

INSTRUCTOR'S NOTE

Answers will vary. Possible answers shown at right.

2. **core sentence:** Eddie shouted.

   Add one prepositional phrase: *Eddie shouted at the girl.*

   Add another prepositional phrase: *Eddie shouted at the girl in the red dress.*

3. **core sentence:** A helicopter hovered.

   Add one prepositional phrase: *During the battle, a helicopter hovered.*

   Add another prepositional phrase: *During the battle, a helicopter hovered above the ground.*

4. **core sentence:** A cat can be amused.

   Add one prepositional phrase: *A cat can be amused by a toy mouse.*

   Add another prepositional phrase: *A cat can be amused by a toy mouse on a string.*

5. **core sentence:** The woman yawned.

   Add one prepositional phrase: *The woman beside me yawned.*

   Add another prepositional phrase: *The woman beside me yawned during the lecture.*

WORD ORDER

When we speak, we often use a very simple word order: first comes the subject, then the verb. For example, someone would say, "I am going to the store." *I* is the subject that begins the sentence; *am going* is the verb that comes after the subject.

But not all sentences are in such a simple word order. Prepositional phrases, for example, can change the word order.

sentence: Among the contestants was an older man.

Step 1: Mark off the prepositional phrase(s) with parentheses: *(Among the contestants) was an older man.* Remember that nothing in a prepositional phrase can be the subject of a sentence.

Step 2: Find the verb: *was*

Step 3: Who or what was? An older *man* was. The subject of the sentence is *man*.

After you change the word order of this sentence, you can see the subject (S) and verb (V) more easily.

           s   **v**

An older *man was* among the contestants.

Exercise 6   **Finding Prepositional Phrases, Subjects, and Verbs in Complicated Word Order**

Start by putting parentheses around the prepositional phrases in the following sentences. Then underline the subjects and verbs and put an *S* above each subject and a *V* above each verb.

TEACHING TIP

Tell students to identify the prepositional phrases first and then pretend that these phrases do not appear. By doing so, they can spot the subjects and verbs more easily.

1. Among my favorite pieces of clothing was an old baseball cap from my high school days.

2. Under my grandmother's bed is a box with old photographs of her and my grandfather in their wild teenage years.

3. Beneath the floorboards lurks a family of the craftiest mice on this continent.

4. Between my house on Daley Road and the corner was a huge old house behind a rusted iron fence.

5. From the back of the classroom came the soft snoring sound of a student in dreamland.

6. Beyond the layers of deception and intrigue was a simple answer to the mystery of the hero's death.

7. Among the most irritating programs on television are a talent show for deluded contestants and a comedy without any jokes.

8. Inside my mother's purse are expired coupons from the supermarket and tattered half-price offers from local restaurants.

                                (   ) V   S   (   )
   9. Behind the school cafeteria <u>lie</u> six huge <u>dumpsters</u> in a row.
                                (   ) V   S   (   )
   10. Through all my struggles <u>runs</u> a small <u>hope</u> for a better life.

More on Word Order

The expected word order of subject first, then verb, changes when a sentence starts with *There is/are, There was/were, Here is/are, Here was/were*. In such cases, look for the subject after the verb.

      v   **s**   **s**
There *are* a *bakery* and a *pharmacy* down the street.

     v   **s**
Here *is* the *man* with the answers.

To understand this pattern, try changing the word order:

     s   **s**   **v**
A *bakery* and a *pharmacy* *are* there, down the street.

     s   **v**
The *man* with the answers *is* here.

TEACHING TIP

Tell students that substituting the appropriate singular or plural pronoun for the complete subject can help them determine the correct verb form.

You should also note that even if the subject comes after the verb, the verb has to "match" the subject. For instance, if the subject refers to more than one thing, the verb must also refer to more than one thing.

There *are* a *bakery* and a *pharmacy* down the road. (Two things, a bakery and a pharmacy, *are* down the road.)

Word Order in Questions

Questions may have a different word order. The main verb and the helping verb may not be next to each other.

question:	Do you like pizza?
subject:	*you*
verbs:	*do, like*

To understand this concept, think of answering the question. If someone accused you of not liking pizza, you might say, "I *do like* it." You would use two words as verbs.

question:	Will he think about it?
subject:	*he*
verbs:	*will, think*

question:	Is Maria telling the truth?
subject:	*Maria*
verbs:	*is, telling*

> **Exercise 7** **Recognizing Subjects and Verbs in Complicated Word Order: A Comprehensive Exercise**

Underline the subjects and verbs, putting an *S* above the subjects and a *V* above the verbs.

           V   *S*   *S*
   1. There <u>were</u> a gray <u>cat</u> and a striped <u>kitten</u> in the garden.

          V   *S*   *V*

2. <u>Will</u> <u>you</u> <u>drive</u> to Biloxi on Saturday?

                                 V   *S*

3. From the end of the long hall <u>came</u> the <u>sound</u> of laughter.

       V   *S*

4. <u>Was</u> there <u>anything</u> in your coat pocket?

      V   *S*   *S*   *V*

5. <u>Have</u> <u>Jimmy</u> and <u>Chris</u> <u>spoken</u> about the boat trip on the

Hudson River?

      V   *S*

6. Here <u>are</u> the most recent <u>photographs</u> of my nephew.

                              V   *S*

7. Among the stores in the strip mall <u>was</u> a tire <u>store</u> with a section

for wheel alignment and balancing.

      V   *S*   *V*

8. <u>Can</u> <u>we</u> <u>think</u> about a reasonable solution to the problem?

                     V   *S*

9. Near the end of the movie <u>came</u> a terrifying <u>scene</u> inside a dark

cave.

                          V   *S*

10. Between the yellowed pages of the book <u>was</u> a thin <u>film</u> of dust.

Words That Cannot Be Verbs

Sometimes there are words that look like verbs in a sentence, but they are not verbs. Such words include adverbs (words like *always, often, nearly, rarely, never, ever*) that are placed close to the verb but are not verbs. Another word that is placed between a helping verb and a main verb is *not*. *Not* is not a verb.

When you are looking for verbs in a sentence, be careful to eliminate words like *often* and *not*.

He *will* not *listen* to me. (The verbs are *will listen*.)
Althea *can* always *find* a bargain. (The verbs are *can find*.)

Be careful with contractions.

They *haven't raced* in years. (The verbs are *have raced*. *Not* is not a part of the verb, even in contractions.)
*Do*n't you *come* from Arizona? (The verbs are *do come*.)
Won't he ever *learn*? (The verbs are *will learn*. *Won't* is a contraction for *will not*.)

Recognizing Main Verbs

If you are checking to see if a word is a main verb, try the *pronoun test*. Combine your word with this simple list of pronouns: *I, you, he, she, it, we, they*. A main verb is a word such as *drive* or *noticed* that can be combined with the words on this list. Now try the pronoun test.

For the word *drive*: I drive, you drive, he drives, she drives, it drives, we drive, they drive

For the word *noticed*: I noticed, you noticed, he noticed, she noticed, it noticed, we noticed, they noticed

But words such as *never* cannot be used alone with the pronouns:

~~I never, you never, he never, she never, it never, we never, they never~~
(Never did what?)

Never is not a verb. *Not* is not a verb either, as the pronoun test indicates:

~~I not, you not, he not, she not, it not, we not, you not, they not~~
(These combinations do not make sense because *not* is not a verb.)

Verb Forms That Cannot Be Main Verbs

TEACHING TIP

Remind students that an *-ing* form of the word can be a noun (gerund) and a singular subject. (Example: *Riding* is Scott's favorite activity.)

There are forms of verbs that cannot be main verbs by themselves either. **An *-ing* verb, by itself, cannot be the main verb,** as the pronoun test shows.

For the word *voting*: ~~I voting, you voting, he voting, she voting, we voting, they voting~~

If you see an *-ing* verb by itself, correct the sentence by adding a helping verb.

Scott ~~riding~~ his motorcycle. (*Riding*, by itself, cannot be a main verb.)
correction: Scott *was riding* his motorcycle.

Another verb form, called an infinitive, also cannot be a main verb. An **infinitive** is the form of the verb that has *to* placed in front of it.

INFO BOX: **Some Common Infinitives**

to care	to play	to stumble
to feel	to reject	to view
to need	to repeat	to vote

Try the pronoun test, and you'll see that infinitives cannot be main verbs:

For the infinitive *to vote*: ~~I to vote, you to vote, he to vote, she to vote, we to vote, they to vote~~

So if you see an infinitive being used as a verb, correct the sentence by adding a main verb.

We ~~to vote~~ in the election tomorrow. (There is no verb, just an infinitive.)
correction: We *are going* to vote in the election tomorrow.
(Now there is a verb.)

The infinitives and the *-ing* verbs just do not work as main verbs. You must put a verb with them to make a correct sentence.

Exercise 8 **Correcting Problems with *-ing* or Infinitive Verb Forms**

Most—but not all—of the sentences below are faulty; an *-ing* verb or an infinitive may be taking the place of a main verb. Rewrite the sentences that have errors.

1. Behind the heavy purple curtains, a little girl in a nightgown hiding from the noise of the thunderstorm.

   rewritten: *Behind the heavy purple curtains, a little girl in a nightgown*

   was hiding from the noise of the thunderstorm.

INSTRUCTOR'S NOTE

Answers will vary. Possible answers shown at left.

2. After dinner, Mr. Stein wants to sit in front of his big-screen television until bedtime.

   rewritten: *OK*

3. The weeds around the stepping stones creeping between the cracks and over the broken stones.

   rewritten: *The weeds around the stepping stones are creeping between*

   the cracks and over the broken stones.

4. After hours of negotiation, an escaped convict from Utah to surrender to police in New Mexico.

   rewritten: *After hours of negotiation, an escaped convict from Utah is*

   going to surrender to police in New Mexico.

5. At a high point in his career, the internationally known tennis star quitting for personal reasons.

   rewritten: *At a high point in his career, the internationally known tennis*

   star quit for personal reasons.

6. On weekends, my sisters to ride their bicycles to the park near our house.

   rewritten: *On weekends, my sisters like to ride their bicycles to the park*

   near our house.

7. After the midterm exam, a few of the students in my science class were complaining about the grading scale.

   rewritten: *OK*

8. Without a second look, I turned my back on my former friend and walked calmly to my car.

   rewritten: *OK*

9. Lindsay and Vince ridiculing the newcomers to the exclusive club.

   rewritten: *Lindsay and Vince were ridiculing the newcomers to the*

   exclusive club.

10. A famous military leader to present the awards at the banquet for the outstanding members of the graduating class.

    rewritten: *A famous military leader plans to present the awards at the*

    banquet for the outstanding members of the graduating class.

Exercise 9 Finding Subjects and Verbs: A Comprehensive Exercise

Underline the subjects and verbs in these sentences and put an *S* above each subject and a *V* above each verb.

1. There $\underset{V}{\underline{\text{were}}}$ a $\underset{S}{\underline{\text{pen}}}$, a $\underset{S}{\underline{\text{pencil}}}$, and a crumpled $\underset{S}{\underline{\text{piece}}}$ of paper in Sophie's book bag.

2. $\underset{S}{\underline{\text{Melanie}}}$ $\underset{V}{\underline{\text{could have been waiting}}}$ for you at the coffee shop.

3. At the front of the classroom $\underset{V}{\underline{\text{is}}}$ a large $\underset{S}{\underline{\text{box}}}$ with a stack of papers in it.

4. My $\underset{S}{\underline{\text{computer}}}$ $\underset{V}{\underline{\text{does}}}$ not $\underset{V}{\underline{\text{offer}}}$ quick access to the Internet.

5. $\underset{S}{\underline{\text{You}}}$ $\underset{V}{\underline{\text{have}}}$ suddenly $\underset{V}{\underline{\text{developed}}}$ an interest in our handsome neighbor on the third floor.

6. $\underset{V}{\underline{\text{Won't}}}$ $\underset{S}{\underline{\text{you}}}$ $\underset{V}{\underline{\text{think}}}$ about a career in mechanical engineering?

7. $\underset{S}{\underline{\text{Alec}}}$ $\underset{V}{\underline{\text{is dreaming}}}$ of making a return visit to Cancun.

8. At the top of my list of worries $\underset{V}{\underline{\text{are}}}$ the $\underset{S}{\underline{\text{fear}}}$ of missing an opportunity and the $\underset{S}{\underline{\text{fear}}}$ of failure.

9. $\underset{V}{\underline{\text{Don't}}}$ $\underset{S}{\underline{\text{you}}}$ ever $\underset{V}{\underline{\text{take}}}$ time for fun and relaxation?

10. In November, $\underset{S}{\underline{\text{they}}}$ $\underset{V}{\underline{\text{are closing}}}$ their shop and $\underset{V}{\underline{\text{starting}}}$ a new business in Iowa.

TEACHING TIP

For Item number 6, remind students that "won't" = "will not." The verb is technically "will."

ESL NOTE

Nonnative speakers often have difficulty recognizing verbs in contracted form. For more examples, see "Contractions and Verbs" on pp. 661–662 of the ESL Appendix.

Exercise 10 Finding Subjects and Verbs: Another Comprehensive Exercise

Underline the subjects and verbs in these sentences and put an *S* above each subject and a *V* above each verb.

1. Before my speech to the scholarship committee, $\underset{S}{\underline{\text{I}}}$ $\underset{V}{\underline{\text{thought}}}$ about my dream of higher education, $\underset{V}{\underline{\text{looked}}}$ into each person's eyes, and $\underset{V}{\underline{\text{hoped}}}$ for the best.

2. In any marriage, there $\underset{V}{\underline{\text{will be}}}$ a $\underset{S}{\underline{\text{period}}}$ of adjustment for both partners.

3. Here <u>is</u> the old <u>scrapbook</u> with the pictures of you in your Little

    League uniform.

    S   V   V
4. <u>Alicia</u> <u>would</u> never <u>ask</u> for help from her brother.

    V   S   V
5. <u>Haven't</u> <u>you</u> always <u>wanted</u> a house near the ocean?

6. With his giant television on the living room wall and his huge collec-
                  S   V
    tion of films, <u>Todd</u> rarely <u>goes</u> to a movie theater for entertainment.

    V   S   V
7. <u>Can't</u> the <u>two</u> of you ever <u>think</u> about anyone except yourselves?

                        S   V
8. In the bright light, the large <u>dog</u> <u>seemed</u> weird and dangerous.

                                  V   S   S
9. Inside the old and yellowed envelope <u>were</u> a <u>letter</u> and a <u>key</u>.

    S   V   V
10. My <u>uncle</u> <u>kissed</u> me on the cheek and <u>led</u> me to a small room

    behind the store.

| Exercise 11 | **Create Your Own Text** |

Collaborate

Complete this activity with two partners. Below is a list of rules you've just studied. Each member of the group should write one example of each rule. When your group has completed three examples for each rule, trade your completed exercise with another group, and check their examples while they check yours.

The first rule has been done for you.

Rule 1: The verb in a sentence can express some kind of action.
examples:

a. *Wanda sleeps late on the weekends.*

b. *On Monday I found a wallet in the street.*

c. *Melted snow covered the sidewalks and steps.*

Rule 2: The verb in a sentence can express some state of being or one of the five senses.
examples:

a. *Christina is a natural athlete.*

b. *My new shampoo smells clean and fresh.*

c. *Susie's favorite books were murder mysteries.*

INSTRUCTOR'S NOTE

Answers will vary. Possible answers shown at left.

Rule 3: The verb in a sentence can consist of more than one word.
examples:

a. *You may have found the way to the stadium.*

b. *The puppy jumped and barked at the sight of his owner.*

c. *A heavy rain could cause a leak in the roof.*

Rule 4: There can be more than one subject of a sentence.
examples:

a. *Marlon and Shakira went to the free concert.*

b. *My car and your van could use a good cleaning.*

c. *Coffee shops and doughnut stores have the best espresso.*

Rule 5: If you take out the prepositional phrases, it is easier to identify the subject of a sentence, since nothing in a prepositional phrase can be the subject of a sentence. (Write sentences with at least one prepositional phrase and put parentheses around the prepositional phrases.)
examples:

a. *Tanya saw a mouse (at the bottom) (of the cellar stairs).*

b. *(Without apologizing,) a man stepped (in front) (of me).*

c. *A woman (from Guatemala) lives (on the first floor).*

Rule 6: Not all sentences have the simple word order of subject first, then verb. (Give examples of more complicated word order.)
examples:

a. *Have you ever seen a tornado?*

b. *There are two good reasons for Diane's choice.*

c. *Under the carpet was a secret compartment.*

Rule 7: Words like *not, never, often, always,* and *ever* are not verbs. (Write sentences using those words, but write "V" above the verb or verbs.)
examples:

         V   V
a. *You will not take the credit for my idea.*

     V   V
b. *I have never liked fancy desserts.*

           V
c. *Gary often calls his parents in China.*

Rule 8: An *-ing* verb form by itself or an infinitive (*to* preceding the verb) cannot be a main verb. (Write sentences with *-ing* verb forms or infinitives, but underline the main verb.)
examples:

      V
a. *Emilio needs to concentrate on his studies.*

          V
b. *The refrigerator was making a strange noise.*

      V
c. *Danielle is being too stubborn about this problem.*

Connect

Exercise 12   Recognizing Subjects and Verbs in a Paragraph

Underline the subjects and verbs in this paragraph and put an *S* above each subject and a *V* above each verb.

   S   V

    Dontrel should have been a comedian. With his long legs, gangly arms, and

          S V   S

wide eyes, he has the appearance of a clown. In addition, his attitude toward life's

$$\overset{V}{}$$

bad days <u>is</u> unusual and creative. In his own bad times, <u>he</u> <u>looks</u> for the funny side
and <u>brings</u> the humor into other people's lives, too. He <u>can</u> <u>tell</u> the story of a frustrating or terrible incident and <u>transform</u> the moment into a comedy. After an hour
with Dontrel, <u>I</u> <u>gain</u> an insight into my own worries. <u>I</u> <u>have</u> never <u>met</u> anyone with
his powerful attitude. Here <u>is</u> a <u>man</u> with a gift.

Exercise 13 **Recognizing Subjects and Verbs in a Paragraph**

Connect

Underline the subjects and verbs in this paragraph and put an *S* above each
subject and a *V* above each verb.

   A <u>day</u> without some kind of treat <u>is</u> a disappointing day. <u>Everyone</u> <u>deserves</u> a
reward for meeting the challenges of a long day at work, home, or school. A <u>treat</u>
<u>can</u> be anything from a walk with a friend to a piece of chocolate. In fact, <u>treats</u>
<u>are</u> often <u>concealed</u> inside particularly bad days. There <u>could be</u> a quick
<u>compliment</u> from the boss beneath the pile of his or her complaints. At the end of
the day, the <u>memory</u> of that compliment <u>can become</u> a reward for surviving the
hectic work hours. <u>Everyone</u> <u>needs</u> to give himself or herself a treat. In a perfect
world, <u>all</u> of us <u>would be thinking</u> of others, too, with words of praise or thanks, a
phone call, a flower, or a cookie. Small <u>rewards</u> <u>can make</u> a big difference.

Chapter Test: The Simple Sentence

Underline the subjects and verbs in these sentences and put an *S* above
each subject and a *V* above each verb.

1. <u>Lack</u> of sleep <u>should</u> not <u>keep</u> you from an important meeting
   with a potential employer.
2. My best <u>friend</u> during my high school days <u>wants</u> to meet me for
   dinner and some talk about old times.
3. Among the cats at the animal shelter <u>was</u> a beautiful calico <u>kitten</u>.
4. The <u>man</u> in the truck behind us <u>must have made</u> a stop at the
   service plaza in Canoe Creek.
5. My <u>grandmother</u> always <u>pulled</u> me into her arms and <u>kissed</u> me
   on the cheek.

6. A cold, gray $\underset{S}{\underline{\text{Saturday}}}$ and a $\underset{S}{\underline{\text{shortage}}}$ of spending money $\underset{V}{\underline{\text{turned}}}$

the day into a dismal one for Billy.

7. $\underset{V}{\underline{\text{Weren't}}}$ $\underset{S}{\underline{\text{you}}}$ nearly $\underset{V}{\underline{\text{killed}}}$ in an avalanche on the ski slopes?

8. Behind the apartment buildings there $\underset{V}{\underline{\text{are}}}$ $\underset{S}{\underline{\text{dumpsters}}}$ and rusted

electrical $\underset{S}{\underline{\text{boxes}}}$.

9. After all our years together, my $\underset{S}{\underline{\text{girlfriend}}}$ $\underset{V}{\underline{\text{left}}}$ me without any

warning.

10. The $\underset{S}{\underline{\text{thought}}}$ of taking another science class $\underset{V}{\underline{\text{is making}}}$ me

nervous.

CHAPTER 16

Quick Question

Which sentence(s) is/are correct?

(A.) Emily took a photograph, and we all smiled.

B. Emily took a photograph and we all smiled.

(After you study this chapter, you will be confident of your answer.)

Beyond the Simple Sentence: Coordination

A group of words containing a subject and verb is called a **clause**. When that group makes sense by itself, it is called a sentence or an independent clause.

The kind of sentence that is one independent clause is called a **simple sentence**. If you rely too heavily on a sentence pattern of simple sentences, you risk writing paragraphs like this:

> I am a college student. I am also a salesperson in a mall. I am always busy. School is time-consuming. Studying is time-consuming. Working makes me tired. Balancing these activities is hard. I work too many hours. Work is important. It pays for school.

Here is a better version:

> I am a college student and a salesperson at a mall, so I am always busy. School and study are time-consuming, and working makes me tired. Balancing these activities is hard. I work too many hours, but that work is important. It pays for school.

OPTIONS FOR COMBINING SIMPLE SENTENCES

Good writing involves sentence variety; it means mixing a simple sentence with a more complicated one, a short sentence with a long one. Sentence variety is easier to achieve if you can combine related, short sentences into one.

Some students avoid such combining because they are not sure how to do it. They do not know how to punctuate the new combinations. It is true that punctuation involves memorizing a few rules, but once you know them, you will be able to use them automatically and write with more confidence. Here are three options for combining simple sentences and the punctuation rules to follow in each case.

OPTION 1: USING A COMMA WITH A COORDINATING CONJUNCTION

You can combine two simple sentences with a comma and a coordinating conjunction. The coordinating conjunctions are *for, and, nor, but, or, yet,* and *so.*

To coordinate means to join equals. When you join two simple sentences with a comma and a coordinating conjunction (CC), each half of the combination remains an independent clause, with its own subject (S) and verb (V).

Here are two simple sentences:

<pre>
 S   V   S   V
He cooked the dinner.   She worked late.
</pre>

Here are the two simple sentences combined with a comma and with the word *for*, a coordinating conjunction (CC):

<pre>
 S   V   , CC S   V
He cooked the dinner, for she worked late.
</pre>

The combined sentences keep the form they had as separate sentences; that is, they are still both independent clauses, with a subject and verb and with the ability to stand alone.

The word that joins them is the **coordinating conjunction**. It is used to join equals. Look at some more examples. These examples use a variety of coordinating conjunctions to join two simple sentences.

sentences combined with *and*:

<pre>
     S   V   , CC S   V
Jennifer likes Italian food, and Mark prefers Korean dishes.
</pre>

sentences combined with *nor*:

<pre>
 S V   V   , CC V S V
I didn't like the book, nor did I like the movie made from the
    book.
</pre>
(Notice what happens to the word order when you use "nor.")

sentences combined with *but*:

<pre>
 S   V   , CC S   V
I rushed to the bank, but I was too late.
</pre>

<pre>
  S   V   , CC S   V
She can write a letter to Jim, or she can call him.
</pre>

sentences combined with *yet*:

    S   V   , CC S   V

Leo tried to please his sister, *yet she* never *seemed* appreciative of his
    efforts.

sentences combined with *so*:

    S V   , CC S V

I was the first in line for the concert tickets, *so I got* the best seats in
    the stadium.

One easy way to remember the coordinating conjunctions is to call them, as
a group, **fanboys** (**f**or, **a**nd, **n**or, **b**ut, **o**r, **y**et, **s**o).

Where Does the Comma Go?

Notice that the comma comes before the coordinating conjunction (*for,
and, nor, but, or, yet, so*). It comes before the new idea, the second independent clause. It goes where the first independent clause ends. Try this
punctuation check. After you've placed the comma, look at the combined
sentences. For example:

    She joined the army, and she traveled overseas.

Then split it into two sentences at the comma:

    She joined the army. And she traveled overseas. (The split makes
        sense.)

If you put the comma in the wrong place, after the coordinating conjunction, your split sentences would be:

    She joined the army and. She traveled overseas. (The split doesn't
        make sense.)

This test helps you see whether the comma has been placed correctly—
where the first independent clause ends. (Notice that you can begin a sentence with *and.* You can also begin a sentence with *but, or, nor, for, yet,* or
so—as long as you're writing a complete sentence.)

    Caution: Do *not* put a comma every time you use the words *and, but,
or, nor, for, yet,* or *so*; put it only when the coordinating conjunction joins
independent clauses. Do not put the comma when the coordinating conjunction joins two words:

    blue and gold   tired but happy   hot or cold

Do not put the comma when the coordinating conjunction joins phrases:

    on the chair or under the table
    in the water and by the shore
    with a smile but without an apology

**The comma is used when the coordinating conjunction joins two inde-
pendent clauses.** Another way to say the same rule is to say, the comma is
used when the coordinating conjunction joins two simple sentences.

Placing the Comma by Using Subject-Verb (S-V) Patterns

An independent clause, or simple sentence, follows one of these basic
patterns:

    S V

He ran.

or

<pre>
  S   S V
He and I ran.
</pre>

or

<pre>
  S   V   V
He ran and swam.
</pre>

or

<pre>
  S   S V   V
He and I ran and swam.
</pre>

Study all four patterns for the simple sentence, and you will notice that you can draw a line separating the subjects on one side and the verbs on the other:

<pre>
  S | V
  SS | V
  S | VV
  SS | VV
</pre>

So whether the sentence has one subject (or more than one) and one verb (or more than one) in the simple sentence, the pattern is subject(s) followed by verb(s)—one simple sentence.

When you combine two simple sentences, the pattern changes:

two simple sentences:

<pre>
  S   V   S V
He swam. I ran.
</pre>

two simple sentences combined:

<pre>
  S   V   S V
He swam, but I ran.
</pre>

In the new pattern, *SVSV*, you cannot draw a line separating all the subjects on one side, and all the verbs on the other. This new pattern, with two simple sentences (or independent clauses) joined into one, is called a **compound sentence**.

Recognizing the *SVSV* pattern will help you place the comma for compound sentences.

Here is another way to remember this rule. If you have this pattern:

<pre>
  SV | SV
</pre>

use a comma in front of the coordinating conjunction. Do not use a comma in front of the coordinating conjunction with these patterns:

<pre>
  S | V
  SS | V
  S | VV
  SS | VV
</pre>

For example, use a comma for this pattern:

<pre>
  S   V   ,   S V
Jane followed directions, but I rushed ahead.
</pre>

Do not use a comma for this pattern:

<pre>
  S   V   V
Carol cleans her kitchen every week but never wipes the top of the
      refrigerator.
</pre>

You have just studied one way to combine simple sentences. If you are going to take advantage of this method, you have to memorize the coordinating conjunctions—*for, and, nor, but, or, yet,* and *so*—so that your use of them, with the correct punctuation, will become automatic.

Exercise 1   **Recognizing Compound Sentences and Adding Commas**

Add commas only where they are needed in the following sentences. Do not add any words.

1. Cruiser Auto Parts offers a wide range of accessories for Toyota Tundras, so Edward spends half his paycheck on gadgets for his truck.

2. Claudia is looking for a two-bedroom apartment in a good neighborhood or a small house with a porch.

3. My mother won't tell me about her trip to the emergency room, nor will she explain her her decision to take a class in self-defense.

4. Antonio seems worried about something but never confides in me or his sister.

5. My best friend can eat every item in the refrigerator, yet he has maintained the same healthy weight for years.

6. The kitchen table is covered in scratches and dents, for the family cuts and carves food on it every day.

7. Michelle rides her bicycle to class every day, so she saves money on gas for her car.

8. Between the rumpled sheets on my bed I found my lost gold earring, and I immediately put the earring in a safe place.

9. The cat under the porch meowed at me, but it refused to come out from its hideout.

10. A heavy rain crushed the spring flowers into a multicolored mess and turned the grass into streaks of green mud.

Exercise 2   **Combining Sentences Using Coordinating Conjunctions.**

Combine each pair of sentences using a coordinating conjunction and the appropriate punctuation.

INSTRUCTOR'S NOTE

Answers will vary. Possible answers shown at left.

1. Jordan was a wonderful father to his three boys.
   He was not a great husband.

   combined: *Jordan was a wonderful father to his three boys, but he was not a great husband.*

2. Kevin made a reservation at the most popular restaurant in town.
   He wanted to please his new girlfriend.

   combined: *Kevin made a reservation at the most popular restaurant in town, for he wanted to please his new girlfriend.*

3. Many of my friends are sick of the congestion of city life.
   They are looking for jobs in the country.

   combined: *Many of my friends are sick of the congestion of city*

   life, so they are looking for jobs in the country.

4. He can buy a new car with great style and huge monthly payments.
   He can settle for a used car with less style and much smaller payments.

   combined: *He can buy a new car with great style and huge monthly*

   payments, or he can settle for a used car with less style and much

   smaller payments.

5. Alicia has suffered through several bad relationships.
   Alicia keeps choosing the same, abusive kind of partner.

   combined: *Alicia has suffered through several bad relationships, yet*

   she keeps choosing the same, abusive kind of partner.

6. Ramon Ramirez played football in high school.
   Hector Ramirez went to college on a baseball scholarship.

   combined: *Ramon Ramirez played football in high school, and Hector*

   Ramirez went to college on a baseball scholarship.

7. My grandfather always wanted to visit his family in Barbados.
   He never saved enough money for the trip.

   combined: *My grandfather always wanted to visit his family in*

   Barbados, but he never saved enough money for the trip.

8. I caught a bad cold at the hockey game last weekend.
   I couldn't go to work yesterday.

   combined: *I caught a bad cold at the hockey game last weekend, so I*

   couldn't go to work yesterday.

9. My current apartment does not have laundry facilities in the building.
   My current apartment does not have an outlet for cable television.

   combined: *My current apartment doesn't have laundry facilities in the*

   building, nor does it have an outlet for cable television.

10. I might send my child to a day-care center.
    I might drop him off at my mother's house.

    combined: *I might send my child to a day-care center, or I might drop*

    him off at my mother's house.

OPTION 2: USING A SEMICOLON BETWEEN TWO SIMPLE SENTENCES

Sometimes you may want to combine two simple sentences (independent clauses) without using a coordinating conjunction. If you want to join two simple sentences that are related in their ideas and you do not use a coordinating conjunction, you can combine them with a semicolon.

two simple sentences:

> S V   S V
> *I cooked* the turkey. *She made* the stuffing.

two simple sentences combined with a semicolon:

> S V   ; S V
> *I cooked* the turkey; *she made* the stuffing.

Here's another example of this option in use:

> S   V V   ; S V
> *Rain can be* dangerous; *it makes* the roads slippery.

Notice that when you join two simple sentences with a semicolon, the second sentence begins with a lowercase letter, not a capital letter.

You need to memorize the seven coordinating conjunctions so that you can make a decision about punctuating your combined sentences. Remember these rules:

- If a coordinating conjunction joins the combined sentences, put a comma in front of the coordinating conjunction.

  > S V   ,   S V
  > *Tom had* a barbecue in his back yard, and the *food was* delicious.

- If there is no coordinating conjunction, put a semicolon in front of the second independent clause.

  > S V   ;   S V
  > *Tom had* a barbecue in his back yard; the *food was* delicious.

OPTION 3: USING A SEMICOLON AND A CONJUNCTIVE ADVERB

Sometimes you may want to join two simple sentences (independent clauses) with a connecting word called a **conjunctive adverb**.

Here is a list of some conjunctive adverbs:

INFO BOX: Some Common Conjunctive Adverbs

also	furthermore	likewise	otherwise
anyway	however	meanwhile	similarly
as a result	in addition	moreover	still
besides	in fact	nevertheless	then
certainly	incidentally	next	therefore
consequently	indeed	now	thus
finally	instead	on the other hand	undoubtedly

You can use a conjunctive adverb (CA) to join simple sentences, but when you do, you still need a semicolon in front of the adverb.

two simple sentences:

     S   V   S V

My *parents checked* my homework every night. *I did* well in math.

two simple sentences joined by a conjunctive adverb and a semicolon:

     S   V   ; CA S V

My *parents checked* my homework every night; *thus I did* well in math.

     S V   ; CA   S V

She gave me good advice; *moreover, she helped* me follow it.

Punctuating after a Conjunctive Adverb

Notice the comma after the conjunctive adverb in the preceding sentence. Here is the generally accepted rule:

> **Put a comma after the conjunctive adverb if the conjunctive adverb is more than one syllable long.**

For example, if the conjunctive adverb is a word like *consequently, furthermore*, or *moreover*, you use a comma. If the conjunctive adverb is one syllable, you do not have to put a comma after the conjunctive adverb. One-syllable conjunctive adverbs are words like *then* or *thus*.

> I saw her cruelty to her staff; *then* I lost respect for her.
> We worked on the project all weekend; *consequently*, we finished a week ahead of the deadline.

Exercise 3 **Combining Simple Sentences with Semicolons and Conjunctive Adverbs**

Some of the following sentences need a semicolon; others need a semicolon and a comma. Do not add, change, or delete any words; just add the correct punctuation.

1. Desmond likes insects in fact he has a pet spider at home.

2. At the end of dinner came an unpleasant surprise it was the bill for our fancy meal.

3. My first year in college is almost over soon I'll be a sophomore with a fairly respectable academic record.

4. Professor Mackenzie talks too fast I can't keep up with his explanations of the math problems.

5. Shane never paid me back for the loan of twenty dollars instead he took me to the movies yesterday.

6. You always leave the kitchen in a mess furthermore you forget to take out the garbage.

7. My hectic work schedule prevents me from having any fun on the other hand the extra hours at my job are paying my bills.

8. I saw a flash of lightning outside my bedroom window last night next I lost electrical power for hours.

9. My mother dislikes her older brother nevertheless she tolerates his constant visits to her home.

10. My room is beginning to look like a storage unit in a row of
    sleazy warehouses'I must get rid of the clutter.

INSTRUCTOR'S NOTE

Answers will vary. Possible
answers shown.

Exercise 4   **Combining Simple Sentences with Semicolons
and Conjunctive Adverbs**

Below are pairs of simple sentences. Combine each pair into one sentence.
You have two options: (1) use a semicolon, or (2) use a semicolon and a
conjunctive adverb (with a comma if it is needed). Pick the option that
makes the most sense for each sentence.

1. Green fuzz covered the leftover chicken and rice.
   The casserole had been in the refrigerator for two weeks.

   combined: *Green fuzz covered the leftover chicken and rice; the*

   casserole had been in the refrigerator for two weeks.

2. The band on the stage started throwing trinkets to the audience.
   A huge crowd pushed toward the first row of seats.

   combined: *The band on the stage started throwing trinkets to the*

   audience; as a result, a huge crowd pushed toward the first row of seats.

3. Amanda bolted the apartment door.
   Connor frantically called an emergency number.

   combined: *Amanda bolted the apartment door; meanwhile, Connor*

   frantically called an emergency number.

4. I wasted three hours on patching and taping a broken lawn chair.
   I bought a new chair at a discount store.

   combined: *I wasted three hours on patching and taping a broken lawn*

   chair; finally, I bought a new chair at a discount store.

5. Tyler refused to speak to me yesterday at school.
   He even avoided eye contact.

   combined: *Tyler refused to speak to me yesterday at school; he even*

   avoided eye contact.

6. The first snow of the year began to fall.
   The white coating transformed the hills and trees into a strange
   scene.

   combined: *The first snow of the year began to fall; soon the white*

   coating transformed the hills and trees into a strange scene.

7. Molly has to do well on her next two Introduction to Sociology
   tests.
   She could fail the course.

   combined: *Molly has to do well on her next two Introduction to*

   Sociology tests; otherwise, she could fail the course.

8. Skip is turning into a fine dog.
   He has learned all the essential skills of obeying commands and
   walking on a leash.

combined: *Skip is turning into a fine dog; he has learned all the essential*
skills of obeying commands and walking on a leash.

9. You don't have to get me a fancy gift for my birthday.
   You can take me to the latest Quentin Tarantino movie.

combined: *You don't have to get me a fancy gift for my birthday; instead,*
you can take me to the latest Quentin Tarantino movie.

10. I passed my driving test yesterday.
    I have to look for a low-priced car.

combined: *I passed my driving test yesterday; now I have to look for a*
low-priced car.

Exercise 5 **Combining Simple Sentences Three Ways**

Add a comma, a semicolon, or a semicolon and a comma to the following
sentences. Do not add, change, or delete any words; just add the correct
punctuation.

1. No one moved; the huge snake remained coiled in the corner.

2. You should apologize to Sean; moreover, you should apologize sincerely and soon.

3. We will get to the electronics store early; thus we will be the first
   ones at the grand opening sale.

4. Kelly buys a lottery ticket every week, yet she has never won a penny.

5. Andrew regretted his angry words to his wife; similarly, his wife
   felt guilty about the cruelty of her responses.

6. I ran into your old girlfriend at the mall yesterday; incidentally,
   she is going to be in your biology class next semester.

7. My five-year-old son spent three hours at the beach; now he is a
   tired but happy child with sand in his hair, toes, and ears.

8. My roommate hasn't paid his share of the rent in two months, nor
   has he paid any part of the other household expenses.

9. Stephen doesn't like coffee; in fact, he's never been inside a
   Starbucks coffee shop.

10. Last night my dog barked at the front door for about twenty
    minutes, but I couldn't see anyone in the yard.

Collaborate

Exercise 6 **Using Three Options to Combine Simple Sentences**

Below are pairs of simple sentences. Working with a partner or partners,
combine each pair into one sentence in two different ways. Remember, you
have three options: (1) use a comma and a coordinating conjunction, (2) use
a semicolon, or (3) use a semicolon and a conjunctive adverb (with a
comma if it is needed). Pick the options that make the most sense for these
sentences. The first one has been done for you.

1. Crystal ran out of money for her electric bill.
   I lent her enough to pay it.
   combinations:

   a. *Crystal ran out of money for her electric bill, so I lent her enough to pay it.*

   b. *Crystal ran out of money for her electric bill; therefore, I lent her enough to pay it.*

2. All of my shoes are worn out.
   My clothes are falling apart.
   combinations:

   a. *All of my shoes are worn out, and my clothes are falling apart.*

   b. *All of my shoes are worn out; my clothes are falling apart.*

INSTRUCTOR'S NOTE

Answers will vary. Possible answers shown.

3. Luis can be an irritating person.
   He deserves a little sympathy at this sad time.
   combinations:

   a. *Luis can be an irritating person; still he deserves a little sympathy at this sad time.*

   b. *Luis can be an irritating person, yet he deserves a little sympathy at this sad time.*

4. Uncle Scott could have gotten stuck in traffic.
   Uncle Scott could have taken a wrong turn off the highway.
   combinations:

   a. *Uncle Scott could have gotten stuck in traffic, or he could have taken a wrong turn off the highway.*

   b. *Uncle Scott could have gotten stuck in traffic; on the other hand, he could have taken a wrong turn off the highway.*

5. My father never paid me a compliment.
   My father never spent much time with me.
   combinations:

   a. *My father never paid me a compliment, nor did he spend much time with me.*

   b. *My father never paid me a compliment; moreover, he never spent much time with me.*

6. We expected a delicious meal at the stylish and expensive restaurant.
   We got food poisoning.
   combinations:

a. *We expected a delicious meal at the stylish and expensive*

restaurant; instead, we got food poisoning.

b. *We expected a delicious meal at the stylish and expensive*

restaurant, but we got food poisoning.

7. Allison will take me to school tomorrow.
She owes me a favor.

combinations:

a. *Allison will take me to school tomorrow; she owes me a favor.*

b. *Allison will take me to school tomorrow, for she owes me a favor.*

8. Nelson Pinder was offered a great job in Boston.
He decided to move there.

combinations:

a. *Nelson Pinder was offered a great job in Boston; as a result, he*

decided to move there.

b. *Nelson Pinder was offered a great job in Boston, so he decided to*

move there.

9. Summer never seems to last long enough.
Winter always seems to last forever.

combinations:

a. *Summer never seems to last long enough; winter always seems to*

last forever.

b. *Summer never seems to last long enough; however, winter always*

seems to last forever.

10. Someone stole my wallet.
I am worried about identity theft.

combinations:

a. *Someone stole my wallet, so I am worried about identity theft.*

b. *Someone stole my wallet; consequently, I am worried about identity*

theft.

Connect

Exercise 7 **Editing a Paragraph for Errors in Coordination**

Edit the following paragraph for errors in coordination. You do not need to
add or change words. Just add, delete, or change punctuation. There are six
errors in the paragraph.

My six-year-old son wants a cell phone, but I cannot make up my mind about

giving him one. A first grader with a cell phone is a ridiculous concept. Six-year-olds are expected to play with toys _; however, some of my son's friends already play with their own cell phones. I do not want my child to grow up too fast _, and the image of him with a box of wires against his ear is frightening. The other side of this question has its good points. My son already uses my cell phone; in fact _, he can teach me all the mysterious options on it. Safety is another concern for, he *no comma needed* should be able to reach me in any emergency. The issue of the cell phone is a generational conflict. My little boy is racing into the adult world; yet _, I want to slow him down.

Exercise 8   **Editing a Paragraph for Errors in Coordination**

Connect

Edit the following paragraph for errors in coordination. You do not need to add or change words. Just add, delete, or change punctuation. There are eight errors in the paragraph.

A cold turns going to class into a miserable experience. The physical aches of a cold make me want to stay in bed _; also, I dread the embarrassment of dragging myself to class. A cold exhausts me; consequently _, I struggle to stay awake during the teacher's lecture. Sometimes I lose the struggle. My head begins to nod, _; my teacher glares at me. The other awful part of having a cold is the sneezing. No one wants to sit near a sneezer _, so I isolate myself in the back of the room. I pray for a sneeze-free hour _; unfortunately _, a sneeze sneaks up on me. Soon I am the victim of a string of loud sneezes _, and everyone is staring at me in pity and horror. I shrink *no comma* into my seat, and cover my face with tissues.

Chapter Test: Beyond the Simple Sentence—Coordination

Add a comma, a semicolon, or a semicolon and a comma to the following sentences. Do not add, change, or delete any words; just add the correct punctuation.

1. I have a big test in Accounting I tomorrow _, so I will be studying this afternoon.

2. Drivers had little visibility in the smoky haze _; some cars slowed down to a crawl.

3. Amanda Chen enjoys the friendliness of her neighbors in the small town _; still she misses the energy of the city.

4. Pine Grove was once a farming community _; now it is known for its huge automobile plant.

5. You do not have time for a shower, nor do you have time to change your clothes.

6. Sugary drinks are unhealthy; instead, I drink water.

7. My grandfather is making a cradle for his newest grandchild; next he will make a child-sized chair.

8. Ryan brags about his mechanical skills, yet he rarely opens the hood of his own car.

9. The deadline for class registration drew near; meanwhile, Brian struggled with a pile of financial aid forms.

10. My boyfriend has little trouble finding a job, for he has seven years of experience as a chef at well-known restaurants.

INSTRUCTOR'S NOTE

Additional options for combining sentences can be found in Chapter 18 (Options 4 and 5), which covers subordination.

Avoiding Run-On Sentences and Comma Splices

RUN-ON SENTENCES

Run-on sentences are independent clauses that have not been joined correctly. This error is also called a *fused sentence*.

> **run-on sentence error:**
> Carol cleans her kitchen every week she shines every pot and pan.
> **run-on sentence error corrected:**
> Carol cleans her kitchen every week; she shines every pot and pan.
>
> **run-on sentence error:**
> I studied for the test all weekend I am well prepared for it.
> **run-on sentence error corrected:**
> I studied for the test all weekend, so I am well prepared for it.
>
> **run-on sentence error:**
> People crowded into the stadium they scrambled for seats.
> **run-on sentence error corrected:**
> People crowded in the stadium. They scrambled for seats.

ESL NOTE

Run-ons are common mistakes for most writing students. Nonnative speakers commonly write run-on sentences as they attempt to combine simple sentences.

STEPS FOR CORRECTING RUN-ON SENTENCES

When you edit your writing, you can correct run-on sentences by following these steps:

Step 1: Check for two independent clauses.

Step 2: Check that the clauses are separated by either a coordinating conjunction and a comma or by a semicolon.

Follow the steps in checking this sentence:

The meeting was a waste of time the club members argued about silly issues.

Step 1: Check for two independent clauses. You can do this by checking for the subject-verb, subject-verb pattern that indicates two independent clauses:

      S   V   S   V

The *meeting was* a waste of time the club *members argued* about silly issues.

The pattern indicates that you have two independent clauses.

Step 2: Check that the clauses are separated either by a coordinating conjunction (*for, and, nor, but, or, yet, so*) and a comma or by a semicolon.

There is no punctuation between the independent clauses, so you have a run-on sentence. You can correct it three ways:

run-on sentence corrected with a coordinating conjunction and a comma:
The meeting was a waste of time, *for* the club members argued about silly issues.

run-on sentence corrected with a semicolon:
The meeting was a waste of time; the club members argued about silly issues.

run-on sentence corrected with a period and a capital letter:
The meeting was a waste of time. The club members argued about silly issues.

Follow the steps once more as you check this sentence:

I had the flu I missed class last week.

Step 1: Check for two independent clauses. Do this by checking for the subject-verb, subject-verb pattern:

S V   S V

I had the flu *I missed* class last week.

Step 2: Check that the clauses are separated either by a coordinating conjunction (*for, and, nor, but, or, yet, so*) and a comma or by a semicolon.

There is no punctuation between the independent clauses, so you have a run-on sentence. You can correct the run-on sentence three ways:

run-on sentence corrected with a period and a capital letter:
I had the flu. I missed class last week.

run-on sentence corrected with a coordinating conjunction and a comma:
I had the flu, *so* I missed class last week.

run-on sentence corrected with a semicolon:
I had the flu; I missed class last week.

Using the steps to check for run-on sentences can also help you avoid unnecessary punctuation. Consider this sentence:

> The manager gave me my schedule for next week and told me about a special sales promotion.

Step 1: Check for two independent clauses. Do this by checking the subject-verb, subject-verb pattern.

>   s   v   v
> The *manager gave* me my schedule for next week and *told* me about a special sales promotion.

The pattern is SVV, not SVSV. The sentence is not a run-on sentence. It does not need any additional punctuation.

Following the steps in correcting run-on sentences can help you avoid a major grammar error.

TEACHING TIP:

This may be a good time to advise your students that computer grammar/style checkers may often designate a sentence a *run-on* solely because of its length. Remind the class that such programs may be beneficial at times, but they cannot guarantee the accuracy of any diagnosis.

Exercise 1   Correcting Run-on (Fused) Sentences

Some of the sentences below are correctly punctuated. Some are run-on (fused) sentences; that is, they are two simple sentences run together without any punctuation. If the sentence is correctly punctuated, write *OK* in the space provided. If it is a run-on sentence, put an *X* in the space provided and correct the sentence above the lines.

INSTRUCTOR'S NOTE

Answers will vary. Possible answers shown at left.

1. ___*X*___ My sister should have been a nurse *;* she is always handing out vitamins and home remedies.

2. ___*OK*___ On hot days I head for the movies and enjoy the comfort of the air-conditioning.

3. ___*OK*___ Mr. Sullivan works in his yard every weekend yet never seems satisfied with his lawn.

4. ___*X*___ The puppy eats anything on the floor *, and* it pulls the toilet paper off the bathroom roller.

5. ___*OK*___ My favorite television show ends each episode with a mystery and keeps viewers in suspense for a week.

6. ___*X*___ The apples in our high school cafeteria tasted mushy *, so* I avoided eating apples for years.

7. ___*OK*___ Professional basketball players become international celebrities but lose any hope of a private life.

8. ___*X*___ Beneath the avalanche were two skiers *. The* the rescuers reached them after hours of searching.

9. ___*X*___ I climbed three flights of stairs *;* then I paused to catch my breath.

10. ___*X*___ Something has been nagging me all day *;* its my promise to my girlfriend.

COMMA SPLICES

A comma splice is an error that occurs when you punctuate with a comma but should use a semicolon instead. If you are joining two independent clauses without a coordinating conjunction (*for, an, nor, but, or, yet, so*) you must use a semicolon. A comma is not enough.

> **comma splice error:**
> The crowd pushed forward, people began to panic.
>
> **comma splice error corrected:**
> The crowd pushed forward; people began to panic.
>
> **comma splice error:**
> I forgot my glasses, thus I couldn't read the small print in the contract.
>
> **comma splice error corrected:**
> I forgot my glasses; thus I couldn't read the small print in the contract.

CORRECTING COMMA SPLICES

When you edit your writing, you can correct comma splices by following these steps:

> **Step 1:** Check for two independent clauses.
>
> **Step 2:** Check that the clauses are separated by a coordinating conjunction (*for, and, nor, but, or, yet, so*). If they are, then a comma in front of the coordinating conjunction is sufficient. If they are not separated by a coordinating conjunction, you have a comma splice. Correct it by changing the comma to semicolon.

Follow the steps to check for a comma splice in this sentence:

> I dropped the glass, it shattered on the tile floor.
>
> **Step 1:** Check for two independent clauses. You can do this by checking for the subject-verb, subject-verb pattern that indicates two independent clauses.

>   **s**   **v**   **s**   **v**
> *I dropped* the glass, *it shattered* on the tile floor.

The pattern indicates that you have two independent clauses.

> **Step 2:** Check that the clauses are separated by a coordinating conjunction.

There is no coordinating conjunction. To correct the comma splice error, you must use a semicolon instead of a comma.

> **comma splice error corrected:** I dropped the glass; it shattered on the tile floor.

Be careful not to mistake a short word like *then* or *thus* for a coordinating conjunction. Only the seven coordinating conjunctions (*for, and, nor, but, or, yet, so*) with a comma in front of them can join independent clauses.

> **comma splice error:** Susie watched television, then she went to bed.
> **comma splice error corrected:** Susie watched television; then she went to bed.

Then is not a coordinating conjunction; it is a conjunctive adverb. When it joins two independent clauses, it needs a semicolon in front of it.

Also remember that conjunctive adverbs that are two or more syllables long (like *consequently, however, therefore*) need a comma after them as well as a semicolon in front of them when they join independent clauses:

> Harry has been researching plane fares to New York; consequently, he knows how to spot a cheap flight.

(For a list of some common conjunctive adverbs, see Chapter 16.)

Sometimes writers see commas before and after a conjunctive adverb and think the commas are sufficient. Check this sentence for a comma splice by following the steps:

> Jonathan loves his job, however, it pays very little.

Step 1: Check for two independent clauses by checking for the subject-verb, subject-verb pattern.

> S   V   S V
> *Jonathan loves* his job, however, *it pays* very little.

The pattern indicates that you have two independent clauses.

Step 2: Check for a coordinating conjunction.

There is no coordinating conjunction. *However* is a conjunctive adverb, not a coordinating conjunction. Because there is no coordinating conjunction, you need a semicolon between the two independent clauses.

> **comma splice error corrected:**
> Jonathan loves his job; however, it pays very little.

Exercise 2   Correcting Comma Splices

Some of the sentences below are correctly punctuated. Some contain comma splices. If the sentence is correctly punctuated, write *OK* in the space provided. If it contains a comma splice, put an *X* in the space provided and correct the sentence above the lines. To correct a sentence, add the necessary punctuation. Do not add any words.

1. __X__ Jenna pulled the heavy quilt off the bed, then she opened every window in the room.

2. __X__ The leather jacket is soft and stylish, however, it is extremely expensive.

3. __OK__ I take an hour-long bus ride to work every day, yet I appreciate the time to wake up slowly.

4. __X__ Aaron has to buy his geography textbook today, otherwise, he can't turn in the first class assignment.

5. __X__ The actor has a reputation for throwing temper tantrums on movie sets, nevertheless, he is good at his craft.

6. __OK__ Paula moved to a town near Miami Beach, but she never went near the ocean.

7. __X__ My wife and I grew up on the same street, thus we share many memories.

8. __X__ It rained here on Saturday morning; then the sun peeked through the clouds minutes before the graduation procession.

9. __X__ My mother needs a new coat; she has been wearing the same one for ten years.

10. __X__ I got rid of the milk; it tasted sour.

Exercise 3 **Completing Sentences**

Collaborate

INSTRUCTOR'S NOTE

Answers will vary. Possible answers shown.

With a partner or group, write the first part of each of the following incomplete sentences. Make your addition an independent clause. Be sure to punctuate your completed sentences correctly. The first one is done for you.

1. *The driver ignored the railroad warning signals,* and his car was hit by the train.

2. *I gambled all night;* then I ran out of money.

3. *You have been lying to me for months;* incidentally, you also told several lies about me to my friends.

4. *Colin is in trouble;* he was arrested for driving under the influence of alcohol.

5. *I have to finish college;* otherwise, I won't be able to get a good job.

6. *Someone called me at 3:00 a.m.,* but the caller hung up.

7. *The city needs to put a traffic light at that intersection,* or someone will get hurt.

8. *My friend's house was burglarized last month;* now my friend has to testify in court.

9. *A terrible storm hit the airport last night,* and lightning struck the control tower.

10. *You don't have to pay any money until the trial offer expires;* besides, you can always change your mind.

Connect

Exercise 4 **Editing a Paragraph for Run-on Sentences and Comma Splices**

Edit the following paragraph for run-on sentences and comma splices. There are nine errors.

Late arrivals are turning my life into a nightmare. Yesterday my car wouldn't start; this happened to me in a mall parking lot. I had to call an automobile repair service to check my car, and the service operator promised service within an hour. One hour extended into two; meanwhile, I stood beside my car with its hood raised. It was hot on the pavement; in addition, I felt idiotic and pitiful in the eyes of the other shoppers. A service person finally arrived and towed my car' yet the wait was frustrating. A similar incident occurred last week' but it involved waiting in my home. My refrigerator began to make a strange grinding sound' soon it simply shut off. I called a repair company and agreed to pay extra for emergency service. It was slow emergency service, in fact, it arrived three hours later. By that time, water had dripped all over the kitchen floor. The refrigerator technician offered a brief apology' then he took a quick look at my refrigerator and gave me the bad news. I wound up with a huge bill for refrigerator parts and a huge headache. I sometimes keep other people waiting and have never thought about their frustrations. Now I have had my own double dose of irritation', *and* I will try harder not to keep others waiting.

Exercise 5   Editing a Paragraph for Run-on Sentences and Comma Splices

Edit the following paragraph for run-on sentences and comma splices. There are nine errors.

My mother tries to be sneaky in her nagging', however, she is ridiculously obvious. She wants my brother to lose weight', *so* she regularly slips obvious hints into the conversation. He may be dropping by for a minute', however, she uses that minute to tell him about a new study on heart attacks and weight control. My brother is about ten pounds overweight', *yet* she cannot talk to him without mentioning diet, exercise, or calories. My mother is also determined to dance at my sister's wedding. My sister has a longtime boyfriend but is not interested in marrying soon. My mother constantly nudges my sister toward marriage. My mother tells my sister about every wedding in the neighborhood', in fact, she shows my sister the wedding pictures. My mother never gives up' she sends copies of <u>Bride</u> magazine to my sister's house. My mother's goal for me is even more ridiculous. She always dreamed of having a doctor in the family and has picked me for the role. Blood makes me sick' still she hasn't given up hope. She urges me to watch medical dramas on television', *for* they might inspire me. My mother loves her children', nevertheless, she wants to shape them into her idea of perfection.

Chapter Test: Avoiding Run-on Sentences and Comma Splices

Some of the sentences below are correctly punctuated. Some are run-on sentences, and some contain comma splices. If a sentence is correctly punctuated, write *OK* in the space provided. If it is a run-on sentence or contains a comma splice, put an *X* in the space provided, and correct the sentence above the lines by adding the necessary punctuation. Do not add any words.

1. __X__ I pleaded with my brother for twenty minutes; finally; he let me borrow his car.

2. __OK__ Kristy could wear a shirt with long sleeves to the job interview, or she could use makeup to conceal the small tattoo on her wrist.

3. __X__ Miguel and I didn't go to Sean's party last night; instead, we stayed home and watched videos.

4. __OK__ My father worked at the airport all night; now he's asleep.

5. __X__ I spent too much time on the first part of the test; consequently, I ran out of time to complete the second part.

6. __OK__ You're late, so you'll have to search for a parking space.

7. __X__ Ashley was hungry; she ate all the leftover chicken.

8. __OK__ The yellow Labrador raced to the three dogs in the backyard and began leaping with joy.

9. __X__ Our apartment is on a busy street; as a result, we hear noise all the time.

10. __X__ Joseph starts the day with a long, hot shower; then he drinks a can of Diet Pepsi.

CHAPTER 18

Beyond the Simple Sentence: Subordination

Quick Question

Which sentence(s) is/are correct?

(A.) Until I found a job, I could not afford college tuition.

(B.) I could not afford college tuition until I found a job.

(After you study this chapter, you will be confident of your answer.)

MORE ON COMBINING SIMPLE SENTENCES

Before you go any further, look back. Review the following:

- A clause has a subject and a verb.
- An independent clause is a simple sentence; it is a group of words, with a subject and verb, that makes sense by itself.

There is another kind of clause called a **dependent clause**. It has a subject and a verb, but it does not make sense by itself. It cannot stand alone. It is not complete by itself. That is, it *depends* on the rest of the sentence to give it meaning. You can use a dependent clause as another option for combining simple sentences.

OPTION 4: USING A DEPENDENT CLAUSE TO BEGIN A SENTENCE

NOTE

Options 1–3 for sentence combining are explained in Chapter 16, which covers coordination.

Often, you can combine simple sentences by changing an independent clause from one sentence into a dependent clause and placing it at the beginning of the new sentence.

two simple sentences:

s v   s v
I was late for work. My *car had* a flat tire.

changing one simple sentence into a beginning dependent clause:

                    s v   s v
Because my *car had* a flat tire, *I was* late for work.

OPTION 5: USING A DEPENDENT CLAUSE TO END A SENTENCE

You can also combine simple sentences by changing an independent clause from one sentence into a dependent clause and placing it at the end of the new sentence:

s v   s v
I was late for work because my *car had* a flat tire.

Notice how one simple sentence can be changed into a dependent clause in two ways:

two simple sentences:

s   s v   s v
Mother and *Dad wrapped* my presents. *I slept.*

changing one simple sentence into a dependent clause:

s   s v   s v
Mother and *Dad wrapped* my presents while *I slept.*

or

                s v   s   s v
While *I slept, Mother* and *Dad wrapped* my presents.

Using Subordinating Conjunctions

Changing an independent clause to a dependent one is called **subordinating**. How do you do it? You add a subordinating word, called a **subordinating conjunction**, to an independent clause, making it dependent—less "important," or subordinate—in the new sentence.

Keep in mind that the subordinate clause is still a clause; it has a subject and a verb, but it does not make sense by itself. For example, let's start with an independent clause:

s   v
Caroline studies.

Somebody (Caroline) does something (studies). The statement makes sense by itself. But if you add a subordinating conjunction to the independent clause, the clause becomes dependent, incomplete, unfinished, like this:

> *When* Caroline studies (When she studies, what happens?)
> *Unless* Caroline studies (Unless she studies, what will happen?)
> *If* Caroline studies (If Caroline studies, what will happen?)

Now, each dependent clause needs an independent clause to finish the idea:

> **dependent clause**   **independent clause**
> When Caroline studies, she gets good grades.

> **dependent clause**   **independent clause**
> Unless Caroline studies, she forgets key ideas.

> **dependent clause**   **independent clause**
> If Caroline studies, she will pass the course.

There are many subordinating conjunctions. When you put any of these words in front of an independent clause, you make that clause dependent. Here is a list of some subordinating conjunctions:

<table>
<tr><td colspan="4">**INFO BOX:** **Subordinating Conjunctions**</td></tr>
<tr><td>after</td><td>before</td><td>so that</td><td>whenever</td></tr>
<tr><td>although</td><td>even though</td><td>though</td><td>where</td></tr>
<tr><td>as</td><td>if</td><td>unless</td><td>whereas</td></tr>
<tr><td>as if</td><td>in order that</td><td>until</td><td>whether</td></tr>
<tr><td>because</td><td>since</td><td>when</td><td>while</td></tr>
</table>

INSTRUCTOR'S NOTE

Students often confuse rules for punctuating subordinating conjunctions with the rules for punctuating conjunctive adverbs. They will need to study the charts carefully.

If you pick the right subordinating conjunction, you can effectively combine simple sentences (independent clauses) into a more sophisticated sentence pattern. Such combining helps you add sentence variety to your writing and helps to explain relationships between ideas.

> **simple sentences:**
>
>   S   V   V   S   V
> *Leo could* not *read* music. His *performance was* exciting.

> **new combination:**
>
> **dependent clause**   **independent clause**
> Although Leo could not read music, his performance was exciting.

> **simple sentences:**
>
> S V   S V
> *I caught* a bad cold last night. *I forgot* to bring a sweater to the base-ball game.

> **new combination:**
>
> **independent clause**   **dependent clause**
>
> I caught a bad cold last night because I forgot to bring a sweater to the baseball game.

Punctuating Complex Sentences

A sentence that has one independent clause and one (or more) dependent clause(s), is called a **complex sentence**. Complex sentences are very easy to punctuate. See if you can figure out the rule for punctuating by yourself. Look at the following examples. All are punctuated correctly.

dependent clause   **independent clause**
Whenever the baby smiles, his mother is delighted.

independent clause   **dependent clause**
His mother is delighted whenever the baby smiles.

dependent clause   **independent clause**
While you were away, I saved your mail for you.

independent clause   **dependent clause**
I saved your mail for you while you were away.

In the examples above, look at the sentences that have a comma. Look at the ones that do not have a comma. Both kinds of sentences are punctuated correctly. Do you see the rule?

> **If the dependent clause comes at the beginning of the sentence, put a comma after the dependent clause. If the dependent clause comes at the end of the sentence, do not put a comma in front of the dependent clause.**

Although we played well, we lost the game.
We lost the game although we played well.

Until he called, I had no date for the dance.
I had no date for the dance until he called.

Exercise 1   **Punctuating Complex Sentences**

All the sentences below are complex sentences; that is, they have one independent and one (or more) dependent clause(s). Add a comma to each sentence that needs one.

1. Until I can afford a new car, I have to keep paying for repairs on my old one.

2. Give me a call if you want me to drive you to school tomorrow.

3. After my parents stopped arguing about my bad behavior, I fell into a restless and troubled sleep.

4. I fell into a restless and troubled sleep after my parents stopped arguing about my bad behavior.

5. Kristin never buys much when she and I spend time at the mall on the weekends.

6. Because my supervisor insists on punctuality, I come to work early every morning.

7. My brother won't come to dinner unless I make his favorite banana cake.

8. The babysitter became absorbed in her telephone conversation while the children discovered the pleasures of their mother's box of makeup.

9. If I go out with Rebecca on Saturday, I will skip the weekend camping trip with my brothers.

10. Before I started college, I was secretly afraid of meeting new people and finding my way around the campus.

Exercise 2   **More on Punctuating Complex Sentences**

All the sentences below are complex sentences; that is, they have one independent clause and one or more dependent clauses. Add a comma to each sentence that needs one.

1. Gina struggled to hold on to her purse as the crowd around her began pushing forward.

2. The dining room was the biggest room in the house so that the large family could sit comfortably for weekly dinners, birthdays, and holiday celebrations.

3. Whether Al joins the U.S. Army or goes to flight school, he will need the support of his old friends.

4. Alicia wouldn't accept a gift from her father because he hasn't been a part of her life for years.

5. While you were wasting your time playing video games, I finished my book report for sociology class.

6. Since we had missed the first part of the movie, we couldn't understand the plot.

7. When an aggressive driver follows my car too closely, I want to scream.

8. I will own my own house even if I have to work and save for ten or twenty years.

9. Although hot pink is not my favorite color, it looks good on the kitchen walls.

10. As the forest fire moved closer to the houses, the residents prepared for evacuation.

TEACHING TIP

Survey recent magazine and newspaper articles and make photocopies of articles that incorporate a variety of sentence patterns. Ask students to spot prepositional phrases, subordinating conjunctions, and coordinating conjunctions.

INFO BOX: **Options for Combining Sentences**

Coordination

| **Option 1**
Independent clause | , for
, and
, nor
, but
, or
, yet
, so | independent clause |

Option 2
Independent clause   ;   independent clause

Option 3
Independent clause

$\left\{\begin{array}{l}\text{; also,} \\ \text{; anyway,} \\ \text{; as a result,} \\ \text{; besides,} \\ \text{; certainly,} \\ \text{; consequently,} \\ \text{; finally,} \\ \text{; furthermore,} \\ \text{; however,} \\ \text{; incidentally,} \\ \text{; in addition,} \\ \text{; in fact,} \\ \text{; indeed,} \\ \text{; instead,} \\ \text{; likewise,} \\ \text{; meanwhile,} \\ \text{; moreover,} \\ \text{; nevertheless,} \\ \text{; next} \\ \text{; now} \\ \text{; on the other hand,} \\ \text{; otherwise,} \\ \text{; similarly,} \\ \text{; still} \\ \text{; then} \\ \text{; therefore,} \\ \text{; thus} \\ \text{; undoubtedly,}\end{array}\right\}$ independent clause

Subordination

Option 4
Dependent clause
(Put a comma at
the end of the
dependent clause.)

$\left\{\begin{array}{l}\text{After} \\ \text{Although} \\ \text{As} \\ \text{As if} \\ \text{Because} \\ \text{Before} \\ \text{Even though} \\ \text{If} \\ \text{In order that} \\ \text{Since} \\ \text{So that} \\ \text{Though} \\ \text{Unless} \\ \text{Until} \\ \text{When} \\ \text{Whenever} \\ \text{Where} \\ \text{Whereas} \\ \text{Whether} \\ \text{While}\end{array}\right\}$ independent clause

	after	
	although	
	as	
	as if	
	because	
	before	
	even though	
	if	
	in order that	
Option 5	since	
Independent clause	so that	dependent clause
	though	
	unless	
	until	
	when	
	whenever	
	where	
	whereas	
	whether	
	while	

Note: In Option 4, words are capitalized because the dependent clause will begin your complete sentence.

Exercise 3 Using the Five Options for Combining Sentences

Add the necessary commas and/or semicolons to the following sentences. Some are correct as they are.

1. After the rain stopped' the plants in the garden looked fresh and new.

2. One of the puppies in the exercise pen began to bark at the visitor' then all the puppies joined in the barking.

3. The cardboard box absorbed the constant drip from the ceiling and gradually turned into a soggy mess.

4. Caleb has a hot temper even though he seems easygoing and calm.

5. Whenever the phone rings in the middle of the night' I expect bad news.

6. Unless Samantha gets a good night's sleep' she is irritable the next day.

7. Give me your answer' I need to know it now.

8. My wild curly hair grows fast' consequently' I spend a significant part of my paycheck on haircuts.

9. Jose spends most of his spare time playing soccer or watching soccer matches on television' so he would love tickets to the World Cup.

10. I can go to the movies with you on Saturday if you meet me for an afternoon show.

Exercise 4 **More on Using the Five Options for Combining Sentences**

Add the necessary commas and/or semicolons to the following sentences. Some are correct as they are.

1. My brother turned my parents' wedding anniversary into something special; he made a video out of their old, forgotten home movies.

2. Because I can't stand the smell of smoke on a person's clothing, I rarely socialize with smokers.

3. My house is not the cleanest house in town, but it is warm and comfortable.

4. My sister doesn't spend money on the latest toys for her children; instead, she takes them to the park, to the zoo, or to the library for new adventures.

5. Some parking lots were designed many years ago, and the parking spaces in them are too small for many of today's large cars.

6. I always feel guilty when I gossip about a friend.

7. Although Raymond drives a tow truck at work, his own car is a tiny Volkswagen.

8. The pot of spaghetti boiled over while I was distracted by my phone conversation with Eli.

9. Expensive chocolates are an acceptable birthday or Valentine's Day gift; however, they're not a very original one.

10. A couple of my friends from high school are going on a cruise next week; they got a great price on a five-day trip to Mexico.

Collaborate

Exercise 5 **Combining Sentences**

Do this exercise with a partner or a group. Below are pairs of sentences. Combine each pair of sentences into one clear, smooth sentence in two different ways. You can add words as well as punctuation. The first pair of sentences is done for you.

1. We always go to Country Ice Cream for a treat.
   The store has the best hot fudge sundaes in the world.

combination 1: *We always go to Country Ice Cream for a treat because the store has the best hot fudge sundaes in the world.*

combination 2: *We always go to Country Ice Cream for a treat; the store has the best hot fudge sundaes in the world.*

2. My cousin wouldn't drive me to the gym.
   I had to take the bus.

combination 1: *My cousin wouldn't drive me to the gym; therefore, I had to take the bus.*

combination 2: *My cousin wouldn't drive me to the gym, so I had to take the bus.*

TEACHING TIP

Advise students not to rely too often on the word *and* when they are combining sentences. By avoiding the overuse of *and*, they can find more effective ways to combine sentences.

INSTRUCTOR'S NOTE

Answers will vary. Possible answers shown.

3. Oil continued to ooze from the overturned tanker truck.
Motorists struggled to avoid the slick and dangerous part of the highway.

combination 1: *As motorists struggled to avoid the slick and dangerous part of the highway, oil continued to ooze from the overturned tanker truck.*

combination 2: *Oil continued to ooze from the overturned tanker truck; meanwhile, motorists struggled to avoid the slick and dangerous part of the highway.*

4. A sleazy towing company grabbed my car from a no-parking zone.
The company demanded a large cash payment.

combination 1: *A sleazy towing company grabbed my car from a no-parking zone; then the company demanded a large cash payment.*

combination 2: *After a sleazy towing company grabbed my car from a no-parking zone, the company demanded a large cash payment.*

5. Charlie wouldn't listen to Tommy's explanation for the delay.
He wouldn't accept Tommy's apology.

combination 1: *Charlie wouldn't listen to Tommy's explanation for the delay, nor would he accept Tommy's apology.*

combination 2: *Charlie wouldn't listen to Tommy's explanation for the delay; moreover, he wouldn't accept Tommy's apology.*

6. I always wake Mark up in the morning.
He sleeps through the sound of the alarm clock.

combination 1: *I always wake Mark up in the morning because he sleeps through the sound of the alarm clock.*

combination 2: *I always wake Mark up in the morning, for he sleeps through the sound of the alarm clock.*

7. My dog has never caught a squirrel.
She begins each day with the dream of catching one.

combination 1: *Although my dog has never caught a squirrel, she begins each day with the dream of catching one.*

combination 2: *My dog has never caught a squirrel; nevertheless, she begins each day with the dream of catching one.*

8. Bill wanted a career in music.
He became a physician's assistant.

combination 1: *Bill wanted a career in music; instead, he became a physician's assistant.*

combination 2: *Bill wanted a career in music, but he became a physician's assistant.*

9. My father lost his wallet.
He became anxious about the possibility of identity theft.

combination 1: *When my father lost his wallet, he became anxious about the possibility of identity theft.*

combination 2: *My father lost his wallet; he became anxious about the possibility of identity theft.*

10. The apartment for rent could be a good deal.
    It could be a dump.

combination 1: *The apartment for rent could be a good deal, or it could be a dump.*

combination 2: *The apartment for rent could be a good deal; on the other hand, it could be a dump.*

Collaborate

Exercise 6 **Create Your Own Text on Combining Sentences**

Below is a list of rules for coordinating and subordinating sentences. Working with a group, write two examples for each rule.

Option 1: You can join two simple sentences (two independent clauses) into a compound sentence with a coordinating conjunction and a comma in front of it. (The coordinating conjunctions are *for, and, nor, but, or, yet, so.*)

INSTRUCTOR'S NOTE

Answers will vary. Possible answers shown.

example 1: *I woke up early, so I made breakfast for my family.*

example 2: *Chrissie could speak Portuguese, and she could also read it.*

Option 2: You can combine two simple sentences (two independent clauses) into a compound sentence with a semicolon between independent clauses.

example 1: *Seafood can be expensive; Maine lobster is particularly expensive.*

example 2: *My grandfather taught me about fishing; he took me on some wonderful fishing trips.*

Option 3: You can combine two simple sentences (two independent clauses) into a compound sentence with a semicolon and a conjunctive adverb between independent clauses. (Some conjunctive adverbs are *also, anyway, as a result, besides, certainly, consequently, finally, furthermore, however, incidentally, in addition, indeed, in fact, instead, likewise, meanwhile, moreover, nevertheless, next, now, on the other hand, otherwise, similarly, still, then, therefore, thus,* and *undoubtedly.*)

example 1: *He is a champion runner; undoubtedly, he will win the race.*

example 2: *I used to love chocolate; now I rarely crave it.*

Option 4: You can combine two simple sentences (two independent clauses) into a complex sentence by making one clause dependent. The dependent clause starts with a subordinating conjunction. Then, if the dependent clause begins the sentence, the clause ends with a comma.

(Some common subordinating conjunctions are *after, although, as, as if, because, before, even though, if, in order that, since, so that, though, unless, until, when, whenever, where, whereas, whether,* and *while.*)

example 1: *Before I started college, I worked at a supermarket.*

example 2: *As the boys argued loudly, a crowd formed around them.*

Option 5: You can combine two simple sentences (two independent clauses) into a complex sentence by making one clause dependent. Then, if the dependent clause comes after the independent clause, no comma is needed.

example 1: *Lorraine will fix the pipes whenever she can get a free weekend.*

example 2: *It's an honor to be nominated even if I do not win.*

Exercise 7	Editing a Paragraph for Errors in Coordination and Subordination

Connect

Edit the following paragraph for errors in coordination and subordination. You do not have to add words to the paragraph; just add, delete, or change punctuation. There are seven errors.

When summer comes , I worry about my children. I worry because , [no comma] they are not

attending school and need supervision. I am a working parent ; in addition, I am a

college student. I can manage all my responsibilities during the school year

because my children spend each weekday in the classroom and in after-school

programs at school. Summer creates a problem ; I need a place for my six-year-old

twins. I cannot afford a full-time babysitter , and my relatives are available only in

emergencies. Most summer camps are expensive; unfortunately , the cheaper, pub-

licly funded ones are rare. I love to see the look on my children's faces on the last

day of school , but I dread the struggle to find safe summer activities.

Exercise 8	Editing a Paragraph for Errors in Coordination and Subordination

Connect

Edit the following paragraph for errors in coordination and subordination. You do not have to add words to the paragraph; just add, delete, or change punctuation. There are seven errors.

A close relationship with a coworker can be wonderful ; however, it is also

risky. Whether the relationship is a close friendship or a romance , it can make

each workday significant. Having a special person at work can be a treat, unless [no comma] some very typical problems intrude. One problem involves dealing with the other

workers. A workplace relationship is hard to keep secret*,* and those involved in a

close friendship or romance are nearly always the subject of gossip. Another prob-

no comma

lem occurs, if the relationship ends. Seeing a former best friend or soul mate every

;

workday can hurt, in addition, everyone at work is watching the drama of two

people's unhappiness. Sometimes a failed relationship at work can lead at least

no comma

one person to quit his or her job. These problems are worth considering, before a

person mixes work life with social life.

Chapter Test: Coordination and Subordination

Some of the following sentences need commas and/or semicolons. Write *X* next to the incorrect sentences and correct the errors above the lines.

1. __X__ My brother complains about the long hours and stressful pace of his work in a hospital emergency room*,* yet he will never quit his job

2. __X__ Two men in the bleachers began to argue about some minor detail of the referee's decision*,* then the two began punching each other.

3. _____ Anthony starts talking about his classic Dodge Charger whenever he wants to impress a new person in the neighborhood.

4. __X__ After the storm knocked out our electricity*,* we sat around and wondered how to get through the night without our computers, television, lights, and heat.

5. __X__ Attending college full time will get me a college degree fairly quickly*,* on the other hand*,* it will cut into my hours at work.

6. __X__ Since Michael will be busy on Saturday*,* I'll take my brother with me to look at paint colors for my kitchen and bedroom.

7. __X__ Patrick was extremely polite and tactful at his parents' anniversary party*,* for he did not want to start an argument at the family gathering.

8. _____ The movie began with two young men on a deserted beach and then became a weird combination of science fiction, cartoon fantasy, and horror.

9. __X__ The loud croaking of the frogs on the pond across the road started at sundown and continued for hours*,* finally*,* the frogs gave up at dawn.

10. _____ The city began to decay when many manufacturing plants and businesses moved into the nearby suburbs and took thousands of jobs with them.

CHAPTER 19

Quick Question

True or False: A group of words that has a subject and a verb but does not make a complete statement is one kind of a sentence fragment.

(After you study this chapter, you will be confident of your answer.)

Avoiding Sentence Fragments

A **sentence fragment** is a group of words that looks like a sentence, is punctuated like a sentence, but is not a sentence. Writing a sentence fragment is a major error in grammar because it reveals that the writer is not sure what a sentence is.

The following groups of words are all fragments:

Because customers are often in a hurry and have little time to look for bargains.
My job being very stressful and fast paced.
For example, the introduction of salads into fast food restaurants.

There are two easy steps that can help you check your writing for sentence fragments.

> **INFO BOX: Two Steps in Recognizing Sentence Fragments**
>
> **Step 1:** Check each group of words punctuated like a sentence, looking for a subject and a verb.
>
> **Step 2:** If you find a subject and a verb, check that the group of words makes a complete statement.

RECOGNIZING FRAGMENTS: STEP 1

Step 1: Check for a subject and a verb. Some groups of words that look like sentences may actually have a subject but no verb, or they may have a verb but no subject, or they may have no subject *or* verb.

The puppy in the pet store window. (*Puppy* could be the subject of a sentence, but there is no verb.)

Doesn't matter to me one way or the other. (There is a verb, *Does matter*, but there is no subject.)

In the back of my mind. (There are two prepositional phrases, *In the back* and *of my mind*, but there are no subject and verb.)

Remember that an *-ing* verb by itself cannot be the main verb in a sentence. Therefore groups of words like the ones below may look like sentences, but they lack a verb and are really fragments:

Your sister having all the skills required of a good salesperson.

The two top tennis players struggling with exhaustion and the stress of a highly competitive tournament.

Jack being the only one in the room with a piece of paper.

An infinitive (*to* plus a verb) cannot be a main verb in a sentence, either. The following groups of words are also fragments:

The manager of the store to attend the meeting of regional managers next month in Philadelphia.

The purpose to explain the fine points of the game to new players.

Groups of words beginning with words like *also*, *especially*, *except*, *for example*, *in addition*, and *such as* need subjects and verbs, too. Without subjects and verbs, these groups can be fragments, like the ones below:

Also a good place to grow up.

Especially the youngest member of the family.

For example, a person without a high school diploma.

Exercise 1 Checking Groups of Words for Subjects and Verbs

Some of the following groups of words have subjects and verbs; these are sentences. Some are missing subjects, verbs, or both; these are fragments. Put an *S* by each sentence and an *F* by each fragment.

1. ___S___ For example, a newcomer might get lost in the maze of city streets.

2. ___F___ For instance, someone with an interest in fixing up old houses and apartments.

3. ___F___ An angry motorist blasting his horn repeatedly and shouting at no one in particular.

   4. __F__   Can't even consider the possibility of the team losing in the finals.

   5. __F__   Especially a lawn chair and a cool drink in the shade of a palm tree.

   6. __S__   Danielle seems calmer and happier lately.

   7. __F__   In a silly attempt to deceive his girlfriend about his week-end trip.

   8. __S__   In addition, the air-conditioning stopped working.

   9. __F__   The weather being an important factor in our plans for the street fair.

   10. __S__   From a box in the back of the pantry came a stream of ants.

RECOGNIZING FRAGMENTS: STEP 2

Step 2: If a group of words has both a subject and a verb, check that it makes a complete statement. Many groups of words that have both a subject and a verb do not make sense by themselves. They are **dependent clauses**. How can you tell if a clause is dependent? After you have checked each group of words for a subject and verb, check to see if it begins with one of the subordinating conjunctions that start dependent clauses. (Here are some common subordinating words: *after, although, as, as if, because, before, even though, if, in order that, since, so that, though, unless, until, when, whenever, where, whereas, whether, while.*)

A clause that begins with a subordinating conjunction is a dependent clause. When you punctuate a dependent clause as if it were a sentence, you have a kind of fragment called a **dependent-clause fragment**.

   After I woke up this morning.
   Because he liked football better than soccer.
   Unless it stops raining by lunchtime.

It is important to remember both steps in checking for fragments:

   Step 1: Check for a subject and a verb.

   Step 2: If you find a subject and a verb, check that the group of words makes a complete statement.

Exercise 2   **Checking for Dependent-Clause Fragments**

Some of the following groups of words are sentences. Some are dependent clauses punctuated like sentences: these are sentence fragments. Put an *S* by each sentence and an *F* by each fragment.

   1. __F__   As the sky cleared and the morning turned unbearably hot.

   2. __S__   Around the parking lot was a chain-link fence.

   3. __F__   Because of the cost of tuition and other fees such as the student activities fee.

   4. __F__   Although we did not have one comfortable chair in the entire house.

   5. __S__   All frozen pizzas taste like cardboard covered with sauce.

6. ___F___ While my car was in the repair shop at the mall.

7. ___S___ Yet someone must have seen a person running from the burning trailer.

8. ___F___ If the college could offer more required courses in the summer terms.

9. ___F___ Since you pay your share of the electric bill.

10. ___F___ Whenever I see a couple with adorable twin babies in a stroller.

Exercise 3   Using Two Steps to Recognize Sentence Fragments

Some of the following are complete sentences; some are fragments. To recognize the fragments, check each group of words by using the two-step process:

Step 1: Check for a subject and a verb.

Step 2: If you find a subject and a verb, check that the group of words makes a complete statement.

INSTRUCTOR'S NOTE

Some students will no doubt need more practice than others when identifying sentences and fragments. They need to break their habit of automatically assuming that a "long" entry is a sentence.

Then put an *S* by each sentence and an *F* by each fragment.

1. ___S___ Behind the apartment building was a mess of filthy mattresses, rusted metal parts, and broken glass.

2. ___S___ Then the waves crashed higher and closer to the concrete seawall.

3. ___F___ Because of Armando's intense fear of heights.

4. ___S___ From the kitchen came the sizzle of water boiling over and hitting the burner on the stove.

5. ___F___ While we all sat around and reminisced about our middle school pranks.

6. ___F___ The head of the accounting department explaining the new system for distributing paychecks.

7. ___F___ A popular comedian to appear at a fundraising event to help homeless families.

8. ___F___ Although Sam had never taken a music lesson.

9. ___F___ For example, not drinking enough water on a hot day.

10. ___F___ Kevin firmly ignoring Tommy at the annual barbecue at Lake Logan.

CORRECTING FRAGMENTS

You can correct fragments easily if you follow the two steps for identifying them.

Step 1: Check for a subject and a verb. If a group of words is a fragment because it lacks a subject or a verb, or both, *add what is missing.*

> **fragment:** My father being a very strong person. (This fragment lacks a main verb.)

corrected: My father *is* a very strong person. (The verb *is* replaces *being*, which is not a main verb.)

fragment: Doesn't care about the party. (This fragment lacks a subject.)

corrected: *Alicia* doesn't care about the party. (A subject, *Alicia*, is added.)

fragment: Especially on dark winter days. (This fragment has neither a subject nor a verb.)

corrected: *I love* a bonfire, especially on dark winter days. (A subject, *I*, and a verb, *love*, are added.)

Step 2: If you find a subject and a verb, check that the group of words makes a complete statement. To correct the fragment, you can turn a dependent clause into an independent one by removing the subordinating conjunction, *or* you can add an independent clause to the dependent one to create a sentence.

fragment: When the rain beat against the windows. (The statement does not make sense by itself. The subordinating conjunction *when* leads the reader to ask, "What happened when the rain beat against the windows?" The subordinating conjunction makes this a dependent clause, not a sentence.)

corrected: The rain beat against the windows. (Removing the subordinating conjunction makes this an independent clause, a sentence.)

corrected: When the rain beat against the windows, *I reconsidered my plans for the picnic.* (Adding an independent clause turns this into a sentence.)

Note: Sometimes you can correct a fragment by linking it to the sentence before it or after it.

fragment (underlined): I have always enjoyed outdoor concerts. Like the ones at Pioneer Park.

corrected: I have always enjoyed outdoor concerts *like the ones at Pioneer Park.*

fragment (underlined): Even if she apologizes for that nasty remark. I will never trust her again.

corrected: *Even if she apologizes for that nasty remark*, I will never trust her again.

You have several choices for correcting fragments: you can add words, phrases, or clauses; you can take words out or combine independent and dependent clauses. You can transform fragments into simple sentences or create compound or complex sentences. To punctuate your new sentences, remember the rules for combining sentences.

Exercise 4   **Correcting Fragments**

Correct each sentence fragment below in the most appropriate way.

1. I spent two hours waiting at the airport. Until Jessica's flight finally arrived.

INSTRUCTOR'S NOTE

Answers will vary. Possible
answers shown.

corrected: *I spent two hours waiting at the airport until Jessica's flight finally arrived.*

2. To earn the money for my little brother's series of operations. My father took a second job.

   corrected: *To earn the money for my little brother's series of operations, my father took a second job.*

3. Colin searched for candles and matches. After the electricity went off.

   corrected: *Colin searched for candles and matches after the electricity went off.*

4. Because a severe drought has struck our area. We are not allowed to water our lawns.

   corrected: *Because a severe drought has struck our area, we are not allowed to water our lawns.*

5. Then took a sharp left turn across oncoming traffic and nearly caused a serious accident.

   corrected: *Then the crazy driver took a sharp left turn across oncoming traffic and nearly caused a serious accident.*

6. One reason for the sharp downturn in the economy being the sharp increase in the price of gasoline.

   corrected: *One reason for the sharp downturn in the economy is the sharp increase in the price of gasoline.*

7. Mosquitoes had bitten every exposed area of David's skin. Especially his neck and feet.

   corrected: *Mosquitoes had bitten every exposed area of David's skin, especially his neck and feet.*

8. Choosing a difficult topic for her speech. Shawna researched her subject for hours.

   corrected: *Choosing a difficult topic for her speech, Shawna researched her subject for hours.*

9. When you eat a substantial meal late in the evening. You may have trouble falling asleep.

   corrected: *When you eat a substantial meal late in the evening, you may have trouble falling asleep.*

10. If a heavy rain falls, the old house has a tendency to leak in several places. Such as the attic and the kitchen.

    corrected: *If a heavy rain falls, the old house has a tendency to leak in several places such as the attic and the kitchen.*

Exercise 5 **Correcting Fragments Two Ways**

Working with a partner or group, correct each fragment below in two ways. The first one is done for you.

1. Whenever I am waiting for an important phone call.

   corrected: *I am waiting for an important phone call.*

   corrected: *Whenever I am waiting for an important phone call, I am* *extremely impatient and nervous.*

INSTRUCTOR'S NOTE

Answers will vary. Possible answers shown.

2. Except for three days of blizzard conditions.

   corrected: *Last winter was mild except for three days of blizzard* *conditions.*

   corrected: *Except for three days of blizzard conditions, my first winter* *in New Hampshire was better than I had expected.*

3. While the hostage negotiators waited.

   corrected: *While the hostage negotiators waited, reporters from the* *local news stations broadcast reports from the scene.*

   corrected: *The sharpshooters sat patiently while the hostage* *negotiators waited.*

4. You will damage your suede jacket. If you wear it in wet weather.

   corrected: *You will damage your suede jacket if you wear it in wet* *weather.*

   corrected: *If you wear your suede jacket in wet weather, you will* *damage it.*

5. On the other side of town, where Tyler lives.

   corrected: *On the other side of town, where Tyler lives, most of the old* *houses have been remodeled*

   corrected: *Tyler lives on the other side of town.*

6. Although no one at the college knew him well.

   corrected: *No one at the college knew him well.*

   corrected: *Although no one at the college knew him well, Sergio* *seemed polite and friendly.*

7. After the returning soldier had hugged his mother and kissed his girlfriend. He noticed the television cameras pointed at him.

   corrected: *After the returning soldier had hugged his mother and* *kissed his girlfriend, he noticed the television cameras pointed at him.*

corrected: *The returning soldier noticed the television cameras pointed at him after he had hugged his mother and kissed his girlfriend.*

8. The defense attorney delivering a strong case for acquittal.

corrected: *The defense attorney delivered a strong case for acquittal.*

corrected: *The accused woman gained hope after the defense attorney delivered a strong case for acquittal.*

9. Until I get my check. I can't buy any gifts for the holidays.

corrected: *Until I get my check, I can't buy any gifts for the holidays.*

corrected: *I can't buy any gifts for the holidays until I get my check.*

10. Matt considering his chances for promotion at the company.

corrected: *Matt is considering his chances for promotion at the company.*

corrected: *While Matt considers his chances for promotion at the company, he is looking at other job possibilities.*

Connect

Exercise 6   **Editing a Paragraph for Sentence Fragments**

Correct the sentence fragments in the following paragraph. There are five fragments.

Memorial Day weekend is special to me because it is the official start of camp-ing season in my town.

Memorial Day weekend is special to me. Because it is the official start of camping season in my town. Few pleasures compare to the joy of loading up the car

and heading into nature. I like to travel with a friend or two and our dogs. We head
Some of my friends do not understand the lure of camping.
for a river or lake to fish, hike, and explore. Some of my friends not understanding the lure of camping. They think being stuck in the country must be boring.
I suppose it can be dull if people are not open to the beauty of the natural world and its creatures.
I suppose it can be dull. If people are not open to the beauty of the natural world and its creatures. The best part of a day of camping is the evening.
When I can lie back and see hundreds of stars and hear the soft sounds of animals break the silence, I am at peace.
When I can lie back and see hundreds of stars and hear the soft sounds of animals break the silence. I am at peace. Nothing can match the feeling.
From Memorial Day until the fall, I live for camping.
From Memorial Day until the fall. I live for camping.

Exercise 7   **Editing a Paragraph for Sentence Fragments**

Correct the sentence fragments in the following paragraph. There are five fragments.

INSTRUCTOR'S NOTE

Answers will vary. Possible answers shown at left.

Once I became a parent, I struggled to understand why children love dirt, espe-
Once I became a parent, I struggled to understand why children love dirt. Espe-
cially mud.   *In order to understand, I*
cially mud. I thought about this question for some time. In order to understand, I
had to look back to my own childhood days.
had to look back. To my own childhood days. I was fortunate enough to live near
                                                                Nothing
the ocean, and one of my greatest pleasures was playing in the sand. Nothing
was more fun than running my hands through piles of sand or grabbing handfuls
being more fun than running my hands through piles of sand or grabbing handfuls
of wet sand.
of wet sand. Sand, for children, is an acceptable kind of dirt. Parents allow chil-

dren at the beach to run in sand, roll in it, and build sand castles. However, chil-
                                                                I remember the pleas-
dren are also drawn to dirt, especially when the dirt is wet. I remember the pleas-
ure of splashing in mud puddles, even slipping in the mud and coming home
ure of splashing in mud puddles. Even slipping in the mud and coming home
covered in it.
covered in it. I can almost relive the lure of forbidden dirt such as mud pies for
                                                Those memories help me to under-
throwing and dry dirt for sliding into home base. My memories help me to under-
stand the lure of dirt for my own children and to be more tolerant when, covered
stand the lure of dirt for my own children. To be more tolerant when, covered in
in mud, they skip into the house and onto my carpet.
mud, they skip into the house and onto my carpet.

Chapter Test: Avoiding Sentence Fragments

Some of the following are complete sentences; some are sentence fragments. Put an *S* by each sentence and an *F* by each fragment.

1. __F__   Two of the officers from the Pinewood Springs Police
Department to talk about starting a neighborhood Crime
Watch program.

2. __S__   Until I met Charles at work, I had no friends in this country.

3. __F__   Even though my evening class is long and is mostly one
endless, boring lecture.

4. __S__   Except in emergencies, no one is allowed to miss work on
Saturday evening.

5. __F__   Learning the basics of Spanish being a requirement for
acceptance into the Summer in Mexico Study Program.

6. __S__   Then a lighted candle dripped hot wax onto the pages of my
research paper.

7. __F__   When an extremely popular group performs at the auditorium and tickets are sold out.

8. __F__   In order that everyone in the office has a chance to participate in the technical training program.

9. __S__   Next to the aspirin in the medicine cabinet is a box of
cough drops.

10. __F__   Behind the heavy chest of drawers a gold hoop earring shining in the piles of dust.

Using Parallelism in Sentences

Parallelism means balance in a sentence. To create sentences with parallelism, remember this rule:

Similar points should get a similar structure.

Often, you will include two or three (or more) related ideas, examples, or details in one sentence. If you express these ideas in a parallel structure, they will be clearer, smoother, and more convincing.

Here are some pairs of sentences with and without parallelism:

not parallel: Of all the sports I've played, I prefer tennis, handball, and playing golf.

parallel: Of all the sports I've played, I prefer *tennis, handball, and golf.* (Three words are parallel.)

not parallel: If you're looking for the car keys, you should look under the table, the kitchen counter, and behind the refrigerator.

parallel: If you're looking for the car keys, you should look *under the table, on the kitchen counter, and behind the refrigerator.* (Three prepositional phrases are parallel.)

not parallel: He is a good choice for manager because he works hard, he keeps calm, and well liked.

parallel: He is a good choice for manager because *he works hard, he keeps calm, and he is well liked.* (Three clauses are parallel.)

From these examples you can see that parallelism involves matching the structures of parts of your sentence. There are two steps that can help you check your writing for parallelism.

INFO BOX: Two Steps in Checking a Sentence for Parallel Structure

Step 1: Look for the list in the sentence.

Step 2: Put the parts of the list into a similar structure. (You may have to change or add something to get a parallel structure.)

ACHIEVING PARALLELISM

Let's correct the parallelism of the following sentence:

sample sentence: The committee for neighborhood safety met to set up a schedule for patrols, coordinating teams of volunteers, and also for the purpose of creating new rules.

To correct this sentence, we'll follow the steps.

Step 1: Look for the list. The committee met to do three things. Here's the list:
1. to set up a schedule for patrols
2. coordinating teams of volunteers
3. for the purpose of creating new rules

Step 2: Put the parts of the list into a similar structure:
1. *to set up* a schedule for patrols
2. *to coordinate* teams of volunteers
3. *to create* new rules

Now revise to get a parallel sentence.

parallel: The committee for neighborhood safety met *to set up* a schedule for patrols, *to coordinate* teams of volunteers, and *to create* new rules.

If you follow Steps 1 and 2, you can also write the sentence like this:

parallel: The committee for neighborhood safety met to *set up* a schedule for patrols, *coordinate* teams of volunteers, and *create* new rules.

But you cannot write a sentence like this:

not parallel: The committee for neighborhood safety met *to set up* a schedule for patrols, *coordinate* teams, and *to create* new rules.

Think of the list again. You can have
The committee met

1. to set up
2. to coordinate   } parallel
3. to create

Or you can have
The committee met to

1. set up
2. coordinate   } parallel
3. create

But your list cannot be
The committee met to

1. set up
2. coordinate   } not parallel
3. to create

In other words, use the *to* once (if it fits every part of the list), or use it with every part of the list.

Caution: Sometimes making ideas parallel means adding something to a sentence because all the parts of the list cannot match exactly.

> **sample sentence:** In his pocket the little boy had a ruler, rubber band, baseball card, and apple.

> **Step 1:** Look for the list. In his pocket the little boy had a
> 1. ruler
> 2. rubber band
> 3. baseball card
> 4. apple

As the sentence is written, the *a* goes with *a ruler, a rubber band, a baseball card*, and *a apple*. But *a* isn't the right word to put in front of *apple*. Words beginning with vowels (*a, e, i, o, u*) need *an* in front of them: *an apple*. So to make the sentence parallel, you have to change something in the sentence.

> **Step 2:** Put the parts of the list into a parallel structure.

> **parallel:** In his pocket the little boy had *a ruler, a rubber band, a baseball card*, and *an apple*.

Here's another example:

> **sample sentence:** She was amused and interested in the silly plot of the movie.

> **Step 1:** Look for the list. She was
> 1. amused
> 2. interested in
>   the silly plot of the movie

Check the sense of that sentence by looking at each part of the list and how it works in the sentence: "She was *interested in* the silly plot of the movie." That part of the list seems clear. But "She was *amused* the silly plot of the movie"? Or "She was *amused in* the silly plot of the movie"? Neither sentence is right. People are not *amused in.*

> **Step 2:** The sentence needs a word added to make the structure parallel.

> **parallel:** She was *amused by* and *interested in* the silly plot of the movie.

ESL NOTE

Nonnative speakers often need additional work on articles. For practice exercises, see the "Nouns and Articles" section on pp. 651–655 of the ESL Appendix.

TEACHING TIP

Ask students what they plan to do on their next school vacation or on a day off from work. List some responses on the board or on your screen. Have students compose several sentences in parallel structure that incorporate information from the list.

When you follow the two steps to check for parallelism, you can write clear sentences and improve your style.

Exercise 1   Revising Sentences for Parallelism

Some of the following sentences need to be revised so that they have parallel structures. Revise the ones that need parallelism.

INSTRUCTOR'S NOTE

Answers will vary. Possible answers shown at left.

1. Billy would rather help people in need than staring at a computer screen all day.

   revised: *Billy would rather help people in need than stare at a computer screen all day.*

2. The wedding reception was the fanciest I have ever attended, also the most expensive, and the biggest of all.

   revised: *The wedding reception was the fanciest, most expensive, and biggest I have ever attended.*

3. At my old school, wearing last year's styles was like when you wear a sign that says "loser."

   revised: *At my old school, wearing last year's styles was like wearing a sign that says "loser."*

4. The car's price, size, and the condition it was in made it a good buy for a college student.

   revised: *The car's price, size, and condition made it a good buy for a college student.*

5. After my father bailed me out of jail, he spent the rest of the evening shouting at me, blaming himself for my behavior, and also he worried about my future.

   revised: *After my father bailed me out of jail, he spent the rest of the evening shouting at me, blaming himself for my behavior, and worrying about my future.*

6. Cleaning out closets, having to throw away junk, and packing endless boxes are all part of moving out of your home.

   revised: *Cleaning out closets, throwing away junk, and packing endless boxes are all part of moving out of your home.*

7. Put the money in the kitchen drawer or on the dresser.

   revised: *OK*

8. Every time I run into Katie, she talks so long that I wind up looking at my watch, making restless motions, and interrupt her before I can get away.

   revised: *Every time I run into Katie, she talks so long that I wind up looking at my watch, making restless motions, and interrupting her before I can get away.*

9. Andrew has good sense, talent that is natural, and intense motivation.

revised: *Andrew has good sense, natural talent, and intense motivation.*

10. The store opens at 7:30 a.m.; 10:00 p.m. is when it closes.

revised: *The store opens at 7:30 a.m. and closes at 10:00 p.m.*

Collaborate

Exercise 2 **Writing Sentences with Parallelism**

Complete this exercise with a partner or a group. First, brainstorm a draft list; then revise the list for parallelism. Finally, complete the sentence in parallel structure. You may want to assign one step (brainstorming a draft list, revising it, etc.) to each group member and then switch steps on the next sentence. The first one is done for you.

1. Three habits I'd like to break are

draft list	**revised list**
a. *worry too much*	a. *worrying too much*
b. *talking on the phone for hours*	b. *talking on the phone for hours*
c. *lose my temper*	c. *losing my temper*

sentence: *Three habits I'd like to break are worrying too much, talking on the phone for hours, and losing my temper.*

2. Three ways to stay healthy are

INSTRUCTOR'S NOTE

Answers will vary. Possible answers shown at right.

draft list	**revised list**
a. *vitamins*	a. *take vitamins*
b. *regular exercise*	b. *exercise regularly*
c. *balanced diet*	c. *eat a balanced diet*

sentence: *Three ways to say healthy are to take vitamins, to exercise regularly, and to eat a balanced diet.*

3. Two reasons why people choose not to marry are

draft list	**revised list**
a. *afraid of commitment*	a. *fear of commitment*
b. *can't trust others*	b. *lack of trust in others*

sentence: *Two reasons why people choose not to marry are a fear of commitment and a lack of trust in others.*

4. Three gifts that money cannot buy are

draft list	**revised list**
a. *kisses from a child*	a. *a child's kisses*
b. *loyalty of a friend*	b. *a friend's loyalty*
c. *a parent praising you*	c. *a parent's praise*

sentence: _Three gifts that money cannot buy are a child's kisses, a friend's loyalty, and a parent's praise._

5. Saving money is important because (add three reasons)

draft list	**revised list**
a. _gives you security_	a. _gives you security_
b. _support for dreams_	b. _supports your dreams_
c. _a focus for daily life_	c. _focuses your daily life_

sentence: _Saving money is important because it gives you security, supports your dreams, and focuses your daily life._

6. Starting a new job can be stressful because (add three reasons)

draft list	**revised list**
a. _policies are unfamiliar_	a. _unfamiliar policies_
b. _a new boss_	b. _a new boss_
c. _coworkers look strange_	c. _strange coworkers_

sentence: _Starting a new job can be stressful because it means dealing with unfamiliar policies, a new boss, and strange coworkers._

7. When I finish college, I want to (add two goals)

draft list	**revised list**
a. _a good job_	a. _get a good job_
b. _move out of the area_	b. _move out of the area_

sentence: _When I finish college, I want to get a good job and move out of the area._

8. People seem to get angry when (add two times or occasions)

draft list	**revised list**
a. _losing an argument_	a. _they lose an argument_
b. _their team loses_	b. _their team loses a game_

sentence: _People seem to get angry when they lose an argument or their team loses a game._

9. Three characteristics of a good friend are

draft list	**revised list**
a. _honest_	a. _honesty_
b. _always loyal_	b. _loyalty_
c. _generosity_	c. _generosity_

sentence: _Three characteristics of a good friend are honesty, loyalty, and generosity._

10. Two household chores most people dislike are

draft list

a. _to clean the bathroom_

b. _making the bed_

revised list

a. _cleaning the bathroom_

b. _making the bed_

sentence: _Two household chores most people dislike are cleaning the bathroom and making the bed._

TEACHING TIP

Remind students that certain paired words used for comparisons require parallel structure. (Examples: _neither ... nor, either ... or, not only ... but also._) On the board, write a few sentences that incorporate such pairings, and then ask students to compose their own. They should see that nouns and verbs will need to be in a "similar" (i.e., parallel) form.

INSTRUCTOR'S NOTE

Answers will vary. Possible answers shown at right.

Exercise 3 **Combining Sentences and Creating a Parallel Structure**

Combine each cluster of sentences below into one clear, smooth sentence that includes some parallel structure. The first one is done for you.

1. Before you buy a used car, you should research what similar models are selling for.
   It would be a good idea to have a mechanic examine the car.
   Also, how much mileage it has racked up is a consideration.

   combination: _Before you buy a used car, you should compare prices of similar models, get a mechanic to examine the car, and think carefully about the mileage._

2. The qualifications for the job include some sales experience.
   Applicants also have to have good telephone skills.
   Another requirement is being trained in computers.

   combination: _The qualifications for the job include some sales experience, good telephone skills, and computer training._

3. Jake was the funniest friend I ever had.
   He was more generous than any other friend I ever had.
   His loyalty was the best, too.

   combination: _Jake was the funniest, most generous, and most loyal friend I ever had._

4. Hundreds of students waited in line to register for their classes.
   They also were paying their tuition fees.
   Their other goal was to see an advisor.

   combination: _Hundreds of students waited in line to register for their classes, pay their tuition fees, and see an advisor._

5. My aunt started as a night security guard at Crescent Rehabilitation Center.
   Then she was promoted to head of the night security shift.
   Eventually she worked her way up to director of security for the center.

   combination: _My aunt started as a night security guard at Crescent Rehabilitation Center, was promoted to head of the night security shift, and eventually worked her way up to director of security._

6. Shopping malls sell goods.
   Contests are often held at shopping malls.
   Santa Claus and the Easter Bunny are presented at the malls.
   Early morning exercise for mall walkers is offered.
   Special events such as celebrity appearances are another
   sponsored feature at malls.

   combination: *Shopping malls sell goods, hold contests, present Santa*

   Claus and the Easter Bunny, offer early morning exercise for mall

   walkers, and sponsor special events such as celebrity appearances.

7. He was tall.
   His skin was dark.
   He looked muscular.
   He dressed fashionably.
   He was the new dean of students.

   combination: *The new dean of students was tall, dark skinned,*

   muscular, and fashionably dressed.

8. When I need advice, I go to Sean, who is a sensible person.
   Sean has insight.
   Perceptiveness is another one of his strengths.

   combination: *When I need advice, I go to Sean, who is sensible,*

   insightful, and perceptive.

9. If you drive me to New York City, we'll go to Times Square.
   Eating Korean food is something else we'll do.
   In addition, we can walk in Central Park.

   combination: *If you drive me to New York City, we'll go to Times*

   Square, eat Korean food, and walk in Central Park.

10. Look in my wallet when you want some spare change.
    You can also check the zippered compartment in my handbag.
    The pile of coins on the hall table is another place to investigate.

    combination: *When you want some spare change, look in my wallet,*

    check the zippered compartment in my handbag, and investigate the

    pile of coins on the hall table.

| Exercise 4 | **Editing a Paragraph for Errors in Parallelism** |

Connect

Correct any errors in parallelism in the following paragraph. There are four
errors.

Lake Irene Park is a perfect spot for observing families at play. Many families
                                                         relaxing
come for the day and enjoy swimming at the lake, relax under the pine trees, and
                                                    most popular and enjoyable
bicycling on the nature trails. Family barbecues are the most popular activity and
activity (or) most enjoyable activity.
also the most enjoyable. As soon as the family members arrive, the children and

teens run to the shore. Babies play in the sand, toddlers splash at the edge of the

water, and older children chase each other in the deeper parts of the lake. Mean-

by flirting (or) flirting and ~~by~~ playing

while, teens amuse themselves by observing other teens, flirting, and by playing

volleyball. Under the pine trees, mothers gather around the picnic tables. They

unload huge bags full of hamburger rolls, hot dog buns, potato chips, cole slaw,

and macaroni salad. As they gossip and laugh, the smell of sizzling meat floats

over from the huge grills where fathers cook. For the fathers, barbecuing is a seri-

ous business, and it requires many cold drinks. When everyone gathers around the

food, the event reaches its peak. Whether they have been playing, swimming, flirt-

setting up

ing, cooking, or they set up, all the family members are tired but happy. Now

they can enjoy the closeness of family and the pleasure of the meal.

Connect

Exercise 5 Editing a Paragraph for Errors in Parallelism

Correct any errors in parallelism in the following paragraph. There are five
errors.

When I was a child, physical education class used to fill me with dread. First, I

was smaller and less coordinated than most children my age. If the teacher called

on two students to serve as captains and to pick the rest of the class as team

members, I was always the last to be chosen. The captain of each team would

past me

look around me, beside me, or look past me to find anybody except me. I feared

cheerful

the gym teacher, who was always loud, with a cheerful attitude, aggressive, and

energetic. I used to suffer through each class, terrified that the teacher would

criticize

make some comment about my awkwardness or to criticize my team spirit. Now

baseball

that I am an adult, I find basketball, baseball games, football, and soccer exciting

to watch. On weekends, I play basketball with some friends. However, whenever I

fear

think of my old gym classes, I feel twinges of anxiety, being afraid, and insecurity

return.

Chapter Test: Using Parallelism in Sentences

Some of the following sentences have errors in parallelism; some are correct. Put an *X* by the sentences with errors in parallelism.

1. __X__ The Teen Task Force's goals are establishment of a youth activities program, creation of a teen help line, and constructing a teen center.

2. __X__ Jason used to be an average student, a basketball player who was superior, and a devoted son.

3. _____ The secretary grew afraid of and offended by the supervisor's temper tantrums.

4. __X__ At the thrift shop, we bought an antique lamp, a brass platter, silk pillow, a pair of coffee mugs, and a wicker basket for our apartment.

5. _____ If it rains hard tomorrow and you are stuck at school, I can pick you up and drive you home.

6. _____ Shopping at Price Mart is always an ordeal because the parking lot is always full, the store aisles are jammed with shoppers, and the checkout lines are long.

7. __X__ An overly critical parent can destroy the confidence, hopes, increase the worries, and intensify the fears of a child.

8. __X__ Because the coach didn't have much energy, skill, a sense of compassion, or backbone, the players did not respect him.

9. __X__ To keep my dog from chewing my pajamas, I tried hiding them under my pillow, at the top of my closet, over the ceiling fan, and the refrigerator.

10. _____ After my divorce, I spent a year panicking about money, hiding from my friends, and dreading the future.

CHAPTER 21

Using Adjectives and Adverbs

WHAT ARE ADJECTIVES?

Adjectives describe nouns (persons, places, or things) or pronouns (words that substitute for nouns).

adjectives:
She stood in a *dark* corner. (*Dark* describes the noun *corner*.)
I need a *little* help. (*Little* describes the noun *help*.)
She looked *happy*. (*Happy* describes the pronoun *she*.)

An adjective usually comes before the word it describes.

He gave me a *beautiful* ring. (*Beautiful* describes *ring*.)
A *small* horse pulled the cart. (*Small* describes *horse*.)

Sometimes an adjective comes after a *being* verb, a verb that tells what something is. Being verbs are words like *is*, *are*, *was*, *am*, and *has been*. Words like *feels*, *looks*, *seems*, *smells*, *sounds*, and *tastes* are part of the group called being verbs.

He seems *unhappy*. (*Unhappy* describes *he* and follows the being verb *seems*.)
Alan was *confident*. (*Confident* describes *Alan* and follows the being verb *was*.)

Exercise 1   **Recognizing Adjectives**

Circle the adjective in each of the following sentences.

1. Larry got caught in a (heavy) rainstorm.
2. Mr. and Mrs. Salazar were (kind) neighbors.
3. A (small) mouse skittered across the floor.
4. The prisoner seems (unhappy) with the judge's decision.
5. The (enormous) snake was curled inside a box.
6. The cough medicine smelled (horrible.)
7. I want your (honest) opinion of my performance.
8. Lucy could be a (superior) singer.
9. A (dirty) blanket covered the bed.
10. That movie had a (weird) ending.

ADJECTIVES: COMPARATIVE AND SUPERLATIVE FORMS

The **comparative** form of an adjective compares two persons or things.
The **superlative** form compares three or more persons or things.

comparative: Your car is *cleaner* than mine.
superlative: Your car is the *cleanest* one in the parking lot.

comparative: Hamburger is *cheaper* than steak.
superlative: Hamburger is the *cheapest* meat on the menu.

comparative: Lisa is *friendlier* than her sister.
superlative: Lisa is the *friendliest* of the three sisters.

For most adjectives of one syllable, add *-er* to form the comparative, and
add *-est* to form the superlative:

The weather is *colder* than it was yesterday, but Friday was the
    coldest day of the year.
Orange juice is *sweeter* than grapefruit juice, but the *sweetest* juice is
    grape juice.

For longer adjectives, use *more* to form the comparative, and *most* to form
the superlative:

I thought algebra was *more difficult* than composition; however,
    physics was the *most difficult* course I ever took.
My brother is *more outgoing* than my sister, but my father is the *most
    outgoing* member of the family.

The three forms of adjectives usually look like this:

Adjective	Comparative	Superlative
	(two)	(three or more)
sweet	sweeter	sweetest
fast	faster	fastest
short	shorter	shortest
quick	quicker	quickest
old	older	oldest

They may look like this instead:

Adjective	Comparative	Superlative
	(two)	(three or more)
confused	more confused	most confused
specific	more specific	most specific
dangerous	more dangerous	most dangerous
confident	more confident	most confident
beautiful	more beautiful	most beautiful

However, there are some irregular forms of adjectives:

Adjective	Comparative	Superlative
	(two)	(three or more)
good	better	best
bad	worse	worst
little	less	least
many, much	more	most

Exercise 2   Selecting the Correct Adjective Form

Write the correct form of the adjective in each of the following sentences:

1. Milk chocolate tastes _____*better*_____ (good) than dark chocolate.

2. After my surgery, I had to make _____*many*_____ (many) calls to my insurance company; in fact, I called the insurance company _____*more*_____ (many) often than I called my boyfriend.

3. Nick's communications class requires _____*less*_____ (little) public speaking than my communications class does.

4. Which of the four games would be the _____*most*_____ (suitable) for a four-year-old boy?

5. My brother did a _____*good*_____ (good) job painting my bathroom, but he would have done a _____*better*_____ (good) job if he had been painting his own bathroom.

6. My sister is learning to cook and has been trying out her creations on me; of the three dishes I've eaten, the broiled swordfish was the _____*worst*_____ (bad).

7. I love both my brothers, but Oscar is _____*more*_____ (loveable) than Malcolm.

8. <u>Pirates of the Caribbean</u>, <u>Spider-Man</u>, and <u>Shrek</u> all produced sequels; I think <u>Spider-Man</u> offers the _____*best*_____ (good) of the sequels.

9. Sticking with a diet is _____*harder*_____ (hard) than starting one; but the _____*most*_____ (discouraging) part of dieting is reaching a plateau when the pounds won't come off any longer.

10. You look _____*good*_____ (good) in short and long hair; however, I think you look much _____*better*_____ (good) in short hair.

Exercise 3 **Writing Sentences with Adjectives**

Collaborate

INSTRUCTOR'S NOTE

Answers will vary. Possible answers shown at left.

Working with a partner or group, write a sentence that correctly uses each of the following adjectives. Be prepared to share your answers with another group or with the class.

1. oldest *Melvin is the oldest of the four sons.*

2. more useful *A truck is more useful than a van.*

3. richest *Uncle Artie is the richest person in my family.*

4. least *I bought the least expensive paint in the hardware store.*

5. most foolish *Mike's prank was the most foolish of all.*

6. stronger *You are a stronger person than I am.*

7. longer *The job took longer than I had expected.*

8. more alert *He is more alert in the morning than at night.*

9. worse *The new road has worse traffic jams than the old one.*

10. much *Kelly never spent much time with her family.*

WHAT ARE ADVERBS?

Adverbs describe verbs, adjectives, or other adverbs.

> **adverbs:**
> As she spoke, Steve listened *thoughtfully*. (*Thoughtfully* describes the verb *listened.*)
> I said I was *really* sorry for my error. (*Really* describes the adjective *sorry.*)
> The cook worked *very* quickly. (*Very* describes the adverb *quickly.*)

Adverbs answer questions like "How?" "How much?" "How often?" "When?" "Why?" and "Where?"

Exercise 4 **Recognizing Adverbs**

Circle the adverbs in the following sentences.

1. The dog across the street is (usually) quiet, but he barks (uncontrollably) at cats.

2. (Sometimes,) Sarah Sanchez can be (very) irritable.

3. The burglar moved (swiftly) and (silently) through the house.

4. Ethan was (extremely) proud of his (lovingly) rebuilt motorcycle.

5. You can (hardly) expect me to forgive Doug for his dishonesty.

6. Mr. Li (regularly) complains about the noise from the construction crew.

7. My English professor is (genuinely) interested in my stories about my childhood in Nigeria.

8. David Dowd's (beautifully) designed furniture won first prize at a decorator's showcase.

9. When Brad showed up (late) for practice, the coach was (really) upset with him.

10. As he reached the finish line, the winning driver smiled (triumphantly.)

Exercise 5   **Writing Sentences with Adverbs**

Working with a partner or group, write a sentence that correctly uses each of the following adverbs. Be prepared to share your answers with another group or with the class.

INSTRUCTOR'S NOTE

Answers will vary. Possible answers shown at right.

1. rarely   *I rarely take long car trips.*

2. completely   *Her story was completely untrue.*

3. never   *Mrs. Evans has never returned to American Samoa.*

4. sadly   *The lost boy was sadly quiet about his parents.*

5. slowly   *The artist slowly began his work on the canvas.*

6. often   *Esther often takes her lunch to work.*

7. viciously   *Angered by the questions, Joe responded viciously.*

8. truly   *Last week I saw a truly inspiring movie.*

9. always   *You always cook beans and rice on the weekend.*

10. really   *Arthur looked really handsome in his new clothes.*

HINTS ABOUT ADJECTIVES AND ADVERBS

TEACHING TIP

Distribute copies of a recent local newspaper article about a prominent person or issue. Ask one group to find adjectives and the words they modify; ask the other group to find adverbs and the words they modify. Then ask each group to find the most descriptive sentence. Discuss why some sentences are more descriptive than others.

Do not use an adjective when you need an adverb. Some writers make the mistake of using an adjective when they need an adverb.

not this: Talk to me ~~honest~~.
but this: Talk to me *honestly*.

not this: You can say it ~~simple~~.
but this: You can say it *simply*.

not this: He was breathing ~~deep~~.
but this: He was breathing *deeply*.

Exercise 6   **Changing Adjectives to Adverbs**

In each pair of sentences, change the underlined adjective in the first sentence to an adverb in the second sentence. The first one is done for you.

1. a. She is a graceful dancer.

   b. She dances *gracefully*.

2. a. Gloria gave an impatient response.

   b. Gloria responded *impatiently*.

3. a. Mrs. Goldstein was a recent visitor to Concord.

   b. Mrs. Goldstein *recently* visited Concord.

4. a. As she drove to the emergency room, Abigail was <u>nervous</u>.

   b. Abigail *nervously* _____ drove to the emergency room.

5. a. After the contestant conquered his stage fright, his singing was <u>magnificent</u>.

   b. After the contestant conquered his stage fright, he sang *magnificently* ____.

6. a. The team's second try for the title had <u>significant</u> differences from its first attempt.

   b. The team's second try for the title was *significantly* _____ different from its first attempt.

7. a. Governor Millburn's defense of his decision was <u>calm</u>.

   b. Governor Millburn *calmly* _____ defended his decision.

8. a. Cristina made a <u>steady</u> advance to the finish line.

   b. Cristina *steadily* _____ advanced to the finish line.

9. a. The store manager's apology seemed <u>sincere</u>.

   b. The store manager apologized *sincerely* _____.

10. a. Ali was a <u>regular</u> contributor to the Children's Home Fund.

    b. Ali *regularly* _____ contributed to the Children's Home Fund.

Don't Confuse *Good* and *Well*, or *Bad* and *Badly*

Remember that *good* is an adjective; it describes nouns. *Well* is an adverb; it describes verbs. (The only time *well* can be used as an adjective is when it means "healthy": *I feel well today.*

> **not this:** You ran that race ~~good~~.
> **but this:** You ran that race *well*.

> **not this:** I cook eggs ~~good~~.
> **but this:** I cook eggs *well*.

> **not this:** How ~~good~~ do you understand grammar?
> **but this:** How *well* do you understand grammar?

Bad is an adjective; it describes nouns. It also follows being verbs like *is*, *are*, *was*, *am*, and *has been*. Words like *feels*, *looks*, *seems*, *smells*, *sounds*, and *tastes* are part of the group called being verbs. *Badly* is an adverb; it describes action verbs.

> **not this:** He feels ~~badly~~ about his mistake.
> **but this:** He feels *bad* about his mistake. (*Feels* is a being verb; it is described by the adjective *bad.*)

> **not this:** That soup smells ~~badly~~.
> **but this:** That soup smells *bad*. (*Smells* is a being verb; it is described by the adjective *bad.*)

> **not this:** He dances ~~bad~~.
> **but this:** He dances *badly*. (*Dances* is an action verb; it is described by the adverb *badly.*)

Exercise 7 Using *Good* and *Well, Bad* and *Badly*

Write the appropriate word in the following sentences.

1. Arthur sold his car to his sister Kathleen, who wanted it *badly* (bad, badly).

2. Teresa skipped her math class yesterday because she didn't feel *well* (good, well).

3. A day after I had my computer repaired, it worked *well* (good, well), but a week later, it started working *badly* (bad, badly) again.

4. The first firefighter on the scene could have been *badly* (bad, badly) hurt by smoke inhalation.

5. When Pete concentrates on his game, he does *well* (good, well) at regional golf tournaments.

6. My sister has never been a *good* (good, well) liar, but my brother has a gift for lying *well* (good, well).

7. No one wanted to buy the house because it was *badly* (bad, badly) decorated.

8. How *good* (good, well) do you think the movie will be?

9. I shouldn't have bought the new shaving gel; it smells *bad* (bad, badly) on my skin.

10. I feel *bad* (bad, badly) about forgetting Charlene's birthday.

Not *More* + *-er* or *Most* + *-est*

Be careful. Never write both an *-er* ending and *more*, or an *-est* ending and *most*.

> **not this:** I want to work with someone ~~more smarter~~.
> **but this:** I want to work with someone *smarter*.

> **not this:** Alan is the ~~most richest~~ man in town.
> **but this:** Alan is the *richest* man in town.

Use *Than*, not *Then*, in Comparisons

When you compare things, use *than*. *Then* means "at a later time."

> **not this:** You are taller ~~then~~ I am.
> **but this:** You are taller *than* I am.

> **not this:** I'd like a car that is faster ~~then~~ my old one.
> **but this:** I'd like a car that is faster *than* my old one.

When Do I Need a Comma between Adjectives?

Sometimes you use more than one adjective to describe a noun.

> I visited a cold, dark cave.
> The cat had pale blue eyes.

If you look at the preceding examples, one uses a comma between the adjectives *cold* and *dark*, but the other does not have a comma between the adjectives *pale* and *blue*. Both sentences are correctly punctuated. To decide whether you need a comma, try one of these tests:

Test 1:   Try to put *and* between the adjectives. If the sentence still makes sense, put a comma between the adjectives.

>   **check for comma:** I visited a cold, dark cave. (Do you need the comma? Add *and* between the adjectives.)
>   **add *and*:** I visited a cold *and* dark cave. (Does the sentence still make sense? Yes. You need the comma.)
>   **correct sentence:** I visited a cold, dark cave.

>   **check for comma:** The cat had pale blue eyes. (Do you need the comma? Add *and* between the adjectives.)
>   **add *and*:** The cat had pale *and* blue eyes. (Does the sentence still make sense? No. You do not need the comma.)
>   **correct sentence:** The cat had pale blue eyes.

Test 2:   Try to reverse the order of the adjectives. If the sentence still makes sense, put a comma between the adjectives.

>   **check for comma:** I visited a cold, dark cave. (Do you need the comma? Reverse the order of the adjectives.)
>   **reverse order:** I visited a dark, cold cave. (Does the sentence still make sense? Yes. You need the comma.)
>   **correct sentence:** I visited a cold, dark cave.

>   **check for comma:** The cat had pale blue eyes. (Do you need the comma? Reverse the order of the adjectives.)
>   **reverse order:** The cat had blue pale eyes. (Does the sentence still make sense? No. You don't need a comma.)
>   **correct sentence:** The cat had pale blue eyes.

You can use Test 1 or Test 2 to determine whether you need a comma between adjectives.

Exercise 8   **Editing for Errors in Adjectives and Adverbs**

Connect

Edit the following paragraph, correcting all the errors in the use of adjectives and adverbs. Write your corrections above the errors. There are seven errors.

    Many of the contests on television are fun to watch, but they have a few dark

good

elements. The winners of a singing contest, for example, feel extremely well at the

terribly

end of competition, but many other contestants suffer terrible. They are called the

losers, and after one last moment of public grief and shame, they must slink off

the stage in disgrace. Even though those who didn't win might have exceptional

talents, their talents seem worthless because they are not winners. The audience

really

for such competitions is left with a disturbing message: unless a person is real

hard, cruel

talented, there is no place for him or her in the hard cruel world of show business.

In addition, the audience for such competitions develops a nasty attitude toward

the contestants. For example, when viewers watch young women struggle to

become a top model, some viewers ridicule any contestant with even a smaller
small

completely
flaw. In the real world, people are rarely complete beautiful or perfectly talented.

However, the impossible standards and cruel process of picking a winner can
bad

make anyone, competing or watching, feel badly.

Connect

Exercise 9 Editing for Errors in Adjectives and Adverbs

Edit the following paragraph, correcting all the errors in the use of adjectives and adverbs. Write your corrections above the errors. There are seven errors.

most
Taking my driving test was the more frightening experience in my life. As soon

easy
as I saw the examiner, I knew this process would not be easily. The man never

smiled or said hello, just hung on to his clipboard and directed me to the driver's

seat. As I started the car, he gave me his first command. One after another, the

directions continued. After I performed each task, the examiner wrote something

really
on his clipboard. After ten minutes of this treatment, I was real scared. I was
desperate
desperately to get a look at his writing, but I couldn't see it. I couldn't understand

~~more~~ *kinder*
why this man couldn't be more kinder. Finally, he stopped giving orders, and we

returned to the license bureau's parking lot. As I sat in the car, facing front, my

well
eyes filled with panic. "You don't have to worry," the examiner said. "You did good.

more
You'll get your license." Suddenly I felt that this flinty-eyed man was most compas-

sionate than anyone else in the world. I wanted to hug him, but his clipboard was

in the way.

Chapter Test: Using Adjectives and Adverbs

Some of the following sentences have errors in the use of adjectives and adverbs. Some are correct. Put an *X* by each sentence with an error.

1. ___X___ The O'Brien family owns two restaurants; the one downtown is the most expensive.

2. ___X___ I couldn't hear Benjamin's speech because he was speaking too quiet.

3. ___X___ When no one compliments my cooking, I feel badly.

4. _____ Of all the hairstyles you have tried, this one is the least attractive.

5. ___X___ Ryan painted the exterior of the house a light, blue color.

6. _____ I can't decide which phone plan is the better buy because they both seem inexpensive.

7. ___X___ All four of my aunts were constant complainers; Aunt Lucy was the worse.

8. ___X___ Do you think I look well in my new jacket?

9. ___X___ Sam had never seen a dog more uglier than his sister's hound.

10. _____ The witness was really nervous when the police questioned him.

Correcting Problems with Modifiers

Modifiers are words, phrases, or clauses that describe (modify) something in a sentence. All the italicized words, phrases, and clauses below are modifiers.

the *blue* van (word)
the van *in the garage* (phrase)
the van *that she bought* (clause)

foreign tourists (word)
tourists *coming to Florida* (phrase)
tourists *who visit the state* (clause)

Sometimes modifiers limit another word. They make another word (or words) more specific.

the girl *in the corner* (tells exactly which girl)
fifty acres (tells exactly how many acres)
the movie *that I liked best* (tells which movie)
He *never* calls. (tells how often)

Exercise 1   **Recognizing Modifiers**

In each sentence below, underline the modifiers (words, phrases, or clauses) that describe the italicized word or phrase.

1. *A* chocolate *sundae* with sprinkles on top makes my nephew smile with pleasure.

2. Walking confidently down the red carpet, *the celebrity* waved to his fans.

3. Ava searched through the debris for family *photographs* lost in the flood.

4. Smiling at me from the back row of the classroom, *my sister* applauded my speech.

5. Mark and Aaron have adopted *a* friendly stray *cat.*

6. *The passengers* waiting at the terminal for hours began to complain loudly.

7. *The woman* selected for the top job once worked at a local bank.

8. My boyfriend was amused by *a* little *boy* playing with a large beach ball.

9. *The truck* with a dent in its rear bumper belongs to Silvio.

10. Danny couldn't help laughing at *the bully* covered in mud.

CORRECTING MODIFIER PROBLEMS

Modifiers can make your writing more specific and more concrete. Used effectively and correctly, modifiers give the reader a clear, exact picture of what you want to say, and they help you to say it precisely. But modifiers have to be used correctly. You can check for errors with modifiers as you revise your sentences.

INFO BOX: **Three Steps in Checking for Sentence Errors with Modifiers**

Step 1:   Find the modifier.

Step 2:   Ask, "Does the modifier have something to modify?"

Step 3:   Ask, "Is the modifier in the right place, as close as possible to the word, phrase, or clause it modifies?"

If you answer no in either Step 2 or Step 3, you need to revise your sentence. Let's use the steps in the following example.

sample sentence: I saw a girl driving a Mazda wearing a bikini.

Step 1: Find the modifier. The modifiers are *driving a Mazda, wearing a bikini.*

Step 2: Ask, "Does the modifier have something to modify?" The answer is yes. The girl is driving a Mazda. The girl is wearing a bikini. Both modifiers go with *a girl*.

Step 3: Ask, "Is the modifier in the right place?" The answer is yes and no. One modifier is in the right place:

I saw a *girl driving a Mazda*

The other modifier is *not* in the right place:

a Mazda wearing a bikini

The Mazda is not wearing a bikini.

> **revised:** I saw a girl *wearing a bikini* and *driving a Mazda.*

Let's work through the steps once more:

> **sample sentence:** Scampering through the forest, the hunters saw two rabbits.

Step 1: Find the modifier. The modifiers are *scampering through the forest,* and *two.*

Step 2: Ask, "Does the modifier have something to modify?" The answer is yes. There are *two rabbits.* The *rabbits* are *scampering through the forest.*

Step 3: Ask, "Is the modifier in the right place?" The answer is yes and no. The word *two* is in the right place:

two rabbits

But *scampering through the forest* is in the wrong place:

Scampering through the forest, the hunters

The hunters are not scampering through the forest—the rabbits are.

> **revised:** The hunters saw two rabbits *scampering through the forest.*

TEACHING TIP

Tell students that misplaced modifiers are common errors, even in newspaper and magazine articles. See if they can write misplaced modifiers intentionally and then have students read their "incorrect" sentences. Ask students to explain how the modifiers are in an illogical place. Some responses may be quite amusing.

Caution: Be sure to put words like *almost, even, exactly, hardly, just, merely, nearly, only, scarcely,* and *simply* as close as possible to what they modify. If you put them in the wrong place, you may write a confusing sentence.

> **sample sentence:** Etienne only wants to grow carrots and zucchini. (The modifier that creates confusion here is *only.* Does Etienne have only one goal in life—to grow carrots and zucchini? Or are these the only vegetables he wants to grow? To create a clearer sentence, move the modifier.)
> **revised:** Etienne wants to grow *only* carrots and zucchini.

The examples you have just worked with show one common error in using modifiers. This error involves **misplaced modifiers**, words that describe something but are not where they should be in the sentence. Here is the rule to remember:

> **Put a modifier as close as possible to the word, phrase, or clause it modifies.**

Exercise 2 **Correcting Sentences with Misplaced Modifiers**

Some of the following sentences contain misplaced modifiers. Revise any sentence that has a misplaced modifier by putting the modifier as close as possible to whatever it modifies.

1. Hanging from the ceiling, I noticed a giant spider.

    revised: *I noticed a giant spider hanging from the ceiling.*

2. The village is well known for its giant garbage dump where I was born.

    revised: *The village where I was born is well known for its giant garbage dump.*

3. Ray lent the tools to a friendly neighbor that he bought at a garage sale.

    revised: *Ray lent the tools that he bought at a garage sale to a friendly neighbor.*

4. Callie and Jeremy were surprised by the sudden appearance of two deer driving in the national forest.

    revised: *Driving in the national forest, Callie and Jeremy were surprised by the sudden appearance of two deer.*

5. Painted a pale green, the old house looked new again.

    revised: *OK*

6. Dipped in chocolate, my aunt enjoyed the large, plump strawberries.

    revised: *My aunt enjoyed the large, plump strawberries dipped in chocolate.*

7. Standing in line at the ticket counter, the children grew restless and bored.

    revised: *OK*

8. Right from the oven, Annie served the cinnamon cookies.

    revised: *Annie served the cinnamon cookies right from the oven.*

9. Tommy was so hungry that he almost ate everything on the table.

    revised: *Tommy was so hungry that he ate almost everything on the table.*

10. The twins nearly waited for an hour before an emergency vehicle came to help them.

    revised: *The twins waited for nearly an hour before an emergency vehicle came to help them.*

Correcting Dangling Modifiers

The three steps for correcting modifier problems can help you recognize another kind of error. Let's use the steps to check the following sentence.

> **sample sentence:** Strolling through the tropical paradise, many colorful birds could be seen.

> **Step 1:** Find the modifier. The modifiers are *Strolling through the tropical paradise* and *many colorful.*

> **Step 2:** Ask, "Does the modifier have something to modify?" The answer is yes and no. The words *many* and *colorful* modify birds. But who or what is strolling through the tropical paradise? There is no person mentioned in this sentence. The birds are not strolling.

This kind of error is called a **dangling modifier**. It is a modifier that does not have anything to modify; it just dangles in the sentence. To correct this kind of error, you cannot just move the modifier:

> **still incorrect:** Many colorful birds could be seen strolling through the tropical paradise. (There is still no person strolling.)

The way to correct this kind of error is to add something to the sentence. If you gave the modifier something to modify, you might come up with several different revised sentences:

> **revised sentences:** *As I strolled through the tropical paradise, I saw* many colorful birds.

or

> Many colorful birds could be seen *when we were strolling through the tropical paradise.*

or

> *While the tourists strolled through the tropical paradise, they saw* many colorful birds.

Try the process for correcting dangling modifiers once more:

> **sample sentence:** Ascending in the glass elevator, the hotel lobby glittered in the light.

> **Step 1:** Find the modifier. The modifiers are *Ascending in the glass elevator* and *hotel.*

> **Step 2:** Ask, "Does the modifier have anything to modify?" The answer is yes and no. The word *hotel* modifies lobby, but *Ascending in the glass elevator* doesn't modify anything. Who is ascending in the elevator? There is nobody mentioned in the sentence.

To revise this sentence, put somebody or something in it for the modifier to describe:

> *As the guests ascended in the glass elevator*, the hotel lobby glittered in the light.

or

Ascending in the glass elevator, she saw the hotel lobby glitter in the light.

Remember that you cannot correct a dangling modifier just by moving the modifier. You have to give the modifier something to modify; you have to add something to the sentence.

Exercise 3 **Correcting Sentences with Dangling Modifiers**

Some of the following sentences use modifiers correctly. Some sentences have dangling modifiers. Revise the sentences with dangling modifiers. To revise, you will have to add words and change words.

INSTRUCTOR'S NOTE

Answers will vary. Possible answers shown at left.

1. When accelerating to make a green light, an accident can occur.

   revised: *Accelerating to make a green light, a careless driver can cause an accident.*

2. While volunteering at an animal shelter on the weekends, Christopher met a beautiful woman.

   revised: *OK*

3. To find a house in a lower price range, looking farther from the city is necessary.

   revised: *To find a house in a lower price range, you have to look farther from the city.*

4. Having trained as a paramedic in the army, Jose's skills would help him to find a job in civilian life.

   revised: *Having trained as a paramedic in the army, Jose believed that his skills would help him to find a job in civilian life.*

5. Unprepared for a hot day, people began shedding their coats and sweaters.

   revised: *OK*

6. Listening to another of his father's rants, anger began to fill David's head.

   revised: *Listening to another of his father's rants, David was filled with anger.*

7. With hard work and a positive attitude, many of the setbacks and disappointments of a new job can be handled.

   revised: *If a person works hard and maintains a positive attitude, he or she can handle many of the setbacks and disappointments of a new job.*

8. At the age of five, my brother was born, and I had some difficulty being the older brother.

revised: *When I was five, my brother was born, and I had some difficulty being the older brother.*

9. After much discussion and some argument, an agreement was reached.

revised: *The council members reached an agreement after much discussion and some argument.*

10. Reading the letter for the second time, the terrible reality of the situation hit Ashley.

revised: *Reading the letter for the second time, Ashley was hit by the terrible reality of the situation.*

REVIEWING THE STEPS AND THE SOLUTIONS

It is important to recognize problems with modifiers and to correct these problems. Modifier problems can result in confusing or even silly sentences. And when you confuse or unintentionally amuse your reader, you are not making your point.

Remember to check for modifier problems in three steps and to correct each kind of problem in the appropriate way.

INFO BOX: **A Summary of Modifier Problems**

Checking for Modifier Problems

Step 1: Find the modifier.

Step 2: Ask, "Does the modifier have something to modify?"

Step 3: Ask, "Is the modifier in the right place?"

Correcting Modifier Problems
If the modifier is in the wrong place (a misplaced modifier), put it as close as possible to the word, phrase, or clause it modifies.

If the modifier has nothing to modify (a dangling modifier), add or change words so that it has something to modify.

Collaborate

Exercise 4 **Revising Sentences with Modifier Problems**

All of the following sentences have modifier problems. Working with a partner or group, write a new, correct sentence for each incorrect one. You may move words, add words, change words, or remove words. The first one is done for you.

1. Written in stone, the archaeologist could not understand the ancient message.

revised: *The archaeologist could not understand the ancient message written in stone.*

2. Looking for a compatible mate, friends and family members may know several potential partners.

   revised: *If someone is looking for a compatible mate, friends and family members may know several potential partners.*

INSTRUCTOR'S NOTE

Answers will vary. Possible answers shown at left.

3. Without time to study and do homework, surviving in college becomes impossible.

   revised: *Without time to study and do homework, a person will not survive in college.*

4. Daniel is so absentminded that he nearly loses a pen every time he goes to class.

   revised: *Daniel is so absentminded that he loses a pen nearly every time he goes to class.*

5. Proudly carrying a shoe in his mouth, Tommy saw his dog Rocco emerge from the closet.

   revised: *Tommy saw his dog Rocco, proudly carrying a shoe in his mouth, emerge from the closet.*

6. Exhausted after a long day at work, Tina only watched half an hour of television before she fell asleep.

   revised: *Exhausted after a long day at work, Tina watched only half an hour of television before she fell asleep.*

7. An angry man stormed into the police station covered in mud.

   revised: *An angry man covered in mud stormed into the police station.*

8. Before buying a new home, the needs of all the family members should be considered.

   revised: *Before buying a new home, parents should consider the needs of all the family members.*

9. To restore the downtown plaza to its place as the center of the community, the support of all the citizens is necessary.

   revised: *Without the support of all the citizens, we cannot restore the downtown plaza to its place as the center of the community.*

10. Covered in fudge icing, I couldn't stop eating the brownies.

    revised: *I couldn't stop eating the brownies covered in fudge icing.*

Exercise 5 **Editing a Paragraph for Modifier Problems**

Connect

Correct any errors in the use of modifiers in the following paragraph. There are five errors. Write your corrections in the space above the line.

I planned carefully for my college expenses, but I missed some important

items. I never anticipated the little things that add up to big money. Of course, I

budgeted for tuition, books, and lab fees. As a result, I thought I was financially

not always
safe. Unfortunately, reality does always not match a person's expectations. For

I need a series of snacks.
example, to survive a long day or night of classes, a series of snacks are essential.

These snacks are not cheap. I find myself feeding several dollars a day into vora-

I have to stretch my budget to pay for items needed in
cious vending machines. Needed in various classes, my budget must stretch to pay

various classes.
for items. For example, I need large note cards so that I can write a research

paper. I need a graphing calculator for my math class. There are other expenses. I

spend hours driving through campus parking lots, looking for a place to park.

When I find one, I take it and race to class at the last minute. Finding an expensive

I want to scream.
parking ticket on my car window later in the day, screaming is what I want.

expected only
I only expected the big costs of college; however, the little ones are killing me.

Connect

Exercise 6   **Editing a Paragraph for Modifier Problems**

Correct any errors in the use of modifiers in the following paragraph. There
are five errors. Write your corrections in the space above the line.

be just
Stuffed animals used to just be for children, but they are nearly universal fig-

ures today. Teenage girls can be seen carrying their teddy bears or Disney figures

Drivers
on airplanes. In the rear windows of their cars, drivers in their twenties, thirties,

in the rear windows of their cars.
or forties place stuffed mascots. Many adults have small plush toys in their cubi-

When people cannot
cles at work. When unable to decide on a gift, stuffed animals become the answer.

Patients in hospitals get them instead of flowers, wives and girlfriends love them

on Valentine's Day, and a huge plush snake, alligator, or lizard will amuse a grown

man. Some stuffed animals have become collectibles. A few years ago, thousands

of people fought to own the latest Beanie Baby. Today, many expensive depart-

ment stores offer a new version of the store's trademark Teddy bear each year.

stuffed animals are irresistible.
Funny looking, soft, and huggable, the appeal of stuffed animals is irresistible.

They comfort the child in every adult.
In every adult, they comfort the child.

Chapter Test: Correcting Problems with Modifiers

Some of the sentences below have problems with modifiers; some are correct. Put an *X* by each sentence with a modifier problem.

1. __*X*__ When fighting a bad cold, getting plenty of rest and drinking plenty of fluids can help.

2. _____ Before purchasing a car, buyers should compare the base prices and costs of options on several makes and models.

3. __*X*__ Lying by the campfire, the stars seemed magnificent and mysterious.

4. _____ Overjoyed at the idea of a walk in the woods, my dog leaped high into the air.

5. __*X*__ Crawling with insects, Joanna tossed the rotten meat into the garbage.

6. _____ Wanting to impress her new friend, Cathy spent nearly half of her paycheck on new clothes.

7. __*X*__ In order to get to Hillcrest, a drive through the suburbs of Parkside is unavoidable.

8. __*X*__ At the age of seven, my older sister got married, and I no longer had to share a bedroom with her.

9. __*X*__ Adrian gave the furniture to a friend that he didn't need anymore.

10. __*X*__ Creeping across my sheets, I saw a large spider.

Using Verbs Correctly

Verbs are words that show some kind of action or being. The following verbs show action or being:

> He *runs* to the park.
> Melanie *is* my best friend.
> The pizza *tastes* delicious.

Verbs also tell about time.

> He *will run* to the park. (The time is future.)
> Melanie *was* my best friend. (The time is past.)
> The pizza *tastes* delicious. (The time is present.)

The time of a verb is called its *tense.* You can say a verb is in the *present tense, future tense,* or many other tenses.

Using verbs correctly involves knowing which form of the verb to use, choosing the right verb tense, and being consistent in verb tense.

USING STANDARD VERB FORMS

Many people use nonstandard verb forms in everyday conversation. But everyone who wants to write and speak effectively should know different levels of language, from the slang and dialect of everyday conversation to the **standard English** of college, business, and professional environments.

In everyday conversation, you may use **nonstandard forms** like these:

I goes	he don't	we was
you was	it don't	she smile
you be	I be	they walks

But these are not correct forms in standard English.

THE PRESENT TENSE

Look at the standard verb forms for the present tense of the word *listen*:

verb: listen

I listen	we listen
you listen	you listen
he, she, it listens	they listen

Take a closer look at the standard verb forms. Only one form is different:

he, she, it *listens*

This is the only form that ends in *s* in the present tense.

> **INFO BOX:** In the present tense, use an *-s* or *-es* ending on the verb only when the subject is *he*, *she*, or *it*, or the equivalent, such as a proper name or a singular noun.

He calls his mother every day.
She chases the cat away from the bird cage.
It runs like a new car.

Jim calls his mother every day.
Samantha chases the cat away from the bird cage.
The jalopy runs like a new car.

Take another look at the present tense. If the verb is a standard verb, it will follow this form in the present tense.

I attend every lecture.
You care about the truth.
He visits his grandfather regularly.
She drives a new car.
The new *album sounds* great.
We follow that team.
You work well when you both compromise.
They buy the store brand of cereal.

Exercise 1 Picking the Correct Verb in the Present Tense

Underline the subject and circle the correct verb form in parentheses in each of the following sentences.

1. <u>Confidence</u> (keep, (keeps)) a person calm in stressful situations.

2. In bright light, my <u>aunt</u> (look, (looks)) tired and worn.

INSTRUCTOR'S NOTE

For more on using the correct verb form in sentences with prepositional phrases, see Chapter 25, "Making Subjects and Verbs Agree."

3. With faith in the future, <u>Ramon</u> (stay, (stays)) cheerful and focused.

4. At the front of the room ((hang), hangs) an American <u>flag</u> and a <u>picture</u> of George Washington.

5. A <u>cookie</u> with chocolate chips (taste, (tastes)) better than a plain cookie.

6. <u>Monica</u> (want, (wants)) a crib for her baby.

7. On a sunny day in October, <u>Portsmouth</u> (seem, (seems)) like the perfect place to live.

8. After a night out with your friends, <u>you</u> always ((become), becomes) more cheerful.

9. <u>Driving</u> to work in the morning always (take, (takes)) me more time in the winter.

10. On sunny days, <u>we</u> ((walk), walks) to a little shop for coconut ice cream.

TEACHING TIP

An easy rule for students to remember is that if a verb ends in *e*, they can just add a *d* for the past tense. If it ends in a consonant plus *y*, they can change the *y* to *i*.

THE PAST TENSE

The past tense of most verbs is formed by adding *-d* or *-ed* to the verb.

verb: listen

I listened	we listened
you listened	you listened
he, she, it listened	they listened

Add *-ed* to *listen* to form the past tense. For some other verbs, you may add *-d*.

The sun *faded* from the sky.
He *quaked* with fear.
She *crumpled* the paper into a ball.

Exercise 2   **Writing the Correct Verb Forms in the Past Tense**

Write the correct past tense form of each verb in parentheses in each sentence below.

1. You ___*ignored*___ (ignore) the slow leak in the basement for months.

2. Last night, Ira ___*played*___ (play) cards for two hours.

3. In sixth grade, I ___*earned*___ (earn) an award for perfect attendance.

4. For many years, my father ___*talked*___ (talk) about coming to America.

5. A truck driver ___*crossed*___ (cross) the center line on the highway.

6. On Friday, someone ___*called*___ (call) me in the middle of the night.

7. After the movie, my friends ___*invited*___ (invite) me to a Chinese restaurant.

8. After getting lost on the highway, we finally ___*discovered*___ (discover) the correct exit to the Miami airport.

9. My husband ___*blamed*___ (blame) me for our recent argument.

10. Like many young men, Michael ___*wanted*___ (want) instant success.

THE FOUR MAIN FORMS OF A VERB: PRESENT, PAST, PRESENT PARTICIPLE, PAST PARTICIPLE

When you are deciding which form of a verb to use, you will probably rely on one of four forms: the present tense, the past tense, the present participle, and the past participle. Most of the time, you will use one of these forms or add a helping verb to it. As an example, look at the four main forms of the verb *listen*.

Present	**Past**	**Present Participle**	**Past Participle**
listen	listened	listening	listened

You use the four verb forms—present, past, present participle, past participle—alone or with helping verbs, to express time (tense). Forms of regular verbs like *listen* are very easy to remember. Use the present form for the present tense:

TEACHING TIP

Remind students that by reading a draft aloud, they may find a missing *d* in some past tense forms. (Examples: "He *used* to play basketball; he was *supposed* to coach us.")

We *listen* to the news on the radio.

The past form expresses past tense:

I *listened* to language tapes for three hours yesterday.

The present participle, or *-ing* form, is used with helping verbs:

He *was listening* to me.
I *am listening* to you.
You *should have been listening* more carefully.

The past participle is the form used with the helping verbs *have*, *has*, or *had*:

ESL NOTE

Nonnative speakers may have trouble remembering the *-ed* on the past participle form. For more practice, see the section on verbs in the ESL Appendix, pp. 656–659.

I *have listened* for hours.
She *has listened* to the tape.
We *had listened* to the tape before we bought it.

Of course, you can add many helping verbs to the present tense:

present tense:
We *listen* to the news on the car radio.

add helping verbs:
We *will* listen to the news on the car radio.
We *should* listen to the news on the car radio.
We *can* listen to the news on the car radio.

When a verb is regular, the past form is created by adding *-d* or *-ed* to the present form. The present participle is formed by adding *-ing* to the present form, and the past participle form is the same as the past form.

IRREGULAR VERBS

Irregular verbs do not follow the same rules for creating verb forms that regular verbs do. Three verbs that we use all the time—*be, have, do*—are irregular verbs. You need to study them closely. Look at the present tense forms for all three, and compare the standard present tense forms to the nonstandard ones. *Remember to use the standard forms for college or professional writing.*

verb: be

Nonstandard	Standard
~~I be~~ or ~~I is~~	I am
~~you be~~	you are
~~he, she, it be~~	he, she, it is
~~we be~~	we are
~~you be~~	you are
~~they be~~	they are

verb: have

Nonstandard	Standard
~~I has~~	I have
~~you has~~	you have
~~he, she, it have~~	he, she, it has
~~we has~~	we have
~~you has~~	you have
~~they has~~	they have

verb: do

Nonstandard	Standard
~~I does~~	I do
~~you does~~	you do
~~he, she, it do~~	he, she, it does
~~we does~~	we do
~~you does~~	you do
~~they does~~	they do

Caution: Be careful when you add *not* to *does*. If you are writing a contraction of *does not*, be sure you write *doesn't*, not *don't*.

not this: ~~The light don't work.~~
but this: The light doesn't work.

Exercise 3　**Choosing the Correct Form of *be*, *have*, or *do* in the Present Tense**

Circle the correct form of the verb in parentheses in each sentence below.

1. A few comments on the plan for the new stadium (be, **are**) appearing in the local newspaper.

2. Sometimes, you (**do**, does) too much of your studying at the last minute.

3. By the end of the spring, we (be, **are**) sick of rainy days and gray skies.

4. Divorced parents (has, **have**) to maintain good relationships for the sake of their children.

5. Carlos' friends ((do), does) his chores when he goes into the hospital for treatment.

6. On business trips, Selina ((has), have) little time to rest.

7. After a bad storm, it (be, (is)) dangerous to touch any fallen wires.

8. My art appreciation class (don't, (doesn't)) require a research paper.

9. Because of his bilingual background, Alan ((has), have) an opportunity to work for an international company.

10. At night, I (be, (am)) often awake until midnight.

The Past Tense of *be*, *have*, and *do*

The past forms of these irregular verbs can be confusing. Again, compare the nonstandard forms to the standard forms. *Remember to use the standard forms for college or professional writing.*

verb: be

Nonstandard	Standard
~~I were~~	I was
~~you was~~	you were
~~he, she, it were~~	he, she, it was
~~we was~~	we were
~~you was~~	you were
~~they was~~	they were

verb: have

Nonstandard	Standard
~~I has~~	I had
~~you has~~	you had
~~he, she, it have~~	he, she, it had
~~we has~~	we had
~~you has~~	you had
~~they has~~	they had

verb: do

Nonstandard	Standard
~~I done~~	I did
~~you done~~	you did
~~he, she, it done~~	he, she, it did
~~we done~~	we did
~~you done~~	you did
~~they done~~	they did

Exercise 4   **Choosing the Correct Form of *be*, *have*, or *do* in the Past Tense**

Circle the correct verb form in parentheses in each of the following sentences.

1. My mother (done, (did)) everything in her power to keep her children safe and strong.

2. Years ago, Kathleen Duval ((was), were) my first girlfriend.

3. At age two, I ((was), were) known for my ability to sing to anyone who would listen.

4. Although I disliked high school, I (done, (did)) well in most of my classes.

5. In October, a good friend and his brother (was, (were)) driving to work when a flash flood occurred

6. On Valentine's Day, I ((had), has) an unexpected call from my former boyfriend.

7. After Suzanne and I visited Disney World, we (was, (were)) determined to save our money for another visit.

8. No one liked to sign up for classes in the old sign building because it (have, (had)) a strange odor.

9. Nicole complained about being unemployed, but she (done, (did)) nothing to change her situation.

10. The surface of the kitchen counter ((was), were) dull and sticky.

More Irregular Verb Forms

Be, *have*, and *do* are not the only verbs with irregular forms. There are many such verbs, and everybody who writes uses some form of an irregular verb. When you write and you are not certain if you are using the correct form of a verb, check the list of irregular verbs on pages 468–470.

For each irregular verb listed below, the *present*, the *past*, and the *past participle* forms are given. The present participle isn't included because it is always formed by adding *-ing* to the present form.

Irregular Verb Forms

Present	Past	Past Participle
(Today I *arise*.)	(Yesterday I *arose*.)	(I have/had *arisen*.)
arise	arose	arisen
awake	awoke, awaked	awoken, awaked
bear	bore	born, borne
beat	beat	beaten
become	became	become
begin	began	begun
bend	bent	bent
bite	bit	bitten
bleed	bled	bled
blow	blew	blown
break	broke	broken
bring	brought	brought
build	built	built
burst	burst	burst
buy	bought	bought
catch	caught	caught
choose	chose	chosen
cling	clung	clung
come	came	come
cost	cost	cost
creep	crept	crept

Present	Past	Past Participle
cut	cut	cut
deal	dealt	dealt
draw	drew	drawn
dream	dreamed, dreamt	dreamed, dreamt
drink	drank	drunk
drive	drove	driven
eat	ate	eaten
fall	fell	fallen
feed	fed	fed
feel	felt	felt
fight	fought	fought
find	found	found
fling	flung	flung
fly	flew	flown
freeze	froze	frozen
get	got	got, gotten
give	gave	given
go	went	gone
grow	grew	grown
hear	heard	heard
hide	hid	hidden
hit	hit	hit
hold	held	held
hurt	hurt	hurt
keep	kept	kept
know	knew	known
lay (means to put)	laid	laid
lead	led	led
leave	left	left
lend	lent	lent
let	let	let
lie (means to recline)	lay	lain
light	lit, lighted	lit, lighted
lose	lost	lost
make	made	made
mean	meant	meant
meet	met	met
pay	paid	paid
ride	rode	ridden
ring	rang	rung
rise	rose	risen
run	ran	run
say	said	said
see	saw	seen
sell	sold	sold
send	sent	sent
sew	sewed	sewn, sewed
shake	shook	shaken
shine	shone, shined	shone, shined
shrink	shrank	shrunk
shut	shut	shut
sing	sang	sung

Present	Past	Past Participle
sit	sat	sat
sleep	slept	slept
slide	slid	slid
sling	slung	slung
speak	spoke	spoken
spend	spent	spent
stand	stood	stood
steal	stole	stolen
stick	stuck	stuck
sting	stung	stung
stink	stank, stunk	stunk
string	strung	strung
swear	swore	sworn
swim	swam	swum
teach	taught	taught
tear	tore	torn
tell	told	told
think	thought	thought
throw	threw	thrown
wake	woke, waked	woken, waked
wear	wore	worn
win	won	won
write	wrote	written

Exercise 5 Choosing the Correct Form of Irregular Verbs

Write the correct form of the verb in parentheses in each sentence below. Be sure to check the list of irregular verbs.

1. Someone had _slung_ (sling) a wet coat over the stair railing.

2. For as long as I have _known_ (know) him, my father has loved soccer.

3. For years, my sister has _clung_ (cling) to the fantasy of becoming a famous singer.

4. Last week's storm _dealt_ (deal) a terrible blow to the town of Crosswell.

5. When she was thirty, Mrs. Franklin _chose_ (choose) to start a new life.

6. After his father died, Anton _grew_ (grow) up fast.

7. People began leaving the stadium when it became clear that the visiting team had _beaten_ (beat) the home team.

8. Matthew was so angry at his sister that he _flung_ (fling) her letter into the trash bin.

9. Michelle and Nestor have _come_ (come) to a decision about moving out of Bakersfield.

10. All the flowers in the yard _froze_ (freeze) during the night.

Exercise 6 **Writing Sentences with Correct Verb Forms**

With a partner or a group, write two sentences that correctly use each of the verb forms below. In writing these sentences, you may add helping verbs to the verb forms, but do not change the verb form itself. The first one is done for you.

1. sent

    a. *He sent her a dozen roses on Valentine's Day.*

    b. *I have sent him all the information he needs.*

2. lie (means to recline)

    a. *Why don't you lie on the sofa while I make dinner?*

    b. *After work, Sam is so tired he has to lie down for an hour.*

3. shrank

    a. *You put my shirt in hot water and shrank it.*

    b. *Over the years, his enormous ego shrank a little bit.*

4. meant

    a. *The coach meant what she said about missing practices.*

    b. *Lenny never meant to hurt you; he was just upset.*

5. paid

    a. *We paid too much for that old Mitsubishi.*

    b. *I have always paid my bills on time.*

6. lain

    a. *That cat has lain on the windowsill all morning.*

    b. *My chemistry textbook had lain in a puddle all night.*

7. shined

    a. *Before the job interview, I shined my best shoes.*

    b. *The sun has shined on us for three straight weeks.*

8. seen

    a. *I have not seen a movie in six months.*

    b. *Has anyone seen Ricardo lately?*

9. wore

    a. *Taking care of the twins last weekend wore me out.*

    b. *When she was a teenager, Michelle never wore bright colors.*

10. born

    a. *I was born in a little town in Maine.*

    b. *No one could have born the heat in the desert for long.*

INSTRUCTOR'S NOTE

Answers will vary. Possible answers shown at left.

Connect

Exercise 7 **Editing a Paragraph for Correct Verb Forms**

Correct the errors in verb forms in the following paragraph. There are six errors.

do
    I does not want to be a millionaire although I would like to have enough

money to pay all my bills regularly. Worrying about credit card payments and my

pile
car loan can keep me up at night. Every month, when the bills piles up, I wonder

how to economize. Maybe I could sell my car and take public transportation to

work and school. Maybe I could find a better-paying job. My needs do not require

have
millions of dollars. In fact, I would never want to be rich. Rich people has their

chosen
own problems. They must worry about whether they have chose the right invest-
found   *is*
ments and finded trustworthy advisors. My goal is more limited; it be to have

enough money to sleep soundly at night.

Connect

Exercise 8 **Editing a Paragraph for Correct Verb Forms**

Correct the errors in verb forms in the following paragraph. There are ten errors.

are
    Unless you be shy, you cannot understand a shy person. Shy people are often

considered snobs because they don't talk to strangers, even in familiar situations.

For example, I have often sat in the same seat in the same classroom for ten
said   *thought*
weeks and not sayed a word. The teacher and the students probably thinked I was
was
arrogant, but I were just scared. In addition, some shy people are considered
get   *find*
dependent or possessive. Shy people gets these labels because they finds it hard
cling
to make friends. Once they do make a friend, shy people clings to that person out
is
of fear of losing him or her. If you are not shy yourself, remember that what be so
feels
easy for you feel nearly impossible for a shy person. Then be patient as the fearful
finds
person find his or her way.

Chapter Test: Using Verbs Correctly

Some of the sentences below use verbs correctly; others do not. Put an *X* by each sentence with an error in using verbs correctly.

1. _____ A strange-looking man led me to a dark, narrow passage.

2. __X__ When Martin has a migraine headache, he lays on the sofa for hours.

3. __X__ Spending a night in jail change my cousin's attitude.

4. _____ Roberto grew up on a farm and has ridden horses for years.

5. __X__ My truck is falling apart, so I be nervous about taking it on a long trip.

6. _____ The wind has blown nearly all the leaves off the oak tree.

7. __X__ Some animal had bit a hole in the wooden fence and gotten into a bag of seeds.

8. __X__ Courtney done nothing wrong when she kept her brother's secret.

9. __X__ For years, we have no thought about the possibility of a murder in our quiet little town.

10. __X__ I need to see a doctor, but my doctor have no appointments available until next week.

More on Verbs: Consistency and Voice

Remember that your choice of verb form indicates the time (tense) of your statements. Be careful not to shift from one tense to another unless you have a reason to change the time.

CONSISTENT VERB TENSES

Staying in one tense (unless you have a reason to change tenses) is called **consistency of verb tense**.

> **incorrect shifts in tense:**
> The waitress *ran* to the kitchen with the order in her hand, *raced* back with glasses of water for her customers, and *smiles* calmly.
> He *grins* at me from the ticket booth and *closed* the ticket window.

You can correct these errors by putting all the verbs in the same tense.

> **consistent present tense:**
> The waitress *runs* to the kitchen with the order in her hand, *races* back with glasses of water for her customers, and *smiles* calmly.
> He *grins* at me from the ticket booth and *closes* the ticket window.

consistent past tense:
The waitress *ran* to the kitchen with the order in her hand, *raced*
    back with glasses of water for her customers, and *smiled* calmly.
He *grinned* at me from the ticket booth and *closed* the ticket
    window.

Whether you correct the errors by changing all the verbs to the present
tense or by changing them to the past tense, you are making the tenses
consistent. Consistency of tense is important in the events you are describing because it helps the reader understand what happened and when it
happened.

Exercise 1   **Correcting Sentences That Are Inconsistent in Tense**

In each sentence following, one verb is inconsistent in tense. Cross it out
and write the verb in the correct tense in the space above.

1. My brother asked me to dinner, picked a fancy restaurant, and
    left
    then ~~leaves~~ me with the entire bill.

2. Tanisha takes evening classes because they don't interfere with

    her work schedule, require attendance only once a week,
    attract
    ~~attracted~~ serious students, and offer a highly concentrated ver-

    sion of the course content.

3. As soon as Rick saved enough money, he packed up his car,
    got
    drove across the country, and ~~gets~~ a job near a ski resort.

4. Because a new version of a popular cell phone was about to be
    lined
    introduced, people ~~line~~ up outside the local phone store and

    camped out overnight.

5. Charlyce slammed the front door on her angry neighbor; then the
    shouted
    neighbor ~~shouts~~ insults at the closed door until Marvin called the

    police.

6. Yesterday, my boss didn't show up at the office; at the same time,
    occurred
    major problems ~~occur~~ in the phone system, and no one knew

    how to handle the emergency.

7. Sometimes Matthew is good natured and open, but occasionally
    loses
    he worries about minor problems, ~~lost~~ his temper, and hurts his

    closest friends.

8. At the courthouse, the police department made plans for the highly publicized trial; it increased the number of security guards, made room for members of the media to file reports, and
blocked
~~blocks~~ many entrances to the building.

9. Every Tuesday and Thursday, I get up at 6:30 a.m., grab a Diet
pull
Pepsi, ~~pulled~~ on some clothes, stagger outside, and ride my bike to my 7:30 a.m. English class.

10. Whenever my dog wants to go for a walk, she jumps on the sofa,
begins
stares right into my eyes, and ~~began~~ licking me until I give in and pick up her leash.

Connect

Exercise 2   **Editing a Paragraph for Consistency of Tenses**

Read the following paragraph. Then cross out any verbs that are inconsistent in tense and write the corrections above. There are seven errors.

Waiting for my final examination grade in my Introduction to Algebra class made me very tense. After the examination, I asked my instructor when I would
said
know my grade. She ~~says~~ the grade would be posted on her office door as soon as
scored
she ~~scores~~ all the examinations in my class. She told me to check the door in two
failed
days. I knew that if I ~~fail~~ this test, I could not pass the course. I did not sleep for two days. Early in the morning of the third day, I went to my instructor's door, but
hadn't   *was*
she ~~hasn't~~ put the grades up. Worse, she ~~is~~ not in her office. Throughout the day, I checked her door so many times that I felt like I was haunting the office. Finally,
saw   *searched*
at 6:00 p.m., I ~~see~~ a list on the door. I ~~search~~ for my name and found my passing grade. The tension left my body, and I breathed freely again.

Connect

Exercise 3   **Editing a Paragraph for Consistency of Tenses**

Read the following paragraph. Then cross out any verbs that are inconsistent in tense and write the corrections above. There are five errors.

The hardest question to answer is "What do you want for your birthday?" How
tells
is anyone supposed to answer it? If a person ~~told~~ his Aunt Michelle that he wants a gift certificate for an electronics store, he is likely to be in trouble. After that

answer, Aunt Michelle suddenly realizes that her nephew hates the sweaters or

shirts she regularly gives him. If another person answers her sister's question by

runs

requesting a satellite radio system as a birthday gift, that person ~~ran~~ the risk of

being called greedy. Friends' questions are even harder to answer. A person about

has

to celebrate a birthday ~~had~~ to decide whether the right answer to the birthday

question is "You don't have to give me anything." Friends can react to this answer

by praising a person's modesty; but, on the other hand, these friends can see it as a

phony answer. The person who answers the question by saying, "I always love your

choose   *picks*

gifts, so whatever you chose is great" picked a wise answer to this tricky question.

Exercise 4   **Writing a Paragraph with Consistent Verb Tenses**

Collaborate

The paragraph following has many inconsistencies in verb tenses; it shifts between past and present tenses. Working with a group, write two versions of the paragraph: write it once in the present tense, and then a second time in the past tense. Divide your activity; half the group can write it in one tense while the other half can write it in the other tense.

After both rewrites are complete, read the new paragraphs aloud to both parts of the team as a final check.

> My best friend took me for a ride in the country and tells me some bad news. He says that in two weeks he was moving to another state. This news is very sudden and shocks me to my core. My friend is more than a friend; he was a brother, a partner in pranks, a teammate in games, and a keeper of secrets. After he told me, we walk in the woods together. We find it hard to say much because we each knew what the other is feeling. After what seems like hours, he stops walking and faces me. He says the move wasn't what he wanted, but he added that his family needs him. I see sadness in his eyes, and I knew he saw the sorrow in mine.

Paragraph Revised for Consistent Tenses:

My best friend takes me for a ride in the country and tells me some bad news. He says that in two weeks he is moving to another state. This news is very sudden and shocks me to my core. My friend is more than a friend; he is a brother, a partner in pranks, a teammate in games, and a keeper of secrets. After he tells me, we walk in the woods together. We find it hard to say much because we each know what the other is feeling. After what seems like hours, he stops walking and faces me. He says the move isn't what he wants, but he adds that his family needs him. I see sadness in his eyes, and I know he sees the sorrow in mine.

My best friend took me for a ride in the country and told me some bad news. He said that in two weeks he was moving to another state. This news was very sudden and shocked me to my core. My friend was more than a friend; he was a brother, a partner in pranks, a teammate in games, and a keeper of secrets. After he told me, we walked in the woods together. We found it hard to say much because we each knew what the other was feeling. After what seemed like hours, he stopped walking and faced me. He said the move wasn't what he wanted, but he added that his family needed him. I saw sadness in his eyes, and I knew he saw the sorrow in mine.

THE PRESENT PERFECT TENSE

When you are choosing the right verb tense, you should know about two verb tenses, the present perfect and the past perfect, that can make your meaning clear.

The **present perfect tense** is made up of the past participle form of the verb plus *have* or *has* as a helping verb. Use this tense to show an action that started in the past but is still going on in the present.

> **past tense:** My father *drove* a truck for five months. (He doesn't drive a truck anymore, but he did drive one in the past.)
> **present perfect tense:** My father *has driven* a truck for five months. (He started driving a truck five months ago; he is still driving a truck.)

> **past tense:** For years, I *studied* ballet. (I don't study ballet now; I used to.)
> **present perfect tense:** For years, I *have studied* ballet. (I still study ballet.)

Remember, use the present perfect tense to show that an action started in the past and is still going on.

> **Exercise 5** **Distinguishing between the Past Tense and the Present Perfect Tense**

Circle the correct verb in parentheses in each of the following sentences. Be sure to look carefully at the meaning of the sentences.

1. Janet (sent, (has sent)) me a text message every morning for months now.

2. After heavy rain hit the area, the brakes on my car ((felt), have felt) less efficient.

3. A burglar ((cut), has cut) a hole in the roof of a jewelry store and managed to steal the safe.

4. The Addison Steak House (won, (has won)) Kansas City's best restaurant award for several years now.

5. One of the instructors in the business department at the college ((was), has been) a well-known banker but now teaches classes in finance.

6. My four-year-old son (was, (has been)) clinging to my leg for five minutes and is still begging me for ice cream.

7. Yesterday I finally confronted my roommate and (demanded, have demanded) an an explanation for the unpaid light bill.

8. Chris and Ben (were, have been) working in an unsafe building, but they won't complain to their supervisor.

9. My mother (volunteered, has volunteered) at the local food bank since it opened last year.

10. In August, Charles (signed, has signed) a contract with a professional hockey team.

THE PAST PERFECT TENSE

The **past perfect tense** is made up of the past participle form of the verb and *had* as a helping verb. You can use the past perfect tense to show more than one event in the past—that is, when two or more things happened in the past but at different times.

> **past tense:** He *washed* the dishes.
> **past perfect tense:** He *had washed* the dishes by the time I came home. (He washed the dishes *before* I came home. Both actions happened in the past, but one happened earlier than the other.)
>
> **past tense:** Susan *waited* for an hour.
> **past perfect tense:** Susan *had waited* for an hour when she gave up on him. (Waiting came first; giving up came second. Both actions are in the past.)

The past perfect tense is especially useful because you write most of your essays in the past tense, and you often need to get further back into the past. Remember, to form the past perfect tense, use *had* with the past participle of the verb.

ESL NOTE

Past perfect tense is difficult for most students, especially for nonnative speakers.

> **Exercise 6** **Distinguishing between the Past Tense and the Past Perfect Tense**

Circle the correct verb in parentheses in each of the following sentences. Be sure to look carefully at the meaning of the sentences.

1. Most of the audience (guessed, had guessed) the ending to the mystery before the movie was half finished.

2. Melissa was not sure whether Jerry (tried, had tried) to call her earlier that morning.

3. On Mother's Day, my daughter (surprised, had surprised) me with a necklace she had made at her preschool arts and crafts class.

4. By the time Nelson remembered the soup, it (boiled, had boiled) over on the stove.

5. As Brianna brushed her hair, she (studied, had studied) her face in the mirror.

6. Jacob looked at the exam questions and wondered if he (read, had read) the right chapters in his textbook.

7. The defense attorney examined the transcripts of the trial that (took, had taken) place two years earlier.

8. On Sunday morning, I took part in a charity walk-a-thon because my sister (was, had been) nagging me about it for weeks.

9. While my boyfriend devoured a breakfast of bacon, eggs, and pancakes, I (limited, had limited) myself to fruit and yogurt.

10. By the time Amber and I got to the movies, a huge crowd (took, had taken) all the good seats for the new Harry Potter film.

PASSIVE AND ACTIVE VOICE

TEACHING TIP

The word *voice* may confuse students. Spend a few minutes discussing how this term applies to grammar.

Verbs not only have tenses, but they also have voices. When the subject in the sentence is doing something, the verb is in the **active voice**. When something is done to the subject, when it receives the action of the verb, the verb is in the **passive voice**.

active voice:
I painted the house. (*I*, the subject, did it.)
The people on the corner made a donation to the emergency fund.
    (The *people*, the subject, did it.)

passive voice:
The house was painted by me. (The *house*, the subject, didn't do anything. It received the action—it was painted.)
A donation to the emergency fund was made by the people on the corner. (The *donation*, the subject, didn't do anything. It received the action—it was given.)

TEACHING TIP

Stress that the passive voice is easily overused. Remind students that using the active voice whenever possible leads to stronger and more precise writing.

Notice what happens when you use the passive voice instead of the active:

active voice: I painted the house.
passive voice: The house was painted by me.

The sentence in the passive voice is two words longer than the one in the active voice. Yet the sentence that uses the passive voice does not say anything different, and it does not say it more clearly than the one in the active voice.

Using the passive voice can make your sentences wordy, it can slow them down, and it can make them boring. The passive voice can also confuse readers. When the subject of the sentence is not doing anything, readers may have to look carefully to see who or what *is* doing something. Look at this sentence, for example:

A decision to fire you was reached.

Who decided to fire you? In this sentence, it is hard to find the answer to that question.

Of course, there will be times when you have to use the passive voice. For example, you may have to use it when you do not know who did something, as in these sentences:

Our house was broken into last night.
A leather jacket was left behind in the classroom.

But in general, you should avoid using the passive voice and rewrite sentences so that they are in the active voice.

Exercise 7   **Rewriting Sentences, Changing the Passive Voice to the Active Voice**

In the following sentences, change the passive voice to the active voice. If the original sentence does not tell you who or what performed the action, add words that tell who or what did it. An example is done for you.

example: Sandy Adams was appointed chief negotiator last night.

rewritten: *The union leaders appointed Sandy Adams chief negotiator last night.*

1. A twenty-two-year-old man from Idaho has been arrested and charged with the kidnapping of Kelly Romano.

   rewritten: *The highway patrol has arrested a twenty-two-year-old man from Idaho and charged him with the kidnapping of Kelly Romano.*

INSTRUCTOR'S NOTE

Answers will vary. Possible answers shown at left.

2. Questions are being asked about the missing funds at the health center.

   rewritten: *County officials are asking questions about the missing funds at the health center.*

3. The true story of his mother's death was never told to Arthur.

   rewritten: *Arthur's grandparents never told him the true story of his mother's death.*

4. Several paintings were donated to the museum by a wealthy woman.

   rewritten: *A wealthy woman donated several paintings to the museum.*

5. Once a month, the kindergarten class is entertained by a professional storyteller.

   rewritten: *Once a month, a professional storyteller entertains the kindergarten class.*

6. Just before takeoff, an airline safety demonstration was conducted by a flight attendant.

   rewritten: *Just before takeoff, a flight attendant conducted an airline safety demonstration.*

7. Due to the rising costs of energy, a slight increase in your cable bill has been instituted.

   rewritten: *Due to the rising costs of energy, the Friendly Cable Company has instituted a slight increase in your cable bill.*

8. Finally, the ringing phone was answered by the man behind the counter.

   rewritten: *Finally, the man behind the counter answered the ringing phone.*

9. Later today, a contract with an international music company will be signed by the popular performer.

   rewritten: *Later today, the popular performer will sign a contract with an international music company.*

10. A search for the missing weapon was conducted last night.

    rewritten: *Local police conducted a search for the missing weapon last night.*

Avoiding Unnecessary Shifts in Voice

Just as you should be consistent in the tense of verbs, you should be consistent in the voice of verbs. Do not shift from active voice to passive voice, or vice versa, without some good reason to do so.

              active   passive

shift: *I designed* the decorations for the dance; *they were put up* by Chuck.

              active   active

rewritten: *I designed* the decorations for the dance; *Chuck put* them *up*.

                              passive

shift: Many *problems were discussed* by the council members, but

      active

they found no easy answers.

                              active   active

rewritten: The council *members discussed* many problems, but *they found* no easy answers.

Being consistent in voice can help you to write clearly and smoothly.

   Exercise 8 **Rewriting Sentences to Correct Shifts in Voice**

Rewrite the following sentences so that all the verbs are in the active voice. You may change the wording to make the sentences clear, smooth, and consistent in voice.

1. I enjoyed the party until red wine was spilled all over my silk shirt.

   rewritten: *I enjoyed the party until a clumsy woman spilled red wine all over my silk shirt.*

2. If a window was broken by my son, I never knew about the incident.

   rewritten: *If my son broke a window, I never knew about the incident.*

3. Esther screamed with rage when she was called a liar.

   rewritten: *Esther screamed with rage when Gloria called her a liar.*

4. My uncle used to be a pilot; airplanes and airports are loved by him.

   rewritten: *My uncle used to be a pilot; he loves airplanes and airports.*

5. Today a shy fisherman was honored by the city council; the fisherman had risked his life to save a drowning woman.

   rewritten: *Today the city council honored a shy fisherman; the*

   fisherman had risked his life to save a drowning woman.

6. The local roads were packed by frustrated drivers when flash floods closed two major highways.

   rewritten: *Frustrated drivers packed the local roads when flash*

   floods closed two major highways.

7. Because Paul is my old friend, he can be trusted by me.

   rewritten: *Because Paul is my old friend, I can trust him.*

8. The county commissioners decided that every section of the budget will be cut next year.

   rewritten: *The county commissioners decided that they will cut*

   every section of the budget next year.

9. The schedule of summer classes is being posted online today; the college will also distribute paper copies of the schedule throughout the campus.

   rewritten: *Today the college is posting the schedule of summer*

   classes online and distributing paper copies of the schedule throughout

   the campus.

10. The cousins wanted to surprise their grandfather with a fancy party, but specific plans for a party were never discussed.

    rewritten: *The cousins wanted to surprise their grandfather with a*

    fancy party, but they never discussed specific plans for a party.

A Few Tips about Verbs

There are a few errors that people tend to make with verbs. If you are aware of these errors, you'll be on the lookout for them as you edit your writing.

Used to: Be careful when you write that someone *used to* do, say, or feel something. It is incorrect to write *use to*.
  not this: Janine ~~use to~~ visit her mother every week.
        They ~~use to~~ like Thai food.
  but this: Janine *used to* visit her mother every week.
        They *used to* like Thai food.

Could Have, Should Have, Would Have: Using *of* instead of *have* is another error with verbs.
  not this: I ~~could of~~ done better on the test.
  but this: I *could have* done better on the test.

  not this: He ~~should of~~ been paying attention.
  but this: He *should have* been paying attention.

not this: The girls ~~would of~~ liked to visit Washington.
but this: The girls *would have* liked to visit Washington.

Would Have/Had: If you are writing about something that might have been possible, but that did not happen, use *had* as the helping verb.

not this: If I ~~would have~~ taken a foreign language in high school, I wouldn't have to take one now.
but this: If I *had* taken a foreign language in high school, I wouldn't have to take one now.

not this: I wish they ~~would have~~ won the game.
but this: I wish they *had* won the game.

not this: If she ~~would have~~ been smart, she would have called a plumber.
but this: If she *had* been smart, she would have called a plumber.

Collaborate

INSTRUCTOR'S NOTE

Answers will vary. Possible answers shown.

Exercise 9   **Writing Sentences with the Correct Verb Forms**

Do this exercise with a partner or a group. Follow the directions to write or complete each sentence below.

1. Complete this sentence and add a verb in the correct tense: My dog had chewed my best pair of shoes before

   I dragged him out of my closet.

   _____

2. Write a sentence that is more than eight words long and that uses the words *would have been happier* in the middle of the sentence.

   Sarah would have been happier if she had found a job close to home.

   _____

3. Write a sentence that uses the past tense form of these words: *act* and *lose*.

   Last night, Christopher acted like a fool and lost the respect of his

   friends.

4. Write a sentence in the passive voice.

   A holiday concert was planned for next month.

5. Write a sentence in the active voice.

   The band planned a holiday concert for next month.

6. Write a sentence that uses *would have* and *had*.

   If Tim had taken a different route to school, he would have seen the

   terrible accident on Fifth Street.

7. Write a sentence that is more than six words long and that uses the words *had decided* and *before*.

   I had decided that nursing was the ideal career for me long before I

   started college.

8. Write a sentence of more than six words that uses the words
   used to.

   In the fall, I used to love crunching the fallen leaves under my feet.

   _____

9. Write a sentence that contains two verbs in the same tense.

   People are becoming impatient, and they are starting to push in line.

   _____

10. Write a sentence that uses the words *should have.*

    You should have called me last night.

    _____

Connect

Exercise 10 **Editing a Paragraph for Errors in Verbs: Consistency, Tense, and Voice**

Edit the following paragraph for errors in verb consistency, tense, or voice. There are seven errors.

  Yesterday, I finally decided to buy an alarm for my car. Several incidents
convinced   *has been*
convince me that I needed one. The street where I live was considered a high-
                                  had never
crime area for years now, yet I never thought about protecting my car until recent

events changed my mind. A month ago, thieves stole two cars off the street in
                              smashed another car's windshield.
broad daylight, and another car's windshield was smashed. Suddenly, I became

nervous; still I avoided taking any precautions. I assumed that my car was too old
                      greedy thieves would overlook it.
to steal and that it would be overlooked by greedy thieves. Unfortunately, I woke

up early yesterday, looked out my apartment window, and saw my car windshield

smashed into a thousand pieces. Running downstairs to the curb, I saw a huge
                            used
hole where my car radio use to be. Later that day, I took my car to be repaired and
                        had bought
bought a car alarm. Maybe if I would have bought the alarm sooner, I would have

saved the money for my new car radio.

Connect

Exercise 11 **Editing a Paragraph for Errors in Verbs: Consistency, Tense, and Voice**

Edit the following paragraph for errors in verb consistency, tense, or voice. There are eight errors.
                                              would have
  If the owners of Coffee Cavern had been smart, they would of studied the
            they opened the shop.
neighborhood before the shop was opened by them. At one time the site of Coffee

                                        was
Cavern has been a magnet for students. Before the building became a coffee shop,
                                                                        opened
students flocked to the hamburger shop located there. When Coffee Cavern has
                                                        the owners
opened, students were ready to visit the same location. Unfortunately, prices have
of the shop have set prices   *used to*
been set too high for students use to cheap snacks and lunches. Some students

are willing to pay two or three dollars for a great cup of coffee, but no students
are
were ready to pay two dollars for a bagel or three dollars for a tiny slice of lemon

cake. Consequently, college students are saving their money and buying their cof-
                                    The owners opened Coffee Cavern in
fee and snacks at the local doughnut store. Coffee Cavern was opened in a location

popular with students, but the owners created a shop for rich people.

Chapter Test: More on Verbs: Consistency and Voice

Some of the sentences below are correct; others have errors in verb consistency, tense, and voice. Put an *X* next to the sentences with errors.

1. _____ You would have enjoyed the movie about penguins.

2. _____ On Saturday mornings, my boyfriend goes out for fresh
doughnuts, makes a pot of coffee, and pours two glasses of
orange juice.

3. __*X*__ A vote for the soccer club president was held, and Sam Ali
won easily.

4. _____ Peter had learned to surf in Mexico before he started surf-
ing off the coast of California.

5. _____ Hallie has lived in Alabama for three years and plans to buy
a house in Birmingham.

6. __*X*__ One of the twins has been a cook at a fancy restaurant
before he became a celebrity chef on television.

7. __*X*__ When I was in the hospital, Courtney sent me flowers, Pre-
ston visits me, and Sean brought a plant.

8. _____ By the time Stacy found her ideal job, she had worked for
two horrible employers.

9. __*X*__ A friend of the family made an emotional speech; it was followed by tears and applause.

10. __*X*__ If Colin had known about the discount, he could of saved
several hundred dollars.

CHAPTER 25

Making Subjects and Verbs Agree

Subjects and verbs have to agree in number. That means a singular subject must be matched to a singular verb form; a plural subject must be matched to a plural verb form.

singular subject, singular verb:
My *sister walks* to work every morning.

plural subject, plural verb:
Mary, *David*, and *Sam believe* in ghosts.

singular subject, singular verb:
That *movie is* too violent for me.

plural subject, plural verb:
Bulky *packages are* difficult to carry.

Caution: Remember that a regular verb has an *s* ending in only one singular form in the present tense—the form that goes with *he*, *she*, *it*, or their equivalents:

He *makes* me feel confident.

She *appreciates* intelligent conversation.
It *seems* like a good buy.
Bo *runs* every day.
That girl *swims* well.
The machine *breaks* down too often.

Exercise 1   **Subject-Verb Agreement: Selecting the Correct Verb Form**

Select the correct form of the verb in each sentence following.

1. My nephew (is, are) a natural athlete with a great future.

2. The camera sometimes (give, gives) a false impression of the size of a room.

3. My five-year-old son and my three-year-old daughter rarely (go, goes) out to eat.

4. That watch (cost, costs) more than you can afford.

5. By 10:00 p.m., the bar (smell, smells) like spilled beer.

6. People in the middle of a crisis may become startled when a phone (ring, rings).

7. Driving a hundred miles for a picnic (seem, seems) silly.

8. Constantly blaming others (appear, appears) to be John's way of avoiding responsibility.

9. If the television is on, Anna (complain, complains) that she can't concentrate on her homework.

10. After a bad day at work, you (need, needs) a quiet place to relax.

Exercise 2   **Correcting Errors in Subject-Verb Agreement in a Paragraph**

There are errors in subject-verb agreement in the paragraph below. If a verb does not agree with its subject, change the verb form. Cross out the incorrect verb form and write the correct one above. There are eight errors in agreement in the paragraph.

On some days, I cannot concentrate on my homework. These days usually
come   *requires*
~~comes~~ after I have been working hard for a long time. When my job ~~require~~ hours
                              insist
of overtime and my teachers ~~insists~~ on assigning huge amounts of homework, I
find
~~finds~~ myself under pressure. I can meet the demands of that pressure, but after-
                        turns
ward, my brain ~~turn~~ off. No matter how hard I try, nothing works. Studying at
                                              leads   *seems*
home puts me to sleep. Reading in the library ~~lead~~ to daydreaming. It ~~seem~~ that
                    has
my brain ~~have~~ a battery and the battery needs recharging. Fortunately, these lazy

spells never last too long, and I become a serious student again.

PRONOUNS AS SUBJECTS

Pronouns can be used as subjects. Pronouns are words that take the place of nouns. When pronouns are used as subjects, they must agree in number with verbs.

Here is a list of the subject pronouns and the regular verb forms that agree with them, in the present tense:

INFO BOX: Subjective Pronouns and a Present Tense Verb

pronoun	verb	
I	listen	
you	listen	all singular forms
he, she, it	listens	
we	listen	
you	listen	all plural forms
they	listen	

In all the sentences below, the pronoun used as the subject of the sentence agrees in number with the verb:

singular pronoun, singular verb:
I make the best omelet in town.

singular pronoun, singular verb:
You dance very well.

singular pronoun, singular verb:
She performs like a trained athlete.

plural pronoun, plural verb:
We need a new refrigerator.

plural pronoun, plural verb:
They understand the situation.

SPECIAL PROBLEMS WITH AGREEMENT

Agreement seems fairly simple: if a subject is singular, you use a singular verb form, and if a subject is plural, you use a plural verb form. However, there are special problems with agreement that will come up in your writing. Sometimes, it is hard to find the subject of a sentence; at other times, it is hard to determine if a subject is singular or plural.

Finding the Subject

When you are checking for subject-verb agreement, you can find the real subject of the sentence by first eliminating the prepositional phrases. To find the real subject, put parentheses around the prepositional phrases. Then it is easy to find the subject because nothing in a prepositional phrase is the subject of a sentence.

prepositional phrases in parentheses:

S   V
One (of my oldest friends) *is* a social worker.

S   V
A *student* (from one)(of the nearby school districts) *is* the winner.

                          S   V
The *store* (across the street) (from my house) *is* open all night.
             S   V
Jim, (with all his silly jokes), *is* a nice person.

> **Note:** Words and phrases such as *along with, as well as, except, in addition to, including, plus,* and *together with* introduce prepositional phrases. The words that follow them are part of the prepositional phrase and cannot be part of the subject.

              S   V   V
My *sister*, (along with her husband), *is planning* a trip to Bolivia.
             S   V
Tom's *house*, (as well as his apartment), *is* part of a family inheritance.

Exercise 3 Finding the Real Subject by Recognizing Prepositional Phrases

Put parentheses around all the prepositional phrases in the sentences below. Put an *S* above each subject and a V above each verb.

1. Jealousy, in addition to lack of trust, threatens the stability of a marriage.

2. Cristina, plus her mother-in-law, is visiting Venezuela over the summer.

3. Without much thought, a loud customer made a cruel comment on the server's appearance.

4. In the early morning, a tall man with a Great Dane jogs through the park.

5. The truth behind the actors' brawl at the nightclub is a simple story of too much alcohol.

6. Yogurt, as well as low-fat cheese, is a good source of calcium in any diet.

7. My best friend from high school arrived a day early for the reunion.

8. A guest speaker from Children in Distress is coming to my psychology class on Tuesday.

9. Two of the men in the car are friends of Alicia's cousin.

10. The old house, including the yard and driveway, is in good condition.

Exercise 4 **Selecting the Correct Verb Form by Identifying Prepositional Phrases**

Put parentheses around all the prepositional phrases in the sentences below. Then circle the verb that agrees with the subject.

1. A motel (with clean rooms), a small pool, and free breakfast (is, are) at the exit (to Masonville).

2. Mr. Kelly's patience, (in addition) (to his years) (of experience), (explain, explains) his popularity (with students).

3. Gossiping (about friends) (is, are) a clear sign (of a deficiency) (in loyalty).

4. One (of the most handsome men) (in town) (is, are) my best friend, Tyler.

5. (Under suspicion) (of murder), the young man, (together with his fiancée), (was, were) the subject (of a police search).

6. The house (with the blue shutters) (has, have) been sold to a family (from Missouri).

7. Tennis players (at summer tournaments) often (compete, competes) (in dangerously hot weather).

8. One (of the judges) (on the daytime television shows) (go, goes) (into a fit) (of anger) (during every episode).

9. Many (of the tests), plus the regular quizzes, (seem, seems) (designed for a higher-level mathematics class).

10. The dirty dishes (on the kitchen table) (need, needs) to be washed and dried (before dinnertime).

Changed Word Order

You are probably used to looking for the subject of a sentence in front of the verb, but not all sentences follow this pattern. Questions, sentences beginning with words like *here* or *there*, and other sentences change the word order. So you have to look carefully to check for subject-verb agreement.

$\quad$ V$\qquad$ S

Where *are* my *friends*?

$\quad$ V S V

When *is he going* to work?

              V   S

Behind the elm trees *stands* a huge *statue.*

     V   S

There *are potholes* in the road.

     V   S

There *is* a *reason* for his impatience.

TEACHING TIP

Before students begin this exercise, remind them that a verb must always agree with its subject and that subjects are not always found at the beginning of a sentence.

Exercise 5 **Making Subjects and Verbs Agree in Sentences with Changed Word Order**

In each of the sentences below, underline the subject; then circle the correct verb in parentheses.

1. Below the stairs (is, are) a storage area with a sloping ceiling and a good amount of room.

2. Along the sides of the building (was, were) a mural in bright colors.

3. Among the celebrities (was, were) notorious rich girls and badly behaved sports stars.

4. Here (is, are) the representative from the Red Cross and the emergency shelter manager.

5. There (is, are) a collection of old and dirty baseball cards at the back of your closet.

6. Behind all the lies and excuses (is, are) two people with a serious gambling problem.

7. There (was, were) some major disagreements in the beginning of our partnership.

8. Near the top of my list of chores (was, were) a trip to the car wash and a few minutes at the bank.

9. Where (is, are) the bills from last month's trip to Colorado Springs?

10. Here (is, are) a cookie with chocolate chips and a small cup of Pepsi.

COMPOUND SUBJECTS

A **compound subject** is two or more subjects joined by *and, or,* or *nor.*

When subjects are joined by *and,* they are usually plural.

   S   S V

Jermaine and *Lisa are* bargain hunters.

     S   S   V

The *house* and the *garden need* attention.

    S   S   V

A *bakery* and a *pharmacy are* down the street.

Caution: Be careful to check for a compound subject when the word order changes.

        V   S   S

There *are* a *bakery* and a *pharmacy* down the street. (Two things, a *bakery* and a *pharmacy, are* down the street.)

       V   *S*   *S*

Here *are* a *picture* of your father and a *copy* of his birth certificate.
    (A *picture* and a *copy*, two things, *are* here.)

When subjects are joined by *or*, *either . . . or*, *neither . . . nor*, *not only . . . but also*, the verb form agrees with the subject closer to the verb.

                singular S   *plural S, plural V*
Not only the restaurant *manager* but also the *waiters were* pleased
    with the new policy.

          plural S   *singular S, singular V*
Not only the *waiters* but also the restaurant *manager was* pleased
    with the new policy.

            plural S   *singular S, singular V*
Either the *parents* or the *boy walks* the dog every morning.

          singular S   *plural S, plural V*
Either the *boy* or the *parents walk* the dog every morning.

           plural S   *singular S, singular V*
Neither the *tenants* nor the *landlord cares* about the parking situation.

          singular S   *plural S, plural V*
Neither the *landlord* nor the *tenants care* about the parking situation.

> **Exercise 6**   **Making Subjects and Verbs Agree: Compound Subjects**

Circle the correct form of the verb in parentheses in each sentence below.

1. Neither a steel rod in his leg nor a fear of heights (keep, (keeps)) Adam from climbing mountains.

2. Most of the time, Simon Fraser or Ruben Melendez (come, (comes)) in early on Saturdays.

3. As soon as I arrive with the pizza, either my roommates or my girlfriend (grab, (grabs)) it out of my hands.

4. There (is, (are)) a big hairy spider and some beetles under the porch.

5. Whenever you complain about the noise, neither your brother nor your sister (pay, (pays)) any attention.

6. Not only my carpet but also my chairs (was, (were)) ruined when my dining room flooded during the recent storm.

7. Here (is, (are)) a letter from the bank and a bill from the phone company.

8. Either a visit to the zoo or an afternoon at the movies (sound, (sounds)) good to me.

9. Within days after Jeff won the lottery, there (was, (were)) appeals for his money from long-lost relatives and friends.

10. On autumn days, neither stress nor worries ((keep), keeps) me from enjoying the beautiful colors of the leaves.

INDEFINITE PRONOUNS

Certain pronouns that come from a group called **indefinite pronouns** always take a singular verb.

INFO BOX: Indefinite Pronouns

one	nobody	nothing	each
anyone	anybody	anything	either
someone	somebody	something	neither
everyone	everybody	everything	

If you want to write clearly and correctly, you must memorize these words and remember that they always take a singular verb. Using your common sense is not enough because some of these words seem plural: for example, *everybody* seems to mean more than one person, but in grammatically correct English, it takes a singular verb. Here are some examples of the pronouns used with singular verbs:

singular S   *singular V*
Everyone in town *is talking* about the scandal.
singular S   *singular V*
Each of the boys *is* talented.
singular S   *singular V*
One of their biggest concerns *is* crime in the streets.
singular S   *singular V*
Neither of the cats *is* mine.

Hint: You can memorize the indefinite pronouns as the *-one, -thing,* and *-body* words (every*one*, every*thing*, every*body*, and so forth) plus *each, either,* and *neither.*

| Exercise 7 | **Making Subjects and Verbs Agree: Using Indefinite Pronouns** |

Circle the correct verb in parentheses in each sentence following.

1. Anybody except a genius (was, were) going to be confused by the famous scientist's explanation.

2. Somebody in the neighborhood (is, are) stealing my mail.

3. Everything in my bedroom (come, comes) from a thrift shop).

4. Something in Billy's explanation and apology (seem, seems) false.

5. Anyone from the tropics (know, knows) how to stay cool on a hot day.

6. (Has, Have) everybody at the daycare center been given a flu shot?

7. Nobody in your group of friends (act, acts) happy to see me.

8. Anything with hot peppers in it (make, makes) my taste buds dance with pleasure.

9. One of the kindest people at the hospital (was, were) a young nurse from Brazil.

10. Here (is, are) everybody from the basketball team.

COLLECTIVE NOUNS

Collective nouns refer to more than one person or thing:

team	company	council
class	corporation	government
committee	family	group
audience	jury	crowd

Most of the time, collective nouns take a singular verb.

singular S, singular V
The *committee is sponsoring* a fund-raiser.

singular S, singular V
The *audience was* impatient.

singular S, singular V
The *jury has reached* a verdict.

The singular verb is used because the group is sponsoring, or getting impatient, or reaching a verdict, *as one unit.*

Collective nouns take a plural verb only when the members of the group are acting individually, not as a unit.

The sophomore *class are fighting* among themselves. (The phrase *among themselves* shows that the class is not acting as one unit.)

Exercise 8   Making Subjects and Verbs Agree: Using Collective Nouns

Circle the correct verb in parentheses in each sentence below.

1. The Green Corporation (give, gives) all its full-time employees ten vacation days.

2. The family from Nevada (is, are) looking for a house to rent for at least one year.

3. Some members of the jury (was, were) falling asleep in the late afternoon sessions.

4. My son's kindergarten class (sing, sings) songs at the start of each day.

5. The Merrill College Student Council (was, were) determined to raise the issue of student fees.

6. The most popular team in baseball history (is, are) deeply divided on the issue of steroid use.

7. Although rain delayed the outdoor concert, the crowd at the park (was, were) patiently cheerful.

8. When a movie is boring or slow, the audience (begin, begins) to talk among themselves.

9. Once a year, the motorcycle club (donate, donates) toys to children in hospitals and orphanages.

10. For years, the board of directors at the computer company (has, have) discussed the problem of overseas competition.

MAKING SUBJECTS AND VERBS AGREE: THE BOTTOM LINE

As you have probably realized, making subjects and verbs agree is not as simple as it first appears. But if you can remember the basic ideas in this section, you will be able to apply them automatically as you edit your own writing. Below is a quick summary of subject-verb agreement.

INFO BOX: Making Subjects and Verbs Agree: A Summary

1. Subjects and verbs should agree in number: singular subjects get singular verb forms; plural subjects get plural verb forms.

2. When pronouns are used as subjects, they must agree in number with verbs.

3. Nothing in a prepositional phrase can be the subject of the sentence.

4. Questions, sentences beginning with *here* or *there*, and other sentences can change word order, making subjects harder to find.

5. Compound subjects joined by *and* are usually plural.

6. When subjects are joined by *or, either . . . or, neither . . . nor,* or *not only . . . but also,* the verb form agrees with the subject closest to the verb.

7. Indefinite pronouns always take singular verbs.

8. Collective nouns usually take singular verbs.

Exercise 9   **A Comprehensive Exercise on Subject-Verb Agreement**

Circle the correct verb form in parentheses in each sentence below.

1. One of the sheets in my roommate's closet (is, are) exactly like my lost blue sheet.

2. Anybody with good instincts (know, knows) how to spot a dishonest salesperson.

3. Each of the children at the preschool (has, have) been through the shock of the first day away from home.

4. If the case is a highly controversial one, the jury (is, are) going to face more stress than usual.

5. The electric company (is, are) working on power outages in three counties.

6. Beyond the railroad tracks (is, are) a row of dilapidated storage units.

7. Here (was, were) my best friend and my worst enemy in the same room.

8. Nothing except a selection of soft drinks (was, were) served at the long meeting.

9. Every Friday night, one of the neighbors (take, takes) turns holding a cookout.

10. Not only the groceries in the back of my car but also the chocolate bar on the dashboard (was, were) covered in ants.

Exercise 10   **Writing Sentences with Subject-Verb Agreement**

Collaborate

With a partner or a group, turn each of the following phrases into a sentence—twice. That is, write two sentences for each phrase. Use a verb that fits, and put the verb in the present tense. Be sure that the verb agrees with the subject.

INSTRUCTOR'S NOTE

Answers will vary. Possible answers shown.

1. A large bag of rocks *is a heavy burden.*

   A large bag of rocks *weighs too much for me to carry.*

2. Either cake or ice cream *makes a great dessert.*

   Either cake or ice cream *is loaded with calories.*

3. The company *needs a new director of human resources.*

   The company *likes to hire people with a background in sales or computer information systems.*

4. Mickey and Minnie *are famous Disney characters.*

   Mickey and Minnie *are the most famous mice in the world.*

5. Everything on the menu *costs a fortune.*

   Everything on the menu *is made with meat.*

6. Someone on the Safe City Council *wants to establish curfews for teenagers.*

   Someone on the Safe City Council *is looking for volunteers to patrol the neighborhood.*

7. Not only my friends but also my brother *dislikes my new haircut.*

   Not only my friends but also my brother *wants me to go back to college.*

8. Anybody from this state *knows about bad weather.*

   Anybody from this state *is used to driving long distances.*

9. One of children's greatest fears _is of being abandoned._

_____

One of children's greatest fears _is a fear of the dark._

_____

10. Neither broccoli nor other green vegetables _appeal to my toddler._

_____

Neither broccoli nor other green vegetables _are widely known for their powerful health benefits._

_____

Collaborate

| Exercise 11 | **Create Your Own Text on Subject-Verb Agreement** |

Working with a partner or a group, create your own grammar handbook. Below is a list of rules on subject-verb agreement. Write one sentence that is an example of each rule. The first one is done for you.

Rule 1: Subjects and verbs should agree in number: singular subjects get singular verb forms; plural subjects get plural verb forms.

example: _A battered old car stands in the front yard._

_____

Rule 2: When pronouns are used as subjects, they must agree in number with verbs.

example: _We practice our dance routine on Friday afternoon._

_____

Rule 3: Nothing in a prepositional phrase can be the subject of the sentence.

example: _One of my brothers is a volunteer at the animal shelter._

_____

Rule 4: Questions, sentences beginning with _here_ or _there_, and other sentences can change word order, making subjects harder to find.

example: _Here are the answers to your questions about the loan._

_____

Rule 5: When subjects are joined by _and_, they are usually plural.

example: _The car and the truck need washing._

_____

Rule 6: When subjects are joined by _or, either . . . or, neither . . . nor_, or _not only . . . but also_, the verb form agrees with the subject closest to the verb.

example: _Neither the girls nor their brother is at home today._

_____

Rule 7: Indefinite pronouns always take singular verbs.

example: *At the shoe store, everything is on sale.*

_____

Rule 8: Collective nouns usually take singular verbs.

example: *The company is recruiting at our college.*

_____

Exercise 12 **Editing a Paragraph for Errors in Subject-Verb Agreement**

Connect

Edit the following paragraph by correcting any verbs that do not agree with their subjects. Write your corrections above the lines. There are eight errors.

are

There is two keys to understanding my father. As children, neither my sisters

was

nor I were aware of how much my father's background influenced his beliefs and

was

behavior. My father's family were from China, and he came to this country as a

little boy. His parents were strong believers in family unity, so my father was raised

to believe that adult children lived at home until they married. He still cannot

wants

believe that today nearly everyone want to leave home and live independently

before marriage. In addition, my father's family was poor and had to struggle to

helps

make a living. An understanding of those struggles help me to accept the way my

teases

father treats money. Everyone tease him about his obsession with saving and his

come

love of bargains, but these values comes from his parents. Each time my father

warns me about spending too much money or cautions me about the dangers of

living on my own, he is repeating the lessons his parents taught him. Yet I am from

is

another generation and another country, so something about my attitudes are

bound to disturb him. As I grow older, I hope my father and I will grow in under-

standing.

Exercise 13 **Editing a Paragraph for Errors in Subject-Verb Agreement**

Connect

Edit the following paragraph by correcting any verbs that do not agree with their subjects. Write your corrections above the lines. There are six errors.

come   *are*

Cats comes in a variety of types. There is outdoor cats, indoor cats, friendly

cats, shy cats, cuddly cats, and adventurous cats. One cat is not at all typical, and that cat is Rudy. Rudy is a cat who loves dogs. Everyone in the neighborhood *has* ~~have~~

seen Rudy, a large Siamese, greet a strange dog. Rudy walks slowly and deliber-

ately toward the dog and makes a few faint sounds as he approaches. Softly, Rudy

sniffs the dog. Nothing in the dog's experience *has* ~~have~~ prepared it for this moment,

so the dog is usually too startled to growl. Next, Rudy rubs his plump, furry body

against the dog. He slinks along the dog's side in the same way most cats will rub

against a person's legs. Finally, Rudy rolls over right under the dog's nose. Rudy

wants to play. At this point, the dog is stunned and *sniffs* ~~sniff~~ the cat. Rudy loves the

attention. The dog still doesn't know how to behave. Dogs expect cats to run away

and to be natural enemies. Generations of dogs *have* ~~has~~ never seen a cat like Rudy, for

he is a true dog lover.

Chapter Test: Making Subjects and Verbs Agree

Some of the sentences below are correct; others have errors in making subjects and verbs agree. Put an *X* next to the sentences with errors.

1. __X__ Neither of the apartments near the college have a large bedroom.

2. _____ My neighbor must be a good cook; on the weekends, a delicious and faintly cinnamon smell floats into my window.

3. __X__ Years ago, when my father got a job at the food processing
plant, there was health insurance and vacation pay for all
the full-time employees.

4. _____ Everyone at the movies was complaining about the broken
air-conditioning system.

5. _____ At the entrance to the school is a huge sign with "Go, Pan-
thers!" and a large cartoon animal painted on it.

6. _____ Not only the rent but also the utility bills require a large
part of my salary.

7. __X__ Either a good book or several magazines keeps my mother
occupied on the long flight to Arizona.

8. __X__ Where is the perpetrators of this horrible crime?

9. __X__ A crowd of happy fans are celebrating in the street.

10. _____ Each of the paramedics at the station has a different way of
coping with the pressure of the job.

Using Pronouns Correctly: Agreement and Reference

NOUNS AND PRONOUNS

Nouns are the names of persons, places, or things.

> *Jack* is a good friend. (*Jack* is the name of a person.)
> The band is from *Orlando*. (*Orlando* is the name of a place.)
> I hated the *movie*. (*Movie* is the name of a thing.)

Pronouns are words that substitute for nouns. A pronoun's **antecedent** is the word or words it replaces.

> *antecedent*   *pronoun*
> *Jack* is a good friend; *he* is very loyal.
>   *antecedent*   *pronoun*
> I hated *the movie* because *it* was too violent.
> *antecedent*   *pronoun*
> *Playing tennis* was fun, but *it* started to take up too much of my
>   time.
> *antecedent*   *pronoun*
> *Mike and Michelle* are sure *they* are in love.

antecedent   *pronoun*
Sharon gave away *her* old clothes.
antecedent   *pronoun*
The dog rattled *its* dish, begging for dinner.

Exercise 1   **Identifying the Antecedents of Pronouns**

Underline the word or words that are the antecedent of the italicized pronoun in each sentence below.

1. <u>A short walk</u> is healthy for workers because *it* takes them away from the workplace and relieves stress.

2. <u>Your brother</u> called me yesterday; *he* seemed a little depressed.

3. Camille looked at <u>two used cars</u> this afternoon; *they* were overpriced and unattractive.

4. My husband loves <u>sushi</u>, but I refuse to eat *it*.

5. <u>The baby</u> can't go outside without *his* down jacket.

6. <u>The television show</u> lost *its* special charm a few episodes ago.

7. <u>Luis</u>, do *you* need a ride to work?

8. <u>The parrots</u> have finally ended *their* conversation.

9. <u>Meeting new people</u> is difficult for me; *it* seems like a scary job interview.

10. <u>Your father and I</u> will talk about moving to Maryland after *we* visit Baltimore.

AGREEMENT OF A PRONOUN AND ITS ANTECEDENT

ESL NOTE

Some nonnative speakers are unaccustomed to using subject pronouns. Refer them to "Nouns or Pronouns Used as Subjects" on pp. 655–656 of the ESL Appendix.

A pronoun must agree in number with its antecedent. If the antecedent is singular, the pronoun must be singular. If the antecedent is plural, then the pronoun must be plural.

singular antecedent   *singular pronoun*
Susan tried to arrive on time, but *she* got caught in traffic.

plural antecedent   *plural pronoun*
Susan and Ray tried to arrive on time, but *they* got caught in traffic.

plural antecedent   *plural pronoun*
The visitors tried to arrive on time, but *they* got caught in traffic.

Agreement of pronoun and antecedent seems fairly simple. If an antecedent is singular, use a singular pronoun. If an antecedent is plural, use a plural pronoun. There are, however, some special problems with agreement of pronouns, and these problems will come up in your writing. If you become familiar with the explanations, examples, and exercises that follow, you will be ready to handle the special problems.

INDEFINITE PRONOUNS

Certain words called **indefinite pronouns** always take a singular verb. Therefore, if one of these indefinite pronouns is the antecedent, the pronoun that replaces it must be singular. Here are the indefinite pronouns:

> **INFO BOX:** **Indefinite Pronouns**
>
> | | | | |
> |---|---|---|---|
> | one | nobody | nothing | each |
> | anyone | anybody | anything | either |
> | someone | somebody | something | neither |
> | everyone | everybody | everything | |

You may think that *everybody* is plural, but in grammatically correct English, it is a singular word. Therefore, if you want to write clearly and correctly, memorize these words as the *-one*, *-thing*, and *-body* words: every*one*, every*thing*, every*body*, and so on, plus *each*, *either*, and *neither*. If any of these words is an antecedent, the pronoun that refers to it is singular.

singular antecedent   *singular pronoun*
Each of the Boy Scouts received *his* merit badge.

singular antecedent   *singular pronoun*
Everyone in the sorority donated *her* time to the project.

Avoiding Gender Bias

Consider this sentence:

Everybody in the math class brought _____ own calculator.

How do you choose the correct pronoun to fill in the blank? If everybody in the class is male, you can write

Everybody in the math class brought *his* own calculator.

Or if everybody in the class is female, you can write

Everybody in the math class brought *her* own calculator.

Or if the class has students of both genders, you can write

Everybody in the math class brought *his or her* own calculator.

In the past, most writers used the pronoun *his* to refer to both men and women. Today, many writers try to use *his or her* to avoid gender bias. If you find using *his or her* is getting awkward or repetitive, you can rewrite the sentence and make the antecedent plural:

correct: *The students* in the math class brought *their* own calculators.

But you cannot shift from singular to plural:

incorrect: ~~Everybody in the math class brought their own calculators.~~

Exercise 2 **Making Pronouns and Antecedents Agree**

Write the appropriate pronoun in the blank in each of the following sentences. Look carefully for the antecedent before you choose the pronoun.

1. Eugene was wearing a new blue sweater, and he looked good in ___*it*___ .

2. Widening the highway next to Sullivan Street has upset the nearby residents because ___*they*___ are suffering from the noise and dirt of construction.

3. No one really knows the little girl in the back row of the kindergarten class; ___she___ is always quiet and still.

4. Most of the employees at the office bring ___their___ lunch to work.

5. Lewis can be irritating when ___he___ talks about himself too much.

6. If you need a place to stay, either of my aunts in Puerto Rico will do ___her___ best to make you feel at home.

7. Everyone in the boys' choir devotes most of ___his___ free time to practicing.

8. A widow may have a hard time adjusting to life without ___her___ husband.

9. Each of my nephews paid for ___his___ college tuition by working long hours.

10. Caroline lost a silver ring when ___it___ slipped off her soapy finger and down the drain.

COLLECTIVE NOUNS

Collective nouns refer to more than one person or thing:

audience	corporation	government
class	council	group
committee	crowd	jury
company	family	team

Most of the time, collective nouns take a singular pronoun.

> *collective noun*   *singular pronoun*
> The *team* that was ahead in the playoffs lost *its* home game.

> *collective noun   singular pronoun*
> The *corporation* changed *its* policy on parental leave.

Collective nouns are usually singular because the group is losing a game or changing a policy as one, as a unit. Collective nouns take a plural pronoun only when the members of the group are acting individually, not as a unit.

> The *class* picked up *their* class rings this morning. (The members of the class pick up their rings individually.)

Exercise 3   **Making Pronouns and Antecedents Agree: Collective Nouns**

Circle the correct pronoun in each sentence below.

1. The commissioners at the Sprucedale City Council gave (its, **their**) approval to the construction of a new teen center.

2. A gang of my brother's army buddies met for (**its**, their) annual picnic at Still Waters Park.

3. Before the court adjourned for the day, the judge gave the jury (**its**, their) directions.

4. A family from China opened (**its**, their) second furniture company in Baton Rouge.

5. After the club meets, one of (its, their) members always suggests adjourning to a nearby restaurant.

6. Marilyn no longer orders movies from the Film Net company because of (its, their) poor delivery record.

7. Several of the drawing and design classes held (its, their) last class meeting outdoors because of the beautiful spring weather.

8. The retreating army disintegrated when the difficult journey caused the leaders to fight among (itself, themselves).

9. After waiting ninety minutes for the star of the show to appear, the audience lost (its, their) patience.

10. Because of the recent scandals about contaminated food, the global corporation has changed (its, their) inspection procedures.

Exercise 4 **Writing Sentences with Pronoun-Antecedent Agreement**

Collaborate

With a partner or a group, write a sentence for each pair of words below, using each pair as a pronoun and its antecedent. The first pair is done for you.

1. women . . . their

   sentence: *Women who work outside the home have to plan their time carefully.*

2. family . . . its

   sentence: *My family takes its traditions seriously.*

   INSTRUCTOR'S NOTE

   Answers will vary. Possible answers shown.

3. anybody . . . his or her

   sentence: *Has anybody lost his or her notebook?*

4. drivers . . . they

   sentence: *Drivers on the turnpike never obey the speed limit; they regularly drive ten to twenty miles an hour above the limit.*

5. security . . . it

   sentence: *My last relationship offered me no security; maybe I will find it with another person.*

6. either . . . her

   sentence: *Either of my aunts will let me stay at her house when I visit St. Louis.*

7. everybody . . . his or her

   sentence: *Everybody in line should be ready to show his or her photo identification.*

8. America . . . it

sentence: *Many people want to live in America; to them, it represents*
hope and opportunity.

9. music videos . . . they

sentence: *I don't like to watch too many music videos; after a while,*
they all start to look the same.

10. identity theft . . . it

sentence: *Identity theft is frightening because the victim may not be*
aware of it for months or years.

Connect

Exercise 5   Editing a Paragraph for Errors in Pronoun-Antecedent Agreement

Read the following paragraph carefully, looking for errors in agreement of
pronouns and their antecedents. Cross out each pronoun that does not
agree with its antecedent and write the correct pronoun above it. There are
six pronouns that need correcting.

Carlotta feels lucky to have found a job at the Treasure Value Company. After

working at a series of part-time, dead-end positions, Carlotta interviewed for an

entry-level position at the Greendale branch of the Treasure Value Company. Two

days later, the company made ~~their~~ *its* offer. While the salary is not great, Carlotta is

pleased because the benefits are quite generous. Once she has worked at the

company for a year, ~~they~~ *it* will give her ten days of paid vacation leave. In addition,

she is allowed five paid sick days per year. Most important, the company offers

health insurance to ~~their~~ *its* full-time employees. A representative of Treasure Value's

human resources department told Carlotta that ~~they~~ *he or she* would soon meet with

Carlotta to explain the company's health plan in more detail. Because Carlotta has

never had health insurance and has had to borrow money to pay her medical bills,

the promise of any insurance makes this job attractive. Carlotta is optimistic

about her employment at the Treasure Value Company because she feels that ~~their~~ *its*

policies indicate a humane attitude toward ~~their~~ *its* employees.

Connect

Exercise 6   Editing a Paragraph for Errors in Pronoun-Antecedent Agreement

Read the following paragraph carefully, looking for errors in agreement of
pronouns and their antecedents. Cross out each pronoun that does not
agree with its antecedent and write the correct pronoun above it. There are
six pronouns that need correcting.

My English class had an adventure yesterday. As the students sat, quietly revising their drafts, one girl shrieked with terror. "A mouse!" she cried. "It's under my desk!" Immediately, everybody in the room jumped on ~~their~~ *his or her* chair. Soon somebody in the back of the room swore ~~they~~ *he or she* saw a large mouse, maybe even a rat, running along the baseboard. This new sighting brought more excitement. "Does anybody have a box or a book bag?" asked one resourceful student. "Somebody could empty the box or bag. Then ~~they~~ *he or she* could use it to trap the mouse." Just as this suggestion was made, the mouse decided to make another dash around the room. Now everybody snatched ~~their~~ *his or her* belongings off the floor so that the rodent would not hide in them. Nobody knew what to do. Even our instructor was left without a way to restore order. "Let's finish class early today," he said. We all filed cautiously out of the room. No one considered the class that comes after ours. ~~They~~ *It* would have to deal with the mouse on ~~their~~ *its* own.

PRONOUNS AND THEIR ANTECEDENTS: BEING CLEAR

Remember that pronouns are words that replace or refer to other words, and the words that are replaced or referred to are antecedents.

Make sure that a pronoun has one clear antecedent. Your writing will be vague and confusing if a pronoun appears to refer to more than one antecedent or if it doesn't have any specific antecedent to refer to. In grammar, such confusing language is called a problem with *reference of pronouns*.

When a pronoun refers to more than one thing, the sentence becomes confusing or silly. The following are examples of unclear reference:

Jim told Leonard his bike had been stolen. (Whose bike was stolen? Jim's? Leonard's?)

She put the cake on the table, took off her apron, pulled up a chair, and began to eat it. (What did she eat? The cake? The table? Her apron? The chair?)

If there is no one clear antecedent, you must rewrite the sentence to make the reference clear. Sometimes the rewritten sentence may seem repetitive, but a little repetition is better than a lot of confusion.

unclear: Jim told Leonard his bike had been stolen.
clear: Jim told Leonard Jim's bike had been stolen.
clear: Jim told Leonard, "My bike has been stolen."
clear: Jim told Leonard Leonard's bike had been stolen.
clear: Jim told Leonard, "Your bike has been stolen."

unclear: She put the cake on the table, took off her apron, pulled up a chair, and began to eat it.
clear: She put the cake on the table, took off her apron, pulled up a chair, and began to eat the cake.

Sometimes the problem is a little more tricky. Can you spot what's wrong with this sentence?

> **unclear:** Bill decided to take a part-time job which worried his parents. (What worried Bill's parents? His decision to work part-time? Or the job itself?)

Be very careful with the pronoun *which*. If there is any chance that using *which* will confuse the reader, rewrite the sentence and get rid of *which*.

> **clear:** Bill's parents were worried about the kind of part-time job he chose.
> **clear:** Bill's decision to work part-time worried his parents.

Sometimes, a pronoun has nothing to refer to; it has no antecedent.

> **no antecedent:** When Bill got to the train station, they said the train was going to be late. (Who said the train was going to be late? The ticket agents? Strangers Bill met on the tracks?)
> **no antecedent:** Maria has always loved medicine and has decided that's what she wants to be. (What does "that" refer to? The only word it could refer to is "medicine," but Maria certainly doesn't want to be a medicine. She doesn't want to be an aspirin or a cough drop.)

If a pronoun lacks an antecedent, add an antecedent or get rid of the pronoun.

> **add an antecedent:** When Bill got to the train station and asked the ticket agents about the schedule, they said the train was going to be late. ("They" refers to the ticket agents.)
> **drop the pronoun:** Maria has always loved medicine and has decided she wants to be a physician.

Note: To check for clear reference of pronouns, underline any pronoun that may not be clear. Then try to draw a line from that pronoun to its antecedent. Are there two or more possible antecedents? Is there no antecedent? In either case, you need to rewrite.

TEACHING TIP

This is a good place to discuss the vague use of *they* and how often it is used incorrectly in conversation and in writing. Stress that vague references can be confusing and misleading. For example, "The management doesn't know what they are doing." Who, exactly, are *they*? Since management is a collective noun, and *they* has no antecedent in the sentence, *they* should be changed to *it* and *are* changed to *is*.

| Exercise 7 | **Rewriting Sentences for Clear Reference of Pronouns** |

Rewrite the following sentences so that the pronouns have clear references. You may add, take out, or change words.

INSTRUCTOR'S NOTE

Answers will vary. Possible answers shown at right.

1. *Stupidly, Leonard took his mother to a violent movie.*
   Leonard took his mother to a violent movie ~~which was stupid~~.

2. Years ago, *superstitious people* ~~they~~ believed that black cats were a sign of bad luck.

3. The heavy bowl fell on the tile floor, and *the tile floor* ~~it~~ cracked.

4. Laura told her best friend Celia that *Celia* ~~she~~ worried too much.

5. I'm glad I didn't go to Emerson High School because *the students at Emerson High are* ~~they're~~ all snobs and phonies.

6. My brother has always been fascinated by spaceflight, and
   he dreams of being an astronaut.
   ~~that's what he dreams of being.~~

7. Most of the conflicts between teenagers and their parents occur
the parents
because ~~they~~ always think age makes people wiser.

Tyler was shocked to find some
8. Searching in his grandparents' attic, ~~Tyler found some old love~~
old love letters.
~~letters which shocked him.~~

the restaurant owners
9. When we go to lunch at Sun Ray, ~~they~~ always offer a daily special.

Marco's
10. Brian discussed ~~his~~ bad temper with Marco.

Exercise 8 **Editing a Paragraph for Errors in Pronoun Agreement
and Reference**

Connect

Correct any errors in pronoun agreement or reference in the following
paragraph. There are six errors. Write your corrections above the line.

The amount of dirt and disorder three people can live in was revealed to me

last week. This revelation came when my roommates, Sean and Patrick, and I got

ready to move out of our rented apartment. One of the many responsibilities of

moving involves getting a refund of our security deposit. That is, we had the
the rental agency
responsibility of cleaning the apartment before they would refund our deposit.
was
Neither my roommates nor I were prepared for the shock of looking closely at the

dirt and trash in our living space. For years, we had lived like a gang of pleasure

seekers. Now we were forced to become a group of housecleaners determined to
its
work hard and earn their security deposit. Everyone in our situation knows the

endless sorting, scraping, wiping, washing, and dusting involved in moving out of
his or her
their rented home. The worst part involved the last hours of the awful chore when

we thought we were minutes from the end. Unfortunately, we kept discovering

dents in the wall, mold in the showers, and stains on the carpet. We couldn't see
the process
an end to it. Eventually, Sean, Patrick, and I gave up on creating a perfectly clean
we were satisfied with a partial
apartment. We lost a bit of our security deposit, but we did get a partial refund
refund.
which satisfied us.

Exercise 9 **Editing a Paragraph for Errors in Pronoun Agreement and
Reference**

Connect

Correct any errors in pronoun agreement or reference in the following
paragraph. There are seven errors. Write your corrections above the line.

My first day at a new school began as a frightening experience for an eight-year-old. My family had just moved from the city to the suburbs, and I faced the challenge of being the new student at midyear, when all the other students had made friends. As soon as my new teacher brought me into the classroom, they stared at *the students* me blankly. I sat at an empty desk, and nobody on either side of me turned their *his or her* head to smile. I felt that everybody had already formed their opinion of me and *his or her* saw me as uninteresting. Possibly, nobody cared enough to waste their time *his or her* looking at me. At lunch, my teacher was kind enough to lead me to a table full of classmates, but I was too shy to start a conversation. The group at the table went *its* on with their lunchtime rituals of laughing and joking. When the bell rang and we *his or her* filed back into the classroom, I wondered if anybody would ever want me for their *his or her* friend. Suddenly, someone behind me pushed me hard. It was a boy with curly *the grin* black hair and a wide grin. I saw it and pushed him back. At that moment, a friendship began.

Chapter Test: Using Pronouns Correctly: Agreement and Reference

Some of the sentences below are correct; others have errors in pronoun agreement or reference. Put an *X* next to the sentences with errors.

1. __X__ A man on the plane told Richard that he was in the wrong seat.

2. _____ Anybody with enough money can fulfill his or her dreams on the vacation island.

3. __X__ Armando was not particularly good at photography in school; now he is going to be one.

4. _____ Everything on the menu lost its appeal after I peeked into the restaurant's kitchen.

5. __X__ Amanda bought me a birthday gift which I liked.

6. _____ Adventure Motors held its Labor Day sale last weekend.

7. _____ Nothing in Colin's long and complicated explanation seemed as if it would convince my mother of his sincerity.

8. __X__ Did somebody in the student lounge leave their jacket on a chair?

9. _____ Neither of my grandparents had much time or money to spend on his or her appearance.

10. __X__ I'm never going to that club again; they were rude to me last night.

Using Pronouns Correctly: Consistency and Case

When you write, you write from a point of view, and each point of view gets its own form. If you write from the first person point of view, your pronouns are in the *I* (singular) or *we* (plural) forms. If you write from the second person point of view, your pronouns are in the *you* form, whether they are singular or plural. If you write from the third person point of view, your pronouns are in the *he*, *she*, or *it* (singular) or *they* (plural) forms.

Different kinds of writing may require different points of view. When you are writing a set of directions, for example, you may use the second person (*you*) point of view. An essay about your childhood may use the first person (*I*) point of view.

Whatever point of view you use, be consistent in using pronouns. That is, do not shift the form of your pronouns without some good reason.

not consistent: Every time *I* go to that mall, the parking lot is so crowded *you* have to drive around for hours, looking for a parking space.

consistent: Every time *I* go to that mall, the parking lot is so crowded *I* have to drive around for hours, looking for a parking space.

Exercise 1   **Consistency in Pronouns**

Correct any inconsistency in point of view in the sentences below. Cross out the incorrect pronoun and write the correct one above it.

1. Taking a long nap doesn't work well for me; ~~you~~ *I* can wake up feeling more tired than ever.

2. After all the arriving airline passengers stare at the empty revolving luggage carousel ten or twenty minutes, a long stream of luggage rolls slowly before ~~you~~ *them*.

3. My favorite aunt is the kind of relative who praises the smallest success ~~you~~ *I* achieve.

4. Drivers on the interstate highways need to be careful about entering the road; ~~you~~ *they* have to be sure to gather enough speed to merge into traffic.

5. Hallie and I like to shop at the Dollar Bargain Bin because ~~you~~ *we* can always find cheap cosmetics or jewelry there.

6. Sometimes I don't return Joe's calls, for once I start talking to him, he keeps ~~you~~ *me* on the phone for hours.

7. My boyfriend and I like camping near Lake Lion, but ~~you~~ *we* have to be prepared for hordes of mosquitoes in the summer.

8. Whenever I take the time to eat breakfast, I realize how a decent breakfast can give ~~you~~ *me* the energy to face a long day.

9. When I learned English at night school, the instructor was always patient with ~~you~~ *me* and gave me confidence in my abilities.

10. After one meeting with Tom, I believed he was a man who would always be honest with ~~you~~ *me* and would invest my money carefully.

Exercise 2   **Correcting Sentences with Consistency Problems**

Rewrite the following sentences, correcting any errors with consistency of pronouns. To make the corrections, you may have to change, add, or take out words.

1. Unless a teenager is strong enough to resist peer pressure and smart enough to recognize true friends, you will not have an easy trip to adulthood.

   rewrite: *Unless a teenager is strong enough to resist peer pressure and smart enough to recognize true friends, he or she will not have an easy trip to adulthood.*

INSTRUCTOR'S NOTE
Answers will vary. Possible answers shown at left.

2. Pierre becomes aware of his mother's sadness whenever she tells you about her childhood in Haiti.

   rewrite: *Pierre becomes aware of his mother's sadness whenever she tells him about her childhood in Haiti.*

3. Children attending Middlebrook Elementary School this fall must bring your certificate of vaccination before they are admitted to class.

   rewrite: *Children attending Middlebrook Elementary School in the fall must bring their certificate of vaccination before they are admitted to class.*

4. Laura and I cannot trust her cousin Miranda; if you tell her a secret, she reveals it to the whole neighborhood.

   rewrite: *Laura and I cannot trust her cousin Miranda; if we tell her a secret, she reveals it to the whole neighborhood.*

5. Students who have never used the college library should not be nervous because, after their library tour, you will discover that everything is easy to find.

   rewrite: *Students who have never used the college library should not be nervous because, after their library tour, they will discover that everything is easy to find.*

6. My seven-year-old likes the first day of school; he likes seeing his old school friends, wearing your new school clothes, and showing off his superiority to the scared kindergartners.

   rewrite: *My seven-year-old likes the first day of school; he likes seeing his old school friends, wearing his new school clothes, and showing off his superiority to the scared kindergartners.*

7. Some people can make friends easily because you know how to listen and are genuinely interested in others.

   rewrite: *Some people can make friends easily because they know how to listen and are genuinely interested in others.*

8. To me, Mrs. Carmichael is a strict teacher; you can give her a million excuses, but she will never let me out of class early.

   rewrite: *To me, Mrs. Carmichael is a strict teacher; I can give her a million excuses, but she will never let me out of class early.*

9. I can't let Cade go outside by himself anymore; since he learned to open the gate, you can't trust him to stay in the yard.

    rewrite: *I can't let Cade go outside by himself anymore; since he* *learned to open the gate, I can't trust him to stay in the yard.*

10. If a man wants a woman to admire him, you shouldn't brag about his money, status, or popularity with the ladies.

    rewrite: *If a man wants a woman to admire him, he shouldn't brag* *about his money, status, or popularity with the ladies.*

CHOOSING THE CASE OF PRONOUNS

Pronouns have forms that show number and person, and they also have forms that show **case**.

Singular Pronouns	Subjective Case	Objective Case	Possessive Case
1st person	I	me	my
2nd person	you	you	your
3rd person	he, she, it	him, her, it	his, her, its
	who, whoever	whom, whomever	whose
Plural Pronouns			
1st person	we	us	our
2nd person	you	you	your
3rd person	they	them	their
	who, whoever	whom, whomever	whose

The rules for choosing the case of pronouns are simple:

1. When a pronoun is used as a subject, use the subjective case.
2. When a pronoun is used as the object of a verb or the object of a preposition, use the objective case.
3. When a pronoun is used to show ownership, use the possessive case.

pronouns used as subjects:
He practices his pitching every day.
Bill painted the walls, and *we* polished the floors.
Who is making that noise?

pronouns used as objects:
Sarah called *him* yesterday.
He gave all his money to *me*.
With *whom* did you argue?

pronouns used to show possession:
I am worried about *my* grade in Spanish.
The nightclub has lost *its* popularity.
I wonder *whose* dog this is.

Pronoun Case in a Related Group of Words

You need to be careful in choosing case when the pronoun is part of a related group of words. If the pronoun is part of a related group of words, isolate the pronoun. Next, try out the pronoun choices. Then decide which pronoun is correct and write the correct sentence. For example, which of these sentences is correct?

> Aunt Sophie planned a big dinner for Tom and *I*.
> > or
> Aunt Sophie planned a big dinner for Tom and *me*.

Step 1: Isolate the pronoun. Eliminate the related words *Tom and*.

Step 2: Try each case:

> Aunt Sophie planned a big dinner for *I*.
> > or
> Aunt Sophie planned a big dinner for *me*.

Step 3: The correct sentence is

> Aunt Sophie planned a big dinner for Tom and me.

The pronoun acts as an object, so it takes the objective case.

Try working through the steps once more to be sure that you understand this principle. Which of the following sentences is correct?

> Last week, *me* and my friend took a ride on the new commuter train.
> > or
> Last week, *I* and my friend took a ride on the new commuter train.

Step 1: Isolate the pronoun. Eliminate the related words *and my friend*.

Step 2: Try each case:

> Last week, *me* took a ride on the new commuter train.
> > or
> Last week, *I* took a ride on the new commuter train.

Step 3: The correct sentence is

> Last week, I and my friend took a ride on the new commuter train.

The pronoun acts as a subject, so it takes the subjective case.

> **Note:** You can also write it this way:
> > Last week, my friend and I took a ride on the new commuter train.

COMMON ERRORS WITH CASE OF PRONOUNS

Be careful to avoid these common errors:

1. *Between* is a preposition, so the pronouns that follow it are objects of the preposition: between *us*, between *them*, between *you and me*. It is never correct to write *between you and I*.

   not this: ~~The plans for the surprise party must be kept a secret between you and I.~~

   but this: The plans for the surprise party must be kept a secret between you and me.

2. Never use *myself* as a replacement for *I* or *me*.

   not this: ~~My father and myself want to thank you for this honor.~~
   but this: My father and I want to thank you for this honor.

   not this: ~~She thought the prize should be awarded to Arthur and myself.~~
   but this: She thought the prize should be awarded to Arthur and me.

3. The possessive pronoun *its* has no apostrophe.

   not this: ~~The car held it's value.~~
   but this: The car held its value.

   not this: ~~The baby bird had fallen from it's nest.~~
   but this: The baby bird had fallen from its nest.

4. Pronouns that complete comparisons can be in the subjective, objective, or possessive case.

   subjective: Christa speaks better than *I*.
   objective: The storm hurt Manny more than *her*.
   possessive: My car is as fast as *his*.

   > **Note:** To decide on the correct pronoun, add the words that complete the comparison and say them aloud.

   Christa speaks better than I *speak*.
   The storm hurt Manny more than *the storm hurt* her.
   My car is as fast as his *car*.

5. *Who* and *whoever* are in the subjective case. *Whom* and *whomever* are in the objective case.

   subjective: *Who* came to the house?
   subjective: *Whoever* wants the books can take them.

   objective: *Whom* did Larry bring to the house?
   objective: You can bring *whomever* you like to the house.

   > **Note:** If you have trouble choosing between *who* and *whom*, or *whoever* and *whomever*, substitute *he* for *who* and *whoever*, and *him* for *whom* and *whomever* to check the correctness of your choice.

Check this sentence:

   Who made the cake?

Is it correct? Change the sentence, substituting *he* in one version, and *him* in another version.

   He made the cake.
   Him made the cake.

If *he* is correct, then *who* is correct.

Check another sentence:

   With whom are you arguing?

Is it correct? Change the sentence, substituting *he* in one version, and *him* in another version. To make your choice simpler, write the sentence as a statement, not a question:

   You are arguing with *he*.
   You are arguing with *him*.
   If *him* is correct, then *whom* is correct.

Exercise 3 **Choosing the Right Case of Pronoun**

Circle the correct pronoun in parentheses in each of the following sentences.

1. My sister and (I, myself) are honored to have won this community service award.

2. I will cooperate with (whoever, whomever) the committee selects to head the team.

3. Ted has a great deal of charm, but your personality is more open than (he, him, his).

4. I know how to make money, but my girlfriend is better at saving money than (I, me).

5. Once the roads were cleared, Keith and (he, him) drove into town to get supplies.

6. I told you that my serious illness was supposed to remain a secret between you and (I, me).

7. (Who, Whom) did the panel choose as the most talented performer?

8. If Technology Haven would lower (its, it's) prices, I would buy all my computer supplies at that store.

9. A drunken driver and (we, us) collided at the intersection of Carlson Boulevard and Fifth Street.

10. Two investors and (I, myself) are considering the purchase and renovation of an old Mexican restaurant on McKinley Road.

Exercise 4 **Write Your Own Text on Pronoun Case**

Collaborate

With a partner or with a group, write two sentences that could be used as examples for each of the following rules. The first one is done for you.

Rule 1: When a pronoun is used as a subject, use the subjective case.

examples: *He complained about the noise in the street.*

Tired and hungry, they stopped for lunch.

Rule 2: When a pronoun is used as the object of a verb or the object of a preposition, use the objective case.

examples: *Jack's remarks hurt her.*

Samuel gave the ticket to me.

Rule 3: When a pronoun is used to show ownership, use the possessive case.

examples: *The cat hurt its paw.*

Anthony lost his temper.

Rule 4: When a pronoun is part of a related group of words, isolate the pronoun to choose the case. (For examples, write two sentences in which the pronoun is part of a related group of words.)

examples: *Jack and he sold the car.*

Mother is making dinner for Denise and me.

Connect

Exercise 5 Editing a Paragraph for Errors in Pronoun Consistency and Case

In the following paragraph, correct any errors in pronoun consistency and case. There are six errors. Write your corrections above the line.

When I cannot think of a gift for my father, I go to the place I call The Men's Gadget and Toy Store. This store, officially called Stonewood, is full of items that no one needs. The items seem to fly off the shelves because men (or the women who shop for men) find these inventions attractive. The staff is mostly male and knows how to operate all the gadgets; however, the shoppers are as likely to be female as male. Maybe the women, like myself [*me*], are desperate to find some gift that isn't a shirt, a tie, a sweater, or some cologne for a husband, boyfriend, brother, grandfather, uncle, or father. Stonewood offers new choices; their [*its*] tricks are luring men into the store and soothing women's anxieties. For example, last year I bought my father a tiny, battery-powered fan. It's [*Its*] size was tiny, but it's [*its*] price was not. This year, I found a small inflatable pillow with a dark blue cloth cover and a tiny valve. Stonewood advertised this pillow as a travel pillow, and I gave it to my father even though he rarely goes anywhere. As far as I know, the pillow has spent its life in a dresser drawer, and the tiny fan sits in a closet. While these gifts appear useless, me [*I*] and my father enjoy looking at them and wondering about the person who invented them. He also likes to show these gifts to friends. Stonewood must make a fortune if there are many people like my father and I [*me*].

Connect

Exercise 6 Editing a Paragraph for Errors in Pronoun Consistency and Case

In the following paragraph, correct any errors in pronoun consistency and case. There are six errors. Write your corrections above the line.

Last month, the vice president of the Volunteers for Safe Streets Club asked Arthur Sansovino and myself [*me*] to prepare a report on the group's financial assets and on it's [*its*] future needs. The work of the report was divided between Arthur and I [*me*] so that both aspects of the report are covered adequately. Arthur's most important finding is that this year's financial statement is better than last year's. This year,

Volunteers for Safe Streets has a balance of $1,250 in the treasury, with no bills left to be paid. However, my research uncovered a need for more money, especially if the club wants to expand its education program for children and expand the night time patrols. Clearly, ~~us~~ *we* members of the club know that working for safe streets is a continuing challenge. In studying the club's future needs, I have learned that an organization must struggle to collect donations when people don't know ~~you~~ *it* well. Therefore, I believe that next year the club should work on becoming better known in the community. To end this summary, I want to say that Arthur and ~~me~~ *I* welcome any questions and will be distributing copies of our complete report.

Chapter Test: Using Pronouns Correctly: Consistency and Case

Some of the sentences below are correct; others have errors in pronoun consistency or case. Put an *X* next to the sentences with errors.

1. _____ Whom did you call about the leak in the roof?

2. _____ I and a few friends spent the day at a small amusement park in High Ridge.

3. __X__ Yesterday I felt so hot that you could not walk barefoot on the pavement.

4. _____ Travis is upset; somebody's photograph in the exhibit was judged better than his.

5. __X__ On behalf of the agency and myself, I am happy to accept this public service award.

6. __X__ For Abigail and I, the chance to visit New Zealand was a great opportunity.

7. __X__ Clifford stopped going to the city swim meets when you had to pay a high price for admission.

8. __X__ Once I got a full-time job, saving for a home became easier for my husband and I.

9. __X__ You can socialize with whoever you like; you don't have to ask my permission.

10. _____ I had a carefree childhood; no child worried less than I.

Punctuation: The Basics

THE PERIOD

Periods are used two ways.

1. Use a period to mark the end of a sentence that makes a statement.

We invited him to dinner at our house.
When Richard spoke, no one paid attention.

2. Use a period after abbreviations.

Mr. Ryan
James Wing, Sr.
10:00 p.m.

> **Note:** If a sentence ends with a period marking an abbreviation, do not add a
> second period.

Exercise 1   **Using Periods**

Add periods where they are needed in each of the following sentences.

1. Oscar bought about fifteen lbs. of special food for his sick terrier.

2. When the elementary school children went on field trips, they were nervous around people like Mr. Carlson, the principal.

3. Isaac wants to get a B.S. degree in biology, and his friend, Dr. Hamilton, told him to prepare by taking many science classes in high school.

4. Tell Ms. Marko or Mr. Scanlon about the parking problems in the gymnasium parking lot.

5. Last night I studied for my social sciences test until nearly 2:00 a.m.

6. Nicholas Anderson, Sr., is a better businessman than his son.

7. Someday, I want to be known as Cecilia Knowles, R.N., so I am going to college to study nursing.

8. We had a traditional Thanksgiving dinner with turkey, stuffing, cranberry sauce, pumpkin pie, etc. at my mother's house.

9. After Sgt. Albury left the scene, people crowded around the yellow tape to see what was left of the burned car.

10. You could have asked Aunt Maya to visit us next September.

THE QUESTION MARK

Use a question mark after a direct question.

> Isn't she adorable?
> Do you have car insurance?

If a question is not a direct question, it does not get a question mark.

> They asked if I thought their grandchild was adorable.
> She questioned whether I had car insurance.

Exercise 2   **Punctuating with Periods and Question Marks**

Add any missing periods and question marks to each sentence below.

1. Fred asked me if I would drive to St. Louis with him.

2. Have the painters finished the bathroom walls yet?

3. Leonard wanted to find out whether his old girlfriend was still single.

4. Is it possible that the people in the house next door have gone away for good?

5. Maybe you can tell me when Mr. Lynch is arriving at the airport.

6. If Javier goes to Dr Nair for the surgery, Javier will be in the hands of an experienced surgeon

7. Wasn't that a terrible experience ?

8. Annabel wanted to know why the cat loved to scratch the rough wood of the picnic table

9. Can anyone tell me where Ms Harris meets her 2:00 p m class ?

10. There is some question about the exact time of the incident

---

Exercise 3   **Editing a Paragraph for Errors in Periods and Question Marks**

In the following paragraph, correct errors in punctuating with periods and question marks. The errors may involve missing or incorrect punctuation. There are ten errors.

Mr.

When I saw Mr Pollack for the first time, I wondered what kind of boss he

?

would be? Would he be easygoing or mean, understanding or inflexible. After a

week of working with him, I realized that he was a mix of all these qualities. On

the first day that he worked at the store, Mr. Pollack seemed to be inflexible. In

his first words to his new employees, he stressed the rules He warned us about

etc.,

lateness, inappropriate dress, absences, etc, and he said that he would enforce the

rules without exceptions Every day of the first week, Mr. Pollack was at the store

a.m.

before the start of the 5:00 am shift. In fact, some of the staff were not sure

whether he spent the night in the storeroom. He seemed to be watching all his

employees, sneaking behind their backs and spying. Quickly, Mr. Pollack became

unpopular. Then, after six days of his supervision, an accident happened. Mrs

Lerner, an older woman who has been with the store for years, slipped and fell on

a wet patch of the newly mopped floor. Mr. Pollack stayed by her side, comforting

her until the ambulance came. He told her not to worry about hospital bills or

missed days at work. He assured her that no matter how long it took for her to get

well, she would have a job waiting for her. On that day, I first saw the human side

of Mr Pollack

Section Test: Punctuation: The Period and the Question Mark

Some of the sentences below are correct; others have errors in the use of periods and question marks. Put an *X* next to the sentences with errors.

1. __X__ After I got to know Dr Stefanovic, I trusted her with my medical care.

2. _____ Carl was not sure whether the restaurant was open for breakfast.

3. _____ The officer could have asked Katy Gomez about the time of the break-in.

4. __X__ Now that Eddie has finished medical school, he has become Edward Obara, M D

5. __X__ At the Crosstown Market, Mr O'Neill was selling two lbs of organic sweet potatoes for two dollars.

6. _____ Will Abraham ever finish restoring his old Ford Mustang?

7. __X__ My roommate woke me up at 6:00 am yesterday so that we could study for our botany test.

8. _____ Uncle Colin has been calling and questioning me about my plans for St. Patrick's Day.

9. _____ Do you think about Nate very often?

10. __X__ Since my father and I share the same first, middle, and last names, he is Calvin B Kiyosaki, Sr.

THE COMMA

There are four main ways to use a comma, as well as other, less important ways. *Memorize the four main ways.* If you can learn and understand these four rules, you will be more confident and correct in your punctuation. That is, you will use a comma only when you have a reason to do so; you will not be scattering commas in your sentences simply because you think a comma might fit, as many writers do.

The four main ways to use a comma are as a lister, a linker, an introducer, or an inserter (use two commas).

Use a Comma as a Lister

Commas support items in a series. These items can be words, phrases, or clauses.

> **comma between words in a list:** Her bedroom was decorated in shades of blue, green, and gold.
>
> **comma between phrases in a list:** I looked for my ring under the coffee table, between the sofa cushions, and behind the chairs.
>
> **comma between clauses in a list:** Last week he graduated from college, he found the woman of his dreams, and he won the lottery.

> **Note:** In a list, the comma before *and* is optional, but most writers use it.

INSTRUCTOR'S NOTE

Printer friendly handouts and self-scoring exercises on comma use and other forms of punctuation can be found at *http://owl.english.purdue.edu/handouts/interactive*, part of a comprehensive "fair use" Web site sponsored by the Purdue University Writing Lab.

Exercise 4   **Using a Comma as a Lister**

Add commas only where they are needed in the following sentences. Do not add any other punctuation or change existing punctuation.

TEACHING TIP

Have volunteers read aloud their punctuated sentences from this exercise. They should soon become aware of the natural pauses and rhythms of the sentences.

1. Meat' fish' cheese' beans' and dairy products are sources of protein.

2. Nicole can do the laundry' Mike can vacuum the house' and I can clean the kitchen.

3. The thief caught with the money was silent' snarling' and slippery.

4. Bargain prices for DVD players' satellite radios' and flat-screen televisions drew shoppers to the electronics store.

5. I will wash' dry' and fold your dirty clothes when you take them off the floor and put them in the laundry basket.

6. My aunt knew she was spending too much time and money on television shopping channels when boxes of glittering jewelry' expensive makeup' and household gadgets started piling up in her house.

7. Eric is self-centered' he lacks any sense of responsibility' and he lies to his friends.

8. Sweaters' pajamas' and scarves are the only gifts my aunt ever gave me.

9. I misplaced my backpack with my chemistry workbook' cell phone' and student ID card in it.

10. There are certain creatures I hope never to see in my house; these include rats' mice' snakes' and lizards.

Use a Comma as a Linker

A comma and a coordinating conjunction link two independent clauses. The coordinating conjunctions are *for, and, nor, but, or, yet, so*. The comma goes in front of the coordinating conjunction:

> I have to get to work on time, or I'll get into trouble with my boss.
> My mother gave me a beautiful card, and she wrote a note on it.

Exercise 5 **Using a Comma as a Linker**

Add commas only where they are needed in the following sentences. Some sentences do not need commas. Do not change words or add any other punctuation.

1. Dr. Pinsky used to clean my teeth' and he would give me a new toothbrush afterward.

2. My daughter can spend the weekend with her father' or she can stay at her grandmother's house.

3. A day with my best friend lets me escape from my worries and act like a child again.

4. Todd wouldn't talk to his wife' nor would he listen to his friend's advice.

5. Sophie must be sick' for she has missed every class this week.

6. George had planned a perfect holiday party' but something went wrong.

7. Jerry has tried several diets and exercise plans yet can't seem to lose weight.

8. Lisa's cousin Lev is quiet and rarely goes out to the movies or sports events.

9. My dog missed me' so he went to sleep with an old sock of mine in his mouth.

10. Tim does all his assignments at the last minute' yet he always manages to turn them in on time.

Use a Comma as an Introducer

Put a comma after introductory words, phrases, or clauses in a sentence.

a comma after an introductory word:
Yes, I agree with you on that issue.
Dad, give me some help with the dishes.

a comma after an introductory phrase:
In the long run, you'll be better off without him.
Before the anniversary party, my father bought my mother a necklace.

a comma after an introductory clause:
If you call home, your parents will be pleased.
When the phone rings, I am always in the shower.

Exercise 6   Using a Comma as an Introducer

Add commas only where they are needed in the following sentences. Some sentences do not need commas. Do not change words or add any other punctuation.

1. In the back of the dark room stood a man from my past.

2. Unless the weather improves' we won't be able to hunt tomorrow.

3. Sure' I can take care of your cat while you are away.

4. Courtney' do you have an extra pencil or pen?

5. On my little brother's birthday' I took him to a water park.

6. While Bernard grills the fish' you can make the rice and beans.

7. Behind the curtains are two children playing hide-and-seek.

8. After a few days' Luisa got used to the noisy city streets.

9. If he calls' tell him I went away for the weekend.

10. Under the circumstances' you should be the one to apologize for the misunderstanding.

Use a Comma as an Inserter

When words or phrases that are *not* necessary are inserted into a sentence, put a comma on *both* sides of the inserted material:

The game, unfortunately, was rained out.
My test score, believe it or not, was the highest in the class.
Potato chips, my favorite snack food, are better-tasting when they're fresh.
James, caught in the middle of the argument, tried to keep the peace.

Using commas as inserters requires that you decide what is essential to the meaning of the sentence and what is nonessential.

> **If you do not need material in a sentence, put commas around the material. If you need material in a sentence, do not put commas around the material.**

For example, consider this sentence:

> The girl who called me was selling magazine subscriptions.

Do you need the words "who called me" to understand the meaning of the sentence? To answer that question, write the sentence without those words:

> The girl was selling magazine subscriptions.

Reading the shorter sentence, you might ask, "Which girl?" The words *who called me* are essential to the sentence. Therefore you do not put commas around them.

> **correct:** The girl who called me was selling magazine subscriptions.

Remember that the proper name of a person, place, or thing is always sufficient to identify it. Therefore any information that follows a proper name is inserted material; it gets commas on both sides.

> Video Views, which is nearby, has the best prices for video and DVD rentals.
> Sam Harris, the man who won the marathon, lives on my block.

Note: Sometimes the material that is needed in a sentence is called *essential* (or *restrictive*), and the material that is not needed is called *nonessential* (or *nonrestrictive*).

TEACHING TIP

To emphasize the difference between essential and nonessential information, write the following sentence on the board: "My grandmother who rides a motorcycle is eighty." Inserting commas implies the writer has one grandmother; omitting commas implies the writer has two grandmothers.

Exercise 7   **Using Commas as Inserters**

Add commas only where they are needed in the following sentences. Some sentences do not need commas.

1. A house full of toys will not always make a troubled child happy.

2. My best friend his eyes red and swollen mourned the loss of his cousin.

3. Mr. Murdock could of course decide to raise the phone rates.

4. Drivers who take the shortcut to the airport can save at least ten minutes and avoid the congestion at the toll plaza.

5. Our neighbor an enthusiastic gardener has transformed his yard into a small park.

6. The Polar Express which both children and adults enjoy was created with an experimental animation process.

7. The little girl at the end of the line has dropped the ice cream out of her cone.

8. Ultimate Books the bookstore in the Midland Mall has the biggest collection of fantasy books and magazines.

9. The woman in the gray suit introduced the guest of honor at the luncheon.

10. Baltimore,where I was born,has changed a great deal since I was a child.

Remember the four main ways to use a comma—as a lister, a linker, an introducer, and an inserter—and you'll solve many of your problems with punctuation.

Exercise 8 **Punctuating with Commas: The Four Main Ways**

Add commas only where they are needed in the following sentences. Do not add any other punctuation, and do not change any existing punctuation. Some sentences do not need commas.

1. Until I get a good job,I have to watch my spending,use public transportation,and take advantage of free entertainment.

2. Byron's house is near the campus,so he can ride his bike to his classes.

3. Shakira will never be lonely,for she has a group of loving,long-time,and loyal friends.

4. No,we can't get the car repaired until we find a mechanic who works on Saturdays.

5. Shocked and happy,Lena reread the winning numbers,and her grip on the lottery ticket tightened.

6. The puppy with the white face is the smartest-looking one in the litter.

7. Ruben stood at the side of the road and waited for Diego to catch up with him.

8. Patrick asked me to return his electric drill,paint brushes,and paint scraper before the weekend.

9. If you want a good used car,go to Edward Motors,the car lot next to the flea market.

10. The Egg Palace,the old place on Route 4,has the cheapest breakfast,the best coffee,and the nicest staff in town.

Other Ways to Use a Comma

There are other places to use a comma. Reviewing these uses will help you feel more confident as a writer.

1. **Use commas with quotations**. Use a comma to set off a direct quotation from the rest of the sentence.

   My father told me, "Money doesn't grow on trees."
   "Let's split the bill," Raymond said.

Note that the comma that introduces the quotation goes before the quotation marks. But once the quotation has begun, commas or periods go inside the quotation marks.

2. **Use commas with dates and addresses**. Use commas between the items in dates and addresses.

> August 5, 1980, is Chip's date of birth.
> We lived at 133 Emerson Road, Lake Park, Pennsylvania, before we
>   moved to Florida.

Notice the comma after the year in the date, and the comma after the state in the address. These commas are needed when you write a date or address within a sentence.

3. **Use commas in numbers**. Use commas in numbers of one thousand or larger.

> The price of equipment was $1,293.

4. **Use commas for clarity**. Put a comma when you need it to make something clear.

> Whoever it is, is about to be punished.
> While hunting, the eagle is swift and strong.
> I don't like to dress up, but in this job I have to, to get ahead.

Exercise 9 Punctuation: Other Ways to Use a Comma

Add commas wherever they are needed in the following sentences. Do not add any other punctuation, and do not change any existing punctuation.

1. "There isn't any milk in the refrigerator" my little boy complained.

2. On January 1 2002 Suzanne and Colin moved into a small house in Clifton New Jersey.

3. Be sure that anything you do you do for the right reasons.

4. The electric bill at my father's restaurant can run as high as $1500 a month.

5. "I have lived at 535 Orchid Place Denver Colorado for more than six years" Alex told me.

6. Kevin graduated from high school on June 15 2007 and soon started work as a landscaper in Mobile Alabama.

7. Melissa stood in front of the clothes in her closet and muttered "I have got to clean out this mess."

8. "Let's talk this over like adults" my cousin pleaded.

9. "It's going to be twins" my wife said on March 22 1999.

10. The car salesman said "The sticker price for that car is only $26299."

Exercise 10 Punctuating with Commas: A Comprehensive Exercise

Add commas only where they are needed in the following sentences. Do not add any other punctuation, and do not change any existing punctuation. Some of the sentences do not need commas.

1. Fortunately I made it to work on time and avoided another lecture from my supervisor.

2. "Never promise more than you can deliver" my father used to say.

3. As I tucked my daughter into bed'she held her teddy bear close to her heart.

4. The man that got arrested was from my neighborhood.

5. It took me a whole day to sort through my bills'finish my math assignment'and study for my accounting test.

6. My sister'the first member of our family to go to college'is a pediatrician.

7. Isaac always complained about his high school science classes but wound up becoming a science teacher.

8. All I can say'Mario'is that you have done me a great favor.

9. Frank was awarded a Purple Heart on May 12'2003'at a special ceremony.

10. China'silver'and glassware are the specialties of the store'so I am going there to look for a wedding gift.

Exercise 11   **Editing a Paragraph for Errors in Commas**

Connect

In the following paragraph, correct any errors related to punctuating with commas. The errors may involve missing or incorrect use of commas. There are eleven errors.

My brother is'in general'a good person'but he has one major flaw. He refuses to

lend me his car. I have asked to borrow his car to go to a movie'to get to school on

time'to go out Saturday night, and even to go to work. In every case, he has

refused. I am not sure why he is so selfish about his car. It isn't a magnificent car.

70,533
It's a dented old KIA and has 70533 miles on it. I have tried to reason with my

brother about his selfishness. Unfortunately'my brother makes the same comment

no comma needed
each time, that I mention the car. "Think about the dent in the car" he says. He

no comma needed   ,
gives me a phony smile, and adds "Remember how the dent got there." Well, I

guess he has a point. I'm the one who dented the car. It happened on the one and

only time he let me borrow it.

Section Test: Punctuation: The Comma

Some of the sentences below are correct; others have errors in punctuating with commas. Put an *X* next to the sentences with errors.

1. __*X*__ Christina Roberts, my best friend since high school was born in Fort Lauderdale, during a powerful hurricane.

2. _____ The damage to the empty house was senseless, and whoever did it, did it out of pure meanness.

3. __X__ No I don't want your old computer, printer, or digital camera.

4. _____ Sam had an enjoyable evening with Cassie last weekend but never bothered to call her again.

5. _____ Super Foods, which is open twenty-four hours a day, is the best place for last-minute grocery shopping.

6. _____ A little girl from the children's hospital led the group in singing a popular song.

7. _____ Angry and frightened, the woman whose purse had been stolen screamed loudly, picked herself off the pavement, and ran after the thief.

8. _____ "No one will criticize you for telling the truth," my brother told me.

9. __X__ Ella, her face shining with happiness, graduated from college on May 22, 2007 with a degree in physical therapy.

10. __X__ Getting my truck repaired cost me $1214, but it was cheaper than making enormous car payments on a new truck.

The Semicolon and the Colon

THE SEMICOLON

There are two ways to use semicolons:

1. **Use a semicolon to join two independent clauses:**

   Michael loved his old Camaro; he worked on it every weekend.
   The situation was hopeless; I couldn't do anything.

> **Note:** If the independent clauses are joined by a conjunctive adverb, you will still need a semicolon. You will also need a comma after any conjunctive adverb that is more than one syllable long.

conjunctive adverb
He was fluent in Spanish; *consequently*, he was the perfect companion for our trip to Venezuela.

conjunctive adverb
I called the hotline for twenty minutes; *then* I called another number.

> **For Your Information:** A list of common conjunctive adverbs is on page 395.

Independent clauses joined by coordinating conjunctions (the words *for, and, nor, but, or, yet,* and *so*) do not need semicolons. Use a comma in front of the coordinating conjunction:

coordinating conjunction
Michael loved his old Camaro, *and* he worked on it every weekend.
coordinating conjunction
He was fluent in Spanish, *so* he was the perfect companion for our trip to Venezuela.

2. **Use semicolons to separate the items on a list that contains commas.** Adding semicolons will make the list easier to read:

> The contestants came from Rochester, New York; Pittsburgh, Pennsylvania; Trenton, New Jersey; and Boston, Massachusetts. (The semicolons show that Rochester is a city in the state of New York, Pittsburgh is a city in the state of Pennsylvania, and so forth.)

> The new officers of the club will be Althea Bethell, president; Francois Riviere, vice president; Ricardo Perez, secretary; and Lou Phillips, treasurer. (The semicolons link the person, Althea Bethell, with the office, president, and so forth.)

Exercise 12   Punctuating with Semicolons

Add any missing semicolons to the following sentences. In some sentences, you may have to change commas to semicolons.

1. The noise of construction workers outside the building grew louder; meanwhile, I was trying to conduct a serious conversation on the telephone.

2. Two years ago, I was terrified of water; now I love to jump into the deep end of the pool.

3. My aunt took me to a fancy restaurant for dinner; in addition, she bought me two new CDs at a music store.

4. Stacey is smart, attractive, and outgoing, yet she longs to be more like her younger sister.

5. Mario, my father; Mark, my older brother; Michael, my younger brother; and Michelle, my sister, all have first names that begin with *M*.

6. Gene is upset about something; you need to talk to him.

7. Arthur was wearing a new jacket and had just gotten a haircut; in fact, he looked quite handsome.

8. I studied hard for my grammar test; thus I didn't think it was too difficult.

9. Sarah will call the cable company or stop by its office for an explanation of the latest bill.

10. I have to pack my suitcase tonight; otherwise, I might forget something in the morning rush to the airport.

THE COLON

A colon is used at the end of a complete statement. It introduces a list or an explanation:

colon introduces a list:

When I went grocery shopping, I picked up a few things: milk, eggs, and coffee.

colon introduces an explanation:

The room was a mess: dirty clothes were piled on the chairs, wet towels were thrown on the floor, and an empty pizza box was tossed in the closet.

Remember that the colon comes after a complete statement. What comes after the colon explains or describes what came before the colon. Look once more at the two examples, and you'll see the point.

When I went grocery shopping, I picked up a few things: milk, eggs, and coffee. (The words after the colon—*milk, eggs, and coffee*—explain what few things I picked up.)

The room was a mess: dirty clothes were piled on the chairs, wet towels were thrown on the floor, and an empty pizza box was tossed in the closet. (In this sentence, all the words after the colon describe what the mess was like.)

Some people use a colon every time they put a list in a sentence, but this is not a good rule to follow. Instead, remember that a colon, even one that introduces a list, must come after a complete statement.

not this: ~~When I go to the beach, I always bring: suntan lotion, a big towel, and a cooler with iced tea.~~

but this: When I go to the beach, I always bring my supplies: suntan lotion, a big towel, and a cooler with iced tea.

A colon may also introduce long quotations.

On December 8, 1941, the day after the Japanese attacked Pearl Harbor, President Franklin Delano Roosevelt summed up the situation: "Hostilities exist. There is no blinking at the fact that our people, our territory, and our interests are in grave danger." (Note that what comes after the colon explains what came before it.)

Exercise 13 Punctuating with Colons

Add colons where they are needed in the following sentences. Some sentences do not need a colon.

1. When you go to the cabin for the weekend, be sure to fill your car with groceries, extra blankets, insect repellent, books, binoculars, and fishing gear.

2. My husband did a superb job of cleaning the bathroom a shining bathtub, a spotless sink, a gleaming toilet, a sink without toothpaste stuck on it, and even a floor free of footprints.

3. Since I had twenty dollars left over at the end of the week, I bought some small surprises for my husband a can of cashews, a bottle of wine, and his favorite magazine.

4. Until we cleaned out the garage, we had a collection of tools, ladders, empty boxes, lawn chairs, broken appliances, and rags crowded into the space.

5. My cat brings me what he thinks are trophies a dead lizard, a mouse, even a small snake.

6. Our neighborhood has several Fourth of July traditions flags flying in people's yards, a parade of small children on their bikes or in strollers, and a community barbecue on a dead-end street.

7. If you want to contribute to the food drive for victims of the storm, you can bring canned food, bread and rolls, bottled water, and paper plates and towels.

8. My grandmother believes that there are two kinds of children the ones who behave and the ones who don't.

9. The bridesmaids had their choice of three colors for their dresses pink, yellow, or lavender.

10. The men looked like rap celebrities lots of jewelry, designer clothes, and shoes that cost more than my monthly salary.

Exercise 14   Using Semicolons and Colons

Add semicolons and colons where they are needed in the following sentences. You might have to change a comma to a semicolon.

1. I will never go to a sushi restaurant the idea of eating raw fish makes me sick.

2. You need floor mats for your car, and be sure to look for the usual auto supplies motor oil, car wax, and windshield wiper fluid.

3. Leroy sent me a get-well card he's always thoughtful.

4. If you go to the drug store, get me some toothpaste, hair gel, and aspirin.

5. Arthur seems like a trustworthy employee, on the other hand, I don't know that much about him.

6. There has been a shake-up in the managerial staff of Tompkins Motors, so the new leaders are Karen Killian, manager, Pierre LaValle, assistant manager, Ron Jessup, service manager, and Lorena Robles, business manager.

7. After my father got a job with a hotel, he took classes in accounting, customer relations, restaurant management, and business law.

8. Your parents love Luisa, also, she is fond of them.

9. Every time I take my father to a good restaurant, he orders the same thing a salad with thousand island dressing, a steak, and a baked potato.

10. Marianne skipped dinner last night then she left the house at 10:00 a.m.

Exercise 15   Editing a Paragraph for Errors in Semicolons and Colons

In the following paragraph, correct any errors related to punctuating with semicolons or colons. The errors may involve missing or incorrect use of semicolons or commas. There are seven errors.

Miscommunication can lead to a pleasant surprise. My surprise began yesterday when I asked my husband to pick up a few items at the supermarket. He was

;

on his way out the door at the last minute, he asked, "Do you need anything?" "Get

no colon needed

something for lunch," I called. I told him to buy: some turkey sandwiches, potato

:

salad, and apples. He came back with all the wrong items a frozen turkey instead

of turkey sandwiches, sweet potatoes instead of potato salad, and an apple pie

instead of apples. He claimed that these items were exactly what I had ordered.

My husband has always loved the turkey, sweet potatoes, and apple pie we eat at

Thanksgiving, and I suspected he had grabbed the chance to buy the ingredients

;

for his favorite meal. At first, I was angry then I calmed down. We couldn't eat a

,   ;

frozen turkey for lunch; so I'd have to adapt. He had brought me food for dinner

as a result, we'd have a lovely dinner. Late that night, after the turkey had baked

for many hours and the sweet potatoes had become candied yams, we had a deli-

:

cious, Thanksgiving-style dinner in June. In addition, I learned a new lesson make

the most of any surprise that comes your way.

Section Test: Punctuation: The Semicolon and the Colon

Some of the following sentences are correct; others have errors in the use of semicolons and colons. Put an *X* next to the sentences with errors.

1. _____ Drawn by the famous country singer's last concert, people came from all over the southern states: Gainesville, Florida; Savannah, Georgia; Huntsville, Alabama; and Jackson, Mississippi.

2. _____ Don't try to convince me; I'm not going anywhere with you.

3. __*X*__ Amanda forgot to pack her medication; so we had to turn around and drive fifty miles back to her house.

4. _____ Carlos will eat just about any cookie in the world: stale cookies, cookie crumbs, half-eaten cookies, even cookies that have fallen on the floor.

5. __*X*__ My cousin got stuck in traffic: then his car overheated.

6. _____ If you go to the Bahamas, be sure to enjoy the natural beauty: the turquoise water, the powdery white beaches, and the amazing undersea creatures.

7. __*X*__ Three of my former teachers have won teaching awards: Mrs. Anthony, my first-grade teacher, Mrs. Evans, my fifth-grade teacher; and Mr. Goldfarb, my tenth-grade history teacher.

8. <u>X</u>   Charlie won't talk to me about his worries; nor will he share them with his mother.

9. _____   When Danny shops for clothes, he buys sneakers, tee shirts, jeans, and hooded jackets; he never buys a dress shirt or slacks.

10. _____   In my first term in college, I took Fundamentals of Mathematics, Introduction to Sociology, and Art Appreciation.

THE APOSTROPHE

Use the apostrophe in the following ways:

1. **Use an apostrophe in contractions to show that letters have been omitted.**

   do not   = don't
   I will   = I'll
   is not   = isn't
   she would = she'd
   will not   = won't

Also use the apostrophe to show that numbers have been omitted:

   the summer of 1998 = the summer of '98

Exercise 16   Using Apostrophes in Contractions

Add apostrophes where they are necessary in each sentence below.

1. Dr. Fanelli is a great veterinarian; she'll tell you what's wrong with your potbellied pig.

2. My grandfather never stops talking about the blizzard of '84 and how he didn't think he'd live through it.

3. The cruise wasn't what I'd expected, but I'll never forget it.

4. How's your new baby doing?

5. Terry won't tell you that there's a problem with the financing for the car.

6. Henry and Lori couldn't make the trip this week; they'll come next month when they've got more time.

7. I haven't seen Monica lately; I hear she's got a new job.

8. If you're sick, you'd better stay home from work today.

9. It's wonderful to see dolphins in their natural habitat.

10. Parents shouldn't argue in front of their small children; the children don't know how to cope with family conflict.

2. **Use an apostrophe to show possession. If a word does not end in s, show ownership by adding an apostrophe and s.**

   the ring belongs to Jill   = Jill's ring
   the wallet belongs to somebody   = somebody's wallet
   the books are owned by my father = my father's books

If two people jointly own something, put the 's on the name of the second person listed.

> Ann and Mike own a house = Ann and Mike's house

If a word already ends in s and you want to show ownership, just add an apostrophe.

the ring belongs to Frances	= Frances' ring
two boys own a dog	= the boys' dog
the house belongs to Ms. Jones	= Ms. Jones' house

Caution: Be careful with apostrophes. These words, the possessive pronouns, do not take apostrophes: *his, hers, theirs, ours, yours, its.*

not this: ~~The pencils were their's.~~
but this: The pencils were theirs.

not this: ~~The steak lost it's flavor.~~
but this: The steak lost its flavor.

Exercise 17   **Using Apostrophes to Show Possession**

Add apostrophes where they are needed in the following sentences. Some sentences do not need apostrophes.

1. Mrs. Noriko promised to improve the company's marketing division and expand its overseas office.

2. I went to Charles and Amy's wedding yesterday, and I thought their wedding cake tasted better than yours.

3. I tried to put the dinner dishes, pots, and pans away quietly, but I dropped one pot's lid against the stove's hood, creating a horrible, clanking sound.

4. Catherine and Anthony are creative people, and the credit for renovating the pediatric wing of the hospital is all theirs.

5. I hope that, when I mentioned the changes at the women's club, I did not hurt anyone's feelings.

6. Be careful when you pack my aunt's photograph albums; her whole life is contained in them.

7. I miss San Diego's weather, but I love Boston's college life and its sense of history.

8. My sister Allison's musical ability is all hers; no one else in the family can sing, play an instrument, or read music.

9. I had to describe the lost suitcase to the airport cargo manager so that he could be sure the bag was ours.

10. In a week or two, the beautiful tree will have lost all its gold and scarlet leaves.

3. Use the apostrophe for special uses of time, and to create a plural of numbers mentioned as numbers, letters mentioned as letters, and words that normally do not have plurals.

special uses of time: It will take a week's work.
numbers mentioned as numbers: Take out the 5's.

INSTRUCTOR'S NOTE

Some students have learned that the "proper" way to indicate possession for proper names ending in s is to add 's. You can assure students that either James' or James's, for example, is correct. However, you can also note that newspapers and magazines have their own style sheets and preferences regarding these options.

INSTRUCTOR'S NOTE

MLA and *Chicago Manual of Style* guides advise writers to avoid the apostrophe in the plural of numbers written as numbers. However, some college-level grammar guides stipulate that 7's or 7s is acceptable, and newspapers and magazines have their own preferences.

letters mentioned as letters: Cross your *t*'s.
words that normally do not have plurals: I want no more *maybe*'s.

Caution: Do not add an apostrophe to a simple plural.

not this: ~~He lost three suitcase's.~~
but this: He lost three suitcases.

Exercise 18 Special Uses of Apostrophes

Add apostrophes where they are needed in the following sentences. Some sentences do not need apostrophes. Do not change or add any words.

1. I have *B*'s on all my science quizzes, so I feel confident about the test.

2. Alice is going to New Zealand for three weeks; she will stay with relatives who live there.

3. Jennifer deserves a day's pay for all the time she spent on cleaning up your office.

4. There are two *e*'s in the word *coffee*.

5. The winner of the lottery won an amount of money with six *0*'s at the end, so it has to be at least one million dollars.

6. It will be several months before I can save up enough vacation days for a trip to Wyoming.

7. My mother writes very fancy capital *A*'s because she used to study calligraphy.

8. The down payment on my new house is less than a year's worth of rent on my old one.

9. Don wants to spend hundreds of dollars on an anniversary party for our parents, but I think we can give them a memorable day for less money.

10. Don't forget your "*excuse me*'s" and "*please*'s" when you visit Aunt Claudia.

Exercise 19 Using Apostrophes: A Comprehensive Exercise

Add apostrophes where they are needed in the following sentences. Some sentences do not need apostrophes. Do not change or add any words.

1. I forgot one book's title and had to ask my friend for the information.

2. Don't get involved in the children's project; let the experience be all theirs.

3. I'll never forget Texas' storms and its blistering summer heat.

4. You pronounce your *r*'s differently than I pronounce mine.

5. Professor Harris' tests are always challenging, so you'll have to study hard for his final exam.

6. Won't you tell me who's been asking questions about me?

7. Some of the mail is hers, and the rest of it is yours.

8. Nothing's worse than having a neighbor's dog barking all night.

9. The club I belong to has an annual awards banquet for its members.

10. It cost me a month's worth of overtime to pay for my daughter's dental work, but her smile is my reward.

Connect

Exercise 20   Editing a Paragraph for Errors in Apostrophes

In the following paragraph, correct any errors related to punctuating with apostrophes. The errors may involve missing or incorrect use of apostrophes. There are ten errors.

My friend visited me last week, and because of the weather, I saw a year's worth of movies in a week. Ryan came from Florida to visit, expecting to see snow and enjoy such winter sports as ice-skating and sledding. However, the weather didn't [*didn't*] cooperate with Ryan's plan's [*plans*]. It rained heavily for seven day's [*days*]. As a result, I had to find activities that interested my friend. Since Ryan love's [*loves*] films, it wasnt [*wasn't*] too difficult to amuse him. We went to every movie in town. For me, the week was unusual since I rarely go to the movies; in fact, its [*it's*] possible for me to spend twelve months without visiting the neighborhood multiplex. Before Ryans [*Ryan's*] visit, the last film I remember seeing was in the fall of 04 [*'04*] when my sister dragged me to see <u>SpongeBob SquarePants</u>. Last week, the weather arranged things so that Id [*I'd*] see many movies. Ryan and I saw two action movies, a horror film, a cartoon adventure, and two comedies. Ryan couldn't have been happier, and I am now an expert on early-bird ticket prices and rocking-chair seating.

Section Test: Punctuation: The Apostrophe

Some of the sentences below are correct; others have errors in using punctuation. Put an *X* by each sentence with an error.

1. __X__   Morris is sure to say his "*thank you*s" when he visits his grandfather's house.

2. _____   I'm not sure if Mark and Maria left behind the serving bowls, but I know the platters are theirs.

3. __X__   The stray kitten has to be somebodys pet, so we'll post the kitten's photo throughout the neighborhood and keep the little cat safe until it's owner shows up.

4. __X__   Although Adam and Jackson look like twins, the brother's personalities are different.

5. __X__   We'll go to Rita's and Carlos' party after we've had dinner.

6. __X__ Tammy got a months salary as a bonus after she'd broken the company's record for sales.

7. _____ I'd like to see a few more *0*'s at the end of my income tax refund check.

8. __X__ There's no one under the bed; the monster is a product of Charles imagination.

9. _____ My father's southern relatives always drop the "*g*'s" when they say words like "fishing" and "running."

10. _____ Years from now, when we've saved enough money, a house in a good neighborhood will be ours.

Other Punctuation and Mechanics

THE EXCLAMATION MARK

The exclamation mark is used at the end of sentences that express strong emotion:

> **appropriate:** You've won the lottery!
> **inappropriate:** We had a great time! (*Great* already implies excitement.)

Be careful not to overuse the exclamation mark. If your choice of words is descriptive, you should not have to rely on the exclamation point for emphasis. Use it sparingly, for it is easy to rely on exclamations instead of using better vocabulary.

THE DASH

Use a dash to interrupt a sentence. It usually indicates a dramatic shift in tone or thought.

> I picked up the crystal bowl carefully, cradled it in my arms, walked softly—and tripped, sending the bowl flying.

Two dashes set off dramatic words that interrupt a sentence.

> Ramon took the life preserver—our only one—and tossed it far out to sea.

Because dashes are somewhat dramatic, use them sparingly.

PARENTHESES

Use parentheses to enclose extra material and afterthoughts.

> I was sure that Ridgefield (the town I'd just visited) was not the place for me.
> Her name (which I have just remembered) was Celestine.

> **Note:** Commas in pairs, dashes in pairs, and parentheses are all used as inserters. They set off material that interrupts the flow of the sentence. The least dramatic and smoothest way to insert material is to use commas.

THE HYPHEN

A hyphen joins two or more descriptive words that act as a single word.

> The old car had a souped-up engine.
> Bill was a smooth-talking charmer.

Use a hyphen in the written form of compound numbers from twenty-one to ninety-nine.

Exercise 1 **Punctuating with Exclamation Marks, Dashes, Parentheses, and Hyphens**

Add any exclamation marks, dashes, parentheses, and hyphens that are needed in the sentences below.

1. Larry took the airline ticket my last chance at freedom and threw it into the incinerator.

2. There's someone hiding in the closet

3. Lenny Montalbano the boy who used to live next door grew up to start his own medical research company.

4. Mr. Okada is a caring, competent, and good natured supervisor.

5. Mr. Thompson is known for his eccentric ways; one day he came to work in a handsome blue blazer, striped silk tie, gray flannel slacks and bright orange sneakers.

6. Get off the train tracks

7. The salesperson said the radio was a top of the line product.

8. The Aces Club where my cousin said all the single people meet turned out to be a loud, dirty bar and grill.

9. The killer drew a breath his last one and fell to the ground.

10. Amanda married a battle weary veteran of the war in Iraq.

QUOTATION MARKS

Use quotation marks for direct quotes, for the titles of short works, and for other special uses.

1. Put quotation marks around direct quotes, a speaker or writer's exact words:

   My mother told me, "There are plenty of fish in the sea."
   "I'm never going there again," said Irene.
   "I'd like to buy you dinner," Peter said, "but I'm out of cash."
   My best friend warned me, "Stay away from that guy. He will break
       your heart."

Look carefully at the preceding examples. Notice that a comma is used to introduce a direct quotation, and that at the end of the quotation, the comma or period goes inside the quotation marks:

   My mother told me, "There are plenty of fish in the sea."

Notice how direct quotes of more than one sentence are punctuated. If the quote is written in one unit, quotation marks go before the first quoted word and after the last quoted word:

   My best friend warned me, "Stay away from that guy. He will break
       your heart."

But if the quote is not written as one unit, the punctuation changes:

   "Stay away from that guy," my best friend warned me. "He will break
       your heart."

Caution: Do *not* put quotation marks around indirect quotations:

   indirect quotation: He asked if he could come with us.
   direct quotation: He asked, "Can I come with you?"
   indirect quotation: She said that she wanted more time.
   direct quotation: "I want more time," she said.

2. Put quotation marks around the titles of short works. If you are writing the title of a short work like a short story, an essay, a newspaper or magazine article, a poem, or a song, put quotation marks around the title:

   In middle school, we read Robert Frost's poem "The Road Not Taken."
   My little sister has learned to sing "Itsy Bitsy Spider."

If you are writing the title of a longer work like a book, movie, magazine, play, television show, or CD, underline the title:

   Last night I saw an old movie, <u>Stand By Me</u>.
   I read an article called "Campus Crime" in <u>Newsweek</u>.

> **Note:** In printed publications such as books or magazines, titles of long works are put in italics. But when you are writing by hand or typing, underline the titles of long works.

3. There are other, special uses of quotation marks. You use quotation marks around words mentioned as words in a sentence.

   When you said "never," did you mean it?
   People from the Midwest pronounce "water" differently than I do.

If you are using a quotation within a quotation, use single quotation marks.

> My brother complained, "Every time we get in trouble, Mom has to say 'I told you so.'"
> Kyle said, "Linda has a way of saying 'Excuse me' that is really very rude."

CAPITAL LETTERS

There are ten main situations in which you capitalize:

1. Capitalize the first word of every sentence:

   Yesterday we saw our first soccer game.

2. Capitalize the first word in a direct quotation if the word begins a sentence:

   My aunt said, "This is a gift for your birthday."
   "Have some birthday cake," my aunt said, "and have some more ice cream." (Notice that the second section of this quote does not begin with a capital letter because it does not begin a sentence.)

3. Capitalize the names of persons:

   Nancy Perez and Frank Murray came to see me at the store.
   I asked Mother to feed my cat.

Do not capitalize words like *mother*, *father*, or *aunt* if you put a possessive in front of them.

> I asked my mother to feed my cat.

4. Capitalize the titles of persons:

   I spoke with Dr. Wilson.
   He has to see Dean Johnston.

Do not capitalize when the title is not connected to a name:

> I spoke with that doctor.
> He has to see the dean.

5. Always capitalize countries, cities, languages, nationalities, religions, races, months, days of the week, documents, organizations, holidays, and historical events or periods:

   In high school, we never studied the Vietnam War.
   The Polish-American Club will hold a picnic on Labor Day.

Use small letters for the seasons:

> I love fall because I love to watch the leaves change color.

6. Capitalize the names of particular places:

   We used to hold our annual meetings at Northside Auditorium in Springfield, Iowa, but this year we are meeting at Riverview Theater in Langton, Missouri.

Use small letters if a particular place is not given:

> We are looking for an auditorium we can rent for our meeting.

7. Use capital letters for geographic locations:

> Jim was determined to find a good job in the West.

But use small letters for geographic directions:

> To get to my house, you have to drive west on the turnpike.

8. Capitalize the names of specific products:

> I always drink Diet Pepsi for breakfast.

But use small letters for a kind of product:

> I always drink a diet cola for breakfast.

9. Capitalize the names of specific school courses:

> I have to take Child Psychology next term.

But use small letters for a general academic subject:

> My advisor told me to take a psychology course.

10. Capitalize the first and last words in the titles of long or short works, and capitalize all other significant words in the titles:

> I've always wanted to read <u>The Old Man and the Sea</u>.
> Whenever we go to see the team play, my uncle sings "Take Me Out to the Ballgame."

Note: Remember that the titles of long works, like books, are underlined; the titles of short ones, like songs, are quoted.

Exercise 2   **Using Quotation Marks, Underlining, and Capital Letters**

Add any missing quotation marks, underlining, and capital letters to the sentences below.

1. When I was growing up, uncle [Uncle] Richard was my favorite relative, but I later discovered my uncle had a dangerous temper.

2. When Melanie signed up for her winter term at college, she registered for classes in social science, writing, and music.

3. I can't stand it, ["] my girlfriend said, ["] when you say ['] maybe ['] instead of giving me a definite answer. ["]

4. I finally found a good pre-school for my son; it's the madison [M] school for early childhood education, [S E C E] and dr. Howard of Miller [D] university is the director. [U]

5. One night, my brother Jason was watching a television show called Dirty Jobs [<u>Dirty Jobs</u>]; I watched it for a minute and said, ["] Ugh! Turn off that disgusting program."

6. David is looking for a job in the midwest [M] because he wants to be near his parents, who live north of Chicago.

7. Whenever Mimi says the word ["] love, ["] she means the word ["] infatuation. ["]

8. Gerry, stop complaining, his father said. It doesn't do any good to complain.
   "   "   "
   "

   Gridiron Gang
9. I took my nephews to see Gridiron gang; afterward, they said it was the best movie in the world.

10. There is nothing funnier than listening to my father sing Marvin Gaye's old song, I heard it Through the Grapevine.
    " H   I   "

NUMBERS

Spell out numbers that take one or two words:

> Alice mailed two hundred brochures.
> I spent ninety dollars on car repairs.

Use the numbers themselves if it takes more than two words to spell them out.

> We looked through 243 old photographs.
> The sticker price was $10,397.99.

Also use numbers to write dates, times, addresses, and parts of a book.

> We live at 24 Cambridge Street.
> They were married on April 3, 1993.
> Chapter 3 had difficult maps to read, especially the one on page 181.

TEACHING TIP

Tell students that newspaper articles do not usually spell out numbers. These rules apply to essays.

ABBREVIATIONS

Although you should spell out most words rather than abbreviate them, you may abbreviate *Mr., Mrs., Ms., Jr., Sr., Dr.* when they are used with a proper name. You should abbreviate references to time and to organizations widely known by initials.

> The moderator asked Ms. Steinem to comment.
> The bus left at 5:00 p.m., and the trip took two hours.
> He works for the FBI.

You should spell out the names of places, months, days of the week, courses of study, and words referring to parts of a book:

> **not this:** ~~I missed the last class, so I never got the notes for Chap. 3.~~
> **but this:** I missed the last class, so I never got the notes for Chapter 3.

> **not this:** ~~He lives on Chestnut Street in Boston, Mass.~~
> **but this:** He lives on Chestnut Street in Boston, Massachusetts.

> **not this:** ~~Pete missed his psych. test.~~
> **but this:** Pete missed his psychology test.

Exercise 3   **Using Numbers and Abbreviations**

Correct any errors in the use of numbers or abbreviations in the following sentences. Some sentences may not need corrections.

                      sociology   *Monday*
1. Ellen came into our soc. class last Mon., carrying her research paper, which looked about three in. thick.
                             inches

2. Mr. and Mrs. Chang sent one hundred fifty *155* five invitations to their daughter's wedding in Minneapolis, Minn. *Minnesota*

3. My parents' apartment on Sunset Ave. *Avenue* had 4 rooms. *four*

4. Matthew left Fla. *Florida* on Mar. third, *March 3* 2004, to begin a job with the Abraham and Braun Co. *Company* in N. Dakota. *North*

5. My phys. ed. *physical education* teacher starts class promptly at 8:30 a.m. every Fri. *Friday*

6. It took me two hrs. *hours* to finish Chap. *Chapter* 3 of my sociology textbook.

7. Gregory charges twenty-five dollars an hour to help people with their computer problems.

8. Charles Woods, Jr., was an executive with the NFL for ten years before he took a job with ABC Sports.

9. My father and his 3 *three* brothers arrived in New York on a cold Feb. *February* day in 1975.

10. Dr. Hoffman used to live on 5723 Elm Street, Boston, Mass., *Massachusetts* until he took a job at the Univ. *University* of Wisconsin in Madison.

> **Note:** Exercises incorporating concepts from both punctuation chapters follow the chapter test.

Chapter Test: Other Punctuation and Mechanics

Some of the sentences below are correct; others have errors in the use of exclamation marks, dashes, parentheses, hyphens, quotation marks, capital letters, numbers, and abbreviations. Put an *X* next to the sentences with errors.

1. __X__ My mother warned, "Before you do anything impulsive, think about your future".

2. __X__ Carlotta spent one thousand and eighty dollars on new curtains for her house even though she owes her brother hundreds of dollars for fixing her roof.

3. __X__ At my aunt's wedding reception, my sister sang "I Will Always love You" as the bride and groom danced.

4. __X__ Dr. Gillespie is teaching an online course in Intro. to Psychology in the summer term.

5. __X__ In our elementary school library, there was a framed copy of The Star-Spangled Banner on the wall.

6. _____ You always say "eventually" when I ask you whether you will ever get married.

7. _____ "Give me a few minutes," Father said, "and I'll take you to the park."

8. __X__ I used to walk down the fashionable streets in Palm Beach, Fl., and stare at the the expensive cars and luxury stores.

9. _____ The spoiled heiress picked up the heavy china plate—a hand-painted antique—and smashed it against the wall.

10. _____ Nathan was so eager to leave Springfield (the town where he was born) that he took a job at a broken-down gas station five hundred miles away.

Exercise 4 **A Comprehensive Exercise on All Punctuation and Mechanics**

Add any missing punctuation to the following sentences. Also, correct any errors in capitalization and in the use of numbers or abbreviations.

1. We had a second rate meal at Frank and Maries house of Ribs *second-rate* *Marie's H* last Sat. night we can't recommend the place to you. *Saturday* *;*

2. I'm looking for a book called the rule of four my friend recommended it. *The Rule of Four;*

3. The five year old boy began to pour chocolate syrup on the kitchen floor meanwhile the babysitter dozed on the living room couch. *;*

4. Lance took 2 spanish courses at National H.S. so he does not have to take a foreign language class at Centenary college. *two S* *High School,* *C*

5. The star athlete wanted to know if she could miss a days practice. *day's*

6. The star athlete asked Can I miss a days practice *, "* *day's* *?"*

7. I love Its a whole new world, the song from the movie Aladdin. *" ,* *W* *N* *W* *"* *Aladdin*

8. Now that we live in Buffalo N.Y. I need some warm clothes sweaters, gloves, hats, and a coat with a heavy lining. *, New York,* *:*

9. Ill keep your secret Bill as long as your secret doesnt hurt anyone elses chance at happiness. *' ' '* *'*

10. An old man with a cane walked slowly down the sidewalk for the ice made the pavement treacherous. *'*

Exercise 5 **A Comprehensive Exercise on All Punctuation and Mechanics**

Add any missing punctuation to the following sentences. Also, correct any errors in capitalization and in the use of numbers or abbreviations.

1. Tonya Brillstein my best friend told me she is sick of Lance and Marcus teasing. *' '* *'*

2. The oral surgery will cost me $2321 nevertheless I intend to have it as soon as possible. *$2,321;* *,*

3. All I can say, dad is that youve hurt Nicoles feelings. *Dad,* *,* *'*

4. Let me see your license, the officer said and give me your registration too. *" "* *' "* *' "*

5. A man with bright red hair was seen leaving the scene of the
   crime , but witnesses could not identify him.

6. The teenagers wonder whether their favorite teacher will ever
   Pennsylvania
   return to the classroom at Penn. State University.
   Friday Night Lights
7. The movie Friday Night Lights was based on a book about a real
   h
   High school football team in Texas.

8. When Vincent takes a trip with his Great Danes, he packs his van
   full of the animals , possessions ; two large dog beds , giant bags of
   dog food , special spill - proof water bowls , and at least a dozen dog
   toys. ,

9. Theres a red Mustang in the parking lot with its lights on ; maybe
   the car is yours.
   The Seven Habits of Highly Effective
10. No , don't buy me that book called The 7 Habits of Highly Effective
    People.
    People ; I have to break my bad habits before I can start developing
    good ones.

Connect

Exercise 6   **Editing a Paragraph for Errors in All Punctuation and Mechanics**

In the following paragraph, correct any errors related to punctuation or mechanics. The errors may involve missing or incorrect punctuation, capitalization, use of numbers, or abbreviations. There are twenty-two errors.

no comma
Babies can be hard to figure out. I made this discovery , when my neighbor

Rosanna asked me for a favor. When she knocked on my door , she looked like

she had just climbed out of bed : her eyes half-open, her hair flat and matted, and

her clothes rumpled. In reality , she wasnt waking up ; she was desperate for sleep.

" Can you do me a big favor? " she asked , " I wouldnt ask you , but its an emergency " .

Rosanna explained that she had been up all night, walking her baby Marcus,

singing to him, and rocking him. Nothing would put Marcus to sleep. "I've got to

get a couple of hours , sleep , " she explained , "before I go to work. All I need is for

"
you to watch the baby until my husband comes home from his job in two hours.

Then, she said, her husband could take over , and she could go to her job. I felt

sorry for her , so I agreed. The strangest part of the story is a happy ending. As

soon as I had Marcus in my arms , he fell asleep. Babies certainly seem to live by
schedules.
their own strange schedule's.

Exercise 7 Editing a Paragraph for Errors in All Punctuation and Mechanics

Connect

In the following paragraph, correct any errors related to punctuation or mechanics. The errors may involve missing or incorrect punctuation, capitalization, use of numbers, or abbreviations. There are twenty-three errors.

In my first year of high school, I signed up for a music class called Introduction
Choral Music   ,
to choral music. I had no idea the class would involve so much singing and even

              ,
worse so much practice. During one class, we sang the first notes of the song
"   "   *thirty*
Summertime at least 30 times before our teacher let us move on. In the early

                              ,
weeks of the semester I became impatient with all the emphasis on perfection. I
                                                          no comma
was happy on the one day when our teacher was sick because, his absence meant
              ,   ,   *Mr. Holland's Opus*
we didnt have to sing. Instead we watched an old movie called Mr Holland's opus.
              months's
After about a months worth of practice, my attitude began to change. The stu-

      ,   ,   ,   ;
dents including me began to form into a group. The groups singing improved
                                                          no comma
meanwhile our teacher prepared us to face an audience. By the end, of the year, I
                    High School
was a proud member of the Eleanor Roosevelt H.S. Chorus. Every time I sang for
              no apostrophe
students, parent's, or community members, I felt the power of music. In addition, I

understood how those hard hours of practice can lead to a special kind of accom-

plishment.

Spelling

No one is a perfect speller, but there are ways to become a better speller. If you can learn a few spelling rules, you can answer many of your spelling questions.

VOWELS AND CONSONANTS

To understand the spelling rules, you need to know the difference between vowels and consonants. **Vowels** are the letters *a, e, i, o, u,* and sometimes *y.* **Consonants** are all the other letters.

The letter *y* is a vowel when it has a vowel sound.
 silly (The *y* sounds like *ee,* a vowel sound.)
 cry (The *y* sounds like *i,* a vowel sound.)

The letter *y* is a consonant when it has a consonant sound.
 yellow (The *y* has a consonant sound.)
 yesterday (The *y* has a consonant sound.)

SPELLING RULE 1: DOUBLING A FINAL CONSONANT

When you add an ending, double the final consonant of a word if all three of the following are true:

1. The word is one syllable, or the accent is on the last syllable,
2. The word ends in a single consonant preceded by a single vowel, and
3. The ending you are adding starts with a vowel.

begin	+	ing	=	beginning
shop	+	er	=	shopper
stir	+	ed	=	stirred
occur	+	ed	=	occurred
fat	+	est	=	fattest
pin	+	ing	=	pinning

Exercise 1 Doubling a Final Consonant

Add *-ed* to the following words by applying the rules for double consonants.

1. hammer *hammered*
2. swat *swatted*
3. trick *tricked*
4. order *ordered*
5. admit *admitted*

6. repel *repelled*
7. uncoil *uncoiled*
8. stop *stopped*
9. excel *excelled*
10. defer *deferred*

SPELLING RULE 2: DROPPING THE FINAL *E*

Drop the final *e* before you add an ending that starts with a vowel.

observe	+	ing	=	observing
excite	+	able	=	excitable
fame	+	ous	=	famous
create	+	ive	=	creative

Keep the final *e* before an ending that starts with a consonant.

love	+	ly	=	lovely
hope	+	ful	=	hopeful
excite	+	ment	=	excitement
life	+	less	=	lifeless

Exercise 2 Dropping the Final *e*

Combine the following words and endings by following the rule for dropping the final *e*.

1. imagine + able *imaginable*
2. care + less *careless*
3. arrange + ment *arrangement*
4. resource + ful *resourceful*
5. behave + ing *behaving*
6. home + less *homeless*
7. expense + ive *expensive*
8. intense + ly *intensely*
9. adore + able *adorable*
10. refuse + ing *refusing*

SPELLING RULE 3: CHANGING THE FINAL *Y* TO *I*

When a word ends in a consonant plus *y*, change the *y* to *i* when you add an ending:

try	+	es	=	tries
silly	+	er	=	sillier
rely	+	ance	=	reliance
tardy	+	ness	=	tardiness

Note: When you add *-ing* to words ending in *y*, always keep the *y*.

cry	+	ing	=	crying
rely	+	ing	=	relying

Exercise 3   Changing the Final *y* to *i*

Combine the following words and endings by applying the rule for changing the final *y* to *i*.

1.	happy	+	er	*happier*
2.	apply	+	ing	*applying*
3.	convey	+	er	*conveyer*
4.	penny	+	less	*penniless*
5.	marry	+	ed	*married*
6.	deny	+	es	*denies*
7.	ally	+	ance	*alliance*
8.	comply	+	ant	*compliant*
9.	ready	+	ness	*readiness*
10.	imply	+	ing	*implying*

SPELLING RULE 4: ADDING *-S* OR *-ES*

Add *-es* instead of *-s* to a word if the word ends in *ch*, *sh*, *ss*, *x*, or *z*. The *es* adds an extra syllable to the word.

box	+	es	=	boxes
witch	+	es	=	witches
class	+	es	=	classes
clash	+	es	=	clashes

Exercise 4   Adding -s or -es

Apply the rule for adding *-s* or *-es* to the following words.

1.	polish	*polishes*	6.	fix	*fixes*
2.	defeat	*defeats*	7.	pass	*passes*
3.	march	*marches*	8.	smash	*smashes*
4.	stock	*stocks*	9.	back	*backs*
5.	distress	*distresses*	10.	tax	*taxes*

SPELLING RULE 5: USING *IE* OR *EI*

Use *i* before *e*, except after *c*, or when the sound is like *a*, as in *neighbor* and *weigh*.

i before *e*:
relief   convenience   friend   piece

e before *i*:
conceive   sleigh   weight   receive

Exercise 5   Using *ie* or *ei*

Add *ie* or *ei* to the following words by applying the rule for using *ie* or *ei*.

1. dec _e i_ t
2. fr _e i_ ght
3. conc _e i_ t
4. bel _i e_ f
5. perc _e i_ ve

6. ch _i e_ f
7. n _i e_ ce
8. f _i e_ ld
9. ingred _i e_ nt
10. sh _i e_ ld

Exercise 6   Spelling Rules: A Comprehensive Exercise

Combine the following words and endings by applying the spelling rules.

1. blur   +   ed   *blurred*
2. carry   +   ed   *carried*
3. fizz   +   s or es   *fizzes*
4. tidy   +   er   *tidier*
5. perch   +   s or es   *perches*
6. harass   +   s or es   *harasses*
7. plan   +   ed   *planned*
8. ready   +   ness   *readiness*
9. ply   +   able   *pliable*
10. concur +   ed   *concurred*
11. unhappy + est   *unhappiest*
12. devote +   ion   *devotion*
13. spite   +   ful   *spiteful*
14. impulse +   ive   *impulsive*
15. confine +   ment   *confinement*
16. rely   +   es   *relies*
17. apply   +   ance   *appliance*
18. catch   +   s or es   *catches*
19. offer   +   ed   *offered*
20. suffer   +   ing   *suffering*

Exercise 7   Editing a Paragraph for Spelling

Correct the spelling errors in the following paragraph. Write your corrections above each error. There are ten errors.

Driving

    Driving above the speed limit is so common that I became angry when I

received   *zipping*

recieved a speeding ticket yesterday. I was ziping down the highway on my way

                                stopped   *implied*

home until a police officer turned on her flashing light and stoped me. She implyed

I had been going twenty miles above the speed limit. What irritates me is that the

                         defiance

traffic situation on that highway encourages defyance of the rules. Everyone

                      enforcement

speeds on that road, and there has been no enforcment of the rules for years. I

exceed the speed limit for two reasons: because everyone disobeys the rules and

gets away with it, and because it's safer to speed than to follow the rules. If I slow

down, I risk an accident as the cars around me tailgate my car, cut me off, or run

me off the road. On a crowded highway, people who observe the speed limit risk

crashes   *believe*

crashs. I know the police officer was doing her job, but I beleive I was doing mine

by keeping up with the flow of traffic. I realize that driving at high speeds in heavy

                                crazier

traffic is crazy, but unfortunately, trying to slow down can be crazyer.

DO YOU SPELL IT AS ONE WORD OR TWO?

Sometimes you can be confused about certain words. You are not sure whether to combine them to make one word or to spell them as two words. The lists below show some commonly confused words.

Words That Should Not Be Combined

a lot	each other	high school	every time
even though	good night	all right	no one
living room	dining room	in front	

Words That Should Be Combined

another	newspapers	bathroom
bedroom	playroom	good-bye, goodbye, or good-by
bookkeeper	roommate	cannot
schoolteacher	downstairs	southeast, northwest, etc.
grandmother	throughout	nearby
worthwhile	nevertheless	yourself, himself, myself, etc.

Words Whose Spelling Depends on Their Meaning

one word: *Already* means "before."
He offered to do the dishes, but I had *already* done them.

TEACHING TIP

Emphasize that computer spell-check programs will not be able to distinguish whether one-word or two-word spellings are correct. Students who claim that their spelling is fine since "I ran it through my spell-check" are usually surprised when the instructor finds several spelling errors.

two words: *All ready* means "ready."
My dog was *all ready* to play Frisbee.

one word: *Altogether* means "entirely."
That movie was *altogether* too confusing.
two words: *All together* means "in a group."
My sisters were *all together* in the kitchen.

one word: *Always* means "every time."
My grandfather is *always* right about baseball statistics.
two words: *All ways* means "every path" or "every aspect."
We tried *all ways* to get to the beach house.
He is a gentleman in *all ways*.

one word: *Anymore* means "any longer."
I do not want to exercise *anymore*.
two words: *Any more* means "additional."
Are there *any more* pickles?

one word: *Anyone* means "any person at all."
Is *anyone* home?
two words: *Any one* means "one person or thing in a special group."
I'll take *any one* of the chairs on sale.

one word: *Apart* means "separate."
Liam stood *apart* from his friends.
two words: *A part* is "a piece or section."
I read *a part* of the chapter.

one word: *Everyday* means "ordinary."
Tim was wearing his *everyday* clothes.
two words: *Every day* means "each day."
Sam jogs *every day*.

one word: *Everyone* means "all the people."
Everyone has bad days.
two words: *Every one* means "all the people or things in a specific group."
My father asked *every one* of the neighbors for a donation to the Red
  Cross.

Exercise 8   Do You Spell It as One Word or Two?

Circle the correct word in parentheses in each sentence below.

1. Jason apologized to me yesterday; he said he wanted to make
   everything (all right, allright) between us.

2. Terry would be happy to own (any one, anyone) of the beautiful
   houses being built on Pinewood Avenue.

3. If you have (all ready, already) seen the new Jamie Fox
   movie, let's go see the one with Denzel Washington and Matt
   Damon.

4. Robin is thinking of moving back to the (North East, Northeast);
   she misses her friends in Vermont.

5. Being snowed in at the airport was an (all together, (altogether)) horrible experience.

6. My father sold insurance, and my mother was a (school teacher, (schoolteacher)) in an elementary school.

7. ((Every time), Everytime) I hear that song, I think of Luis.

8. My math professor says he doesn't want to hear ((any more), anymore) complaints about the homework.

9. Lynn told me to return ((every one), everyone) of the CDs I borrowed from her.

10. Tom will have to get a new (room mate, (roommate)) if Bernard leaves town.

Connect

Exercise 9   **Do You Spell It as One Word or Two? Correcting Errors in a Paragraph**

The following paragraph contains errors in word combinations. Correct the errors in the space above each line. There are nine errors.

high school   *already*
Even in my first year of highschool, I was all ready certain that I wanted to

attend college and earn a degree. Seven years later, I am starting to make my
            A lot   *throughout*
dream come true. Alot happened in those seven years. First, I struggled through

out my teens, dropping out of high school in my junior year. At that time, I was

having a hard time coping with my parents' divorce. The divorce caused my

mother to lose much of the family income, and I was angry at my father and at

much of the world. I also hated being the student without money in a school
            everyone
where every one else had new clothes, expensive jewelry, and the latest in cell

phones. I worked at a series of jobs to help support my mother, and I fell into a

routine of meaningless work, bursts of rage, and a sense of hopelessness.

Suddenly, two years ago, hope returned in the form of a new friend. She urged me

to take steps, even if they were small ones, to change my life. It was hard to
            altogether
change my life all together, but small steps led me to earn my G.E.D. Next month,
                        nearby   *good-bye, goodbye, or good-by*
I will begin my first class at a near by college. I can say good by to a dead-end life.
                                    nevertheless
I will be working hard and taking a big chance; never the less, I will be moving

toward my seven-year-old dream.

A LIST OF COMMONLY MISSPELLED WORDS

Following is a list of words you use often in your writing. Study this list and use it as a reference.

1. absence
2. absent
3. accept
4. ache
5. achieve
6. acquire
7. across
8. actually
9. advertise
10. again
11. a lot
12. all right
13. almost
14. always
15. amateur
16. American
17. answer
18. anxious
19. apology
20. apparent
21. appetite
22. appreciate
23. argue
24. argument
25. asked
26. athlete
27. attempt
28. August
29. aunt
30. author
31. automobile
32. autumn
33. avenue
34. awful
35. awkward
36. balance
37. basically
38. because
39. becoming
40. beginning
41. behavior
42. belief
43. believe
44. benefit
45. bicycle
46. bought
47. breakfast
48. breathe
49. brilliant
50. brother
51. brought
52. bruise
53. build
54. bulletin
55. bureau
56. buried
57. business
58. busy
59. calendar
60. cannot
61. career
62. careful
63. catch
64. category
65. caught
66. cemetery
67. cereal
68. certain
69. chair
70. cheat
71. chicken
72. chief
73. children
74. cigarette
75. citizen
76. city
77. college
78. color
79. comfortable
80. committee
81. competition
82. conscience
83. convenient
84. conversation
85. copy
86. cough
87. cousin
88. criticism
89. criticize
90. crowded
91. daily
92. daughter
93. deceive
94. decide
95. definite
96. dentist
97. dependent
98. deposit
99. describe
100. desperate
101. development
102. different
103. dilemma
104. dining
105. direction
106. disappearance
107. disappoint
108. discipline
109. disease
110. divide
111. doctor
112. doesn't
113. don't
114. doubt
115. during
116. dying
117. early
118. earth
119. eighth
120. eligible
121. embarrass
122. encouragement
123. enough
124. environment
125. especially
126. etc.
127. every
128. exact
129. exaggeration
130. excellent
131. except
132. excite
133. exercise
134. existence
135. expect
136. experience
137. explanation
138. factory

139. familiar
140. family
141. fascinating
142. February
143. finally
144. forehead
145. foreign
146. forty
147. fourteen
148. friend
149. fundamental
150. general
151. generally
152. goes
153. going
154. government
155. grammar
156. grateful
157. grocery
158. guarantee
159. guard
160. guess
161. guidance
162. guide
163. half
164. handkerchief
165. happiness
166. heavy
167. height
168. heroes
169. holiday
170. hospital
171. humorous
172. identity
173. illegal
174. imaginary
175. immediately
176. important
177. independent
178. integration
179. intelligent
180. interest
181. interfere
182. interpretation
183. interrupt
184. irrelevant
185. irritable
186. iron
187. island
188. January

189. jewelry
190. judgment
191. kindergarten
192. kitchen
193. knowledge
194. laboratory
195. language
196. laugh
197. leisure
198. length
199. library
200. listen
201. loneliness
202. lying
203. maintain
204. maintenance
205. marriage
206. mathematics
207. meant
208. measure
209. medicine
210. million
211. miniature
212. minute
213. muscle
214. mysterious
215. naturally
216. necessary
217. neighbor
218. nervous
219. nickel
220. niece
221. ninety
222. ninth
223. occasion
224. o'clock
225. often
226. omission
227. once
228. operate
229. opinion
230. optimist
231. original
232. parallel
233. particular
234. peculiar
235. perform
236. perhaps
237. permanent
238. persevere

239. personnel
240. persuade
241. physically
242. pleasant
243. possess
244. possible
245. potato
246. practical
247. prefer
248. prejudice
249. prescription
250. presence
251. president
252. privilege
253. probably
254. professor
255. psychology
256. punctuation
257. pursue
258. quart
259. really
260. receipt
261. receive
262. recognize
263. recommend
264. reference
265. religious
266. reluctantly
267. remember
268. resource
269. restaurant
270. rhythm
271. ridiculous
272. right
273. sandwich
274. Saturday
275. scene
276. schedule
277. scissors
278. secretary
279. seize
280. several
281. severely
282. significant
283. similar
284. since
285. sincerely
286. soldier
287. sophomore
288. strength

289. studying
290. success
291. surely
292. surprise
293. taught
294. temperature
295. theater
296. thorough
297. thousand
298. tied

299. tomorrow
300. tongue
301. tragedy
302. trouble
303. truly
304. twelfth
305. unfortunately
306. unknown
307. until
308. unusual

309. using
310. variety
311. vegetable
312. Wednesday
313. weird
314. which
315. writing
316. written
317. yesterday

Words That Sound Alike/Look Alike

WORDS THAT SOUND ALIKE/LOOK ALIKE

Words that sound alike or look alike (often called *homonyms*) can be confusing. Here is a list of some of the confusing words. Study this list, and make a note of any words that give you trouble.

a/an/and *A* is used before a word beginning with a consonant or consonant sound:

> Jason bought *a* car.

An is used before a word beginning with a vowel or vowel sound:

> Nancy took *an* apple to work.

And joins words or ideas:

> Pudding *and* cake are my favorite desserts.
> Fresh vegetables taste delicious, *and* they are nutritious.

accept/except *Accept* means "to receive":

> I *accept* your apology.

Except means "excluding":

> I'll give you all my books *except* my dictionary.

addition/edition An *addition* is something that is added:

> My father built an *addition* to our house in the form of a porch.

An *edition* is an issue of a newspaper or one of a series of printings of a book:

> I checked the latest *edition* of the *Daily News* to see if my advertisement is in it.

advice/advise *Advice* is an opinion offered as a guide; it is what you give someone:

> Betty asked for my *advice* about finding a job.

Advise is what you do when you give an opinion offered as a guide:

> I couldn't *advise* Betty about finding a job.

affect/effect *Affect* means "to influence something":

> Getting a bad grade will *affect* my chances for a scholarship.

Effect means "a result" or "to cause something to happen":

> Your kindness had a great *effect* on me.
> The committee struggled to *effect* a compromise.

allowed/aloud *Allowed* means "permitted":

> I'm not *allowed* to skateboard on those steps.

Aloud means "out loud":

> The teacher read the story *aloud*.

all ready/already *All ready* means "ready":

> The dog was *all ready* to go for a walk.

Already means "before":

> David had *already* made the salad.

altar/alter An *altar* is a table or place in a church:

> They were married in front of the *altar*.

Alter means "to change":

> My plane was delayed, so I had to *alter* my plans for the evening.

angel/angle An *angel* is a heavenly being:

> That night, I felt an *angel* guiding me.

An *angle* is the space within two lines:

> The road turned at a sharp *angle*.

are/our *Are* is a verb, the plural of *is*:

> We *are* friends of the mayor.

Our means "belonging to us":

> We have *our* family quarrels.

beside/besides *Beside* means "next to":

He sat *beside* me at the concert.

Besides means "in addition":

I would never lie to you; *besides*, I have no reason to lie.

brake/break *Brake* means "to stop" or "a device for stopping":

That truck *brakes* at railroad crossings.
When he saw the animal on the road, he hit the *brakes*.

Break means "to come apart", or "to make something come apart":

The eggs are likely to *break*.
I can *break* the seal on that package.

breath/breathe *Breath* is the air you take in, and it rhymes with *death*:

I was running so fast, I lost my *breath*.

Breathe means "to take in air":

He found it hard to *breathe* in high altitudes.

buy/by *Buy* means "to purchase something":

Sylvia wants to *buy* a shovel.

By means "near," "by means of," or "before":

He sat *by* his sister.
I learn *by* taking good notes in class.
By ten o'clock, Nick was tired.

capital/capitol *Capital* means "city" or "wealth":

Albany is the *capital* of New York.
Jack invested his *capital* in real estate.

A *capitol* is a building where a legislature meets:

The city has a famous *capitol* building.

cereal/serial *Cereal* is a breakfast food or type of grain:

My favorite *cereal* is Cheerios.

Serial means "in a series":

Look for the *serial* number on the appliance.

choose/chose *Choose* means "to select." It rhymes with *snooze*:

Today I am going to *choose* a new sofa.

Chose is the past tense of *choose*:

Yesterday I *chose* a new rug.

close/clothes/cloths *Close* means "near" or "intimate." It can also mean "to end or shut something":

We live *close* to the train station.
James and Margie are *close* friends.
Noreen wants to *close* her eyes for ten minutes.

Clothes are wearing apparel:

Eduardo has new *clothes*.

Cloths are pieces of fabric:

>I clean the silver with damp *cloths* and a special polish.

coarse/course *Coarse* means "rough" or "crude":

>The top of the table had a *coarse* texture.
>His language was *coarse*.

A *course* is a direction or path. It is also a subject in school:

>The hurricane took a northern *course*.
>In my freshman year, I took a *course* in drama.

complement/compliment Complement means "complete" or "make better":

>The colors in that room *complement* the style of the furniture.

A *compliment* is praise:

>Trevor gave me a *compliment* about my cooking.

conscience/conscious Your *conscience* is your inner, moral guide:

>His *conscience* bothered him when he told a lie.

Conscious means "aware" or "awake":

>The accident victim was not fully conscious.

council/counsel A *council* is a group of people:

>The city *council* meets tonight.

Counsel means "advice" or "to give advice":

>I need your *counsel* about my investments.
>My father always *counsels* me about my career.

decent/descent *Decent* means "suitable" or "proper":

>I hope Mike gets a *decent* job.

Descent means "going down, falling, or sinking":

>The plane began its *descent* to the airport.

desert/dessert A *desert* is dry land. To *desert* means "to abandon":

>To survive a trip across the *desert*, people need water.
>He will never *desert* a friend.

Dessert is the sweet food we eat at the end of a meal.

>I want ice cream for *dessert*.

do/due *Do* means "perform":

>I have to stop complaining; I *do* it constantly.

Due means "owing" or "because of":

>The rent is *due* tomorrow.
>The game was canceled *due* to rain.

does/dose *Does* is a form of *do*:

>My father *does* the laundry.

A *dose* is a quantity of medicine.

>Whenever I had a cold, my mother gave me a *dose* of cough syrup.

fair/fare *Fair* means "unbiased." It can also mean "promising" or "good":

> The judge's decision was *fair*.
> Jose has a *fair* chance of winning the title.

A *fare* is the amount of money a passenger must pay.

> I couldn't afford the plane *fare* to Miami.

farther/further *Farther* means "a greater physical distance":

> His house is a few blocks *farther* down the street.

Further means "greater" or "additional." Use it when you are not describing a physical distance:

> My second French class gave me *further* training in French conversation.

flour/flower *Flour* is ground-up grain, an ingredient used in cooking:

> I use whole-wheat *flour* in my muffins.

A *flower* is a blossom:

> She wore a *flower* in her hair.

forth/fourth *Forth* means "forward":

> The pendulum on the clock swung back and *forth*.

Fourth means "number four in a sequence":

> I was *fourth* in line for tickets.

hear/here *Hear* means "to receive sounds in the ear":

> I can *hear* the music.

Here is a place:

> We can have the meeting *here*.

heard/herd *Heard* is the past tense of *hear*:

> I *heard* you talk in your sleep last night.

A *herd* is a group of animals:

> The farmer has a fine *herd* of cows.

hole/whole A *hole* is an empty place or opening:

> I see a *hole* in the wall.

Whole means "complete" or "entire":

> Silvio gave me the *whole* steak.

isle/aisle An *isle* is an island:

> We visited the *isle* of Capri.

An *aisle* is a passageway between sections of seats:

> The flight attendant came down the *aisle* and offered us coffee.

its/it's *Its* means "belonging to it":

> The car lost *its* rear bumper.

TEACHING TIP

Remind students that possessive pronouns (*his, hers, its, ours, theirs,* and *yours*) are exceptions to the rules governing apostrophes used to show possession.

It's is a shortened form of *it is* or *it has*:

> *It's* a beautiful day.
> *It's* been a pleasure to meet you.

knew/new   *Knew* is the past tense of *know*:

> I *knew* Teresa in high school.

New means "fresh, recent, not old":

> I want some *new* shoes.

know/no   *Know* means "to understand":

> They *know* how to play soccer.

No is a negative:

> Carla has *no* fear of heights.

Exercise 1   Words That Sound Alike/Look Alike

Circle the correct words in parentheses in each sentence below.

1. I need to look (farther, *further*) into the circumstances of the crime before I can (advice, *advise*) you about possible suspects.

2. The rich investment banker collects first (additions, *editions*) of famous books; he has an expert tell him which ones to (*buy*, by).

3. Edward must have no (*conscience*, conscious), for he was willing to (*desert*, dessert) his children in order to satisfy his own desires.

4. Whenever Kim (complements, *compliments*) me, I (*hear*, here) a hint of insincerity in her voice.

5. Eric needs a (does, *dose*) of reality before he makes plans to walk to the (*altar*, alter) with Sabrina.

6. I spent a (hole, *whole*) lot of money on dresses and other (close, *clothes*, cloths) last month, and now payment is (do, *due*).

7. When I had to speak in front of the town (*council*, counsel), I was so nervous I could hardly (breath, *breathe*).

8. One of (are, *our*) trees was struck by lightning; a huge branch fell at a crazy (angel, *angle*).

9. A large man crowded in (*beside*, besides) me on the bus right before I tried to reach the (isle, *aisle*).

10. I'm lazy, and I don't know how to cook, so I live on (*cereal*, serial) and Pop Tarts unless someone cooks me a (*decent*, descent) meal.

Collaborate

Exercise 2   Words That Sound Alike/Look Alike

Working with a partner or group, write one sentence for each word below.

1. a. its   *The elephant raised its trunk and screeched.*

   b. it's   *It's too late to call Nelson.*

INSTRUCTOR'S NOTE

Answers will vary. Possible answers shown.

2. a. coarse | *The blanket was a coarse woolen cloth.*

b. course | *I need three more courses to graduate.*

3. a. fair | *We need a fair assessment of the situation.*

b. fare | *Subway fares have gone up recently.*

4. a. forth | *We will go forth into the world with confidence.*

b. fourth | *Jasmine was the fourth speaker at the luncheon.*

5. a. capital | *I lost all my capital in a failed restaurant.*

b. capitol | *There is a beautiful dome on the capitol building.*

6. a. accept | *I hope the homeowners accept our offer.*

b. except | *Everyone except Ramon likes country music.*

7. a. brake | *Something is wrong with the brakes on my car.*

b. break | *Be careful with that vase; you'll break it.*

8. a. affect | *Robin's decision will affect my plans.*

b. effect | *My pleading had no effect on Uncle Oscar.*

9. a. know | *You know how I feel about lying.*

b. no | *There is no reason to worry.*

10. a. flour | *Making a pie, I got flour all over my shirt.*

b. flower | *I bought a bunch of flowers at the market.*

Exercise 3   Editing a Paragraph for Words That Sound Alike/Look Alike

The following paragraph has errors in words that sound alike/look alike. Correct each error in the space above it. There are twelve errors.

advice   heard

The secret to losing weight is a healthy diet. I used to believe the advise I herd on

television: try this quick weight-loss product, or take these pills and watch the

pounds melt away. I also convinced myself that I really didn't eat much, anyway, so I

had no reason to change my diet. I would skip meals and live on snacks from the

addition   buy dessert

vending machine at my workplace. In edition, I would by desert foods like cake and

cookies to reward myself after a long day. I justified these treats by telling myself I

clothes

had barely eaten all day, so I could afford the calories. Meanwhile, my cloths were

knew

getting tight, and I was constantly tired. Deep down, I new I was not living a healthy

accepted   *conscious*

life. Eventually, I excepted the fact that I had to make a conscience choice to change

aisle choose

my eating habits. Today, when I walk down the supermarket isle, I chose carefully. I

plan my meals so that I do not have to resort to chips and candy bars for energy. I

whole

do not focus on shedding pounds but concentrate on a hole new approach to food.

MORE WORDS THAT SOUND ALIKE/LOOK ALIKE

lead/led When *lead* rhymes with *need*, it means "to give directions, to take charge." If *lead* rhymes with *bed*, it is a metal:

> The marching band will *lead* the parade.
> Your bookbag is as heavy as *lead*.

Led is the past form of *lead* when it means "to give directions, to take charge":

> The cheerleaders *led* the parade last year.

lessen/lesson *Lessen* means make less or reduce:

> I took an aspirin to *lessen* the pain of my headache.

A *lesson* is something to be learned or studied.

> I had my first guitar *lesson* yesterday.

loan/lone A *loan* is something you give on the condition that it be returned:

> When I was broke, I got a *loan* of fifty dollars from my aunt.

Lone means "solitary, alone":

> A lone *shopper* stood in the checkout line.

loose/lose *Loose* means "not tight":

> In the summer, *loose* clothing keeps me cool.

To *lose* something means "to be unable to keep it":

> I'm afraid I will *lose* my car keys.

moral/morale *Moral* means "upright, honorable, connected to ethical standards":

> I have a *moral* obligation to care for my children.

Morale is confidence or spirit:

> After the game, the team's *morale* was low.

pain/pane *Pain* means "suffering":

> I had very little *pain* after the surgery.

A *pane* is a piece of glass:

> The girl's wild throw broke a window *pane*.

pair/pear A *pair* is a set of two:

> Mark has a *pair* of antique swords.

A *pear* is a fruit:

> In the autumn, I like a *pear* for a snack.

passed/past *Passed* means "went by." It can also mean "handed to":

> The happy days *passed* too quickly.
> Janice *passed* me the mustard.

Past means "the time that has gone by":

> Let's leave the *past* behind us.

patience/patients *Patience* is calm endurance:

When I am caught in a traffic jam, I should have more *patience*.

Patients are people under medical care:

There are too many *patients* in the doctor's waiting room.

peace/piece *Peace* is calmness:

Looking at the ocean brings me a sense of *peace*.

A *piece* is a part of something:

Norman took a *piece* of coconut cake.

personal/personnel *Personal* means "connected to a person." It can also mean "intimate":

Whether to lease or own a car is a *personal* choice.
That information is too *personal* to share.

Personnel are the staff in an office:

The Digby Electronics Company is developing a new health plan for its *personnel*.

plain, plane *Plain* means "simple, clear, or ordinary." It can also mean "flat land":

The restaurant serves *plain* but tasty food.
Her house was in the center of a windy *plain*.

A *plane* is an aircraft:

We took a small *plane* to the island.

presence/presents Your *presence* is your attendance, your being somewhere:

We request your *presence* at our wedding.

Presents are gifts:

My daughter got too many birthday *presents*.

principal/principle *Principal* means "most important." It also means "the head of a school":

My *principal* reason for quitting is the low salary.
The *principal* of Crestview Elementary School is popular with students.

A *principle* is a guiding rule:

Betraying a friend is against my *principles*.

quiet/quit/quite *Quiet* means "without noise":

The library has many *quiet* corners.

Quit means "stop":

Will you *quit* complaining?

Quite means "truly" or "exactly":

Victor's speech was *quite* convincing.

rain/reign/rein *Rain* is wet weather:

> We have had a *week* of rain.

To *reign* is to rule; *reign* is royal rule:

> King Arthur's *reign* in Camelot is the subject of many poems.

A *rein* is a leather strap in an animal's harness:

> When Charlie got on the horse, he held the *reins* very tight.

right/rite/write *Right* is a direction (the opposite of left). It can also mean "correct":

> To get to the gas station, turn *right* at the corner.
> On my sociology test, I got nineteen out of twenty questions *right*.

A *rite* is a ceremony:

> I am interested in the funeral *rites* of other cultures.

To *write* is to set down in words:

> Brian has to *write* a book report.

sight/site/cite A *sight* is something you can see:

> The truck stop was a welcome *sight*.

A *site* is a location:

> The city is building a courthouse on the *site* of my old school.

Cite means "to quote an authority." It can also mean "to give an example":

> In her term paper, Christina wanted to *cite* several computer experts.
> When my father lectured me on speeding, he *cited* the story of my
>   best friend's car accident.

sole/soul A *sole* is the bottom of a foot or shoe:

> My left boot needs a new *sole*.

A *soul* is the spiritual part of a person:

> Some people say meditation is good for the *soul*.

stair/stare A *stair* is a step:

> The toddler carefully climbed each *stair*.

A *stare* is a long, fixed look:

> I wish that woman wouldn't *stare* at me.

stake/steak A *stake* is a stick driven into the ground:

> The gardener put *stakes* around the tomato plants.

A *steak* is a piece of meat or fish:

> I like my *steak* cooked medium rare.

stationary/stationery *Stationary* means "standing still":

> As the speaker presented his speech, he remained *stationary*.

Stationery is writing paper:

> For my birthday, my uncle gave me some *stationery* with my name
>   printed on it.

steal/steel To *steal* means "to take someone else's property without permission or right":

> Last night, someone tried to *steal* my car.

Steel is a form of iron:

> The door is made of *steel*.

than/then *Than* is used to compare things:

> My dog is more intelligent *than* many people.

Then means "at that time":

> I lived in Buffalo for two years; *then* I moved to Albany.

their/there/they're *Their* means "belonging to them":

> My grandparents donated *their* old television to a women's shelter.

There means "at that place." It can also be used as an introductory word:

> Sit *there*, next to Simone.
> *There* is a reason for his happiness.

They're is a contraction of *they are*:

> Jaime and Sandra are visiting; *they're* my cousins.

thorough/through/threw *Thorough* means "complete":

> I did a *thorough* cleaning of my closet.

Through means "from one side to the other." It can also mean "finished":

> We drove *through* Greenview on our way to Lake Western.
> I'm *through* with my studies.

Threw is the past tense of *throw*:

> I *threw* the ball to him.

to/too/two *To* means "in a direction toward." It is also a word that can go in front of a verb:

> I am driving *to* Miami.
> Selena loves *to* write poems.

Too means "also." It also means "very":

> Anita played great golf; Adam did well, *too*.
> It is *too* kind of you to visit.

Two is the number:

> Mr. Almeida owns *two* clothing stores.

vain/vane/vein *Vain* means "conceited." It also means "unsuccessful":

> Victor is *vain* about his dark, curly hair.
> The doctor made a *vain* attempt to revive the patient.

A *vane* is a device that moves to indicate the direction of the wind:

> There was an old weather *vane* on the barn roof.

A *vein* is a blood vessel:

> I could see the *veins* in his hands.

waist/waste The *waist* is the middle part of the body:

>He had a leather belt around his *waist*.

Waste means "to use carelessly." It also means "thrown away because it is useless":

>I can't *waste* my time watching trashy television shows.
>That manufacturing plant has many *waste* products.

wait/weight *Wait* means "to hold yourself ready for something":

>I can't *wait* until my check arrives.

Weight means "heaviness":

>He tested the *weight* of the bat.

weather/whether *Weather* refers to conditions outside.

>If the *weather* is warm, I'll go swimming.

Whether means "if":

>*Whether* you help me or not, I'll paint the hallway.

were/we're/where *Were* is the past form of *are*:

>Only last year, we *were* scared freshmen.

We're is the contraction of *we are*:

>Today *we're* confident sophomores.

Where refers to a place:

>Show me *where* you used to play basketball.

whined/wind/wined *Whined* means "complained":

>Polly *whined* about the weather because the rain kept her
>   indoors.

Wind (if it rhymes with *find*) means "to coil or wrap something" or "to turn a key":

>*Wind* that extension cord, or you'll trip on it.

Wind (if it rhymes with *sinned*) is air in motion:

>The *wind* blew my cap off.

If someone *wined* you, he or she treated you to some wine:

>My brother *wined* and dined his boss.

who's/whose *Who's* is a contraction of *who is* or *who has*:

>*Who's* driving?

Whose means "belonging to whom":

>I wonder *whose* dog this is.

woman/women *Woman* means "one adult female person":

>A *woman* in the supermarket gave me her extra coupons.

Women means "more than one woman":

Three *women* from Missouri joined the management team.

wood/would *Wood* is a hard substance made from trees:

I have a table made of a polished *wood*.

Would is the past form of *will*:

Albert said he *would* think about the offer.

your/you're *Your* means "belonging to you":

I think you dropped *your* wallet.

You're is the short form of *you are*:

You're not telling the truth.

Exercise 4   **More Words That Sound Alike/Look Alike**

Circle the correct words in each sentence below.

1. During the (rain, reign) of King George III of England, the American colonies lost (patience, patients) with the king's restrictive laws and fought for (their, there, they're) freedom.

2. (Moral, Morale) at the fraternity has declined since the group was criticized for its reckless initiation (rights, rites, writes).

3. In these negotiations, the ambassador's (principal, principle) goal is to maintain the (peace, piece) and not (loose, lose) the support of our allies.

4. It was (quiet, quit, quite) noisy in the library today until the librarian asked the three elderly men to (quiet, quit, quite) laughing and chatting at the computers.

5. We thought we were lost at first, but eventually Diane's directions (lead, led) us to a large red barn with a (weather, whether)(vain, vane, vein).

6. The (whined, wind, wined) swept the rain against the car with such force that we hardly knew (were, we're, where) we (were, we're, where) going.

7. I want to know (who's, whose) responsible for making that (woman, women) wait for an hour and (than, then) giving her the wrong prescription.

8. If (your, you're) looking for a (loan, lone) to start your business, you will have to (sight, site, cite) similar projects that have been successful.

9. Edward knew he (wood, would) be (to, too, two) busy to stop for a meal, so he put a (pair, pear), a bottle of water, and a granola bar in his briefcase.

10. It will take time to (lessen, lesson) the heartache of Rick's loss, but eventually he will find (peace, piece).

Exercise 5 **More Words That Sound Alike/Look Alike**

INSTRUCTOR'S NOTE

Answers will vary. Possible answers shown at left.

Working with a partner or group, write one sentence for each of the words below.

1. a. loose   *One of the shutters on the window is loose.*

   b. lose   *Be careful not to lose that ticket.*

2. a. stationary   *Ellie exercises on a stationary bike.*

   b. stationery   *He wrote me on company stationery.*

3. a. wander   *I am afraid my new puppy will wander away.*

   b. wonder   *I wonder if Serena has a boyfriend.*

4. a. passed   *We passed my old house.*

   b. past   *I miss the old parties of our past.*

5. a. plain   *Tell me the plain truth.*

   b. plane   *Regina always travels by plane.*

6. a. thorough   *The police made a thorough investigation.*

   b. through   *The cat ran through the house.*

   c. threw   *Sherman threw the Frisbee across the park.*

7. a. sole   *A nail is stuck in the sole of your shoe.*

   b. soul   *Don't sell your soul for money or fame.*

8. a. stake   *There was a stake with a sign on it in the front yard.*

   b. steak   *Julio cooked a thick, juicy steak.*

9. a. wait   *Arthur has to wait for his wife.*

   b. weight   *You are losing too much weight.*

10. a. stair   *Claudia ran up the stairs.*

    b. stare   *The crowd began to stare at the newcomer.*

Exercise 6 **Editing a Paragraph for Errors in More Words That Sound Alike/Look Alike**

Connect

The following paragraph has errors in words that sound alike or look alike. Correct each error in the space above it. There are eleven errors.

   For months, I envied my roommate's remarkable luck in college. Tony is one of

those students who never seems to study until the last minute and yet always

       right
seems to have the rite answers on a test. I, on the other hand, study regularly and

                  than
steadily for all my tests and quizzes. Yet Tony always got better grades then I did.

  wondered   *steal*
Sometimes I wandered if he had managed to steel a copy of the test, but I realized

                        steel
he had two talents: a knack for memorizing facts quickly, and nerves of steal that

             whine
allowed him to remain cool under pressure. I used to wind to my sister that it

Then
wasn't fair. Than, one day, Tony and I, who were in the same history class, took
thorough
our final exam. My preparation for the test had been through; Tony hadn't had the
patience
patients to do anything but skim the textbook. As I worked on my exam, I saw
stare
Tony stair blankly. Later, he began to fidget. After the exam, Tony asked me, "Wasn't
quite
that a terrible test?" "No," I answered, "I thought it was quiet easy." When our

instructor posted the results of the exam, I stopped envying Tony.

Exercise 7 **Words That Sound Alike/Look Alike: A Comprehensive Exercise**

Circle the correct words in parentheses in each sentence below.

1. As the officer began to (advice, **advise**) Lucy of her (**rights**, rites, writes), Lucy remained (**stationary**, stationery).

2. Mrs. Kowalski is such a good (sole, **soul**) that I sometimes feel she is an (**angel**, angle) (hear, **here**) on earth.

3. (Its, **It's**) a sad day when a Tom Cruise movie loses (**its**, it's) power to entertain me, but this movie is a (waist, **waste**) of my time.

4. Liam's shirt (**complements**, compliments) the color of his eyes, and that color (wood, **would**) look good on you, (to, **too**, two).

5. I was not (conscience, **conscious**) of Anita's bad temper until she jerked hard on her horse's (rains, reigns, **reins**) and (than, **then**) kicked the poor animal.

6. It was so cold that I could see my (**breath**, breathe) on the window (**pane**, pain) and (**knew**, new) that winter had arrived.

7. Bart was not willing to (**accept**, except) his brother's (council, **counsel**) about applying for financial aid.

8. (**Your**, You're) behavior in court can (**affect**, effect) the outcome of the trial, no matter how (**fair**, fare) the jury tries to be.

9. As I walked down the (isle, **aisle**) with my bride, I suddenly realized that we were about to go (**forth**, fourth) into a (knew, **new**) life.

10. My doctor is encouraging his (patience, **patients**) to try a (does, **dose**) of an over-the-counter cold medicine instead of overusing antibiotics.

11. My brother's class is taking a trip to Tallahassee, the (**capital**, capitol) of Florida, as part of a (coarse, **course**) in political science.

12. I hope that the loss of his home will have no (farther, **further**) (affect, **effect**) on the (all ready, **already**) unhappy child.

13. Larry doesn't follow fashion trends; when he needs (close, **clothes**, cloths), he buys (**plain**, plane) old jeans and flannel shirts from discount stores.

14. My first goal is to find a (decent, descent) apartment; (then, than) I want to meet someone (who's, whose) (principals, principles) are the same as mine.

15. I (wander, wonder) if I should go to the (personal, personnel) department of Satellite Services and apply for a job; I've (heard, herd) that (moral, morale) is high among the staff.

16. The actress is so (vain, vane, vein) that she expects fresh (flours, flowers) in her dressing room every night.

17. I want to take my toddler to Felipe's wedding, but I don't (know, no) (weather, whether) children are (aloud, allowed) at the ceremony.

18. Residents of the area are nervous about the rumors of a (cereal, serial) killer; (their, there, they're) locking (their, there, they're) doors at night.

19. It was difficult for the employees at the plant to (wait, weight) for a decision from the company president when so many jobs (were, we're, where) at (stake, steak).

20. The famous athlete's (presence, presents) at the local basketball game caused many people to (stair, stare).

Exercise 8 **Editing a Paragraph for Errors in Words That Sound Alike/ Look Alike: A Comprehensive Exercise**

The following paragraph has errors in words that sound alike or look alike. Correct each error in the space above it. There are nineteen errors.

        right
There are a rite way and a wrong way to make important decisions. The wrong
          choose
way is to act on impulse and to chose immediately. Decisions made this way can
                      pain
prove to be the correct ones, but more frequently they lead to pane and regret. A
        patience   *personal   principles*
better way to decide is to use patients and be true to personnel principals. It takes
                                    advice
time to reach a conclusion, and some of that time can be spent seeking advise
    whose   *morals*
from people who's knowledge, experience, or morales you respect. Another step
       further   *effects*
in decision-making is to look farther than the immediate affects of a choice. Get-

ting married on a whim, for example, can bring instant happiness. However, once
      aisle   *passed*
the joyful trip down the isle is complete and a blissful period has past, there are
                          Besides
problems like money and education to consider. Beside, any life-changing deci-
                       angles It's
sion deserves to be looked at from all the angels. Its better to consider your
      than   *wondering*   *would*
options carefully then to spend years wandering how your life wood have been

different if you'd made another choice.

Word Choice

One way to improve your writing is to pay close attention to your choice of words. As you revise and edit, be careful to use precise language and avoid wordiness, clichés, and slang.

PRECISE LANGUAGE

Try to be as specific as you can in explaining or describing. Replace vague, general words or phrases with more precise language.

> **not this:** Last night, I made ~~a lot~~ of money in tips.
> **but this:** Last night, I made *fifty dollars* in tips.

> **not this:** He gave me a ~~nice~~ smile.
> **but this:** He gave me a *friendly* smile.
> **or this:** He gave me a *reassuring* smile.
> **or this:** He gave me a *welcoming* smile.

> **not this:** Maggie is a ~~good~~ friend.
> **but this:** Maggie is a *loyal* friend.
> **or this:** Maggie is a *devoted* friend.

Exercise 1   Using Precise Language

In the following sentences, replace each italicized word or phrase with a more precise word or phrase. Write your revisions above the lines.

INSTRUCTOR'S NOTE

Answers will vary. Possible answers shown at left.

1. I had a *nice* weekend with my folks. *(relaxing)*
2. You need to buy *a lot* of potato chips for the party. *(six large bags)*
3. I think about you *often*. *(every day)*
4. Take Mr. Benson for English; he's *nice*. *(kind and easygoing)*
5. Mitchell had another *bad* day at work. *(discouraging)*
6. This time, let's go to an *interesting* movie. *(action-packed)*
7. I am going to need *a lot* of help with this course. *(three hours a week)*
8. I tried to practice my speech, but it sounds *stupid*. *(disorganized)*
9. What's wrong? You sound *funny* today. *(upset)*
10. You will make a *great* father someday. *(loving)*

WORDINESS

As you revise and edit your work, check for *wordiness*: the use of extra words. If you can convey the same idea in fewer words, do so. You can be precise *and* direct.

not this: After the accident, ~~I thought in my mind that~~ I was to blame.
but this: After the accident, *I thought* I was to blame.

not this: ~~In my opinion,~~ I think children should exercise daily.
but this: *I think* children should exercise daily.

not this: Jorge bought a CD ~~for the price of~~ $10.95.
but this: Jorge bought a CD *for* $10.95.

Here is a list of some wordy expressions and possible substitutes:

Wordy Expressions	Possible Substitutes
alternative choices	alternatives, choices
asset group	assets
attach together	attach
at a later date and time	later
at a future date	later
at that time	then
at the present moment	now, presently
at the present time	now, presently
at this point in time	now, today
basic essentials	essentials
blend together	blend
bring together	unite
by means of	by
by the fact that	because
change out	replace
combine together	combine

consider the fact that	consider
continue on	continue
day in and day out	daily
deep down inside he believed	he believed
due to the fact that	because
each and every one	each one
end result	result
for all intents and purposes	realistically
for the reason that	because
gather together	gather
have a need for	need
have a realization of	realize
I felt inside	I felt
I personally feel	I feel
I thought in my head	I thought
in the field of art (music, etc.)	in art (music, etc.)
in the near future	soon
in this day and age	today
in this modern world	today
in my mind, I think	I think
in my opinion, I think	I think
in order to	to
in today's society	today
join together	join
maximum amount	maximum
mix together	mix
of a remarkable kind	remarkable
on a daily basis	daily
on and on	endlessly
on a regular basis	regularly
past experience	experience
point in time	time
reached a decision	decided
really and truly	really
reason why	reason
refer back	refer
reflect back	reflect
repeat again	repeat
separate out	separate
shadow of a doubt	doubt
share in common	share
short in stature	short
small in size	small
skills set	skills
start off	start
switch out	replace
the reason being	because
things of that nature	similar traits/objects
top priority	priority
true facts	facts
two different kinds	two kinds
unite together	unite
until and unless	until, unless
very unique	unique

Exercise 2   **Revising for Wordiness**

Revise the following sentences, eliminating the wordiness. Write your revisions in the space above the lines.

1. *Today*
   ~~At this point in time~~, I ~~personally~~ feel that better office technology should be the company's ~~top~~ priority.

2. I cannot approve a promotion for Walter Ford because ~~in my opinion~~ I think that his skills ~~set~~ would not be adequate in the new position.

3. By ~~means of~~ researching the alternatives, our committee has
   decided
   ~~reached a decision~~ to continue the office's contract with the
   because
   Info-Fix computer maintenance company ~~due to the fact that~~
   Info-Fix offers us ~~the~~ maximum ~~amount of~~ service at a reasonable price.

4. *Today*
   ~~In this day and age~~, consumers are willing to spend their money
   remarkable
   on some computer products ~~of a remarkable kind~~.

5. *thought*   *regularly*
   I ~~thought to myself~~ that I had better start studying ~~on a regular basis~~ if I really ~~and truly~~ wanted to finish college.

6. Todd asked me to repeat my refusal ~~again~~ because ~~deep down inside~~ he believed that I would never say "no" to him.

7. Christina is small ~~in size~~ and short ~~in stature~~, yet she has a powerful personality and a ~~very~~ unique ability to motivate others.

8. *Experience*   *today*
   ~~Past~~ experience has taught me that ~~in today's society~~ we can blend ~~together~~ two ~~different~~ kinds of music and create a popular and profitable sound.

9. *Because*
   ~~By the fact that~~ I plan to be an artist, I would rather not take a course in ~~the field of~~ mathematics, but I have to learn the ~~basic~~ essentials as a college requirement.

10. I want to know the ~~true~~ facts of the store's bankruptcy, but you just refer ~~back~~ to gossip and rumors.

CLICHÉS

Clichés are worn-out expressions. Once they were a new way of making a point, but now they are old and tired. You should avoid them in your writing.

> **not this:** I know that Monica will always ~~be there for me~~.
> **but this:** I know that Monica will always support me.

> **not this:** Alan experienced the ~~trials and tribulations~~ of late registration.
> **but this:** Alan experienced the difficulties of late registration.

Following are some common clichés. If you spot clichés in your writing, replace them with more direct or thoughtful statements of your own.

ESL TIP

If you have nonnative speakers, ask them to list some commonly used clichés from their native language. Ask them to give the common meaning of the cliché, and then ask them for the literal translation. This may be an amusing way for all students to spot clichés in their own writing. (For example: "Estas tomando el pelo" is a Spanish cliché that means, "You're kidding me." However, the literal translation is "You're drinking my hair." The expression is analogous to "You're pulling my leg.")

Some Common Clichés

acting like there's no tomorrow	in the blink of an eye
all in all	in the final analysis
all the time in the world	information superhighway
at the end of the day	I wouldn't be where I am today
avoid like the plague	kick the bucket
beat around the bush	last but not least
between a rock and a hard place	let bygones be bygones
break the ice	light as a feather
break new ground	live life to the fullest
by the same token	make ends meet
can't hold a candle to	on the same page
climb the ladder of success	on top of the world
cold as ice	one day at a time
cry my eyes out	over the hill
cutting edge	pure as the driven snow
dead tired	quick as a wink
dead as a doornail	ready on day one
down in the dumps	rock solid
down on his luck	shoulder to cry on
a drop in the bucket	sick as a dog
few and far between	slept like a log
free as a bird	smooth as silk
first and foremost	state of the art
fresh as a daisy	the ball's in your court
give it your best shot	the sky's the limit
go the distance	through thick and thin
go the extra mile	trials and tribulations
grass is always greener	tried and true
hard as a rock	up at the crack of dawn
he (she) is always there for me	when all is said and done
hit the ground running	when the rubber hits the road
hit the nail on the head	when things get rough
hot under the collar	worked and slaved
hustle and bustle	worked like a dog

Exercise 3   Revising Clichés

The following sentences contain clichés (italicized). Working with a partner or a group, rewrite the sentences, replacing the clichés with more direct or thoughtful words or phrases. Write in the space above the lines.

Collaborate

INSTRUCTOR'S NOTE

Answers will vary. Possible answers shown at left.

1. When I lost my best friend, I was ready to *cry my eyes out.*
   cry for hours

2. Kind neighbors are *few and far between.*
   rare

3. *I wouldn't be where I am today* without Professor Miyori's
   I would never have become a doctor

   inspiring classes.

4. Since I lost my weekend job at the hospital, I am struggling to

   make ends meet.
   pay the bills

5. Hank has a *tried and true* method of repairing leaky windows.
   reliable

6. When I take my dog for a walk, she acts like she is *on top of the*
   completely
   world.
   happy

7. If you want to be on our management team, you have to be able

   to *go the distance.*
   endure hard work

8. Tanika has been *down in the dumps* ever since she had an argu-
   depressed

   ment with her sister.

9. If I am not qualified for the job, *don't beat around the bush* about
   be honest

   the situation.

10. Some people might have envied my family, but that's only because

    they believed *the grass is always greener* in somebody else's home.
    life is always better

Exercise 4   Identifying Clichés

Underline all the clichés in the following paragraph. There are nine clichés.

   Last month my husband faced so many problems that he had no choice but to take things <u>one day at a time</u>. First, Geraldo was <u>as sick as a dog</u> with the flu for ten days, but that illness proved to be <u>a drop in the bucket</u> compared to his other difficulties. His truck broke down just when Geraldo was most needed at work and he had already missed several work days because of the flu. His boss told him to show up for work or lose his job, putting Geraldo <u>between a rock and a hard place</u>. To repair the truck, Geraldo got a loan from his brother and returned to work. He <u>worked like a slave</u>, <u>getting up at the crack of down</u> and working until late in the evening to make up for the days he had missed. <u>Last but not least,</u> Geraldo learned that his niece had been injured in a car accident in Miami. <u>All in all</u>, it was a tough time for Geraldo, but he proved that he knows how to cope <u>through thick and thin</u>.

Connect

Exercise 5   **Editing for Imprecise Language, Wordiness, and Clichés**

Edit the following paragraph for imprecise language, wordiness, and
clichés. Write your revisions above the lines. There are twelve places that
need editing.

                                                                fashionable
    When Nina finished high school, she expected to find a job at a ~~nice~~ clothing
                          achieve success
store and quickly ~~climb the ladder of success~~. ~~Deep down inside~~, Nina believed
                              dozens
that because she had ~~a lot~~ of good ideas about fashion, she could really ~~and truly~~

become a famous designer in two or three years. She felt that her designs would

be ~~very~~ unique, and without ~~a shadow of~~ a doubt, she would soon be a star in the

fashion world. Once she found a job in a clothing store at the mall, however, Nina

learned that anyone who wants to learn how to create fashion first has to learn
                    Daily   *worked hard*
how to sell fashion. ~~Day in and day out~~, she ~~worked and slaved~~ until she became
                                                            pay her bills
an assistant manager. Once her salary was enough to allow her to ~~make ends~~

~~meet~~, Nina made an important decision. She enrolled in college, where she is tak-

ing classes in ~~the fields of~~ fashion design and business. Although she can afford
                              fully committed
only part-time attendance, she is ~~giving her best shot~~ to an education that can lead

her closer to her dreams.

SLANG

Slang is an informal vocabulary frequently used during conversations
among friends. It is also used by fiction writers when they try to create
realistic dialogue. Slang expressions and their meanings can change frequently. "Cool" and "hot" can both mean "popular," while "bad" as a slang
term can mean "good." Today, "guys" as slang refers to males and females.
Slang expressions change often, and because they can easily be misunderstood, you should avoid them in formal writing assignments that require
precise word choice.

    The following list may contain slang that you use in everyday conver-
sation, but you may also notice several expressions that are now considered outdated.

Slang	Standard English
awesome	terrific
All bets are off.	The future is uncertain.
back in the day	in the past (or when I was younger)
bent out of shape	upset
big time	major
bounce (verb)	leave
Bring it on.	Challenge me.
bummed	disappointed

chill (or chill out)	relax (or calm down)
creeps me out	makes me uneasy
don't have a clue	have no idea
Don't mess with me.	Don't bother me.
Dial it back.	Be less intense.
ditch (verb)	throw away
Don't go there.	Don't talk about it.
Do you know what I'm saying?	Do you understand?
Feel me?	Do you understand?
For real?	Really?
for sure	certainly
get his/her act together	become more organized or focused
get his/her groove on	regain momentum or confidence
gets me down	upsets me, saddens me
get (or wrap) my head around	understand (or imagine)
Get real.	Be realistic.
give it up for; give a shout out	applaud for; recognize
Give me a break.	Be more lenient with me.
got game	has excellent skills
he/she goes	he/she says
Hold up.	Wait.
I got your back.	I'll protect you. (or I'll look out for you.)
I'm down with that.	I agree with that; I accept that.
I'm into	I'm interested in
I'm not buying it.	I don't believe it.
It's all good.	Everything is fine.
It's on you.	It's your fault. (or It's your responsibility.)
Lighten up.	Be less serious.
mess up	make a mistake
my bad	my mistake
No problem. (after "Thank you.")	You're welcome.
party (verb)	socialize (or celebrate)
seal (or close) the deal	reach an agreement (or win)
set of wheels	automobile
Show me some love.	Be considerate (or kind) to me.
That's on you.	That's your fault.
They got served.	They were soundly defeated (or insulted).
They're tight.	They are close friends.
totaled	destroyed
tripping	acting strangely (or irrationally)
True story?	Is it true?
true that	definitely
wasted	inebriated
What's up with that?	What does that mean?

Exercise 6 **Identifying Slang**

Collaborate

Working with a partner or group, write your own examples of slang that you and your friends use today. After each example of slang, write its meaning in standard English.

INSTRUCTOR'S NOTE

Answers will vary. Possible answers shown at right.

1. slang: *bling*

   standard English: *expensive jewelry*

2. slang: *give props to*

   standard English: *give recognition to*

3. slang: *dude*

   standard English: *man*

4. slang: *Cut me some slack.*

   standard English: *Don't be so strict with me.*

5. slang: *That won't cut it.*

   standard English: *That won't work.*

Collaborate

Exercise 7 **Revising Slang**

Working with a partner or group, revise each sentence to eliminate slang. For smoother style, you can change the word order as well as wording that is not slang.

INSTRUCTOR'S NOTE

Answers will vary. Possible answers shown at right.

1. My brother was really bummed about losing his job, so I told him he should just chill for a few days until he could get his act together and be ready to look for another job.

   My brother was very upset about losing his job, so I told him to relax for

   a few days until he could focus on finding work again.

   _____

2. Driving down a dark, deserted road creeps me out at times, but my sister can't even lighten up enough to drive at night.

   Driving down a dark, deserted road occasionally makes me uneasy, but

   my sister can't even relax enough to drive at night.

   _____

3. Kesha hopes to win a lead role in our civic center's production of Rent, but she knows that all bets are off if professional actors are allowed to audition.

   Kesha hopes to win a lead role in our civic center's production of Rent,

   but she knows her chances are narrow if professional actors are allowed

   to audition.

4. Back in the day, my father was the starting quarterback for his high school, and he often brags that he's still got game.

   Years ago in high school, my father was the starting quarterback, and

   he often brags that he still has excellent athletic skills.

   _____

5. At the academic awards ceremony, I gave a shout out to my parents because they had always been there for me.

At the academic awards ceremony, I thanked my parents for constantly

supporting and motivating me.

6. Whenever Jenna drinks too much, she starts tripping and shouting at strangers, "Bring it on!"

   Whenever Jenna drinks excessively, she acts irrationally and even

   challenges strangers to a fight.

7. I really messed up when I lied to my manager about my accounting skills; unfortunately, any spreadsheet mistakes will now be all
   on me.

   Lying to my manager about my accounting skills was a major mistake

   because I will now have to take responsibility for any spreadsheet

   mistakes.

8. Before we started camping, we had no clue how to pitch a tent
   and couldn't get our heads around the idea of sleeping outdoors.

   Before we started camping, we had no idea how to pitch a tent and

   couldn't imagine sleeping outdoors.

9. My little brother and I are tight, so I told him that he should get
   real about living on his own since he works only part-time and
   barely has enough money for the security deposit on a small
   apartment.

   My little brother and I are close, so I told him he should be realistic

   about living on his own since he works only part-time and barely has

   enough money for the security deposit on a small apartment.

10. Sometimes it gets me down when my parents argue, but I know
    they will always have each other's back.

    Sometimes I become sad when my parents argue, but I know they will

    always look out for each other.

Connect

Exercise 8 **Editing for Imprecise Language, Wordiness, Clichés, and Slang**

Edit the following paragraph for imprecise language, wordiness, clichés,
and slang. Write your revisions above the lines. There are ten places that
need editing.

INSTRUCTOR'S NOTE

Answers will vary. Possible
answers shown at left.

During my senior year of high school, I worked as a delivery person for an auto

                                      at least twenty

parts store. The job was never boring because I had ~~a lot of~~ deliveries to make

                          difficult   man

each day, but some customers could be ~~rough.~~ One ~~dude~~ owned a body shop, and he always complained to me about the prices of the parts he ordered. He always

upset

acted ~~all bent out of shape~~ and accused my boss of overcharging, but I just

reminded him that I didn't set the prices. Another regular customer owned a gas

station, and he liked to do some of the car repairs himself. He always wanted to

time to spare

show me what he was doing and thought that I had ~~all the time in the world.~~

regularly

However, I was on a strict schedule and couldn't afford to chat ~~on a regular basis.~~

exhausted

Sometimes I was ~~dead tired~~ after a long day of making deliveries, but at least I

car

was able to save money for college and buy a used ~~set of wheels.~~ Maybe my old

give me a discount

boss and some of the customers on my old route will ~~give me a break~~ on parts and

wait for one.

repairs, but I won't ~~hold my breath.~~

CHAPTER 33

Sentence Variety

Quick Question

In the following sentence, find the adverb and move it to the beginning of the sentence.

The old man foolishly gave the saleswoman his social security number.

(After you study this chapter, you will feel more confident of your answer.)

One way to polish your writing is to work on *sentence variety*, the use of different lengths and kinds of sentences. You can become skilled in sentence variety by (1) revising your writing for a balance of short and long sentences and for a mix of sentence types, and (2) being aware of the kinds of sentences you can use.

BALANCING LONG AND SHORT SENTENCES

There are no grammar errors in the following paragraph, but it needs revision for sentence variety.

> I have a routine for waking up. First, I grab a can of Diet Pepsi. I gulp it down. I turn on the TV at the same time. I watch cartoons. I sit for about half an hour. Then the caffeine in the Pepsi starts working. I move to the shower. I make the water temperature very hot. Steam fills the bathroom. My muscles come alive. I begin to feel fully awake.

The paragraph is filled with short sentences. Read it aloud, and you will notice the choppy, boring style of the writing. Compare it to the

587

following revised paragraph, which contains a variety of short and long sentences:

> I have a routine for waking up. First, I grab a can of Diet Pepsi and gulp it down while I turn on the TV. Then I watch cartoons for about half an hour. When the caffeine in the Pepsi starts working, I move to the shower. I make the water temperature so hot that steam fills the bathroom. My muscles come alive as I begin to feel fully awake.

The revised paragraph balances short and long sentences. Read it aloud, and you will notice the way the varied lengths create a more flowing, interesting style.

Some writers rely too heavily on short sentences; others use too many long sentences. The following paragraph contains too many long sentences.

> Randall wanted to make new friends because his old friends had become a bad influence. Randall loved his old friends, especially Michael, but they had begun to be involved in some dangerous activities, and Randall didn't want to be part of these crimes because Randall wanted to apply to the police academy, and he knew that having a record would destroy his chances of admission. Consequently, Randall was honest with Michael, and Randall told him that Randall couldn't risk his future by mixing with people who liked to joyride in stolen cars or steal from neighborhood stores. Soon Randall's friends stopped asking him out, and for a while Randall felt lonely and isolated, but eventually, Randall formed some new friendships, and he was happy to be part of a new group and happy it was one that didn't break the law.

Read the previous paragraph aloud, and you will notice that the sentences are so long and complicated that part of their meaning is lost. Piling on one long sentence after another can make a paragraph boring and difficult to follow. Compare the previous paragraph to the following revised version.

> Randall wanted to make new friends because his old friends had become a bad influence. Randall loved his old friends, especially Michael. However, they had begun to be involved in some dangerous activities, and Randall didn't want to be a part of these crimes. He wanted to apply to the Police Academy and knew that having a record would destroy his chances of admission. Consequently, Randall spoke honestly to Michael. Randall explained that he couldn't risk his future by mixing with people who liked to joyride in stolen cars or steal from neighborhood stores. Soon Randall's friends stopped asking him out, and for a while, Randall felt lonely and isolated. Eventually, Randall formed some new friendships and was happy to be part of a new, law-abiding group.

Read the revised paragraph aloud, and you will notice the combination of long and short sentences makes the paragraph clearer and smoother. Careful revision helps you achieve such a mix.

Exercise 1   Revising Short Sentences

The following paragraph is composed entirely of short sentences. Rewrite it so that it contains a mix of short and long sentences. Write your revisions above the lines.

She works five

My great aunt leads an active life for a woman of seventy-five. She works at a

days a week at the same drug store she has worked at for thirty years.

drug store. She has worked there for thirty years. She works five days a week.

Every Friday night, she meets her friends to drink coffee, play cards, and gossip

Every Friday night she meets her friends. They drink coffee and play cards. They

about their neighbors.   Each weekend, she sings in a choir and then

also gossip about their neighbors. Each weekend, she sings in a choir. After-

joins the members of the choir for brunch.

wards, the members of the choir go out for brunch. My great aunt also keeps up

She is known for her style, which is clearly expressed in her

with the latest fashions. She is well known for her style. It is clearly expressed in

elaborate hats.   She is a young woman of seventy-five, the kind I'd like to be

her elaborate hats. She is a young woman of seventy-five. I'd like to be like her

someday.

someday.

INSTRUCTOR'S NOTE

Answers will vary. Possible answers shown at left.

Exercise 2 **Revising Long Sentences**

The following paragraph is composed entirely of long sentences. Rewrite it so that it contains a mix of short and long sentences. Write your revisions above the lines.

I am still upset about it

Yesterday I heard a conversation that hurt me deeply. I am still upset about it

because I cannot figure out why people would be so unkind about me when they

because I cannot figure out why people would be so unkind about me when they

hardly know me. I don't know how casual friends have any right to assess me so

hardly know me or have any right to assess me so negatively. It all began at work

negatively. It all began at work as I was about to enter the break room. I heard two

as I was about to enter the break room and I heard two people I considered to be

people I considered friends talking. All I heard was my name, and then someone

my friends talking. All I heard was my name, and then someone laughed as if I

laughed as if I were a joke of some kind. At this point, I decided to stay outside

were a joke of some kind, and by this point I decided to stay outside the door and

the door and listen.

listen. Soon I heard one of my so-called friends say, "Jerome? He's not invited."

I decided to walk away from the room so the two wouldn't notice me outside. Also, I

I decided to walk away from the room so the two wouldn't notice me outside and

couldn't walk in without them wondering what I might have heard. I have spent hours

since I couldn't walk in without them wondering what I might have heard. I have

trying to understand why they laughed at me. Even worse, I don't know why I'm being

spent hours trying to understand why they laughed at me and, even worse, why

left out of some party or other event. I know I'm being silly, and I tell myself I heard

I'm being left out of some party or other event. I know I'm being silly, and I tell

only part of a conversation that could be interpreted in a different way. Nevertheless, I

myself I heard only part of a conversation that could be interpreted in a different

still feel that hearing others discuss me was a terrible experience.

way, but I still feel that hearing others discuss me was a terrible experience.

INSTRUCTOR'S NOTE

Answers will vary. Possible answers shown at left.

USING DIFFERENT WAYS TO BEGIN SENTENCES

Most of the time, writers begin sentences with the subject. However, if you change the word order, you can break the monotony of using the same pattern over and over.

Begin with an Adverb

One way to change the word order is to begin with an adverb, a word that describes verbs, adjectives, or other adverbs. (For more on adverbs, see Chapter 21.) You can move adverbs from the middle to the beginning of the sentence as long as the meaning is clear.

> **adverb in middle:** Ricky opened the package *carefully* and checked the contents.
> **adverb at beginning:** *Carefully*, Ricky opened the package and checked the contents.

> **adverb in middle:** The policewoman *calmly* issued a ticket to the aggressive driver.
> **adverb at beginning:** *Calmly*, the policewoman issued a ticket to the aggressive driver.

Exercise 3 **Writing Sentences That Begin with an Adverb**

In the following sentences, move the adverb to the beginning of the sentence.

Slyly, Isabel smiled at the unsuspecting new team member.
1. Isabel smiled slyly at the unsuspecting new team member.
Frantically, Emilio searched for his concert tickets.
2. Emilio searched frantically for his lost concert tickets.
Angrily, the big dog barked at the strange man in the yard.
3. The big dog barked angrily at the strange man in the yard.
Rhythmically, Ernie stroked the horse to calm it.
4. Ernie stroked the horse rhythmically to calm it.
Frequently, my mother spends her Saturdays at garage sales.
5. My mother frequently spends her Saturdays at garage sales.
Carefully, Amber walked between the shelves filled with antiques.
6. Amber walked carefully between the shelves filled with antiques.
Cruelly, the evil scientist in the film laughed at his victim.
7. The evil scientist in the film laughed cruelly at his victim.
Thoughtlessly, Andrew revealed his sister's infatuation with his new friend.
8. Andrew thoughtlessly revealed his sister's infatuation with his new friend.
Silently, Charlie accepted the blame for the incident.
9. Charlie silently accepted the blame for the incident.
Blissfully, the little boy slept in his father's arms.
10. The little boy slept blissfully in his father's arms.

Begin with a Prepositional Phrase

A prepositional phrase contains a preposition and its object. (For more on prepositions, see Chapter 15.) You can change the usual word order of a sentence by moving a prepositional phrase from the end of a sentence to the beginning. You can do this as long as the meaning of the sentence remains clear.

> **prepositional phrase at the end:** A gleaming silver convertible suddenly passed me *in the left lane.*
> **prepositional phrase at the beginning:** *In the left lane*, a gleaming silver convertible suddenly passed me.

> **prepositional phrase at the end:** The bulldog growled and snarled *with fierce intensity.*
> **prepositional phrase at the beginning:** *With fierce intensity*, the bulldog growled and snarled.

> **Note:** Most of the time, you put a comma after a prepositional phrase that begins a sentence. However, you do not need a comma if the prepositional phrase is short.

Exercise 4   **Writing Sentences That Begin with a Prepositional Phrase**

Rewrite the following sentences, moving a prepositional phrase to the beginning of the sentence. Write your revisions above the lines.

During most of spring break, Oscar was in bed with the flu.
1. Oscar was in bed with the flu during most of spring break.

In the alley, the white van with a dented rear panel remained abandoned.
2. The white van with a dented rear panel remained abandoned in the alley.

On the weekends, Daniel felt most lonely.
3. Daniel felt most lonely on the weekends.

At the Superior Bakery, you can get homemade lemon cake.
4. You can get homemade lemon cake at the Superior Bakery.

Without her dictionary, Ardeese can't write a letter or an essay.
5. Ardeese can't write a letter or an essay without her dictionary.

Before I go to work, I'll do the laundry.
6. I'll do the laundry before I go to work.

From hundreds of strangers, the heroic soldier received letters and gifts.
7. The heroic soldier received letters and gifts from hundreds of strangers.

Inside a dusty leather book, an old letter was concealed.
8. An old letter was concealed inside a dusty leather book.

Underneath Vinnie's rough exterior, there is a kind person.
9. There is a kind person underneath Vinnie's rough exterior.

After the rain stopped, we swam in the ice-cold lake.
10. We swam in the ice-cold lake after the rain stopped.

Exercise 5   **Creating Sentences That Begin with Prepositional Phrases**

Collaborate

Working with a partner or group, write sentences that begin with the following prepositional phrases.

1. In a year , *I will be a sophomore in college.*

2. On long weekends , *I often sleep late.*

3. After the accident , *the police caught the driver who fled.*

4. For amusement , *I like to watch reality television shows.*

5. Under too much pressure , *Ted lost his temper.*

6. Between us , *we have enough money to go to lunch.*

7. Near my house *is a great place for Korean barbecue.*

8. With no regret , *Michael quit his job at the plant nursery.*

9. Before you go , *give me your phone number.*

10. At the end of class , *everyone races out the door.*

INSTRUCTOR'S NOTE

Answers will vary. Possible answers shown at left.

USING DIFFERENT WAYS TO JOIN IDEAS

Another way to create sentence variety is to try different methods of combining ideas. Among these methods are (1) using an *-ing* modifier, (2) using an -*ed* modifier, (3) using an appositive, and (4) using a *who, which,* or *that* clause.

Use an -*ing* Modifier

You can avoid short, choppy sentences by using an -*ing* modifier. This way, one of the short sentences becomes a phrase. (For more on modifiers, see Chapter 22.)

> **two short sentences:** Sarah was talking on her cell phone. She drove into a tree.
> **combined with an -*ing* modifier:** Talking on her cell phone, Sarah drove into a tree.

> **Note:** If the modifier begins the sentence, be sure that the next word is the one the modifier describes.

> **two short sentences:** Mr. Martinez loves to read travel books. He plans his next vacation.
> **combined with an -*ing* modifier:** Mr. Martinez loves to read travel books, *planning his next vacation.*

Exercise 6 Using -*ing* Modifiers

INSTRUCTOR'S NOTE

Answers will vary. Possible answers shown at right.

Following are pairs of sentences. Combine each pair by using an -*ing* modifier.

1. A fat black cat sat by the window. It was licking its paws.
   combined: *Licking its paws, a fat black cat sat by the window.*

2. The earrings gleamed in the velvet box. They invited me to try them on.
   combined: *Inviting me to try them on, the earrings gleamed in the velvet box.*

3. Tonya wiped her little boy's tears. She struggled to comfort the child.
   combined: *Wiping her little boy's tears, Tonya struggled to comfort the child.*

4. The sound of my neighbor's television blasted through my apartment walls. It irritated me all weekend.
   combined: *Irritating me all weekend, the sound of my neighbor's television blasted through my apartment walls.*

5. One of my friends hoped to get good tips. She took a job at a popular restaurant.
   combined: *Hoping to get good tips, one of my friends took a job at a popular restaurant.*

6. Aggressive drivers tailgate at high speeds. They risk their own and others' lives.
   combined: *Risking their own and others' lives, aggressive drivers tailgate at high speeds.*

7. My mother worried about my first job away from home. She
called me three times a day.
combined: *Worrying about my first job away from home, my mother*
called me three times a day.

8. Philip Delgado needed a favor. He showed up at my house last
night.
combined: *Needing a favor, Philip Delgado showed up at my house*
last night.

9. Carrie Swenson dreamed of a career as a dancer. She enrolled in
a high school dedicated to the arts.
combined: *Dreaming of a career as a dancer, Carrie Swenson enrolled*
in a high school dedicated to the arts.

10. The bride wore a black dress. She shocked all the wedding
guests.
combined: *Shocking all the wedding guests, the bride wore a black*
dress.

Use an *-ed* Modifier

You can also avoid short, choppy sentences by using an *-ed* modifier. This
way, one of the short sentences becomes a phrase. (For more on modifiers,
see Chapter 22.)

> **two short sentences:** The fish was broiled with lemon and butter.
> The fish was delicious.
> **combined with an *-ed* modifier:** *Broiled with lemon and butter*,
> the fish was delicious.

> **Note:** If the modifier begins the sentence, be sure that the next word is the
> one the modifier describes.

> **two short sentences:** Sam gave me a jewelry box. It was painted
> with silver and blue flowers.
> **combined with an *-ed* modifier:** Sam gave me a jewelry box
> *painted with silver and blue flowers.*

Exercise 7 Using *-ed* Modifiers

Following are pairs of sentences. Combine each pair, using an *-ed*
modifier.

1. The chicken was stuffed with herb dressing. The chicken was
delicious.
combined: *Stuffed with herb dressing, the chicken was delicious.*

2. Armand's boat was a total loss. Armand's boat was wrecked in a
fierce storm.
combined: *Wrecked in a fierce storm, Armand's boat was a total loss.*

INSTRUCTOR'S NOTE

Answers will vary. Possible
answers shown.

3. Alan followed every rule. Alan was motivated by fear of his supervisor.

combined: *Motivated by fear of his supervisor, Alan followed every rule.*

4. I lost a beautiful bracelet. The bracelet was studded with coral beads.

combined: *I lost a beautiful bracelet studded with coral beads.*

5. My new belt had a large silver buckle. The buckle was engraved with an elaborate design.

combined: *My new belt had a large silver buckle engraved with an elaborate design.*

6. Sergeant Thomas Levy was named Officer of the Year. He risked his life to save a woman drowning in a canal.

combined: *Named Officer of the Year, Sergeant Thomas Levy risked his life to save a woman drowning in a canal.*

7. The old house was designed for a large family. It was converted into three spacious apartments.

combined: *Designed for a large family, the old house was converted into three spacious apartments.*

8. Patrick is inspired by his famous mother. He is studying to become a child psychologist.

combined: *Inspired by his famous mother, Patrick is studying to become a child psychologist.*

9. Samantha was married at eighteen. She has never experienced living on her own.

combined: *Married at eighteen, Samantha has never experienced living on her own.*

10. Now that I have my own place, I miss my mother's kitchen. It was stocked with snacks and treats.

combined: *Now that I have my own place, I miss my mother's kitchen stocked with snacks and treats.*

Collaborate

Exercise 8 **Completing Sentences with *-ing* or *-ed* Modifiers**

Working with a partner or group, complete each sentence below.

1. Stranded in the airport *, the passengers began to complain to the airline staff.*

2. Looking for trouble *, David started an argument with Isaac.*

3. Taking the wrong turn *, we got lost in the city.*

INSTRUCTOR'S NOTE

Answers will vary. Possible answers shown.

4. Suspected of murder , *the young woman hired a lawyer.*

5. Deprived of sleep , *the student couldn't concentrate in class.*

6. Smiling at me , *the baby stretched out his arms.*

7. Trapped in the cave , *the explorers began to dig frantically.*

8. Dropping the ball , *the child refused to play any longer.*

9. Excited by the news , *my parents began to smile.*

10. Trusting his friend , *Anthony lent him the money.*

Use an Appositive

Another way to combine short, choppy sentences is to use an appositive. An **appositive** is a phrase that renames or describes a noun. Appositives can go in the beginning, middle, or end of a sentence. Use commas to set off the appositive.

> **two short sentences:** Chocolate milk contains calcium and vitamins. It is a favorite of children.
> **combined with an appositive:** Chocolate milk, *a favorite of children*, contains calcium and vitamins.

> **two short sentences:** Richard is my best friend. He has been a wrestler for several years.
> **combined with an appositive:** Richard, *my best friend*, has been a wrestler for several years.

> **two short sentences:** I am looking forward to Thanksgiving. It is my favorite holiday.
> **combined with an appositive:** I am looking forward to Thanksgiving, *my favorite holiday*.

TEACHING TIP

If you remind students that an appositive gives "extra information" about a noun, they should easily see why commas are used to separate the additional material from the core sentence.

Exercise 9   Using Appositives

Following are pairs of sentences. Combine each pair by using an appositive.

1. Inez is an accountant. She is helping me with my taxes.
   combined: *Inez, an accountant, is helping me with my taxes.*

2. Island Theaters is an old movie house. It is being sold to a restaurant chain.
   combined: *Island Theaters, an old movie house, is being sold to a restaurant chain.*

INSTRUCTOR'S NOTE

Answers will vary. Possible answers shown.

3. I want to take you to Electronics Unlimited. It is the cheapest computer store in the area.

combined: *I want to take you to Electronics Unlimited, the cheapest computer store in the area.*

4. My new boyfriend took me to dinner at Sunflower. It is the fanciest restaurant in the city.

combined: *My new boyfriend took me to dinner at Sunflower, the fanciest restaurant in the city.*

5. Kima is a warm-hearted person. She adopted a shelter cat last week.

combined: *Kima, a warm-hearted person, adopted a shelter cat last week.*

6. Arrogance and impatience are my brother's worst qualities. They show up whenever he is under stress.

combined: *Arrogance and impatience, my brother's worst qualities, show up whenever he is under stress.*

7. Yesterday, I heard the buzz of a mosquito. It is a sure sign of summer.

combined: *Yesterday, I heard the buzz of a mosquito, a sure sign of summer.*

8. Dr. Harjo dresses like a college student. He is a world-renowned scientist.

combined: *Dr. Harjo, a world-renowned scientist, dresses like a college student.*

9. Chicken nuggets and French fries are full of fat. They are my son's favorite foods.

combined: *Chicken nuggets and French fries, my son's favorite foods, are full of fat.*

10. Lucille Okara is a respected negotiator. She is heading an international peace conference in Guatemala.

combined: *Lucille Okara, a respected negotiator, is heading an international peace conference in Guatemala.*

Use a *Who, Which,* or *That* Clause

Clauses beginning with *who, which,* or *that* can combine short sentences.

two short sentences: Jacob is my favorite cousin. He won the golf tournament.

combined with a *who* clause: Jacob, *who is my favorite cousin,* won the golf tournament.

two short sentences: Good running shoes can be expensive. They make running easier.

combined with a *which* clause: Good running shoes, *which can be expensive*, make running easier.

two short sentences: The cinnamon buns were delicious. I tasted them.

combined with a *that* clause: The cinnamon buns *that I tasted* were delicious.

Punctuating *who, which,* or *that* clauses requires some thought. Decide whether the information in the clause is *essential* or *nonessential.* If the information is essential, do not put commas around it:

> **essential clause:** Students *who like history* will love the movie. (Without the clause *who like history,* the sentence would not have the same meaning. Therefore the clause is essential and is not set off by commas.)
>
> **nonessential clause:** Mel, *who has been singing for years,* deserves to win. (The clause *who has been singing for years* is not essential to the meaning of the sentence. Therefore, it is set off by commas.)

If you have to choose between *which* and *that, which* usually begins a nonessential clause, and *that* usually begins an essential clause.

> **essential clause:** The car *that he was driving* is expensive.
>
> **nonessential clause:** The car, *which I've had for years,* needs a new muffler.

> **Note:** Essential and nonessential clauses are also referred to as *restrictive* and *nonrestrictive* clauses.

Exercise 10   Using *Who, Which,* or *That* Clauses

Following are pairs of sentences. Combine each pair by using a *who, which,* or *that* clause.

1. Sharon told me a secret. The secret shocked me.

   combined: *Sharon told me a secret that shocked me.*

INSTRUCTOR'S NOTE

Answers will vary. Possible answers shown.

2. Belgian chocolate is available in the United States. Some consider it the best chocolate in the world.

   combined: *Belgian chocolate, which some consider the best in the world, is available in the United States.*

3. Clara works with a young man. The young man teaches yoga in the evening.

   combined: *Clara works with a young man who teaches yoga in the evening.*

4. Tyler Nelson is married to my sister. He used to play baseball on a minor league team.

   combined: *Tyler Nelson, who used to play baseball on a minor league team, is married to my sister.*

5. People love their pets. They will spend a great deal of money to keep their animals healthy and happy.

   combined: *People who love their pets will spend a great deal of money to keep their animals healthy and happy.*

6. Pocket scooters are popular with children. The scooters can be dangerous on public roads.

   combined: *Pocket scooters, which are popular with children, can be dangerous on public roads.*

7. Joanna bought a new coffeemaker. The coffeemaker brews one cup of coffee at a time.

   combined: *Joanna bought a new coffeemaker that brews one cup of coffee at a time.*

8. Selena wants to go back to Albuquerque. Albuquerque is her favorite vacation spot.

   combined: *Selena wants to go back to Albuquerque, which is her favorite vacation spot.*

9. I need to thank my father. He worked at two jobs to help me finish college.

   combined: *I need to thank my father, who worked at two jobs to help me finish college.*

10. Talking to strangers once made me nervous. Talking to strangers is now an important part of my job.

    combined: *Talking to strangers, which once made me nervous, is now an important part of my job.*

Connect

Exercise 11 **Revising for Sentence Variety: A Comprehensive Exercise**

Rewrite the following paragraph, combining each pair of underlined sentences using one of the following: an *-ing* modifier, an *-ed* modifier, an appositive, or a *who*, *which*, or *that* clause. Write your revisions in the spaces above the lines.

                               My last girlfriend was a beautiful woman who swore
   Jealousy is like a poison. <u>My last girlfriend was a beautiful woman. She swore</u>
she had not a drop of jealous blood.
<u>she had not a drop of jealous blood.</u> At first, she was understanding and tolerant
                                                              Checking my eyes
of the time I spent without her. Then I noticed a slight change. <u>She would check</u>
carefully, she tried to detect any lies about my social activities.
<u>my eyes carefully. She tried to detect any lies about my social activities.</u> This sub-
                                         Antonio, my best friend, advised me
tle surveillance made me somewhat uneasy. <u>Antonio was my best friend. He</u>
to break off the relationship.
<u>advised me to break off the relationship.</u> Antonio said I would soon see my girl-
                                         Blinded by my infatuation, I hoped that my
friend become more possessive. <u>I was blinded by my infatuation. I hoped that my</u>
girlfriend would change.
<u>girlfriend would change.</u> She did, but the change made me jealous. She left me

when she found someone she liked better.

Readings for Writers

WRITING FROM READING: THE WRITING PROCESS

Getting Carded

David Migoya

"Getting carded" usually means getting checked for identification at bars, restaurants, or clubs, but <u>Denver Post</u> writer David Migoya uses it to mean getting one's first credit card, a milestone for many college students. He warns that the card, a symbol of maturity, has its dangers.

Words You May Need to Know (Corresponding paragraph numbers are in parentheses.)

bombard (1): attack
entice (1): draw on by exciting hope or desire
"maxed out" (3): slang for "used to the maximum amount allowed"
rescinded (4): taken back
droves (5): herds
savvy (6): knowledgeable
jalopy (6): an old car that is falling apart

travesty (6): grotesque imitation (in this case, of graduating with a bright future)
cavalier (7): free and easy
pitfalls (8): hidden dangers
vulnerable (8): liable to be hurt
ultimately (9): eventually
perks (10): slang for "perquisites" (extra payments)

1   They remember their first love, their first car, and, if financial institutions have it right, their first credit card. Because the result could be a commitment that outlasts the first two, banks bombard college students with credit offers designed to entice them to sign up and start charging. And the unsuspecting will be lured by methods ranging from free tee shirts and university-logo coffee mugs to inconceivably low interest rates and high spending limits. "Every year, there's a fresh pack of prospects called freshmen," said Kim McGrigg of Consumer Credit Counseling Services in Denver. "College students are the largest identifiable segment of new customers."

2   It didn't take long for the credit-card offers to land at Jeffrey Kaczmarek's feet. "It seemed like they showed up the moment I moved into the dorm," said Kaczmarek, an Iowa State University graduate. "Most of the problems I created have been behind me for only two years." The thirty-three-year-old computer programmer recalls a freshman year filled with important purchases— "pizza, beer, cigarettes, and other really useful things for college," he said with sarcastic tone—all of them on a $500-limit credit card, his first.

3   With one card "maxed out," Kaczmarek said, getting a second card was easy. "It was a chain reaction," the Denver resident said. "And when all was said and done, I was into it for $4,500." Not only did the debt follow him, but the creditors did, too. "When you're in school and the creditors are calling all the time, it's stress you don't need," he said. "I turned off my phone; I screened calls; it was a terrible way to live."

4   The time after college wasn't any better because a poor credit history affected interest rates Kaczmarek was offered on car loans. He said he even suspects a job offer was rescinded because of it. "As a freshman, I had no way to pay the $500 card," he said, "but it looked *soooo* good."

5   As colleges and universities begin the new school year, the credit offers come in droves. More than fifty-eight percent of college students said they saw credit-card marketers on campus for two or more days at the beginning of a semester, and seventy-eight percent of all students say they have a card, according to the U.S. Public Interest Research Group. "There's significant data supporting the theory that if you can be the first card in their wallet, they'll remain loyal, " said John Ulzheimer, president of education services at Credit.com. "Some issuers mail over a billion pieces a year."

6   The savvy student will use the new card to build credit responsibly so that it later comes in handy to rent an apartment, get a car loan, obtain a mortgage, or even land a job. Used improperly, though, a credit card can cause more heartache to a student than a breakup and cost a lot more than a tune-up. In the end, some students learn it's easier to part ways with a jalopy than with the bad credit they got from buying it. "That low credit score is the grade they never thought about or wanted to earn," Ulzheimer said. "The students spend their time working on an impressive GPA, and they get a degree in one hand and a bad credit score in the other. It's a sad travesty."

7   The worst problems occur not from overspending or maxing out credit limits—which typically are kept low to start—but from fees associated with late payments or interest rates. Put simply, a student who consistently pays only the monthly minimum is likely to hit financial ruin quickly. In fact, the number of eighteen- to twenty-four-year-olds who filed for bankruptcy has ballooned by ninety-six percent in the past decade, according to the Richmond Credit Abuse Resistance Education Program. "The biggest issue is in the attitude toward using the card, and it's usually very cavalier," McGrigg of Consumer Credit Counseling said. "It's a tool of convenience, not an extension of your income."

8   Problems come from a lack of understanding about how credit cards work and the everlasting pitfalls of abuse. Some students just aren't ready for them, said Judy McKenna, a Fort Collins-based financial planner. "It's a particularly vulnerable population that may not come from much money, or it's a group of the temporarily poor," McKenna said. "The pulls to use the

cards can be very strong." The average college student has a credit-card balance of $552, according to the Credit Research center at Georgetown University. Yet forty-five percent of students say they're in serious debt with balances averaging $3,000, Jumpstart Coalition reports.

9   Despite the possible long-term association, why do credit card issuers pursue students if they pose such a financial risk? The answer, according to experts, is Mom and Dad. "Ultimately, the cards get paid by parents who swoop in and save them," said Susan Black, director of financial planning at eMoney Advisor. Said Ulzheimer, "It's actually a safer bet to sign up a student than what common sense tells you."

10   The experts offer several approaches to avoiding problems. The easiest, McKenna said, is simply to avoid the cards, at least until a student gets a full-time job. "Living on a checkbook or cash is smarter," she said. If a student must have a card, he or she should shop around for the best offer, including a competitive interest rate, low or no annual fee, a payment grace period, and user perks such as bonus points or cash back. Sometimes, the perks can pay for a student's trip home or a spring break destination. "Credit isn't for you if you're not serious enough about your financial future to take the time and research which card is best," McGrigg said.

11   Alternatives to credit cards and good ways to build a student's credit history include secured cards—those that require a deposit equaling the credit limit—and charge cards, which require full payment for all purchases each month. Prepaid cards, known as "stored-value cards," are popular because they limit spending. They are accepted like a credit card but are more like a gift certificate. They owner buys an amount on the card and spends it down, either by purchases or cash advances. "They're easy to control and can't be abused," Ulzheimer said.

Comprehension Check

1. What are some of the methods banks use to lure college students to sign up for credit cards? *(See paragraph 1.)*

2. When Jeffrey Kaczmarek was a freshman in college, what kind of purchases did he make with his credit card? *(See paragraph 2.)*

3. According to the United States Public Interest Research Group, what percentage of college students say they have a credit card? *(See paragraph 5.)*

4. What is likely to happen to a student who pays only the monthly minimum on his or her credit card? *(See paragraph 7.)*

5. What, according to "Getting Carded," are some alternatives to credit cards and good ways to build a student's credit history? *(See paragraph 11.)*

Discussion Prompts/Writing Options

If you write on any of the following topics, work through the stages of the writing process in preparing your assignment.

1. "Getting Carded" discusses the dangers that shadow a student getting his or her first credit card. Write a summary of the article. Describe the short-term and long-term dangers, and explain how a student bombarded with credit card offers can avoid "maxing out" or can find a better alternative to a credit card.

2. If you have one or more credit cards, write about how well (or badly) you cope with the temptations to spend beyond your limit.

3. Write about three items (small or large) that many people pay for with a credit card, but that should be bought only with cash or a check. Explain why these items should not be purchased on credit.

4. Write about a purchase that you regret making. Did you buy the item on impulse? Did you buy it to cheer yourself up? To impress someone? To reward yourself? To fit in? How did you feel at the time you made the purchase? How did you feel later?

Collaborate

5. Although college students must cope with the dangers and temptations of credit cards, students also enjoy the advantages of having at least one credit card. Working with a partner or group, brainstorm some examples of these advantages. When you have at least five examples, work individually on writing about these advantages.

Critical Thinking: Topics for Discussion and Writing

If you write on any of the following topics, work through the stages of the writing process in preparing your assignment.

1. If you were the parent of a college student, would you advise him or her to get a credit card? Why or why not?

2. Why do so many college students fall into debt? What financial pressures make the college years a difficult time?

3. As you read "Getting Carded," did you notice some of the phrases that revealed the attitudes of some financial experts? For example, Judy McKenna, a Fort Collins-based financial planner, called first-year college students "a particularly vulnerable population that may not come from much money," or "a group of the temporarily poor." Do you believe these are valid descriptions? Another expert, Susan Black, director of financial planning at eMoney Advisor, said that credit card issuers pursue student business even when the companies expect many students to fall into debt because "the cards get paid by parents who swoop in and save them." In your experience, do parents save their college freshmen from credit card debt? Are these experts creating an accurate picture of freshmen?

WRITING FROM READING: ILLUSTRATION

Spanglish

Janice Castro, with Dan Cook and Cristina Garcia

The authors of this article discuss the "free-form blend of Spanish and English" that has developed from a mix of cultures. They explain this blend by using many examples.

Words You May Need to Know (Corresponding paragraph numbers are in parentheses.)

bemused (1): confused
Quiero un **(1):** I want a. . . .
cerveza: **(1):** beer
linguistic currency (2): way of speaking
syntax (3): word order
patter (3): quick talk
Anglo (3): native-born Americans
ir al **(4):** go to the

counterparts (5): duplicates
phenomena (5): remarkable things
implicit (5): contained
languorous (5): lacking energy
almuerzo **(5):** lunch
hybrids (6): blends
wielded (9): used
gaffes (9): social mistakes

1   In Manhattan a first-grader greets her visiting grandparents, happily exclaiming, "Come here, *sientate*!" Her bemused grandfather, who does not speak Spanish, nevertheless knows she is asking him to sit down. A Miami personnel officer understands what a job applicant means when he says, "*Quiero un* part time." Nor do drivers miss a beat reading a billboard alongside a Los Angeles street advertising *CERVEZA—SIX-PACK!*

2   This free-form blend of Spanish and English, known as Spanglish, is common linguistic currency wherever concentrations of Hispanic Americans are found in the U.S. In Los Angeles, where fifty-five percent of the city's three million inhabitants speak Spanish, Spanglish is as much a part of daily life as sunglasses. Unlike the broken-English efforts of earlier immigrants from Europe, Asia, and other regions, Spanglish has become a widely accepted conversational mode used casually—even playfully—by Spanish-speaking immigrants and native-born Americans alike.

3   Consisting of one part Hispanicized English, one part Americanized Spanish and more than a little fractured syntax, Spanglish is a bit like a Robin Williams comedy routine: a crackling line of cross-cultural patter straight from the melting pot. Often it enters Anglo homes and families through the children, who pick it up at school or at play with their young Hispanic contemporaries. In other cases, it comes from watching TV; many an Anglo child has learned *uno dos tres* almost as quickly as one two three.

4   Spanglish takes a variety of forms, from the Southern California Anglos who bid farewell with the utterly silly "*hasta la* bye-bye" to the Cuban-American drivers in Miami who *parquean* their *carros* (park their

cars). Some Spanglish sentences are mostly Spanish, with a quick detour for an English word or two. A Latino friend may cut short a conversation by glancing at his watch and excusing himself with the explanation that he must "*ir al* supermarket."

5   Many of the English words transplanted this way are simply handier than their Spanish counterparts. No matter how distasteful the subject, for example, it is still easier to say "income tax" than *impuesto sobre la renta*. At the same time, many Spanish-speaking immigrants have adopted such terms as VCR, microwave and dishwasher for what they view as largely American phenomena. Still other English words convey a cultural context that is not implicit in the Spanish. A friend who invites you to *lonche* most likely has in mind the brisk American custom of "doing lunch" rather than the languorous afternoon break traditionally implied by *almuerzo*.

6   Mainstream Americans exposed to similar hybrids of German, Chinese, or Hindi might be mystified. But even Anglos who speak little or no Spanish are somewhat familiar with Spanglish. Living among them, for one thing, are nineteen million Hispanics. In addition, more American high school and university students sign up for Spanish than for any other foreign language.

7   Only in the past ten years, though, has Spanish begun to turn into a national slang. Its popularity has grown with the explosive increases in U.S. immigration from Latin American countries. English has increasingly collided with Spanish in retail stores, offices and classrooms, in pop music and on street corners. Anglos whose ancestors picked up such Spanish words as *rancho*, *bronco*, *tornado*, and *incommunicado*, for instance, now freely use such Spanish words as *gracias*, *bueno*, *amigo*, and *por favor*.

8   Among Latinos, Spanglish conversations often flow easily from Spanish into several sentences of English and back. Spanglish is a sort of code for Latinos: the speakers know Spanish, but their hybrid language reflects the American culture in which they live. Many lean to shorter, clipped phrases in place of the longer, more graceful expressions their parents used. Says Leonel de la Cuesta, an assistant professor of modern languages at Florida International University in Miami: "In the U.S., time is money, and that is showing up in Spanglish as an economy of language." Conversational examples: *taipiar* (type) and *winshi-wiper* (windshield wiper) replace *escribir a maquina* and *limpiaparabrisas*.

9   Major advertisers, eager to tap the estimated $134 billion in spending power wielded by Spanish-speaking Americans, have ventured into Spanish to promote their products. In some cases, attempts to sprinkle Spanish through commercials have produced embarrassing gaffes. A Braniff Airlines ad that sought to tell Spanish-speaking audiences they could settle back *en* (in) luxuriant *cuero* (leather) seats, for example, inadvertently said they could fly without clothes (*encuero*). A fractured translation of the Miller Lite slogan told readers the beer was "Filling, and less delicious." Similar blunders

are often made by Anglos trying to impress Spanish-speaking pals. But if Latinos are amused by mangled Spanish, they also recognize these goofs as a sort of friendly acceptance. As they might put it, *no problema.*

Comprehension Check

1. Define "Spanglish" and describe how it becomes commonly used in both Anglo and Hispanic homes. *(See paragraph 3.)*

2. What do you think is the most interesting Spanglish word or phrase in the essay? Why? *(Answers will vary.)*

3. According to the professor quoted in the article, how does Spanglish reflect the idea that "time is money"? *(See paragraph 8.)*

4. Give some humorous examples from the essay of how major advertisers have made mistakes in trying to reach Spanish-speaking audiences. *(See paragraph 9.)*

Discussion Prompts/Writing Options

If you write on any of the following topics, work through the stages of the writing process in preparing your assignment.

1. "Spanglish" gives several reasons for the growth of this blend of languages. In a paragraph, explain how and why Spanglish has become so widespread.

2. Groups often share their own special language. Computer users, for example, use many terms that a non-user would not understand. Police officers, health-care workers, restaurant workers, musicians, bloggers, and others all use words or terms that are understood only by their group. For a writing assignment, describe four key words or phrases used by a specific group. Focus it with a topic sentence like the following:

   There are four key terms in the language of _____ (name the group.)

   You can write from your own experience, brainstorm with classmates, or interview a member of a specific group.

3. Describe the blending of two languages in your daily life. You can discuss the language of two cultures or countries (like English and Creole, or English and Portuguese), or of two parts of your life (like the formal language you use at work and the informal language you use at home). Give several specific examples of each language.

4. For class discussion or for a writing assignment, describe how two cultures can blend in a person's choice of clothing, music, or family rituals.

5. The authors of "Spanglish" say that "English has increasingly collided with Spanish in retail stores, offices and classrooms, in pop music and on street corners." Working with a partner or group, brainstorm examples to support that statement. For example, ask and answer such questions as "Where and how does Spanish appear in music popular with both Anglos and Hispanics?" and

Collaborate

"How is Spanish appearing in offices?" When you have at least five examples, work individually on a writing assignment that is based on the authors' statement.

6. If English is not your native language, describe the problems you have learning English. Give specific examples of each problem.

7. Write about one of the following main ideas:

> What we think of as "American" food really includes food from many cultures.
>
> or
>
> Americans regularly use words or phrases from other languages. (If you use this idea, avoid using the examples given in "Spanglish.")

To support your main idea, be sure to use as many specific examples as you can.

Critical Thinking: Topics for Discussion and Writing

If you write on any of the following topics, work through the stages of the writing process in preparing your assignment.

1. A widely discussed question today is whether English should become the official language of the United States. Consider this question and as you do, think about these questions:

> What are the advantages of an official language?
> What are the disadvantages?
> What practical issues would arise if English were to become the official language?
> Would all government documents be available only in English?
> What about pamphlets and forms about health, public safety, education, and so forth?
> What about emergency directions issued during a natural disaster?

2. Many children from other countries enter United States schools with limited English language skills. There are two common ways to help speakers of other languages learn a new language in school: (1) total immersion, in which the student learns the new language by hearing and using only that language in all his or her classes and in all school activities, and (2) bilingual education, in which the student learns through a mix of his or her first language and the new one. Which way, total immersion or bilingual education, seems most effective. Why?

   If there are nonnative speakers in your class, you may want to ask them about their experiences learning English and what methods worked well for them.

3. How much does a person's accent matter in his or her ability to succeed? Does accent, whether it is a sign of a person's country of origin, region of the United States, or social status, keep some people from moving up socially or progressing in certain careers? Whether you believe a person's accent doesn't matter, matters a little, or has a significant impact, give specific examples to support your belief.

WRITING FROM READING: DESCRIPTION

A Present for Popo

Elizabeth Wong

The child of Chinese immigrants, Elizabeth Wong was born in Los Angeles, California. She has a master of fine arts degree and has worked as a writer for newspapers and television. She has also written several plays. In "A Present for Popo," Wong describes a beloved grandmother.

Words You May Need to Know (Corresponding paragraph numbers are in parentheses.)

nimbly (1): quickly, gracefully
problematic (2): difficult, or leading to problems
vain (2): proud of your appearance
co-opted (3): taken over
niggling (4): unimportant
dim sum **(6):** a light meal

terrarium (7): a small container where plants and small creatures are kept alive under conditions imitating their natural environment
tenuous (12): weak, or fragile
cohesive (12): binding

1   When my Popo opened a Christmas gift, she would shake it, smell it, listen to it. She would size it up. She would open it nimbly, with all enthusiasm and delight, and even though the mittens were ugly or the blouse too small or the card obviously homemade, she would coo over it as if it were the baby Jesus.

2   Despite that, buying a gift for my grandmother was always problematic. Being in her late 80s, Popo didn't seem to need any more sweaters or handbags. No books certainly, as she knew only six words of English. Cosmetics might be a good idea, as she was just a wee bit vain.

3   But ultimately, nothing worked. "No place to put anything anyway," she used to tell me in Chinese. For in the last few years of her life, Popo had a bed in a room in a house in San Gabriel owned by one of her sons. All her belongings, her money, her very life was now co-opted and controlled by her sons and their wives. Popo's daughters had little power in this matter. This was a traditional Chinese family.

4   For you see, Popo had begun to forget things. Ask her about something that happened twenty years ago, and she could recount the details in the heartbeat of a New York minute. But it was those niggling everyday matters that became so troubling. She would forget to take her heart medicine. She would forget where she put her handbag. She would forget she talked to you just minutes before. She would count the few dollars in her billfold, over and over again. She would ask me for the millionth time, "So when are you going to get married?" For her own good, the family decided she should give up her beloved one-room Chinatown flat. Popo herself recognized she might be a danger to herself. "I think your grandmother is going crazy," she would say.

5   That little flat was a bothersome place, but Popo loved it. Her window had a view of several import-export shops below, not to mention the grotesque plastic hanging lanterns and that nasty loudspeaker serenading tourists with eighteen hours of top-40 popular hits.

6   My brother Will and I used to stand under her balcony on Mei Ling Way, shouting up, "Grandmother on the Third Floor! Grandmother on the Third Floor!" Simultaneously, the wrinkled faces of a half-dozen grannies would peek cautiously out their windows. Popo would come to the balcony and proudly claim us. "These are my grandchildren coming to take me to *dim sum*." Her neighbors would cluck and sigh, "You have such good grandchildren. Not like mine."

7   In that cramped room of Popo's, I could see past Christmas presents. One was a full-wall collage of family photos that my mother and I made together and presented one year with lots of fanfare. Popo had attached additional snapshots by way of paper clips and Scotch tape. And there, on the window sill, sat a little terrarium to which Popo had tied a small red ribbon. "For good luck," as she gleefully pointed out the sprouting buds. "See, it's having babies."

8   Also, there were the utility shelves on the wall, groaning from a wide assortment of junk, stuff, and whatnot. Popo was fond of salvaging discarded things. After my brother had installed the shelving, she did a little jig, then took a whisk broom and lightly swept away any naughty spirits that might be lurking on the walls. "Shoo, shoo, shoo, away with you, Mischievous Ones!" That apartment was her independence, and her pioneer spirit was everywhere in it.

9   Popo was my mother's mother, but she was also a second mother to me. Her death was a great blow. The last time I saw her was Christmas 1990, when she looked hale and hearty. I thought she would live forever. Last October, at ninety-one, she had her final heart attack. The next time I saw her, it was at her funeral.

10   There she was in an open casket, with a shiny new penny poised between her lips, a silenced warrior woman. Her sons and daughters placed colorful pieces of cloth in her casket. They burned incense and paper money. A small marching band led a New Orleans-like procession through the streets of Chinatown. Popo's picture, larger than life, stood in a flatbed truck to survey the world of her adopted country.

11   This little four-foot, nine-inch woman had been the glue of our family. She wasn't perfect, she wasn't always even nice, but she learned from her mistakes, and, ultimately, she forgave herself for being human. It is a lesson of forgiveness that seems to have eluded her own sons and daughters.

12   And now she is gone. And with her—the tenuous, cohesive ties of blood and duty that bound us to family. My mother predicted that once the distribution of what was left of Popo's estate took place, no further words would be exchanged between Popo's children. She was right.

13   But this year, six of the twenty-seven grandchildren and two of the eighteen great-grandchildren came together for a holiday feast of honey-baked ham and mashed potatoes. Not a gigantic family reunion. But I think, for now, it's the one yuletide present my grandmother might have truly enjoyed.

Comprehension Check

1. Despite Popo's excitement at Christmas, what was "problematic" for the narrator? *(See paragraph 2.)*

2. Where did Popo spend her last years, and who was in charge of her life? *(See paragraph 3.)*

3. What were three indications of Popo's forgetfulness? *(See paragraph 4.)*

4. What do you think is the most descriptive sentence in the essay? Why? *(Answers will vary.)*

5. What did Popo do with a small red ribbon? Why? *(See paragraph 7.)*

6. What superstitious act did Popo perform after her son installed shelving? *(See paragraph 8.)*

7. Describe what you feel is the most intriguing part of Popo's funeral ritual. *(Answers will vary; see paragraph 10.)*

8. What passage suggests that Popo's children were not close to each other? *(See paragraph 12.)*

Discussion Prompts/Writing Options

If you write on any of the following topics, work through the stages of the writing process in preparing your assignment.

1. Elizabeth Wong uses many details about her grandmother's apartment to describe the woman. With as many details as possible, describe how a person's environment (for example, her office, his apartment) reflects that person.

2. Wong's essay includes a description of a funeral in a Chinese-American family. Write a description of some custom or ritual in your family. You could write, for instance, about a wedding, funeral, celebration of a holiday, or religious occasion.

3. "A Present for Popo" is a tribute to a beloved person. Write a description of someone who holds a special place in your life.

4. The grandmother in Wong's essay is an immigrant, a Chinese woman who moved to America. Describe an immigrant that you know. Focus on how the person reflects a combination of two countries or cultures.

5. Describe an elderly person you know well. In your description, you can use details of appearance and behavior. Focus on how these details reveal personality.

6. Describe yourself at age ninety. Use your imagination to give details of your appearance, behavior, and family relationships at that stage of your life.

Critical Thinking: Topics for Discussion and Writing

If you write on any of the following topics, work through the stages of the writing process in preparing your assignment.

1. This tribute to a grandmother has a dark side in its hints of generational changes and family conflicts. Consider the details that point to the dark side.

2. Is Popo's story typical of the fate of many older Americans? Consider what her early life must have been like (her granddaughter talks of Popo's "enthusiasm and delight" at receiving a gift and calls her a "warrior woman"). Then consider how she spent her last days.

3. With all the relocations and migrations of family members today, are there still elders (male and female) who lead a family and keep it together? If you believe that the days of matriarchs and patriarchs (female and male heads of families) are over, explain why. If you believe many families are still guided and united by a person like Popo, give examples.

WRITING FROM READING: NARRATION

The Good Father

Alisa Valdes-Rodriguez

In this essay, best-selling author Alisa Valdes-Rodriguez writes about her father. He was orphaned, shipped to one foster home after another, and later abandoned by his wife to raise their children alone. Yet, despite it all, this Latino father maintained an open heart and became his only daughter's hero and best friend.

Words You May Need to Know (Corresponding paragraph numbers are in parentheses.)

elitist (2): people who believe they belong to a superior group and deserve special treatment
tantamount (2): equal to
scarlet letter (2): a sign of shame; the term comes from Nathaniel Hawthorne's novel about a woman forced to wear a scarlet letter as punishment for committing adultery
transplanted (4): moved or relocated from one place to another
confronted (4): stood in front of, faced
***arroz con pollo* (6):** chicken with rice

1   For years I have sent my father a Mother's Day card. I'm not trying to insult him, and I'm not trying to make a joke. Rather, I am acknowledging the fact that from the time I was eleven, when my parents divorced and my mother left us, my father served as both a mother and a father to me. A single father raising a daughter through her adolescence is unusual. But that my Cuban dad raised me to be strong, confident, and brave is all the more remarkable considering the details of his early life.

2   The story begins in Santa Clara, Cuba, in the 1940s. My grandmother Eugenia Leyba was a beautiful teenager, the maid in the home of a wealthy

family. The family had two sons. The sons made a bet, each thinking that he would be the first to sleep with the maid. My grandfather Ricardo Hernandez "won" that bet (no one knows whether by force or through charm). What we do know is that my father, Nelson, was the product of this unhappy union, and Ricardo, now living in Miami, never claimed him. When Ricardo's parents discovered that the maid was pregnant by their son, they did what most class- and color-conscious elitists would have done at the time: they fired Eugenia and spread rumors about her around town, rumors that made it impossible for her to find work. Being a single mother—and a single teen mother from the working class—is difficult anywhere in Latin America, even today; in the 1940s it was tantamount to wearing a scarlet letter.

3   The young Eugenia gave birth to my father on the kitchen table in her mother's house. She then moved to Havana, shamed, and took jobs as a domestic servant. When my father was seven, his mother married. The man's name was Elpidio Valdes. In those days it was scandalous for a man to marry a woman who had a child, so Eugenia and Elpidio pretended that he was my dad's father, even changing my dad's last name to Valdes. When my dad was nine, Eugenia died of leukemia. No one told him she was dead until the funeral. Elpidio stood at the grave with my father as the casket was lowered and said simply, "That's your mother. Men don't cry."

4   When my dad was fifteen, Elpidio heard about Operation Pedro Pan, a U.S.-based program that arranged for children to be taken out of the newly communist Cuba, and thought it was a marvelous idea. He sent my father, alone, to the United States. (Ultimately the program transplanted 14,000 children.) Unlike many of the other kids, however, my father never saw his family again. Elpidio did not come after him or even try to reach him. At fifteen my father was on his own in a new country, placed in the fourth grade because he knew no English, and shuffled from one foster home to another until he was eighteen. Then he fell in love with a tall American woman, married her, and had a son. He took a job as a janitor at the University of New Mexico at Albuquerque and started reading student papers he found on teachers' desks. He thought the papers in the sociology department were particularly interesting and confronted the head of the department, saying that he, the lowly janitor, could do a better job than the students.

5   The department head took my father under his wing, and within six years, during which time I was born, my dad had a Ph.D. in sociology. He eventually became a professor at the same university where he had once cleaned toilets. My mother, a woman with a history of picking low-life men to scandalize her parents and to match her terrible self-esteem, did not have as much interest in a successful academic as she'd had in an immigrant janitor with limited English. She moved out of the state with scarcely a second thought—leaving behind my brother, Ricardo, and me.

6   My father, despite his own troubled history, embraced the opportunity to raise me. He taught himself to cook, and some of my fondest memories are of him whipping up *arroz con pollo* in the kitchen of our house near the university. And when I was twelve and got my period, my dad—an orphan boy from the mean streets of Havana—celebrated by buying me flowers and having a female friend of his take me out for ice cream.

7   When I wanted to be a jazz saxophonist, my father bought me the most expensive tenor sax he could find. He listened as I practiced and came to my room with tears in his eyes to tell me how talented I was. When I decided that I wanted to be a journalist, my dad told me to apply to Columbia University, which had the best graduate school for journalism in the nation. I was afraid I wouldn't get in, but Dad told me I would. He was right. When I decided to leave newspapers—and my steady salary—to write novels, my dad opened his home to me and told me to stay as long as I needed to. I was thirty-two years old, married, with a baby. My dad did not care; he knew I could do it. He read pages of what I'd written and told me it was great. As always, my father believed in me before I believed in myself, and helped guide me toward publication of my first novel and a whole new career as an author.

8   I hear so many Latinas bashing our men as if somehow this will help move us to equality. And I know that many men are rotten to women. But many are not. Many are like my father: wonderful, sensitive human beings who stand behind their daughters. Papi, I love you. Happy Father's Day.

Comprehension Check

1. According to the author, what was remarkable about the way her father, Nelson Valdez, raised her? *(See paragraph 1.)*

2. What job did Valdez-Rodriguez's grandmother hold as a teenager, and how did she become a victim of a cruel bet? *(See paragraph 2.)*

3. Whom did Eugenia marry, and what did her husband do to avoid the appearance of a scandal? *(See paragraph 3.)*

4. What sad event happened when Nelson was nine, and what so-called advice did his stepfather give him at the time? *(See paragraph 3.)*

5. What was Operation Pedro Pan, and how did the program change Nelson's life when he was fifteen? *(See paragraph 4.)*

6. What was Nelson's first job at the University of New Mexico, and who became a mentor for him? *(See paragraphs 4 and 5.)*

7. What does Valdez-Rodriguez suggest was the reason her mother abandoned the family? *(See paragraph 5.)*

8. Nelson supported his daughter's various career goals and provided much encouragement. Describe three specific examples of such encouragement. *(See paragraph 7.)*

Discussion Prompts/Writing Options

If you write on any of the following topics, work through the stages of the writing process in preparing your assignment.

1. One of the author's fondest memories is of her father "whipping up *arroz con pollo*," a chicken and rice dish. What is one of your fondest memories of a family ritual? If you write a narrative of this memory, be sure to arrange the details in a clear, logical order.

2. When he was a janitor at a university, Nelson Valdes was brave enough to confront the head of the sociology department. Write a narrative about the first time you tried to conquer a particular fear, such as speaking in front of an audience, flying for the first time, asking someone out on a first date, and so forth.

3. When Nelson Valdes was only fifteen years old, he was sent to the United States all alone and was placed in the fourth grade because he could not speak English. Write about an experience that seemed negative for you at the time but that proved to be a positive turning point in your life. Although you will be writing your narrative in time order, try to use a variety of transitional words and phrases. (Avoid repetitive use of "then" and "next.")

4. Nelson Valdes supported his daughter's changing career goals even when she had to give up a steady salary and move back home with a husband and baby. Recall the first time you realized that a friend or family member would accept you, no matter how risky your choices may have seemed.

Critical Thinking: Topics for Discussion and Writing

If you write on any of the following topics, work through the stages of the writing process in preparing your assignment.

1. Valdes-Rodriguez doesn't write much about her mother (saying only that she "had a history of picking low-life men to scandalize her parents" and suffered from "terrible self-esteem"). Imagine this story from her mother's point of view: do you think the mother felt the loss of her children and guilt about her choices?

2. Why was Nelson Valdes able to suffer such abandonment and pain yet still have the strength to become a loving, caring parent? Are there any clues in his daughter's descriptions of his childhood, early struggles, and ultimate success? What qualities emerge as he finds his way to a good life?

3. In many ways, "The Good Father" is about people trapped in roles: the servant girl who has no power, the single teen mother, the janitor who is invisible to most people on a university campus, and so forth. Consider how roles—being a victim of or breaking out of such roles—create the conflicts in this essay.

WRITING FROM READING: PROCESS

Breath of Life

Judith Sachs

Judith Sachs, an expert on stress management, has taught the subject in places from universities and corporate settings to holistic health centers. She is also the author or coauthor of more than twenty books on preventive health and stress management. In this excerpt from her book, <u>Twenty-Minute Vacations</u>, Sachs explains how a simple process—breathing correctly—can give us a vacation from stress.

Words You May Need to Know (Corresponding paragraph numbers are in parentheses.)

ledge (2): rim
slack (2): loose
pubic bone (3): the front bone of the pelvis

sternum (3): the breastbone
stray (10): wander
acknowledge (10): recognize

1   Inhaling and exhaling—you probably aren't even conscious of those precious breaths that occur over and over during the course of each day and night. You can turn this involuntary physical activity into a meaningful twenty-minute vacation that will get you in touch with the deeper sense of yourself that you probably ignore most of the time.

2   Find a place you like: it may be a corner of your living room, or out in the sun on a warm rock or on a ledge of a pool near an office building. Get as comfortable as possible and lie down. Loosen your belt and take off your shoes. You want your head in line with your neck, the chin slightly tucked in. Let your shoulders go slack, draining into the floor or ground under you.

3   In order to breathe—really let go and breathe!—you have to allow the stomach muscles to release. Just for a minute, hold your breath, and tighten everything, from your pubic bone to your xiphoid process (the small bone beneath the sternum). Now let it out with a huge sigh. Roll your head from side to side, yawning as you do so. Okay, you're ready to begin.

4   It's important to become aware of the way you breathe normally, something of which you probably never were conscious. So start your vacation as an observer of the process. Watch what happens as you take breath in and let it out. Do you breathe quickly or slowly? Are your inhalations and exhalations even, or does one take more time than the other? Do you stop and catch your breath, then inhale some more? Do you draw your nostrils closed in an attempt to take in more air? Does your chest rise as you do this? Do you pause after you've exhaled, getting ready to breathe again? Do you hold your breath? Do you sigh a lot?

5   Don't judge yourself or decide that your breathing is "wrong" or "right." You're on vacation and should be enjoying yourself. As you get deeper into the process, you'll find that it becomes easier and easier to fill and empty all the various cavities of your body—not just your lungs, nose,

and mouth, but also, if you can imagine them clearly enough, your heart, your liver, and your bones.

6   Breathing should come right from your belly. Don't worry about your lungs; they'll get oxygen no matter what you do. Put your hand on your lower abdomen and push against it with your stomach muscles as though you were pushing the air out. See your belly as a balloon, expanding and growing as you inhale, deflating as you exhale. Be sure you inhale and exhale at the same pace, in the same rhythm. Loosen all your limbs and allow them to be stirred by your breath. Breathe in and out through your nose, keeping your mouth lightly closed.

7   For the next part of this vacation, breathe normally, which probably will give you rather shallow breaths (this is the way most people breathe most of the time). Then, as your belly opens up and you are able to take in more air, let the breaths deepen and intensify. If at any point in this vacation you feel lightheaded or dizzy, just go back to your regular breathing.

8   Now you are going to get creative with your breathing by dividing it into three parts. In the first part, inhale into your belly just a little; then bring the air up into your chest, and finally all the way into your throat. When you have as much air as you can possibly take, begin the three-part exhale: first, let the air out from the throat, then from the chest, then from the stomach. Continue this pattern as long as it feels comfortable. You can always switch back to your normal breathing at any point if the three-part breathing is too intense.

9   While you are on vacation, you are going to think of nothing but the breath: how cool the inhalation feels as it rushes in through your nostrils, how warm the exhalation feels on your upper lip as you let the air escape. The gentle in and out of breathing is like a wave, never really ending and never really beginning. There is always just a little left in your lungs, even when you've exhaled completely, and always a small gap at the top when you think you can't take in any more.

10   Your thoughts doubtless will stray in the midst of this journey; if you find yourself thinking about anything else at all, simply acknowledge the thought, let it go, and return to your focus on the breath. You want to feel like a passenger in a car, watching the scenery go by, acknowledging each view but attaching to none. A twenty-minute session of breathing will leave you refreshed and relaxed, ready for the rest of your day.

Comprehension Check

1. What, according to Sachs, is the greatest benefit of the "Breath of Life" exercise? *(See paragraph 1.)*

2. Sachs suggests several places where a person can begin the exercise. What are the places? *(See paragraph 2.)*

3. In what part of the body, according to Sachs, should proper breathing originate? *(See paragraphs 6.)*

4. Sachs explains that "creative breathing" involves dividing the breathing process into three parts? What are the three parts? *(See paragraph 8.)*

5. What are the three parts of "creative exhaling"? *(See paragraph 8.)*

6. How should you react if your thoughts wander while you are trying to concentrate on your breathing? *(See paragraph 10.)*

Discussion Prompts/Writing Options

If you write on any of the following topics, work through the stages of the writing process in preparing your assignment.

1. Almost everyone engages regularly in a stressful process. Write about one process that adds to your daily stress. For instance, you may write about the stress of opening your e-mail at work each morning, or about cleaning up your children's mess at the end of the day. As you write about the steps of the process, be sure to include details about your stress level building or decreasing.

2. Exercise is considered an effective stress-buster. Do you regularly engage in some physical activity (anything from walking to boxing) that helps you to relax? If so, describe the process involved in relieving your stress while you are engaged in this exercise.

3. Do you allow yourself a brief "vacation" during a busy day? That is, do you take a ten- or twenty-minute break to clear your head and catch your breath? What do you do during that break? Describe the steps of your "vacation" process.

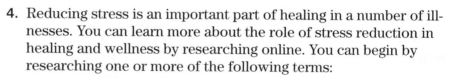

Computer

4. Reducing stress is an important part of healing in a number of illnesses. You can learn more about the role of stress reduction in healing and wellness by researching online. You can begin by researching one or more of the following terms:

> meditation and strokes
> meditation and heart attacks
> alternative medicine
> stress and cancer
> guided imagery and pain management
> mind-body connection
> mind-body medicine

After you have explored the role of stress reduction in healing and wellness, write about one process that minimizes pain or helps heal illness by reducing stress.

Critical Thinking: Topics for Discussion and Writing

If you write on any of the following topics, work through the stages of the writing process in preparing your assignment.

1. Do you believe that a breathing exercise can help a person relieve stress? Would you feel silly trying the "Breath of Life" activity? Explain why or why not.

2. For five minutes, focus only on your breathing. If after five minutes, you realize that you found yourself being distracted often,

ask yourself why it is difficult to focus only on your breathing. Does it take discipline to maintain that focus? Is it possible that modern life, with its constant multitasking and ever-present electronic stimulation, makes focusing on one thing more difficult for most people than it used to be? If you agree, write about one typical process (such as studying, planning, or decision-making) that can be made more difficult by distractions.

3. How much of our daily stress would disappear if we changed our lifestyles? For example, would life be less stressful if we spent less, bought less, cut back on unnecessary driving, chose a smaller living space, and found meaningful work that might pay less? What stands in the way of most people who would like to make such changes? Could it be financial demands, career ambitions, or family pressures?

WRITING FROM READING: COMPARISON OR CONTRAST

Honesty and Dishonesty

Jo-Ellan Dimitrius and Mark Mazzarella

Although Jo-Ellan Dimitrius is not a lawyer, she has been closely connected to some of the most famous trials of the past twenty-five years. Dimitrius' gift for decoding the hidden messages in the appearance, facial expression, tone of voice, and personal habits of jurors, witnesses, lawyers, and judges has enabled her to predict their behavior. Her book, Reading People, which contains the section "Honesty and Dishonesty," applies the skills she uses in the courtroom to everyday life so that readers can learn how to "read people" and learn how others "read" us.

Words You May Need to Know (Corresponding paragraph numbers are in parentheses.)

furrowed (4): wrinkled
brow (4): forehead
deviations (6): departures from customary behavior

subtle (8): delicate, difficult to notice or understand
disbelief (8): refusal to believe

1 Imagine a young boy insisting to his mother that he wasn't the one who took the cookies out of the cookie jar. He can't bring himself to look her in the eye for more than an instant. He's shifting from foot to foot, and stuttering to beat the band. Honest people are generally relaxed and open. Dishonest people aren't.

2 Any trait that shows tension, nervousness, or secretiveness indicates possible dishonesty. There are four different types of liars: occasional, frequent, habitual, and professional. Two of those types, habitual and professional, are difficult to spot by their body language alone. The habitual liar is so accustomed to lying that he may not care or fully realize he's lying, so he usually won't show it. The professional liar has rehearsed his lies so well that his behavior will give little away.

3 Like drug and alcohol abusers, people who lie won't usually admit it. But lying is often easy to detect when you know what to look for. The symp-

toms listed here are reliable tip-offs to the occasional and frequent liar. These physical clues generally appear only when someone knows he's lying and is at least somewhat troubled when he does. Luckily, most people are at worst occasional liars and reveal their discomfort in many ways.

4   Symptoms of dishonesty include shifty or wandering eyes, any type of fidgeting, rapid speech, change in voice, shifting back and forth on one's feet or in a chair, any signs of nervousness, an exaggerated version of the "sincere," furrowed-brow look, sweating, and shaking. Other symptoms include any activity that obscures the eyes, face, or mouth, such as putting the hand over the mouth while talking, rubbing the nose, or blinking the eyes. Symptoms may also be licking the lips, running the tongue over the teeth, leaning forward, and inappropriate familiarity, such as backslapping, other touching, and getting too close (invading personal space).

5   The signs of honesty are just the opposite of those listed above. Honest people are relaxed and calm. They usually meet your gaze. A sincere smile and the warm, kind eyes that most of us know when we see them also indicate honesty.

6   When things get stressful, it can be difficult to tell the difference between honest nervousness or defensiveness and dishonesty. If your employee has made a horrible mistake and you've asked him to explain it, chances are he'll look nervous and defensive no matter how truthful he is. I've watched hundreds of nervous witnesses, and I've found the surest way to detect a lie in a stressful situation is to watch for their patterns of behavior, looking for consistencies and deviations.

7   Several years ago, I worked on a case in which the owner of a real estate development company was being sued by his partner for fraud. One of the key witnesses was an employer who had worked closely with both men. A very nervous woman under the best of circumstances, she shook like a leaf from the moment she was sworn in until the moment she left the witness stand. She showed all the classic signs of dishonesty: failing to maintain eye contact, shaking, fidgeting in her chair, and fussing with small paper cups on the witness stand. But I couldn't conclude from this that she was lying because had she simply been dishonest, she probably would have been more comfortable during at least some portion of her testimony—when describing her personal background, for instance. The fact that this woman's discomfort was constant revealed that she was nervous, not necessarily dishonest.

8   You have to pay close attention to someone's normal pattern in order to notice a deviation from it when he or she lies. Sometimes the variation is as subtle as a pause. Other times it's obvious and abrupt. I recently saw a news interview with an acquaintance who I was certain was going to lie about a few sensitive issues, and lie she did. During most of her interview she was calm and direct, but when she started lying, her manner changed dramatically: she threw her head back, laughed in "disbelief," and shook

her head back and forth. It's true the questions dealt with very personal issues, but I've found that *in general, if a person is telling the truth, his or her manner will not change significantly or abruptly.* But you won't see those changes if you're not watching carefully.

Comprehension Check

1. According to Jo-Ellan Dimitrius, what can signs of tension, nervousness, or secretiveness indicate? *(See paragraph 2.)*

2. Dimitrius divides liars into four types. What are the four types? *(See paragraph 2.)*

3. Her analysis focuses on only two types of liars. What are the two types? *(See paragraph 2 or 3.)*

4. How, according to Dimitrius, does a stressful situation affect an observer's ability to spot a liar? *(See paragraphs 6 and 7.)*

5. Before an observer can spot a person who is telling a lie, what must the observer know about the person? *(See paragraph 8.)*

Discussion Prompts/Writing Options

If you write on any of the following topics, work through the stages of the writing process in preparing your assignment.

1. According to Dimitrius, what body language is a sign of an honest person, and what body language may signal a liar? Write a summary of her article, and include her warnings about confusing nervousness with dishonesty and about the need to know a person's normal behavior patterns before judging his or her honesty.

2. Contrast the body language of two celebrities who have recently been in trouble with the law. Which celebrity appeared to be more honest, and why?

3. Have you ever "misread" a person's body language? Contrast how you interpreted the person's signals with the reality of the person's intentions.

4. Write about the different body languages of the attentive student and the inattentive student in a college classroom.

5. Reread the signs or symptoms of dishonesty in paragraph 4 of Dimitrius' essay. Pick any five of them, and show how these signs may indicate a trait or emotion different from dishonesty.

Critical Thinking: Topics for Discussion and Writing

If you write on any of the following topics, work through the stages of the writing process in preparing your assignment.

1. Why do some people lie more than others? Consider whether fear, insecurity, greed, a desire to feel powerful, or other traits can prompt a person to lie.

2. Dimitrius stresses that knowing the background and setting of an action is essential to judging it. That is, a person may appear dishonest because he or she is nervous, but, Dimitrius warns, "nervousness can be an honest response to a difficult situation." Can you think of times in which a person might be misjudged because the background or setting of his behavior was misunderstood? For example, a person who runs at the sight of a police officer may have grown up in a country where terror squads in uniform administered justice, or a person might laugh inappropriately in a serious setting because he or she is nervous.

3. Are there situations in everyday life in which people *expect* to hear lies? Buying or trading a car is one such situation. Can you think of others? Think about business, legal, or personal interactions in which most people are accustomed to dishonesty.

WRITING FROM READING: CLASSIFICATION

Three Disciplines for Children

John Holt

John Holt is an educator and activist who believes our system of education needs a major overhaul. In this essay, he classifies the ways children learn from three fundamental disciplines, and he warns against overusing one kind of discipline.

Words You May Need to Know (Corresponding paragraph numbers are in parentheses.)

discipline (1): the training effect of experience

impersonal (2): without personal or human connection

impartial (2): fair

indifferent (2): not biased, not prejudiced

wheedled (2): persuaded by flattery or coaxing

ritual (3): an established procedure, a ceremony

yield (5): give in to, submit

impotent (5): powerless

1   A child, in growing up, may meet and learn from three different kinds of disciplines. The first and most important is what we might call the Discipline of Nature or of Reality. When he is trying to do something real, if he does the wrong thing or doesn't do the right one, he doesn't get the results he wants. If he doesn't pile one block right on top of another, or tries to build on a slanting surface, his tower falls down. If he hits the wrong key, he hears the wrong note. If he doesn't hit the nail squarely on the head, it bends, and he has to pull it out and start with another. If he doesn't measure properly what he is trying to build, it won't open, close, fit, stand up, fly, float, whistle, or do whatever he wants it to do. If he closes his eyes when he swings, he won't hit the ball. A child meets this kind of discipline every time he tries to *do* something, which is why it is so important in school to give children more chances to do things, instead of just reading or listening to someone talk (or pretending to).

2   This discipline is a great teacher. The learner never has to wait long for his answer; it usually comes quickly, often instantly. Also it is clear, and very often points to the needed correction; from what happened he can not only see what he did was wrong, but also why, and what he needs to do instead. Finally, and most important, the giver of the answer, call it Nature, is impersonal, impartial, and indifferent. She does not give opinions or make judgments; she cannot be wheedled, bullied, or fooled; she does not get angry or disappointed; she does not praise or blame; she does not remember past failures or hold grudges. With her one always gets a fresh start; this time is the one that counts.

3   The next discipline we might call the Discipline of Culture, of Society, of What People Really Do. Man is a social, cultural animal. Children sense around them this culture, this network of agreements, customs, habits, and rules binding the adults together. They want to understand it and be a part of it. They watch very carefully what people around them are doing and want to do the same. They want to do right, unless they become convinced they can't do right. Thus children rarely misbehave seriously in church, but sit as quietly as they can. The example of all those grown-ups is contagious. Some mysterious ritual is going on, and children, who like rituals, want to be part of it. In the same way, the little children I see at concerts or operas, though they may fidget a little or perhaps take a nap now and then, rarely make any disturbance. With all those grownups sitting there, neither moving or talking, it is the most natural thing in the world to imitate them. Children who live among adults who are habitually courteous to each other, and to them, will soon learn to be courteous. Children who live surrounded by people who speak a certain way will speak that way, however much we may try to tell them that speaking that way is bad or wrong.

4   The third discipline is the one that most people mean when they speak of discipline—the Discipline of Superior Force, of sergeant to private, of "you do what I tell you, or I'll make you wish you had." There is bound to be some of this in a child's life. Living as we do surrounded by things that can hurt children, or that children can hurt, we cannot avoid it. We can't afford to let a small child find out from experience the danger of playing in a busy street, or of fooling with the pots on top of a stove, or of eating up the pills in the medicine cabinet. So, along with other precautions, we say to him, "Don't play in the street, or touch things on the stove, or go into the medicine cabinet, or I'll punish you." Between him and the danger too great for him to imagine we put a lesser danger, but one he can imagine and maybe therefore want to avoid. He can have no idea of what it would be like to be hit by a car, but he can imagine being shouted at, or spanked, or sent to his room. He avoids these substitutes for the greater danger until he can understand it and avoid it for its own sake.

5   However, we ought to use this discipline only when it is necessary to protect the life, health, safety, or well-being of people or other living creatures, or to prevent destruction of things that people care about. We

ought not to assume too long, as we usually do, that a child cannot understand the real nature of the danger from which we want to protect him. The sooner he avoids the danger, not to escape our punishment, but as a matter of good sense, the better. He can learn that faster than we think. In Mexico, for example, where people drive their cars with a good deal of spirit, I saw many children no older than five or four walking unattended on the streets. They understood about cars; they knew what to do. A child whose life is full of the threat and fear of punishment is locked into babyhood. There is no way for him to grow up, to learn to take responsibility for his life and acts. Most important of all, we should not assume that having to yield to the threat of our superior force is good for the child's character. It is never good for anyone's character. To bow to superior force makes us feel impotent and cowardly for not having had the strength or courage to resist. Worse, it makes us resentful and vengeful. We can hardly wait to make someone pay for our humiliation, yield to us as we were once made to yield. No, if we cannot always avoid using the Discipline of Superior Force, we should at least use it as seldom as we can.

Comprehension Check

1. According to Holt's "Discipline of Nature or of Reality," why should schools give children more "chances to do things"? *(See paragraph 1.)*
2. Why is the Discipline of Nature such a great teacher? *(See paragraph 2.)*
3. What does Holt feel is most important about the Discipline of Nature? *(See paragraph 2.)*

4. Holt states that the Discipline of Culture involves children imitating adults because children want to understand this world and "be part of it." What are three specific examples Holt gives of this type of discipline? *(See paragraph 3.)*

5. How would an adult use the Discipline of Superior Force to protect a child from a greater danger? Give some specific examples. *(See paragraph 4.)*

6. Holt says that adults sometimes use the Discipline of Superior Force to protect children from dangers the young cannot understand. While Holt agrees that this discipline is occasionally necessary, he warns parents not to rely on one assumption for too long. What is that assumption? *(See paragraph 5.)*

Discussion Prompts/Writing Options

If you write on any of the following topics, work through the stages of the writing process in preparing your assignment.

1. John Holt writes a very clear classification with a clear purpose: he is trying to explain how children should learn. Write a summary of the types of discipline Holt explains. In your summary, include

definitions and examples for each type of discipline. Your examples can come from Holt's article as well as from your own experiences.

Collaborate

2. Holt says that it is very important "in school to give children more chances to do things, instead of just reading or listening to someone talk."

   Classify your elementary or high school classes according to how much they allowed you to do. Include your opinion of each category.

   If your instructor agrees, begin this assignment with an interview. Ask a writing partner to interview you about your learning experiences as a way of gathering ideas for this topic. Then do the same for your partner. Before any interviewing begins, write at least seven questions to ask your partner.

Collaborate

3. Holt says children want to understand society and to be a part of it. "They watch very carefully what people around them are doing and want to do the same."

   Classify children according to the behavior they have learned from their parents. If your instructor agrees, freewrite on this topic, and then share your freewriting with a writing partner or group, for reaction and further ideas.

4. Classify the types of school discipline you experienced on the basis of how effective each type was in changing your behavior or attitude.

Computer

5. Visit *www.home-school.com/group* to gain some knowledge about the growing trend of home-schooling. Classify types of home-schooling programs according to one of the following bases: accreditation standards, innovative curricula, or interactive activities offered by state or local home-schooling clubs and organizations.

Critical Thinking: Topics for Discussion and Writing

If you write on any of the following topics, work through the stages of the writing process in preparing your assignment.

1. Holt says, "Children who live among adults who are habitually courteous to each other, and to them, will soon learn to be courteous. Children who live surrounded by people who speak a certain way will speak that way, however much we may try to tell them that speaking that way is bad or wrong." In other words, children imitate what they see and hear. Consider whether what children see (and learn) at home is powerful enough to withstand the outside influences of peers, school, and the playground.

2. Holt describes children in Mexico who, at age four or five, have learned to walk alone and safely on busy streets. His point is that we (American parents) should not "assume too long, as we usually do, that a child cannot understand the real nature of the danger from which we want to protect him." Do you think American parents are too protective?

3. At what age should a child be warned about child predators? About drugs?

WRITING FROM READING: DEFINITION

Breaking the Bonds of Hate

Virak Khiev

Virak Khiev, who immigrated to America at age ten, wrote this essay when he was a nineteen-year-old senior at The Blake School in Minneapolis, Minnesota. As you read his essay, you will notice how he defines The American Dream and two kinds of war.

Words You May Need to Know (Corresponding paragraph numbers are in parentheses.)

carrion (4): dead flesh
stereotype (5): an established image of someone or something, believed in by many people
unscrupulous (5): without a conscience
mentality (6): attitude, way of thinking

adversaries (7): enemies
immortalized (9): given the ability to live forever
"the melting pot" (10): an image of America in which all the races and ethnic groups blend in harmony
mind-set (10): attitude

1   Ever since I can remember, I wanted the ideal life: a big house, lots of money, cars. I wanted to find the perfect happiness that so many people have longed for. I wanted more than life in the jungle of Cambodia. America was the place, the land of tall skyscrapers, televisions, cars and airplanes.

2   In the jungles of Cambodia I lived in a refugee camp. We didn't have good sanitation or modern conveniences. For example, there were no inside bathrooms—only ones made from palm-tree leaves, surrounded by millions of flies. When walking down the street, I could smell the aroma of the outhouse; in the afternoon, the five- and six-year-olds played with the dirt in front of it. It was the only thing they had to play with, and the "fragrance" never seemed to bother them, and it never bothered me. Because I smelled it every day, I was used to it.

3   The only thing that bothered me was the war. I have spent half of my life in war. The killing is still implanted in my mind. I hate Cambodia. When I came to America nine years ago at the age of ten, I thought I was being born into a new life. No more being hungry, no more fighting, no more killing. I thought I had escaped the war.

4   In America, there are more kinds of material things than Cambodians could ever want. And here we don't have to live in the jungle like monkeys, we don't have to hide from mortar bombing and we don't have to smell the rotten human carrion. But for the immigrant, America presents a different type of jungle, a different type of war and a smell as bad as the waste of Cambodia.

5   Most Americans believe the stereotype that immigrants work hard, get a good education and have a very good life. Maybe it used to be like that, but

not anymore. You have to be deceptive and unscrupulous in order to make it. If you are not, then you will end up like most immigrants I've known: living in the ghetto in a cockroach-infested house, working on the assembly line or in the chicken factory to support your family, getting up at three o'clock in the morning to take the bus to work and not getting home until 5:00 p.m.

6   If you're a kid my age, you drop out of school to work because your parents don't have enough money to buy you clothes for school. You may end up selling drugs because you want cars, money and parties, as all teenagers do. You have to depend on your peers for emotional support because your parents are too busy working in the factory trying to make money to pay the bills. You don't get along with your parents because they have a different mentality: you are an American, and they are Cambodian. You hate them because they are never there for you, so you join a gang as I did.

7   You spend your time drinking, doing drugs and fighting. You beat up people for pleasure. You don't care about anything except your drugs, your beers and your revenge against adversaries. You shoot at people because they've insulted your pride. You shoot at the police because they are always bothering you. They shoot back, and then you're dead like my best friend Sinerth.

8   Sinerth robbed a gas station. He was shot in the head by the police. I'd known him since the sixth grade from my first school in Minneapolis. I can still remember his voice calling me from California. "Virak, come down here, man," he said. "We need you. There are lots of pretty girls down here." I promised him that I would be there to see him. The following year he was dead. I felt sorry for him. But as I thought it over, maybe it is better for him to be dead than to continue with the cycle of violence, to live with hate. I thought, "It is better to die than live like an angry young fool, thinking that everybody is out to get you."

9   When I was like Sinerth, I didn't care about dying. I thought that I was on top of the world, being immortalized by drugs. I could see that my future would be spent working on the assembly line like most of my friends, spending all my paycheck on the weekend and being broke again on Monday morning. I hated going to school because I couldn't see a way to get out of the endless cycle. My philosophy was "Live hard and die young."

10   I hated America because, to me, it was not the place of opportunities or the land of "the melting pot," as I had been told. All I had seen were broken beer bottles on the street and homeless people and drunks using the sky as their roof. I couldn't walk down the street without someone yelling out, "You gook" from his car. Once again I was caught in the web of hatred. I'd become a mad dog with the mind-set of the past: "When trapped in the corner, just bite." The war mentality of Cambodia came back: get what you can and leave. I thought I came to America to escape war, poverty, fighting, to escape the violence, but I wasn't escaping; I was being introduced to a newer version of war—the war of hatred.

11   I was lucky. In Minneapolis, I dropped out of school in the ninth grade to join a gang. Then I moved to Louisiana, where I continued my life of "immortality" as a member of another gang. It came to an abrupt halt when I crashed a car. I wasn't badly injured, but I was underage, and the fine took all my money. I called a good friend of the Cambodian community in Minneapolis for advice (she'd tried to help me earlier). I didn't know where to go or whom to turn to. I saw friends landing in jail, and I didn't want that. She promised to help me get back in school. And she did.

12   Since then I've been given a lot of encouragement and caring by American friends and teachers who've helped me turn my life around. They opened my eyes to a kind of education that frees us all from ignorance and slavery. I could have failed so many times except for those people who believed in me and gave me another chance. Individuals who were willing to help me have taught me that I can help myself. I'm now a twelfth grader and have been at my school for three years; I plan to attend college in the fall. I am struggling to believe I can reach the other side of the mountain.

Comprehension Check

1. Describe the conditions of the refugee camp where Khiev once lived. *(See paragraph 2.)*

2. Khiev states that for an immigrant, "America presents a different type of jungle, a different type of war and a smell as bad as the waste of Cambodia." What are some examples Khiev gives of trying to survive this new jungle? *(See paragraphs 6 and 7.)*

3. How was Khiev once like his friend Sinerth, and what happened to his friend? *(See paragraph 8.)*

4. What was Khiev's stereotype of America before he arrived in the United States, and how did this image differ from the "newer version of war" he experienced in his new country? *(See paragraph 10.)*

5. What was a major turning point for Khiev, and to whom did he turn for help? *(See paragraph 11.)*

6. What does Khiev say "frees us all from ignorance and slavery"? *(See paragraph 12.)*

Discussion Prompts/Writing Options

If you write on any of the following topics, work through the stages of the writing process in preparing your assignment.

1. Trace the turning points in Virak Khiev's life. Consider all the changes in his life and whether they made his life better or worse.

2. Khiev defines "the bonds of hate," a hate that kept him from achieving a good life. He says that he was a prisoner of his hatred

for the country that denied him what he hoped for and of his hatred for his parents. He hated the endless cycle of poverty and struggle he found in the ghetto.

Define the term "bonds of hate" by providing examples you have observed (or experienced) of the kind of hatred that can keep a person in chains.

3. By explaining what a gang does and why he joined one, Khiev defines the term "gang." Write your own definition of a gang. When you brainstorm about this word, remember that "gang" can have both positive and negative associations. For example, the late actor Paul Newman established a camp called "The Hole-in-the Wall Gang" for children with cancer, so he used the word in a positive way. On the other hand, a "gang" of thieves has a negative association.

4. Write your personal definition of The American Dream. Use examples from your life or from the lives of others you know well.

5. Khiev says, "for the immigrant, America presents a different type of jungle, a different type of war and a smell as bad as the waste of Cambodia."

Define "The Immigrant's Experience of America." Define the term using the experiences of one or more immigrants as examples. Your definition does not have to be similar to Khiev's. If you are an immigrant to America, you can use your own experiences as examples. If you are not an immigrant, interview one or more immigrants, taking notes and/or taping the interviews to gather details. Your classmates or teachers may include people to interview. Before you interview, have at least six questions to ask.

6. Khiev defines the luck in his life as the help of other people, particularly one woman who was a friend to the Cambodian community. Define the luck in your life.

Critical Thinking: Topics for Discussion and Writing

If you write on any of the following topics, work through the stages of the writing process in preparing your assignment.

1. Why are many young people drawn to the philosophy, "Live hard and die young"? Do movies, music, and advertising promote the philosophy? What are other reasons for the young's fascination with danger, excitement, and death?

2. At one point, Khiev says, "You have to be deceptive and unscrupulous in order to make it." Later, he says that there is "a kind of education that frees us all from ignorance and slavery." He also credits the people "who believed in me and gave me another chance" with helping him turn his life around. Which of his three statements reflects your experience or beliefs? Why?

3. Could Virak Khiev's essay convince a teenager to leave behind a life of violence, drugs, and crime? Why or why not?

WRITING FROM READING: CAUSE AND EFFECT

Students in Shock

John Kellmayer

In this 1989 essay, John Kellmayer, an educator, explores the reasons why college students are stressed beyond their limits. He also discusses how colleges are reacting to student problems.

Words You May Need to Know (Corresponding paragraph numbers are in parentheses.)

warrant (6): demand, call for, require
magnitude (9): great importance
biofeedback (10): a method of monitoring your blood pressure, heart rate, etc. as a way of monitoring and controlling stress

1   If you feel overwhelmed by your college experiences, you are not alone—many of today's college students are suffering from a form of shock. Going to college has always had its ups and downs, but today the "downs" of the college experience are more numerous and difficult, a fact that schools are responding to with increased support services.

2   Lisa is a good example of a student in shock. She is an attractive, intelligent twenty-year-old college junior at a state university. Having been a straight-A student in high school and a member of the basketball and softball teams there, she remembers her high school days with fondness. Lisa was popular then and had a steady boyfriend for the last two years of school.

3   Now, only three years later, Lisa is miserable. She has changed her major four times already and is forced to hold down two part-time jobs in order to pay her tuition. She suffers from sleeping and eating disorders and believes she has no close friends. Sometimes she bursts out crying for no apparent reason. On more than one occasion, she has considered taking her own life.

4   Dan, too, suffers from student shock. He is nineteen and a freshman at a local community college. He began college as an accounting major but hated that field. So he switched to computer programming because he heard the job prospects were excellent in that area. Unfortunately, he discovered that he had little aptitude for programming and changed majors again, this time to psychology. He likes psychology but has heard horror stories about the difficulty of finding a job in that field without a graduate degree. Now he's considering switching majors again. To help pay for school, Dan works nights and weekends as a sales clerk at K-Mart. Dan feels he has no choice except to stay on the job. A few months ago, his girlfriend of a year and a half broke up with him.

5   Not surprisingly, Dan has started to suffer from depression and migraine headaches. He believes that in spite of all his hard work, he just

isn't getting anywhere. He can't remember ever being this unhappy. A few times he considered talking to somebody in the college psychological counseling center. He rejected that idea, though, because he didn't want people to think there was something wrong with him.

6   What is happening to Lisa and Dan happens to millions of college students each year. As a result, one-quarter of the student population at any time will suffer from symptoms of depression. Of that group, almost half will experience depression intense enough to warrant professional help. At schools across the country, psychological counselors are booked up months in advance. Stress-related problems such as anxiety, migraine headaches, insomnia, anorexia, and bulimia are epidemic on college campuses. Suicide rates and self-inflicted injuries among college students are higher now than at any other time in history. The suicide rate among college youth is fifty percent higher than among non-students of the same age. It is estimated that each year more than five hundred college students take their own lives. College health officials believe these reported problems represent only the tip of the iceberg. They fear that most students, like Lisa and Dan, suffer in silence.

7   There are three reasons today's college students are suffering more than in earlier generations. First is a weakening family support structure. The transition from high school to college has always been difficult, but in the past, there was more family support to help get through it. Today, with divorce rates at a historical high and many parents experiencing their own psychological difficulties, the traditional family is not always available for guidance and support. And when students who do not find stability at home are bombarded with new and stressful experiences, the results can be devastating.

8   Another problem college students face is financial pressure. In the last decade tuition costs have skyrocketed—up about sixty-six percent at public colleges and ninety percent at private schools. And at the same time that tuition costs have been rising dramatically, there has been a cutback in federal aid to students. College loans are now much harder to obtain and are available only at near-market interest rates. Consequently, most college students must work at least part-time. And for some students, the pressure to do well while holding down a job is too much to handle.

9   A final cause of student shock is the large selection of majors available. Because of the magnitude and difficulty of choosing a major, college can prove a time of great indecision. Many students switch majors, some a number of times. As a result, it is becoming commonplace to take five or six years to get a degree. It can be depressing to students not only to have taken courses that don't count toward a degree but also to be faced with the added tuition costs. In some cases, these costs become so high that they force students to drop out of college.

10   While there is no magic cure for all student shock, colleges have begun to recognize the problem and are trying in a number of ways to help students cope with the pressures they face. First of all, many colleges are upgrading their psychological counseling centers to handle the greater demand for services. Additional staff is being hired, and experts are doing research to learn more about the psychological problems of college students. Some schools even advertise these services in student newspapers and on campus radio stations. Also, third- and fourth-year students are being trained as peer counselors. These peer counselors may be able to act as a first line of defense in the battle for students' well-being by spotting and helping to solve problems before they become too big for students to handle. In addition, stress management workshops have become common on college campuses. At these workshops, instructors teach students various techniques for dealing with stress, including biofeedback, meditation, and exercise.

11   Finally, many schools are improving their vocational counseling services. By giving students more relevant information about possible majors and career choices, colleges can lessen the anxiety and indecision often associated with choosing a major.

12   If you ever feel that you're "in shock," remember that your experience is not unique. Try to put things in perspective. Certainly, the end of a romance or failing an exam is not an event to look forward to. But realize that rejection and failure happen to everyone sooner or later. And don't be reluctant to talk to somebody about your problems. The useful services available on campus won't help you if you don't take advantage of them.

Comprehension Check

1. How did Lisa's high school experience differ from her college experience? *(See paragraphs 2 and 3.)*

2. What are some pressures facing Dan, and why is he considering changing his major again? *(See paragraph 4.)*

3. Why did Dan decide against getting some psychological counseling at his college? *(See paragraph 5.)*

4. What are some common "stress-related problems" facing college students? *(See paragraph 6.)*

5. What three reasons does the author give for students "suffering more than in earlier generations"? *(See paragraphs 7, 8, and 9.)*

6. Describe some financial pressures students face. *(See paragraph 8.)*

7. Even though colleges offer students a wide choice of majors, what problems do some students experience regarding their choice of majors? *(See paragraph 9.)*

8. What are some of the steps colleges have taken to help students who feel overwhelmed by college pressures? What is the role of peer counselors? *(See paragraph 10.)*

Discussion Prompts/Writing Options

If you write on any of the following topics, work through the stages of the writing process in preparing your assignment.

1. Based on "Students in Shock," write a summary of the three significant reasons college students are in distress, and then give an overview of how colleges are reacting to student stress. Remember to use logical and effective transitions throughout your summary.

2. Make a list of all the reasons this 1989 article gives for college students feeling "in shock." Working with a group or on your own, list some pressures that the article does not mention. Then, working alone, select one of these pressures and describe its effects.

3. For discussion or for a paragraph or short essay, describe either the positive or negative effects of your college experience thus far. Be sure you have at least three effects.

4. Write a letter to your college instructors. Your letter will be a paragraph giving at least three reasons why students seem tired in class.

5. Stress has different effects on different people. Freewrite about the effects of college stress on you and people you know. Use your freewriting to plan and write a paragraph or short essay on the effects of college stress. Use your and your friends' experiences as examples of the different effects of college stress.

6. If your campus offers peer counseling, contact your counseling department to learn more about the program. See if you can interview a peer counselor and find out what some of the positive effects have been for him or her and the students who seek help. Bring your notes to class for discussion, or write an essay that explains the program's goals, and then, based on your interview, describe some of the positive effects of this program.

Critical Thinking: Topics for Discussion and Writing

If you write on any of the following topics, work through the stages of the writing process in preparing your assignment.

1. How does the image of what the college experience is supposed to be and the resulting disillusion lead to student stress? You can think about how older people tell younger ones that "your college years are the best of your life," and current students brag about their wild social lives. Also consider the role of advertising, movies, and the Internet in creating a false picture of college.

2. "Students in Shock," written in 1989, describes students suffering from depression and other stress-related illnesses such as anorexia, bulimia, anxiety, and insomnia. Why, after so many years, are college students still suffering from the same ailments?

3. Consider people you know who are your age but who do not attend college. Are their lives as stressful as yours? Why or why not?

WRITING FROM READING: ARGUMENT

Sidewalks Can Make a Town a Neighborhood

Carolyn V. Egan

"When I was little, the world was mine," says Carolyn V. Egan. On the sidewalks of her town, she walked to school and got to know the streets, seasons, people, and pets of the community. She argues that today's suburbs, with their fortress-like homes and lack of sidewalks, deny children the pleasures of exploring and create a false sense of safety for worried parents.

Words You May Need to Know (Corresponding paragraph numbers are in parentheses.)

odometer (1): an instrument for measuring the distance traveled by a car or truck

emerging (1): developing

mere (1): only

spasm (1): a brief burst of feeling

self-recrimination (1): accusations and counteraccusations against oneself

quirky (1): peculiar

incautious (1): careless

cocoons (2): protective structures or coverings

scurrying (3): hurrying

grammar school (3): elementary school

roiling (4): stirring up the mud

quickened (4): became alive, revived

meandering (5): turning or winding

indigo (5): deep violet blue

trudged (5): walked wearily

beckoning (6): tempting, attracting

technological portals (7): doors or entrances created by inventions such as computers and the Internet

abstraction (7): something unreal

predators (8): people who victimize others

discern (8): recognize

chauffeuring (8): driving

parochialism (8): an extreme narrowness in interests or views

nostalgic (9): expressing a longing for the experiences of the past

artifacts (9): man-made objects

bequeath (9): pass down

1   According to my odometer, the grocery store is exactly 1.1 miles down the road from where I live in an emerging suburb that was a stretch of largely uninterrupted tobacco fields a mere twenty-five years ago. I walked this distance once in a spasm of self-recrimination, only to find my life at risk at every quirky bend along the route where cars are accustomed to their incautious rule.

2   My adventure yielded this startling revelation: I need a car to safely navigate my town because—apart from a few new developments that sit like isolated cocoons—it lacks sidewalks. Most of us drive everywhere, no matter how near our destination. But in my childhood during the 1960s and '70s, the world was still accessible to pedestrians.

3   Some of my earliest memories are of me scurrying to keep pace with my mother as she pushed my sister in her baby carriage along the sidewalks across town. When I was older, I memorized every crack in the half mile of

sidewalk linking my home to my grammar school. No school bus stopped traffic at every block to pick up children at their front doors. Nor did a parade of mothers wait in idling automobiles to cart their children home when the school bell sounded.

4   When I was little, the world was mine. I knew where the rainwater carved rivers in sand beds at the bottom of the hill before roiling to its final plunge down the storm drain. I knew the best street for a running slide in my winter boots. I knew the smell and look of spring as it quickened green upon the front lawns I passed. And I remember my heart quickening with it, in anticipation.

5   As I grew, I walked farther. I walked to and from more-distant schools. I walked to my first jobs, to my friends' houses, to the movies. Sidewalks enabled these humming, skipping, thoughtful journeys, during which I came to know the corner stores, the old factory buildings, the smiling ladies hunched over their gardens along the meandering paths that twisted toward home. I knew the seasons of the geese that pierced the indigo sky and the seasons of the squirrels that clicked in solemn contest with hungry birds in gray branches. I knew which dogs would greet me and which would bark a warning; the cats that curled sweet tails around my legs; the mailmen who trudged—heads down—from house to house. All these things I knew and counted on.

6   I am told that nobody really cares about sidewalks; nobody wants to shovel them. Yet sidewalks—those evenly spaced concrete blocks—stitch a town into a neighborhood. They allow a physical experience of community while beckoning children to explore, to discover, to make friends three blocks away. For kids today, geography is understood from the back seat of a car, rather than through the scents and textures of heart-beating, muscle-flexing, self-motivated expeditions that connect one place to another, one person to another. The destination has displaced the journey.

7   Parents have become slaves to their children's schedules, terrified to let their offspring out of sight. New houses are huge, enclosing all of life. They're connected by technological portals to the outside world, making an abstraction of everything beyond their walls.

8   We worry about the safety of our children if we let them loose to wander sidewalks, even while we hear more and more stories of predators on the highways and byways of the Internet. We have forgotten that we cannot protect our children by telling them to hop in and buckle up. Our children do not develop the instincts to discern and avoid danger from the back seat of an automobile. We deprive them of self-mastery by insulating them from very cold and very hot temperatures, from rain, from wind. They do not know who they are without a plan, without a ride. While we encourage dependence in our children by chauffeuring them everywhere, we also

encourage in them habits of selfishness and parochialism. Adult maturity is rooted in the unstructured roaming of childhood.

9   Sidewalks are becoming nostalgic artifacts of a time before three- or four-car families. To me, their absence represents disturbing changes in the way we connect to one another—and the habits, values, and capacities we bequeath to our children. It troubles me to wonder where the sidewalk really ends.

Comprehension Check

1. Carolyn V. Egan currently lives in a suburb that is still growing. Before this land was developed for housing, what was it used for? *(See paragraph 1.)*

2. Recently, as she tried to walk from her home to the grocery store, Egan realized two things. What were they? *(See paragraph 2.)*

3. When Egan grew up in the 1960s and 1970s, how did she get to school? *(See paragraph 3.)*

4. Egan says, "When I was little, the world was mine." What examples does she use to support this statement? *(See paragraphs 4 and 5.)*

5. Egan says she has been told that "nobody really cares about sidewalks" today. What makes them a nuisance to some people? *(See paragraph 6.)*

6. Egan describes children isolated inside their houses, relying on one way of connecting to the outside world. What is the one means of connection? *(See paragraph 7.)*

7. Egan warns that by spending too much of their time being chauffeured everywhere, today's children fail to develop certain skills. What are those skills? *(See paragraphs 7 and 8.)*

Discussion Prompts/Writing Options

If you write on any of the following topics, work through the stages of the writing process in preparing your assignment.

1. Is a big, secure house (complete with a two- or three-car garage) in the suburbs the American dream? Argue for the advantages of living in such a community.

2. Consider a family with one or more young children. What do you believe is the safest living environment for them? Is it the city, the country, or the suburbs? Write an argument that is aimed at convincing such a family to live in this environment.

3. Egan discusses Americans' fear of child predators. Argue for the best way to keep children safe from such predators.

4. Argue for one of the following: It is possible/no longer possible for children today to fully explore and experience their community.

5. Do you believe that children today need more direct experiences in the natural world? Why or why not?

Critical Thinking: Topics for Discussion and Writing

If you write on any of the following topics, work through the stages of the writing process in preparing your assignment.

1. What does Egan mean when she says, "Adult maturity is rooted in the unstructured roaming of childhood"? Do you believe that "unstructured roaming" is essential to growing up? Are there also experiences available to a suburban child, safe in a structured routine and a secure house, that will help the child to grow to adulthood?

2. Egan describes two kinds of neighborhoods: (1) the sidewalk-lined, generally safe but adventure-filled neighborhood of her childhood, and (2) the automobile-dominated, sidewalk-free, isolating neighborhood of today's suburbs. Have you ever lived in either of these types of neighborhoods? If so, assess the neighborhood. If you have not lived in either kind of neighborhood, assess the type of neighborhood you grew up in. Consider the safety, sociability, and appeal to children of whatever neighborhood you describe.

3. What connections to a wider world are available to a child today who plays mainly indoors and often alone? Do "technological portals" link him to others and to the world beyond his home?

4. Is Egan's description of the ideal childhood a fantasy? Has life changed so much that her vision of childhood freedom is unrealistic and unsafe?

WRITING FROM READING: THE ESSAY

The Longest Day

Danna L. Walker

In 2007, professor Danna L. Walker gave her Understanding Mass Media class at American University a challenging assignment: the students had to live without any kind of electronic media for twenty-four hours. "Could a class of college students survive without iPods, cell phones, computers, and television from one sunrise to the next?" she asked. How they handled "the e-media fast" and what they and their professor learned from the experience is the subject of this <u>Washington Post</u> article.

Words You May Need to Know (Corresponding paragraph numbers are in parentheses.)

painstakingly (1): carefully
gospel (1): absolute truth
media (2): means of communication, such as television or e-mail, that reach a large number of people
saturated (2): soaked
balk (2): refuse to act
e-media fast (3): a voluntary refraining from using any electronic media

discourse (3): a formal discussion, serious conversation, or written treatment of a subject
cavernous (4): like a cave
futile (6): useless, ineffective
ad nauseam (6): to the extent of causing disgust or boredom
unconventional (6): unusual, not conforming to ordinary rules or roles
borne witness to (6): personally seen

tsunami (6): a giant wave caused by an earthquake under the sea

watchdogging (6): warning

ensued (7): followed

crescendo (7): a gradual increase in loudness

in retrospect (16): looking back

contemporaries (16): people growing up during the same time period

binary code (16): a two-part code

grueling (17): severe

dawned (18): began

baby boomers (18): Americans born between 1946 and 1964, when there was a huge spike in birth rates

static (19): unchanging, unmoving

analog map (19): an older system of representing data

malleable (19): adaptable

terrain (19): land

came of age (19): grew up

demographic (19): age group

court (19): try to gain the favor of

elusive (19): hard to catch or attract

old media (19): print media such as books and newspapers

savvy (20): intelligent, knowing

articulate (20): able to use language easily and fluently

inopportune (25): inappropriate

elaborate (30): add details

bite (30): accept an offer

luxuriating (31): indulging, enjoying

adrift (33): lost, without direction

negotiate (34): deal with

evoking (34): producing

complied (34): obeyed

ubiquitous (35): existing everywhere

benchmark (35): marked point

thought police (35): In the world of *1984*, thought police spied on and punished citizens whose thoughts were considered unsuitable or dangerous to society

totalitarianism (35): absolute control by the government

scenario (35): plot outline

mass consumption (35): enormous numbers of people focused on spending money on goods and services

escapism (35): avoiding reality by focusing on entertainment

constraining (35): preventing, restraining

musings (35): thoughts

relevant (35): significant in a new time

indulgences (36): gratifications of desire

trivial (36): unimportant

minute (36): extremely small

necessarily (39): inevitably

frivolous (39): silly, lacking seriousness

constraint (40): restraint, limit

logistics (40): in the military, the science of transporting, buying, and supplying

stupor (40): mental fog

Lincoln-Douglas debates (40): in 1858, a series of seven debates between Abraham Lincoln, a Republican, and Stephen A. Douglas, a Democrat, during a campaign for an Illinois seat in the U.S. Senate. The main subject of all the debates was slavery. The debates were covered by newspapers across the nation.

sphere (40): field of activity

1   I was wondering if I could really pull it off, making undergraduates do without any kind of electronic media for twenty-four hours. I hesitated as I wrote the assignment painstakingly into my fourteen-page syllabus for the spring semester. The syllabus is considered a contract with the students. If the assignment is there, they can't get around it. If it's there, it's gospel, so I put it in.

2   This would be a good way, I thought, to get my students in my "Understanding Mass Media" class at American University to think about the media-saturated world they live in and what its effects on them might be. I wondered if they would balk or even refuse to do it.

3   Their faces looked skeptical when we finally got to the e-media fast about halfway through the semester. No television, computers, iPods or other MP3 devices, radio, video games, CD players, records or cell phones (or land lines) for twenty-four hours. If they slipped up or cheated—and I said with faked confidence that I'd be able to tell from their papers if they had—they'd have to start the twenty-four hours over. I gave them the option of doing the fast during spring break, to make it easier and to see how their family and friends would interact with the assignment. They were to write a short report about their experience and include a reflection on the assigned reading, *Amusing Ourselves to Death: Public Discourse in the Age of Show Business*, by the late New York University communications professor Neil Postman.

4   I stepped down from the podium in the dimly lit and cavernous Wechsler Theater, where my class is held, to stand in the center aisle among my students—the better to look them in the eye if they challenged me.

5   "No cell phones?" they asked in pleading voices, looking around at one another with wide eyes and open mouths.

6   "How are cell phones media?" another student protested, but she could sense that resistance was futile. We had talked ad nauseam in class about how individuals' use of digital devices, including cell phone photos, video, and texting, has created an army of unconventional citizen journalists who have borne witness to the 9/11 attacks, the 2004 Indian Ocean tsunami, the Iraq war, Hurricane Katrina and more, changing the face of journalism through their media watchdogging blogs and online social networks.

7   "I'll be doing it, too," I offered reassuringly. A few seconds of silence ensued as they appeared to consider whether that made a difference. A crescendo of audible desperation followed.

8   "When we're driving around, can't we listen to the radio?" a student asked.

9   "No," I said as steadfastly as I could.

10   "It's only for, like, twenty-four hours, right?" asked a student near the back.

11   "Yes," I said quickly. Then came the moment when my growing experience with college students paid off.

12   "And what can you do for a lot of that time?" I asked loudly with a big smile, bending at the knees and opening my arms like an overly optimistic cheerleader when the junior varsity is down by thirteen points in the fourth quarter.

13   "Sleep!" came the chorus of voices after barely a beat.

14   "Yes!" I responded. "You can sleep, you can read, you can have conversations. In person!"

15   "Can we eat?" some asked, to laughter.

16   In retrospect, perhaps that last question wasn't as ridiculous as it sounded. Eighteen- to twenty-year-olds know in their hearts that electronic media are nearly as dear to their lives as physical nourishment. They have vague memories of a time before iTunes, personalized ring tones, Facebook, Google, Rocketboom, "MySpace: The Movie," and www. i-am-bored. com. But like their contemporaries, the Olsen twins, whom they watched grow up in the media, they are no longer innocent. They have tasted the pleasures brought by binary code, and, like most of us, they're not into deprivation.

17   Could my students, in fact, survive "the grueling pain that was the twenty-four-hour, e-media fast" as one self-described iPod and computer addict would later write in her paper?

18   The fifty young women and men in my class at American University are what are called digital natives or "millennials," those born between 1980 and 2000, many of whom graduated from high school as the twenty-first century dawned. Researchers say they will constitute the largest generation in American history, outnumbering baby boomers by as much as thirty-three percent.

19   Millennials grew up thinking that computers were as much a part of the family room furniture as my generation thought televisions were. While we boomers have had to change our thinking entirely from its static analog map of reality, their generation has always been comfortable with the malleable, non-physical terrain of electronic networks. They started life with VCRs and CDs and led the charge to digital video and MP3s. They were the first to link up through cell phones and instant messages. Personal computers came of age as they were born, and they grew up with the World Wide Web and e-mail, not to mention Nintendo, Game Boy, Sony PlayStation, GameCube, and Xbox. They are the demographic that marketers love to court, but they can be elusive to advertisers tied to old media.

20   And yet, even though they are savvy, articulate, emotionally attached and educated consumers of electronic media, millennials don't actually think much about it. At the beginning of the semester, my students seemed surprised to learn that they are trailblazers in a time of upheaval in the media world. But they became painfully aware once they were forced to unplug.

21   "I was in shock," wrote one student. "I honestly did not think I could accomplish this task. The twenty-four hours I spent in what seemed like complete isolation became known as one of the toughest days I had to endure."

22   Another student apparently did not see the irony in this statement: "I felt like I would be wasting my time doing the project. I did not want to give up my daily schedule, which mainly includes lying on my couch, watching television and playing The Sims2—a [life simulator] computer game."

23   Back in Wechsler Theater after spring break, with my students' ordeal over and their papers written, I asked them to tell me what had occurred in their lives for twenty-four media-free hours.

24   "What was good about it?" I asked, somewhat hopefully.

25   "Your cellphone, like, it always rings at the most inopportune times, so it was nice for a day to not have it constantly ringing," someone piped up.

26   Said another, "The peace and quiet. I realized how I depended on e-media because I don't pick up a newspaper. The way I get my news is either talk to people or watch TV."

27   "Every single one of these people in here," one student said, looking around the classroom, "we can't deal with silence anymore. We always have to have at least two things going on, whether it's the TV or the computer or iPod or cell phone."

28   On they went as I scribbled down their comments.

29   "I really felt productive. I thought that I would just be, ah, no stress. But I was nonstop all day, cleaning, cooking, weed-whacking, yardwork."

30   Two students spent extra time with their mothers. They wouldn't elaborate in front of their peers, but one later wrote in his paper, "My mother is thrilled that I'm doing this fast. To her it means I get to spend the day with her. I bite, and we walk into town for some brunch. I draw out the brunch as long as possible."

31   Many students said they got out more than usual. If they heard someone leaving from across the dormitory hall, they jumped at the chance to join in. A lot of them said they got more sleep, some of them luxuriating in a rare afternoon nap, and enjoyed reading a book.

32   They had to be creative about everyday activities. "I actually had to go out and get a newspaper, which I normally don't do," one student said. "It wasn't that bad, but I almost felt like I wasn't getting all the news" without Internet updates. "I realized I couldn't be around any of my friends because they weren't willing to do this with me. They would blast the radio if I was in the car or try to make me play video games," said another. Some had their friends hide their cell phones, and one put Post-it notes around saying, "NO TECHNOLOGY," to avoid reflexive television and Internet use.

33   Some were completely adrift. "There was a moment in my day when I felt homeless," one student said. "I couldn't go home because I knew that would be too tempting. I couldn't be with my friends because that would be too tempting. I had just eaten, so I couldn't just sit in a restaurant all day. I was walking down the street literally with nowhere to go, and I just didn't know what I was going to do." Several students realized their circle of daily friends included many who were nowhere near them geographically. "I found it hard because a lot of the people I talk to aren't in my immediate area, so they didn't relate to it," said one student.

34   Others realized the Internet helps them negotiate relationships. "I started thinking about the idea that we've given up responsibility by relying on technology because it's a lot easier to send a text message to say I'm sorry," said one student. A student's cell phone interrupted the class, evoking laughter. Then I asked them all to turn their cell phones on, and they eagerly complied.

35   Postman, the author of our assigned book, became alarmed by the growing influence of media in 1985. It was during the second term of the first Hollywood actor to become president, as the first television generation came of age, and as live news, MTV, cable television, and videocassette recorders were soon to become ubiquitous. The world had passed by one year the benchmark of George Orwell's *1984*, the futuristic novel published in 1949 that foretold of Big Brother, the thought police, and totalitarianism. But Postman believed that Aldous Huxley's 1932 scenario in *Brave New World* was more compelling—one in which society is destroyed by its worship of mass consumption and escapism. Postman believed television, in particular, was constraining higher thought and "and transforming our culture into one vast arena for show business" without our realizing it. He thought that, because we are engineered to avoid our own imprisonment, we just needed to be aware of what our growing addiction to media was doing to us. But were an intellectual's twenty-year-old musings about the future of our media world still relevant?

36   In their papers, a surprising number of students said Postman had convinced them of his argument or at least made them feel guilty about their e-media indulgences. "A day without electronic media showed me how dependent society and I were upon it," one student wrote. "Without that distraction, I can discover new things in the real world, or at least be more productive. Neil Postman was right when he said that American society has become obsessed with the trivial and the minute."

37   One student related the lessons of the book to her own upbringing. "The fact that the media trivialize information and turn public discourse into pure entertainment are both things my father tried to explain to me as a young child that I'm only now starting to understand," she wrote.

38   But some of my students jumped to defend their media habits. "Blogs, online newspapers, and Web sites all use more typed language than images when distributing news media. This puts a hole in Postman's argument," wrote one. Another student put it thoughtfully. "I think we have over-media medicated ourselves," she said. But "I don't feel ashamed at all. It's part of our culture, and I am completely addicted to it. I mean, the media fast was pretty much impossible for me. As long as our generation maintains a level of personable skills and we remain responsible, I think that we're okay. It's fine. It's not an epidemic. It's okay. It's okay."

39   Part way through the semester the students seemed to be getting defensive about their media habits. A little earlier, some of them took my lecture on David Mindich's book *Tuned Out: Why Americans Under Forty Don't*

Follow the News to mean I thought less of them for not reading the newspaper or even knowing that traditional network news still exists. I don't, necessarily. There are a number of reasons why the age of the average newspaper and network news viewer is over fifty, not the least of which include trends that began when I was my students' age. Many of the reasons lie with the failures of the media themselves. But I sense my students want to shout, "We're not frivolous just because we like to IM and go on Facebook! Or, even if we are frivolous, we don't care because we're college students!"

40   I'm not from the we're-all-going-to-hell-in-a-handbasket school of media thought. I use most of the electronic gadgets my students do. E-media keep us up to the minute on information, facilitate relationships without geographic constraint, make logistics easier, and sometimes help us relax and fight boredom. But I do know a world my students haven't inhabited—a world in which we may have had less ready access to information but had more power to turn it off and reflect. I hold on to the hope that we're not too far gone in our media stupor to recapture the idealistic vision of the Lincoln-Douglas debates, meaningful discourse, and human-to-human interaction in the public sphere.

41   Perhaps my students don't totally disagree with me. They would say there is a town square of the twentieth-first century. It's just that it's a rectangle—a glowing LCD screen in their pockets, on their desk, or dominating an entire room. And while they may have enjoyed some parts of their journey to a bygone era during the e-media fast, they couldn't wait to press the power button and get back to the present.

Comprehension Check

1. The "e-media fast" assignment had two parts. One part was a twenty-four-hour period without any e-media. What was the other part? *(See paragraph 3.)*

2. What book was assigned reading? *(See paragraph 3.)*

3. Danna L. Walker refers to several events covered by "citizen journalists" using digital devices. Name one of these events. *(See paragraph 6.)*

4. How old were the students in Walker's Understanding Mass Media class? *(See paragraph 16.)*

5. What are "millenials"? *(See paragraph 18.)*

6. One student complained that "doing the [media fast] project" would be a waste of time. How did the student's description of his or her daily schedule make the student's complaint seem ironic? *(See paragraph 22.)*

7. One student praised the "peace and quiet" of the media fast. However, another student commented on silence and its effect on "every single" class member. What was the comment? *(See paragraph 27.)*

8. Walker praised the electronic media, saying that it served many useful purposes. Name one of the useful purposes Walker mentions. *(See paragraph 40.)*

9. When people lived without e-media, Walker says, they had "less ready access to information," but they also had one power that her students seem to lack. What is that power? *(See paragraph 40.)*

10. Walker says that, for her students, the town square that used to serve as the center of public conversation has been replaced by a twenty-first century version of the town square. What is the new version? *(See paragraph 41.)*

Discussion Prompts/Writing Options

If you write on any of the following topics, work through the stages of the writing process in preparing your assignment.

1. How do you get news? How familiar are you with national or world issues and events? Do you feel that you are sufficiently informed? Why or why not?

2. Consider the amount of trivial "news" that appears on television or online. You can think about the personalities (such as athletes, actors, musicians, and people "famous for being famous") and scandals that receive enormous coverage in the media and fascinate the public. Once you have a list of these trivial "news" stories, pick three. Explain why they fascinate the public.

3. Using Walker's article, find one student comment about e-media, the e-media fast, the effects of the e-media fast, or the lessons learned. Then explain why you found the comment insightful or true.

4. When you are alone at home, what e-media keeps you company? For example, is your cell phone on? Your television? Your computer? Why? What does each form of e-media do for you?

5. Do you ever seek a quiet place such as your room or a place in nature? Why or why not?

Critical Thinking: Topics for Discussion and Writing

If you write on any of the following topics, work through the stages of the writing process in preparing your essay.

1. Do you think that Walker's analysis of e-media and its role in the lives of millennials is unrealistic or overly critical? If so, why?

2. Do you think that an older generation, which may feel confused and threatened by the power of new technology such as e-mail, the Internet, and iPods, is overreacting to inevitable and even positive changes in society?

3. One of Walker's students wrote, "I think we have over-medicated ourselves" (with e-media) but "I don't feel ashamed at all. It's part of our culture. And I am completely addicted to it. I mean, the media fast was pretty much impossible for me. As long as our generation maintains a level of personable [attractive in manner and

appearance] skills and we remain responsible, we're okay. It's fine. It's not an epidemic. It's okay. It's okay."

React to her statement. Do you think we are addicted to electronic media? Is it an epidemic? Is it "okay"?

WRITING FROM READING: THE ESSAY

A Brother's Murder

Brent Staples

In 1984, writer Brent Staples received news of his younger brother's murder. In this essay, he explores how two black men growing up in poverty and pain can take such different paths. As he traces his escape from anger and desperation, he grieves the loss of the brother he could not rescue.

Words You May Need to Know (Corresponding paragraph numbers are in parentheses.)

emerged (1): came out of
massive (1): large
inseparable (1): very close
escalated (1): increased
posturing (1): trying to look tough
assailant (1): attacker
wrenched (2): suddenly pulled
light-years (2): a long way
mortality (2): death
brash (2): fast-moving, impulsive
donned (2): put on
noncommissioned officer (3): an enlisted member of the armed forces appointed to lead other enlisted men and women
affluent (3): prosperous
paranoia (3): extreme irrational distrust of others
machismo (3): a strong sense of manhood that includes

aggressiveness, domination of women, and physical courage
incursions (3): attacks, violations
upwardly mobile (4): likely to move up in wealth and status
ensconced (4): securely settled
grim (4): gloomy
umbilical (4): a connection between family members
desolate (5): deserted, lifeless
idle (5): unemployed, inactive
embittered (5): made bitter
forays (5): trips, ventures
terrain (5): ground
dive (6): a rundown bar or nightclub
affected (6): imitated, put on
alarm (7): sudden fear
earnestly (8): seriously
recurrent (8): occurring repeatedly

1   It has been more than two years since my telephone rang with the news that my younger brother Blake—just twenty-two years old—had been murdered. The young man who killed him was only twenty-four. Wearing a ski mask, he emerged from a car, fired six times at close range with a massive .44 Magnum, then fled. The two had once been inseparable friends. A senseless rivalry—beginning, I think, with an argument over a girlfriend—escalated from posturing to threats, to violence, to murder. The way the two were living, death could have come to either of them from anywhere. In fact, the assailant had already survived multiple gunshot wounds from an incident much like the one in which my brother lost his life.

2   As I wept for Blake, I felt wrenched backwards into events and circumstances that had seemed light-years gone. Though a decade apart, we both were raised in Chester, Pennsylvania, an angry, heavily black, heavily poor, industrial city southwest of Philadelphia. There, in the 1960s, I was introduced to mortality, not by the old and failing, but by beautiful young men who lay wrecked after sudden explosions of violence. The first, I remembered from my fourteenth year—Johnny, brash lover of fast cars, stabbed to death two doors from my house in a fight over a pool game. The next year, my teenage cousin, Wesley, whom I loved very much, was shot dead. The summers blur. Milton, an angry neighbor, shot a crosstown rival, wounding him badly. William, another teenage neighbor, took a shotgun blast to the shoulder in some urban drama and displayed his bandages proudly. His brother, Leonard, severely beaten, lost an eye and donned a black patch. It went on.

3   I recall not long before I left for college, two local Vietnam veterans— one from the Marines, one from the Army—arguing fiercely, nearly at blows about which outfit had done the most in the war. The most killing, they meant. Not much later, I read a magazine article that set that dispute in a context. In the story, a noncommissioned officer—a sergeant, I believe— said he would pass up any number of affluent, suburban-born recruits to get hard-core soldiers from the inner city. They jumped into rice paddies with "their manhood on their sleeves," I believe he said. These two items—the veterans arguing and the sergeant's words—still characterize for me the circumstances under which black men in their teens and twenties kill one another with such frequency. With a touchy paranoia born of living battered lives, they are desperate to be *real* men. Killing is only machismo taken to the extreme. Incursions to be punished by death were many and minor, and they remain so: they include stepping on the wrong toe, literally; cheating in a drug deal; simply saying "I dare you" to someone holding a gun; crossing territorial lines in a gang dispute. My brother grew up to wear his manhood on his sleeve. And when he died he was in that group—black, male, and in its teens and early twenties—that is far and away the most likely to murder or be murdered.

4   I left the East Coast after college, spent the mid- and late 1970s in Chicago as a graduate student, taught for a time, then became a journalist. Within ten years of leaving my hometown, I was overeducated and "upwardly mobile," ensconced on a quiet, tree-lined street where voices raised in anger were scarcely ever heard. The telephone, like some grim umbilical, kept me connected to the old world with news of deaths, imprisonings, and misfortune. I felt emotionally beaten up. Perhaps to protect myself, I added a psychological dimension to the physical distance I had already achieved. I rarely visited my hometown. I shut it out.

5   As I fled the past, so Blake embraced it. On Christmas of 1983, I traveled from Chicago to a black section of Roanoke, Virginia, where he then lived. The desolate public housing projects, the hopeless, idle young men crashing against one another—these reminded me of the embittered town we'd grown up in. It was a place where once I would have been comfortable, or at least sure of myself. Now, hearing of my brother's forays into crime, his scrapes with police and street thugs, I was scared, unsteady on foreign terrain.

6   I saw that Blake's romance with the street life and the hustler image had flowered dangerously. One evening that late December, standing in some Roanoke dive among drug dealers and grim, hair-trigger losers, I told him I feared for his life. He had affected the image of the tough he wanted to be. But behind the dark glasses and the swagger, I glimpsed the baby-faced toddler I'd once watched over. I nearly wept. I wanted desperately for him to live. The young think themselves immortal, and a dangerous light shone in his eyes as he spoke laughingly of making fools of the policemen who had raided his apartment looking for drugs. He cried out as I took his right hand. A line of stitches lay between the thumb and index finger. Kickback from a shotgun, he explained, nothing serious. Gunplay had become part of his life.

7   I lacked the language simply to say: Thousands have lived this for you and died. I fought the urge to lift him bodily and shake him. This place and the way you are living smells of death to me, I said. Take some time away, I said. Let's go downtown tomorrow and buy a plane ticket anywhere, take a bus trip, anything to get away and cool things off. He took my alarm casually. We arranged to meet the following night—an appointment he would not keep. We embraced as though through glass. I drove away.

8   As I stood in my apartment in Chicago holding the receiver that evening in February 1984, I felt as though part of my soul had been cut away. I questioned myself then, and I still do. Did I not reach back soon enough or earnestly enough, for him? For weeks I awoke crying from a recurrent dream in which I chased him, urgently trying to get him to read a document I had, as though reading it would protect him from what had happened in waking life. His eyes shining like black diamonds, he smiled and danced just beyond my grasp. When I reached for him, I caught only the space where he had been.

Comprehension Check

1. Brent Staples says that his brother's murder was a result of a senseless rivalry. Who killed his brother, and what was the reason behind the rivalry? *(See paragraph 1.)*

2. How old was the author when he was "introduced to mortality"? Describe some of the fatal shootings of teenagers whom Staples knew. *(See paragraph 2.)*

3. Describe the type of recruit the noncommissioned officer was seeking, and explain why many of the teenagers Staples grew up with were perfect recruits. *(See paragraph 3.)*

4. Staples believes that angry inner city teens like his brother possess a "touch of paranoia born of living battered lives," and are "desperate to be *real* men." What are some of the seemingly simple acts that can lead to killing among this group of young men? *(See paragraph 3.)*

5. During Staples' ten-year absence from his hometown, he became "upwardly mobile" but felt "emotionally beaten up." How did he try to cope with the distance he had put between himself and his roots? *(See paragraph 4.)*

6. How did Blake's path differ from his brother's, and why did Brent fear for his brother's life? *(See paragraph 6.)*

7. Describe Staples' recurrent dream after his brother was murdered. *(See paragraph 8.)*

8. What do you think is the most effective description (phrase or sentence) in this article? Be prepared to explain your choice. *(Answers will vary.)*

Discussion Prompts/Writing Options

If you write on any of the following topics, work through the stages of the writing process in preparing your assignment.

1. Brent Staples tried to connect emotionally with his brother. He warned Blake about the dangers of staying on a violent path. Do you think Staples did everything he could to save his brother? Use specific details from the article to support your point of view.

2. If you have witnessed or experienced a particularly disturbing or violent event in your neighborhood, describe the event and its consequences. You can include its immediate impact on you and your neighbors as well as its lasting effects.

3. Although "A Brother's Murder" was first published in 1986, some of Staples' descriptions, such as "idle young men crashing against one another," can apply to some violent and angry young males today. Select three or four descriptions or statements from the article that are still relevant and accurate. Be sure to include specific connections to senseless violence today.

4. Imagine all that could have happened in Staples' recurrent dream. What was the chase like, why is he "urgently" trying to get his brother to read a document, what did the document say, how did his brother react, and so forth. Focus on creating a clear picture of what each man sees and feels.

Critical Thinking: Topics for Writing and Discussion

If you write on any of the following topics, work through the stages of the writing process in preparing your assignment.

1. Put yourself in Blake Staples' shoes. Why do you think his life took such a different turn than his brother's?

2. How would you define a "real" man? How do you think Brent Staples defined it? How did Blake Staples define it?

3. How many people who live in relatively safe areas become numb to daily reports of violence locally or nationally? What kinds or instances of violence can shock people used to tuning out the daily crime news?

WRITING FROM READING: THE ESSAY

Navajo Code Talkers: The Century's Best Kept Secret

Jack Hitt

In this essay, Jack Hitt talks of the secret heroism of a group of Native Americans during World War II. By using the language of their tribe, the Navajo code talkers made an "incredible contribution" to "winning history's biggest war."

Words You May Need to Know (Corresponding paragraph numbers are in parentheses.)

decisive (1): unmistakable
Iwo Jima (1): a Japanese Island in the Pacific
momentous (1): important
guttural (1): harsh, grating
intonations (1): tones
baffled (1): confused
infuriated (1): made angry
conformed (1): followed the rules of
linguistic (1): language
cryptographers (1): people who study secret codes
decipher (1): solve or decode
clandestine (1): secret
cryptographic (2): secret code
intercepted (2): stopped, interrupted, or turned aside

proficient (2): expert
sabotage (2): destroy
the Pentagon (2): the United States military establishment
gambits (2): maneuvers
virtually (3): practically
artillery (3): weapons
coined (3): created
neologisms (3): new words
pyrotechnic (4): resembling fireworks
elite (5): high status
solemnly (5): gravely
messaging apparatus (6): means for sending messages

1   During World War II, on the dramatic day when Marines raised the American flag to signal a key and decisive victory at Iwo Jima, the first word of this momentous news crackled over the radio in odd guttural noises and complex intonations. Throughout the war, the Japanese were repeatedly baffled and infuriated by these seemingly inhuman sounds. They conformed to no linguistic system known to the Japanese. The curious sounds were the military's one form of conveying tactics and strategy that the master cryptographers in Tokyo were unable to decipher. This perfect code was the language of the Navajo tribe. Its application in World War II as a clandestine system of communications was one of the twentieth century's best-kept secrets.

2   After a string of cryptographic failures, the military in 1942 was desperate for a way to open clear lines of communication that would not be intercepted by the enemy. In the 1940s, there was no such thing as a "secure line." All talk had to go out onto the public airwaves. Standard codes were an option, but the cryptographers in Japan could quickly crack them. And there was another problem: the Japanese were proficient at intercepting short-distance communications, on walkie-talkies for example, and then having well-trained English-speaking soldiers either sabotage the message or send out false commands to set up an ambush. That was the situation in 1942 when the Pentagon authorized one of the boldest gambits of the war.

3   The solution was conceived by the son of missionaries to the Navajos, a former Marine named Philip Johnston. His idea: station a native Navajo speaker at every radio station. Since Navajo had never been written down or translated into any other language, it was an entirely self-contained human communication system restricted to Navajos alone; it was virtually indecipherable without Navajo help. Without some key or way into a language, translation is virtually impossible. Not long after the bombing of Pearl Harbor, the military dispatched twenty-nine Navajos to Camp Elliott and Camp Pendleton in California to begin a test program. These first recruits had to develop a Navajo alphabet since none existed. And because Navajo lacked technical terms of military artillery, the men coined a number of neologisms specific to their task and war.

4   According to Chester Nez, one of the original code talkers, "Everything we used in the code was what we lived with on the reservation every day, like the ants, the birds, bears." Thus, the term for a tank was "turtle," a tank destroyer was "tortoise killer." A battleship was "whale." A hand grenade was "potato," and plain old bombs were "eggs." A fighter plane was "hummingbird," and a torpedo plane "swallow." A sniper was "pick 'em off." Pyrotechnic was "fancy fire."

5   It didn't take long for the original twenty-nine recruits to expand to an elite corps of Marines, numbering at its height 425 Navajo Code Talkers, all from the American Southwest. Each Talker was so valuable, he traveled everywhere with a personal bodyguard. In the event of capture, the Talkers had solemnly agreed to commit suicide rather than allow America's most valuable war code to fall into the hands of the enemy. If a captured Navajo did not follow that grim instruction, the bodyguard's instructions were understood: shoot and kill the Code Talker.

6   The language of the Code Talkers, their mission, and every detail of their messaging apparatus were secrets they were all ordered to keep, even from their own families. They did. It wasn't until 1968, when the military felt convinced that the Code Talkers would not be needed for any future wars, that America learned of the incredible contribution a handful of Native Americans made to winning history's biggest war. The Navajo Code Talkers,

sending and receiving as many as 800 errorless messages at fast speed during "the fog of battle," are widely credited with giving U.S. troops the decisive edge at Guadalcanal, Tarawa, Saipan, Iwo Jima, and Okinawa.

Comprehension Check

1. Why was the Navajo tribe's language considered a "perfect code" for the United States to use for conveying "tactics and strategy" during World War II? *(See paragraph 1.)*

2. Before the United States started using the Navajo language as a secret code of communication, why were standard codes ineffective? *(See paragraph 2.)*

3. Who was Philip Johnston, what was his idea concerning Navajo speakers, and why was the Navajo language such a perfect choice for secret communication? *(See paragraph 3.)*

4. What did the first group of Navajo recruits have to develop in order to use their language as code? *(See paragraph 3.)*

5. The Navajo Code Talkers became "an elite corps of Marines." How many recruits did this corps have at its height, and where were they all from? *(See paragraph 5.)*

6. What were some indications that each Talker was extremely valuable to the United States? *(See paragraph 5.)*

7. If the Navajo Code Talkers were captured by the enemy, what were they expected to do? *(See paragraph 5.)*

8. When did America finally learn about "the incredible contribution a handful of Native Americans made to winning history's biggest war"? *(See paragraph 6.)*

Discussion Prompts/Writing Options

If you write on any of the following topics, work through the stages of the writing process in preparing your assignment.

1. The language of the Navajo tribe was the perfect language to use for secret code. Are you familiar with any regional language or slang that would be hard to decipher by anyone unfamiliar with this form of communication? If so, describe where this language developed, how often it is used, and why it would be so difficult to decipher or translate.

2. The Navajo Code Talkers could be considered unsung heroes because their heroic contributions during World War II went unrecognized for so many years. Write a short essay about someone whom you regard as an unsung hero in your school, community, city, or state.

3. Jack Hitt, author of "Navajo Code Talkers," states that the Talkers "are widely credited with giving U.S. troops the decisive edge at Guadalcanal, Tarawa, Saipan, Iwo Jima, and Okinawa." Conduct an online search for information about one or more of these battles, and see if the contributions of the Navajo Code Talkers

Computer

are mentioned. If so, summarize the specific contributions of the Talkers. If not, summarize the main points of the article(s); you may want to include details about the purpose of the battle, the length of the battle, the number of casualties, and the degree of success.

> **Note:** If you choose to summarize one article, refer to "Writing a Summary of a Reading," on pp. 332–337 in Chapter 13, "Writing from Reading."

Critical Thinking: Topics for Writing And Discussion

If you write on any of the following topics, work through the stages of the writing process in preparing your assignment.

1. As the creators of a secret code, the "elite corps of Marines" known for many years as the Navajo Code Talkers were secret heroes. Consider what benefits and rewards (from family, society, and the government) this group of Native Americans were denied because of this secrecy.

2. The members of the Navajo Code Talkers had to promise to commit suicide if they were ever captured by the enemy. Would you want a loved one to join a similar secret group and make a similar promise?

3. The Navajo Code Talkers' most valuable skill came from their brains, not from their physical abilities. How much does winning a war depend on physical strength, troop numbers, and weapons, and how much does it depend on mental abilities? In considering these questions, give examples of the power of all these components of battle.

ESL APPENDIX
Grammar Practice for Nonnative Students

NOUNS AND ARTICLES

A noun names a person, place, or thing. There are nouns and noncount nouns.

> **Count nouns** refer to persons, places, or things that can be counted:
> three *doughnuts*, two *kittens*, five *pencils*
> **Noncount** nouns refer to things that can't be counted: *medicine,*
> *housework, mail*

Here are some more examples of count and noncount nouns.

count	noncount
rumor	gossip
violin	music
school	intelligence
suitcase	luggage

One way to remember the difference between count and noncount nouns is to put the word *much* in front of the noun. For example, if you can say *much luggage*, then *luggage* is a noncount noun.

Exercise 1 Practice: Identifying Count and Noncount Nouns

Write *count* or *noncount* next to each word below.

1. *count* gift
2. *count* fence
3. *noncount* gossip
4. *noncount* toothpaste
5. *count* coin

6. *noncount* safety
7. *noncount* ice cream
8. *noncount* money
9. *count* toothbrush
10. *count* cookie

Exercise 2 More on Identifying Count and Noncount Nouns

Write *count* or *noncount* next to each word below.

1. *noncount* determination
2. *noncount* cleanliness
3. *noncount* torture
4. *noncount* compassion
5. *count* elevator

6. *count* discussion
7. *count* magazine
8. *noncount* wool
9. *count* sweater
10. *count* victim

Using Articles with Nouns

Articles point out nouns. Articles are either **indefinite** (*a, an*) or **definite** (*the*). There are several rules for using these articles.

1. Use *a* in front of consonant sounds, and use *an* before vowel sounds:

a card	an orange
a radio	an answer
a button	an entrance
a thread	an invitation
a nightmare	an uncle

2. Use *a* or *an* in front of singular count nouns (*a* or *an* means any one):

   I ate *an* egg.
   James planted *a* tree.

3. Do not use *a* or *an* with noncount nouns:

   not this: Selena filled the tank with a̶ gasoline.
   but this: Selena filled the tank with gasoline.

   not this: I am studying a̶n̶ algebra.
   but this: I am studying algebra.

4. Use *the* before both singular and plural count nouns whose specific identify is known to the reader:

   The dress with the sequins on it is my party dress.
   Most of *the* movies I rent are science fiction films.

5. Use *the* before noncount nouns only when they are specifically identified:

   not this: I need t̶h̶e̶ help. (Whose help? What help? The noncount noun *help* is not specifically identified.)
   but this: I need *the help* of a good plumber. (Now *help* is specifically identified.)

   not this: K̶i̶n̶d̶n̶e̶s̶s̶ of the people who took me in was remarkable. (The noncount noun *kindness* is specifically identified, so you need *the*.)
   but this: *The kindness* of the people who took me in was remarkable.

Exercise 3 Using *a* or *an*

Put *a* or *an* in the spaces where it is needed. Some sentences are correct as they are.

1. Mr. Kaminsky lent us __*a*__ flashlight.

2. Kelly received _____ criticism for her behavior.

3. The lake near my house has __*an*__ alligator in it.

4. Tamsin drew __*a*__ picture of __*an*__ elephant.

5. He admires _____ honesty in his friends.

6. Nina should take __*a*__ class in _____ biology if she wants to become __*a*__ nurse.

7. We visited __*an*__ island with __*a*__ reputation for beautiful beaches.

8. What Brian needs is _____ ambition and _a_ set of goals.

9. The swimmer got caught in _an_ undertow and called for _a_ lifeguard.

10. Tommy was lucky to have had _an_ aunt with _an_ appetite for _____ fun.

Exercise 4 **More on Using *a* or *an***

Put *a* or *an* in the spaces where it is needed. Some sentences are correct as they are.

1. Lilly gave me _an_ idea for my first speech in my communications class.

2. After breakfast, I often take _a_ walk before my first class.

3. To become _a_ soldier, a person needs _____ courage.

4. My father always tries to avoid _an_ argument with _a_ customer in the store.

5. Charles has _a_ craving for _an_ ice cream sundae.

6. The children drank _____ milk every morning.

7. Mr. Slezak always has _____ patience with his new employees.

8. Can you use _an_ old blanket as _a_ bed for _a_ puppy?

9. My sixty-year-old uncle relies on _____ exercise and _a_ vegetarian diet to keep him healthy.

10. Last night, _an_ owl in _a_ tree near my house kept me awake with its loud hooting.

Exercise 5 **Using *the***

Put *the* in the spaces where it is needed. Some sentences are correct as they are.

1. Ryan dreamed of _the_ adventures of his teen years.

2. If you stay focused, you will find _the_ strength to finish _____ college.

3. Arthur never listened to _____ advice or bothered to consider _the_ consequences of his actions.

4. Charlene is interested in _____ art, but she has no interest in _the_ business of selling art.

5. My parents have never attended _____ concerts, yet they love _____ music.

6. Tests show that my six-year-old has _the_ intelligence of a much older child.

7. Thanks to _the_ dedication of _the_ people at _the_ Family Harvest Food Bank, we have been able to serve 1,200 more Thanksgiving dinners to _the_ needy parents and children of our community.

8. Finding the right career takes _the_ insight to know your strengths and weaknesses and ____ careful investigation into _the_ demands and rewards of various jobs.

9. Whenever Ian feels overcome by ____ stress, he watches ____ soccer on ____ television.

10. An over-the-counter cream from _the_ drugstore took _the_ sting out of _the_ ant bites I got in _the_ backyard.

Exercise 6   **More on Using *the***

Put *the* in the spaces where it is needed. Some sentences are correct as they are.

1. An old scrapbook from a box in _the_ basement took me back to _the_ first days of basic training.

2. My success is due to _the_ support of my family and friends.

3. A long talk with a counselor gave Delilah _the_ courage that she needed to change _the_ destructive patterns of her romantic life and replace them with ____ healthy behavior.

4. Every time Rocco senses ____ panic invading his thoughts, he takes ____ deep breaths.

5. Growing up means accepting ____ responsibility for your choices and developing _the_ sense to avoid ____ foolish impulses.

6. Under _the_ direction of Dr. Ortega, _the_ clinic at South Glade has brought ____ affordable health care to _the_ farm workers who live nearby.

7. Sarah rarely enjoyed ____ gossip and ignored _the_ resentment and jealousy of her peers.

8. Ben wants to major in ____ business, and he is especially ____ interested in ____ international business.

9. My sister took a class in ____ ceramics, and now she wants to take one in _the_ study of pre-Colombian pottery.

10. I hope Luke has _the_ sense to avoid drugs and alcohol.

Connect

Exercise 7   **Correcting a Paragraph with Errors in Articles**

Correct the errors with *a*, *an*, or *the* in the following paragraph. You may need to add, change, or eliminate articles. Write the corrections in the space above the errors. There are fourteen errors.

My older brother Sam has the ability to assess ~~the~~ people after only one meet-

ing. He can recognize who is telling ~~the~~ lies and who is shy but good-hearted. Sam

has *a* gift; he can read *the* body language of strangers who are trying to present ~~the~~ *a*

good image. This talent is useful to him when he has to deal with salespeople or

others trying to get ~~a~~ money from him. Sometimes, his talent helps me. When Sam met my new boyfriend, he warned me that the man was ~~the~~ *a* manipulator. I was

fooled because my boyfriend had ~~a~~ *the* charm of ~~the~~ *a* movie star. Weeks later, I saw

the truth of Sam's warning and felt like ~~a~~ *an* idiot to be so trusting. It took me *a* few months

to realize that I don't have Sam's rare gift and must rely on ~~the~~ experience, not ~~the~~

insight, in order to choose my friends.

Connect

| Exercise 8 | Correcting Another Paragraph with Errors in Articles |

Correct the errors with *a*, *an*, or *the* in the following paragraph. You may need to add, change, or eliminate articles. There are eight errors.

I want to become *a* physical therapist because the demands of the work match my

personality. I enjoy meeting ~~the~~ people and getting to know them. In addition, when

people are suffering, I want to help them by treating the causes of their misery. ~~A~~

Physical ~~physical~~ therapy helps people recover from the pain caused by ~~a~~ *an* injury such as a fall

on an icy sidewalk or a chronic condition such as arthritis. More important, I have

always done well in science and biology classes, and I am now studying ~~the~~ physiol-

ogy. Next semester, I plan to register for *a* class in anatomy. My interests in ~~a~~ health

and my desire to help people make physical therapy ~~a~~ *the* right career for me.

NOUNS OR PRONOUNS USED AS SUBJECTS

A noun or a pronoun (a word that takes the place of a noun) is the subject of each sentence or dependent clause. Be sure that all sentences or dependent clauses have a subject.

> **not this:** Drives to work every day.
> **but this:** *He* drives to work every day.

> **not this:** My sister is pleased when gets a compliment.
> **but this:** My sister is pleased when *she* gets a compliment.

Be careful not to *repeat* the subject.

> **not this:** The police officer ~~she~~ said I was speeding.
> **but this:** The police officer said I was speeding.

> **not this:** The car that I needed ~~it~~ was a sports car.
> **but this:** The car that I needed was a sports car.

| Exercise 9 | Correcting Errors with Subjects |

Correct any errors with subjects in the sentences below. Write your corrections above the errors.

1. Danielle ~~she~~ never calls me unless *she* gets in trouble.

2. When it rains, my hair ~~it~~ often gets frizzy.

3. In December, small oranges from Spain ~~they~~ are a delicious gift.

4. In a strange city, *it* is easy to get lost.

5. Cotton clothes are cool in the summer; *they* also let your skin breathe.

6. Your brother Raoul ~~he~~ gave me a ride to work yesterday.

7. Last year Michelle and I ~~we~~ drove to Nashville, Tennessee.

8. *He* Rarely mentions his childhood and avoids talking about his family.

9. Every time *she* gets a test back in math class, she reviews her mistakes.

10. The happiest day of my life ~~it~~ was when you were born.

Exercise 10 More on Correcting Errors with Subjects

Correct any errors with subjects in the sentences below. Write your corrections above the errors.

1. My cat ~~she~~ got into the garage yesterday and knocked over a can of paint.

2. Once *she* finishes work at the hotel, Laura stops at a fast food restaurant on her way home.

3. *Caitlin* Sometimes forgets to take out the garbage on Monday nights.

4. A few weeks ago, my brother and his friends ~~they~~ donated blood at the bloodmobile.

5. Next time *he* runs into a member of the highway patrol, David will be more polite.

7. Fried chicken has the tasty combination of crispness outside and tenderness inside; *it* has a spicy flavor, too.

8. Wanting to make friends, *the child* was too trusting around strangers.

9. After a thunderstorm, the air ~~it~~ feels fresh and cool.

10. My wife and I ~~we~~ need to rent a truck because we have to move our furniture to a new apartment.

VERBS

Necessary Verbs

Be sure that a main verb isn't missing from your sentences or dependent clauses.

not this: My boyfriend very ambitious.
but this: My boyfriend *is* very ambitious.

not this: Sylvia cried when the hero in the movie.
but this: Sylvia cried when the hero in the movie died.

-s Endings

Be sure to put the -s on present tense verbs in the third person singular:

not this: He ~~run~~ in the park every morning.
but this: He *runs* in the park every morning.

not this: The concert ~~start~~ at 9:00 p.m.
but this: The concert *starts* at 9:00 p.m.

-ed Endings

Be sure to put -ed endings on the past participle form of a verb. There are three main forms of a verb:

present: Today I walk.
past: Yesterday I walked.
past participle: I *have* walked. He *has* walked.

The past participle form is also used after *were, was, had,* and *has.*

not this: He has ~~call~~ me every day this week.
but this: He has *called* me every day this week.

not this: My neighbor was ~~surprise~~ by the sudden storm.
but this: My neighbor was *surprised* by the sudden storm.

Do not add -ed endings to infinitives. An infinitive is the verb form that uses *to* plus the present form of the verb:

infinitives: to consider, to obey

not this: Dean wanted me to ~~considered~~ the proposal.
but this: Dean wanted me to *consider* the proposal.

not this: I taught my dog to ~~obeyed~~ commands.
but this: I taught my dog to *obey* commands.

Exercise 11   Correcting Errors in Verbs: Necessary Verbs, Third-Person Present Tense, Past Participles, and Infinitives

Correct any errors in verbs in the sentences below. Write your corrections in the space above the lines. Some sentences do not need any corrections.

1. After Ellen <u>start</u> *(starts)* to <u>cooked</u> *(cook)*, she <u>concentrate</u> *(concentrates)* on the food and <u>pay</u> *(pays)* no attention to her family's conversation.

2. Obsessive jealousy *(is)* a sign of danger in any romantic relationship.

3. Before Roy was <u>introduce</u> *(introduced)* to Joanne, he had never <u>meet</u> *(met)* a woman from Australia.

4. Every morning, my dog kisses my face and begs for a walk.

5. Three of the smartest babies at the daycare center *(are)* Jonelle, Hedrick, and Tyrese, my niece and nephews.

6. Lucy was <u>flatter</u> *(flattered)* by the attention she received at Wynona's wedding reception.

7. Monique urged Roberto to <u>refused</u> *(refuse)* the offer from his father.

8. Will had expected a different gift from the one his family gave him.

9. Once I got my driver's license, I wanted to *explore* explored new places every weekend.

10. Parts of the movie were *filmed* film at an amusement park where my friend *sells* sell souvenirs.

Exercise 12 **More on Correcting Errors in Verbs: Necessary Verbs, Third-Person Present Tense, Past Participles, and Infinitives**

Correct any errors in verbs in the sentences below. Write your corrections in the spaces above the lines. Some sentences do not need any corrections.

1. The wedding cake was so big that it was *baked* bake in a special oven to *guarantee* guaranteed that the cake pans would fit.

2. After the storm, the electricity *was/went* off for several days, and all the food in my refrigerator was *spoiled* spoil.

3. On summer nights, my cat *leaves* leave my yard and meets other cats in the neighborhood.

4. My older sister has *warned* warn me about falling in love too fast.

5. Adrienne and Leo were delighted with the surprise gift; they *had* has not expected Leo's uncle to remember their anniversary.

6. Oliver, Owen, and Luke *were* my best friends in elementary and middle school.

7. Sometime my life seems like a bad soap opera, and I want to *change* changed the channel.

8. My roommates have stopped paying the rent, so I am caught in a difficult situation.

9. For years, my nephew has talked about going back to Texas, and last month he packed his bags and drove to Corpus Christi.

10. I like to eat dinner late, but at my grandparents' house, dinner *begins* begin at 5:00 p.m.

Exercise 13 **Correcting a Paragraph with Errors in Necessary Verbs, Third-Person Present Tense, Past Participles, and Infinitives**

Correct the verb errors in the following paragraph. Write your corrections above the lines. There are thirteen errors.

My dog *is* very old, yet he still likes to *walk* ~~walked~~ every morning. At 7:00 a.m., he *wakes* ~~wake~~ me up by kissing me. He *sleeps* ~~sleep~~ at the foot of my bed, but he is too elderly to *jump* ~~jumped~~ off the high bed, so he must wait until I can help him. I remember when my dog was a puppy; then he could jump a foot off the floor. Now that he is older, he has *lost* ~~lose~~ some of his strength but none of his spirit. As soon as he *hears* ~~hear~~ the

wags
jingle of his leash, he ~~wag~~ his tail with joy. Although he is a senior dog, he loves to

pull   *drag*   *means*
~~pulled~~ on his leash and to ~~dragged~~ me to his favorite spots. Because he ~~mean~~ so

am   *follow*
much to me, I happy to ~~followed~~ my dog on his morning adventures.

Exercise 14   **Correcting Another Paragraph with Errors in Necessary Verbs, Third-Person Present Tense, Past Participles, and Infinitives**

Correct the verb errors in the following paragraph. Write your corrections above the lines. There are eight errors.

is   *worked*
It difficult to grow up without a permanent home. My parents have ~~work~~ in six

towns since I was born, and I have lived in ten different houses or apartments.

was
When I was very young, the most frightening part of moving getting lost in a

to
strange place. Later, I had deal with the terrors of making friends in a strange

school. To the students, I was the stranger, and they did not make it easy for me to

fit in. For years, I coped by acting like a tough, arrogant loner; however, I was

scared
~~scare~~ and hungry for friendship. Since my mother and father worked long hours at

were   *inherited*
their jobs, they not able to give me much attention. Fortunately, I ~~inherit~~ their

strong will to survive. As a result, I can look back on my childhood and recognize

sits
that a permanent home ~~sit~~ at the center of my dreams. Next, I can vow to work

hard for that home.

Two-Word Verbs

Two-word verbs contain a verb plus another word, a preposition or adverb. The meaning of each word by itself is different from the meaning the two words have when they are together. Look at this example:

> Sometimes Consuelo *runs across* her sister at the park.

You might check *run* in the dictionary and find that it means "to move quickly." *Across* means "from one side to the other." But *run across* means something different:

> **not this:** Sometimes Consuelo ~~moves quickly from one side to the other of~~ her sister at the park.
> **but this:** Sometimes Consuela *encounters* her sister at the park.

Sometimes a word or words come between the words of a two-word verb:

> On Friday night, I *put* the garbage *out*; the Sanitation Department collects it early Saturday morning.

Here are some common two-word verbs:

ask out:	Jamal wants to *ask* Teresa *out* for dinner.
break down:	I hope my car doesn't *break down*.
bring in:	Advertising will *bring in* more customers.
bring up:	Don't *bring up* Carmella's divorce.
call off:	You can *call* the party *off*.
call on:	I need to *call on* you for help.
call up:	Jim will *call* Ken *up* tomorrow.
come across:	I often *come across* bargains at thrift shops.
drop in:	Let's *drop in* on Claude.
drop off:	My father will *drop* the package *off*.
fill in:	You can *fill in* your name.
fill out:	Danny has to *fill out* a complaint form.
get up:	Gill has to *get up* early tomorrow.
give in:	Zack won't *give in* to Leo's demands.
give up:	Keith won't *give up* on getting a promotion.
hand in:	We have to *hand in* our assignments.
hand out:	I hope the theater *hands out* free passes.
hang up:	Just *hang up* the telephone.
keep on:	You must *keep on* practicing your speech.
keep up:	Gary can't *keep up* with the math assignments.
let out:	My brother *let* the secret *out*.
look into:	Jonelle will *look into* the situation.
look over:	Jake needs to *look* the plans *over*.
look up:	I had to *look* the word *up* in the dictionary.
make up:	Can I *make up* the test I missed?
open up:	I can't wait to *open up* my gifts.
pack up:	Rick is going to *pack up* his old clothes.
pick up:	Tomorrow I *pick up* my first paycheck.
put down:	I want to *put* this box *down*.
put on:	Wait until I *put on* a coat.
quiet down:	The teacher told the class to *quiet down*.
run into:	Nancy will *run into* Alan at the gym.
run out:	The family has *run out* of money.
send off:	Chris can *send* Mike *off* to get pizza.
take down:	Ted will *take down* the old window shades.
take off:	It's time to *take off* that silly hat.
take out:	I have to *take out* the garbage.
think over:	I like your idea; let me *think* it *over*.
think through:	We have to *think through* this problem.
throw out:	It's time to *throw out* these old magazines.
try on:	Before you buy the shirt, *try* it *on*.
try out:	She wants to *try* the lawnmower *out*.
turn down:	Sal thinks Wayne should *turn* the job *down*.
turn in:	Dwayne forgot to *turn in* his homework.
turn off:	I forgot to *turn* the oven *off*.
turn on:	*Turn* the television *on*.
turn out:	I wonder how this story will *turn out*.
turn up:	Nick is sure to *turn up* at the party.
write down:	You can *write down* your address.

Exercise 15 Writing Sentences with Two-Word Verbs

Write a sentence for each of the following two-word verbs. Use the list of common two-word verbs as a guide, but consult a dictionary if you are not sure what the verbs mean.

INSTRUCTOR'S NOTE

Answers will vary. Possible answers shown at left.

1. take out   *I offered to take my parents out for dinner.*

2. turn on   *It's so cold that I want to turn on the heat.*

3. keep up   *Don't walk fast; I can't keep up with you.*

4. fill in   *Al can fill in the missing parts of the story.*

5. hand in   *Robin wants to hand her paper in early.*

6. turn out   *I think this conflict will turn out badly.*

7. write down   *You can write the directions down for me.*

8. think over   *Before I decide, I want to think my options over.*

9. break down   *My old refrigerator can break down at any time.*

10. put on   *When it snowed, I put my boots on.*

Exercise 16 More on Writing Sentences with Two-Word Verbs

Write a sentence for each of the following two-word verbs. Use the examples as a guide, but consult a dictionary if you are not sure what the verbs mean.

INSTRUCTOR'S NOTE

Answers will vary. Possible answers shown at left.

1. pack up   *Lynn can pack up the old dishes and give them to charity.*

2. make up   *Jeremy wants to make up the day he missed at his job.*

3. take off   *Take the coffee cups off the table.*

4. turn on   *Will you turn on the fan?*

5. send off   *When Tom annoys me, I want to send him off to the moon.*

6. open up   *Go ahead; open up the envelope.*

7. try out   *Todd always wants to try his new jokes out on me.*

8. call on   *Lori calls on me for advice about her financial problems.*

9. come across   *Do you ever come across any of my old CDs?*

10. keep on   *Kelly should not keep on lying to her mother.*

Contractions and Verbs

Contractions often contain verbs you may not recognize in their shortened forms.

contraction: *I'm* losing weight.
long form: I am losing weight.

contraction: *She's* been my best friend for years.
long form: *She has* been my best friend for years.

contraction: *He's* leaving tomorrow.
long form: *He is* leaving tomorrow.

contraction: *They'll* never know.
long form: *They will* never know.

contraction: The *truck's* in the garage.
long form: The *truck is* in the garage.

> **Note:** The use of contractions may be discouraged in your composition classes. Always check with your instructor.

Exercise 17   Contractions and Verbs

In the space above each contraction, write its long form. The first one is done for you.

1. *You would*
   You'd be unhappy in a place with constant rain.
2. *We have*
   We've never been to a Greek restaurant.
3. *We are*
   We're going to a Greek restaurant.
4. *She will*
   She'll be home by nine or ten.
5. *dog is*
   The *dog's* sleeping on your bed.
6. *day has*
   The *day's* had some surprises for me.
7. *They will*
   They'll find a cheaper apartment near the turnpike.
8. *she would*
   I am sure *she'd* quit her job.
9. *will not*
   Robert *won't* sell his motorcycle.
10. *could have*
    You *could've* called me this morning.

Exercise 18   More on Contractions and Verbs

In the space above each contraction, write its long form. The first one is done for you.

1. *you had*
   I wish that *you'd* called me before you drove all the way to Cleveland.
2. *should have*
   The men *should've* taken Mr. Wing's advice.
3. *There is*
   There's nothing wrong with the computer.
4. *They had*
   They'd never seen an alligator or a sea turtle.
5. *We would*
   We'd be the only ones dressed casually at a formal dinner.
6. *he will*
   Do you think *he'll* call me?
7. *game is*
   The *game's* over for me.
8. *they have*
   On several occasions, *they've* lent me money.
9. *I will*
   On Saturday, *I'll* meet you at the mall.
10. *You have*
    You've given me a good idea.

PREPOSITIONS

Prepositions are little words such as *with, for, of, around,* or *near.* Some prepositions can be confusing; these are the ones that show time and place.

Prepositions That Show Time

1. Use *at* to show a specific or precise time:
   I will call you *at* 7:30 p.m.
   The movie starts *at* midnight.

2. Use *on* with a specific day or date:
   The meeting is *on* Friday.
   Frances begins basic training *on* June 23.

3. Use *by* when you mean "no later than that time":
   Jean has to be at work *by* 8:00 a.m.
   We should be finished with the cleaning *by* 5:00 p.m.

4. Use *until* when you mean "continuing up to a time":
   Yesterday I slept *until* 10:00 a.m.
   The dentist cannot see me *until* tomorrow.

5. Use *in* when you refer to a specific time period (minutes, hours, days, months, years):
   I'll be with you *in* a minute.
   Nikela works *in* the morning. (You can also say *in* the afternoon, or *in* the morning, or *in* the evening, but *at* night.)

6. Use *during* when you refer to a continuing time period or within the time period:
   I fell asleep *during* his speech.
   My sister will study management *during* the summer.

7. Use *for* to tell the length of a period of time:
   We have been married *for* two years.
   Wanda and Max cleaned the attic *for* three hours.

8. Use *since* to tell the starting time of an action:
   He has been calling *since* 9:00 a.m.
   We have been best friends *since* third grade.

Prepositions That Show Place

1. Use *in* to refer to a country, area, state, city, or neighborhood:
   He studied *in* Ecuador.
   Mr. Etienne lives *in* Houston.

2. Use *in* to refer to an enclosed space:
   He put the money *in* his wallet.
   Delia waited for me *in* the dining room.

3. Use *at* to refer to a specific address:
   The repair shop is *at* 7330 Glades Road.
   I live *at* 7520 Maple Lane.

4. Use *at* to refer to the corner or intersection:
   We went to a garage sale *at* the corner of Spring Street and Lincoln Avenue.
   The accident occurred *at* the intersection of Madison Boulevard and Temple Road.

5. Use *on* to refer to a street or a block:
   Dr. Lopez lives *on* Hawthorne Street.
   Malcolm bought the biggest house *on* the block.

6. Use *on* to refer to a surface:
   Put the sandwiches *on* the table.
   There was a bright rug *on* the floor.

7. Use *off* to refer to a surface:
   Take the sandwiches *off* the table.
   She wiped the mud *off* the floor.

8. Use *into* and *out of* for small vehicles such as cars:
   Our dog leaped *into* the convertible.
   The children climbed *out of* the car.

9. Use *on* and *off* for large vehicles like planes, trains, buses, and boats:
   I was so seasick, I couldn't wait to get *off* the ship.
   I like to ride *on* the bus.

Exercise 19 Correcting Errors in Prepositions

Correct any errors in prepositions in the following sentences. Write your corrections above the lines.

1. We used to live on 770 Third Avenue, but now we live on Appleton Way.
   [at above "on 770"]

2. Lisa found her kitten on the kitchen, sleeping at a shelf.
   [in above "on", on above "at"]

3. Our flight was so bumpy, I couldn't wait to get out of the plane.
   [off above "out of"]

4. Pierre lived at Haiti until he was a teenager.
   [in above "at"]

5. The restaurant on the intersection of Lincoln Road and Green
   Street has been in business until 1991.
   [at above "on", since above "until"]

6. Clean out the mess on your closet and put your dirty clothes at the
   washing machine during 6:00 p.m.
   [in above "on", in above "at", by above "during"]

7. The surprise birthday party is at Saturday night; you have to
   arrive during 7:30 p.m.
   [on above "at", by above "during"]

8. I had to scrub in an hour to get the tomato sauce stains in the floor.
   [for above "in", off above "in"]

9. Sean helped his mother on the car and put her suitcase at the trunk.
   [into above "on", in above "at"]

10. James took the twenty-dollar bill off the table and put the money
    on his wallet.
    [in above "on"]

Exercise 20 More on Correcting Errors in Prepositions

Correct any errors in prepositions in the following sentences. Write your corrections above the lines.

1. Josh and Gloria have lived in New York City in ten years.
   [for above "in"]

2. Jesse has a burst of energy on the morning, but he gets sleepy at
   the afternoon.
   [in above "on", in above "at"]

3. By the weekend, José will be sitting in a beach at Miami.
   [on above "in", in above "at"]

4. I don't like to travel on a car when I am used to gliding in the
   sidewalk with my skateboard.
   [in above "on", on above "in"]

5. We have been hiding the birthday cake into the kitchen cabinet
   since three hours.
   [in above "into", for above "since"]

Text Credits

Page 325: Gwinn Owens, "A Ridiculous Addiction," from *Newsweek*, December 4, 1989. Copyright © 1989 by Gwinn Owens. Reprinted with permission.

Page 599: David Migoya, "Getting Carded." *The Denver Post* (August 23, 2007) c-01, Business Section. Reprinted by permission of *The Denver Post*.

Page 603: Janice Castro with Dan Cook and Cristina Garcia, "Spanglish" from "Spanish Spoken Here." *TIME* July 11, 1998. Copyright © 1988 by Time Inc. Reprinted with permission.

Page 607: Elizabeth Wong, "A Present for Popo," from the *Los Angeles Times*, December 30, 1992. Copyright © 1992 by Elizabeth Wong. Reprinted with permission.

Page 610: Alisa Valdes-Rodriguez, "The Good Father." *Latina*, June 2004, pp. 79–80.

Page 614: Judith Sachs, "Breath of Life," from *Twenty-Minute Vacations*. 4255 West Touhy Avenue, Lincolnwood (Chicago) IL 60712. A Stonesong Press Book. Copyright © 2001 by The Stonesong Press, Inc. and Judith Sachs. Reprinted by permission.

Page 617: From READING PEOPLE by Jo-Ellan Dimitrius, Ph.D. and Mark Mazzarella. Copyright © 1998, 1999 by Jo-Ellan Dimitrius, Ph.D. and Mark Mazzarella. Used by permission of Random House, Inc.

Page 620: John Holt, "Three Disciplines for Children," from Freedom and Beyond. (New York: E.P. Dutton, 1972). Copyright © 1972 by John Holt. Reprinted with permission of Holt Associates; Heinemann, a division of Reed Elsevier, Inc., Portsmouth, NH.

Page 624: Virak Khiev, "Breaking the Bonds of Hate," from *Newsweek*, April 22, 1992. Copyright © 1992. Reprinted with permission.

Page 628: John Kellmayer, "Students in Shock," from David Daniels, Janet M. Goldstein, and Christopher G. Hayes, *A Basic Reader for College Writers*. Reprinted with permission of the author.

Page 632: Carolyn V. Egan, "Sidewalks Can Make a Town a Neighborhood." *Newsweek*, April 24, 2006. Copyright © 2006. Reprinted with permission.

Page 635: Danna L. Walker, "The Longest Day: Could a Class of College Students Survive without iPods, Cell Phones, Computers and TV from One Sunrise to the Next?" *The Washington Post*, August 5, 2007, magazine section W20. Column: The Education Review. Reprinted by permission of the author.

Page 643: Brent Staples, "A Brother's Murder." *The New York Times*, March 30, 1986, "About Men" column. Copyright © 1986 by the New York Times Company.

Page 647: Jack Hitt, "Navajo Code Talkers: The Century's Best Kept Secret" from Robert Wilson, *American Greats*. Copyright © 1999 Robert A. Wilson. Reprinted by permission of Public Affairs, a member of Perseus Books Group.

Photograph Credits

Page 2: www.photos.com/Jupiter Images; **Page 35 (top):** Michael Newman/PhotoEdit Inc.; **(bottom):** Bill Bachmann/PhotoEdit Inc.; **Page 36:** Meredith Parmelee/Getty Images, Inc.—Stone Allstock; **Page 38:** Tom Stillo/Omni-Photo Communications, Inc.; **Page 55 (top):** Peter Arnold, Inc./Alamy Images; **(bottom):** Ann Boyajian/Getty Images, Inc.—Artville LLC; **Page 57:** www.photos.com/Jupiter Images; **Page 77 (top):** www.photos.com/Jupiter Images; **(bottom):** Ryan McVay/Getty Images, Inc.—Photodisc; **Page 79:** www.photos.com/Jupiter Images; **Page 101:** David Yopung-Wolff/PhotoEdit Inc.; **Page 102:** AP Wide World Photos; **Page 104:** www.photos.com/Jupiter Images; **Page 122:** Todd Bigelow/Aurora Photos, Inc.; **Page 123:** Getty Images, Inc. **Page 125:** RON CHAPPLE/Getty Images, Inc.—Taxi; Page 150: Peter Wilson © Dorling Kindersley; **Page 151:** © Joseph Sohm/ChromoSohm Inc./CORBIS; **Page 153 (left):** Altrendo Images/Getty Images, Inc.; **(middle):** Doug Menuez/Photodisc/Getty Images, Inc. ;**(right):** Kevin Mackintosh/Getty Images, Inc.—Stone Allstock; **Page 169:** Gary Conner/PhotoEdit Inc.; **Page 171:** © Ellen B. Senisi; **Page 190:** Getty Images, Inc. **Page 192:** A. Ramey/PhotoEdit Inc.; **Page 212:** China Tourism Press.Xie, Guang Hui/Getty Images, Inc.—Image Bank; **Page 213:** Jose Luis Pelaez/Corbis/Betmann; **Page 215:** Rudi Von Briel/PhotoEdit Inc.; **Page 234 (top):** Bill Bachman/Photo Researchers, Inc.; **(bottom):** Alex L. Fradkin/Getty Images, Inc.—Photodisc; **Pages 236, 273:** www.photos.com/Jupiter Images; **Page 323:** Joe Sohm/Chrom sohm/ Stock Connection; **Page 346:** www.photos.com/Jupiter Images; **Page 372:** Will & Deni McIntyre/Photo Researchers, Inc.; **Page 389:** Doug Menuez/Getty Images, Inc.—Photodisc; **Page 403:** Getty Images, Inc.—Photodisc; **Page 411:** www.photos.com/Jupiter Images; **Page 423:** Getty Images -Stockbyte, Royalty Free; **Pages 432, 442, 452, 462,474, 487, 501, and 511:** www.photos.com/Jupiter Images; **Page 520:** Doug Menuez/Getty Images, Inc.—Photodisc; **Pages 540, 550, 560, 576, and 587:** www.photos.com/Jupiter Images.

INDEX

Note: Readings are listed under "reading selections." Each selection contains vocabulary definitions, comprehension checks, and critical-thinking questions for discussion or writing topics.